Explore the World

A informational guide to 261 countries and territories

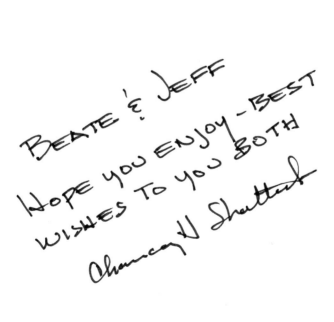

Beate & Jeff
Hope you enjoy – best
wishes to you both
Chauncey N Shattuck

December 1996

Explore the World

Copyright © 1996 by Chauncey H Shattuck

International Standard Book Number: 0-9655265-0-X
Library of Congress Catalog Card Number: 96-90762
Dewey Decimal System Number: 910 SHA 1996

Manufactured in the United States of America
Whipsaw Publishing
P O Box 21124
Reno, Nevada, 89515-1124

Published for domestic and foreign distribution
First Edition

PREFACE

This is, so far as I know, the only book ever to appear in print that presents an overview of 261 countries and territories, 4 oceans, and the world. A map is included for each country and territory with the longitude and latitude for easy orientation.

Where available the address for newspapers, tourist information and diplomatic representation are presented for those who perhaps would like to travel or do business in a particular country; also the appendix contains the telephone numbers of the US State Department of Consular Affairs Automated Fax System and the World Business Directory (over 140,000 businesses involved in international trade).

Environment and travel conditions have been excluded because all countries have similar problems.

My wish is for you to explore the countries and territories of the world, using this book as a guide to assist in expanding your knowledge.

Chauncey

It is a pleasure to acknowledge the help of my family:
my wife Virginia, our children Greg, Janet and Alan
and others in preparation of this handbook

Contents

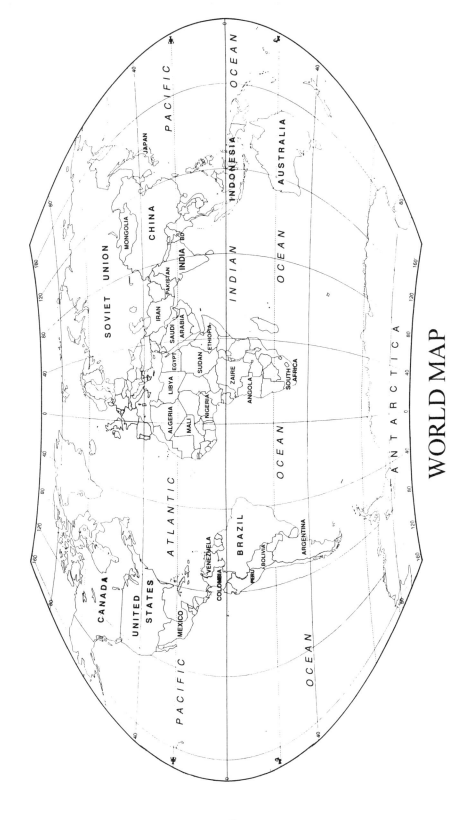

WORLD MAP

Afghanistan

300 km

Capital: Kabul   longitude: 69.13 E   latitude: 34.31 N   elevation: 5,955 ft
Government: Islamic republic - transitional
Flag: NA: note - the flag has changed at least twice since 1992

Geography

Location: Southern Asia, north of Pakistan
Total Area: 647,500 sq km (250,000 sq miles) slightly smaller than Texas.
Boundaries: China, Iran, Pakistan, Tajikistan, Turkmenistan, Uzbekistan
Climate: arid to semiarid; cold winters and hot summers
Temperature (F): High/Low Jan. 36/18, Apr. 66/43, July 92/61, Oct. 73/42
Average annual precipitation: 12 inches
Terrain: rugged mountains; plains in north and southwest.
Highest point is Nowshak 7,485 m (24,557 ft)
Natural resources: natural gas, petroleum, coal, copper, talc, barites,
sulphur, lead, zinc, iron ore, salt, precious and semiprecious stones
Natural hazards: damaging earthquakes occur in Hindu Kush mountains;
flooding

People

Population: 21,251,900 (July 1995 est.)
Life expectancy at birth: total population 45.37 years
Nationality: Afghan
Ethnic divisions: Pashtum 38%, Tajik 25%, Uzbek 6%, Hazara 19%, minor
ethnic groups (Chahar Aimaks, Turkmen, Baloch, and others)
Religions: Sunni Muslim 84%, Shi'a Muslim 15%, other 1%
Languages: Pashtu 35%, Afghan Persian (Dari) 50%, Turkic languages
(primarily Uzbek and Turkmen) 11%, 30 minor languages (primarily Balochi
and Pashai) 4%, much bilingualism
Literacy: total population 29%

1

Economy

Imports: food and petroleum products; most consumer goods

Exports: fruits and nuts, hand woven carpets, wool, cotton, hides and pelts, precious and semiprecious gems

Industries: production of textiles, soap, furniture, shoes, fertilizer, and cement; hand woven carpets; natural gas, oil, coal, copper

Agriculture: largely subsistence farming and nomadic animal husbandry; cash products - wheat, fruits, nuts, karakul pelts, wool, mutton

Currency: 1 afghani (Af) = 100 puls

Afghanis per US$1 - 1900 (Jan. 1994)

Transportation:

Railroads: total 24.6 km

Roads: total 21,000 km paved and unpaved

Ports: Keleft, Kheyrabad, Shir Khan

Airports: 48 total paved and unpaved. The international airports are located at Kabul and Qandahar

The Press: daily newspapers

Anis: Kabul, evening, circ. 25,000

Kabul New Times: POB 983, Ansari Wat, Kabul telephone (93) 61-847 English, circ. 5,000.

Tourism:

Tourist attractions are the painted caves and high statue of Buddha at Bamian; Mosque and minarets throughout the country; Bandi Amir, with its suspended lakes; high mountains of the Hindu Kush

Afghan Tourist Organization: Ansari Wat, Shar-i-Nau, Kabul telephone (93) 30-323

Diplomatic representation in US:

chief of mission (vacant); Charge d'Affaires Abdul Rahim

chancery: 2341 Wyoming Avenue NW, Washington, D.C. 20008

telephone: [1] (202) 234-3770, 3771

FAX: [1] (202) 328-3516

US diplomatic representation: none; embassy was closed in January 1989

Albania

Capital: Tirane   longitude: 41.20 N   latitude: 19.49 E   elevation: 292 ft
Government: emerging democracy
    Flag: red with a black two-headed eagle in the center
Geography:
    Location: Southeastern Europe, bordering the Adriatic Sea, between Greece
    and Serbia and Montenegro
    Total Area: 28,750 sq km (11,100 sq mi) slightly larger than Maryland
    Boundaries: Greece, The Former Yugoslav Republic of Macedonia, Serbia
    and Montenegro
    Climate: mild temperate: cool, cloudy, wet winters: hot clear, dry summers:
    interior is cooler and wetter
    Temperature (F) High/Low Jan. 53/36, Apr. 65/47, July 87/63, Oct. 73/50
    Average annual precipitation: 40 inches, about 100 inches in the north
    mountains
    Terrain: mostly mountains and hills: small plains along coast. Highest point
    is Mt. Columbia 3,747 m (12,294 ft)
    Natural resources: petroleum, natural gas, coal, chromium, copper, timber,
    nickel
    Natural hazards: destructive earthquakes; tsunami occur along southeastern
    coast.
    Note: strategic location along Strait of Otranto (links Adriatic Sea to Ionian
    Sea and Mediterranean Sea)
People:
    Population: 3,413,900 (July 1995 est)
    Life expectancy at birth: total population 73.81 years
    Nationality: Albanian
    Ethnic division: Albanian 95%, Greeks 3%

Religions: Muslim 70%, Albanian 20%, Roman Catholic 10%

Languages: Albanian (Tosk is the official dialect), Greek

Literacy: total population 72%

Economy

Imports: machinery, consumer goods, grains

Exports: asphalt, metals and metallic ores, electricity, crude oil, vegetables, fruits, tobacco

Industries: food processing, textiles and clothing, lumber, oil, cement, chemicals, mining, basic metals, hydropower

Agriculture: wheat, corn, potatoes, sugar beets, cotton, tobacco

Currency: 1 lek (L) = 100 qintars   leke per US$1 - 100 (Jan 1995)

Transportation:

Railroads: total 543 km

Roads: total 18,450 km paved and unpaved

Ports: Durres, Sarande, Shergjin, Vlore

Airports: 11 total paved and unpaved. There is a small international airport at Rinas, about 25 km from Tirana. Albania has air links with several other countries but, no regular internal service.

The Press: daily newspapers   Rilindja Demokratike: Rp. Fortuzi, Tirana; circ. 30,000

Zeei i Popullit: Bulevardi Deshmoret e Kombit. Tirina. circ. 50,000   telephone (42) 27-808 fax (42) 27-813

Tourism: There are important archaeological sites and one of the largest Roman amphitheaters at Durres.

Albturist: Bulevardi Deshmoret e Kombit 6, Tirana telephone (42) 23-860, fax (42) 27-956

Diplomatic representation in US:

chief of mission: Ambassador Lublin Hasan Dilja

chancery: Suite 1010, 1511 K Street NW, Washington DC 20005

telephone: [1] (202) 223-4942, 8187

FAX: [1] (202) 628-7342

US Diplomatic representation:

chief of mission: Ambassador Joseph E. Lake

embassy: Rruga E. Elbansanit 103, Tirane

mailing address: PSC 59, Box 100 (A), APO AE 09624

telephone: [355] (42) 32-875, 33-520

FAX: [355] (42) 32-222

Algeria

Capital: Algiers   longitude: 3.00 E   latitude: 36.50 N   elevation: 194 ft

Government: republic

Flag: red with a black two-headed eagle in the center

Geography:

Location: Northern Africa, bordering the Mediterranean Sea, between Morocco and Tunisia

Total Area: 2,381,740 sq km (919,590 sq mi) slightly less than 3.5 times the size of Texas

Boundaries: Libya, Mali, Mauritania, Morocco, Niger, Tunisia, Western Sahara

Climate: arid to semiarid; mild, wet winters with hot, dry summers along coast; drier with cold winters and hot summers on high plateau; sirocco is hot, dust/sand-laden wind especially common in summer

Temperature: (F) High/Low Jan. 59/49, Apr. 68/55, July 83/70, Oct. 74/63

Average annual precipitation: 27 inches north, 12 inches high plateau, Sahara has less than 5 inches

Terrain: mostly high plateau and desert; some mountains; narrow, discontinuous coastal plain.

Highest point is Tahat 3,003 m (9,852 ft)

Natural resources: petroleum, natural gas, iron ore, phosphates, uranium, lead, zinc

Natural hazards: mountainous areas subject to severe earthquakes; mud slides

People:

Population: 28,539,321 (July 1995 est)

Life expectancy at birth: total population 68.01 years

Nationality: Algerian

Ethnic division: Arab-Berber 99%, European less than 1%

Religions: Sunni Muslim (state religion) 99%, Christian and Jewish 1%

Languages: Arabic (official) French, Berber dialects

Literacy: total population 57%

Economy

Algeria has the fifth largest reserves of natural gas in the world and ranks fourteenth in oil.

Imports: capital goods, food and beverages, consumer goods

Exports: petroleum and natural gas

Industries: petroleum, light industries, natural gas, mining, electrical, petrochemical, food processing

Agriculture: wheat, barley, oats grapes, olives, citrus, fruits, sheep, cattle

Currency: 1 Algerian dinars (DA) = 100 centimes

Algerian dinars per US$1 - 42.71

Transportation:

Railroads: total 4,733 km

Roads: total paved and unpaved 95,576 km

Ports: Algiers, Annaba, Arzew, Bejaia, Beni Saf, Dellys, Djendjene, Ghazaouet, Jijel, Mostaganem, Oran, Skikda, Tenes

Airports: 139 total paved and unpaved, the main international airport is at Dar-el-Bieda, about 20 km from Algiers.

The Press: daily newspapers **An-Nasr:** BP 388, Zone Industrielle, La Palma, Constantine; telephone (4) 93-92-16 circ. 340,000

Horizons: 20 rue de la Liberte, Algiers telephone (2) 73-67-24; fax (2)73-61-34 evening, French circ. 300,000

Tourism: attractions are along the Mediterranean coast, the mountains and desert. Roman ruins of Tipasa, Constantine, Oran, Tamanrasset. Atlas mountains

Office National du Tourisme: 8 ave de Pekin Alger-Gare, Algiers telephone (2) 60-59-60 fax (2) 59-13-15

Diplomatic representation in US:

chief of mission: Ambassador Osmane Bencherif

chancery: 2118 Kalorama Road, Washington, DC 20008

telephone: [1] (202) 265-2800

US Diplomatic representation:

chief of mission: Ambassador Ronald E. Neumann

embassy: 4 Chemin Cheikh Bachir El-Ibrahimi, Algiers

mailing address: B.P. Box 549, Alger-Gare. 16000 Algiers

telephone: [213] (2) 69-11-86, 69-18-54, 69-38-75

FAX: [213] (2) 69-39-79

American Samoa

Capital: Pago Pago   longitude: 170.42 W latitude: 14.16 S elevation: 29 ft

Government: unincorporated and unorganized territory of the US; administered by the US Department of Interior, Office of Territorial and International Affairs

Flag: blue with a white triangle edged in red that is based on the fly side and extends to the hoist side; a brown and white American bald eagle flying toward the hoist side is caring two traditional Samoan symbols of authority, a staff and a war club

Geography

Location: Oceania, group of islands in the South Pacific Ocean, about one-half of the way from Hawaii to New Zealand

Total Area: 199 sq km (77 sq mi) slightly larger than Washington, DC

Boundaries: no land boundaries

Climate: tropical marine, moderated by southeast trade winds.

Temperature (F): High/Low Jan. 81/80, Apr. 81/79, July 79/78, Oct. 80/79

Average annual precipitation: 124 inches

Terrain: five volcanic islands with rugged peaks and limited coastal plains, two coral atolls (Rose Island, Swains Island)

Highest point is Lata Mountain on Tau Island 1100 m (3,609 ft)

Natural resources: pumice, pumicite

Natural hazards: typhoons common from December to March

People

Population: 57,366 (July 1995 est.)

Life expectancy at birth: total population 72.91 years

Nationality: American Samoan

Ethnic division: Samoan (Polynesian) 89%, Caucasian 2%, Tongan 4%, other 5%

Religions: Christian Congregationalist 50%, Roman Catholic 20%, Protestant denominations and others 30%

Languages: Samoan (closely related to Hawaiian and other Polynesian languages), English; most people are bilingual

Literacy: 97% total population

Economy

Imports: materials for canneries, food, petroleum products, machinery and parts

Exports: canned tuna

Industries: tuna canneries (largely dependent on foreign fishing vessels), meat canning, handicraft

Agriculture: bananas, coconuts, vegetables, taro, breadfruit, yams, copra, pineapples, papayas, dairy farming

Currency: 1 United States dollar = 100 cents   US currency is used

Transportation

Railroads: none

Roads: 350 km total paved and unpaved

Ports: Aanu'u, Auasi, Faleosao, Ofu, Pago Pago, Ta'u

Airports: 4 paved. The main airport is located at Pago Pago

Note: small airstrips on Fituita and Ofu

Tourism: Blunt's Point, Virgin Falls, Mount Alava, Assu village, the Library of American Samoa

Diplomatic representation in US: none (territory of the US)

US Diplomatic representation: none (territory of the US)

Andorra

Capital: Andorra La Vella   longitude: 1.30 E   latitude: 42.30 N
elevation: 3,545 ft

Government: parliamentary democracy

Flag: three equal vertical bands of blue (hoist side), yellow, and red with the national coat of arms centered in the yellow band; the coat of arms features a quartered shield; similar to the flags of Chad and Romania that do not have a national coat of arms in the center

Geography:

Location: Southwestern Europe, between France and Spain in the eastern Pyrenees

Total Area: 450 sq km (174 sq mi) slightly more than 2.5 times the size of Washington, DC

Boundaries: France and Spain

Climate: temperate; snowy, cold winters and warm, dry summers
Temperature (F): High/Low Jan. 43/36, Apr. 58/39, July 79/54, Oct. 60/42
Average annual precipitation: 32 inches

Terrain: rugged mountains dissected by narrow valleys. The country is drained by the Valira River
Highest point is in the Pyrenees mountains 2700 m (8860 ft)

Natural resources: hydropower, mineral water, timber, iron ore, lead

Natural hazards: snow slides, avalanches

People:

Population: 65,780 (July 1995 est)

Life expectancy at birth: total population 78.52 years

Nationality: Andorran

Ethnic division: Spanish 61%, Andorran 30%, French 6%

Religions: Roman Catholic

Languages: Catalan (official) French, Castilian

Literacy: total population 86%

Economy

Imports: consumer goods, food

Exports: electricity, tobacco products, furniture

Industries: tourism (particularly skiing), sheep, timber, tobacco, banking

Agriculture: sheep raising, tobacco, rye, wheat, barley, oats and some vegetables

Currency: 1 French franc (F) = 100 centimes; 1 peseta Pta) = 100 centimos; the French and Spanish currencies are used. French francs per US$1 - 5.29

Transportation:

Railroads: none

Roads: 96 km

Ports: none

Airports: none. The closest airport is at Seo de Urgel in Spain, about 20 km form Andorra de Vella

The Press: daily newspapers

Correu Andorra: Avinguda Meritxell 114, Andorra la Vella
telephone 22-500: fax 22-938   circ. 2,000

Diari d' Andorra: Avinguda Riberaygua 39,
Andorra la Vella; telephone 63-700; fax 63-800   circ. 3,000

Tourism: attractive mountain scenery. Five facilities are available for winter skiing. Romanesque churches and bridges. Trout fishing. Duty free goods

Ministeri de Turisme i Esports: Carrer Prat de la Creu, 62-64 Andorra la Vella   telephone 28-345   fax 60-184

Diplomatic representation in US:
Andorra has no mission in the US

US Diplomatic representation:
Andorra is included within the Barcelona (Spain) Consular District, and the US Consul General visits Andorra periodically

Angola

Capital: Luanda   longitude: 13.15 E   latitude: 8.50 S elevation: 194 ft

Government: transitional government nominally a multiparty democracy with a strong presidential system

Flag: two equal horizontal bands of red (top) and black with a centered yellow emblem consisting of a five-pointed star within half a cogwheel crossed by a machete (in the style of a hammer and sickle)

Geography:

Location: Southern Africa, bordering the South Atlantic Ocean, between Namibia and Zaire

Total Area: 1,246,700 sq km. (481,351 sq mi) slightly less than twice the size of Texas

Boundaries: Congo, Namibia, Zaire, Zambia

Climate: semiarid in the south and along the coast of Luanda: north is cool, dry season (May to October) and hot, rainy season (November to April) Temperature (F): High/Low Jan. 83/74, Apr. 85/75, July 74/65, Oct. 79/71 Average annual precipitation: 13 inches

Terrain: narrow coastal plain rises abruptly to vast interior plateau Highest point is Mt. Moco 2,620 m (8,593 ft)

Natural resources: petroleum, diamonds, iron ore, phosphates, copper, feldspar, gold, bauxite, uranium

Natural hazards: locally heavy rainfall causes periodic flooding on the plateau

People:

Population: 10,070,000 (July 1995 est.)

Life expectancy at birth: total population 46.28 years

Nationality: Angolan

Ethnic division: Ovimbundu 37%, Kimbundu 25%, Bakongo 13%, mestico (mixed European and Native African) 2%, European 1%, other 22%

Religions: indigenous beliefs 47%, Roman Catholic 38%, Protestant 15%

Languages: Portuguese (official), Bantu and other African languages

Literacy: total population 42%

Economy

Imports: capital equipment (machinery and electrical equipment), food, vehicles and spare parts, textiles and clothing, medicines

Exports: oil, diamonds, refined petroleum products, gas, coffee, sisal, fish and fish products, timber, cotton

Industries: petroleum; mining - diamonds, iron ore, phosphates, feldspar, bauxite, uranium, and gold; fish processing; food processing; brewing; tobacco; sugar; textiles; cement; basic metal products

Agriculture: cash crops - bananas, sugarcane, coffee, sisal, corn, cotton, cane, manioc, tobacco; food crops - cassava, corn, vegetables, plantains; livestock production accounts for 20%, fishing 4%, forestry 2%

Currency: 1 new kwanza (NKz) = 100 lwei
new kwanza per US1$ - 900,000 (official rate 25 April 1995)

Transportation:

Railroads: 3,189 km

Roads: 73,828 km total paved and unpaved

Ports: Ambriz, Cabinda, Lobito, Luanda, Malogo, Namibe, Porto Amboim, Soyo

Airports: 289 total paved and unpaved. The major airport is at Luanda

The Press: daily newspaper   **O jornal de Angola:** CP 1312, Luanda
telephone 33-16-23   circ. 41,000

Tourism: Luanda, tourist facilities are limited

National tourist Agency:
Palacic de Vidro, CP 1240, Luanda
telephone 37-27-50

Diplomatic representation in US:
chief of mission: Ambassador Antonio Franca
embassy: 1050 Connecticut Avenue NW,
Washington, DC 20036   Suite 760
telephone: [1] (202) 785-1156
FAX: [1] (202) 785-1258

US Diplomatic representation:
chief of mission: Ambassador Edmund T DeJarnette
embassy: 32 Rua Houari Boumedienne, Miramar, Luanda
mailing address: C.P. 6484, Luanda; American Embassy, Luanda,
Department of State, Washington, DC 20521-2550
telephone: [244] (2) 345-481, 346-418
FAX: [244] (2) 347-884

Anguilla

20 km

Sombrero

Caribbean
Sea

Prickly Pear Cays   Scrub Island

THE VALLEY

Blowing Point

Anguilla

Capital: The Valley   longitude: 63.20 W   latitude: 18.30 N
Government: dependent territory of the UK

Flag: two horizontal bands of white (top, almost triple width) and light blue
with three orange dolphins in an interlocking circular design centered in the
white band

Geography

Location: Caribbean, island in the Caribbean Sea, east of Puerto Rico

Total Area: 91 sq km (35 sq mi) about half the size of Washington, DC

Boundaries: no land boundaries

Climate: tropical; moderated by northeast trade winds

Temperature (F): average 80 degrees

Average annual precipitation: 36 inches

Terrain: flat and low lying island of coral and limestone

Highest point is 61 m

Natural resources: negligible; salt, fish, lobster

Natural hazards: frequent hurricanes and other tropical storms (July to October)

People

Population: 7,099 (July 1995 est.)

Life expectancy at birth: total population 74.1 years

Nationality: Anguillan

Ethnic division: black African

Religions: Anglican 40%, Methodist 33%, Seventh-Day Adventist 7%, Baptist 5%, Roman Catholic 3%, other 12%

Languages: English (official)

Literacy: total population 95%

Economy

Imports: NA

Exports: lobster and salt

Industries: tourism, boat building, salt

Agriculture: pigeon peas, corn, sweet potatoes, sheep, goats, pigs, cattle, poultry, fishing (including lobster)

Currency: 1 EC dollar (EC$) = 100 cents

East Caribbean dollars per US1$ - 2.70

Transportation

Railroads: none

Roads: 105 km paved and unpaved

Ports: Blowing Point, Road Bay

Airports: 3 total paved and unpaved. Wallblake Airport has a paved runway and is located near The Valley

The Press: monthly news-sheet

Official Gazette: The Valley telephone 497-3080

Tourism: soft sandy scenic beaches, crystal clear water, perfect for snorkeling

Department of Tourism: The Secretariat The Valley telephone 497-2759 fax 497-3389

Antarctica

1000 km

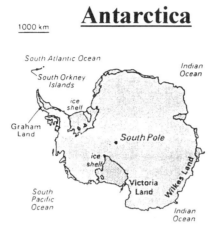

Government: Antarctic Treaty: The Antarctic Treaty, establishes the legal framework for the management of Antarctica. Administration is carried out through consultative member meetings. Currently, there are 42 treaty member nations

Geography

Location: continent mostly south of the Antarctic Circle

Total Area: 14,000,000 sq km (5,405,400 sq mi) (est.) slightly less than 1.5 times the size of the US

Note: second-smallest continent (after Australia)

Land Boundaries: none

Climate: severe low temperatures vary with latitude, elevation, and distance from the ocean; East Antarctica is colder than West Antarctica because it is higher in elevation; Antarctic Peninsula has the most moderate climate; higher temperatures occur in January along the coast and average slightly below freezing

Terrain: about 98% thick continental ice sheet and 2% barren rock, with average elevations between 2,000 and 4,000 meters; mountain ranges up to 4,897 meters high; (highest point - Vinson Massif Sentinel Range, 16,863 ft) ice free coastal areas include parts of southern Victoria Land, Wilkes Land, the Antarctic Peninsula area, and parts of Ross Island on McMurdo Sound; glaciers form ice shelves along about half of the coastline, and floating ice shelves constitute 11% of the area on the continent

Natural resources: none presently exploited; iron ore, chromium, copper, gold, nickel, platinum and other minerals, and coal and hydrocarbons have been found in small, uncommercial quantities

Environment

Current issues: in October 1991 it was reported that the ozone shield, which protects the Earth's surface from harmful ultraviolet radiation, had dwindled to the lowest level recorded over Antarctica since 1975 when measurements were first taken

Natural hazards: katabatic (gravity-driven) winds blow coastward from the higher interior; frequent blizzards form near the foot of the plateau; cyclonic storms form over the ocean and move clockwise along the coast; volcanism on Deception Island and isolated areas of West Antarctica; other seismic activity rare and weak

Note: the coldest, windiest, highest, and driest continent; during summer more solar radiation reaches the surface at the South Pole than is received at the Equator in an equivalent period; mostly uninhabitable

Population: no indigenous inhabitants; note - there are seasonally staffed research stations

Economy

Overview: no economic activity at present except for fishing off the coast and small-scale tourism, both based abroad

Transportation

Ports: none; offshore anchorage

Airports: 42 landing facilities at different locations operated by 15 national governments party to the Treaty

Antigua and Barbuda

20 km

Barbuda

Caribbean Sea

SAINT JOHN'S   Antigua

₀ Redonda

Capital: Saint John's   longitude: 61.50 W   latitude: 17.08 N   elevation: 40 ft

Government: parliamentary democracy

Flag: red with inverted isosceles triangle based on the top edge of the flag; the triangle contains three horizontal bands of black (top), light blue, and white with a yellow rising sun in the black band

15

Geography:

    Location: Caribbean, islands between the Caribbean Sea and the North Atlantic Ocean, east-southeast of Puerto Rico

    Total Area: 440 sq km (170 sq mi) (includes Redonda 1.6 sq km) slightly less than 2.5 times the size of Washington, DC

    Boundaries: no land boundaries

    Climate: tropical marine; little seasonal temperature variation.

    Temperature (F): High/Low Jan. 83/73, Apr. 85/75, July 86/78, Oct. 86/76

    Terrain: mostly low-lying limestone and coral islands with some higher volcanic areas.

    Highest point is Boggy Peak 1,447 m (4,747 ft)

    Natural resources: negligible

    Natural hazards: hurricanes and tropical storms (July to October); periodic droughts

People:

    Population: 65,176 (July 1995 est)

    Life expectancy at birth: 73.4 years

    Nationality: Antiguan and Barbudan

    Ethnic division: black African, British, Portuguese, Lebanese, Syrian

    Religions: Anglican (predominant) other Protestant sects, some Roman Catholic

    Languages: English (official), local dialects

    Literacy: total population 89%

Economy

    Imports: food and live animals, machinery and transport equipment, manufactures, chemicals, oil

    Exports: petroleum products, manufactures, food and live animals, machinery and transport equipment

Industries: tourism, construction, light manufacturing (clothing, alcohol, household appliances)

Agriculture: cotton, fruits, vegetables, and livestock; other crops - bananas, coconuts, cucumbers, mangoes, sugarcane

Currency: 1 EC dollar (EC$) = 100 cents

    East Caribbean dollars (EC$) per US1$ - 2.70

Transportation:

    Railroads: total 77 km

    Roads: total 240 km paved and unpaved

    Ports: Saint John's

Airports: 3 total paved and unpaved. Antigua's (V.C. Bird) International Airport is located about 9 km north-east of St John's and can accommodate jet-engined aircraft. There is a small airstrip at Codrington on Barbuda

The Press: weekly newspapers   **The Herald:** Redcliffe House, 2nd Floor, Cross and Redcliffe Streets, St John's telephone 462-3752   circ. 2,500

The Nation: Ministry of Information, Cross Street, POB 590, St John's telephone 462-0010   circ. 1500

Tourism: tourism is the country's main industry, it is a duty free center and has facilities for cruise-ships. Over 300 beaches, sailing and water sports

Antigua Department of Tourism:
Long and Thames Streets, POB 363, St John's
telephone 462-0029   fax 462-2483

Diplomatic representation in US:
chief of mission: Ambassador Patrick A Lewis
chancery: 3216 New Mexico Avenue NW, Washington DC 20016
telephone: [1] (202) 362-5211, 5266, 5122
FAX: [1] (202) 362-5225

US Diplomatic representation: the post was closed 30 June 1994; the US Ambassador to Barbados is accredited to Antigua and Barbuda

Arctic Ocean

Geography
Location: body of water mostly north of the Arctic Circle
Area: 14,056,000 sq km (5,427,022 sq mi) slightly more than 1.5 time the size of the US; smallest of the world's four oceans.

17

Note: includes Baffin Bay, Barents Sea, Beaufort Sea, Chuchi Sea, East Siberian Sea, Greenland Sea, Hudson Bay, Hudson Strait, Kara Sea, Northwest Passage, and other tributary water bodies

Climate: polar climate characterized by persistent cold and relatively narrow annual temperature ranges; winters characterized by continuous darkness, cold and stable weather conditions, and clear skies; summers characterized by continuous daylight, damp and foggy weather, weak cyclones with rain and snow

Terrain: central surface covered by a perennial drifting polar icepack that averages about 3 meters in thickness, although pressure ridges may be three times that size; clockwise drift pattern in the Beaufort Gyral Stream, but nearly straightline movement from the New Siberian Islands (Russia) to Denmark Strait (between Greenland and Iceland); the ice pack is surrounded by open seas during the summer, but more than doubles in size during the winter and extends to the encircling land masses; the ocean floor is about 50% continental shelf (highest percentage of any ocean) with the remainder a central basin interrupted by three submarine ridges; maximum depth is 4,665 meters in the Fram Basin

Natural resources: sand and gravel aggregates, placer deposits, polymetallic nodules, oil and gas fields, fish, marine mammals (seals and whales)

Environment

Current issues: endangered marine species include walruses and whales; fragile ecosystem slow to recover from disruption or damage

Natural hazards: ice islands occasionally break away from northern Ellesmere Island; icebergs calved from glaciers in western Greenland and extreme northeastern Canada; permafrost in islands; virtually ice blocked from October to June; ships subject to superstructure icing from October to May

Transportation

Ports: Churchill (Canada), Murmansk (Russia), Prudhoe Bay (US)

Argentina

Capital: Buenos Aires longitude: 58.30 W latitude: 34.40 S elevation: 89 ft

Government: republic

Flag: three equal horizontal bands of light blue (top), white, and light blue; centered in the white band is a radiant yellow sun with a human face known as the Sun of May

Geography:

Location: Southern South America, bordering the South Atlantic Ocean, between Chile and Uruguay

Total Area: 2,766,890 sq km (1,068,296 sq mi) slightly less than three-tenths the size of the US

Boundaries: Bolivia, Brazil, Chile, Paraguay, Uruguay

Climate: mostly temperate; arid in southeast; subantarctic in southwest
Temperature (F): High/Low Jan. 85/63, Apr. 72/53, July 57/42, Oct. 69/50
Average annual precipitation: 37 inches

Terrain: rich plains of the Pampas in the northern half, flat to rolling plateau of Patagonia in south, rugged Andes along western border
Highest point is Cerro Aconcagua 6,959 m (22,831 ft)

Natural resources: fertile plains of the pampas, lead, zinc, tin, copper, iron ore, manganese, petroleum, uranium

Natural hazards: Tucuman and Mendoza areas in the Andes subject to earthquakes; pamperos are violent windstorms that can strike the Pampas and northeast; heavy flooding

People:

Population: 34,292,742 (July 1995 est)

Life expectancy at birth: 71.51 years

Nationality: Argentine

Ethnic division: white 85%, mestizo, indian, or other nonwhite groups 15%

19

Religions: nominally Roman Catholic 90% (less than 20% practicing), Protestant 2%, Jewish 2%, others 6%

Languages: Spanish (official) English, Italian, German, French

Literacy: total population: 95%

Economy

Argentina is rich in natural resources.

Imports: machinery and equipment, chemicals, metals, fuels and lubricants, agricultural products

Exports: meat, corn, oilseed, manufactures

Industries: food processing, motor vehicles, consumer durables, textiles, chemicals and petrochemicals, printing, metallurgy, steel

Agriculture: among world's top five exporters of grain and beef; principal crops - wheat, corn, sorghum, soybeans, sugar beets

Currency: 1 nuevo peso argentino = 100 centavos   peso per US1$ - 0.99

Transportation:

Railroads: total 34,572 km

Roads: total paved and unpaved 208,350 km

Ports: Bahia Blanca, Buenos Aires, Comodoro Rivadavia, Concepcion del Uruguay, La Plata, Mar del Plata, Necochea, Rio Gallegos, Rosario, Santa Fe, Ushuaia

Airports: 1,602 total paved and unpaved. Argentina has 10 international airports.

The Press: daily newspapers   **Clarin:** Piedras 1743, 1140 Buenos Aires; telephone (1) 27-00-61
circ. 480,000 (daily) 750,000 (Sunday)
Cronica: Garay 130, 1063 Buenos Aires; telephone (1) 361-1001
circ. 330,000 (morning)   450,000 (Sunday)

Tourism: tourist attractions are numerous, the Andes mountains , Atlantic beaches, Iguazu Falls, Perito Moreno Glacier

Secretaria de Turismo de la Nacion:
Calle Suipacha 1111, 21 , 1368 Buenos Aires
telephone (1) 312-5621 fax (1) 313-6834

Diplomatic representation in US:

chief of mission: Ambassador Raul Enrique Granillo Ocampo

chancery: 1600 New Hampshire Avenue NW, Washington, DC 20009

telephone: [1] (202) 939-6400 through 6403

US Diplomatic representation:
chief of mission: Ambassador James R. Cheek
embassy: 4300 Columbia, 1425 Buenos Aires
mailing address: Unit 4334; APO AA 34034
telephone: [54] (1) 777-4533, 4534
FAX: [54] (1) 777-0197

Armenia

Capital: Yerevan   longitude: 44.30 E   latitude: 40.11 N
Government: republic
Flag: three equal horizontal bands of red (top), blue, and gold
Geography:
Location: Southwestern Asia, east of Turkey
Total Area: 29,800 km (11,505 sq mi) slightly larger than Maryland
Boundaries: Azerbaijan, Georgia, Iran, Turkey
Climate: high land continental, hot summers average 77 F, cold winters average 26F
Average annual precipitation: 12.6 inches
Terrain: high Armenian Plateau with mountains; little forest land; fast flowing rivers; good soil in Aras River valley
Highest point is Mt. Aragats 4,095 m (13,435 ft)
Natural resources: small deposits of gold, copper, molybdenum, zinc, alumina
Natural hazards: occasionally severe earthquakes; droughts
People:
Population: 3,557,290 (July 1995 est)
Life expectancy at birth: total population 72.36 years
Nationality: Armenian
Ethnic division: Armenian 93%, Azeris 3%, Russian 2%

21

Religions: Armenian Orthodox 94%

Languages: Armenian 96%, Russian 2%

Literacy: total population 99%

Economy

Imports: grains other foods, fuel, other energy

Exports: gold and jewelry, aluminum, transport equipment, electrical equipment

Industries: machine tools, electric motors, tires, knitted wear, hosiery, shoes, silk fabric, washing machines, chemicals, trucks, watches, instruments and micro electronics

Agriculture: fruits (especially grapes) and vegetables farming, minor live stock sector, vineyards near Yerevan are famous for brandy and other liquors

Currency: 1 dram = 100 luma   dram per US1$ - 406

Transportation:

Railroads: total 840 km

Roads: total paved and unpaved 11,300 km

Ports: none

Airports: total paved and unpaved 11

The Press: daily newspaper   **Ankakhutiun:** 375013 Yerevan, Gregory the Illuminator Street 15; telephone (8852) 58-18-64

Hayk: 375019 Yerevan, Marshal Baghramyan Street 14; telephone (8852) 56-34-56   circ. 30,000 weekly

Tourism: NA

Diplomatic representation in US:

chief of mission: Ambassador Ruben Shugarian

chancery: Suite 210, 1660 L Street NW, Washington, DC 20036

telephone: [1] (202) 628-5766

FAX: [1] (202) 628-5769

US Diplomatic representation:

chief of mission: Ambassador Harry J. Gilmore

embassy: 18 Gen Bagramian, Yerevan

mailing address: use embassy street address

telephone: [7] (8852) 15-11-44, 52-46-61

FAX: [7] (8852) 15-11-38

Aruba

Capital: Oranjestad   longitude: 70.06 W   latitude: 12.33 N
Government: part of the Dutch realm
   Flag: blue with two narrow horizontal yellow stripes across the lower portion and a red, four-pointed star outlined in white in the upper hoist-side corner
Geography
   Location: Caribbean, island in the Caribbean Sea, north of Venezuela
   Total Area: 193 sq km (74.5 sq mi) slightly larger than Washington, DC
   Boundaries: no land boundaries
   Climate: tropical marine; little seasonal temperature variation
   Temperature (F): High/Low Jan. 89/75, Apr. 94/77, July 96/79, Oct. 94/79
   Average annual precipitation: 20 inches
   Terrain: flat with a few hills; scant vegetation
   Highest point is 50.9 m (167 ft)
   Natural resources: negligible; white sandy beaches
   Natural hazards: lies outside the Caribbean hurricane belt
People
   Population: 65,974 (July 1995 est.)
   Life expectancy at birth: total population 76.56 years
   Nationality: Aruban
   Ethnic division: mixed European/Cribbean Indian 80%
   Religions: Roman Catholic 82%, Protestant 8%, Hindu, Muslim, Confucian, Jewish
   Languages: Dutch (official), Papiamento (a Spanish, Portuguese, Dutch, English dialect), English (widely spoken), Spanish
   Literacy: NA%
Economy
   Imports: food, consumer goods, manufactures, petroleum products, crude oil for refining and re-export

23

Exports: mostly refined petroleum products

Industries: tourism, transshipment facilities, oil refining

Agriculture: poor quality soils and low rainfall limit agriculture activity to the cultivation of aloes, some livestock, and fishing

Currency: 1 Aruban florin (Af) = 100 cents

Aruban florins per US1$ - 1.79

Transportation

Railroads: none

Roads: NA

Ports: Barcadera, Oranjestad, Sint Nicolaas

Airports: 2 paved. The Queen Reina Beatrix international airport is about 2 miles east of Oranjestad

The Press: daily newspapers   **The News:** Italiestraat 5, Oranjestad

telephone (8) 24-725 fax (8) 26-125 circ. 8,300

La Prensa: Bachstraat 6, POB 566 Oranjestad

telephone (8) 21-199   fax (8) 28-634

Tourism: white sandy beaches

Aruba Tourism Authority:

L.C. Smith Blvd 172, Oranjestad

telephone (8) 23-777   fax (8) 34-702

Diplomatic representation in US: none (self-governing part of the Netherlands)

US Diplomatic representation: none (self-governing part of the Netherlands)

Ashmore and Cartier Islands

20 km

Indian   Ocean

Capital: none; administered from Canberra, Australia

longitude: 121.00 E   latitude: 12.05 S

Government: territory of Australia

Geography:

Location: Southeastern Asia, islands in the Indian Ocean, northwest of Australia

Total Area: 5 sq km (1.93 sq mi) about 8.5 times the size of The Mall in Washington, DC

Boundaries: no land boundaries

Climate: tropical

Terrain: low with sand and coral

Highest point is about 2.5 m above sea level

Natural resources: fish

Natural hazards: surrounded by shoals and reefs which can pose maritime hazards

People:

Population: no indigenous inhabitants; there are only seasonal caretakers

Ports: none; offshore anchorage only

Diplomatic representation in US: none (territory of Australia)

US Diplomatic representation: none (territory of Australia)

Atlantic Ocean

Geography

Location: body of water between Africa, Antarctica, and the Western Hemisphere

Area: 82,217,000 sq km (31,743,984 sq mi) slightly less than nine times the size of the US; second-largest of the world's four oceans

Note: includes Baltic Sea, Black Sea, Caribbean Sea, Davis Strait, Denmark Strait, Drake Passage, Gulf of Mexico, Mediterranean Sea, North Sea, Norwegian Sea, Scotia Sea, Weddell Sea, and other tributary water bodies

Climate: tropical cyclones (hurricanes) develop off the coast of Africa near Cape Verde and move westward into the Caribbeans Sea; hurricanes can occur from May to December, but are most frequent from August to November

Terrain: surface usually covered with sea ice in Labrador Sea, Denmark Strait, and Baltic Sea from October to June; clockwise warm water gyre (broad, circular system of currents) in the northern Atlantic, counterclockwise warm water gyre in the southern Atlantic; the ocean floor is dominated by the Mid-Atlantic Ridge, a rugged north-south center line for the entire Atlantic basin; maximum depth is 8,605 meters in the Puerto Rico Trench

Natural resources: oil and gas fields, fish, marine mammals (seals and whales), sand and gravel aggregates, placer deposits, polymetallic nodules, precious stones

Environment

Current issues: endangered marine species include the manatee, seals, sea lions, turtles, and whales; driftnet fishing is exacerbating declining fish stocks and contributing to international disputes; municipal sludge pollution off eastern US, southern Brazil, and eastern Argentina; oil pollution in Caribbean Sea, Gulf of Mexico, Lake Maracaibo, Mediterranean Sea, and North Sea; industrial waste and municipal sewage pollution in Baltic Sea, North Sea, and Mediterranean Sea

Natural hazards: icebergs common in Davis Strait, Denmark Strait, and the northwestern Atlantic Ocean from February to August and have been spotted as far south as Bermuda and the Madeira Islands; icebergs from Antarctica occur in the extreme southern Atlantic Ocean; ships subject to superstructure icing in extreme northern Atlantic from October to May and extreme southern Atlantic from May to October; persistent fog can be a maritime hazard from May to September

Transportation

Ports: Alexandria (Egypt), Algiers (Algeria), Antwerp (Belgium), Barcelona (Spain), Buenos Aires (Argentina), Casablanca (Morocco), Colon (Panama), Copenhagen (Denmark), Dakar (Senegal), Gdansk (Poland), Hamburg (Germany), Helsinki (Finland), Las Palmas (Canary Islands, Spain), Le Havre (France), Lisbon (Portugal), London (UK), Marseille (France), Montevido (Uruguay), Montreal (Canada), Naples (Italy), New Orleans, (US), New York (US), Oran (Algeria), Oslo (Norway), Piraeus (Greece), Rio de Janeiro (Brazil), Rotterdam (Netherlands), Saint Petersburg (Russia, Stockholm (Sweden)

Australia

Capital: Canberra   longitude: 149.08 E   latitude: 35.18 S   elevation: 1,886 ft

Government: federal parliamentary state

Flag: blue with the flag of the UK in the upper hoist-side quadrant and a large seven-pointed star in the lower hoist-side quadrant; the remaining half is a representation of the Southern Cross constellation in white with one small five-pointed star and four, larger, seven-pointed stars

Geography:

Location: Oceania, continent between the Indian Ocean and the South Pacific Ocean

Total Area: 7,686,850 sq km (2,967,893 sq mi) slightly smaller than the US

Boundaries: no land boundaries

Climate: generally arid to semiarid; temperate south and east; tropical in north

Temperature (F): High/Low   Jan. 83/55, Apr. 62/44, July 52/33, Oct. 68/43

Average annual precipitation: 23 inches

Terrain: mostly low plateau with deserts; fertile plain southwest

Highest point is Mt. Kosciusko 2,228 m (7,310 ft)

Natural resources: bauxite, coal, iron ore, copper, tin, silver, uranium, nickel, tungsten, mineral sands, lead, zinc, diamonds, natural gas, petroleum

Natural hazards: cyclones along the coast; severe droughts

People:

Population: 18,322,240 (July 1995 est.)

Life expectancy at birth: total population 77.78 years

Nationality: Australian

Ethnic division: Caucasian 95%, Asian 4%, aboriginal and other 1%

Religions: Anglican 26.1%, Roman Catholic 26%, other Christian 24.3%

Languages: English, native languages

27

Literacy: total population 100%

Economy

Imports: machinery and transport equipment, computers and office machines, crude oil and petroleum products

Exports: coal, gold, meat, wool, alumina, wheat, machinery and transport equipment

Industries: mining, industrial and transportation equipment, food processing, chemicals, steel

Agriculture: world's largest exporter of beef and wool, second largest for mutton, and among the top wheat exporters; major crops - wheat, barley, sugarcane, fruit; livestock - cattle, sheep, poultry

Currency: 1 Australian dollar ($A) = 100 cents
Australian dollars per US1$ - 1.30

Transportation:

Railroads: 40,478 km

Roads: total 837,872 paved and unpaved

Ports: Adelaide, Brisbane, Cairns, Darwin, Devonport, Fremantle, Geelong, Hobart (Tasmania), Launceton (Tasmania), Mackay, Melbourne, Sydney, Townsville

Airports: 480 paved and unpaved. The country is well served by international airlines.

The Press: daily newspapers **The Australian:** News Ltd, 2 Holt Street, Surry Hills 2010 POB 4245 circ. 153,000
telephone (2) 288-3000   fax (2) 280-2282

The Sydney Morning Herald: 235 Jones Street, Broadway, POB 506
telephone (2) 282-2833   fax (2) 282-1640

Tourism: Main attractions are swimming and surfing on the Pacific beaches. Skin diving along the Great Barrier Reef. Alice Springs and Ayers Rock are among the attraction of the interior desert. Australia's unique wildlife.
Note: world's smallest continent but sixth-largest country; population concentrated along the eastern and southern coasts; regular, tropical, invigorating, sea breeze known as "the Doctor" occurs along the west coast in the summer

Australian Tourist Commission: Level 3, 80 Willian Street
Wooloomooloo, Sydney, NSW 2011;
POB 2721, Sydney, NSW 2001
telephone (2) 360-1111   fax (2) 331-6469

28

Diplomatic representation in US:

   chief of mission: Ambassador Donald Eric Russell
   chancery: 1601 Massachusetts Avenue NW, Washington, DC 20036
   telephone: [1] (202) 797-3000
   FAX: [1] (202) 797-3168

US Diplomatic representation:

   chief of mission: Ambassador Edward J Perkins
   embassy: Moonah Place, Yarralumla, Canberra,
            Australian Capital Territory 2600
   mailing address: APO AP 96549
   telephone: [61](6) 270-5000
   FAX: [61] (6) 270-5970

Austria

Capital: Vienna   longitude: 16.22 E   latitude: 48.13 N elevation: 664 ft

Government: federal republic

Flag: three equal horizontal bands of red (top), white, and red

Geography:

   Location: Central Europe, north of Italy

   Total Area: 83,850 sq km (32,374 sq mi) slightly smaller than Maine

   Boundaries: Czech Republic, Germany, Hungary, Italy, Liechtenstein, Slovakia, Slovenia, Switzerland

   Climate: temperate; continental, cloudy; cold winters with frequent rain in lowlands and snow in mountains; cool summers with occasional showers
   Temperature (F): High/Low Jan. 34/25, Apr. 58/42, July 76/60, Oct. 56/44
   Average annual precipitation: 25 inches

   Terrain: in the west and south mostly mountains (Alps); along the eastern and northern margins mostly flat or gently sloping

29

Highest point is Grossglockner 3,797 m (12,457 ft)

Natural resources: iron ore, petroleum, timber, magnesite, aluminum, lead, coal, lignite, copper, hydropower

Natural hazards: NA

People:

Population: 7,986,665 (July 1995 est.)

Life expectancy at birth: total population 76.9 years

Nationality: Austrian

Ethnic division: German 99.4%, Croatian 0.03%

Religions: Roman Catholic 85%, Protestant 6%

Languages: German

Literacy: total population 99%

Economy

Imports: petroleum, foodstuffs, machinery and equipment, vehicles, chemicals, textiles and clothing, pharmaceuticals

Exports: machinery and equipment, iron and steel, lumber, textiles, paper products, chemicals

Industries: food, iron and steel, machines, textiles, chemicals, electrical, paper and pulp, tourism, mining, motor vehicles

Agriculture: grains, fruit, potatoes, sugar beets, sawn wood, cattle, pigs, poultry

Currency: 1 Austrian schilling (S) = 100 groschen

Austrian schilling per US1$ - 10.7

Transportation:

Railroads: 5,624 km

Roads: total 110,000 km paved and unpaved

Ports: Linz, Vienna

Airports: total 55 paved and unpaved. The main international airport is at Schwechat, near Vienna.

The Press: daily newspapers   **Wiener Zeitung:** 1037 Vienna, Rennweg 12A
telephone (1) 79-78-98   fax (1) 79-789-433
Wiener Zeitung, is the oldest daily paper published in the world, founded in 1703. circ. 26,900

Neue Kronen-Zeitung: 1190 Vienna, Muthgrasse 2
telephone (1) 36-010   fax (1) 36-83-85
circ. 580,000 weekdays, Sunday 778,000

Tourism: the country's mountain scenery attracts visitors in both summer and winter. Lake Beusiedler seashore, Danube valley

Note: landlocked; strategic location at the crossroads of central Europe with many easily traversable Alpine passes and valleys; major river is the Danube; population is concentrated on eastern lowlands because of steep slopes, poor soils, and low temperature elsewhere.

> **Osterreich Werbung** (Austrian National Tourist Office)
> 1040 Vienna, Margaretenstr, 1
> telephone (1) 58-866,   fax (1) 588-6620

Diplomatic representation in US:
> *chief of mission:* Ambassador Helmut Tuerk
> *chancery:* 3524 International Court NW, Washington, DC 20008-3035
> *telephone:* [1] (202) 895-6700
> *FAX:* [1] (202) 895-6750

US Diplomatic representation:
> *chief of mission:* Ambassador Swanee G. Hunt
> *embassy:* Boltzmanngasse 16, A-1091, Vienna
> *mailing address:* use embassy street address
> *telephone:* [43] (1) 31-339
> *FAX:* [43] (1) 310-0682

Azerbaijan

150 km

Capitol: Baku   longitude: 16.22 E   latitude: 48.13 N

Government: republic

Flag: three equal horizontal bands of blue (top), red, and green; a crescent and eight-pointed star in white are centered in red band

Geography:

Location: Southwestern Asia, bordering the Caspian Sea, between Iran and Russia

31

Total Area: 86,600 sq km (33,436 sq mi) slightly larger than Maine
Boundaries: Armenia, Georgia, Iran, Russia, Turkey
Climate: dry, semiarid steppe
Temperature: average winter (F) 29 (14 F in the mountains)
average summer 79 F
Average annual precipitation: 10 inches (69 inches on the Caspian coast)
Terrain: large, flat Kur-Araz Lowland (much of it below sea level) with
Great Caucasus Mountains to the north, Qarabag (Karabakh) Upland in west;
Baku lies on Abseron (Apsheron) Peninsula that juts into the Caspian Sea
Highest point is Bazardiuzi Peak 4,466 m (14,652 ft)
Natural resources: petroleum, natural gas, iron ore, nonferrous metals,
alumina
Natural hazards: droughts; some lowland areas threatened by rising levels
of the Caspian Sea

People:

Population: 7,789,890 (July 1995 est.)
Life expectancy at birth: total population 71.09 years
Nationality: Azerbaijani
Ethnic division: Azeri 90%, Dagestani Peoples 3.2%, Russian 2.5%
Armenian 2.3%
Religions: Muslim 93.4%, Russian Orthodox 2.5%,
Armenian Orthodox 2.3%
Languages: Azeri 89%, Russian 3%, Armenian 2%
Literacy: total population 97%

Economy

Imports: machinery and parts, consumer durables, foodstuffs, textiles
Exports: oil and gas, chemicals, oilfield equipment, textiles, cotton
Industries: petroleum and natural gas, petroleum products, oil field equipment;
steel, iron ore, cement; chemicals and petrochemicals; textiles
Agriculture: cotton, grain, rice, grapes, fruit, vegetables, tea, tobacco; cattle, pigs,
sheep and goats
Currency: 1 manat = 100 gopik   manats per US1$ - 4,500
Transportation:

Railroads: 2,090 km in common carrier service
Roads: 36,700 total km paved and unpaved
Ports: Baku
Airports: total 69 paved and unpaved. The major airport is located at Baku
The Press: daily newspaper   **Azadlyg:** (Liberty) Baku, Akademik Sh.
Azizbeyov St 62   circ. 142,000

Tourism: the ancient city of Shaki, Gobustan Museum, which features prehistoric dwellings and cave paintings over 10,000 years old. Khudafarin Bridge, the village of Lahij

Diplomatic representation in US:
> *chief of mission:* Ambassador Hafiz Mir Jalal Pashayev
> *chancery:* (temporary) Suite 700, 927 15th Street NW,
> Washington, DC 20005
> *telephone:* [1] (202) 842-0001
> *FAX:* [1] (202) 842-0004

US Diplomatic representation:
> *chief of mission:* Ambassador Richard D. Kauzlarich
> *embassy:* Azadliq Prospect 83, Baku
> *mailing address:* use embassy street address
> *telephone:* [9] (9412) 96-00-19, 98-03-37
> *FAX:* [9] (9412) 98-37-55

The Bahamas

Capital: Nassau   longitude: 72.20 W   latitude: 25.05 N elevation: 12 ft

Government: commonwealth

> **Flag:** three equal horizontal bands of aquamarine (top), gold, and aquamarine with a black equilateral triangle based on the hoist side

Geography:

> **Location:** Caribbean, chain of islands in the North Atlantic Ocean, southeast of Florida
> **Total Area:** 13,940 sq km (5,382 sq mi) slightly larger than Connecticut
> **Boundaries:** no land boundaries

Climate: tropical marine; moderated by warm waters of Gulf Stream
Temperature (F): High/Low Jan. 77/65, Apr. 81/69, July 88/75, Oct. 85/73
Average annual precipitation: 46 inches
Terrain: long, flat coral formations with some low rounded hills
Highest point is Mt. Alvernia 63m (206 ft)
Natural resources: salt, aragonite, timber
Natural hazards: hurricanes and other tropical storms that cause extensive
flood and wind damage

People:

Population: 256,620 (July 1995 est.)
Life expectancy at birth: total population 72.12 years
Nationality: Bahamian
Ethnic division: black 85%, white 15%
Religions: Baptist 32%, Anglican 20%, Roman Catholic 19%,
Methodist 6%, Church of God 6%
Languages: English, Creole (among Haitian immigrants)
Literacy: total population 90%

Economy

Imports: foodstuffs, manufactured goods, crude oil, vehicles, electronics
Exports: pharmaceuticals, cement, rum, crawfish, refined petroleum
products
Industries: tourism, banking, cement, oil refining and transshipment, salt
production, rum, aragonite, pharmaceuticals, spiral welded steel pipe
Agriculture: citrus fruit, vegetables, poultry
Currency: 1 Bahamian dollar (B$) = 100 cents   Bahamian dollar per US1$ - 1.00
Transportation:

Railroads: none
Roads: 2,400 km total paved and unpaved
Ports: Freeport, Matthew Town, Nassau
Airports: total 60 paved and unpaved. Nassau International Airport and
Freeport International Airport are the main terminals for international and
internal services.
The Press: newspapers   **Nassau Daily Tribune:** Shirly Street, POB N-3011,
Nassau   telephone 322-1986   fax 328-2398   circ. 12,600
Nassau Guardian: 4 Carter Street, Oakes Field,
POB N-3011, Nassau   telephone 323-5654
fax 325-3379   circ. 14,200
Tourism: Mild climate and beautiful beaches attract many tourist. Fishing, scuba
diving and island boat trips

Diplomatic representation in US:
chief of mission: Ambassador Timothy Baswell Donaldson
chancery: 2220 Massachusetts Avenue NW, Washington, DC 20008
telephone: [1] (202) 319-2660   *FAX:* [1] (202) 319-2668
US Diplomatic representation:
chief of mission: Ambassador Sidney Williams
embassy: Mosmar Building, Queen Street, Nassau
mailing address: P O Box N-8197, Nassau
telephone: [1] (809) 322-1181,   328-2206
FAX: [1] (809) 328-7838

Bahrain

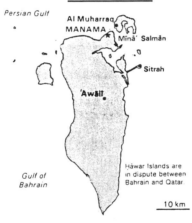

Capital: Manama   longitude: 50.38 E   latitude: 26.12 N elevation: 18 ft
Government: traditional monarchy
Flag: red with a white serrated band (eight white points) on the hoist side
Geography:
Location: Middle East, archipelago in the Persian Gulf, east of Saudi Arabia
Total Area: 620 sq km. (239 sq mi) slightly less than 3.5 times the size of Washington, DC
Boundaries: no land boundaries
Climate: arid; mild, pleasant winters; very hot, humid summers
Temperature (F): High/Low Jan. 68/57, Apr. 84/70, July 95/85, Oct. 90/75
Average annual precipitation: 3.2 inches
Terrain: mostly low plain rising gently to low central escarpment
Natural resources: oil, associated and non associated natural gas, fish

Natural hazards: periodic droughts; dust storms

People:

    Population: 575,930 (July 1995 est.)

    Life expectancy at birth: total population 73.94 years

    Nationality: Bahraini

    Ethnic division: Bahraini 63%, Asian 13%, other Arab 10%, Iranian 8%

    Religions: Shi'a Muslim 70%, Sunni Muslim 30%

    Languages: Arabic, English, Farsi, Urdu

    Literacy: total population 84%

Economy

    Imports: crude oil, foodstuffs, consumer goods, textiles

    Exports: petroleum and petroleum products, aluminum

Industries: petroleum processing and refining, aluminum smelting, offshore banking, ship repairing

Agriculture: fruit, vegetables, poultry, dairy products, shrimp, fish

Currency: 1 Bahraini dinar (BD) = 1,000 fils   Bahraini dinars per US1$ - 0.376

Transportation:

    Railroads: none

    Roads: total 2,670 km paved and unpaved

    Ports: Manama, Mina' Salman, Sitrah

    Airports: 4 total paved and unpaved. Bahrain International Airport is capable of taking the largest aircraft in use.

The Press: daily newspapers   **Akhbar al-Khalij:** (Gulf News) POB 5300, Manama   circ. 22,000
telephone 62-01-11, fax 62-15-66

        Gulf Daily News: POB 5300, Manama,
telephone 62-02-22, fax 62-21-41   circ. 12,000

Tourism: archaeological sites, burial mounds, Portuguese Fort, Bahrain National Museum

        Bahrain Tourism Co: POB 5831, Manama
telephone 53-05-30, fax 53-08-67

Diplomatic representation in US:

    chief of mission: Ambassador Muhammad Abd Al-Ghaffar al-Abdallah

    chancery: 3502 International Drive NW, Washington, DC 20008

    telephone: [1] (202) 342-0741, 342-0742

US Diplomatic representation:

chief of mission: Ambassador David M. Ransom

embassy: Building No. 979, Road 3119 (next to Ahli Sports Club), Zinj District, Manama

mailing address: FPO AE 09834-5100; P O Box 26431 Manama

telephone: [973] 27-33-00; after hours [973] 27-51-26

FAX: [973] 27-25-94

Baker Island

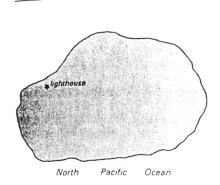

300 m

lighthouse

North   Pacific   Ocean

Capital: none; administered from Washington, DC

longitude: 173.20 W   latitude: 2.00 N

Government: unincorporated territory of the US administrated by the Fish and Wildlife Service of the Department of the Interior as part of the National Wildlife Refuge system

Geography

Location: Oceania, atoll in the North Pacific Ocean, about one-half of the way from Hawaii to Australia

Total Area: 1.4 sq km (0.54 sq mi) about 2.3 times the size of The Mall in Washington, DC

Boundaries: no land boundaries

Climate: equatorial; scant rainfall, constant wind, burning sun

Terrain: low, nearly level coral island surrounded by a narrow fringing reef

Natural resources: guano

Environment

Current issues: no natural fresh water resources

Natural hazards: the narrow fringing reef surrounding the island can be a maritime hazard.

Note: treeless, sparse, and scattered vegetation consisting of grasses, prostrate vines, and low growing shrubs; primarily a nesting, roosting, and foraging habitat for seabirds, shorebirds, and marine wildlife

People

Population: uninhibited; public entry is by special-use permit only and generally restricted to scientist and educators; a cemetery and cemetery ruins are located near the middle of the west coast

Economy

no economic activity

Transportation

Ports: none; offshore anchorage only; note - there is one boat landing area along the middle of the west coast

Airports: 1 abandoned World War II runway of 1,665 m

Note: there is a day beacon near the middle of the west coast

Bangladesh

Capital: Dhaka   longitude: 90.22 E   latitude: 23.42 N   elevation: 26 ft

Government: republic

Flag: green with a large red disk slightly to the hoist side of center; green is the traditional color of Islam

Geography:

Location: Southern Asia, bordering the Bay of Bengal, between Burma and India

Total Area: 144,000 sq km. (55,598 sq mi) slightly smaller than Wisconsin

Boundaries: Burma, India

Climate: tropical; cool, dry winter (October to March); hot, humid summer (March to June); cool, rainy monsoon (June to October)

Temperature (F): High/Low Jan. 77/54, Apr. 95/73, July 88/79, Oct. 88/75

Average annual precipitation: 76 inches

38

Terrain: mostly flat alluvial plain; hilly in southeast
Highest point is Keokradong 1,230 m (4,034 ft)
Natural resources: natural gas, arable land, timber
Natural hazards: droughts, cyclones; much of the country routinely flooded during the summer monsoon season

People:

Population: 128,095,000 (July 1995 est.)
Life expectancy at birth: total population 55.46 years
Nationality: Bangladeshi
Ethnic division: Bengali 98%
Religions: Muslim 83%, Hindu 16%, Buddhist, Christian, other
Languages: Bangla (official), English
Literacy: total population 35%

Economy

Imports: capital goods, petroleum, food, textiles
Exports: garments, jute and jute goods, leather, shrimp
Industries: jute manufacturing, cotton textiles, food processing, steel, fertilizer
Agriculture: jute, rice, wheat, tea, sugarcane, potatoes, beef, milk, poultry
Currency: 1 taka = 100 poiska   taka per US1$ - 40.25

Transportation:

Railroads: 2,892 km
Roads: total 7,240 km paved and unpaved
Ports: Barisal, Chandpur, Chittagong, Cox's Bazar, Dacca, Khulna, Mongla (includes Chalna), Narayanganj
Airports: 16 total paved and unpaved. Zia International Airport is near Dhaka.

The Press: daily newspapers   **Dainik Bangla:** 1 Rajuk Avenue, Dhaka 1000
telephone (2) 86-47-48   circ. 65,000
Dainin Ittefaq: 1 Ramkrishna Road, Dhaka 1203
telephone (2) 25-60-75   circ. 195,000

Tourism: Tourist attractions include the cities of Dhaka, Chittagong and Cox's Bazar which has the worlds longest beach. Sundarbans wildlife reserve

Bangladesh Parjatan Corporation
233 Old Airport Road, Tejgaon, Dhaka 1215
telephone (2) 32-51-55

Diplomatic representation in US:

chief of mission: Ambassador Humayun Kabir
chancery: 2201 Wisconsin Avenue NW, Washington, DC 20007
telephone: [1] (202) 342-8372 through 8376

chief of mission: Ambassador David N. Merrill

embassy: Diplomatic Enclave, Madani Avenue, Baridhara, Dhaka

mailing address: G.P.O. Box 323, Dhaka 1212

telephone: [880] (2) 88-47-00 through 88-47-22

FAX: [880] (2) 88-37-44

Barbados

Capital: Bridgetown longitude: 59.37 W latitude: 13.06 N elevation: 181 ft

Government: parliamentary democracy

Flag: three equal vertical bands of blue (hoist side), yellow, and blue with the head of a black trident centered on the gold band; the trident head represents independence and a break with the past (the colonial coat of arms contained a complete trident)

Geography:

Location: Caribbean, island between the Caribbean Sea and the North Atlantic Ocean, northeast of Venezuela

Total Area: 430 sq km. (166 sq mi) slightly less than 2.5 times the size of Washington, DC

Boundaries: no land boundaries

Climate: tropical; rainy season (June to October)

Temperature (F): High/Low Jan. 83/70, Apr. 86/72, July 86/74, Oct. 86/73

Average annual precipitation: 50 inches

Terrain: relatively flat; rises gently to central highland region

Highest point is Mount Hillaby 340m (1,115 ft)

Natural resources: petroleum, fishing, natural gas

Natural hazards: hurricanes (especially June to October); periodic landslides

People:

Population: 256,400 (July 1995 est.)

Life expectancy at birth: total population 74.16 years

Nationality: Barbadian

Ethnic division: African 80%, European 4%, other 16%

Religions: Protestant 67%, Anglican 40%, Pentecostal 8%, Methodist 7%, Roman Catholic 4%, none 17%

Languages: English

Literacy: total population 99%

Economy

Import: consumer goods, machinery, foodstuffs, construction materials, chemicals, fuel, electrical components

Export: sugar and molasses, rum, other foods and beverages, chemicals, electrical components, clothing

Industries: tourism, sugar, light manufacturing, component assembly for export

Agriculture: sugarcane, vegetables, cotton

Currency: 1 Barbadian dollar (Bds$) = 100 cents

Bardadian dollars per US1$ = 2.01

Transportation:

Railroads: none

Roads: total 1,570 km paved and unpaved

Ports: Bridgetown

Airports: Grantly Adams International Airport, at Seawell, is the one and only airport, located about 18 km from Bridgetown.

The Press: daily newspapers   **Bardados Advocate:** Fontabelle, POB 230, St. Micheal   circ. 15,000
telephone 426-1210 fax 429-7045

Caribbean Week: Lefferts Place, River Road, St. Micheal
telephone 436-1902   fax 436-1904   circ. 60,000

Tourism: Healthy climate, varied scenery and outdoor sports of all kinds, beaches, tropical gardens

Barbados Tourism Authority: Harbour Road, POB 242, Bridgetown. telephone 427-2623   fax 426-4080

Diplomatic representation in US:

chief of mission: Ambassador Courtney Blackman

chancery: 2144 Wyoming Avenue NW, Washington, DC 20008

telephone: [1] (202) 939-9218, 9219

FAX: [1] (202) 332-7467

US Diplomatic representation:

chief of mission: Ambassador Jeanette W. Hyde

embassy: Canadian Imperial Bank of Commerce Building
Broad Street, Bridgetown

mailing address: P.O. Box 302, Bridgetown; FPO AA 34055

telephone: [1] (809) 436-4950

FAX: [1] (809) 429-5246

Bassas da India

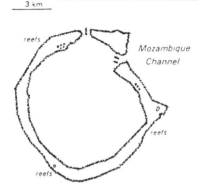

3 km

Capital: none; administered by France from Reunion

longitude: 40.00 E   latitude: 22.00 S

Government: French possession administered by a Commissioner of the Republic, resident in Reunion

Geography

Location: Southern Africa, islands in the southern Mozambique Channel, about one-half of the way from Madagascar to Mozambique

Total Area: 0.2 sq km (.08 sq mi)

Boundaries: no land boundaries

Climate: tropical

Terrain: a volcanic rock 2.4 meters high

Natural resources: none

Environment

Current issues: NA

Natural hazards: maritime hazard since it is usually under water during high tide and surrounded by reefs; subject to periodic cyclones

People

Population: uninhibited

Economy

Overview: no economic activity

Belarus

150 km

Capital: Minsk   longitude: 27.30 E   latitude: 53.51 N elevation: 738 ft

Government: republic

Flag: three horizontal bands of white (top), red, and white

Geography:

Location: Eastern Europe, east of Poland

Total Area: 207,600 sq km (80,154 sq mi) slightly smaller than Kansas

Boundaries: Latvia, Lithuania, Poland, Russia, Ukraine

Climate: cold winters, cool and moist summers; transitional between continental and maritime

Temperature (F): High/Low Jan. 19/8, Apr. 46/33, July 70/48, Oct. 48/39

Average annual precipitation: 28.2 inches

Terrain: generally flat and contains much marshland

Highest point is Mount Dzerzhin 341 m (1,119 ft)

Natural resources: forest land, peat deposits, small quantities of oil and natural gas

Natural hazards: NA

People:

Population: 10,438,000 (July 1995 est.)

Life expectancy at birth: total population 71.03 years

Nationality: Belarusian

Ethnic division: Byelorussian 77.9%, Russian 13.2%, Polish 4.1%, Ukrainian 2.9%

Religions: Eastern Orthodox, other

Languages: Byelorussian, Russian, other

Literacy: total population 97%

Economy

    Imports: fuel, natural gas, industrial raw materials, textiles, sugar

    Exports: machinery and transport equipment, chemicals, foodstuffs

Industries: Trucks, tractors, earthmoving equipment, equipment for animal husbandry and livestock feeding, motorcycles, television sets, chemical fibers, fertilizer, linen fabric, wool fabric, radios, refrigerators

Agriculture: grain, potatoes, vegetables, meat, milk

Currency: Belarusian rubel (BR)   Belarusian rubles per US1$ - 10,600

Transportation:

    Railroads: total 5,570 km

    Roads: total 98,200 km paved and unpaved

    Ports: Mazyr

    Airports: total 118 paved and unpaved

The Press: daily newspapers   **Belorusskaya Niva:**

    220041 Minsk, pr. F. Skariny 77

    telephone (0172) 32-38-95 circ. 150,000 5 days a week

    Sovetskaya Belorossiya: 220041 Minsk, pr F. Skariny 77

    telephone (0172) 32-23-52 circ. 674,000

Tourism: scenic country, especially the wild flowers, straw inlaying handicraft, folklore group of traveling musicians from Minsk "Yanka"

    Belintourist: 220078 Minsk, pr. Masherava 19

    telephone (0172) 26-98-40   fax (0172) 23-11-43

Diplomatic representation in US:

    chief of mission: Ambassador Seergey Nikolayvich Martynov

    chancery: 1619 New Hampshire Avenue NW, Washington, DC 20009

    telephone: [1] (202) 986-1604

    FAX: [1] (202) 986-1805

US Diplomatic representation:

    chief of mission: Ambassador Kenneth Spencer Yalowitz

    embassy: Starovilenskaya # 46, Minsk

    mailing address: use embassy street address

    telephone: [7] (0172) 34-65-37

Belgium

Capital: Brussels   longitude: 4.21 E   latitude: 50.50 N   elevation: 328 ft

Government: constitutional monarchy

Flag: three equal vertical bands of black (hoist side), yellow, and red; the design was based on the flag of France

Geography:

Location: Western Europe, bordering the North Sea, between France and the Netherlands

Total Area: 30,510 sq km (11,779 sq mi) slightly larger than Maryland

Boundaries: France, Germany, Luxembourg, Netherlands

Climate: temperate; mild winters, cool summers; rainy, humid, cloudy
Temperature (F): High/Low Jan. 40/30, Apr. 58/41, July 73/54, Oct. 60/45
Average annual precipitation: 34 inches

Terrain: flat coastal plains in northwest, central rolling hills, rugged mountains of Ardennes Forest in southeast
Highest point is Botrange 694 m (2,277 ft)

Natural resources: coal, natural gas

Natural hazards: flooding is a threat in areas of reclaimed coastal land, protected from the sea by concrete dikes

People:

Population: 10,082,000 (July 1995 est.)

Life expectancy at birth: total population 77.21 years

Nationality: Belgian

Ethnic division: Fleming 55%, Walloon 33%, mixed or other 12%

Religions: Roman Catholic 75%, Protestant 25%

Languages: Dutch 56%, French 32%, German 1%

Literacy: total population 99%

Economy

Imports: fuels, grains, chemicals, foodstuffs

45

Exports: iron and steel, transportation equipment, tractors, diamonds, petroleum products

Industries: engineering and metal products, motor vehicle assembly, processed food and beverage, chemicals, basic metals, textiles, glass, petroleum, coal

Agriculture: beef, veal, pork, milk; major crops are sugar beets, fresh vegetables, fruits, grain, tobacco

Currency: 1 Belgian franc (BF) = 100 centimes   Belgian francs per US1$ - 31.54

Transportation:

Railroads: total 3,410 km

Roads: 137,912 km total paved and unpaved

Ports: Antwerp, Brugge, Gent, Hasselt, Liege, Mons, Namur, Oostende, Zeebrugge

Airports: 43 total paved and unpaved. The main international airport is at Brussels. There are also international airports at Antwerp, Liege, Charleroi and Ostend.

The Press: daily newspapers

De Nieuwe Gazet: 10 Leopoldstraat, 2000 Antwerp   circ. 296,250 telephone (3) 231-9680   fax (3) 234-1666

La Derniere Heure/Les Sports: 127 blvd Emile Jacqmain, 1000 Brussels telephone (2) 211-2888   fax (2) 211-2870

Tourism: The country's seaside attract many visitors, many towns have rich and cultural interest. The Ardennes region is excellent for mountain hiking. North Sea Coast

Tourist Information Brussels: Hotel de Ville, Grand-Place, 1000 Brussels. telephone (2) 513-8940   fax (2) 514-4538

Diplomatic representation in US:

chief of mission: Ambassador Andre Adam

chancery: 3330 Garfield Street NW, Washington, DC 20008

telephone: [1] (202) 333-6900

FAX: [1]1(202) 333-3079

US Diplomatic representation:

chief of mission: Ambassador Alan J. Blinken

embassy: 27 Boulevard du Regent, B-1000 Brussels

mailing address: APO AE 09724; PSC 82, Box 002, Brussels

telephone: [32] (2) 513-3830

FAX: [32] (2) 511-2725

Belize

Capital: Belmopan   longitude: 88.48 W   latitude: 17.13 N
elevation: at Belize City is 17 ft

Government: parliamentary democracy

Flag: blue with a narrow red stripe along the top and bottom edges; centered is a large white disk bearing the coat of arms; the coat of arms features a shield flanked by two workers in front of a mahogany tree with the related motto SUB UMBRA FLOREO (I Flourish in the Shade) on a scroll at the bottom, all encircled by a green garland

Geography:

Location: Middle America, bordering the Caribbean Sea, between Guatemala and Mexico

Total Area: 22,960 sq km (8,864 sq mi) slightly larger than Massachusetts

Boundaries: Guatemala and Mexico

Climate: tropical; very hot and humid; rainy season (May to February)
Temperature (F): High/Low Jan. 81/67, Apr. 86/74, July 87/75, Oct. 86/72
Average annual precipitation: 75 inches

Terrain: flat, swampy coastal plain; low mountains south
Highest point is Victoria Peak 1,122 m (3,681 ft)

Natural resources: arable land potential, timber, fish

Natural hazards: frequent, devastating hurricanes (September to December) and coastal flooding (especially in the south)

People:

Population: 214,100 (July 1995 est.)

Life expectancy at birth: total population 68.32 years

Nationality: Belizean

Ethnic division: mestizo 44%, Creole 30%, Maya 11%, Garifuna 7%

47

Religions: Roman Catholic 62%, Protestant 30%, Anglican 12%
Methodist 6%, Mennonite 4%, Seventh-Day Adventist 3%, Pentecostal 2%,
Jehovah's Witnesses 1%

Languages: English (official), Spanish, Maya, Garifuna (Carib)

Literacy: total population 91%

Economy

Imports: machinery and transportation equipment, food, manufactured
goods, fuels, chemicals, pharmaceuticals

Exports: sugar, citrus fruits, bananas, clothing, fish products, molasses,
wood

Industries: garment production, food processing, tourism, construction

Agriculture: bananas, cocoa, citrus fruits, fish, cultured shrimp, lumber

Currency: 1 Belizian dollar = 100 cents   Belizean dollars per US1$ - 2.00

Transportation:

Railroads: none

Roads: 2,710 km paved and unpaved

Ports: Belize City, Big Creek, Corozol, Punta Gorda

Airports: 46 total paved and unpaved. Philip S.W. Goldson International
Airport is about 14 km from Belize City, and can accommodate
medium-sized jet-engined aircraft.

The Press: weekly newspapers   **Amandala:** Amandala Press, 3304
Partridge Street, POB 15, Belize City
telephone (2) 77-276   fax (2) 75-934 circ. 45,000
The Belize Times: 3 Queen Street, POB 506
Belize City   circ. 6,000
telephone (2) 45-757   fax (2) 31-940

Tourism: The main attractions are the beaches, cays, and barrier reef. The
governments policy is to develop 'eco-tourism', based on unspoiled natural
environment. There are nine major wildlife reserves including the worlds
only reserves for jaguar and the red-footed booby

Belize Tourist Board: 83 North Front Street,
POB 325 Belize City;
telephone (2) 77-213 fax (2) 77-490

Diplomatic representation in US:

chief of mission: Ambassador Dean R. Lindo

chancery: 2535 Massachusetts Avenue NW, Washington, DC 20008

telephone: [1] (202) 332-9636

FAX: [1] (202) 332-6888

US Diplomatic representation:

chief of mission: Ambassador George Charles Bruno

embassy: Gabourel Lane and Hutson Street, Belize

mailing address: P.O. Box 286, Belize City;

APO: Unit 7401, APO AA 34025

telephone: [501] (2) 77-161 through 77-163

FAX: [501] (2) 30-802

Benin

Capital: Porto-Novo   longitude: 2.47 E   latitude: 6.30 N   elevation: 23 ft

Government: multiparty system

Flag: two equal horizontal bands of yellow (top) and red with a vertical green band on the hoist side

Geography:

Location: Western Africa, bordering the North Atlantic Ocean, between Nigeria and Togo

Total Area: 112,620 sq km (43,483 sq mi) slightly smaller than Pennsylvania

Boundaries: Burkina Faso, Niger, Nigeria, Togo

Climate: tropical; hot, humid in south; semiarid in north

Temperature (F): High/Low Jan. 80/74, Apr. 83/78, July 78/74, Oct. 80/75

Average annual precipitation: 52 inches

Terrain: mostly flat to undulating plain; some hills and low mountains

Highest point is Atakora Mountains 635 m (2,083 ft)

Natural resources: small offshore oil deposits, limestone, marble, timber

Natural hazards: hot, dry, dusty harmattan wind may affect north in winter

People:

Population: 5,522,680 (July 1995 est.)

Life expectancy at birth: total population 52.24 years

Nationality: Beninese

Ethnic division: African 99% (42 ethnic groups, most important being Fon, Adja, Yoruba, Bariba) Europeans 5,500

Religions: indigenous beliefs 70%, Muslim 15%, Christian 15%

Languages: French (official), Fon and Yoruba (most common vernaculars in south), at least six major tribal languages in north

Literacy: total population 23%

Economy

Imports: foodstuffs, beverages, tobacco, petroleum products, intermediate goods, capital goods, light consumer goods

Exports: cotton, crude oil, palm products, cocoa

Industries: textiles, cigarettes, construction material, beverages, food, petroleum

Agriculture: food crops: corn, sorghum, cassava, yams, beans, rice; cash crops include cotton, palm oil, peanuts, poultry and livestock

Currency: 1 CFA franc (CFAF) = 100 centimes

Communaute Financiere Africaine francs per US1$ - 529.43

Transportation:

Railroads: 578 km

Roads: total 8,435 km total paved and unpaved

Ports: Cotonou, Porto-Novo

Airports: 7 total paved and unpaved. The International Airport is at Cotonou

The Press: newspapers   **La Gazette du Golfe:** Carre 961 'J' Etoile Rouge, BP 03-1624, Cotonou

circ. national edition 18,000, international edition 15,000

telephone 31-35-58   fax 30-01-99

Tam-Tam-Express: BP 2302, Cotonou

telephone and fax 30-12-05   circ. 15,000

Tourism: National parks and game reserves, Royal Palace in Abomey, boat tours to Ganvie fishing villages

Conseil National du Tourisme: Cotonou

Diplomatic representation in US:

chief of mission: Ambassador Lucien Edgar Tonoukouin

chancery: 2737 Cathedral Avenue NW, Washington, DC   20008

telephone: [1] (202) 232-6656, 6657, 6658

FAX: [1] (202) 265-1996

US Diplomatic representation:

chief of mission: Ambassador Ruth A. Davis

embassy: Rue Caporal Bernard Anani, Cotonou

mailing address: B.P. 2012, Cotonou

telephone: [229] 30-06-50, 30-05-13, 30-17-92

FAX: [229] 41-15-22

Bermuda

Capital: Hamilton   longitude: 64.48 W   latitude: 32.18 N   elevation: 151 ft

Government: dependent territory of the UK

Flag: red with the flag of the UK in the upper hoist-side quadrant and the Bermudian coat of arms (white and blue shield with a red lion holding a scrolled shield showing the sinking of the ship Sea Venture off Bermuda in 1609) centered on the outer half of the flag

Geography

Location: North America, group of islands in the North Atlantic Ocean, east of North Carolina (US)

Total Area: 50 sq km (19.3 sq mi) about 0.3 times the size of Washington, DC

Boundaries: no land boundaries

Climate: subtropical; mild, humid; gales, strong winds common in winter Temperature (F): High/Low Jan. 68/58, Apr. 71/59, July 85/73, Oct. 79/69 Average annual precipitation: 58 inches

Terrain: low hills separated by fertile depressions

Natural resources: limestone, pleasant climate fostering tourism

Natural hazards: hurricanes (June to November)

People

Population: 62,200 (July 1995 est.)

Life expectancy at birth: total population 75.03 years

51

Nationality: Bermudian

Ethnic division: black 61%, white and others 39%

Religions: Anglican 37%, Roman Catholic 14%, African Methodist Episcopal (Zion) 10%, Methodist 6%, Seventh-Day Adventist 5%, other 28%

Languages: English

Literacy: total population 98%

Economy

Bermuda enjoys one of the highest per capita incomes in the world, having successfully exploited its location by providing luxury tourist facilities and financial services.

Imports: fuel, foodstuffs, machinery

Exports: semitropical produce, light manufactures, re-export of pharmaceuticals

Industries: tourism, finance, structural concrete products, paints, pharmaceuticals, ship repairing

Agriculture: most basic foods must be imported; produces bananas, vegetables, citrus fruits, flowers, dairy products

Currency: 1 Bermudian dollar (Bd$) = 100 cents

Bermudian dollar per US1$ - 1.00

Transportation

Railroads: none

Roads: total 210 km paved and unpaved

Ports: Hamilton, Saint George

Airports: 1 with paved runway

The Press: newspapers   **Burmuda Sun**

Royal Gazette

Tourism: Island consists mainly of limestone formed by seashells and coral. High rocks along the shore sculptured by wind and water. Fortresses in St George

Diplomatic representation in US: none (dependent territory of the UK)

US Diplomatic representation:

chief of mission: Ambassador Robert A. Farmer

consulate general: Crown Hill, 16 Middle Road, Devonshire, Hamilton

mailing address: P O Box HM325, Hamilton HMBX; PSC 1002,
FPO AE 09727-1002

telephone: [1] (809) 295-1342

Bhutan

75 km

Capital: Thimphu   longitude: 89.45 E   latitude: 27.32 N   elevation 4,388 ft

Government: monarchy; special treaty relationship with India

Flag: divided diagonally from the lower hoist side corner; the upper triangle is orange and the lower triangle is red; centered along the dividing line is a large black and white dragon facing away from the hoist side

Geography:

Location: Southern Asia, between China and India

Total Area: 47,000 sq km (18,147 sq mi) slightly more than half the size of Indiana

Boundaries: China, India

Climate: varies; tropical in southern plains; cool winters and hot summers in central valleys; severe winters and cool summers in Himalays

Temperature (F): High/Low Jan. 65/35, Apr. 83/53, July 84/68, Oct. 80/56

Average annual precipitation: 56 inches

Terrain: mostly mountainous with some fertile valleys and savanna

Highest point is Kula Kangri 7,554 m (24,784 ft)

Natural resources: timber, hydropower, gypsum, calcium carbide

Natural hazards: violent storms coming down from the Himalayas are the source of the country's name which translates as Land of the Thunder Dragon; frequent landslides during the rainy season

Note: Bhutan is a small land-locked Himalayan nation with a monarchy. It is a protectorate of India.

People:

Population: 1,780,640 (July 1995 est.)

Life expectancy at birth: total population 51.03 years

Nationality: Bhutanese

Ethnic division: Bhote 50%, ethnic Nepalese 35%, indigenous or migrant tribes 15%

Religions: Lamaistic Buddhism 75%, Indian and Nepalese-influenced Hinduism 25%

Languages: Dzongkha (official) Bhotes speak various Tibetan dialects; Nepalese speak various Nepalese dialects

Literacy: NA

Economy

Import: fuel and lubricants, grain, machinery and parts, vehicles, fabrics, rice

Export: cardamom, gypsum, timber, handicrafts, cement, fruit, electricity (to India), precious stones, spices

Industries: cement, wood products, processed fruits, alcoholic beverages, calcium carbide

Agriculture: rice, corn, root crops, citrus fruit, dairy products, food grains, eggs

Currency: 1 ngultrum (Nu) - 100 chetrum; note - Indian currency is also legal tender.   Ngultrum per US1$ - 31,37

Transportation:

Railroads: none

Roads: 2,165 km paved and unpaved

Ports: none

Airports: There are two airports, The International Airport at Paro is paved, the other is unpaved

The Press: weekly newspaper   **Kuensel Corporation:** POB 204, Thimphu
telephone 23-043   fax 22-975
circ. 680 (Nepali), 8,400 (English), 3,000 (Dzongkha)

Tourism: fortified monasteries, museums, temples, handicraft centers

Tourism Authority of Bhutan; Ministry of Communications, Thimphu
telephone 23-252, fax 23-695

Diplomatic representation in US:

Bhutan has no embassy in the US, but does have a Permanent Mission to the UN, headed by Ugyen Taering, located at 2 United Nations Plaza, 7th Floor, New York, NY 10017, telephone [1] (212) 826-1919.

US Diplomatic representation:

No formal diplomatic relations, although informal contact is maintained between Bhutanese and US Embassy in New Delhi (India)

Bolivia

Capital: La Paz (seat of government)   longitude: 68.10 W
Sucre (legal capital and seat of judiciary)   latitude: 16.30 S
elevation: 12,001 ft (3,658 m) * See tourism note

Government: republic

    Flag: three horizontal bands of red (top), yellow, and green with the coat of arms centered on the yellow band; similar to the flag of Ghana, which has a large black five-pointed star centered in the yellow band

Geography:

    Location: Central South America, southwest of Brazil

    Total Area: 1,098,580 sq km (424,162 sq mi) slightly less than three times the size of Montana

    Boundaries: Argentina, Brazil, Chile, Paraguay, Peru

    Climate: varies with altitude; humid and tropical to cold and semiarid
Temperature (F): High/Low Jan. 63/43, Apr. 65/40, July 62/33, Oct. 66/40
Average annual precipitation: 22.6 inches

    Terrain: rugged Andes Mountains with a highland plateau (Altiplano), hills, lowland plains of the Amazon Basin
Highest point is Nevada Ancohuma 6,550 m (21,489 ft)

    Natural resources: tin, natural gas, petroleum, zinc, tungsten, antimony, silver, iron, lead, gold, timber

    Natural hazards: cold, thin air of high plateau is obstacle to efficient fuel combustion, as well as to physical activity by those unaccustomed to it from birth; flooding in the northeast (March to April)

People:

    Population: 7,896,254 (July 1995 est.)
    Life expectancy at birth: total population 63.85 years
    Nationality: Bolivian

Ethnic division: Quechua 30%, Aymara 25%, mestizo (mixed European and Indian ancestry) 25%-30%, European 5%-15%

Religions: Roman Catholic 95% Protestant (Evangelical Methodist)

Languages: Spanish (official), Quechua (official), Aymara (official)

Literacy: total population 80%

Economy

Imports: capital goods, chemicals, petroleum, food

Exports: metals, natural gas, soybeans, jewelry, wood

Industries: mining, smelting, petroleum, food and beverages, tobacco, handicrafts, clothing

Agriculture: coffee, cocoa, cotton, corn, sugarcane, rice, potatoes, timber

Currency: 1 boliviano ($B) = 100 centavos   bolivianos per US1$ - 4.72

Transportation:

Railroads: 3,684 km

Roads: total 42,815 km paved and unpaved

Ports: none; however, Bolivia has free port privileges in the maritime ports of Argentina, Brazil, Chile, and Paraguay

Airports: 1,382 total paved and unpaved. There are two international airports, one at La Paz and the other at Santa Cruz.

The Press:　　　**El Diario:** Calle Loayza 118, Casilla 5, La Paz
　　　　　　telephone (2) 39-09-00   fax (2) 36-38-46   circ. 55,000
　　　　Presencia: Avda Mariscal Santa Cruz 1295, Casilla 3276, La Paz
　　　　　　telephone (2) 37-23-44   fax (2) 39-10-40

Tourism: The Andes peaks include Chacaltaya, which has the highest ski-run in the world. There are pre-Incan ruins at Tiwanaku. Excellent lake fishing.

Direccion Nacional de Turismo:
Calle Mercado 1328, Casilla 1868, La Paz
telephone (2) 36-74-63   fax (2) 37-46-30

Note: Atmospheric pressure is about two-thirds that at sea level. Reduced pressure causes problems for visitors who suffer from mountain sickness. Acclimation takes a few days to a week. This area not recommend for those who suffer from weak heart or lung complaints

Diplomatic representation in US:

chief of mission: Ambassador Andres Petricevic Raznatovic

chancery: 3014 Massachusetts Avenue NW, Washington, DC 20008

telephone: [1] (202) 483-4410 through 4412

FAX: [1] (202) 328-3712

US Diplomatic representation:
chief of mission: Ambassador Curt Warren Kamman
embassy: Avenida Arce 2780, San Jorge, La Paz
mailing address: P.O. Box 425, La Paz; APO AA 34032
telephone: [591] (2) 43-02-51
FAX: [591] (2) 43-39-00

Bosnia and Herzegovina

Capital: Sarajevo   longitude: 18.26 E   latitude: 43.52 N

Government: emerging democracy. The Federation of Bosnia and Herzegovina, formed by Muslims and Croats in March 1994, remains in the implementation stages.

Flag: white with a large blue shield; the shield contains white Roman crosses with a white diagonal band running from the upper hoist corner to the lower fly side

Geography:

Location: Southeastern Europe, bordering the Adriatic Sea and Croatia

Total Area: 51,233 sq km (19,781 sq mi) slightly larger than Tennessee

Boundaries: Croatia, Serbia, Montenegro

Climate: hot summers and cold winters; areas of high elevation have short, cool summers and long, severe winters; mild, rainy winters along the coast
Temperature (F): High/Low Jan. 37/26, Apr. 64/45, July 83/62, Oct. 64/47

Terrain: mountains and valleys

Natural resources: coal, iron, bauxite, manganese, timber, wood products, copper, chromium, lead, zinc

Natural hazards: frequent and destructive earthquakes

People:

Population: 3,201,825 (July 1995 est.)

Life expectancy at birth: total population 75.47 years

Nationality: Bosnian, Herzegovian

Ethnic division: Muslim 38%, Serb 40%, Croat 22%

Religions: Muslim 40%, Orthodox 31%, Catholic 15%, Protestant 4%

Languages: Serbo-Croatian 99%

Literacy: NA

Economy

Imports: NA

Exports: NA

Industries: steel production, mining (coal, iron ore, lead, zinc, manganese, bauxite) manufacturing (vehicle assembly, textiles, tobacco products, wooden furniture, domestic appliances) oil refining

Agriculture: regularly produces less than 50% of food needs; the foothills of northern Bosnia support orchards, vineyards, livestock, and some wheat and corn; long winters and heavy precipitation leach soil fertility reducing agricultural output in the mountains

Currency: 1 dinar = 100 para; Croatian dinar used in Croat-held area, presumably to be replaced by the new Croatian kuna; old and new Serbian dinars used in Serb-held area; hard currencies probably supplanting local currencies in areas held by Bosnian government.

Transportation:

Railroads: 1,021 km

Roads: 21,168 paved and unpaved

Ports: Bosanski Brod

Airports: 27 total paved and unpaved. The international airport is at Sarajevo.

The Press: daily newspapers

Oslobodjenje: 71000 Sarajevo, Dzemala Bijedica 185.

telephone (71) 45-41-44   circ. 49,800

Vecernje novine: 71000 Sarajevo, Borise Goranina 13

telephone (71) 51-84-97, fax (71) 27-18-79

Tourism: NA

Diplomatic representation in US:

chief of mission: Ambassador Sven Alkalaj

chancery: Suite 760, 1707 L Street NW, Washington, DC 20036

telephone: [1] (202) 833-3612, 3613, 3615

FAX: [1] (202) 833-2061

US Diplomatic representation:

chief of mission: Ambassador Victor Jackovich

embassy: address NA

mailing address: American Embassy Bosnia, c/o AmEmbassy Vienna
Boltzmangasse 16, A-1091, Vienna, Austria; APO: (Bosnia) Vienna,
Department of State, Washington, DC 20521-9900

telephone: [43] (1) 31-339

FAX: [43] (1) 310-0682

Botswana

Capital: Gaborone   longitude: 25.25 E   latitude: 24.45 S
elevation: at Francistown is 3,294 ft. (long. 27.30 E   lat. 21.13 S)

Government: parliamentary republic

Flag: light blue with a horizontal white-edged black stripe in the center

Geography:

Location: Southern Africa, north of South Africa

Total Area: 600,370 sq km (231,803 sq mi) slightly smaller than Texas

Boundaries: Namibia, South Africa, Zimbabwe

Climate: semiarid; warm winters and hot summers.
Temperature (F): High/Low Jan. 88/65, Apr. 83/56, July 75/41, Oct. 90/61
Average annual precipitation: 17.6 inches

Terrain: predominately flat to gently rolling tableland; Kalahari Desert in
southwest. Average elevation 1,000 m (3,281 ft)

Natural resources: diamonds, copper, nickel, salt, soda ash, potash, coal,
iron ore, silver

Natural hazards: periodic droughts; seasonal August winds blow from the
west, carrying sand and dust across the country, which can obscure visibility

People:

Population: 1,392,414 (July 1995 est.)

59

Life expectancy at birth: total population 63.56 years

Nationality: Motswana (Singular) Batswana (plural)

Ethnic division: Batswana 95%, Kalanga, Basarwa, and Kgalagadi 4%, white 1%

Religions: indigenous beliefs 50%, Christian 50%

Languages: English (official), Setswana

Literacy: total population 23%

Economy

Imports: foodstuffs, vehicles and transport equipment, textiles, petroleum products

Exports: diamonds, copper and nickel, meat

Industries: mining of diamonds. copper, nickel, coal, salt, soda ash, potash, live stock processing

Agriculture: sorghum, maize, millet, pulses, groundnuts, beans, cowpeas, sunflower seeds, livestock

Currency: 1 pula (P) = 100 thebe   pula per US1$ - 1.70

Transportation:

Railroads: 888 km

Roads: total 11,514 km paved and unpaved

Ports: none

Airports: total 100 paved and unpaved. The main international airport is at Gaborone.

The Press: daily newspaper

Dikgang tsa Gompieno: Private Bag 0060, Gaborone.

telephone 35-25-41   circ. 40,000

Department of information and Broadcasting; Setswana and English

Tourism: There are five game reserves and three national parks including Chobe, near Victoria Falls. Okavango swamps

Tourism Development Unit,
Ministry of Commerce and Industry
Private Bag 004, Gaborone.
telephone 35-30-24, fax 37-15-39

Diplomatic representation in US:

chief of mission: Ambassador Botsweletse Kingsley Sebele

chancery: Suite 7M, 3400 International Drive NW, Washington, DC 20008

telephone: [1] (202) 244-4990, 4991

FAX: [1] (202) 244-4164

US Diplomatic representation:

chief of mission: Ambassador Howard F. Jeter

embassy: no address available

mailing address: P.O. Box 90, Gaborone

telephone: [267] 35-39-82

FAX: [267] 35-69-47

— 2 km — **Bouvet Island**

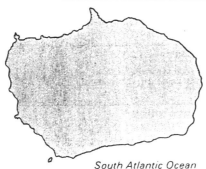

South Atlantic Ocean

Capital: none; administered from Oslo, Norway

longitude: 3.00 E   latitude: 55.00 S

Government: territory of Norway

Geography

Location: Southern Africa, island in the South Atlantic Ocean, south-southwest of the Cape of Good Hope (South Africa)

Total Area: 58 sq km (23 sq mi) about 0.3 times the size of Washington, DC

Boundaries: no land boundaries

Climate: antarctic

Terrain: volcanic; maximum elevation about 800 meters; coast is mostly inaccessible

Natural resources: none

Natural hazards: NA

Note: covered by Glacial ice

People

Population: uninhabited

Economy

no economic activity

Transportation

Ports: none; offshore anchorage only

61

Brazil

Capitol: Brasilia   longitude: 47.55 W   latitude: 15.45 S
elevation: 853 ft at Parana (long. 48.06 W, lat. 12.26 S)

Government: federal republic

    Flag: green with a large yellow diamond in the center bearing a blue celestial globe with 27 white five-pointed stars (one for each state and the Federal District) arranged in the same pattern as the night sky over Brazil; the globe has a white equatorial band with the motto ORDEM E PROGRESSO (Order of Progress)

Geography:

    Location: Eastern South America, bordering the Atlantic Ocean
    Total Area: 8,511,965 sq km (3,286,470 sq mi) slightly smaller than the US
    Boundaries: Argentina, Bolivia, Columbia, French Guiana, Guyana, Paraguay, Peru, Suriname, Uruguay, Venezuela
    Climate: mostly tropical, but temperate south
    Temperature (F): High/Low Jan. 84/73, Apr. 80/69, July 75/63, Oct. 72.66
    Average annual precipitation: 62.2 inches
    Terrain: mostly flat to rolling lowlands north; some plains, hills, mountains, and narrow coastal belt
    Highest point is Pico da Neblina 3,014 m (9,889 ft)
    Natural resources: bauxite, gold, iron ore, manganese, nickel, phosphates, platinum, tin, uranium, petroleum, hydropower, timber
    Natural hazards: recurring droughts in northeast; floods and occasional frost in south

People:

    Population: 160,737,489 (July 1995 est.)
    Life expectancy at birth: total population 61.82 years
    Nationality: Brazilian

Ethnic division: Caucasian (includes Portuguese, German, Italian, Spanish, Polish) 55%, mixed Caucasian and African 38%, African 6%, other (includes Japanese, Arab, Amerindian) 1%

Religions: Roman Catholic (nominal) 70%

Languages: Portuguese (official), Spanish, English, French

Literacy: total population 80%

Economy

Imports: crude oil, capital goods, chemical products, foodstuffs, coal

Exports: iron ore, soybean bran, orange juice, footwear, coffee, motor vehicle parts

Industries: textiles, shoes, chemicals, cement, lumber, mining (iron ore, tin), steel making, machine building - including aircraft, motor vehicles, motor vehicle parts and assemblies, and other machinery and equipment

Agriculture: world largest producer and exporter of coffee and orange juice concentrates and second-largest exporter of soybeans; other products - rice, corn, sugarcane, cocoa, beef, some wheat

Currency: 1 real (R$) = 100 centavos   real per US1$ - 0.85

Transportation:

Railroads: 30,612 km

Roads: total 1,670,148 km paved and unpaved

Ports: Belem, Fortaleza, Ilheus, Imbituba, Manaus, Paranagua, Porto Alegre, Recife, Rio de Janeiro, Rio Grande, Salvador, Santos, Vitoria

Airports: 3,467 total paved and unpaved. 21 are international, although most international traffic is handled by two airports in Rio de Janeiro and two in Sao Paulo

The Press: daily newspapers **Dairio da Trade:** Rua Goias 36
30190 Belo Horizonte, Mg   circ. 150,000 evenings
telephone (31) 273-2322   fax (31) 273-4400

Zero Hora: Av. Ipiranga 1075, 90160-093 Porto Alegre, RS
telephone (51) 223-4400   fax (51) 229-5848
circ. 120 weekdays, 250,000 sundays

Tourism: Rio de Janerio with its famous beaches, is the center of tourist attractions. Other attractions are the tropical forests of the Amazon basin, the wildlife of the Pantanal, and the great Iguacu Falls

Centro Brasileiro de Informacao Turistica: Rua Mariz e Barros 13
6 andar, Praca da Bandeira, 20270 Rio de Janeiro, RJ
telephone (21) 293-1313   fax (21) 273-9290

Diplomatic representation in US:

    chief of mission: Ambassador Paulo Tarso Flecha de Lima

    chancery: 3006 Massachusetts Avenue NW, Washington, DC 20008

    telephone: [1] (202) 745-2700

    FAX: [1] (202) 745-2827

US Diplomatic representation:

    chief of mission: Ambassador Melvin Levitsky

    embassy: Avenida das Nacoes, Lote 3, Brasilia, Distrito Federal

    mailing address: Unit 3500; APO AA 34030

    telephone: [55] (61) 321-7272

    FAX: [55] (61) 225-9136

British Indian Ocean Territory

Capital: none   longitude: 39.50 E   latitude: 21.30 S

Government: dependent territory of the UK

    Flag: white with the flag of the UK in the upper hoist-side quadrant and six blue wavy horizontal strips bearing a palm tree and yellow crown centered on the outer half of the flag

Geography

    Location: Southern Asia, archipelago in the Indian Ocean, about one-half way from Africa to Indonesia

    Total Area: 60 sq km (23 sq mi) about 0.3 time the size of Washington, DC

    Boundaries: no land boundaries

    Climate: tropical marine; hot, humid, moderated by trade winds

    Terrain: flat and low (up to 4 meters in elevation)

    Natural resources: coconuts, fish

    Natural hazards: NA

Note: archipelago of 2,300 islands; Diego Garcia, largest and southernmost island, occupies strategic location in central Indian Ocean; island is site of joint US-UK military facility

People

Population: no indigenous inhabitants

Economy

There are no industrial or agricultural activities on the islands

Transportation

Roads: short stretch of paved road between port and airfield on Diego Garica

Ports: Diego Garcia

Airports: 1 with paved runway

Diplomatic representation in US: none (dependent territory of the UK)

US Diplomatic representation: none (dependent territory of the UK)

British Virgin Islands

Capital: Road Town   longitude: 64.37 W   latitude: 18.27 N

Government: dependent territory of UK

Flag: blue with the flag of the UK in the upper hoist-side quadrant and the Virgin Islander coat of arms centered in the outer half of the flag; the coat of arms depicts a woman flanked on either side by a vertical column of six oil lamps above a scroll bearing the Latin word VIGILATE (Be Watchful)

Geography

Location: Caribbean, between the Caribbean Sea and the North Atlantic Ocean, east of Puerto Rico

Total Area: 150 sq km (58 sq mi) about 0.8 times the size of Washington, DC

Boundaries: no land boundaries

Climate: subtropical; humid; temperatures moderated by trade winds

Temperature (F): High/Low Jan. 78/75, Apr. 81/77, July 83/81, Oct. 83/79
Average annual precipitation: 39 inches
Terrain: coral islands relatively flat; volcanic islands steep, hilly
Highest point is Sage Mountain 543 m (1,781 ft)
Natural resources: negligible
Natural hazards: hurricanes and tropical storms (July to October)

People

Population: 13,027 (July 1995 est.)
Life expectancy at birth: total population 72.73 years
Nationality: British Virgin Islander
Ethnic division: black 90%, white, Asian
Religions: Protestant 86%, (Methodist 45%, Anglican 21%, Church of God 7%, Seventh-Day Adventist 5%, Baptist 4%, Jehovah's Witnesses 2%, other 2%) Roman Catholic 6%, none 2%, other 6%
Languages: English (official)
Literacy: 98% total population

Economy

Imports: building materials, automobiles, foodstuffs, machinery
Exports: rum, fresh fish, gravel, sand, fruits, animals
Industries: tourism, light industry, construction, rum, concrete block, offshore financial center
Agriculture: livestock (including poultry), fish, fruit, vegetables
Currency: 1 United States dollar (US$) = 100 cents
US currency is used

Transportation

Railroads: none
Roads: 106 km total paved and unpaved
Ports: Road Town
Airports: 3 total paved and unpaved. The main airport is Beef Island, about 10 miles from Road Town

The Press: weekly newspapers   **The Island Sun:** POB 21, Road Town, Tortola
telephone 42-476   fax 44-540   circ. 2,600
The BVI Beacon: POB 3030, Road Town, Tortola
telephone 43-767   fax 46-267   circ. 3,000

Tourism: water sports; sailing, diving, fishing
British Virgin Islands Tourist Board
Waterfront Drive, POB 134, Road Town
Tortola   telephone 43-134   fax 43-866

Diplomatic representation in US: none (dependent territory of the UK)
US Diplomatic representation: none (dependent territory of the UK)

Brunei

25 km

Capital: Bandar Seri Begawan   longitude: 114.58 E   latitude: 4.56 N
Elevation: 10 ft

Government: constitutional sultanate

Flag: yellow with two diagonal bands of white (top, almost double width) and black starting from the upper hoist side; the national emblem in red is superimposed at the center; the emblem includes a swallow-tailed flag on top of a winged column within an upturned crescent above a scroll and flanked by two upraised hands

Geography:

Location: Southeastern Asia, bordering the South China Sea and Malaysia
Total Area: 5,770 sq km (2,228 sq mi) slightly larger than Delaware
Boundaries: Malaysia
Climate: tropical; hot, humid, rainy
Temperature (F): High/Low   Jan. 86/76, Apr. 89/76, July 88/77, Oct. 87/76
Average annual precipitation: 131 inches
Terrain: flat coastal plain rises to mountains in east; hilly lowland in west
Highest point is Pagom 1,850 m (6,070 ft)
Natural resources: petroleum, natural gas, timber
Natural hazards: typhoons, earthquakes, and severe flooding are very rare

People:

Population: 292,266 (July 1995 est.)
Life expectancy at birth: total population 71.24 years
Nationality: Bruneian
Ethnic division: Malay 64%, Chinese 20%, other 16%

Religions: Muslim (official) 63%, Buddhism 14%, Christian 8%, indigenous beliefs and others 15%

Languages: Malay (official), English, Chinese

Literacy: total population 88%

Economy

Imports: machinery and transport equipment, manufactured goods, food, chemicals

Exports: crude oil, liquefied natural gas, petroleum products

Industries: petroleum, petroleum refining, liquefied natural gas, construction

Agriculture: principal crops and livestock include rice, cassava, bananas, buffaloes, and pigs

Currency: 1 Bruneian dollar (B$) = 100 cents   Burneian dollars per US1$ - 1.45

Transportation:

Railroads: 13 km private line

Roads: 1,090 km total paved and unpaved

Ports: Bandar Seri Begawan, Kuala Belait, Muara, Seria, Tutong

Airports: 5 total paved and unpaved. There is an international airport near Bandar Seri Begawan

The Press: newspapers   **Borneo Bulletin:** 74 Jalan Sungei, POB 69, Kuala Belait 6000   circ. 30,000
telephone (3) 33-43-44,   fax (3) 33-44-00

Pelita Brunei: Department of Information, Prime Minister's Office, Istana Nurul Iman, Bandar Seri Begawan 1100
fax (2) 22-59-42 weekly government newspaper; distributed free. circ. 45,000

Tourism: Sultan Omar Ali Saifuddin Mosque, Churchill Memorial Museum, Hassanal Balkiah Aquarium

Information Bureau: **Department of Information**
Prime Minister's Office, Bandar Seri Begawan 2041;
telephone (2) 24-04-00   fax (2) 24-41-04

Diplomatic representation in US:

chief of mission: Ambassador Haji Jaya bin Abdul Latif

chancery: Watergate, Suite 300, 3rd floor, 2600 Virginia Avenue, Washington, DC 20037

telephone: [1] (202) 342-0159

FAX: [1] (202) 342-0158

US Diplomatic representation:
chief of mission: Ambassador Theresa A. Tull
embassy: Third Floor, Teck Guan Plaza, Jalan Sultan, Banar Seri Begawan
mailing address: American Embassy Box B, APO AP 96440
telephone: [673] (2) 22-96-70
FAX: [673] (2) 22-52-93

Bulgaria

Capital: Sofia   longitude: 23.18 E   latitude: 42.40 N elevation: 1,805 ft
Government: emerging democracy
Flag: three equal horizontal bands of white (top), green, and red; the national emblem formerly on the hoist side of the white stripe has been removed - it contained a rampant lion within a wreath of wheat ears below a red five-pointed star and above a ribbon bearing the dates 681 (first Bulgarian state established) and 1944 (liberation from Nazi control)

Geography:

Location: Southeastern Europe, bordering the Black Sea, between Romania and Turkey
Total Area: 110,910 sq km (42,822 sq mi) slightly larger than Tennessee
Boundaries: Greece, The Former Yugoslav Republic of Macedonia, Romania, Serbia and Montenegro (all with Serbia), Turkey
Climate: temperate; cold, damp winters; hot dry summers
Temperature (F): High/Low Jan. 35/25, Apr. 60/42, July 81/60, Oct. 63/46
Average annual precipitation: 28 inches
Terrain: mostly mountains with lowlands in north and southeast
Highest point is Mount Musala 2,925 m (9,596 ft)
Natural resources: bauxite, copper, lead, zinc, coal, timber, arable land
Natural hazards: earthquakes, landslides

People:

Population: 8,775,198 (July 1995 est.)

Life expectancy at birth: total population 73.68 years

Nationality: Bulgarian

Ethnic division: Bulgarian 85.3%, Turk 8.5%, Gypsy 2.6%, Macedonian 2.5%, Armenian 0.3%, Russian 0.2%

Religions: Bulgarian Orthodox 85%, Muslim 13%, Jewish 0.8%, Roman Catholic 0.5%, Uniate Catholic 0.2%, Protestant-Armenian and other 0.5%

Languages: Bulgarian; secondary languages closely correspond the ethnic breakdown

Literacy: total population 98%

Economy

Imports: fuels, minerals, and raw materials, machinery and equipment, manufactured goods, agricultural products

Exports: machinery and equipment, agricultural products, manufactured consumer goods, fuels, minerals, raw materials, and metals

Industries: machine building and metal working, food processing, chemicals, textiles, building materials, ferrous and nonferrous metals

Agriculture: climate and soil conditions support livestock raising and the growing of various grain crops, oil seeds, vegetables, fruits, and tobacco; more than one-third of the arable land devoted to grain; worlds forth-largest tobacco exporter.

Currency: 1 lev (Lv) = 100 stotinki   leva per US1$ - 67.04

Transportation:

Railroads: 4,294 km

Roads: 36,932 km total paved and unpaved

Ports: Burgas, Lom, Nesebur, Ruse, Varna, Vidin

Airports: 355 total paved and unpaved airports. The three international airports are at Sofia, Varna and Burgas

The Press: daily newspapers   **24 Chasa:** (24 Hours): 1000 Sofia, Blvd Tsarigradsko shosse 47 circ. 330,000 telephone (2) 44-19-45   fax (2) 43-39-339

Demokratsiya: 1000 Sofia, Rakoski Street 134 telephone (2) 39-01-86 fax (2) 39-02-12   circ. 106,000

Tourism: Bulgaria's tourist attractions include the resorts on the Black Sea coast, mountain scenery and historic centers.

Bulgarian Tourist Chamber: Sofia, Triaditza Street 5 telephone (2) 87-40-59

Diplomatic representation in US:
> *chief of mission:* Ambassador Snezhana Damianova Botusharova
> *chancery:* 1621 22nd Street NW, Washington, DC 20008
> *telephone:* [1] (202) 387-7969
> *FAX:* [1] (202) 234-7973

US Diplomatic representation:
> *chief of mission:* Ambassador Willian D. Montgomery
> *embassy:* 1 Saborna Street, Sofia
> *mailing address:* Unit 1335, Sofia; APO .\E09213-1335
> *telephone:* [359] (2) 88-48-01 through 05
> *FAX:* [359] (2) 80-19-77

Burkina

Capital: Ouagadougou   longitude: 1.40 W   latitude: 12.20 N
elevation: 991 ft

Government: parliamentary

Flag: two equal horizontal bands of red (top) and green with a yellow five-pointed star in the center; uses the popular pan-African colors of Ethiopia

Geography:

Location: Western Africa, north of Ghana

Total Area: 274,200 sq km (105,869 sq mi) slightly larger than Colorado

Boundaries: Benin, Ghana, Cote d'Ivoire

Climate: tropical; warm, dry winters; hot, wet summers

Temperature (F): High/Low Jan. 92/60, Apr. 103/79, July 91/74, Oct. 95/70

Average annual precipitation: 35.2 inches

Terrain: mostly flat to dissected, undulating plains; hills in west and southeast

Highest point is 717 m (2,352 ft)

Natural resources: manganese, limestone, marble; small deposits of gold, antimony, copper, nickel, bauxite, lead, phosphates, zinc, silver

Natural hazards: recurring droughts

People:

Population: 10,422,828 (July 1995 est.)

Life expectancy at birth: total population 46.6 years

Nationality: Burkinabe

Ethnic division: Mossi (about 2.5 million) Gurunsi, Senufo, Lobi, Bobo, Mande, Fulani

Religions: indigenous beliefs 40%, Muslim 50%, Christian (mainly Roman Catholic) 10%

Languages: French (official), tribal languages belonging to Sudanic family, spoken by 90% of the population

Literacy: total population 18%

Economy

Imports: machinery, food products, petroleum

Exports: cotton, gold, animal products

Industries: cotton lint, beverages, agricultural processing, soap, cigarettes, textiles, gold mining and extraction

Agriculture: peanuts, shea nuts, sesame, cotton; food crops - sorghum, millet, corn, rice, some food grains; livestock

Currency: 1 CFA franc (CFAF) = 100 centimes

Communaute Financiere Africaine francs per US1$ - 529.43

Transportation:

Railroads: 620 km

Roads: 16,500 km total paved and unpaved

Ports: none

Airports: 48 total paved and unpaved. There are international airports at Ouagadougou and Bobo-Dioulasso

The Press: daily newspapers   **Observteur Paalga:** 01 BP 584, Ouagadougou 01
telephone 33-27-05   fax 31-45-79   circ. 8,500

Sidwaya: 5 rue du Marche', 01 BP 507, Ouagadougou 01
State-owned.   circ. 5,000

Tourism: There is a wide variety of wild animals in the game reserves. Some big game hunting in the east and southwest, along the banks of the Mouhoun river. National museum in Ougadougou

Direction de l'Administration Touristique et Hoteliere:
BP 624, Ouagadougou   telephone 30-63-96

Diplomatic representation in US:
    chief of mission: Ambassador Gaetan R. Ouedraogo
    chancery: 2340 Massachusetts Avenue NW, Washington, DC 20008
    telephone: [1] (202) 332-5577, 6895
US Diplomatic representation:
    chief of mission: Ambassador Donald J. McConnell
    embassy: Avenue Raoul Follerau, Ouagadougou
    mailing address: 01 B.P. 35, Ouagadougou
    telephone: [226] 30-67-23 through 30-67-25
    FAX: [226] 31-23-68

Burma

Capital: Rangoon (regime refers to the capital as Yangon)
elevation: 18 ft   longitude: 96.10 E   latitude: 16.47 N
Government: military regime
    Flag: red and blue rectangle in the upper hoist-side corner bearing, all in
    white, 14 five-pointed stars encircling a cogwheel containing a stalk of rice;
    the 14 stars represent the 14 administrative divisions
Geography
    Location: Southern Asia, bordering the Andaman Sea and the Bay of
    Bengal, between Bangladesh and Thailand
    Total Area: 678,500 sq km (261,969 sq mi) slightly smaller than Texas
    Boundaries: Bangladesh, China, India, Loas, Thailand
    Climate: tropical monsoon; cloudy, rainy, hot, humid summers (southwest
    monsoon, June to September); less cloudy, scant rainfall, mild temperatures,
    lower humidity during winter (northeast monsoon, December to April)
    Temperature (F): High/Low Jan. 89/65, Apr. 97/76, July 85/76, Oct. 88/76
    Average annual precipitation: 105 inches
    Terrain: central lowlands ringed by steep, rugged highlands

Highest point is Hkakabo Razi 5,881 m (19,296 ft)

Natural resources: petroleum, timber, tin, antimony, zinc, copper, tungsten, lead, coal, some marble, limestone, precious stones, natural gas

Natural hazards: destructive earthquakes and cyclones; flooding and landslides common during rainy season (June to September); periodic droughts

People

Population: 45,103,809 July 1995 est.)

Life expectancy at birth: total population 60.47 years

Nationality: Burmese

Ethnic division: Burman 68%, Shan 9%, Karan 7%, Rakhine 4%, Chinese 3%, Mon 2%, Indian 2%, other 5%

Religions: Buddhist 89%, Christian 4%, (Baptist 3%, Roman Catholic 1%), Muslim 4%, animist beliefs 1%, other 2%

Languages: Burmese; minority ethnic groups have their own language

Literacy: total population 81%

Economy

Imports: machinery, transport equipment, chemicals, food products

Exports: pulses and beans, teak, rice, hardwood

Industries: agricultural processing; textiles and footwear; wood and wood products; petroleum refining; mining of copper, tin, tungsten, iron; construction materials; pharmaceuticals; fertilizer

Agriculture: self-sufficient in food; principal crops - paddy rice, corn, oilseed, sugarcane, pulses; world's largest stand of hardwood trees

Currency: 1 kyat (K) = 100 pyas

kyats per US1$ - 5.86

Transportation

Railroads: 3,991 km

Roads: 27,000 km paved and unpaved

Ports: Bassein, Bhamo, Chauk, Mandalay, Moulmein, Myitkyina, Rangoon, Sittwe, Tavoy

Airports: 80 total paved and unpaved. International Airport, near Yangon

The Press: daily newspapers

Myanma Alin: 212 Theinbyu Road, Botahtaung POB 40, Yangon
telephone (1) 73-182   circ. 400,000

New Light of Myanmar: 22-30 Stand Road, Yangon
telephone (1) 89-190   circ. 14,500

Tourism: Buddhist temples and shrines, outstanding palaces in the larger cities. Beaches at Sandoway

Myanmar Travels and Tours: 77-91 Sule Pagoda Road
POB 559, Yangon   telephone (1) 75-828   fax (1) 89-588

Diplomatic representation in US:

chief of mission: Ambassador U Thaung

chancery: 2300 S Street NW, Washington, DC 20008

telephone: [1] (202) 332-9044, 9045

US Diplomatic representation:

chief of mission: Ambassador (vacant) Charge d'Affaires Marilyn A. Meyers

embassy: 581 Merchant Street, Rangoon (GPO 521)

mailing address: American Embassy, Box B, APO AP 96546

telephone: [95] (1) 82-055, 82-182

FAX: [95] (1) 80-409

Burundi

Capital: Bujumbura   longitude: 29.19 E   latitude: 3.22 S
elevation: 2,640 ft

Government: republic

Flag: divided by a white diagonal cross into red panels (top and bottom) and green panels (hoist side and outer side) with a white disk superimposed at the center bearing three red six-pointed stars outlined in green arranged in a triangular design (one star above, two stars below)

Geography:

Location: Central Africa, east of Zaire

Total Area: 27,830 sq km (10,745 sq mi) slightly larger than Maryland

Boundaries: Rwanda, Tanzania, Zaire

Climate: temperate; warm; occasional frost in uplands; dry season from June to September

Temperature (F): High/Low Jan. 82/66, Apr. 82/66, July 84/63, Oct. 86/68

Average annual precipitation: 33 inches

Terrain: hilly and mountainous, dropping to a plateau in east, some plains
The north south ranges rise more than 2,438 m (8,000 ft)
Natural resources: nickel, uranium, rare earth oxide, peat, cobalt, copper, platinum (not yet exploited), vanadium
Natural hazards: flooding, landslides

People:

Population: 6,262,429 (July 1995 est.)
Life expectancy at birth: total population 39.86
Nationality: Burundian
Ethnic division: *Africans:* Hutu (Bantu) 85%, Tutsi (Hamitic) 14%, Twa (Pygmy) 1%
non-Africans: Europeans 3,000, South Asians 2,000
Religions: Christian 67% (Roman Catholic 62%, Protestant 5%), indigenous beliefs 32%, Muslim 1%
Languages: Kirundi (official), French (official), Swahili (along Lake Tanganyika and in the Bujumbura area)
Literacy: total population 50%

Economy

Imports: capital goods, petroleum products, foodstuffs, consumer goods
Exports: tea, cotton, hides, and skins
Industries: light consumer goods such as blankets, shoes, soap; assembly of imported components; public works construction; food processing
Agriculture: cash crops - coffee, cotton, tea; food crops - corn, sorghum, sweet potatoes, bananas, manoic; livestock - meat, milk, hides and skins
Currency: 1 Burundi franc (FBu) = 100 centimes
Burundi francs per US1$ - 248.51

Transportation:

Railroads: none
Roads: 5,900 km paved and unpaved
Inland waterways: Lake Tanganyika
Ports: Bujumbura
Airports: 4 total paved and unpaved. The international airport is at Bujumbura and is equipped to take large jet-engined aircraft

The Press: newspapers   **Le Renouveau du Burundi:** BP 2870, Bujumbura
daily; French;   circ. 20,000
Ubumwe: BP 1400, Bujumbura
telephone (2) 23-929   weekly   circ. 20,000

Tourism: Kilemba Hot Springs, wildlife reserves and parks, bird watching, Lake Tanganyika, over 400 species of fish

Office National du Tourisme: BP 902, Bujumbura
telephone (2) 22-202

Diplomatic representation in US:
  chief of mission: post vacant
  chancery: Suite 212, 2233 Wisconsin Avenue NW, Washington DC, 20007
  telephone: [1] (202) 342-2574
US Diplomatic representation:
  chief of mission: Ambassador Robert C. Krueger
  embassy: Avenue des Etats-Unis, Bujumbura
  mailing address: B.P. 1720, Bujumbura
  telephone: [257] (2) 23-454
  FAX: [257] (2) 22-926

Cambodia

Capital: Phnom Penh   longitude: 104.55 E   latitude: 11.35 N
  elevation: 39 ft
Government: multiparty liberal democracy under a constitutional monarchy
  established in September 1993
  Flag: horizontal band of red separates two equal horizontal bands of blue
  with a white three-towered temple representing Angkor Wat in the center
Geography:
  Location: Southeastern Asia, bordering the Gulf of Thailand, between
  Thailand and Vietnam
  Total Area: 181,040 sq km (69,900 sq mi) slightly smaller than Oklahoma
  Boundaries: Laos, Thailand, Vietnam
  Climate: tropical; rainy, monsoon season (May to November); dry season
  (December to April); little seasonal temperature variation
  Temperature (F): High/Low Jan. 87/70, Apr. 94/76, July 89/76, Oct. 87/76

Average annual precipitation: 55.3 inches

Terrain: mostly low, flat plains; mountains in southwest and north
Highest point is 1,813 m (5,948 ft)
Note: a land of paddies and forests dominated by the Mekong River and Tonle Sap

Natural resources: timber, gemstones, some iron ore, manganese, phosphates, hydropower potential

Natural hazards: monsoonal rains (June to November); flooding; occasional droughts

People:

Population: 10,561,373 (July 1995 est.)

Life expectancy at birth: total population 49.46 years

Nationality: Cambodian

Ethnic division: Khmer 90%, Vietnamese 5%, Chinese 1%

Religions: Theravada Buddhism 95%, other 5%

Languages: Khmer (official), French

Literacy: total population 35%

Economy

Imports: cigarettes, construction materials, petroleum products, machinery

Exports: timber, rubber, soybeans, sesame

Industries: rice milling, fishing, wood and wood products, rubber, cement, gem mining

Agriculture: mainly subsistence farming except for rubber plantations; main crops - rice, rubber, corn, food shortages - rice, meat, vegetables, dairy products, sugar, flour

Currency: 1 new riel (CR) = 100 sen   riels per US1$ - 2,470

Transportation:

Railroads: 655 km

Roads: 34,100 km total paved and unpaved

Ports: Kampong Saom (Sihanoukville), Kampot, Krong Kaoh Kong, Phnom Penh

Airports: 22 total paved and unpaved. The international airport is at Pochentong near Phnom Penh

The Press: newspapers   **Kampuchea:** 158 blvd Tou Samouth, Phnom Penh telephone (23) 25-559   weekly, circ. 55,000

Pracheachon: 101 blvd Tou Samouth, Phnom Penh twice a week   circ. 50,000

Tourism: 12th century temples at Angkor Wat

General Directorate for Tourism: Phnom Penh

Diplomatic representation in US:
Ambassador Sisowath Sirirath represents Cambodia at the United Nations
US Diplomatic representation:
chief of mission: Ambassador Charles H. Twining
embassy: 27 EO Street 240, Phnom Penh
mailing address: Box P, APO AP 96546
telephone: [855] (23) 26-436, 26-438
FAX: [855] (23) 26-437

Cameroon

Capital: Yaounde
longitude: 11.31 E   latitude: 3.51 N   elevation: 2,526 ft
Government: unitary republic; multiparty presidential regime (oppositional parties legalized 1990)
Flag: three equal bands of green (hoist side), red, and yellow with a yellow five-pointed star centered in the red band; uses the popular pan-African colors of Ethiopia
Geography:
Location: Western Africa, bordering the North Atlantic Ocean, between Equatorial Guinea and Nigeria
Total Area: 475,440 sq km (183,567 sq mi) slightly larger than California
Boundaries: Central African Republic, Chad, Congo, Equatorial Guinea, Gabon, Nigeria
Climate: varies with terrain, from tropical along coast to semiarid and hot in north
Temperature (F): High/Low Jan. 85/67, Apr. 85/66, July 80/66, Oct. 81/65
Average annual precipitation: 61.2 inches
Terrain: diverse, with coastal plain in southwest, dissected plateau in center, mountains in west, plains in north

Natural resources: petroleum, bauxite, iron ore, timber, hydropower potential

Natural hazards: recent volcanic activity with release of poisonous gases

People:

Population: 13,521,000 (July 1995 est.)

Life expectancy at birth: total population 57.48 years

Nationality: Cameroonian

Ethnic division: Cameroon Highlanders 31%, Equatorial Bantu 19%, Kirdi 11%, Fulani 10%, Northwestern Bantu 8%, Eastern Nigritic 7%, other African 13%, non-African less than 1%

Religions: indigenous beliefs 51%, Christian 33%, Muslim 16%

Languages: 24 major African language groups, English (official), French (official)

Literacy: total population 55%

Economy

Imports: machines and electrical equipment, food, consumer goods, transport equipment

Exports: petroleum products, lumber, cocoa beans, aluminum, coffee, cotton

Industries: petroleum production and refining, food processing, light consumer goods, textiles, lumber

Agriculture: commercial and food crops include coffee, cocoa, timber, bananas, oilseed, grains, livestock, root starches

Currency: 1 CFA franc (CFAF) = 100 centimes

Communaute Financiere Africaine francs (CFAF) per US1$ - 529.43

Transportation:

Railroads: 1,111 km

Roads: 65,000 km total paved and unpaved

Ports: Bonaberi, Douala, Garoua, Kribi, Tiko

Airports: 60 total paved and unpaved. The international airports are at Douala, Garoua, Yaounde and Bafoussam

The Press: newspapers   **Cameroon Tribune:** BP 1218, Yaounde telephone 30-40-12   fax 30-43-62   daily,   circ. 20,000
Cameroon Post: Yaounde; weekly, English

Tourism: Tourist are attracted by the national parks, game reserves, sandy beaches and the cultural diversity of local customs. Museum of African Art in Bamenda

Societe Camerounaise de Tourisme: BP 7138, Yaounde telephone 23-32-19

Diplomatic representation in US:
>*chief of mission*: Ambassador Jerome Mendouga
>*chancery*: 2349 Massachusetts Avenue NW, Washington, DC 20008
>*telephone:* [1] (202) 265-8790 through 8794

US diplomatic representation:
>*chief of mission:* Ambassador Harriet W. Isom
>*embassy:* Rue Nachtigal Yaounde
>*mailing address:* B.P. 817 Yaounde
>*telephone:* [237] 23-40-14
>*FAX:* [237] 23-07-53

Canada

Capital: Ottawa   longitude: 75.43 W latitude: 45.25 N elevation: 339 ft

Government: confederation with parliamentary democracy

>**Flag:** three vertical bands of red (hoist side), white (double width, square), and red with a red maple leaf centered in the white band

Geography:
>**Location:** Northern North America, bordering the North Atlantic Ocean and North Pacific Ocean, north of the conterminous US
>**Total Area:** 9,976,140 sq km (3,851,788 sq mi) slightly larger than US
>**Boundaries:** US
>**Climate:** varies from temperate in south to subarctic and arctic in north
>Temperature (F): High/Low Jan. 21/3, Apr. 51/31, July 81/58, Oct. 54/37
>Average annual precipitation: 34.3 inches
>**Terrain:** mostly plains with mountains in west and lowlands is southeast
>Highest point is Mt. Logan 6,050 m (19,850 ft)
>Note: second-largest country in world (after Russia); strategic location between Russia and US via north polar route; nearly 90% of the population is concentrated in the region near the US/Canada border.

Natural resources: nickel, zinc, copper, gold, lead, molybdenum, potash, silver, fish, timber, wildlife, coal, petroleum, natural gas

Natural hazards: continuous permafrost in north is a serious obstacle to development; cyclonic storms form east of the Rocky Mountains, a result of the mixing of air masses from the Arctic, Pacific, and American interior, and produce most of the country's rain and snow

People:

Population: 28,434,545 (July 1995 est.)

Life expectancy at birth: total population 78.29 years

Nationality: Canadian

Ethnic division: British Isles origin 40%, French origin 27%, other European 20%, indigenous Indian and Eskimo 1.5%

Religions: Roman Catholic 46%, United Church 16%, Anglican 10%, other 28%

Languages: English (official), French (official)

Literacy: total population 97%

Economy

Imports: crude oil, chemicals, motor vehicles and parts, durable consumer goods, electronic computers; telecommunications equipment and parts

Exports: newsprint, wood pulp, timber, crude petroleum, machinery, natural gas, aluminum, motor vehicles and parts; telecommunications equipment

Industries: processed and unprocessed minerals, food products, wood and paper products, transportation equipment, chemicals, fish products, petroleum and natural gas

Agriculture: one of the world's major producers and exporters of grain (wheat and barley), key source of US agricultural imports; large forest resources cover 35% of total land area; commercial fisheries provide annual catch of 1.5 million metric tons, of which 75% is exported

Currency: 1 Canadian dollar (Can$) = 100 cents
Canadian dollars per US1$ - 1.41

Transportation:

Railroads: 78,148 km

Roads: total 849,404 km paved and unpaved

Ports: Becancour, Churchill, Halifax, New Westminister, Prince Rupert, Quebec, Saint John (New Brunswick), Saint John's (Newfoundland) Seven Islands, Sydney, Three Rivers, Toronto, Windsor

Airports: 1,386 paved and unpaved, with international airports in all major cities

The Press: daily newspapers   **Edmonton Journal:** POB 2421, Edmonton, AB T5J 7W9   circ. 152,000
telephone (403) 429-5400   fax (403) 498-5604
The Vancouver Sun: 2250 Granville Street, Vancouver, BC V6H 3G2   circ. 205,000
telephone (604) 732-2111, fax (604) 732-2323

Tourism: national parks, Calgary Stampede
Tourism Industry Association of Canada
130 Albert Street, Suite 1016, Ottawa, ON K1P 5G4
telephone (613) 238-3883   fax (613) 238-3878

Diplomatic representation in US:
chief of mission: Ambassador Raymond A.J. Chretien
chancery: 501 Pennsylvania Avenue NW, Washington, DC 20001
telephone: [1] (202) 682-1740
FAX: [1] (202) 682-7726

US Diplomatic representation:
chief of mission: Ambassador James Johnston Blanchard
embassy: 100 Wellington Street, K1P 5T1, Ottawa
mailing address: P.O. Box 5000, Ogdensburg, NY 13669-0430
telephone: [1] (613) 238-5335, 4470
FAX: [1] (613) 238-5720

Cape Verde

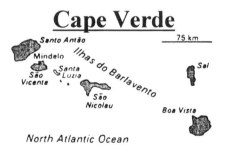

Capital: Praia   longitude: 23.30 W   latitude: 14.55 N elevation: 112 ft
Government: republic

Flag: three horizontal bands of light blue (top, double width), white (with a horizontal red stripe in the middle third), and light blue; a circle of 10 yellow five-pointed stars is centered on the hoist end of the red stripe and extends into the upper and lower blue bands

Geography:

Location: Western Africa, group of islands in the North Atlantic Ocean, west of Senegal

Total Area: 4,030 sq km (1,556 sq mi) slightly larger than Rhode Island

Boundaries: no land boundaries

Climate: temperate; warm, dry, summer; precipitation very erratic
Temperature (F): High/Low Jan. 77/68, Apr. 79/69, July 83/75, Oct. 85/76
Average annual precipitation: 10.2 inches

Terrain: steep, rugged, rocky, volcanic
Highest point is 2,829 m (9,281 ft)

Natural resources: salt, basalt rock, pozzolana, limestone, kaolin, fish

Natural hazards: prolonged droughts; harmattan wind can obscure visibility; volcanically and seismically active

People:

Population: 435,983 (July 1995 est.)

Life expectancy at birth: total population 63.01 years

Nationality: Cape Verdean

Ethnic division: Creole (mulatto) 71%, African 28%, European 1%

Religions: Roman Catholicism fused with indigenous beliefs

Languages: Portuguese, Crioulo, a blend of Portuguese and West African words

Literacy: total population 53%

Economy

Imports: foodstuffs, consumer goods, industrial products, transport equipment

Exports: fish, bananas, hides and skins

Industries: fish processing, salt mining, garment industry, ship repair, construction materials, food and beverage production

Agriculture: largely subsistence farming; bananas are the only export crop; other crops - corn, beans, sweet potatoes, coffee; growth potential of agriculture sector limited by poor soils and scanty rainfall; annual food imports required; fish catch provides for both domestic consumption and small exports

Currency: 1 Cape Verdean escudo (CVEsc) = 100 centavos
Cape Verdean escudos per US1$ - 85.53

Transportation:

Railroads: none

Roads: 1,100 km total paved and unpaved

Ports: Mindelo, Praia, Tarrafal

Airports: 6 total paved and unpaved. The Amilcar Cabral international airport is at Espargos on Sal Island A second international airport on Sai Tiago is scheduled for completion in late 1996.

The Press: newspapers   **Agaviva:** Sao Vicente   telephone 31-21-21
                              monthly   circ. 4,000
                              A Semana: CP 36c, Avda Cidade de Lisboa,
                              Sao Tiago, telephone 61-25-69   fax 61-39-50
                              weekly   circ. 5,000

Tourism: The islands offer attractive mountain scenery, and white sandy beaches.
                    Instituto Nacional do Turismo: CP 294, Praia, Sao Tiago
                              telephone 61-44-73   fax 61-32-10

Diplomatic representation in US:

chief of mission: Vacant

chancery: 3415 Massachusetts Avenue NW, Washington, DC 20007

telephone: [1] (202) 965-6820

FAX: [1] (202) 965-1207

US Diplomatic representation:

chief of mission: Ambassador Joseph M. Segars

embassy: Rua Abilio Macedo 81, Praia

mailing address: C.P. 201, Praia

telephone: [238] 61-56-16

FAX: [238] 61-13-55

Cayman Islands

50 km

Caribbean Sea

Cayman
Brac
Little
Cayman

Grand Cayman
GEORGE TOWN

Caribbean Sea

Capital: George Town   longitude: 81.23 W   latitude: 19.18 N

Government: dependent territory of the UK

Flag: blue, with the flag of the UK in the upper hoist-side quadrant and the Caymanian coat of arms on a white disk centered on the outer half of the flag; the coat of arms includes a pineapple and turtle above the shield with three stars (representing the three islands) and a scroll at the bottom bearing the motto HE HATH FOUNDED IT UPON THE SEAS

Geography

Location: Caribbean, island in Caribbean Sea, nearly one-half of the way from Cuba to Honduras

Total Area: 260 sq km (100.4 sq mi) slightly less than 1.5 time the size of Washington, DC

Boundaries: no land boundaries

Climate: tropical marine; warm, rainy summers (May to October) and cool, relatively dry winters (November to April)

Temperature (F): High/Low Jan. 77/73, Apr. 80/76, July 83/81, Oct. 81/79

Average annual precipitation: 60 inches

Terrain: low-lying limestone base surrounded by coral reefs

Natural resources: fish, climate and beaches that foster tourism

Natural hazards: hurricanes (July to November)

People

Population: 33,192 (July 1995 est.)

Life expectancy at birth: total population 77.1 years

Nationality: Caymanian

Ethnic division: mixed 40%, white 20%, black 20%, expatriates of various ethnic groups 20%

Religions: United Church (Presbyterian and Congregational), Anglican, Baptist, Roman Catholic, Church of God, other Protestant denominations

Languages: English

Literacy: total population 98%

Economy

Imports: foodstuffs, manufactured goods

Exports: turtle products, manufactured consumer goods

Industries: tourism, banking, insurance and finance, construction, building materials, furniture making

Agriculture: minor production of vegetables, fruit, livestock; turtle farming

Currency: 1 Caymanian dollar (CI$) = 100 cents

Caymanian dollars per US1$ - 0.83

Transportation

Railroads: none

Roads: 160 km total paved and unpaved

Ports: Cayman Brac, George Town

Airports: 3 total paved and unpaved. There are two international airports, Owen Roberts, near George Town, and Gerard Smith Airport on Cayman Brac

The Press: newspapers   **The Daily Caymanian Compass:**
POB 1365, Grand Cayman   circ. 8,000   5 a week
telephone 949-5111   fax 949-7033
     The New Caymanian: POB 1139, George Town, Grand Cayman
telephone 949-7414   fax 949-0036   weekly

Tourism: beaches, diving in off shore reefs, Pedro's Castle, Rum Point, Kiemanus Museum

Cayman Islands Department of Tourism:
Harbor Center, POB 67, George Town,   Grand Cayman
telephone   949-0623   fax   949-4053

Diplomatic representation in US: none (dependent territory of the UK)

US Diplomatic representation: none (dependent territory of the UK)

The Central African Republic

400 km

Capital: Bangui   longitude: 18.37 E   latitude: 4.23 N   elevation: 1,270 ft

Government: republic

Flag: four equal horizontal bands of blue (top), white, green, and yellow with a vertical red band in center; there is a yellow five-pointed star on the hoist side of the blue band

Geography

Location: Central Africa

Total Area: 622,980 sq km (240,533 sq mi) slightly smaller than Texas

Boundaries: Cameroon, Chad, Congo, Sudan, Zaire

Climate: tropical; hot, dry winters; mild to hot, wet summers

Temperature (F): High/Low   Jan. 90/68, Apr. 91/71, July 85/69, Oct. 87/69

Average annual precipitation: 60.8 inches

Terrain: vast, flat to rolling, monotonous plateau; scattered hills in northeast and southwest

Natural resources: diamonds, uranium, timber, gold, oil

Natural hazards: hot, dry, dusty harmattan winds affect northern areas; floods are common

People

Population: 3,209,780 (July 1995 est.)

Life expectancy at birth: total population 42.15 years

Nationality: Central African

Ethnic division: Baya 34%, Banda 27%, Sara 10%, Mandjia 21%, Mboum 4%, M'Baka 4%, other Europeans and French

Religions: indigenous beliefs 24%, Protestant 25%, Roman Catholic 25% Muslim 15%, other 11%

Note: animistic beliefs and practices strongly influence the Christian majority

Languages: French (official), Sangho (lingua franca and national language), Arabic, Hunsa, Swahili

Literacy: total population 38%

Economy

Imports: food, textiles, petroleum products, machinery, electrical equipment, motor vehicles, chemicals, pharmaceuticals, consumer goods, industrial products

Exports: diamonds, timber, cotton, coffee, tobacco

Industries: diamond mining, sawmills, breweries, textiles, footwear, assembly of bicycles and motorcycles

Agriculture: self-sufficient in food production except for grain; commercial crops - cotton, coffee, tobacco, timber; food crops - manioc, yams, millet, corn, bananas

Currency: 1 CFA franc (CFAF) = 100 centimes
Communaute Financiere Africaine francs per US1$ - 529.43

Transportation

Railroads: none

Roads: 22,000 km total paved and unpaved

Ports: Bangui, Nola

Airports: 61 total paved and unpaved. The international airport is at Bangui-Mpoko

The Press: newspapers   **E Le Songo:** Sango;   daily   circ. 250

Journal officiel de la Republic Centrafricaine:
BP 739, Bangui   fortnightly

Tourism: The main tourist attractions are the waterfalls, tropical forest and wildlife

Office National Centrafricain du Tourisme

BP 655, Bangui   telephone 61-45-66

Diplomatic representation in US:

chief of mission: Ambassador Henri Koba

chancery: 1618 22nd Avenue NW, Washington, DC 20008

telephone: [1] (202) 483-7800, 7801

FAX: [1] (202) 332-9893

US Diplomatic representation:

chief of mission: Ambassador Robert E. Gribbin III

embassy: Avenue David Dacko, Bangui

mailing address: BP 924, Bangui

telephone: [236] 61-02-00, 61-25-78, 61-02-10

FAX: [236] 61-44-94

Chad

400 km

Capital: N'Djamena   longitude: 14.59 E   latitude: 12.10 N
elevation: 968 ft

Government: republic

Flag: three equal vertical bands of blue (hoist side), yellow, and red; similar to the flag of Romania; also similar to the flag of Andorra, which has a national coat of arms featuring a quartered shield centered in the yellow band; design was based on the flag of France

Geography

Location: Central Africa, south of Libya

Total Area: 1,284,000 million sq km (495,752 sq mi) slightly more than three times the size of California

Boundaries: Cameroon, Central African Republic, Libya, Niger, Nigeria, Sudan

Climate: tropical in south, desert in north

Temperature (F): High/Low   Jan. 93/57, Apr. 107/74, July 92/72, Oct. 97/70

Average annual precipitation: 29.3 inches

Terrain: broad, arid plains in center, desert in north, mountains in northwest, lowlands in south

Highest point is Emi Koussi 3,415 m (11,204 ft)

Natural resources: petroleum (unexploited but exploration under way), uranium, natron, kaolin, fish (Lake Chad)

Natural hazards: hot, dry, dusty harmattan winds occur in north; periodic droughts; locust plagues

People

Population: 5,586,500 (July 1995 est.)

Life expectancy at birth: total population 41.19 years

Nationality: Chadian

Ethnic division:

north and center: Muslims (Arabs, Toubou, Hadjerai, Kotoko, Kanembou, Baguirmi, Boulala, Zaghawa, and Maba)

south: non-Muslims (Sara, Ngambaye, Mbaye, Goulaye, Moundang, Moussei, Massa) non indigenous 150,000, of whom 1,000 are French

Religions: Muslim 50%, Christian 25%, indigenous beliefs; animism 25%

Languages: French (official), Arabic (official), Sara (in south), Sango (in south), more than 100 different languages and dialects are spoken

Literacy: total population 30%

Economy

Imports: machinery and transportation equipment , industrial goods, petroleum products, foodstuff

Exports: cotton, cattle, textiles, fish

Industries: cotton textile mills, slaughterhouses, brewery, natron (sodium carbonate), soap, cigarettes

Agriculture: largely subsistence farming; cotton most important cash crop; food crops include sorghum, millet, peanuts, rice, potatoes, manioc; livestock - cattle, sheep, goats, camels; self-sufficient in food in years of adequate rainfall

Currency: 1 CFA franc (CFAF) = 100 centimes

Communaute Finaciere Africaine Francs per US1$ - 529.43

Transportation

Railroads: none

Roads: 31,322 km total paved and unpaved

Ports: none

Airports: 66 total paved and unpaved. The international airport is at N'Djamena

The Press: newspapers   **Al-Watan:** BP 407, N'Djamena

telephone 51-47-05   weekly

Contact: N'Dkamena   current affairs

Tourism: Tourist attractions include scenery from the dense forests of the south to the deserts of the north, Lake Chad

Direction du Tourisme, des Parcs Nationaux et Reserves de Faune:

BP 86, N'Djamena   telephone (51) 23 03,   fax (57) 22 61

Diplomatic representation in US:

chief of mission: Ambassador Mahamat Saleh Ahmat

chancery: 2002 R Street NW, Washington, DC 20009

telephone: [1] (202) 462-4009

FAX: [1] (202) 265-1937

US Diplomatic representation:

chief of mission: Ambassador Laurence E. Pope II

embassy: Avenue Felix Eboue, N'Djamena

mailing address: BP 413, N'Djamena

telephone: [235] (51) 62-18, (51) 40-09, (51) 47-59

FAX: [235] (51) 33-72

Chile

Capital: Santiago   longitude: 70.40 W latitude: 33.30 S elevation: 1,706 ft

Government: republic

Flag: two equal horizontal bands of white (top) and red; there is a blue square the same height as the white band at the hoist-side end of the white band; the square bears a white five-pointed star in the center; design was based on the US flag

Geography

Location: Southern South America, bordering the South Atlantic Ocean and South Pacific Ocean, between Argentina and Peru

Total Area: 756,950 sq km (292,258 sq mi) slightly smaller than twice the size of Montana

Boundaries: Argentina, Bolivia, Peru

Climate: temperate, desert in north; cool and damp south

Temperature (F): High/Low Jan. 85/53, Apr. 74/45, July 59/37, Oct. 72/45
Average annual precipitation: 14.2 inches

Terrain: low coastal mountains; fertile central valley; rugged Andes in east
Highest point is Ojos del Salado 6,880 m (22,572 ft)

Natural resources: copper, timber, iron ore, nitrates, precious metals, molybdenum

Natural hazards: severe earthquakes; active volcanism; tsunamis

People

Population: 14,161,216 (July 1995 est.)

Life expectancy at birth: total population 74.88 years

Nationality: Chilean

Ethnic division: European and European-Indians 95%, Indian 3%

Religions: Roman Catholic 89%, protestant 11%, Jewish

Languages: Spanish

Literacy: total population 94%

Economy

Chile is the world's largest producer and exporter of copper.

Imports: capital goods, spare parts, raw materials petroleum, foodstuffs

Exports: copper, other metals and minerals, wood products, fish and fishmeal, fruits

Industries: copper, other minerals, foodstuffs, fish processing, iron and steel, wood and wood products, transport equipment, cement, textiles

Agriculture: major exporter of fruit, fish, and timber products; major crops - wheat, corn, grapes, beans, sugar beets, potatoes, deciduous fruit; livestock products - beef, poultry, wool

Currency: 1 Chilean peso (Ch$) = 100 centavos
Chilean pesos per US1$ - 408

Transportation

Railroads: 7,766 km

Roads: 79,599 km total paved and unpaved

Ports: Antofagasta, Arica, Chanarol, Coquimbo, Iquique, Puerto Montt, Punta Arenas, San Antonio, San Vicente, Talcahuano, Valparaiso

Airports: 390 total paved and unpaved. The principal international airports are Chacalluta, about 14 km northeast of Arica, and Arturo Merino Benitez about 20 km northeast of Santiago

The Press: daily newspapers

El Mercurio: Avda Santa Maria 5542
Casilla 13-D, Santiago
telephone (2) 330-1111   fax (2) 228-7541
circ. 124,000 weekdays, 285,000 Sundays

La Tercera de la Hora: Vicuna Mackenna 1870, Santiago
telephone (2) 551-7067   fax (2) 556-1017
circ. 200,000 morning

Tourism: Chile has a variety of attractions, fine beaches, ski resorts in the Andes, hunting and fishing in the southern archipelago

Servicio Nacional de Turismo: Avda Providencia 1550
Casilla 14082, Santiago
telephone (2) 236-0531   fax (2) 236-1417

Diplomatic representation in US:

chief of mission: Ambassador Gabriel Guerra-Mondragon
chancery: 1732 Massachusetts Avenue NW, Washington, DC 20036
telephone: [1] (202) 785-1746
FAX: [1] (202) 887-5579

US Diplomatic representation:

chief of mission: Ambassador Gabriel Guerra-Mondragon
embassy: Codina Building, 1343 Agustinas, Santiago
mailing address: Unit 4127, Santiago; APO AA 34033
telephone: [56] (2) 232-2600
FAX: [56] (2) 330-3710

China

Capital: Beijing   longitude: 116.26 E   latitude: 35.55 N   elevation: 171 ft

Government: communist state

Flag: red with a large yellow five-pointed star and four smaller yellow five-pointed stars (arranged in a vertical arc toward the middle of the flag) in the upper hoist-side corner

Geography

Location: Eastern Asia, bordering the East China Sea, Korea Bay, Yellow Sea, and South China Sea, between North Korea and Vietnam

Total Area: 9,596,960 sq km (3,705,386 sq mi) slightly larger than the US

Boundaries: Afghanistan, Bhutan, Burma, Hong Kong, India, Kazakhstan, North Korea, Kyrgyzstan, Loas, Macau, Mongolia, Nepal, Pakistan, Russia, Tajikistan, Vietnam

Climate: extremely diverse; tropical in south to subarctic in north

Temperature (F): High/Low Jan. 34/14, Apr. 70/45, July 88/70, Oct. 68/43

Average annual precipitation: 24.5 inches

Terrain: mostly mountains, high plateaus, deserts in west; plains, deltas, and hills in east

Highest point is Mt Muztagh 7,282 m (23,891 ft)

Natural resources: coal, iron ore, petroleum, mercury, tin, tungsten, antimony, manganese, molybdenum, vanadium, magnetite, aluminum, lead, zinc, uranium, hydropower potential (world's largest)

Natural hazards: frequent typhoons (about 5 per year along the southern and eastern coasts); damaging floods; tsunamis; earthquakes; droughts

People

Population: 1,203,097,300 (July 1995 est.)

Life expectancy at birth: total population 68.08 years

Nationality: Chinese

Ethnic division: Han Chinese 91.9%, Zhuang, Uygur, Hui, Yi, Tibetan, Miao, Manchu, Mongol, Buya, Korean, and other nationalities 8.1%

Religions: Daoism (Taoism), Buddhism, Muslim 2%-3%, Christian 1% Note: officially atheist, but traditionally pragmatic and eclectic

Languages: Standard Chinese or Mandarin (Putonghua, based on the Beijing dialect), Yue (Cantonese), Wu (Shanghainese), Minbei (Fuzhou), Minnan (Hokkien-Taiwanese), Xiang, Gan, Hakka dialects

Literacy: total population 87%

Economy

Imports: rolled steel, motor vehicles, textile machinery, oil products, aircraft

Exports: textiles, garments, footwear, toys, machinery and equipment, weapon systems

Industries: iron and steel, coal, machine building, armaments, textiles and apparel, petroleum, cement, chemical fertilizers, consumer durables, food processing, autos, consumer electronics, telecommunications

Agriculture: Among the world's largest producers of rice, potatoes, sorghum, peanuts, tea, barley, and pork; commercial crops include cotton, other fibers, and oilseeds, fish (including fresh water and pond raised)

Currency: 1 yaun (Y) = 10 jiao   yaun per US1$ - 8.44

Transportation

Railroads: 65,780 km

Roads: total 1,029,000 million km paved and unpaved

Ports: Aihui, Changsha, Dalian, Fuzhou, Guangzhou, Hangzhou, Harbin, Huangpu, Nanning, Ningbo, Qingdao, Qinhuangdao, Shinghai, Shantou, Tanggu, Xiamen, Xingang, Zhanjiang

Airports: 204 total paved and unpaved. 47 airports are capable of handling Boeing 737 and larger aircraft.

The Press: daily newspapers

Beijing Wanbao: 34 Xi Biaobei Hutong, Dongdan, Beijing 100743   circ. 800,000 telephone (1) 513-2233   fax (1) 512-6581

Chengdu Evening News: Qingyum Nan Jie, Chengdu 610017   circ. 700,000 telephone 66-45-01   fax 66-65-97

Tourism: Attractions include dramatic scenery and places of historical interest such as the Great Wall, the Ming Tombs, and the Forbidden City of Beijing. Tibet with its monasteries and temples, has been opened to tourist.

China International Travel Service:
103 Fuxingmenbei Dajie, Beijing 100800
telephone (1) 601-1122   fax (1) 601-2013

Diplomatic representation in US:
chief of mission: Ambassador Li Daoyu
chancery: 2300 Connecticut Avenue NW, Washington, DC 20008
telephone: [1] (202) 328-2500 through 2502
Fax: [1] (202) 328-2500
US Diplomatic representation:
chief of mission: Ambassador J. Stapleton Roy
embassy: Xiu Shui Bei Jie 3, 100600 Beijing
mailing address: PSC 461, Box 50, Beijing: FPO AP 96521-0002
telephone: [86] (1) 532-3831
FAX: [86] (1) 532-3178

Christmas Island

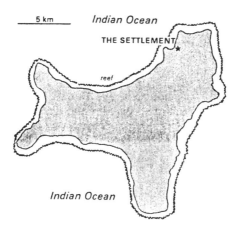

Capital: The Settlement   longitude: 104.40 E   latitude: 10.30 S
Government: territory of Australia
    Flag: the flag of Australia is used
Geography:
    Location: Southeastern Asia, island in the Indian Ocean, south of Indonesia
    Total Area: 135 sq km (52 sq mi) about 0.8 times the size of
    Washington, DC
    Boundaries: no land boundaries
    Climate: tropical; heat and humidity moderated by trade winds
    Terrain: steep cliffs along coast rise abruptly to central plateau
    Highest point is Ross Hill 98.45 m (323 ft)
    Natural resources: phosphate
    Natural hazards: almost completely surrounded by a reef which can be a
    maritime hazard

People:

Population: 889 (July 1995 est). All workers are employees of the Phosphate Mining Company of Christmas Island, Ltds.

Life expectancy at birth: NA

Nationality: Christmas Islander

Ethnic division: Chinese 61%, Malay 25%, European 11% others% no indigenous population

Religions: Buddhist 36.1%, Muslim 25.4%, Christian 17.7% (Roman Catholic 8.2%)

Languages: English

Literacy: NA

Industries: phosphate extraction

Agriculture: NA

Currency: 1 Australian dollar = 100 cents   Australian dollars per US1$ - 1.30

Transportation:

Railroads: none

Roads: NA

Ports: Flying Fish Cove

Airports: one

Tourism: Efforts are being made to develop the island's considerable potential for tourism.   **Christmas Island Resort Pty Ltd:** POB 888, Christmas Island 6798, Indian Ocean telephone 84-81   fax 84-80

Diplomatic representation in US: none (territory of Australia)

US Diplomatic representation: none (territory of Australia)

Clipperton Island

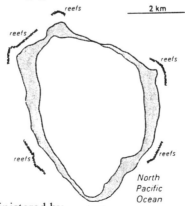

Capital: none; administered by France from French Polynesia   longitude: 110.06 W   latitude: 10.10 N

Government: French possession administered by France from French Polynesia by High Commissioner of the Republic

Geography

Location: Middle America, atoll in the North Pacific Ocean, southwest of Mexico

Total Area: 7 sq km (2.7 sq mi) about 12 times the size of The Mall in Washington, DC

Boundaries: no land boundaries

Climate: tropical

Terrain: coral atoll

Natural resources: none

Natural hazards: NA

Note: reef about 8 km in circumference

People

Population: uninhabited

Economy

The only economic activity is a tuna fishing station

Transportation

Ports: none; offshore anchorage only

Diplomatic representation in US: none (possession of France)

US Diplomatic representation: none (possession of France)

Cocos (Keeling) Island

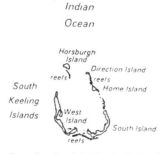

Capital: West Island   longitude: 96.53 E   latitude: 12.05 S elevation: 10 ft

Government: territory of Australia

Geography

Location: Southeastern Asia, group of islands in the Indian Ocean, south of Indonesia, about one-half of the way from Australia to Sri Lanka

Total Area: 14 sq km (5.4 sq mi) about 24 times the size of The Mall in Washington, DC

Note: includes the two main islands of West Island and Home Island

Boundaries: no land boundaries

Climate: pleasant, modified by the southeast trade wind for about nine months of the year; moderate rain fall

Temperature (F): High/Low Jan. 86/77, Apr. 85/78, July 82/76, Oct. 84/76

Average annual precipitation: 78.2 inches

Terrain: flat, low lying coral atolls

Natural resources: fish

Natural hazards: cyclones may occur in the early months of the year

Note: two coral atolls thickly covered with coconut palms and other vegetation

People

Population: 604 (July 1995 est.)

Life expectancy at birth: NA

Nationality: Cocos Islanders

Ethnic division: West Island; Europeans

Home Island: Cocos Malays

Religions: Sunni Muslims

Languages: English

Economy

Imports: foodstuffs

Exports: copra

Industries: copra products

Agriculture: gardens provide vegetables, bananas, pawpaws, coconuts

Currency: 1 Australian dollar ($A) = 100 cents

Australian dollars per US1$ - 1.30

Transportation

Railroads: none

Roads: NA

Ports: none; lagoon anchorage only

Airports: 1 paved

Diplomatic representation in US: none (territory of Australia)

US Diplomatic representation: none (territory of Australia)

Columbia

Capital: Bogota   longitude: 75.04 W   latitude: 4.38 N   elevation: 8,678 ft
Government: republic; executive branch dominates government structure
Flag: three horizontal bands of yellow (top, double-width), blue, and red; similar to the flag of Ecuador, which is longer and bears the Ecuadorian coat of arms superimposed in the center

Geography

Location: Northern South America, bordering the Caribbean Sea, between Panama and Venezuela, bordering the North Atlantic Ocean, between Ecuador and Panama
Total Area: 1,138,910 sq km (439,733 sq mi) slightly less than three times the size of Montana
Boundaries: Brazil, Ecuador, Panama, Peru, Venezuela
Climate: tropical along coast and eastern plains; cooler in highlands
Temperature (F): High/Low Jan. 67/48, Apr. 67/51, July 64/50, Oct. 66/50
Average annual precipitation: 41.9 inches
Terrain: flat coastal lowlands, central highlands, high Andes Mountains, eastern lowland plains
Highest point is Pico Cristobal Colon 5,800 m   (19,029 ft)
Natural resources: petroleum, natural gas, coal, iron ore, nickel, gold, copper, emeralds
Natural hazards: highlands subject to volcanic eruptions; occasional earthquakes; periodic droughts

People

Population: 36,200,251 (July 1995 est)
Life expectancy at birth: total population 72.48 years
Nationality: Colombian

Ethnic division: mestizo 58%, white 20%, mulatto 14%, black 4%, mixed black-Indian 3%, Indian 1%

Religions: Roman Catholic 95%

Languages: Spanish

Literacy: total population 88%

Economy

Imports: industrial equipment, transportation equipment, consumer goods, chemicals, paper products

Exports: petroleum, coffee, coal, bananas, fresh cut flowers

Industries: textiles, food processing, oil, clothing and footwear, beverages, chemicals, metal products, cement; mining - gold, coal, emeralds, iron, nickel, silver, salt

Agriculture: crops make up two-thirds and livestock one-third of agricultural output; climate and soils permit a wide variety of crops, such as coffee, rice, tobacco, corn, sugarcane, cocoa beans, oilseeds, vegetables; forest products and shrimp farming are becoming more important

Currency: 1 Columbian peso (COl$) = 100 centavos
Columbian peso per US1$ - 846.67

Transportation

Railroads: 3,386 km

Roads: total 107,377 km paved and unpaved

Ports: Barranquilla, Buenaventura, Cartagena, Leticia, Puerto Bolivar, San Andres, Santa Marta, Tumaco, Turbo

Airports: 1,307 total paved and unpaved. There are a total of 11 international airports serving the larger cities

The Press: daily newspapers   **El Espectador:** Avda 68, No 22-71, Apdo Aereo 3441, Santa Fe de Bogota, DC telephone (1) 260-6044   circ. 220,000

El Tiempo: Avda El Dorado No 59-70
Apdo Aereo 3633, Santa Fe de Bogoto, DC
telephone (1) 295-9555   circ. 200,000 weekdays,   350,000 Sundays

Tourism: Principal tourist attractions are the Caribbean coast, the 16th century walled city of Cartagena, the Amazon town of Leticia, columbian relics and monuments of colonial art. Andes mountains, extensive jungles and forests.

Corporacion Nacional de Turismo: Calle 28, N0 13a-15, 16-18
Apdo Aereo 8400, Santa Fe de Gogota, DC
telephone (1) 283-9466   fax (1) 284- 3818

Diplomatic representation in US:

   chief of mission: Ambassador Carlos Lleras de la Fuente

   chancery: 2118 Leroy Place NW, Washington, DC 20008

   telephone: [1] (202) 387-8338   *FAX:* [1] (202) 232-8643

US Diplomatic representation:

   chief of mission: Ambassador Myles R.R. Frechette

   embassy: Calle 38, No. 8-61, Bogota

   mailing address: Aparto Aereo 3813, Bogota; APO AA 34038

   telephone: [57] (1) 320-1300

   FAX: [57] (1) 288-5687

Comoros

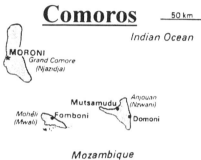

Capital: Moroni   longitude: 43.16 E   latitude: 11.40 S

Government: independent republic

   Flag: green with a white crescent in the center of the field, its points facing upward; there are four white five-pointed stars placed in a line between the points of the crescent; the crescent, stars, and color green are traditional symbols of Islam; the four stars represent the four main islands of the archipelago

Geography

   Location: Southern Africa, group of islands in the Mozambique Channel, about two-thirds of the way between northern Madagascar and northern Mozambique

   Total Area: 2,170 sq km (838 sq mi) slightly more than 12 times the size of Washington, DC

   Boundaries: no land boundaries

   Climate: tropical marine; rainy season (November to May)

   Temperature (F): High/Low Jan. 82/80, Apr. 81/79, July 75/72, Oct. 78/76

   Terrain: volcanic islands, interiors vary from steep mountains to low hills

   Natural resources: negligible

Natural hazards: cyclones and tsunamis possible during rainy season (December to April); Mount Kartala on Grand Comore is an active volcano

People

Population: 549,338 (July 1995 est)

Life expectancy at birth: total population 58.27 years

Nationality: Comoran

Ethnic division: Antalote, Cafre, Makoa, Oimatsaha, Sakalava

Religions: Sunni Muslim 86%, Roman Catholic 14%

Languages: Arabic (official), French (official), Comoran (a blend of Swahili and Arabic)

Literacy: total population 48%

Economy

Imports: rice and other foodstuffs, petroleum products, cement, consumer goods

Exports: vanilla, ylang-ylang, cloves, perfume oil, copra

Industries: perfume distillation, textiles, furniture, jewelry, construction materials, soft drinks

Agriculture: subsistence agriculture and fishing; plantation produce cash crops for export - vanilla, cloves, perfume essences, copra; principal food crops - coconuts, bananas, cassava; world's leading producer of essence of ylang-ylang (for perfumes) and second-largest producer of vanilla

Currency: 1 Comoran franc (CF) = 100 centimes

Comoran francs per US1$ - 297.07

Transportation

Railroads: none

Roads: total 750 km paved and unpaved

Ports: Fomboni, Moroni, Mutsamudu

Airports: 4 total paved and unpaved. The international airport is at Moroni-Hahaya on Njazidja

The Press: newspaper   **Al Watwany:** M'tsangani, BP 984, Moroni

telephone (73) 08-61   state owned   circ. 1,500 weekly

Tourism: Principal attractions are beaches, underwater fishing and mountain scenery   **Societe Comorienne de Tourisme et d'Hotellerie:** Itsandre Hotel, Njazidja   telephone (73) 23-65

Diplomatic representation in US:

chief of mission: Ambassador Mohamed Ahamadu Djimbanao

chancery: (temporary) care of the Permanent Mission of the Federal and Islamic Republic of the Comoros to the United Nations, 336 East 45th Street, 2nd Floor, New York, NY 10017

telephone: [1] (212) 972-8010   *FAX:* [1] (212) 983-4712

US Diplomatic representation: none; ambassador to Port Louis, Mauritius, is accredited to Comoros

Congo

Capital: Brazzaville   longitude: 15.14 E   latitude: 4.14 S elevation: 1,043 ft

Government: republic

Flag: red, divided diagonally from the lower hoist side by a yellow band; the upper triangle (hoist side) is green and the lower triangle is red; uses the popular pan-African colors of Ethiopia

Geography

Location: Western Africa, bordering the South Atlantic Ocean, between Angola and Gabon

Total Area: 342,000 sq km (132,046 sq mi) slightly smaller than Montana

Boundaries: Angola, Cameroon, Central African Republic, Gabon, Zaire

Climate: tropical; rainy season (March to June); dry season (June to October); constantly high temperatures and humidity; particularly enervating climate astride the Equator

Temperature (F): High/Low Jan. 88/69, Apr. 91/71, July 82/63, Oct. 89/70

Average annual precipitation: 58 inches

Terrain: coastal plain, southern basin, central plateau, northern basin

Natural resources: petroleum, timber, potash, lead, zinc, uranium, copper, phosphates, natural gas

Natural hazards: seasonal flooding

People

Population: 2,504,996 (July 1995 est.)

Life expectancy at birth: total population 47.09 years

Nationality: Congolese

Ethnic division: south: Kongo 48%

north: Sangha 20%, M'Bochi 12%

center: Teke 17%, Europeans 8,500 (mostly French)

Religions: Christian 50%, animist 48%, Muslim 2%

Languages: French (official), African languages (Lingala and Kikongo are the most widely used)

Literacy: total population 60%

Economy

Imports: intermediate manufactures, capital equipment, construction materials, foodstuffs

Exports: crude oil, lumber, plywood, sugar, cocoa, coffee, diamonds

Industries: petroleum, cement, lumbering, brewing, sugar milling, palm oil, soap, cigarette

Agriculture: cassava accounts for 90% of food output; other crops - rice, corn, peanuts, vegetables; cash crops include coffee and cocoa; forest products

Currency: 1 CFA franc (CFAF) = 100 centimes

Communaute Financiere Africaine francs per US1$ - 529.4

Transportation

Railroads: total 797 km

Roads: 11,960 km total paved and unpaved

Ports: Brazzaville, Impfondo, Ouesso, Oyo, Pointe-Noire

Airports: 41 total paved and unpaved. There are international airports at Brazzaville and Pointe-Noire, and smaller airports at six regional capitals.

The Press: newspapers   **ACI:** BP 2144 Brazzaville   telephone 83-05-91

circ, 1,000   daily

Mweti: BP 991 Brazzaville   telephone 81-10-87   circ. 8,000

Tourism: limited. Mbamou Island

Direction Generale du Tourisme et des Loisirs:

BP 456, Brazzaville   telephone 83-09-53

Diplomatic representation in US:

chief of mission: Ambassador Pierre Damien Boussoukou-Boumba

chancery: 4891 Colorado Avenue NW, Washington, DC 20011

telephone: [1] (202) 726-0825

FAX: [1] (202) 726-1860

US Diplomatic representation:

chief of mission: Ambassador William C Ramsey

embassy: Avenue Amilcar Cabral, Brazzaville

mailing address: BP 1015, Brazzaville

telephone: [242] 83 20 70

FAX: [242] 83 63 38

Cook Island

Rakahanga
Penrhyn
Pukapuka
Manihiki
Nassau Island
Suwarrow

South Pacific Ocean

Palmerston
Aitutaki Manuae
Takutea Mitiaro
Mauke
400 km
Rarotonga ★AVARUA
Mangaia

Capital: Avarua   longitude: 162.00 W   latitude: 11.00 S

Government: self-governing parliamentary government in free association with New Zealand

Flag: blue, with the flag of the UK in the upper hoist-side quadrant and a large circle of 15 white five-pointed stars (one for every island) centered in the outer half of the flag

Geography

Location: Oceania, group of islands in the South Pacific Ocean, about one-half of the way from Hawaii to New Zealand

Total Area: 240 sq km (93 sq mi) slightly less than 1.3 times the size of Washington, DC

Boundaries: no land boundaries

Climate: tropical; moderated by trade winds

Temperature (F): High/Low Jan. 89/75, Apr. 87/74, July 84/71, Oct. 86/73

Average annual precipitation: 84 inches

Terrain: low coral atolls in north; volcanic, hilly islands in south

Natural resources: negligible

Natural hazards: typhoons (November to March)

People

Population: 19,343 (July 1995 est)

Life expectancy at birth: total population 71.14 years

Nationality: Cook Islander

Ethnic division: Polynesian (full blood) 81.3%, Polynesian and European 7.7%, Polynesian and other 7.7%, European 2.4%, other 0.9%

Religions: Christian (majority of populace members of Cook Islands Christian Church)

Languages: English (official), Maori

Literacy: NA%

106

Economy
    Imports: foodstuffs, textiles, fuels, timber
    Exports: copra, fresh and canned fruit, clothing
Industries: fruit processing, tourism
Agriculture: export crops - copra, citrus fruits, pineapples, tomatoes, bananas;
    subsistence crops - yams, taro
Currency: 1 New Zealand dollar (NZ$) = 100 cents
           New Zealand dollars per US1$ - 1.56
Transportation
    Railroads: none
    Roads: 187 km total paved and unpaved
    Ports: Avarua, Avatiu
    Airports: 7 total paved and unpaved
The Press: daily newspaper   **Cook Island News:** POB 15, Avarua, Rarotonga
        telephone 22-999   fax 25-303   circ. 2,600
Tourism: beautiful beaches, barrier reefs, wild orchids
        Cook Islands Tourist Authority: POB 14, Rarotonga
        telephone 29-435 fax 21-435
Diplomatic representation in US: none (self-governing in free association with
    New Zealand)
US Diplomatic representation: none (self-governing in free association with New
    Zealand)

Coral Sea Islands

Capital: none; administered from Canberra, Australia
      longitude: 156.06 E   latitude: between 12.00 S and 24.00 S
Government: territory of Australia administered by the Ministry of Environment,
    Sport, and Territories

Geography:

    Location: Oceania, islands in the Coral Sea, northeast of Australia

    Total Area: less than 3 sq km (1.16 sq mi) includes numerous small islands and reefs scattered over a sea area of about 1 million sq km, with Willis Islets the most important

    Boundaries: no land boundaries

    Climate: tropical

    Terrain: sand and coral reefs and islands (or cays)

    Natural resources: negligible

    Natural hazards: occasional, tropical cyclones

People:

    Population: no indigenous inhabitants

Transportation:

    Roads: none

    Ports: none; offshore anchorage only

    Airports: none

Diplomatic representation in US: none (territory of Australia)

US Diplomatic representation: none (territory of Australia)

Costa Rica

Capital: San Jose   longitude: 84.04 W   latitude: 9.59 N   elevation: 3,760 ft

Government: democratic republic

    Flag: five horizontal bands of blue (top), white, red (double width), white, and blue, with the coat of arms in a white disk on the hoist side of the red band

Geography

    Location: Middle America, bordering both the Caribbean Sea and the North Pacific Ocean, between Nicaragua and Panama

Total Area: 51,100 sq km (19,730 sq mi) slightly smaller than West Virginia
note: includes Isla del Coco
Boundaries: Nicaragua and Panama
Climate: tropical; dry season (December to April); rainy season (May to November)
Temperature (F): High/Low Jan. 75/58, Apr. 79/62, July 77/62, Oct. 77/60
Average annual precipitation: 70.7 inches
Terrain: coastal plains separated by rugged mountains
Highest point is Chirripo Grande 3,819 m (12,530 ft)
Natural resources: hydropower potential
Natural hazards: occasional earthquakes, hurricanes along Atlantic coast; frequent flooding of lowlands at onset of rainy season; active volcanoes

People

Population: 3,419,114 (July 1995 est.)
Life expectancy at birth: total population 78.11 years
Nationality: Costa Rican
Ethnic division: white (including mestizo) 96%, black 2%, Indian 1%, Chinese 1%
Religions: Roman Catholic 95%
Languages: Spanish (official), English; spoken around Puerto Limon
Literacy: total population 93%

Economy

Imports: raw materials, consumer goods, capital equipment, petroleum
Exports: coffee, bananas, textiles, sugar
Industries: food processing, textiles and clothing, construction materials, fertilizer, plastic products
Agriculture: cash commodities - coffee, beef, bananas, sugar; other food crops include corn, rice, beans, potatoes; normally self-sufficient in food except for grain.
Currency: 1 Costa Rican colon (C) = 100 centimos
Costa Rican colones per US1$ - 164.4

Transportation

Railroads: total 950 km
Roads: 35,560 km total paved and unpaved
Ports: Caldera, Golfito, Moin, Puerto Limon, Puerto Quepos, Puntarenas
Airports: 174 total paved and unpaved. Juan Santamaria, Costa Rica's international airport is located at El Coco, about 16 km from San Jose

The Press: daily **newspapers**

La Nacion: Llorente de Tibas,
Apdo 10.138, San Jose
telephone 87-48-48 fax 40-64-80
circ. 110,000 morning

La Republica: Barrio Tournon, Guadelupe, Apdo 2.130, San Jose
telephone 23-02-66 fax 55-39-50   circ. 60,000 morning

Tourism: Main tourist features are the Irazu and Poas volcanoes. Caribbean
beaches of Limon, and the Pacific beaches at Guanacaste and Puntarenas.
Unique reserves and natural parks. Jungle train to Limon

Instituto Costarricense de Turismo:
Calle 5 y 7, Avda 4a 777, 1000 San Jose
telephone 23-17-33   fax 23-54-52

Diplomatic representation in US:
chief of mission: Ambassador Sonia Picado
chancery: 2114 S Street NW, Washington, DC 20008
telephone: [1] (202) 234-2945
FAX: [1] (202) 265-4795

US Diplomatic representation:
chief of mission: US Ambassador to Costa Rica Peter De Vos
embassy: Pavas Road, San Jose
mailing address: APO AA 34020
telephone: [506] 220-3939 *FAX:* [506] 220-2305

Cote d'Ivoire

Capital: Yamoussoukro longitude: 4.01 W latitude: 5.19 N elevation: 65 ft
Note: Abidjan is administrative center

Government: republic; multiparty

Flag: three equal vertical bands of orange (hoist side), white, and green; similar to the flag of Ireland, which is longer and has the colors reversed - green (hoist side), white, and orange; also similar to the flag of Italy, which is green (hoist side), white, and red; design was based on the flag of France

Geography

Location: Western Africa, bordering the North Atlantic Ocean, between Ghana and Liberia

Total Area: 322,460 sq km (124,502 sq mi) slightly larger than New Mexico

Boundaries: Kurkina, Ghana, Guinea, Liberia, Mali

Climate: tropical along coast, semiarid in far north; three seasons - warm and dry (November to March), hot and dry (March to May), hot and wet (June to October)

Temperature (F): High/ Low Jan. 88/73, Apr. 90/75, July 83/73, Oct. 85/74

Average annual precipitation: 77.1 inches

Terrain: mostly flat to undulating plains; mountains in northwest

Highest point is 1,751 m (5,745 ft)

Natural resources: petroleum, diamonds, manganese, iron ore, cobalt, bauxite, copper

Natural hazards: coast has heavy surf and no natural harbors; during rainy season torrential flooding is possible

People

Population: 14,791,257 (July 1995 est.)

Life expectancy at birth: total population 48.87 years

Nationality: Ivorian

Ethnic division: Baoule 23%, Bete 18%, Senoufou 15%, Malinke 11%, Angi, foreign Africans (mostly Burkinabe and Malians, about 3 million), non-Africans 130,000 to 330,000 (French 30,000 and Lebanese 100,000 to 300,000)

Religions: indigenous 25%, Muslim 60%, Christian 12%

Languages: French (official), 60 native dialects; Dioula is the most widely spoken

Literacy: total population 34%

Economy

Cote d'Ivoire is among the world's largest producers and exporters of coffee, cocoa beans, and palm-kernal oil

Imports: food, capital goods, consumer goods, fuel

Exports: cocoa, coffee, tropical woods, petroleum, cotton, bananas, pineapples, palm oil

Industries: foodstuffs, wood processing, oil refining, automobile assembly, textiles, fertilizer, beverages

Agriculture: cash crops include coffee, cocoa beans, timber, bananas, palm kernels, rubber; food crops - corn, rice, manioc, sweet potatoes; not self-sufficient in bread grain and dairy products

Currency: 1 CFA franc (CFAF) = 100 centimes
Communaute Financiere Africaine francs per US1$ - 529.43

Transportation

Railroads: total 660 km

Roads: 46,600 km total paved and unpaved

Ports: Abidjan, Aboisso, Dabou, San-Pedro

Airports: 40 total paved and unpaved. There are two international airports, Abidjan-Houphouet-Boigny and Yamoussoukro

The Press: daily newspapers **Fraternite-Matin:** blvd du General de Gaulle, 01 BP 1807, Abidjan 01 telephone 21-27-27 circ. 80,000

La Chronique du Soir: 09 Bp 150, Abidjan 09 telephone 22-15-12

Tourism: Of interest to the tourist are game reserves, forests, rich tribal folklore and the lively city of Abidjan. Beaches

Direction de la Promotion Touristique: BP V184, Abidjan telephone 21-49-70, fax 21-73-06

Diplomatic representation in US:

chief of mission: Ambassador Moise Koumoue-Koffi
chancery: 2424 Massachusetts Avenue NW, Washington, DC 20008
telephone: [1] (202) 797-0300
FAX: [1] (202) 387-6381

US Diplomatic representation:

chief of mission: Ambassador Hume A. Horan
embassy: 5 Rue Jesse Owens, Abidjan
mailing address: 01 BP 1712, Abidjan
telephone: [225] 21-09-79, 21-46-72
FAX: [225] 22-23-59

Croatia

100 km

Capital: Zagreb   longitude: 15.58 E   latitude: 45.48 N
Government: parliamentary democracy
Flag: red, white and blue horizontal bands with Croatian coat of arms
(red and white checkered)

Geography
Location: Southeastern Europe, bordering the Adriatic Sea, between Bosnia
and Herzegovina and Solvenia
Total Area: 56,538 sq km (21,829 sq mi) slightly smaller than West Virginia
Boundaries: Bosnia and Herzegovina, Hungary, Serbia and Montenegro,
Solvenia
Climate: Mediterranean and continental; continental climate predominant
with hot summers and cold winters; mild winters, dry summers along coast
Average annual precipitation: 35 inches
Terrain: geographically diverse; flat plains along Hungarian border, low
mountains and highlands near Adriatic coast, coastline, and islands
Natural resources: oil, some coal, bauxite, low-grade iron ore, calcium,
natural asphalt, silica, mica, clays, salt
Natural hazards: frequent and destructive earthquakes

People
Population: 4,665,821 (July 1995 est.)
Life expectancy at birth: total population 74.02 years
Nationality: Croat
Ethnic division: Croat 78%, Serb 12%, Muslim 0.9%, Hungarian 0.5%,
Slovenian 0.5%, others 10.8% (1991)
Religions: Catholic 76.5%, Orthodox 11.1%, Slavic Muslim 1.2%,
Protestant 0.5%, others and unknown 10.8%
Languages: Serbo-Croatian 96%, other 4%
Literacy: total population 97%

Economy

Imports: machinery and transport equipment, fuels and lubricants, food and live animals, chemicals, manufactured goods, miscellaneous manufactured articles, raw materials, beverages and tobacco

Exports: machinery and transport equipment, other manufacturers, chemicals, food and live animals, raw materials, fuels and lubricants

Industries: chemical and plastics, machine tools, fabricated metal, electronics, pig iron and rolled steel products, aluminum reduction, paper, wood products (including furniture), building materials (including cement), textiles, shipbuilding, petroleum and petroleum refining, food processing and beverages

Agriculture: central Croatian highlands are less fertile but support cereal production, orchards, vineyards, livestock breeding, and dairy farming; coastal areas and offshore islands grow olives, citrus fruits, and vegetables

Currency: 1 Croatian kuna = 100 paras

Croatian kuna per US1$ - 6.51

Transportation

Railroads: 2,699 km

Roads: 27,368 km total paved and unpaved

Ports: Dubrovnik, Omis, Ploce, Pula, Rijeka, Sibenik, Split, Zadar

Airports: 76 total paved and unpaved. There are eight international airports in Croatia

The Press: daily newspapers

Glas Slavonije: 54000 Osijek, Prolaz Carla Bende 2   circ. 22,500 telephone (52) 12-67-22   fax (54) 12-11-00

Glas Istre: 52000 Pula, Obala Marsala Tita br. 10 telephone (52) 42-969   fax (52) 41-434   circ. 25,000   morning

Tourism: The Adriatic coast particularly made Croatia a very popular tourist destination. Historic cities

Generalturist: 41000 Zagreb, Praska 5 telephone (41) 45-08-88   fax (41) 42-26-33

Diplomatic representation in US:

chief of mission: Ambassador Petar A. Sarcevic

chancery: 2343 Massachusetts Avenue NW, Washington, DC 20008

telephone: [1] (202) 588-5899

FAX: [1] (202) 588-8936

US Diplomatic representation:

chief of mission: Ambassador Peter W. Galbraith

embassy: Andrije Hebranga 2, Zagreb

mailing address: US Embassy, Zagreb, Unit 1345, APO AE 09213-1345

telephone: [385] (41) 45-60-00

FAX: [385] (41) 44-02-35

Cuba

Capital: Havana (La Habana)   longitude: 82.25 W   latitude: 23.07 N elevation: 80 ft

Government: Communist state

Flag: five equal bands of blue (top and bottom) alternating with white; a red equilateral triangle based on the hoist side bears a white five-pointed star in the center

Geography

Location: Caribbean, island between the Caribbean Sea and the North Atlantic Ocean.

Total Area: 110,860 sq km. (42,803 sq mi) slightly smaller than Pennsylvania.

Note: largest country in Caribbean.

Boundaries: None. US Naval Base at Guantanamo Bay is a part of Cuba and leased by the US Government.

Climate: tropical; moderated by trade winds; dry season (November to April); rainy season (May to October)

Temperature (F) High/Low Jan. 79/65, Apr. 84/69, July 89/75, Oct. 85/73

Average annual precipitation: 48.2 inches

Terrain: mostly flat to rolling plains with rugged hills and mountains in the southeast.

Highest point is Pico Turquino 2,000m (6,561 ft)

115

Natural resources: cobalt, nickel, iron ore, copper, manganese, salt, timber, silica, petroleum.

Natural hazards: the east coast is subject to hurricanes f rom August to October; droughts are common.

People

Population: 10,937,640 (July 1995 est.)

Life expectancy at birth: total population 77.05 years.

Nationality: Cuban

Ethnic division: mulatto 51%, white 37%, black 11%, Chinese 1%

Religions: nominally Roman Catholic 85%

Languages: Spanish

Literacy: total population 98%

Economy

Imports: petroleum, food, machinery, chemicals

Exports: sugar, nickel, shellfish, tobacco, medical products, citrus, coffee

Industries: sugar milling and refining, petroleum refining, food and tobacco processing, textiles, chemicals, paper and wood products, metal (particularly nickel), cement, fertilizers, consumer goods, agricultural machinery

Agriculture: key commercial crops - sugar cane, tobacco, and citrus fruits; other products - coffee, rice, potatoes, meat, beans

Currency: 1 Cuban peso = 100 centavos.   Pesos per US$1 - 1.00

Transportation

Railroads: total 12,623 km

Roads: 26,477 km total paved and unpaved

Ports: Cienfuegos, La Habana, Manzanillo, Mariel, Matanzas, Nuevitas, Santiago de Cuba

Airports: 181 total paved and unpaved. There are international airports at Havana, Santiago de Cuba, Camaguey and Varadero.

The Press: Granma is the only nation wide daily newspaper

Granma: Avda General Suarez y Calle Territorial, Plaza de la Revolucion Jose Marti, Apdo 6187, Havana; telephone (7) 79-33-61   fax (7) 70-90-06

Tourism: Santo Tomas Caverns, National Parks, beaches

Cubanacan: Calle 148, entre 11 y 13, Apdo 16046, Havana; telephone (7) 20-25-78,   fax (7) 33-60-46

Diplomatic representation in US:

chief of mission: Principal Officer Alfonso Fraga Perez represented by the Cuban Interests Section of the Swiss Embassy in Washington, DC

chancery: 2630 and 2639 16th Street NW, Cuban Interests Section, Swiss Embassy, Washington, DC 20009   Telephone (202) 797-8609, 8610, 8615

US diplomatic representation:

chief of mission: Principal Officer Joseph G. Sullivan

US Interests Section: USINT, Swiss Embassy, Calzada Entre L Y M .
Vedado Seccion, Havana

telephone: 33-35-51 through 33-35-59, 33-37-00 (operator assistance
required)

Cyprus

Mediterranean Sea

Capital: Nicosia   longitude: 33.21 E   latitude: 35.09 N elevation: 574 ft

Government: republic

Flag: white with a copper-colored silhouette of the island (the name Cyprus
is derived from the Greek work for copper) above two green olive braches in
the center of the flag; the branches symbolize the hope for peace and
reconciliation between Greek and Turkish communities.

Note: the Turkish Cypriot flag has a horizontal red stripe at the top and
bottom between which is a red crescent and red star on a white field

Geography

Location: Middle East, island in the Mediterranean Sea, south of Turkey

Total Area: 9,250 sq km (3,571 sq mi) about 0.7 times the size of
Connecticut

Boundaries: no land boundaries

Climate: temperate, Mediterranean with hot, dry summers and cool, wet
winters

Temperature (F): High/Low Jan. 59/42, Apr. 75/50, July 98/70, Oct. 83/58

Average annual precipitation: 13.7 inches

Terrain: central plain with mountains to north and south; scattered but
significant plains along southern coast

Highest point is 1,953 m (6,406 ft)

117

Natural resources: copper, pyrites, asbestos, gypsum, timber, salt, marble, clay earth pigment

Natural hazards: moderate earthquake activity

People

Population: 736,636 (July 1995 est.)

Life expectancy at birth: total population 76.47 years

Nationality: Cypriot

Ethnic division: Greek 78%, Turkish 18%, others 4%

Religions: Greek Orthodox 78%, Muslim 18%, Maronite, Armenian Apostolic, and others 4%

Languages: Greek, Turkish, English

Literacy: total population 94%

Economy

Imports: consumer goods, petroleum and lubricants, food and feed grains, machinery

Exports: citrus, potatoes, grapes, wine, cement, clothing and shoes

Industries: food, beverages, textiles, chemicals, metal products, tourism, wood products

Agriculture: major crops - potatoes, vegetables, barley, grapes, olives, citrus fruits; vegetables and fruit provide 25% of export revenues

Currency: 1 Cypriot pound (#C) = 100 cents; 1 Turkish lira (TL) = 100 kurus
Cypriot pounds per US1$ - 0.47   Turkish liras per US1$ - 37,444.1

Transportation

Railroads: none

Roads: Greek area total 10,448 km paved and unpaved
Turkish area total 6,116 km paved and unpaved

Ports: Famagusta, Kyrenia, Larnaca, Limassol, Vasilikos Bay

Airports: 15 total paved and unpaved. Two international airports, Larnaca and Paphos.

The Press: daily newspapers   **Apogevmatini:** POB 5603, 5 Aegaleo Street, Strovolos, Nicosia   circ. 10,000
telephone (2) 35-36-03, fax (2) 35-32-23

Haravghi: POB 1556, ETAK Bldg, 6 Akamantos Street, Nicosia
telephone (2) 47-63-56   fax (2) 36-51-54
circ. 13,500   morning

Tourism: Cyrpus is a developed Mediterranean island nation divided "de facto" into two areas. Greek Cypriot southern part of the island and the Turkish Republic of Northern Cyprus.

Cyprus Tourism Organization: POB 4535, 19 Limassol Ave, Nicosia
telephone (2) 31-57-15   fax (2) 31-30-22
Cyprus Turkish Tourism Enterprises, Ltd: Kyreni, Mersin 10, Turkey
telephone (81) 52-165   fax (81) 52-073
Diplomatic representation in US:
chief of mission: Ambassador Andreas J. Jacovides
chancery: 2211 R Street NW, Washington, DC 20008
telephone: [1] (202) 462-5772
Note: Representative of the Turkish area in the US is Namik Korman, office at
1667 K Street NW, Washington, DC,   telephone [1] (202) 887-6198
US Diplomatic representation:
chief of mission: Ambassador Richard A. Boucher
embassy: corner of Metochiou and Ploutarchou Streets, Engomi, Nicosia
mailing address: PO Box 4536 APO AE 09836
telephone: [357] (2) 47-61-00
FAX: [357] (2) 46-59-44

Czech Republic

Capital: Prague   longitude: 14.26 E   latitude: 50.06 N elevation: 860 ft
Government: parliamentary democracy
Flag: two equal horizontal bands of white (top) and red with a blue isosceles
triangle based on the hoist side (almost identical to the flag of the former
Czechoslovakia)
Geography
Location: Central Europe, southeast of Germany
Total Area: 78,703 sq km (30,387 sq mi) slightly smaller than South
Carolina
Boundaries: Austria, Germany, Poland, Slovakia

Climate: temperate; cool summers; cold, cloudy, humid winters
Temperature (F): High/Low Jan. 49/7, Apr. 73/29, July 91/49, Oct. 71/29
Average annual precipitation: 16.8 inches
Terrain: two main regions: Bohemia in the west, consisting of rolling plains, hills, and plateaus surrounded by low mountains; and Moravia in the east, consisting of very hilly country
Natural resources: hard coal, soft coal, kaolin, clay, graphite
Natural hazards: NA

People

Population: 10,432,774 (July 1995 est.)
Life expectancy at birth: total population 73.54 years
Nationality: Czech
Ethnic division: Czech 94.4%, Slovak 3%, polish 0.6%, German 0.5%, Gypsy 0.3%, Hungarian 0.2%, other 1%
Religions: atheist 39.8%, Roman Catholic 39.2%, Protestant 4.6%, Orthodox 3%, other 13.4%
Languages: Czech, Slovak
Literacy: total population 99%

Economy

Imports: machinery and transport equipment, manufactured goods, chemicals, fuels and lubricants, raw materials, agricultural products
Exports: manufactured goods, machinery and transport equipment, chemicals, fuels, minerals, metals, agricultural products
Industries: fuels, ferrous metallurgy, machinery and equipment, coal, motor vehicles, glass, armaments
Agriculture: largely self-sufficient in food production; diversified crop and livestock production, including grains, potatoes, sugar beets, hops, fruit, hogs, cattle, and poultry; exporter of forest products
Currency: 1 koruna (Kc) - 100 haleru
koruny (Kcs) per US1$ - 27.76

Transportation

Railroads: 9,434 km
Roads: 55,890 km total paved and unpaved
Ports: Decin, Prague, Usti and Labem
Airports: 116 total paved and unpaved. The main civil airports are at Prague, Brno, Karlovy Vary and Ostrava
The Press: daily newspapers **Prace:** Vaclavske nam. 17, 112 58 Prague 1
telephone (2) 2422-4969   fax (2) 2422-6475
circ 220,000

Rude pravo: Na Florenci 19, 111 21 Prague 1
telephone (2) 2422-5503   fax (2) 2481-1607   circ. 375,000

Tourism: Tourist attractions are magnificent scenery, winter sports, historic towns, famous castles and cathedrals. Resorts and spas with natural mineral springs
Cedok: Na prikope 18, 111 35 Prague 1
telephone (2) 2419-7111   fax (2) 2321-1656

Diplomatic representation in US:
  chief of mission: Ambassador Michael Zantovsky
  chancery: 3900 Spring of Freedom Street NW, Washington, DC 20008
  telephone: [1] (202) 363-6315 6316
  FAX: [1] (202) 966-8540
US Diplomatic representation:
  chief of mission: Ambassador Adrian A Basora
  embassy: Trziste 15, 11801 Prague 1
  mailing address: Unit 1330; APO AE 09213-1330
  telephone: [42] (2) 2451-0847
  FAX: [42] (2) 2451-1001

Denmark

Capital: Copenhagen   longitude: 12.35 E latitude: 55.40 N elevation: 33 ft
Government: constitutional monarchy
  Flag: red with a white cross that extends to the edges of the flag; the vertical part of the cross is shifted to the hoist side, and that design element of the DANNEBROG (Danish flag) was subsequently adopted by the other Nordic countries of Finland, Iceland, Norway, and Sweden

Geography

Location: Northern Europe, bordering the Baltic Sea and the North Sea, on a peninsula north of Germany

Total Area: 43,070 sq km (16,629 sq mi) slightly more than twice the size of Massachusetts

Boundaries: Germany

Climate: temperate; humid and overcast; mild, windy winters and cool summers

Temperature (F): High/Low Jan. 36/28, Apr. 51/38, July 71/57, Oct. 54/44

Average annual precipitation: 23.6 inches

Terrain: low and flat to gentle rolling plains

Highest point is Yding Skovhoj 173 m (568 ft)

Natural resources: petroleum, natural gas, fish, salt, limestone

Natural hazards: flooding is a threat in some areas of the country (e.g., parts of Jutland, along the southern coast of the island of Lolland) that are protected from the sea by a system of dikes

People

Population: 5,199,437 (July 1995 est)

Life expectancy at birth: total population 76.11 years

Nationality: Dane

Ethnic division: Scandinavian, Eskimo, Faroese, German

Religions: Evangelical Lutheran 91%, other Protestant and Roman Catholic 2%, other 7%

Languages: Danish, Faroese, Greenlandic (an Eskimo dialect), German (small minority)

Literacy: total population 99%

Economy

Imports: petroleum, machinery and equipment, chemicals, grain and foodstuffs, textile, paper

Exports: meat and meat products, dairy products, transport equipment (shipbuilding), fish, chemicals, industrial machinery

Industries: food processing, machinery and equipment, textiles and clothing, chemical products, electronics, construction, furniture, and other wood products, shipbuilding

Agriculture: principal products - meat, dairy, grain, potatoes, rape, sugar beets, fish

Currency: 1 Danish krone (DKr) = 100 oere

Danish kroner per US1$ - 6.03

Transportation

Railroads: 2,838 km

Roads: 71,042 km total, concrete, asphalt, stone block

Ports: Alborg, Arhus, Copenhagen, Esbjerg, Fredericia, Grenaa, Koge, Odense, Struer

Airports: 118 total paved and unpaved. The international airport is at Copenhagen

The Press: daily newspapers **Berlingske Tidende:** Pilestraede 34, 1147 Copenhagen K
telephone 33-75-75-75   fax 33-75-20-20
circ. 135,000 weekdays, 185,000 Sundays

B.T.: Kr. Bernikowsgade 6, 1147 Copenhagen K
telephone 33-75--75-33   fax 33-75-20-33
circ. 195,000 weekdays, 226,000 Sundays

Tourism: Beautiful old towns and countryside and the sophisticated Copenhagen, Kronburg Castle at Elsinore, Viking Museum in Roskilde

Danmarks Turistrad: Vesterbrogade 6d,
1620 Copenhagen V telephone 33-11-14-15 fax 33-93-14-16

Diplomatic representation in US:

chief of mission: Ambassador Knud-Erik Tygessen

chancery: 3200 Whitehaven Street NW, Washington, DC

telephone: [1] (202) 234-4300

FAX: [1] (202) 328-1470

US Diplomatic representation:

chief of mission: Ambassador Edward E. Elson

embassy: Dag Hammarskjolds Alle 24, 2100 Copenhagen O

mailing address: APO AE 09716

telephone: [45] (31) 42-31-44

FAX: [45] (35) 43-02-23

Djibouti

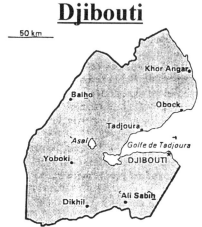

Capital: Djibouti   longitude: 43.09 E   latitude: 11.36 N   elevation: 23 ft

Government: republic

Flag: two equal horizontal bands of light blue (top) and light green with a white isosceles triangle based on the hoist side bearing a red five-pointed star in the corner

Geography

Location: Eastern Africa, bordering the Gulf of Aden and the Red Sea, between Eritrea and Somalia

Total Area: 22,000 sq km (8,494 sq mi) slightly larger than Massachusetts

Boundaries: Eritrea, Ethiopia, Somalia

Climate: desert; torrid, dry

Temperature (F): High/Low Jan. 84/73, Apr. 90/79, July 106/87, Oct. 92/80

Average annual precipitation: 5.1 inches

Terrain: coastal plain and plateau separated by central mountains

Highest point is Moussa Ali 2,063 m (6,768 ft)

Natural resources: geothermal areas

Natural hazards: earthquakes; droughts; occasional cyclonic disturbance from the Indian Ocean bring heavy rains and flash floods

People

Population: 421,320 (July 1995 est)

Life expectancy at birth: total population 49.7 years

Nationality: Djiboutian

Ethnic division: Somali 60%, Afar 35%, French, Arab, Ethiopian, and Italian 5%

Religions: Muslim 94%, Christian 6%

Languages: French (official) Arabic (official), Somali, Afar

Literacy: total population 48%

Economy

Imports: foods, beverages, transport equipment, chemicals, petroleum products

Exports: hides and skins, coffee (in transit)

Industries: limited to a few small-scale enterprises, such as dairy products and mineral water bottling

Agriculture: mostly fruit and vegetables; herding of goats, sheep, and camels

Currency: 1 Djiboutian franc (DF) = 100 centimes

Djiboutian francs per US1$ - 177.72

Transportation

Railroads: 97 km

Roads: 2,900 km total paved and unpaved

Ports: Djibouti

Airports: 13 total paved and unpaved. The international airport is at Ambouli, about 6 km from Djibouti

The Press: newspapers   **Carrefour Africain:** BP 393, Djibouti

fax 35-49-16   fortnightly

La Nation: place du 27 juin, BP 32, Djibouti

telephone 35-22-01   weekly

Tourism: Principal attractions are the desert scenery and water sports facilities on the coast

Office National du Tourisme et de l'Artisanat:

place du 27 juin, BP 1938, Djibouti, telephone 35-37-90   fax 35-63-22

Diplomatic representation in US:

chief of mission: Ambassador Roble Olhaye

chancery: Suite 515, 1156 15th Street, NW, Washington, DC 20005

telephone: [1] (202) 331-0270

FAX: [1] (202) 331-0302

US Diplomatic representation:

chief of mission: Ambassador Martin L. Cheshes

embassy: Plateau du Serpent, Boulevard Marechal Joffre, Djibouti

mailing address: BP 185, Djibouti

telephone: [253] 35-39-95

FAX: [253] 35-39-40

Dominica

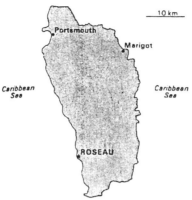

Capital: Roseau   longitude: 43.09 E latitude: 15.18 N elevation: 60 ft

Government: parliamentary democracy

Flag: green with a centered cross of three equal bands - the vertical part is yellow (hoist side), black, and white - the horizontal part is yellow (top), black, and white; superimposed in the center of the cross is a red disk bearing a sisserou parrot encircled by 10 green five-pointed stars edged in yellow; the 10 stars represent the 10 administrative divisions (parishes)

Geography

Location: Caribbean, island between the Caribbean Sea and the North Atlantic Ocean, about one-half of the way from Puerto Rico to Trinidad and Tobago

Total Area: 750 sq km (290 sq mi) slightly more than four times the size of Washington, DC

Boundaries: no land boundaries

Climate: tropical; moderated by northeast trade winds; heavy rainfall
Temperature (F): High/Low Jan. 84/68, Apr. 88/69, July 98/72, Oct. 89/72
Average annual precipitation: 77.9 inches

Terrain: rugged mountains of volcanic origin
Highest point is Morne Diablotin 1,447 m (4,747 ft)

Natural resources: timber

Natural hazards: flash floods are a constant threat; destructive hurricanes can be expected during the late summer months

People

Population: 82,608 (July 1995 est.)

Life expectancy at birth: total population 77.2 years

Nationality: Dominican

Ethnic division: black, Carib Indians

Religions: Roman Catholic 77%, Protestant 15% (Methodist 5%, Pentecostal 3%, Seventh-Day Adventist 3%, Baptist 2%, other 2%), none 2%, unknown 1% other 5%

Languages: English (official), French patois

Literacy: total population 94%

Economy

Imports: manufactured goods, machinery and equipment, food, chemicals

Exports: bananas, soap, bay oil, vegetables, grapefruit, oranges

Industries: soap, coconut oil, tourism, copra, furniture, cement blocks, shoes

Agriculture: principal crops - bananas, citrus, mangoes, root crops, coconuts; bananas provide the bulk of export earnings; forestry and fisheries potential not exploited

Currency: 1 EC dollar (EC$) = 100 cents

East Caribbean dollars per US1$ - 2.70

Transportation

Railroads: none

Roads: 750 km total paved and unpaved

Ports: Portsmouth, Roseau

Airports: 2 paved airports. Canefield Airport at Roseau and Melville Hall Airport about 64 km from Roseau

The Press: newspapers   **New Chronicle:** Wallhouse, POB 1724, Roseau telephone 82-121   fax 88-031   circ. 4,600   Friday

Official Gazette: Government Printery, Roseau telephone 82-401   circ. 600   weekly

Tourism: To preserve the beautiful, lush scenery the Government has designated areas of the island as nature reserves. There are also two marine reserves. Birdlife includes several endangered species.

National Development Corporation:
Valley Road, POB 73, Roseau
telephone 82-351   fax 85-840

Diplomatic representation in US: Dominica has no embassy in the US

US Diplomatic representation: no official residence since the Ambassador resides in Bridgetown (Barbados), but travels frequently to Dominica

Dominican Republic

North Atlantic Ocean

Caribbean Sea

Capital: Santo Domingo   longitude: 69.57 W latitude: 18.30 N
elevation: 57 ft

Government: republic

    Flag: a centered white cross that extends to the edges, divides the flag into
four rectangles - the top ones are blue (hoist side) and red, the bottom ones
are red (hoist side) and blue; a small coat of arms is at the center of the cross

Geography

    Location: Caribbean, eastern two-thirds of the island of Hispaniola, between
the Caribbean Sea and the North Atlantic Ocean, east of Haiti

    Total Area: 48,730 sq km (18,815 sq mi) slightly more than twice the size
of New Hampshire

    Boundaries: Haiti

    Climate: tropical maritime; little seasonal temperature variation; seasonal
variation in rainfall

    Temperature (F): High/Low Jan. 84/66, Apr. 88/69, July 88/72, Oct. 87/72
Average annual precipitation: 57.8 inches

    Terrain: rugged highlands and mountains with fertile valleys interspersed
Highest point is Pico Duarte 3,175 m (10,417 ft)

    Natural resources: nickel, bauxite, gold, silver

    Natural hazards: occasional hurricanes (July to October)

    Note: shares island of Hispaniola with Haiti (eastern two-thirds is the
Dominican Republic, western one-third is Haiti)

People

    Population: 7,511,263 (July 1995 est.)

    Life expectancy at birth: total population 68.73 years

    Nationality: Dominican

    Ethnic division: white 16%, black 11%, mixed 73%

    Religions: Roman Catholic 95%

Languages: Spanish

Literacy: total population 83%

Economy

Imports: foodstuffs, petroleum, cotton and fabrics, chemicals and pharmaceuticals

Exports: ferronickel, sugar, gold, coffee, cocoa

Industries: tourism, sugar processing, ferronickel and gold mining, textiles, cement, tobacco

Agriculture: commercial crops - sugarcane, coffee, cotton, cocoa, and tobacco; food crops - rice, beans, potatoes, corn, bananas; animal output - cattle, hogs, dairy products, meat, eggs; not self-sufficient in food

Currency: 1 Dominican pesos (RD$) = 100 centavos
Dominican pesos per US1$ - 13.25

Transportation

Railroads: 1,655 km

Roads: 12,000 km total paved and unpaved

Ports: Barahona, La Romana, Puerto Plata, San Pedro de Macoris, Santo Domingo

Airports: 36 total paved and unpaved. The international airports are located at Santa Domingo and Puerto Plata

The Press: daily newspapers **Listin Diario:** Paseo de los Periodistas 52, Ensanche Miraflores, Santo Domingo, DN
telephone 686-6688 fax 686-6595 circ. 55,000

Ultima Hora: Paseo de los Periodistas 52, Ensanche Miraflores, Santos Domingo, DN
telephone 688-3361 fax 688-3019 circ. 52,000

Tourism: beaches, casinos

Secretaria de Estado de Turismo:
Avda Mexico esq. 30 de Marzo, Santo Domingo
telephone 687-3655 fax 682-3806

Diplomatic representation in US:

chief of mission: Ambassador Jose del Carmen Ariza Gomez

chancery: 1715 22nd Street NW, Washington, DC 20008

telephone: [1] (202) 332-62280

FAX: [1] (202) 265-8057

US Diplomatic representation:

chief of mission: Ambassador Donna Jean Hrinak

embassy: corner of Calle Cesar Nicolas Penson and Calle Leopoldo Navarro, Santo Domingo

mailing address: Unit 5500, Santo Domingo; APO AA 34041

telephone: [1] (809) 541-2171, 8100

FAX: [1] (809) 686-7437

Ecuador

Galapagos Islands

Capital: Quito   longitude: 78.30 W   latitude: 0.14 S elevation: 9,446 ft

Government: republic

Flag: three horizontal bands of yellow (top, double width), blue, and red with a coat of arms superimposed at the center of the flag; similar to the flag of Columbia that is shorted and does not bear a coat of arms

Geography

Location: Western South America, bordering the Pacific Ocean at the Equator, between Columbia and Peru

Total Area: 283,560 sq km (109,483 sq mi) slightly smaller than Nevada

Boundaries: Columbia, Peru

Climate: tropical along coast becoming cooler inland

Temperature (F): High/Low Jan. 72/46, Apr. 70/47, July 72/44, Oct. 72/46

Average annual precipitation: 43.9 inches

Terrain: coastal plain (costa), inter-Andean central highlands (sierra), and flat to rolling eastern jungle (oriente)

Highest point is Chimborazo 6,267 m (20,561 ft)

Natural resources: petroleum, fish, timber

Natural hazards: frequent earthquakes, landslides, volcanic activity; periodic droughts

People

Population: 10,890,950 (July 1995 est.)

Life expectancy at birth: total population 70.35 years

Nationality: Ecuadorian

Ethnic division: mestizo (mixed Indian and Spanish) 55%, Indian 25%, Spanish 10%, black 10%

Religions: Roman Catholic 95%

Languages: Spanish (official), Indian languages (especially Quechua)

Literacy: total population 87%

Economy

Imports: transport equipment, consumer goods, vehicles, machinery, chemicals

Exports: petroleum, bananas, shrimp, cocoa, coffee

Industries: petroleum, food processing, textiles, metal work, paper products, wood products, chemicals, plastics, fishing, lumber

Agriculture: leading producer and exporter of bananas and balsawood; other agricultural exports - coffee, cocoa, fish, shrimp; other crops - rice, potatoes, manioc, plantains, sugarcane; livestock products - cattle, sheep, hogs, beef, pork, dairy products; net importer of food grains, dairy products, and sugar

Currency: 1 sucre (S/) = 100 centavos

sucres per US1$ - 1,198.1

Transportation

Railroads: 965 km

Roads: 43,709 km paved and unpaved

Ports: Esmeraldas, Guayaquil, La Libertad, Manta, Puerto Bolivar, San Lorenzo

Airports: 175 total paved and unpaved. The international airports are at Mariscal Sucre, near Quito, and Simon Bolivar, near Guayaquil

The Press: daily newspapers   **El Comercio:** Kilometro 6 Sur, Apdo 57, Quito   circ. 135,000
telephone (2) 26-00-20   fax (2) 61-44-66

El Tiempo: Avda America y Villalengua, Apdo 3117, Quito circ. 36,000

Tourism: Pre-Columbian artifacts, tropical rain forests, Cotopaxi volcano and national park with dwarf wildflowers, the Amazon

Associacion Ecuatoriana de Agencias de Viajes y Turismo: Edif. Banco del Pacifico, 5, Avda Amazonas 720 y Veintimilla, Casilla 9421, Quito   telephone (2) 50-36-69   fax (4) 28-58-72

Diplomatic representation in US:

    chief of mission: Ambassador Edgar Teran Teran

    chancery: 2535 15th Street NW, Washington, DC 20009

    telephone: [1] (202) 234-7200

US Diplomatic representation:

    chief of mission: Ambassador Peter F. Romero

    embassy: Avenida 12 de Octubre y Avenida Patria, Quito

    mailing address: APO AA 34039-3420

    telephone: [593] (2) 56-28-90, 56-16-24, 56-17-49

    FAX: [593] (2) 50-20-52

Egypt

Capital: Cairo   longitude: 31.15 E   latitude: 30.03 N elevation: 381 ft

Government: republic

    Flag: three equal horizontal bands of red (top), white, and black with the national emblem (a shield superimposed on a golden eagle facing the hoist side above a scroll bearing the name of the country in Arabic) centered in the white band; similar to the flag of Yemen, which has a plain white band; also similar to the flag of Syria that has two green stars and to the flag of Iraq, which has three green stars (plus an Arabic inscription) in a horizontal line centered in the white band

Geography

    Location: Northern Africa, bordering the Mediterranean Sea, between Libya and the Gaza Strip

    Total Area: 1,001,450 sq km (386,660 sq mi) slightly more than three times the size of New Mexico

    Boundaries: Gaza Strip, Israel, Libya, Sudan

    Climate: desert; hot, dry summers with moderate winters

Temperature (F): High/Low Jan. 65/47, Apr. 83/57, July 96/70, Oct. 86/65

Average annual precipitation: 1.1 inches

Terrain: vast desert plateau interrupted by Nile valley and delta

Highest point is Mount Katherina 2,637 m (8,651 ft)

Natural resources: petroleum, natural gas, iron ore, phosphates, manganese, limestone, gypsum, talc, asbestos, lead, zinc

Natural hazards: periodic droughts; frequent earthquakes, flash floods, landslides, volcanic activity; hot, driving windstorm called khamsin occurs in spring; duststorms, sandstorms

People

Population: 62,359, 623 (July 1995 est.)

Life expectancy at birth: total population 61.12 years

Nationality: Egyptian

Ethnic division: Eastern Hamitic stock (Egyptians, Bedouins, and Berbers) 99%, Greek, Nubian, Armenian, other European (primarily Italian and French) 1%

Religions: Muslim (mostly Sunni) 94% (official estimate), Coptic Christian and other 6%

Languages: Arabic (official), English and French widely understood by educated classes

Literacy: total population 48%

Economy

Imports: machinery and equipment, foods, fertilizers, wood products, durable consumer goods, capital goods

Exports: crude oil and petroleum products, cotton yarn, raw cotton, textiles, metal products, chemicals

Industries: textiles, food processing, tourism, chemicals, petroleum, construction, cement, metals

Agriculture: cotton, rice, corn, wheat, beans, vegetables; cattle, water buffalo, sheep, goats; annual fish catch about 140,000 metric tons

Currency: 1 Egyptian pound (#E) = 100 piasters

Egyptian pounds per US1$ - 3.4

Transportation

Railroads: 4,895 km

Roads: 47,387 km total paved and unpaved

Ports: Alexandria, Al Ghurdaqah, Aswan, Asyut, Bur Safajah, Damietta, Marsa Matruh, Port Said, Suez

Airports: 91 total paved and unpaved. The main international airports are at Heliopolis about 20 km from Cairo, and Alexandria

The Press: daily newspapers

Al-Ahram: Sharia al-Galaa, Cairo
telephone (2) 574-7011 fax (2) 574-7089
circ. 900,000

Al-Akhbar: Dar Akhbar al-Yawn, Sharia as-Sahafa, Cairo
telephone (2) 574-8100   circ. 980,000

Tourism: famous pyramids, the Sphinx, Nile, Suez Canel, diving in the Red Sea, fish filled reef, coral gardens

Ministry of Tourism: Misr Travel Tower, Abbassia Square, Cairo
telephone (2) 282-8430   fax (2) 282-9771

Diplomatic representation in US:

chief of mission: Ambassador Ahmed Maher El Sayed
chancery: 3521 International Court NW, Washington, DC 20008
telephone: [1] (202) 895-5400
FAX: [1] (202) 244-4319, 5131

US Diplomatic representation:

chief of mission: Ambassador Edward S. Walker, Jr
embassy: (North Gate) 8, Kamel El-Din Salah Street, Garden City, Cairo
mailing address: APO AE 09839-4900
telephone: [20] (2) 355-7371
FAX: [20] (2) 357-3200

El Salvador

North Pacific Ocean

Capital: San Salvador   longitude: 89.10 W   latitude: 13.40 N
elevation. 2,238 ft

Government: republic

Flag: three equal horizontal bands of blue (top), white, and blue with the national coat of arms centered in the white band; the coat of arms features a round emblem encircled by the words REPUBLICA DE EL SALVADOR EN LA AMERICA CENTRAL; similar to the flag of Nicaragua, which has a different coat of arms centered in the white band - it features a triangle encircled by the words REPUBLICA DE NICARAGUA on top and AMERICA CENTRAL on the bottom; also similar to the flag of Honduras, which has five blue stars arranged in an X pattern centered in the white band

Geography

Location: Middle America, bordering the North Pacific Ocean, between Guatemala and Honduras

Total Area: 21,040 sq km (8,124 sq mi) slightly smaller than Massachusetts

Boundaries: Guatemala, Honduras

Climate: tropical; rainy season (May to October); dry season (November to April)

Temperature (F): High/Low Jan. 90/60, Apr. 93/65, July 89/65, Oct. 87/65

Average annual precipitation: 70 inches

Terrain: mostly mountains with narrow coastal belt and central plateau

Highest point is Santa Ana 2,385 m (7,825 ft)

Natural resources: hydropower, geothermal power, petroleum

Natural hazards: known as the land of volcanoes; frequent and sometimes very destructive earthquakes and volcanic activity

People

Population: 5.870,481 (July 1995 est.)

Life expectancy at birth: total population 67.5 years

Nationality: Salvadoran

Ethnic division: mestizo 94%, Indian 5%, white 1%

Religions: Roman Catholic 75%

Languages: Spanish, Nahua (among some Indians)

Literacy: total population 73%

Economy

Imports: raw materials, consumer goods, capital goods

Exports: coffee, sugarcane, shrimp

Industries: food processing, beverages, petroleum, nonmetallic products, tobacco, chemicals, textiles, furniture

Agriculture: coffee most important commercial crop; other products - sugarcane, corn, rice, beans, oilseed, beef, dairy products, shrimp; not self-sufficient in food

Currency: 1 Salvadoran colon (C) = 100 centavos

Salvadoran colones per US1$ - 8.76

Transportation

Railroads: 602 km

Roads: 10,000 km paved and unpaved

Ports: Acajutla, Puerto Cutuco, La Libertad, La Union, Puerto El Triunfo

Airports: 106 total paved and unpaved

The Press: daily newspapers **El Diario de Hoy:** 11a Calle Oriente y Avda Cuscatancingo 271, Apdo 495, San Salvador telephone 71-01-00 fax 22-94-41 circ. 87,000

El Mundo: 2a Avda Norte 211, Apdo 368, San Salvador telephone 71-44-00 circ. 60,000 weekdays, 62,000 Sundays

Tourism: Tourist attractions are the volcanoes, upland lakes with beautiful scenery, ancient Mayan ruined temples and wonderful beaches along the Pacific coast

Comite Nacional de Turismo: San Salvador telephone 23-45-66

Diplomatic representation in US:

chief of mission: Ambassador Ana Cristina Sol

chancery: 2308 California Street NW, Washington, DC 20008

telephone: [1] (202) 265-9671, 9672

US Diplomatic representation:

chief of mission: Ambassador Alan H. Flanigan

embassy: Final Boulevard, Station Antiguo Cuscatlan, San Salvador

mailing address: Unit 3116, San Salvador; APO AA 34023

telephone: [503] 78-44-44

FAX: [503] 78-60-11

Equatorial Guinea

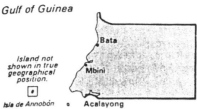

Gulf of Guinea

Island not shown in true geographical position.

Isla de Annobón ▫ Acalayong

Capital: Malabo   longitude: 8.48E   latitude: 3.45 N

Government: republic in transition to multiparty democracy

Flag: three equal horizontal bands of green (top), white, and red with a blue isosceles triangle based on the hoist side and the coat of arms centered in the white band; the coat of arms has six yellow six-pointed stars (representing the mainland and five offshore islands) above a gray shield bearing a silk-cotton tree and below which is a scroll with the motto UNIDAD, PAZ, JUSTICIA (Unity, Peace, Justice)

Geography

Location: Western Africa, bordering the North Atlantic Ocean, between Cameroon and Gabon

Total Area: 28,050 sq km (10,830 sq mi) slightly larger than Maryland

Boundaries: Cameroon, Gabon

Climate: tropical; always hot, humid

Temperature (F): High/Low Jan. 87/67, Apr. 89/70, July 84/69, Oct. 86/70

Average annual precipitation: 71.8 inches

Terrain: coastal plains rise to interior hills; islands are volcanic

Natural resources: timber, petroleum, small unexploited deposits of gold, manganese, uranium

Natural hazards: violent windstorms

People

Population: 420,293 (July 1995 est.)

Life expectancy at birth: total population 52.56 years

Nationality: Equatorial Guinean

Ethnic division: Bioko (primarily Bubi, some Fernandinos), Rio Muni (primarily Fang), Europeans less than 1,000, mostly Spanish

Religions: nominally Christian and predominantly Roman Catholic, pagan practices

Languages: Spanish (official), pidgin English, Fang, Bubi, Ibo

Literacy: total population 62%

Economy

Imports: petroleum, food, beverages, clothing, machinery

Exports: coffee, timber, cocoa beans

Industries: fishing, sawmilling

Agriculture: cash crops - rice, yams, cassava, bananas, oil palm nuts, manioc, livestock

Currency: 1 CFA franc (CFAF) = 100 centimes

Communaute Financiere Africaine francs per US1$ - 529.43

Transportation

Railroads: none

Roads: 2,760 km total paved and unpaved

Ports: Bata, Luba, Malabo

Airports: 3 total paved. There is an international airport at Malabo, and a smaller airport at Bata.

The Press: newspapers   **Ebano:** Malabo; Spanish   circ. 1,000

            Hoja Parroquial: Malabo;   weekly

Tourism: beaches at Bioko, Malabo

Diplomatic representation in US:

chief of mission: (vacant) Charge d'Affaires ad interim
Theodoro Biyogo Nsue

chancery: (temporary) 57 Magnolia Avenue, Mount Vernon, NY 10553

telephone: [1] (914) 738-9584, 667-6913

FAX: [1] (914) 667-6838

US Diplomatic representation:

chief of mission: Charge d'Affaires Joseph P. O'neill

embassy: Calle de Los Ministros, Malabo

mailing address: P O Box 597, Malabo

telephone: [240] (9) 21-85, 24-06, 25-07

FAX: [240] (9) 21-64

Eritrea

Capital: Asmara   longitude: 39.20 E   latitude: 16.02 N

Government: transitional government

   Flag: red isosceles triangle (based on the hoist side) dividing the flag into two right triangles; the upper triangle is green, the lower one blue; a gold wreath encircling a gold olive branch is centered on the hoist side of the red triangle

Geography

   Location: Eastern Africa, bordering the Red Sea, between Djibouti and Sudan

   Total Area: 121,320 sq km (46,842) slightly larger than Pennsylvania

   Boundaries: Djibouti, Ethiopia, Sudan

   Climate: hot, dry desert strip along Red Sea coast, cooler and wetter in the central highlands (up to 61 cm of rainfall annually); semiarid in western hills and lowlands; rainfall heaviest during June-September except on coastal desert

   Terrain: dominated by extension of Ethiopian north-south trending highlands, descending on the east to a coastal desert plain, on the northwest to hilly terrain and on the southwest to flat-to-rolling plains

   Natural resources: gold, potash, zinc, copper, salt, probably oil (petroleum geologists are prospecting for it), fish

   Natural hazards: frequent droughts

People

   Population: 3,578,709 (July 1995 est.)

   Life expectancy at birth: total population 50 years

   Nationality: Eritrean

Ethnic division: ethnic Tigrays 50%, Tigre and Kunama 40%, Afar 4%, Saho (Red Sea coast dwellers) 3%
Religions: Muslim, Coptic Christian, Roman Catholic, Protestant
Languages: Tigre and Kunama, Cushitic dialects, Tigre, Nora Bana, Arabic
Literacy: total population 23%
Economy
Imports: NA
Exports: NA
Industries: food processing, beverages, clothing and textiles
Agriculture: products - sorghum, livestock (including goats), fish, lentils, vegetables, maize, cotton, tobacco, coffee, sisal (for making rope)
Currency: 1 birr (Br) = 100 cents; at present Ethiopian currency used
       1 birr per US1$ - 5.95
Transportation
Railroads: 307 km
Roads: 3,845 km total paved and unpaved
Ports: Assab (Aseb), Massawa (Mits'swa)
Airports: 20 total paved and unpaved. The international airport is at Asmara
The Press: newspapers   **Chamber News:** POB 856, Asmara
                        Tigrinya and English   telephone 11-13-88
               Hadas Eritrea: Asmara, twice a week Tigrinya and Arabic
                        circ. 25,000
Tourism: Tourist attractions are the Dahlak Islands, a coral archipelago rich in marine life, wildlife, massive cliffs formed by erosion rising from the coastal plains

Diplomatic representation in US:
chief of mission: Ambassador Amdemichael Berhane Khasai
chancery: Suite 400, 910 17th Street NW, Washington, DC 20006
telephone: [1] (202) 429-1991
FAX: [1] (202) 429-9004
US Diplomatic representation:
chief of mission: Ambassador Robert G. Houdek
embassy: 34 Zera Yacob Street, Asmara
mailing address: P O Box 211, Asmara
telephone: [291] (1) 12-00-04
FAX: [291] (1) 12-75-84

Estonia

150 km

Capital: Tallinn   longitude: 24.70 E   latitude: 59.50 N
Government: republic
  Flag: pre-1940 flag restored by Supreme Soviet in May 1990 - three equal
    horizontal bands of blue (top), black, and white
Geography
  Location: Eastern Europe, bordering the Baltic Sea and Gulf of Finland,
  between Latvia and Russia
  Total Area: 45,100 sq km (17,413 sq mi) slightly larger than New
  Hampshire and Vermont combined
  Boundaries: Latvia, Russia
  Climate: maritime, wet, moderate winters, cool summers
  Temperature (F): 23 degrees in January and 62.6 degrees in July
  Average annual precipitation: 22.3 inches
  Terrain: marshy, lowlands
  Natural resources: shale oil, peat, phosphorite, amber
  Natural hazards: flooding occurs frequently in the spring
People
  Population: 1,625,399 (July 1995 est.)
  Life expectancy at birth: total population 70.17 years
  Nationality: Estonian
  Ethnic division: Estonian 61.5%, Russian 30.3%, Ukrainian 3.17%,
  Byelorussian 1.8%, Finn 1.1%, other 2.13%
  Religions: Lutheran
  Languages: Estonian (official), Latvian, Lithuanian, Russian, other
  Literacy: total population 100%
Economy
  Imports: machinery, fuels, vehicles, textiles

Exports: textiles, food products, vehicles, metals

Industries: oil shale, shipbuilding, phosphates, electric motors, excavators, cement, furniture, clothing, textiles, paper, shoes, apparel

Agriculture: very efficient by Soviet standards; net exports of meat, fish, dairy products, and potatoes; imports of feed grains for livestock; fruits and vegetables

Currency: 1 Estonian kroon (EEK) = 100 cents

kroons per US1$ - 12.25

Transportation

Railroads: 1,030 km

Roads: 30,300 km total paved and unpaved

Ports: Haapsalu, Narva, Novotallin, Paldiski, Parnu, Tallinn

Airports: 22 total paved and unpaved. Estonia has air links with most major cities in Russia and several western European cities

The Press: newspapers   **Eesti Ekspress:** Tatari 21B, Tallinn 0001

telephone (6) 31-31-53, fax (6) 31-31-54

weekly, circ. 40,000

Rahva Haal: Parnu mnt. 67A, Tallinn 0090

telephone (2) 68-12-02 fax (2) 44-85-34 circ. 65,000 daily

Tourism: Tourist attractions are historic towns, nature reserves and coastal resorts

Estonian Tourist Board: pikk 71, Tallinn 0101

telephone (2) 60-17-00   fax (2) 45-28-83

Diplomatic representation in US:

chief of mission: Ambassador Toomas Hendrik Ilves

chancery: 1030 15th Street NW, Washington, DC 20005, Suite 1000

telephone: [1] (202) 789-0320

FAX: [1] (202) 789-0471

US Diplomatic representation:

chief of mission: (vacant); Charge d'Affaires Kieth Smith

embassy: Kentmanni 20, Tallinn EE 0001

mailing address: use embassy street address

telephone: [372] (2) 31-20-21 through 24

FAX: [372] (2) 31-20-25

Ethiopia

Capital: Addis Ababa   longitude: 38.50 E   latitude: 9.03 N
elevation: 8,038 ft

Government: transitional government

Flag: three equal horizontal bands of green (top), yellow, and red; Ethiopia is the oldest independent country in Africa, and the colors of her flag were so often adopted by other African countries upon independence that they become known as the pan-African colors

Geography

Location: Eastern Africa, west of Somalia

Total Area: 1,127,127 sq km (435,184 sq mi) slightly less than twice the size of Texas

Boundaries: Djibouti, Eritrea, Kenya, Somalia, Sudan

Climate: tropical monsoon with wide topographic-induced variation
Temperature (F): High/Low Jan. 75/43, Apr. 77/50, July 69/50, Oct. 75/45
Average annual precipitation: 48.7 inches

Terrain: high plateau with central mountain range divided by Great Rift Valley
Highest point is Ras Dashan 4,620 m (15,157 ft)

Natural resources: small reserves of gold, platinum, copper, potash

Natural hazards: geologically active Great Rift Valley susceptible to earthquakes, volcanic eruptions; frequent droughts

People

Population: 55,979,018 (July 1995 est.)

Life expectancy at birth: total population 50 years

Nationality: Ethiopian

Ethnic division: Oromo 40%, Amhara and Tigrean 32%, Sidamo 9%, Shankella 6%, Somali 6%, Afar 4%, Gurage 2%, other 1%

Religions: Muslim 48%, Ethiopian Orthodox 38%, animist 12%

Languages: Amharic (official), Tiginya, Orominga, Somali, Arabic, English (major foreign language taught in schools)

Literacy: total population 24%

Economy

Imports: capital goods, consumer goods, fuel

Exports: coffee, leather products, gold

Industries: food processing, beverages, textiles, chemicals, metals processing, cement

Agriculture: export crops of coffee and oilseeds are grown partly on state farms; principal crops and livestock - cereals, pulses, coffee, oilseeds, sugarcane, potatoes, and other vegetables, hides and skins, cattle, sheep, goats

Currency: 1 birr (Br) = 100 cents
birr per US1$ - 5.95

Transportation

Railroads: 681 km

Roads: 24,127 km total paved and unpaved

Ports: none

Airports: 98 total paved and unpaved. The international airports are located at Addis Ababa and Bahir Dar

The Press: daily newspapers **Addis Zemen:** POB 30145, Addis Ababa
circ. 40,000

Ethiopian Herald: POB 30701, Addis Ababa
telephone 11-90-50 English circ. 38,000

Tourism: Tourist attractions are national parks, the Blue Nile Falls, early Christian monuments and churches

Ethiopian Tourism Commission: POB 2183, Addis Ababa
telephone 51-74-70 fax 51-38-99

Diplomatic representation in US:

chief of mission: Ambassador Berhane Gebre-Christos

chancery: 2134 Kalorama Road NW, Washington, DC 20008

telephone: [1] (202) 234-2281, 2282

FAX: [1] (202) 328-7950

US Diplomatic representation:

chief of mission: Ambassador Irvin Hicks

embassy: Entoto Street, Addis Ababa

mailing address: P O Box 1014, Addis Ababa

telephone: [251] (1) 55-06-66

FAX: [251] (1) 55-21-91

Europa Island

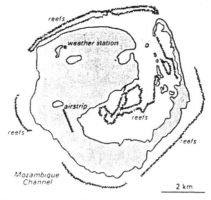

Capital: none; administered by France from Reunion

longitude: 41.20 E   latitude: 22.20 N

Government: French possession administered by Commissioner of the Republic; resident in Reunion

Geography

Location: Southern Africa, island in the Mozambique Channel, about one-half of the way from southern Madagascar to southern Mozambique

Total Area: 28 sq km (10.8 sq mi) about 0.2 times the size of Washington, DC

Boundaries: no land boundaries

Climate: tropical

Terrain: NA

Natural resources: negligible

Natural hazards: NA

People

Population: uninhabited

Ports: none; offshore anchorage only

Airports: 1 with unpaved runway

Falkland Islands

Capital: Stanley longitude: 57.51 W latitude: 51.42 S elevation: 6 ft

Government: dependent territory of UK

Flag: blue with the flag of the UK in the upper hoist-side quadrant and the Falkland Island coat of arms in a white disk centered on the outer half of the flag; the coat of arms contains a white ram (sheep raising is the major economic activity) above the sailing ship Desire (whose crew discovered the islands) with a scroll at the bottom bearing the motto DESIRE THE RIGHT

Geography

Location: Southern South America, islands in the South Atlantic Ocean, east of southern Argentina

Total Area: 12,170 sq km (4,699 sq mi) slightly smaller than Connecticut

Boundaries: no land boundaries

Climate: cold marine; strong westerly winds, cloudy, humid; rain occurs on more than half of days in year; occasional snow all year, except in January and February, but does not accumulate

Temperature (F): High/Low Jan. 56/42, Apr. 49/37, July 40/31, Oct. 48/35

Average annual precipitation: 26.8 inches

Terrain: rocky, hilly, mountainous with some boggy, undulating plains

Natural resources: fish, wildlife

Natural hazards: strong winds persist throughout the year

People

Population: 2,317 (July 1995 est.)

Life expectancy at birth: NA

Nationality: Falkland Islander

Ethnic division: British

146

Religions: primarily Anglican, Roman Catholic, United Free Church, Evangelist Church, Jehovah's Witnesses, Lutheran, Seventh-Day Adventist

Languages: English

Literacy: NA

Economy

Imports: food, clothing, timber, and machinery

Exports: wool, hides and skins, and meat

Industries: wool and fish processing

Agriculture: predominantly sheep farming; small dairy herds, some fodder and vegetable crops

Currency: 1 Falkland pound (#F) = 100 pence

Falkland pound per US1$ - 0.63

Transportation

Railroads: none

Roads: 510 km total paved and unpaved

Ports: Stanley

Airports: 5 total paved and unpaved. The main airport is located at Stanley

The Press: weekly newspaper **Penguin News:** Ross Road, Stanley

fax 22-238

Tourism: bird watching and hiking

Falkland Islands Tourist Board:

56 John Street, Stanley

telephone 22-215   fax 22-619

Diplomatic representation in US: none (dependent territory of the UK)

Diplomatic representation: none (dependent territory of the UK)

Faroe Islands

Capital: Torshavn   longitude: 6.45 W   latitude: 62.02 N   elevation. 82 ft

Government: part of Danish realm; self-governing overseas administrative division of Denmark

Flag: white with a red cross outlined in blue that extends to the edges of the flag; the vertical part of the cross is shifted to the hoist side in the style of the DANNEBROG (Danish flag)

Geography

Location: Northern Europe, island group between the Norwegian Sea and the North Atlantic Ocean, about one-half of the way from Iceland to Norway

Total Area: 1,400 sq km (540.5 sq mi) slightly less than eight times the size of Washington, DC

Boundaries: no land boundaries

Climate: mild winters, cool summers; usually overcast; foggy, windy. Temperature (F): High/Low Jan. 42/33, Apr. 45/36, July 56/47, Oct. 58/40 Average annual precipitation: 56.2 inches

Terrain: rugged, rocky, some low peaks; cliffs along most of coast

Natural resources: fish

Natural hazards: NA

Note: archipelago of 18 inhabited islands and a few uninhabited islets; strategically located along important sea lanes in northeastern Atlantic; precipitous terrain limits habitation to small coastal lowlands

People

Population: 48,871 (July 1995 est.)

Life expectancy at birth: total population 78.29 years

Nationality: Faroese

Ethnic division: Scandinavian

Religions: Evangelical Lutheran

Languages: Faroese (derived from Old Norse), Danish

Literacy: NA

Economy

Imports: machinery and transport equipment, manufactures, food and livestock

Exports: fish and fish products, animal feedstuffs, transport equipment (ships)

Industries: fishing, shipbuilding, handicrafts

Agriculture: principal crops - potatoes and vegetables; livestock - sheep

Currency: 1 Danish krone (DKr) = 100 oere

Danish kroner per US1$ - 6.03

Transportation

Railroads: none

Roads: 200 km total paved and unpaved

Ports: Klaksvick, Torshavn, Tvoroyri

Airports: 1 paved runway. The airport is on Vagar.

The Press: newspapers   **Friu Foroyar:** Argjavegur 26, POB 2055, 165 Argir
telephone 16-444   fax 18-813   circ. 1,000   weekly

Tidindabladid Sosialurin: POB 76, 110 Torshavn
telephone 11-820   fax 14-720   circ. 6,500   5 a week

Tourism: NA

Ferdarad Foroya: Reyngota 17, 100 Torshav
telephone 16-055   fax 10-858

Diplomatic representation in US: none (self-governing overseas administrative division of Denmark)

US Diplomatic representation: none (self-governing overseas administrative division of Denmark)

Fiji

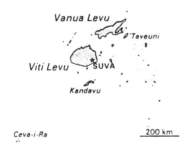

South Pacific Ocean

Capital: Suva   longitude: 178.25 E   latitude: 18.08 S   eolevation: 20 ft

Government: republic

Flag: light blue with the flag of the UK in the upper hoist-side quadrant and the Fijian shield centered on the outer half of the flag; the shield depicts a yellow lion above a white field quartered by the cross of Saint George featuring stalks of sugarcane, a palm tree, and a white dove

Geography

Location: Oceania, island group in the South Pacific Ocean, about two-thirds of the way from Hawaii to New Zealand

Total Area: 18,270 sq km (7,054 sq mi) slightly smaller than New Jersey

Boundaries: no land boundaries

Climate: tropical marine; only slight seasonal temperature variation
Temperature (F): High/Low Jan. 86/74, Apr. 84/73, July 79/68, Oct. 81/70
Average annual precipitation: 117 inches
Terrain: mostly mountains of volcanic origin
Highest point is Tomaniivi 1,323 m (4,341 ft)
Natural resources: timber, fish, gold, copper, offshore oil potential
Natural hazards: cyclonic storms can occur from November to January
Note: includes 332 islands of which approximately 110 are inhabited

People

Population: 772,891 (July 1995 est.)
Life expectancy at birth: total population 65.42 years
Nationality: Fijian
Ethnic division: Fijian 49%, Indian 46%, European, other Pacific Islanders, overseas Chinese, and others 5%
Religions: Christians 52%, (Methodist 37%, Roman Catholic 9%), Hindu 38%, Muslim 8%, other 2%
Languages: English (official), Fijian, Hindustani
Literacy: total population 87%

Economy

Imports: machinery and transport equipment, petroleum products, food. consumer goods, chemicals
Exports: sugar, clothing, gold, processed fish, lumber
Industries: sugar, tourism, copra, gold, silver, clothing, lumber, small cottage industries
Agriculture: principal cash crop is sugarcane; coconuts, cassava, rice, sweet potatoes, bananas; small livestock sector includes cattle, pigs, horses, and goats, fish
Currency: 1 Fijian dollar (F$) = 100 cents
Fijian dollars per US1$ - 1.41

Transportation

Railroads: 644 km
Roads: 3,300 km paved and unpaved
Ports: Labasa, Lautoka, Levuka, Savusavu, Suva
Airports: 23 total paved and unpaved. There is an international airport at Nadi, about 200 km from Suva (west)

The Press: newspapers   **Daily Post:** 422 Fletcher Road, POB 2971, Government Bldgs. Suva   English daily
     Fiji Times: 20 Gordon street, POB 1167, Suva telephone 30-41-11 fax 30-15-21 circ. 27,600 English daily

Tourism: Climate, scenery, fishing, and diving.

Fiji Visitors Bureau: POB 92, Suva

telephone 30-24-33   fax 30-09-70

Diplomatic representation in US:

chief of mission: Ambassador Pita Kewa Nacuva

chancery: Suite 240, 2233 Wisconsin Avenue NW, Washington, DC 20007

telephone: [1] (202) 337-8320

FAX: [1] (202) 337-1996

US Diplomatic representation:

chief of mission: (vacant) Charge d'Affaires Michael W. Marine

embassy: 31 Loftus Street, Suva

mailing address: P O Box 218, Suva

telephone: [679] 31-44-66

FAX: [679] 30-00-81

Finland

Capital: Helisinki   longitude: 25.00 E latitude: 60.08 N elevation. 151 ft

Government: republic

Flag: white with blue cross that extends to the edges of the flag; the vertical part of the cross is shifted to the hoist side in the style of the DANNEBROG (Danish flag)

Geography

Location: Northern Europe, bordering the Baltic Sea, Gulf of Bothnia, and Gulf of Finland, between Sweden and Russia

Total Area: 337,030 sq km (130,127 sq mi) slightly larger than Montana

Boundaries: Norway, Sweden, Russia

151

Climate: cold temperate; potentially subarctic, but comparatively mild because of moderating influence of the North Atlantic Current, Baltic Sea, and more than 60,000 lakes

Temperature (F): High/Low Jan. 26/17, Apr. 44/30, July 71/55, Oct. 47/37

Average annual precipitation: 27.1 inches

Terrain: mostly low, flat to rolling plains interspersed with lakes and low hills

Highest point is Haltiatunturi 1,324 m (4,343 ft)

Natural resources: timber, copper, zinc, iron ore, silver

Natural hazards: NA

Note: long boundary with Russia; Helsinki is northernmost national capital on European continent; population concentrated on small southwestern coastal plain

People

Population: 5,085,206 (July 1995 est.)

Life expectancy at birth: total population 76.22 years

Nationality: Finn

Ethnic division: Finn, Swede, Lapp, Gypsy, Tatar

Religions: Evangelical Lutheran 89%, Greek Orthodox 1%, none 9%, other 1%

Languages: Finish (official), Swedish, (official), small Lapp-and Russian-speaking minorities

Literacy: total population 100%

Economy

Imports: foodstuffs, petroleum and petroleum products, chemicals, transport equipment, iron and steel, machinery, textile yarn and fabrics, fodder grains

Exports: paper and pulp. machinery, chemicals, metals, timber

Industries: metal products, shipbuilding, forestry and wood processing (pulp, paper), copper refining, foodstuffs, chemicals, textiles, clothing

Agriculture: livestock production, especially dairy cattle, predominates; main crops - cereals, sugar beets, potatoes; self-sufficient, but short of food grains and fodder grains; annual fish catch about 160,000 metric tons

Currency: 1 markka (FMk) or Finmark = 100 pennia
markka per US1$ - 4.73

Transportation

Railroads: 5,864 km

Roads: 76,755 km total paved and unpaved

Ports: Hamina, Helsinki, Kokkola, Kotka, Loviisa, Oulu, Pori, Rauma, Turku, Uusikaupunki, Varkaus

Airports: 159 total paved and unpaved. The international airport is about 18 km outside Helsinki

The Press: daily newspapers

Helsingin Sanomat: Ludviginkatu 2-10, POB 975, 00101 Helsinki
telephone (90) 12-21
circ. 482,000 weekdays, 572,000 Sunday

Iltalehti: POB 372, 00101 Helsinki
telephone (90) 50-77-21 fax (90) 53-35-12
circ. 120,000 weekdays, 140,000 Sundays

Tourism: Europe's largest inland water system, magnificent scenery, vast forests.

Matkailun edistamiskeskus: POB 625, 00101 Helsinki
telephone (90) 40-30-11 fax (90) 40-30-13-33

Diplomatic representation in US:
chief of mission: Ambassador Jukka Valtasaari
chancery: 3301 Massachusetts Avenue NW, Washington, DC 20008
telephone: [1] (202) 298-5800
FAX: [1] (202) 298-6030

US Diplomatic representation:
chief of mission: Ambassador Derek N. Shearer
embassy: Itainen Puistotic 14A, Fin-00140, Helsinki
mailing address: APO AE 09723
telephone: [358] (0) 17-19-31
FAX: [358] (0) 17-46-81

France

Capital: Paris   longitude: 2.20 E   latitude: 48.52 N elevation: 246 ft
Government: republic

Flag: three equal vertical bands of blue (hoist side), white, and red; known as the French Tricouleur (Tricolor); the design and colors are similar to a number of other flags, including Belgium, Chad, Ireland, Cote d'Ivoire, and Luxembourg; the official flag for all French dependent areas

Geography

Location: Western Europe, bordering the Bay of Biscay and English Channel, between Belgium and Spain southeast of the UK; bordering the Mediterranean Sea, between Italy and Spain

Total Area: 547,030 sq km (211,208 sq mi) slightly more than twice the size of Colorado

Boundaries: Andorra, Belgium, Germany, Italy, Luxembourg, Monaco, Spain, Switzerland

Climate: generally cool winters and mild summers, but mild winters and hot summers along the Mediterranean

Temperature (F): High/Low Jan. 43/34, Apr. 60/43, July 76/58, Oct. 60/46

Average annual precipitation: 24.4 inches

Terrain: mostly flat plains or gently rolling hills in north and west; remainder is mountainous, especially Pyrenees in south, Alps in east

Highest point is Mont Blanc 4,807 m (15,771 ft)

Natural resources: coal, iron ore, bauxite, fish, timber, zinc, potash

Natural hazards: flooding

People

Population: 58,109,160 (July 1995 est.)

Life expectancy at birth: total population 78.37 years

Nationality: Frenchman

Ethnic division: Celtic and Latin with Teutonic, Slavic, North African, Indochinese, Basque minorities

Religions: Roman Catholic 90%, Protestant 2%, Jewish 1%, Muslim (North African workers) 1%, unaffiliated 6%

Languages: French 100%, rapidly declining regional dialects and languages

Literacy: total population 99%

Economy

Imports: crude oil, machinery and equipment, agricultural products, chemicals, iron and steel products

Exports: machinery and transportation equipment, chemicals, foodstuffs, agricultural products, iron and steel products, textiles and clothing

Industries: steel, machinery, chemicals, automobiles, metallurgy, aircraft, electronics, mining, textiles, food processing, tourism

Agriculture: one of the world's top five wheat producers; other principal products - beef, dairy products, cereals, sugar beets, potatoes, wine grapes; self-sufficient for most temperate zone foods; shortages includes fats and oils and tropical produce

Currency: 1 French franc (F) = 100 centimes
French francs per US1$ - 5.92

Transportation

Railroads: 34,975 km

Roads: 1,511,200 km total paved and unpaved

Ports: Bordeaux, Boulogne, Cherbourg, Dijon, Dunkerque, La Pallice, Le Havre, Lyon, Marseille, Mullhouse, Nantes, Paris, Rouen, Saint Nazaire, Saint Malo, Strasbourg

Airports: 476 total paved and unpaved. The international airports are at Orly, Roissy and Le Bourget (Paris), Bordeaux, Lille, Lyon, Marseille, Nice, Strasbourg, Toulouse

The Press: daily newspapers

Le Figaro: 37 rue du Louvre, 75002 Paris
telephone (1) 42-21-62-00   fax (1) 42-21-64-05
circ. 435,000

Le Monde: 15 rue Falguiere, 75501 Paris Cedex 03
telephone (1) 40-65-25-25   fax (1) 40-65-25-99
circ. 310,000

Tourism: Paris is famous for its historic buildings, theaters, art treasures, fashion shows, restaurants and night clubs. Tourist resorts on the Atlantic and Mediterranean coasts.

Observatoire National du Tourisme: 2 rue Linois, 75015 Paris
telephone (1) 44-37-36-49   fax (1) 44-37-38-51

Diplomatic representation in US:

chief of mission: Ambassador Jacques Andreani
chancery: 4101 Reservoir Road NW, Washington, DC 20007
telephone: [1] (202) 944-6000

US Diplomatic representation:

chief of mission: Ambassador Pamela C. Harriman
embassy: 2 Avenue Gabriel, 75382 Paris Cedex 08
mailing address: Unit 21551, Paris APO AE 09777
telephone: [33] (1) 42-96-12-02,   42-61-80-75
FAX: [33] (1) 42-66-97-83

French Guiana

North
Atlantic
Ocean
100 km

Saint-Laurent du Maroni

Kourou

CAYENNE

Saint-Georges

Saül

Capital: Cayenne   longitude: 52.18 W   latitude: 4.55 N elevation: 20 ft

Government: overseas department of France

Flag: the flag of France is used

Geography

Location: Northern South America, bordering the North Atlantic Ocean, between Brazil and Suriname

Total Area: 91,000 sq km (35,135 sq mi) slightly smaller than Indiana

Boundaries: Brazil, Suriname

Climate: tropical; hot, humid; little seasonal temperature variation
Temperature (F): High/Low Jan. 84/74, Apr. 86/75, July 88/73, Oct. 91/74
Average annual precipitation: 126.1 inches

Terrain: low-lying coastal plains rising to hills and small mountains
Highest point 830 m (2,723 ft)

Natural resources: bauxite, timber, gold (widely scattered), cinnabar, kaolin, fish

Natural hazards: high frequency of heavy showers and severe thunderstorms; flooding

People

Population: 145,270 (July 1995 est.)

Life expectancy at birth: total population 75.52 years

Nationality: French Guianese

Ethnic division: black or mulatto 66%, Caucasian 12%, East Indian, Chinese, Amerindian 12%, other 10%

Religions: Roman Catholic

Languages: French

Literacy: total population 83%

Economy

    Imports: food (grains, processed meat), other consumer goods, producer goods, petroleum

    Exports: shrimp, timber, rum, rosewood essence

Industries: construction, shrimp processing, forestry products, rum, gold mining

Agriculture: some vegetable for local consumption; rice, corn, manioc, cocoa, bananas, sugar; livestock - cattle, pigs, poultry

Currency: 1 French franc (F) = 100 centimes

               French francs per US1$ - 5.92

Transportation

    Railroads: 22 km

    Roads: 1,137 km total paved and unpaved

    Ports: Cayenne, Degrad des Cannes, Saint-Laurent du Maroni

    Airports: 11 total paved and unpaved. Rochambeau International Airport is located about 16 km from Cayenne

The Press: newspapers   **France-Guyane:** 88 bis ave du General de Gaulle, 97300 Cayenne telephone 31-48-80 fax 31-11-57 circ. 6,000   5 times a week

                        La Presse de Guyane: 26 rue Lieutenant Brasse, BP 6012, 97300 Cayenne telephone 31-15-59 circ. 1,200 daily

Tourism: tropical scenery, Devil's Island penal colony

Agence Regionale de Developpement du Tourisme et des Loisirs de la Guyane

                  Pavillon du Tourisme, Jardin Botanique, 12 rue Lalouette, BP 801, 97338 Cayenne Cedex telephone 30-09-00

Diplomatic representation in US: none (overseas department of France)

US Diplomatic representation: none (overseas department of France)

French Polynesia

Capital: Papeete   longitude: 149.34 W   latitude: 17.32 S

Government: overseas territory of France

Flag: the flag of France is used

Geography

Location: Oceania, archipelago in the South Pacific Ocean, about one-half of the way from South America to Australia

Total Area: 3,941 sq km (1,522 sq mi) slightly less than one-third the size of Connecticut

Boundaries: no land boundaries

Climate: tropical, but moderate

Temperature (F): High/Low Jan. 89/72, Apr. 89/72, July 86/68, Oct. 87/70

Average annual precipitation: 64 inches

Terrain: mixture of rugged high islands and low islands with reefs

Natural resources: timber, fish, cobalt

Natural hazards: occasional cyclonic storms in January

Note: included five archipelagoes; Makatea in French Polynesia, is one of the three great phosphate rock islands in the Pacific Ocean - the others are Banaba (Ocean Island) in Kiribati and Nauru

People

Population: 219, 999 (July 1995 est.)

Life expectancy at birth: total population 70.75 years

Nationality: French Polynesian

Ethnic division: Polynesian 78%, Chinese 12%, local French 6%, metropolitan French 4%

Religions: Protestant 54%, Roman Catholic 30%, other 16%

Languages: French (official), Tahitian (official)

Literacy: total population 98%

Economy

Imports: fuels, foodstuffs, equipment

Exports: coconut products, mother of pearl, vanilla, shark meat

Industries: tourism, pearls, agricultural processing, handicrafts

Agriculture: coconut and vanilla plantations; vegetables and fruit; poultry, beef, dairy products

Currency: 1 CFP franc (CFPF) = 100 centimes

Comptoirs Francais du Pacifique francs per US1$ - 96.25

Transportation

Railroads: none

Roads: 600 km total paved and unpaved

Ports: Mataura, Papeete, Rikitea, Uturoa

Airports: 43 total paved and unpaved. There is one international airport (Faaa) about 5 km from Papeete

The Press: newspaper   **Depeche de Tahiti:** Societe Polynesienne de Presse, BP 50, Papeete   daily circ. 15,000
telephone 42-43-43   fax 42-18-20

Tourism: bluegreen lagoons, coral reefs, swim and snorkle, the Gaugin Museum
   Service du Tourisme: Fare Manihini, blvd Pomare, BP 4527, Papeete   telephone 42-93-30   fax 43-66-19

Diplomatic representation in US: none (overseas territory of France)

US Diplomatic representation: none (overseas territory of France)

French Southern and Antarctic Lands

700 km

Indian
Ocean

Île Amsterdam
Île Saint-Paul

Îles Crozet

Îles Kerguelen

Capital: none; administered from Paris, France
longitude: 53.60 W   latitude: 62.50 N

Government: overseas territory of France

Flag: the flag of France is used

Geography

Location: Southern Africa, islands in the southern Indian Ocean, about equidistant between Africa, Antarctica, and Australia.

Total Area: 7,781 sq km (3,004 sq mi) slightly less than 1.5 times the size of Delaware

Boundaries: no land boundaries

Climate: antarctic

Terrain: volcanic

Natural resources: fish, crayfish

Natural hazards: Ile Amsterdam and Ile Saint-Paul are extinct volcanoes
Note: remote location in the southern Indian Ocean

People

    Population: no indigenous inhabitants - there are researchers in summer and winter.

Economy

    Economic activity is limited to servicing meteorological and geophysical research stations and French and other fishing fleets

Transportation

    Ports: none; offshore anchorage only

Gabon

    Capital: Libreville   longitude: 9.25 E   latitude: 0.23 N elevation: 115 ft

Government: republic; multiparty presidential regime

    Flag: three equal horizontal bands of green (top), yellow, and blue

Geography

    Location: Western Africa, bordering the Atlantic Ocean at the Equator, between Congo and Equatorial Guinea

    Total Area: 267,670 sq km (103,347 sq mi) slightly smaller than Colorado

    Boundaries: Cameroon, Congo, Equatorial Guinea

    Climate: tropical; always hot, humid

    Temperature (F): High/Low Jan. 87/73, Apr. 89/73, July 83/68, Oct. 86/71

    Average annual precipitation: 98.8 inches

    Terrain: narrow coastal plain; hilly interior; savanna in east and south

    Highest point is Ibounzi 1,574 m (5,165 ft)

    Natural resources: petroleum, manganese, uranium, gold, timber, iron ore

    Natural hazards: NA

People

    Population: 1,155,800 (July 1995 est.)

    Life expectancy at birth: total population 55.14 years

Nationality: Gabonese

Ethnic division: Bantu tribes including four major tribal groupings (Fang, Eshira, Bapounou, Bateke), other Africans and Europeans 100,000, including 27,000 French

Religions: Christian 55%-75%, Muslim less than 1%

Languages: French (official) Fang, Myene, Bateke, Bapounou/Eschira, Bandjabi

Literacy: total population 61%

Economy

Imports: foodstuffs, chemical products, petroleum products, construction materials, manufactures, machinery

Exports: crude oil, timber, manganese, uranium

Industries: food and beverages, lumbering and plywood, textiles, cement, petroleum refining, mining - manganese, uranium, gold, petroleum

Agriculture: cash crops - cocoa, coffee, palm oil; livestock raising not developed, small fishing operation; okoume (a tropical softwood) is the important timber product

Currency: 1 CFA franc (CFAF) = 100 centimes

Communaute Financiere Africaine francs per US1$ - 529.43

Transportation

Railroads: 649 km

Roads: 7,500 km total paved and unpaved

Ports: Cape Lopez, Kango, Lambarene, Libreville, Owendo, Port-Gentil

Airports: 69 total paved and unpaved. The international airports are located at Libreville, Port-Gentil and Franceville

The Press: newspapers   **Gabon-Matin:** BP 168, Libreville
daily circ. 18,000

L'Union: BP 3849, Libreville   daily circ. 15,000
telephone 73-21-84   fax 73-83-26

Tourism: National parks, Pointe-Denis Resort

Office National Gabonais du Tourisme: BP 161, Libreville
telephone 72-21-82

Diplomatic representation in US:

chief of mission: Ambassador Paul Boundoukou-Latha

chancery: 2233 Wisconsin Avenue NW, Washington, DC

telephone: [1] (202) 797-1000

US Diplomatic representation:
   chief of mission: Ambassador Joseph C. Wilson IV
   embassy: Boulevard de la Mer, Libreville
   mailing address: BP 4000, Libreville
   telephone: [241] 76-20-03 through 76-20-04, 74-34-92
   FAX: [241] 74-55-07

The Gambia

Capital: Banjul   longitude: 16.39 W   latitude: 13.28 N   elevation: 90 ft
Government: republic under multiparty democratic rule
   Flag: three equal horizontal bands of red (top), blue with white edges, and green

Geography
   Location: western Africa, bordering the North Atlantic Ocean and Senegal
   Total Area: 11,300 sq km (4,363 sq mi) slightly more than twice the size of Delaware
   Boundaries: Senegal
   Climate: tropical; hot, rainy season (June to November); cooler, dry season (November to May)
   Temperature (F): High/Low Jan. 88/59, Apr. 91/65, July 86/74, Oct. 89/72
   Average annual precipitation: 49 inches
   Terrain: flood plains of the Gambia River flanked by some low hills
   Highest point is 30 m (98.4 ft)
   Natural resources: fish
   Natural hazards: rainfall has dropped by 30% in the last thirty years
   Note: almost an enclave of Senegal; smallest country on the continent of Africa

People
   Population: 989,300 (July 1995 est.)

Life expectancy at birth: total population 50.55 years

Nationality: Gambian

Ethnic division: African 99%, (Mandinka 42%, Fula 18%, Wolof 16%, Jola 10%, Serahuli 9%, other 4%) non-Gambian 1%

Religions: Muslim 90%, Christian 9%, indigenous beliefs 1%

Languages: English (official), Mandinka, Wolof, Fula, other indigenous vernaculars

Literacy: total population 27%

Economy

Imports: foodstuffs, manufactures, raw materials, fuel, machinery and transport equipment

Exports: peanuts and peanuts products, fish, cotton lint, palm kernels

Industries: peanut processing, tourism, beverages, agricultural machinery assembly, woodworking, metalworking, clothing

Agriculture: major export crop is peanuts; other principal crops - millet, sorghum, rice, corn, cassava, palm kernels; livestock - cattle, sheep, goats; forestry and fishing resources not fully exploited

Currency: 1 dalasi (D) = 100 butut

salasi per US1$ - 9.56

Transportation

Railroads: none

Roads: 3,083 km total paved and unpaved

Ports: Banjul

Airports: 1 international airport at Yundum, about 26 km from Banjul

The Press: newspapers   **The Daily Observer:** PMB 131, Banjul

telephone 49-66-08   fax 49-68-78   daily

The Gambian Times: 21 OAU Blvd, POB 698, Banjul

fortnightly

Tourism: Beautiful beaches and abundant birdlife

Ministry of Information and Tourism:

The Quadrangle, Banjul   telephone 22-84-96

Diplomatic representation in US:

chief of mission: (vacant) Charge d'Affaires Aminatta Dibba

chancery: Suite 1000, 1155 15th Street NW, Washington, DC

telephone: [1] (202) 785-1399, 1379, 1425

FAX: [1] (202) 785-1430

US Diplomatic representation:

chief of mission: Ambassador Andrew J. Winter

embassy: Fajara, Kairaba Avenue, Banjul

mailing address: PMB No. 19, Banjul

telephone: [220] 39-28-56, 39-28-58, 39-19-70, 39-19-71

FAX: [220] 39-24-75

Gaza Strip

The Gaza Strip is Israeli occupied with interim status subject to Israeli/Palestinian negotiations -- final status to be determined. Boundary representation is not necessarily authorative.

Capital: none   longitude: 34.40 E   latitude: 31.50 N

Government: Under the Israeli-PLO Declaration of Principles on Interim Self-Government Arrangements, Israel agreed to transfer certain powers and responsibilities to the Palestinian Authority, and subsequently to an elected Palestinian Council, as part of interim self-governing arrangements in the West Bank and Gaza Strip

Flag: NA

Geography

Location: Middle East, bordering the Mediterranean Sea, between Egypt and Israel

Total Area: 360 sq km (139 sq mi) slightly more than twice the size of Washington, DC

Boundaries: Egypt, Israel

Climate: temperate, mild winters, dry and warm to hot summers

Terrain: flat to rolling, sand- and dune-covered coastal plain

Natural resources: negligible

Natural hazards: NA

Note: there are 24 Jewish settlements and civilian land use sites in the Gaza Strip

People

Population: 813,400 (July 1995 est.)

Note; in addition, there are 4,800 Jewish settlers in the Gaza Strip

Life expectancy at birth: total population 71.09 years

Nationality: NA

Ethnic division: Palestinian Arab and other 99.4%, Jewish 0.6%

Religions: Muslim (predominantly Sunni) 98.7%, Christian 0.7%, Jewish 0.6%

Languages: Arabic, Hebrew (spoken by Israeli settlers), English (widely understood)

Literacy: NA

Economy

Overview: Gaza depends upon Israel for nearly 90% of its external trade. About 40% of Gaza Strip workers are employed across the border by Israeli industrial, construction, and agricultural enterprises.

Imports: food, consumer goods, construction material

Exports: citrus

Industries: generally small family businesses that produce textiles, soap, olive-wood carvings, and mother of pearl souvenirs; the Israelis have established some small-scale modern industries in an industrial center

Agriculture: olives, citrus and other fruits; vegetables; beef and dairy products

Currency: 1 new Israeli shekel (NIS0 = 100 new agorot

new Israeli shekels per US1$ - 3.02

Transportation

Railroads: one line, abandoned and in disrepair, little trackage remains

Roads: NA

Ports: Gaza

Airports: 1 with paved runways

Georgia

150 km

Capital: T'bilisi   longitude: 44.48 E   latitude: 41.43 N   elevation: 1,325 ft

165

Government: republic

   Flag: maroon field with small rectangle in upper hoist side corner; rectangle divided horizontally with black on top, white below

Geography

   Location: Southwestern Asia, bordering the Black Sea, between Turkey and Russia

   Total Area: 69,700 sq km (26,911 sq mi) slightly larger than South Carolina

   Boundaries: Armenia, Azerbaijan, Russia, Turkey

   Climate: warm and pleasant; Mediterranean-like on the Black Sea coast

   Temperature (F): High/Low   Jan. 39/26, Apr. 61/44, July 83/65, Oct. 64/48

   Average annual precipitation: 21.4 inches

   Terrain: largely mountainous with Great Caucasus Mountains in the north and Lesser Caucasus Mountains in the south; Kolkhida Lowlands opens to the Black Sea in the west; Mtkvari River Basin in the east; good soils in river valley flood plains, foothills of Kolhida Lowland

   Highest point is Kazbek Peak 5,047 m (16,558 ft)

   Natural resources: forest lands, hydropower, manganese deposits, iron ore, copper, minor coal and oil deposits; coastal climate and soils allow for important tea and citrus growth

   Natural hazards: NA

People

   Population: 5,726,000 (July 1995 est.)

   Life expectancy at birth: total population 73.1 years

   Nationality: Georgian

   Ethnic division: Georgian 70.1%, Armenian 8.1%, Russian 6.3%, Azeri 5.7%, Ossetian 3%, Abkhaz 1.8%, other 5%

   Religions: Georgian Orthodox 65%, Russian Orthodox 10%, Muslim 11%, Armenian Orthodox 8%, unknown 6%

   Languages: Armenian 7%, Azeri 6%, Georgian 71% (official), Russian 9%, other 7%

   Literacy: total population 99%

Economy

   Imports: fuel, grain and other foods, machinery and parts, transport equipment

   Exports: citrus fruits, tea, wine, other agricultural products; diverse types of machinery; ferrous and nonferrous metals; textiles; chemicals; fuel re-exports

Industries: heavy industrial products include raw steel, rolled steel, airplanes; machine tools, foundry equipment, electric locomotives, tower cranes, electric welding equipment, machinery for food preparation and meat packing, electric motors, process control equipment, including cloth, hosiery, and shoes; chemicals; wood-working industries; the most important food industry is wine

Agriculture: important producer of citrus fruits, tea, grapes; also cultivates vegetables and potatoes; dependent on imports for grains, dairy products, sugar; small livestock sector

Currency: coupons introduced in April 1993 to be followed by introduction of the lari at undetermined future date; in July 1993 use of the Russian ruble was banned

coupons per US1$ - 1,280,000 (end December 1994)

Transportation

Railroads: 1,570 km

Roads: 33,900 km total paved and unpaved

Ports: Bat'umi, P'ot'i, Sokhumi

Airports: 28 total paved and unpaved. The main airport is located at Orbi

The Press: newspapers   **Literaturuli Sakartvelo:** 380004 Tbilisi, Rustaveli telephone (8832) 99-84-04   weekly

Sakartvelos Respublika: Tbilisi   5 a week

Tourism: NA

Diplomatic representation in US:

chief of mission: Ambassador Tedo Japaridze

chancery: (temporary) Suite 424, 1511 K Street NW, Washington, DC 20005

telephone: [1] (202) 393-6060, 5959

US Diplomatic representation:

chief of mission: Ambassador Kent N. Brown

embassy: #25 Antoneli Street, T'bilisi 380026

mailing address: use embassy street address

telephone: [7] (8832) 98-99-67, 93-38-03

FAX: [7] (8832) 93-37-59

Germany

Capital: Berlin   longitude: 13.25 E   latitude: 52.32 N   elevation: 180 ft

Government: federal republic

Flag: three equal horizontal bands of black (top), red, and yellow

Geography

Location: Central Europe, bordering the Baltic Sea and the North Sea, between the Netherlands and Poland, south of Denmark

Total Area: 356,910 sq km (137,803 sq mi) slightly smaller than Montana

Boundaries: Austria, Belgium, Czech Republic, Poland, Switzerland

Climate: temperate and marine; cool, cloudy, wet winters and summers; occasional warm, tropical foehn wind; high relative humidity
Temperature (F): High/Low Jan. 35/26, Apr. 56/39. July 75/57, Oct. 56/42
Average annual precipitation: 23.8 inches

Terrain: lowlands in north, uplands in center, Bavarian Alps in south
Highest point is Fichtelberg 1,214 m (3,983 ft)

Natural resources: iron ore, coal, potash, timber, lignite, uranium, copper, natural gas, salt, nickel

Natural hazards: NA

People

Population: 81,337,600 (July 1995 est.)

Life expectancy at birth: total population 76.62 years

Nationality: German

Ethnic division: German 95.1%, Turkish 2.3%, Italian 0.7%, Greeks 0.4%, Poles 0.4% other 1.1% (made up largely of people fleeing the war in the former Yugoslavia)

Religions: Protestant 45%, Roman Catholic 37%, unaffiliated or other 18%

Languages: German

Literacy: total population 99%

Economy

Imports: manufactures, agricultural products, fuels, raw materials

Exports: manufactures (including machines and machine tools, chemicals, motor vehicles, iron and steel products), agricultural products, raw materials, fuels

Industries:

Western: among world's largest and technologically advanced producers of iron, steel, coal, cement, chemicals, machinery, vehicles, machine tools, electronics; food and beverages, textiles, petroleum refining

Eastern: metal fabrication, chemicals, brown coal, shipbuilding, machine building, food and beverages, textiles, petroleum refining

Agriculture:

Western: diversified crop and livestock farming; principal crops and livestock include potatoes, wheat, barley, sugar beets, fruit, cabbage, cattle, pigs, poultry; net importer of food; fishing and forestry

Eastern: principal crops - wheat, rye, barley, potatoes, sugar beets, fruit; livestock products include pork, beef, chicken, milk, hides and skins; net importer of food; fishing and forestry

Currency: 1 deutsche mark (DM) = 100 pfennige

deutsche marks per US1$ - 1.53

Transportation

Railroads: 43,457 km

Roads: 636,282 km total paved and unpaved

Ports: Berlin, Bonn, Brake, Breman, Bremerhaven, Cologne, Dresden, Duisburg, Emden, Hamburg, Karlsruhe, Lubeck, Magdeburg, Mannheim, Rostock, Stuttgart

Airports: 660 total paved and unpaved. The major international airports are at Berlin, (East and West), Koln-Bonn, Dresden, Dusseldorf, Frankfurt, Hamburg, Hannover, Leipzig, Munchen, and Stuttgart

The Press: daily newspapers   Der Tagesspiegel: 10785 Berlin,Potsdamer Str. 87, 10723 Berlin, Postfach 3304330   circ. 1,325,000 telephone (30) 26-00-90   fax (30) 26-00-93-32

Rheinische Post: 40196 Dusseldorf, Zulpicherstr, 10 telephone (211) 50-50   fax (211) 504-7562   circ. 390,000 daily

Tourism: Tourist attractions include medieval towns and castles, summer and winter resorts, the North Sea and Baltic Sea coasts

Deutsche Zentrale fur Tourismus eV:

60325 Frankfurt a.M., Beethovenstr. 69

telephone (69) 75-720 fax (69) 75-19-03

Diplomatic representation in US:

chief of mission: Ambassador Juergen Chrobog

chancery: 4645 Reservoir Road NW, Washington, DC 20007

telephone: [1] (202) 298-4000

FAX: [1] (202) 298-4249

US Diplomatic representation:

chief of mission: Ambassador Charles E. Redman

embassy: Deichmanns Aue 29, 53170 Bonn

mailing address: Unit 21701, Bonn; APO AE 09080

telephone: [49] (228) 33-91

FAX: [49] (228) 339-2663

Ghana

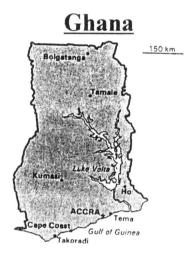

Capital: Accra   longitude: 0.15 W   latitude: 5.33 N elevation: 88 ft

Government: constitutional democracy

Flag: three equal bands of red (top), yellow, and green with a large black five-pointed star centered in the yellow band; uses the popular pan-African colors of Ethiopia; similar to the flag of Bolivia, which has a coat of arms centered in the yellow band

Geography

Location: Western Africa, bordering the North Atlantic Ocean, between Cote d'Ivoire and Togo

Total Area: 238,540 sq km (92,100 sq mi) slightly smaller than Oregon

Boundaries: Burkina, Cote d'Ivoire, Togo

Climate: tropical; warm and comparatively dry along southeast coast; hot, humid in southwest; hot and dry in north

Temperature (F): High/Low Jan. 87/73, Apr. 88/76, July 81/73, Oct. 85/74

Average annual precipitation: 28.5 inches

Terrain: mostly low plains with dissected plateau in south-central area
Highest point is Togo Hills 884 m (2,900 ft)
Natural resources: gold, timber, industrial diamonds, bauxite, manganese, fish, rubber
Natural hazards: dry, dusty, harmattan winds occur from January to March; droughts

People

Population: 17,763,200 (July 1995 est.)
Life expectancy at birth: total population 55.85 years
Nationality: Ghanaian
Ethnic division: black African 99.8% (major tribes - Akan 44%, Moshi-Dagomba 16%, Ewe 13%, Ga 8%0), European and other 0.2%
Religions: indigenous beliefs 38%, Muslim 30%, Christian 24%, other 8%
Languages: English (official), African languages (including Akan, Moshi-Dagomba, Ewe, Ga)
Literacy: total population 60%

Economy

Imports: petroleum, consumer goods, foods, intermediate goods, capital equipment
Exports: cocoa, gold, timber, tuna, bauxite, and aluminum
Industries: mining, lumbering, light manufacturing, aluminum, food processing
Agriculture: major cash crop is cocoa; other principal crops - rice, coffee, cassava, peanuts, corn, shea nuts, timber; (including fish and forestry); normally self-sufficient in food
Currency: 1 new cedi (C) = 100 pesewas
new cedis per US1$ - 1,046.74

Transportation

Railroads: 953 km
Roads: 32,250 km total paved and unpaved
Ports: Takoradi, Tema
Airports: 12 total paved and unpaved. The main international airport is at Accra
The Press: daily newspapers   **Daily Graphic:** Graphic Road, POB 742, Accra
telephone (21) 22-89-11   circ. 100,000
The Ghanaian Times: Ring Road West, POB 2638, Accra
telephone (21) 22-82-82   circ. 42,000

Tourism: Tourist attractions are old trading forts, castles, game reserves, nice beaches

Ghana Tourist Development Co. Ltd:
POB 8710, Accra   telephone (21) 77-20-84   fax (21) 77-20-93

Diplomatic representation in US:

chief of mission: Ambassador Ekwow Spio-Garbrah

chancery: 3512 International Drive NW, Washington, DC 20008

telephone: [1] (202) 686-4520

FAX: [1] (202) 686-4527

US Diplomatic representation:

chief of mission: Ambassador Kenneth L. Brown

embassy: Ring Road East, East of Danquah Circle, Accra

mailing address: P O Box 194, Accra

telephone: [233] (21) 77-53-48, 77-53-49, 77-52-97, 77-52-98

FAX: [233] (21) 77-60-08

Gibraltar

Capital: Gibraltar   longitude: 5.21 W   latitude: 36.09 N elevation: 7 ft

Government: dependent territory of the UK

Flag: two horizontal bands of white (top, double width) and red with a three-towered red castle in the center of the white band; hanging from the castle gate is a gold key centered in the red band

Geography

Location: Southwestern Europe, bordering the Strait of Gibraltar, which links the Mediterranean Sea and the North Atlantic Ocean, on the southern coast of Spain

Total Area: 6.5 sq km (2.5 sq mi) about 11 times the size of The Mall in Washington, DC

Boundaries: Spain

Climate: mediterranean with mild winters and warm summers

Temperature (F): High/Low Jan. 60/50, Apr. 68/56, July 83/68, Oct. 73/62
Average annual precipitation: 30.3 inches
Terrain: a narrow coastal lowland borders The Rock
Natural resources: negligible
Natural hazards: NA

People

Population: 31,900 (July 1995 est.)
Life expectancy at birth: total population 76.61 years
Nationality: Gibraltarian
Ethnic division: Italian, English, Maltese, Portuguese, Spanish
Religions: Roman Catholic 74%, Protestant 11%, (Church of England 8%, other 3%), Moslem 8%, Jewish 2%, none or other 5%
Languages: English (used in schools and for official purposes), Spanish, Italian, Portuguese, Russian
Literacy: NA

Economy

Imports: fuels, manufactured goods, and foodstuffs
Exports: (principally re-exports) petroleum, manufactured goods
Industries: tourism, banking and finance, construction, commerce; support to large UK naval and air base; transit trade and supply depot in the port; light manufacturing of tobacco, roasted coffee, ice, mineral waters, candy, beer, and canned fish
Agriculture: none
Currency: 1 Gibraltar pound (#G) = 100 pence
Gilbraltar pounds per US1$ - 0.63

Transportation

Railroads: NA
Roads: 50 km paved
Ports: Gibraltar
Airports: 1 with paved runways
The Press: newspapers (English) **Gibraltar Chronicle:** 2 Library Gardens
telephone 78-589 fax 79-927
circ. 6,300 daily
Panorama: 93-95 Irish Town   telephone 79-797
circ. 3,600 weekly
Tourism: climate, beaches

Gibraltar National Tourist Board:
POB 303, Cathedral Square
telephone 76-400   fax 79-980

Diplomatic representation in US: none (dependent territory of the UK)

US Diplomatic representation: none (dependent territory of the UK)

Glorioso Islands

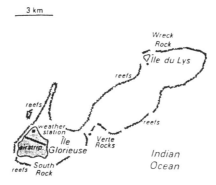

Capital: none; administered by France

longitude: 37.80 E   latitude: 10.00 S

Government: French possession administered by Commissioner of the Republic, resident in Reunion

Geography

Location: Southern Africa, group of islands in the Indian Ocean, northwest of Madagascar

Total Area: 5 sq km (1.93 sq mi) about 8.5 time the size of The Mall in Washington, DC

Boundaries: no land boundaries

Climate: tropical

Terrain: NA

Natural resources: guano, coconuts

Natural hazards: periodic cyclones

People

Population: uninhabited

Diplomatic representation in US: none (possession of France)

US Diplomatic representation: none (possession of France)

Greece

Capital: Athens   longitude: 23.44 E   latitude: 38.00 N   elevation: 351 ft

Government: presidential parliamentary government

> **Flag:** nine equal horizontal stripes of blue alternating with white; there is a blue square in the upper hoist-side corner bearing a white cross; the cross symbolizes Greek Orthodoxy, the established religion of the country

Geography

> **Location:** Southern Europe, bordering the Aegean Sea, Ionian Sea, and the Mediterranean Sea, between Albania and Turkey
>
> **Total Area:** 131,940 sq km (50,942 sq mi) slightly smaller than Alabama
>
> **Boundaries:** Albania, Bulgaria, Turkey, The Former Yugoslav Republic of Macedonia
>
> **Climate:** temperate; mild, wet winters; hot, dry summers
>
> Temperature (F): High/Low Jan. 55/44, Apr. 68/52, July 92/73, Oct. 75/60
>
> Average annual precipitation: 16.1 inches
>
> **Terrain:** mostly mountains with ranges extending into the sea as peninsulas or chains of islands
>
> Highest point is Olympus 2,917 m (9,570 ft)
>
> **Natural resources:** bauxite, lignite, magnesite, petroleum, marble
>
> **Natural hazards:** severe earthquakes

People

> **Population:** 10,647,511 (July 1995 est.)
>
> **Life expectancy at birth:** total population 77.92 years
>
> **Nationality:** Greek
>
> **Ethnic division:** Greek 98%, other 2%
>
> Note: the Greek Government states there are no ethnic divisions in Greece
>
> **Religions:** Greek Orthodox 98%, Muslim 1.3%, other 0.7%
>
> **Languages:** Greek (official), English, French
>
> **Literacy:** total population 95%

Economy

>   **Imports:** manufactured goods, foodstuffs, fuels
>
>   **Exports:** manufactured goods, foodstuffs, fuels

Industries: tourism, food and tobacco processing, textiles, chemicals, metal products, mining, petroleum

Agriculture: principal products - wheat, corn, barley, sugar beets, olives, tomatoes, wine, tobacco, potatoes; self-sufficient in food except meat, dairy products, and animal feedstuffs; fishing and forestry

Currency: 1 drachma (Dr) = 100 lepta

>   1 drachmae per US1$ - 238.20

Transportation

>   **Railroads:** 2,503 km
>
>   **Roads:** 130,000 km total paved and unpaved
>
>   **Ports:** Alexandroupolis, Elevsis, Iraklion (Crete), Kavala, Kerkira, Khalkis, Igoumenitsa, Lavrion, Pirtrai, Piraievs, Thessaloniki, Volos
>
>   **Airports:** 79 total paved and unpaved. There are international airports at Athens, Thessaloniki, Alexandroupolis, Corfu, Lesbos, Andravida, Rhodes, Kos and Heraklion

The Press: newspapers

>   **Apogevmatini:** Odos Phidiou 12, 106 78 Athens
>   telephone (1) 643-0011 fax (1) 360-9876
>   circ. 74,000
>
>   **Eleftheros Typos:** Odos Mitropoleos 1, 105 57 Athens
>   telephone (1) 323-7671   fax (1) 323-3142   circ. 168,000

Tourism: Sunny climate, beaches, natural beauty, traditions and history, archaeological sites.

>   **Ellinikos Organismos Tourismou:** Odos Amerikis 2B, 105 64 Athens
>   telephone (1) 322-3111   fax (1) 322-4148

Diplomatic representation in US:

>   *chief of mission:* Ambassador Loucas Tsilas
>   *chancery:* 2221 Massachusetts Avenue NW, Washington, DC 20008
>   *telephone:* [1] (202) 939-5800
>   *FAX:* [1] (202) 939-5824

US Diplomatic representation:

>   *chief of mission:* Ambassador Thomas M.T. Niles
>   *embassy:* 91 Vasilissis Sophias Boulevard, 10160 Athens
>   *mailing address:* PSC 108, Athens; APO AE 09842
>   *telephone:* [30] (1) 721-2951, 8401
>   *FAX:* [30] (1) 645-6282

Greenland

Capital: Nuuk (Godthab)   longitude: 51.43 W   latitude: 64.11 N
elevation: 66 ft

Government: part of Danish realm; self-governing overseas administrative division

Flag: two equal horizontal bands of white (top) and red with a large disk slightly to the hoist side of center - the top half of the disk is red, the bottom half is white

Geography

Location: Northern North America, island between the Arctic Ocean and the North Atlantic Ocean, northeast of Canada

Total Area: 2,175,600 sq km (839,999 sq mi) slightly more than three times the size of Texas

Boundaries: no land boundaries

Climate: arctic to subarctic; cool summers, cold winters

Temperature (F): High/Low Jan. 19/10, Apr. 31/20, July 52.38, Oct. 35/26

Average annual precipitation: 23.5 inches

Terrain: flat to gradually sloping icecap covers all but a narrow, mountainous, barren, rocky coast

Natural resources: zinc, lead, iron ore, coal, molybdenum, cryolite, uranium, fish

Natural hazards: continuous permafrost over northern two-thirds of the island

Note: dominates North Atlantic Ocean between North America and Europe; sparse population confined to small settlements along coast

People

Population: 57,611 (July 1995 est.)

Life expectancy at birth: total population 67.65 years

Nationality: Greenlander

177

Ethnic division: Greenlander 86%, (Eskimos and Greenland-born Caucasians), Danish 14%

Religions: Evangelical Lutheran

Languages: Eskimo dialects, Danish

Literacy: NA

Economy

Imports: manufactured goods, machinery and transport equipment, food and live animals, petroleum products

Exports: fish and fish products

Industries: fish processing (mainly shrimp), lead and zinc mining, handicrafts, some small shipyards, potential for platinum and gold mining

Agriculture: sector dominated by fishing and sheep raising; crops limited to forage and small gardens vegetables.

Currency: 1 Danish krone (DKr) = 100 oere

Danish kroner per US1$ - 6.03

Transportation

Railroads: none

Roads: 150 km total paved and unpaved

Ports: Faeringehavn, Frederikshaab, Holsteinsborg, Nanortalik, Narsaq, Nuuk (Godthab), Sondrestrom

Airports: 10 total paved and unpaved. Air service to the 19 principal centers in Greenland

The Press: newspapers **Atuagagdliutit/Gronlandsposten:** POB 39, 3900 Nuuk telephone 25-483 3 times a week **Sermitsiaq:** POB 150, 3900 Nuuk telephone 21-902 fax 22-499 weekly

Tourism: snow capped mountains, remote villages, incredible icebergs, deep fjords

Diplomatic representation in US: none (self-governing overseas administrative division of Denmark)

Diplomatic representation: none (self-governing overseas administrative division of Denmark)

Grenada

Capital: Saint George's   longitude: 61.44 W   latitude: 12.04 N

Government: parliamentary democracy

Flag: a rectangle divided diagonally into yellow (top and bottom) and green triangles (hoist side and outer side) with a red border around the flag; there are seven yellow five-pointed stars with three centered in the top red border, three centered in the bottom red border, and one on a red disk superimposed at the center of the flag; there is also a symbolic nutmeg pod on the hoist-side triangle (Grenada is the world's second largest producer of nutmeg, after Indonesia); the seven stars represent the seven administrative divisions

Geography

Location: Caribbean, island in the Caribbean Sea, north of Trinidad and Tobago

Total Area: 340 sq km (131.3 sq mi) slightly less than twice the size of Washington, DC

Boundaries: no land boundaries

Climate: tropical; tempered by northeast trade winds

Temperature (F): High/Low Jan. 82.80. Apr. 85/81, July 84/83, Oct. 85/83

Average annual precipitation: NA

Terrain: volcanic in origin with central mountains

Highest point is Mt. Saint Catherine 840 m (2,757 ft)

Natural resources: timber, tropical fruit, deepwater harbors

Natural hazards: lies on edge of hurricane belt; hurricane season lasts from June to November

People

Population: 94,500 (July 1995 est.)

Life expectancy at birth: total population 70.67 years

Nationality: Grenadian

Ethnic division: black African

179

Religions: Roman Catholic, Anglican, other Protestant sects

Languages: English (official), French patois

Literacy: total population 98%

Economy

Imports: manufactured goods, machinery, chemicals, fuel

Exports: bananas, cocoa, nutmeg, fruit and vegetables, clothing, mace

Industries: food and beverages, textile, light assembly operations, tourism, construction

Agriculture: bananas, cocoa, nutmeg, and mace account for two-thirds of total crop production; world's second-largest producer and forth-largest exporter of nutmeg and mace; small-sized farms predominate, growing a variety of citrus fruits, avocados, root crops, sugarcane, corn, and vegetables

Currency: 1 EC dollar (EC$) = 100 cents

East Caribbean dollars per US1$ - 2.70

Transportation

Railroads: none

Roads: 1.000 km total paved and unpaved

Ports: Grenville, Saint George's

Airports: 3 paved. Point Salines International Airport is about 8 km from Saint George's

The Press: weekly newspapers   **Grenada Guardian:** Upper Lucas Street, Saint George's tel. (444) 3823 fax (444) 2873

The Grenada Times: Market Hill, POB 622, Saint George's telephone (440) 1530 fax (440) 4117

Tourism: extensive rain forests, white sandy beaches, site of historical interest

Grenada Board of Tourism: POB 293, Saint George's telephone (440) 2001 fax (440) 6637

Diplomatic representation in US:

chief of mission: Ambassador Denneth Modeste

chancery: 1701 New Hampshire Avenue NW, Washington, DC 20009

telephone: [1] (202) 265-2561

US Diplomatic representation:

chief of mission: (vacant); Charge d'Affaires Ollie P. Anderson, Jr.

embassy: Point Salines, Saint George's

mailing address: P O Box 54, Saint George's, Grenada, WI

telephone: [1] (809) 444-1173 through 1178

FAX: [1] (809) 444-4820

Guadeloupe

Capital: Basse-Terre   longitude: 61.44 W   latitude: 16.00 N

Government: overseas department of France

Flag: the flag of France is used

Geography

Location: Caribbean, islands in the eastern Caribbean Sea, southeast of Puerto Rico

Total Area: 1,780 sq km (687 sq mi) 10 times the size of Washington, DC

Boundaries: no land boundaries

Climate: subtropical tempered by trade winds; relatively high humidity Temperature (F): High/Low Jan. 77/64, Apr. 79/65, July 82.69, Oct. 81/68

Terrain: Basse-Terre is volcanic in origin with interior mountains; Grand-Terre is low limestone formation; most of the seven other islands are volcanic in origin

Natural resources: cultivable land, beaches and climate that foster tourism

Natural hazards: hurricanes (June to October); La Soufriere is an active volcano

People

Population: 402,900 (July 1995 est.)

Life expectancy at birth: total population 77.2 years

Nationality: Guadeloupian

Ethnic division: black or mulatto 90%, white 5%, East Indian, Lebanese, Chinese less than 5%

Religions: Roman Catholic 95%, Hindu and Pagan African 5%

Languages: French, Creole patois

Literacy: total population 90%

Economy

Imports: foodstuffs, fuels, vehicles, clothing and other consumer goods, construction materials

181

Exports: bananas, sugar, rum

Industries: construction, cement, rum, sugar, tourism

Agriculture: cash crops - bananas, sugarcane; other products include tropical fruits and vegetables; livestock - cattle, pigs, goats; not self-sufficient in food

Currency: 1 French franc (F) = 100 centimes

French francs per US1$ - 5.92

Transportation

Railroads: total km not available; privately owned, narrow-gauge plantation lines

Roads: 1,940 km total paved and unpaved

Ports: Basse-Terre, Gustavia, Marigot, Pointe-a-Pitre

Airports: 9 total paved and unpaved. Raizet International Airport is located about 3 km from Pointe-a-Pitre

The Press: newspapers   **France-Antilles:** 1 rue Hincelin, BP 658, 97159 Pointe-a-Pitre
telephone 90-25-25 fax 91-78-31
daily   circ. 25,000

Jakata: 18 rue Conde, 97110 Pointe-a-Pitre
fortnightly   circ. 6,000

Tourism: an increasingly large number of cruise ships visit the islands. The main attractions are mountainous scenery and beaches, diving. Some of the Caribbean's tamest fish

Office du Tourisme: 5 square de la Banque, POB 1099, 97181 Pointe-a-Pitre
telephone 82-09-30 fax 83-89-22

Diplomatic representation in US: none (overseas department of France)

US Diplomatic representation: none (overseas department of France)

Guam

Capital: Agana   longitude: 144.45 E   latitude: 13.28 N   elevation: 361 ft

Government: organized, unincorporated territory of the US with policy relations between Guam and the US under jurisdiction of the Office of Territorial and International Affairs, US Department of Interior

Flag: territorial flag is dark blue with a narrow red border on all four sides; centered is a red-bordered, pointed, vertical ellipse containing a beach scene, outrigger canoe with sail, and a palm tree with the word GUAM superimposed in bold red letters; US flag is the national flag

Geography

Location: Oceania, island in the North Pacific Ocean, about three-quarters of the way from Hawaii to the Philippines

Total Area: 541.3 sq km (209 sq mi) slightly more than three times the size of Washington, DC

Boundaries: no land boundaries

Climate: tropical marine; generally warm and humid, moderated by northeast trade winds; dry season from January to June, rainy season from July to December; little seasonal temperature variation

Temperature (F): High/Low Jan. 80/78, Apr. 82/80, July 83/80, Oct. 82/80

Average annual precipitation: 88.5 inches

Terrain: volcanic origin, surrounded by coral reefs; relatively flat coraline limestone plateau (source of fresh water) with steep coastal cliffs and narrow coastal plains in north, low rising hills in center, mountains in south

Highest point is Mount Lamlam 406 m (1332 ft)

Natural resources: fishing (largely undeveloped) tourism (especially from Japan)

Natural hazards: frequent squalls during rainy season; relatively rare, but potentially very destructive typhoons (especially in August)

Note: largest and southernmost island in the Mariana Islands archipelago; strategic location in western North Pacific Ocean

People

Population: 153,400 (July 1995 est.)

Life expectancy at birth: total population 74.29 years

Nationality: Guamanian

Ethnic division: Chamorro 47%, Philippino 25%, Caucasian 10%, Chinese, Japanese, Korean, and other 18%

Religions: Roman Catholic 98%, other 2%

Languages: English, Chamorro, Japanese

Literacy: total population 99%

Economy

Imports: petroleum and petroleum products, food, manufactured goods

Exports: mostly transshipment's of refined petroleum products, construction materials, fish, food and beverages products

Industries: US military, tourism, construction, transshipment services, concrete products, printing and publishing, food processing, textiles

Agriculture: relatively undeveloped with most food imported; fruits, vegetables, eggs, pork, poultry, beef, copra

Currency: 1 United Stated dollar (US$) = 100 cents
US currency is used

Transportation

Railroads: none

Roads: 674 km total paved and unpaved

Ports: Apra Harbor

Airports: 5 all paved. The international airport is at Agana

The Press: daily newspaper   **Pacific Daily News:**
POB DN, Agana, GU 96910
telephone 477-9712 fax 472-1512

Tourism: Agana, Micronesian Area Research Center, coral reefs

Guam Visitors Bureau: 1270 North Marine Drive
POB 3520, Agana, GU 96911
telephone 646-5278 fax 646-8861

Diplomatic representation in US: none (territory of the US)

US Diplomatic representation: none (territory of the US)

Guatemala

Capital: Guatemala   longitude: 90.31 W   latitude: 14.38 N
elevation: 4,855 ft

Government: republic

Flag: three equal bands of light blue (hoist side), white, and light blue with the coat of arms centered in the white band; the coat of arms include a green and red quetzal (the national bird) and a scroll bearing the inscription LIBERTAD 15 DE SEPTIEMBER DE 1821 (the original date of independence from Spain) all superimposed on a pair of crossed rifles and a pair of crossed swords and framed by a wreath

Geography

Location: Middle America, bordering the Caribbean Sea, between Honduras and Belize and bordering the North Pacific Ocean, between El Salvador and Mexico

Total Area: 108,890 sq km (42,042 sq mi) slightly smaller than Tennessee

Boundaries: Belize, El Salvador, Honduras, Mexico

Climate: tropical; hot, humid in lowlands; cooler in highlands

Temperature (F): High/Low Jan. 73/53, Apr. 82/58. July 78/60, Oct. 76/60

Average annual precipitation: 51.8 inches

Terrain: mostly mountains with narrow coastal plains and rolling limestone plateau

Highest point is Atitan Volcano 3,537 m (11,604 ft)

Natural resources: petroleum, nickel, rare woods, fish, chicle

Natural hazards: numerous volcanoes in mountains, with frequent violent earthquakes; Caribbean coast subject to hurricanes and other tropical storms

Note: no natural harbors on west coast

People

Population: 10,998,700 (July 1995 est.)

Life expectancy at birth: total population 64.85 years

185

Nationality: Guatemalan

Ethnic division: Mestizo - mixed Amerindian-Spanish ancestry (in local Spanish called Ladino) 56%, Amerindian or predominantly Amerindian 44%

Religions: Roman Catholic, Protestant, traditional Mayan

Languages: Spanish 60%, Indian language 40% (23 Indian dialects, including Quiche, Cakchiquel, Kekchi)

Literacy: total population 55%

Economy

Imports: fuel and petroleum products, machinery, grain, fertilizer, motor vehicles

Exports: coffee, sugar, bananas, cardamom, beef

Industries: sugar, textiles and clothing, furniture, chemicals, petroleum, metals, rubber, tourism

Agriculture: principal crops - sugarcane, corn, bananas, coffee, beans, cardamom; livestock - cattle, sheep, pigs, chickens; food importer

Currency: 1 quetzal (Q) = 100 centavos
free market quetzales per US1$ - 5.73

Transportation

Railroads: 1,019 km

Roads: 26,429 km total paved and unpaved

Ports: Champerico, Puerto Barrios, Puerto Quetzal, San Jose, Santo Tomas de Castilla

Airports: 528 total paved and unpaved. International airport at Guatemala City

The Press: daily newspapers

El Grafico: 14a Avda 9-18, Zona 1, Guatemala City telephone (2) 51-00-21 morning   circ. 60,000

Prensa Libre: 13a Calle 9-31, Zona 1, Guatemala City telephone (2) 21-368   fax (2) 24-297

Tourism: Mayan ruins, ruins of the old capital of Antigua, scenic lakes

Guatemala Tourist Commission: Centro Civico, 7a Avda 1-17, Zona 4, Guatemala City telephone (2) 31-13-33   fax (2) 31-88-93

Diplomatic representation in US:

chief of mission: Ambassador Edmond Mulet

chancery: 2220 R Street NW, Washington, DC 20008

telephone: [1] (202) 745-4952 through 4954

FAX: [1] (202) 745-1908

chief of mission: Ambassador Marilyn McAfee
embassy: 7-01 Avenida de la Reforma, Zone 10, Guatemala City
mailing address: APO AA 34024
telephone: [502] (2) 31-15-41
FAX: [502] (2) 31-88-85

Guernsey

5 km

Burhou

Alderney

English Channel

Guernsey
St. Sampson
Lihou Island
Herm
ST. PETER PORT
Jethou
Brecqhou *Sark*
Little Sark

Capital: Saint Peter Port   longitude: 2.65 W   latitude: 49.50 N
Government: British crown dependency
Flag: white with the red cross of Saint George (patron saint of England) extending to the edges of the flag
Geography
Location: Western Europe, islands in the English Channel, northwest of France
Total Area: 194 sq km (74.9 sq mi) slightly larger than Washington, DC
Boundaries: no land boundaries
Climate: temperate with mild winters and cool summers; about 50% of the days are overcast
Terrain: mostly level with low hills in southwest
Natural resources: cropland
Natural hazards: NA
People
Population: 64,400 (July 1995 est.)
Life expectancy at birth: total population 78.34 years
Nationality: Channel Islander
Ethnic division: UK and Norman-French descent
Religions: Anglican, Roman Catholic, Presbyterian, Baptist, Congregational, Methodist

Languages: English, French; Norman-French dialect spoken in country districts

Literacy: NA

Economy

Imports: coal, gasoline, and oil

Exports: tomatoes, flowers and ferns, sweet peppers, eggplant, other vegetables

Industries: tourism, banking

Agriculture: tomatoes, flowers (mostly grown in greenhouses), sweet peppers, eggplants, other vegetables, fruit; Guernsey cattle

Currency: 1 Guernsey (#G) pound = 100 pence

Guernsey pounds per US1$ -0.63

Transportation

Railroads: none

Roads: NA

Ports: Saint Peter Port, Saint Sampson

Airports: 2 with paved runways

The Press: newspaper

Guernsey Evening Press and Star: POB 57, Braye Road, Vale
telephone (481) 45-866   fax (481) 48-972
Circ. 16,400

Tourism: scenic country side

Guernsey Tourist Board: POB 23, St Peter Port
telephone (481) 72-661 fax (481) 72-12-46

Diplomatic representation in US: none (British crown dependency)

US Diplomatic representation: none (British crown dependency)

Guinea

Capital: Conakry   longitude: 13.43 W   latitude: 9.31 N   elevation: 23 ft

Government: republic

    Flag: three equal bands of red (hoist side), yellow, and green; uses the popular pan-African colors of Ethiopia; similar to the flag of Rwanda, which has a large black letter R centered in the yellow band

Geography

    Location: Western Africa, bordering the North Atlantic Ocean, between Guinea-Bissau and Sierra Leone

    Total Area: 245,860 sq km (94,927 sq mi) slightly smaller than Oregon

    Boundaries: Guinea-Bissau, Cote d'Ivoire, Liberia, Mali, Senegal, Sierra Leone

    Climate: generally hot and humid; monsoonal-type season (June to November) with southwesterly winds; dry season (December to May) with northeasterly harmattan winds

    Temperature (F): High/Low Jan. 88/72, Apr. 90/73, July 83/72, Oct. 87/73

    Average annual precipitation: 169 inches

    Terrain: generally flat coastal plain, hilly to mountainous interior

    Highest point is Nimba Mountains 1,850 m (6,070 ft)

    Natural resources: bauxite, iron ore, diamonds, gold, uranium, hydropower. fish

    Natural hazards: hot, dry, dusty harmattan haze may reduce visibility during dry season

People

    Population: 6,549,336 (July 1995 est.)

    Life expectancy at birth: total population 44.6 years

    Nationality: Guinean

    Ethnic division: Peuhl 40%, Malinke 30%, Soussou 20%, smaller tribes 10%

    Religions: Muslim 85%, Christian 8%, indigenous beliefs 7%

    Languages: French (official); each tribe has its own language

    Literacy: total population 24%

Economy

    Imports: petroleum products, metals, machinery, transport equipment, foodstuffs, textiles, and other grains

    Exports: bauxite, alumina, diamonds, gold, coffee, pineapples, bananas, palm kernels

Industries: mining - bauxite, gold, diamonds, alumina refining; light manufacturing and agricultural processing industries

Agriculture: mostly subsistence farming; principal products - rice, coffee, pineapples, palm kernels, cassava, bananas, sweet potatoes, timber, fishing; livestock - cattle, sheep and goats; not self-sufficient in food grains

Currency: 1 Guinean franc (FG) = 100 centimes

Guinean francs per US1$ - 810.94

Transportation

Railroads: 1,048 km

Roads: 30,100 km total paved and unpaved

Ports: Boke, Conakry, Kamsar

Airports: 15 total paved and unpaved. There is an international airport at Conakry

The Press: newspapers   **Horoya:** BP 191, Conakry   weekly

               Journal Officiel de Guinee: BP 156, Conakry   fortnightly

Tourism: mountains of Futa Djalon

               Secretariat d'Etat au Tourisme et a l'Hotellerie:
square des Martyrs, BP 1304, Conakry telephone 44-26-06

Diplomatic representation in US:

chief of mission: Ambassador Elhadj Boubacar Barry

chancery: 2112 Leroy Place NW, Washington, DC 20008

telephone: [1] (202) 483-9420

FAX: [1] (202) 483-8688

US Diplomatic representation:

chief of mission: Ambassador Joseph A. Saloom III

embassy: 2nd Boulevard and 9th Avenue, Conakry

mailing address: BP 603, Conakry

telephone: [224] 44-15-20 through 44-15-23

FAX: [224] 44-15-22

Guinea-Bissau

North Atlantic Ocean

Capital: Bissau   longitude: 15.39 W   latitude: 11.52 N

Government: republic

Flag: two equal bands of yellow (top) and green with a vertical red band on the hoist side; there is a black five-pointed star centered in the red band; uses the popular pan-African colors of Ethiopia; similar to the flag of Cape Verde, which has the black star raised above the center of the red band and is framed by two corn stalks and a yellow clam shell

Geography

Location: Western Africa, bordering the North Atlantic Ocean, between Guinea and Senegal

Total Area: 36,120 sq km (13,946 sq mi) slightly less than three times the size of Connecticut

Boundaries: Guinea, Senegal

Climate: tropical; generally hot and humid; monsoonal-type rainy season (June to November) with southwesterly winds; dry season (December to May) with northeasterly harmattan winds

Temperature (F): High/Low Jan. 83/62, Apr. 86/65, July 87/75, Oct. 89/74

Terrain: mostly low coastal plain rising to savanna in east

Highest point is 210 m (689 ft)

Natural resources: unexploited deposits of petroleum, bauxite, phosphates, fish, timber

Natural hazards: hot, dry, dusty harmattan haze may reduce visibility during dry season; brush fires

People

Population: 1,124,600 (July 1995 est.)

Life expectancy at birth: total population 47.87 years

Nationality: Guinea-Bissauan

Ethnic division: African 99%, (Balanta 30%, Fula 20%, Manjaca 14%, Mandinga 13%, Papel 7%), European and mulatto less than 1%

Religions: indigenous beliefs 65%, Muslim 30%, Christian 5%

Languages: Portuguese (official), Criolo, African languages

Literacy: total population 36%

Economy

Imports: foodstuffs, transport equipment, petroleum products, machinery and equipment

Exports: cashews, fish, peanuts, palm kernels

Industries: agricultural processing, beer, soft drinks

Agriculture: rice is the staple food; other crops include corn, beans, cassava, cashew nuts, peanuts, palm kernels, and cotton; not self-sufficient in food; fishing and forestry potential not fully exploited

Currency: 1 Guinea-Bissauan peso (PG) = 100 centavos

Guinea-Bissauan peso per US1$ - 14,482

Transportation

    Railroads: none

    Roads: 3,218 km total paved and unpaved

    Ports: Bissau

    Airports: 32 total paved and unpaved. There is an international airport at Bissalanca

The Press: newspapers   **Expresso-Bissau:** Bissau weekly

        No Pintcha: Bissau daily circ. 6,000

Tourism: Island of Babaque

        Centro de Informacao e Turismo: CP 294, Bissau

Diplomatic representation in US:

    chief of mission: Ambassador Alfredo Lopes Cabral

    chancery: 918 16th Street NW, Mezzanine Suite, Washington, DC 20006

    telephone: [1] (202) 872-4222

    FAX: [1] (202) 872-4226

US Diplomatic representation:

    chief of mission: Ambassador Roger A. McGuire

    embassy: Bairro de Penha, Bissau

    mailing address: CP 297, 1067 Bissau Codex, Bissau, Guinea-Bissau

    telephone: [245] 25-22-73, 25-22-74, 25-22-75, 25-22-76

    FAX: [245] 25-22-83

Guyana

Capital: Georgetown   longitude: 58.10 W latitude: 6.46 N elevation: 6 ft

Government: republic

Flag: green with a red isosceles triangle (based on the hoist side) superimposed on a long yellow arrowhead; there is a narrow black border between the red and yellow, and a narrow white border between the yellow and the green

Geography

Location: Northern South America, bordering the North Atlantic Ocean, between Suriname and Venezuela

Total Area: 214,970 sq km (83,000 sq mi) slightly smaller than Idaho

Boundaries: Brazil, Suriname, Venezuela

Climate: tropical; hot, humid, moderated by northeast trade winds; two rainy seasons (May to August, mid-November to mid-January)

Temperature (F): High/Low Jan. 84/74, Apr. 85/76, July 85/75, Oct. 87/76

Average annual precipitation: 88.6 inches

Terrain: mostly rolling highlands; low coastal plain; savanna in south

Highest point is Mt. Roraima 2,772 m (9,094 ft)

Natural resources: bauxite, gold, diamonds, hardwood timber, shrimp, fish

Natural hazards: flash floods are a constant threat during rainy seasons

People

Population: 723,800 (July 1995 est.)

Life expectancy at birth: total population 65.1 years

Nationality: Guyanese

Ethnic division: East Indian 51%, black and mixed 43%, Amerindian 4%, European and Chinese 2%

Religions: Christians 57%, Hindu 33%, Muslim 9%, other 1%

Languages: English, Amerindian dialects

Literacy: total population 96%

Economy

Imports: manufactures, machinery, petroleum, food

Exports: sugar, bauxite/alumina, rice, shrimp, molasses

Industries: bauxite mining, sugar, rice milling, timber, fishing (shrimp), textiles, gold mining

Agriculture: sugar and rice are key crops; development potential exists for fishing and forestry; not self-sufficient in food, especially wheat, vegetable oils, and animal products

Currency: 1 Guyanese dollar (G$) = 100 cents

Guyanese dollars per US1$ - 142.7

Transportation

Railroads: 100 km

Roads: 7,665 km total paved and unpaved

Ports: Bartica, Georgetown, Linden, New Amsterdam, Parika
Airports: 54 total paved and unpaved. Timehri International Airport is about 40 km from Georgetown

The Press: newspapers   **Guyana Chronicle:** 2a Lama Ave, Bel Air Park,
POB 11, Georgetown
telephone (2) 61-576   fax (2) 60-658
circ. 60,000 weekdays,   100,000 Sundays
Stabroek News: 46-47 Robb St, Lacytown, Georgetown
telephone (2) 57-473   fax (2) 54-637
Circ. 18,000 weekdays, 28,000 Sundays

Tourism: beautiful scenery in the interior of the country.
Tourism Association of Guyana: Georgetown

Diplomatic representation in US:
chief of mission: Ambassador Dr. Ali Odeen Ishmael
chancery: 2490 Tracy Place NW, Washington, DC 20008
telephone: [1] (202) 265-6900, 6901
US Diplomatic representation:
chief of mission: Ambassador George F. Jones
embassy: 99-100 Young and Duke Streets, Kingston, Georgetown
mailing address: P O Box 10507, Georgetown
telephone: [592] (2) 54-900 through 54-909, 57-960 through 57-969
FAX: [592] (2) 58-497

Haiti

Capital: Port-au-Prince   longitude: 72.20 W   latitude: 18.33 N
elevation: 121 ft
Government: republic

Flag: two equal bands of blue (top) and red with a centered white rectangle bearing the coat of arms, which contains a palm tree flanked by flags and two cannons above a scroll bearing the motto 'UNION FAIT LA FORCE (Union makes Strength)

Geography

Location: Caribbean, western one-third of the island of Hispaniola. between the Caribbean Sea and the North Atlantic Ocean, west of the Dominican Republic

Total Area: 27,750 sq km (10,714 sq mi) slightly larger than Maryland

Boundaries: Dominican Republic

Climate: tropical; semiarid where mountains in east cut off trade winds

Temperature (F): High/Low Jan. 87/68, Apr. 89/71, July 94/74, Oct. 90/72

Average annual precipitation: 53.3 inches

Terrain: mostly rough and mountainous

Highest point is Chaine de la Selle 2,680 m (8,793 ft)

Natural resources: bauxite

Natural hazards: lies in the middle of the hurricane belt and subject to severe storms from June to October; occasional flooding and earthquakes; periodic droughts

People

Population: 6,540,000 (July 1995 est.)

Life expectancy at birth: total population 44.77 years

Nationality: Haitian

Ethnic division: black 95%, mulatto and European 5%

Religions: Roman Catholic 80% (of which an overwhelming majority also practice Voodoo), Protestant 16% (Baptist 10%, Pentecostal 4%, Adventist 1%, other 1%) none 1%, other 3%

Languages: French (official) 10% Creole

Literacy: total population 35%

Economy

Imports: machine and manufactures, food and beverages, petroleum products, chemicals, fats and oils

Exports: light manufactures, coffee, other agriculture

Industries: sugar refining, textiles, flour milling, cement manufacturing, tourism, light assembly industries based on imported parts

Agriculture: mostly small-scale subsistence farms; commercial crops - coffee, mangoes, sugarcane, wood; staple crops - rice, corn, sorghum; shortage of wheat

Currency: 1 gourde (G) = 100 centimes

gourdes per US1$ - 14.10

Transportation

Railroads: 40 km

Roads: 4,000 km total paved and unpaved

Ports: Cap-Haitien, Gonaives, Jacmel, Jeremie, Cayes, Miragone, Port-au-Prince, Port-de-Paix, Saint-Marc

Airports: 14 total paved and unpaved. The international airport is located about 8 km outside Port-a-Prince

The Press: daily newspapers **Le Matin:** 88 rue du Quai, Port-au-Prince
telephone 22-20-40 circ. 5,000

Le Nouvelliste: 198 rue du Centre, BP 1013, Port-au-Prince
telephone 22-21-14 circ. 6,000

Tourism: Saint Trinite, Museum of Art, mountains and beaches

Office National du Tourisme d'Haiti:
ave Marie-Jeanne, Port-au-Prince telephone 22-17-29

Diplomatic representation in US:

chief of mission: Ambassador Jean Casimir

chancery: 2311 Massachusetts Avenue NW, Washington, DC 20008

telephone: [1] (202) 332-4090 through 4092

FAX: [1] (202) 745-7215

US Diplomatic representation:

chief of mission: Ambassador William Lacy Swing

embassy: Harry Truman Boulevard, Port-au-Prince

mailing address: P O Box 1761, Port-au-Prince

telephone: [509] 22-03-54, 22-03-68, 22-02-00, 22-06-12

FAX: [509] 231-1641

Territory of **Heard Island** an the **McDonald Islands**

20 km

McDonald
Islands

Flat Island
McDonald Island

Shag Island

Indian
Ocean

Heard Island

Capital: none; administered from Canberra, Australia

elevation: 16 ft   longitude: 73.23 E   latitude: 53.01 S

Government: territory of Australia administered by the Australian Ministry for the Environment, Sport, and Territories

Geography:

Location: Southern Africa, islands in the Indian Ocean, about two-thirds of the way from Madagascar to Antarctic

Total Area: 412 sq km (159 sq mi) slightly less than 2.5 times the size of Washington, DC

Boundaries: no land boundaries

Climate: antarctic; almost entirely covered in ice

Temperature (F): High/Low Jan. 41/35, Apr. 39/33, July 34/27, Oct. 35/28

Average annual precipitation: 54.3 inches

Terrain: Heard Island - bleak and mountainous, with a quiescent volcano; McDonald Islands - small and rocky

Natural resources: none

Natural hazards: Heard Island is dominated by a dormant volcano called Big Ben

People:

Population: uninhabited - used primarily for research stations

Transportation:

Ports: none; offshore anchorage only

Diplomatic representation in US: none (territory of Australia)

US Diplomatic representation: none (territory of Australia)

Holy See (Vatican City)

250 meters

Capital: Vatican City   longitude: 12.40 E   latitude: 41.80 N
elevation: 56 ft

Government: monarchical-sacerdotal state

Flag: two vertical bands of yellow (hoist side) and white with the crossed keys of Saint Peter and the papal miter centered in the white band

Geography

Location: Southern European enclave of Rome (Italy)

Total Area: 0.44 sq km (.17 sq mi) about 0.7 times the size of The Mall in Washington, DC

Boundaries: Italy

Climate: temperate; mild, rainy winters (September to mid-May) with hot, dry summers (May to September)

Temperature (F): High/Low Jan. 52/40, Apr. 66/50, July 87/67, Oct. 71/55 average annual precipitation: 30.1 inches

Terrain: low hill

Natural resources: none

Natural hazards: NA

Note: urban; landlocked; enclave of Rome, Italy; world's smallest state; outside the Vatican City, 13 buildings in Rome and Castel Gandolfo (the Pope's summer residence) enjoy extra territorial rights

People

Population: 830 (July 1995 est.)

Life expectancy at birth: NA

Nationality: none

Ethnic division: Italians, Swiss

Religions: Roman Catholic

Languages: Italian, Latin, various other languages

Economy

This unique, non commercial economy is supported financially by contributions (known as Peter's Pence) from Roman Catholics throughout the world, the sale of postage stamps and tourist mementos, fees for admission to museums, and the sale of publications.

Industries: printing and production of small amount of mosaics and staff uniforms; worldwide banking and financial activities

Agriculture: none

Currency: 1 Vatican lira (VLit) = 100 centesimi
Vatican lira per US1$ - 1,609.5

Transportation

Railroads: 862 meters; note - connects to Italy's network at Rome's Saint Peter's station

Roads: none; all city streets

Diplomatic representation in US:

chief of mission: Ambassador Apostolic Pro-Nuncio
Archbishop Agostino Cacciavillan
chancery: 3339 Massachusetts Avenue NW, Washington, DC 20008
telephone: [1] (202) 333-7121

US Diplomatic representation:

chief of mission: Ambassador Raymond L. Flynn
embassy: Via Delle Terme Deciane 26, Rome 00153
mailing address: PSC 59, APO AE 09624
telephone: [39] (6) 46-741
FAX: [39] (6) 638-0159

Honduras

Capital: Tegucigalpa   longitude: 87.14 W   latitude: 14.05 N
elevation: 3,304 ft

Government: republic

Flag: three equal horizontal bands of blue (top), white, and blue with five blue five-pointed stars arranged in an X pattern centered in the white band; the stars represent the members of the former Federal Republic of Central America - Costa Rica, El Salvador, Guatemala, Honduras, and Nicaragua; similar to the flag of Il Salvador, which features a round emblem encircled by the words REPUBLICA DE EL SALVADOR EN LA AMERICA CENTRAL centered in the white band; also similar to the flag of Nicaragua, which features a triangle encircled by the word REPUBLICA DE NICARAGUA on the top and AMERICA CENTRAL on the bottom, centered in the white band

Geography

Location: Middle America, bordering the Caribbean Sea, between Guatemala and Nicaragua and bordering the North Pacific Ocean, between El Salvador and Nicaragua

Total Area: 112,090 sq km (43,278 sq mi) slightly larger than Tennessee

Boundaries: Guatemala, El Salvador, Nicaragua

Climate: subtropical in lowlands, temperate in mountains

Temperature (F): High/Low Jan. 77/57, Apr. 86/62, July 81/64, Oct. 80/63

Average annual precipitation: 32.7 inches

Terrain: mostly mountains in interior, narrow coastal plains

Natural resources: timber, gold, silver, copper, lead, zinc, iron ore, antimony, coal, fish

Natural hazards: frequent, but generally mild, earthquakes; damaging hurricanes and floods along Caribbean coast

People

Population: 5,459,800 (July 1995 est.)

Life expectancy at birth: total population 68.04 years

Nationality: Honduran

Ethnic division: mestizo (mixed Indian and European) 90%, Indian 7%, black 2%, white 1%

Religions: Roman Catholic 97%, Protestant minority

Languages: Spanish, Indian dialects

Literacy: total population 73%

Economy

Imports: machinery and transport equipment, chemical products, manufactured goods, fuel and oil, foodstuffs

Exports: bananas, coffee, shrimp, lobster, minerals, meat, lumber

Industries: agricultural processing (sugar and coffee), textiles, clothing, wood products

Agriculture: principal products include bananas, coffee, timber, beef, citrus fruit, shrimp; importers of wheat

Currency: 1 lempira (L) = 100 centavos

lempiras per US1$ - 9.12

Transportation

    Railroads: 785 km

    Roads: 8,950 km total paved and unpaved

    Ports: La Ceiba, Puerto Castilla, Puerto Cortes, San Lorenzo, Tela, Puerto Lempira

    Airports: 159 total paved and unpaved. There are three international airports

The Press: daily newspapers   **El Tiempo:** 7a Avda No 6, Calle SO 55, Apdo 450, San Pedro Sula;   circ. 70,000

           La Tribuna: Apdo 1501, Tegucigalpa   circ. 60,000

Tourism: Mayan ruins at Copan, boating and fishing

Diplomatic representation in US:

    chief of mission: Ambassador Roberto Flores Bermudez

    chancery: 3007 Tilden Street NW, Washington, DC 20008

    telephone: [1] (202) 966-7702, 2604, 5008, 4596

    FAX: [1] (202) 966-9751

US Diplomatic representation:

    chief of mission: Ambassador William T. Pryce

    embassy: Avenida La Paz, Apartado Postal No 3453, Tegucigalpa

    mailing address: American Embassy, APO AA 34022, Tegucigalpa

    telephone: [504] 36-93-20, 38-51-14

    FAX: [504] 36-90-37

Hong Kong

Lema Channel

Capital: Victoria   longitude: 114.09 E   latitude: 22.19 N   elevation: 109 ft

Government: dependent territory of the UK scheduled to revert to China in 1997

Flag: blue with the flag of the UK in the upper hoist-side quadrant with the Hong Kong coat of arms on a white disk centered on the outer half of the flag; the coat of arms contains a shield (bearing two junks below the crown) held by a lion (representing the UK) and a dragon (representing China) with another lion above the shield and a banner bearing the words HONG KONG below the shield

Geography

Location: Eastern Asia, bordering the South China Sea and China

Total Area: 1,040 sq km (401.5 sq mi) slightly less than six times the size of Washington, DC

Boundaries: China

Climate: tropical monsoon; cool and humid in winter, hot and rainy from spring through summer, warm and sunny in fall

Temperature (F): High/Low Jan. 64/56, Apr. 75.67, July 87/78, Oct. 80/63

Average annual precipitation: 85.1 inches

Terrain: hilly to mountainous with steep slopes; lowland in north

Natural resources: outstanding deepwater harbor, feldspar

Natural hazards: occasional typhoons

People

Population: 5,543,000 (July 1995 est.)

Life expectancy at birth: total population 80.18 years

Nationality: Chinese

Ethnic division: Chinese 95%, other 5%

Religions: eclectic mixture of local religions 90%, Christian 10%

Languages: Chinese (Cantonese) English

Literacy: total population 77%

Economy

Imports: foodstuffs, transport equipment, raw materials, semi-manufactures, petroleum; a large share is re-exported

Exports: clothing, textiles, yarn and fabric, footwear, electrical appliances, watches and clocks, toys

Industries: textiles, clothing, tourism, electronics, plastic toys, watches, clocks

Agriculture: minor role in the economy; local farmers produce fresh vegetables and live poultry. 8% of land is suitable for farming

Currency: 1 Hong Kong dollar (HK$) = 100 cents

Hong Kong dollars per US1$ - 7.80

Transportation

Railroads: 35 km

Roads: 1,100 km total paved and unpaved

Ports: Hong Kong

Airports: 3 with paved runways

The Press: English newspapers   **Hong Kong Standard:** Sing Tao Building, 4th Floor, 1 Wang Kwong Road Kowloon Bay, Kowloon   circ. 48,000 telephone 798-2798   fax 795-3027

South China Morning Post: Tong Chong St. POB 47 telephone 565-2222   fax 811-1278   circ. 120,000

Tourism: Hong Kong, a British Crown Colony, is made up of three geographic areas; The New Territories, Kowloon peninsula, and Hong Kong Island. It is a cosmopolitan, highly developed territory. Chinatown, Kowloon's Space Museum, shops

Hong Kong Tourist Association: Jardine House 35th Floor 1 Connaught Place, Central, POB 2597 telephone 801-7111   fax 810-4877

Diplomatic representation in US: none (dependent territory of the UK)

US Diplomatic representation: none (dependent territory of the UK)

Howland Island

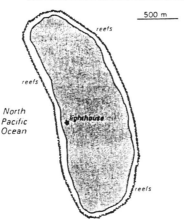

Capital: none; administered from Washington, DC

longitude: 174.00 W   latitude: 2.10 N

Government: unincorporated territory of the US administered by the Fish and Wildlife Service of the US Department of the Interior as part of the National Wildlife Refuge System

Geography

Location: Oceania, island in the North Pacific Ocean, about one-half of the way from Hawaii to Australia

Total Area: 1.6 sq km (.618 sq mi) about 2.7 times the size of The Mall in Washington, DC

Boundaries: no land boundaries

Climate: equatorial; scant rainfall, constant wind, burning sun

Terrain: low-lying, nearly level, sandy, coral island surrounded by a narrow fringing reef, depressed central area

Natural resources: guano

Natural hazards: the narrow fringing reef surrounding the island can be a maritime hazard

Note: almost totally covered with grasses, prostrate vines, and low-growing shrubs; small area of trees in the center; primarily a nesting, roosting, and foraging habitat for sea birds, shore birds, and marine wildlife; feral cats

People

Population: uninhabited; public entry is by special-use permit only and generally restricted to scientists and educators

Economy

no economic activity

Transportation

Ports: none; offshore anchorage only; note - there is one boat landing area along the middle of the west coast

Airports: airstrip constructed in 1937 for scheduled refueling stop on the round-the-world flight of Amelia Earhart and Fred Noonan - they left Lae, New Guinea, for Howland Island, but were never seen again; the airstrip is no longer serviceable.

Hungary

125 km

Capital: Budapest   longitude: 19.03 E   latitude: 47.30 N   elevation: 456 ft
Government: republic

Flag: three equal horizontal bands of red (top), white, green

Geography

Location: Central Europe, northwest of Romania

Total Area: 93,030 sq km (35,919 sq mi) slightly smaller than Indiana

Boundaries: Austria, Croatia, Romania, Serbia and Montenegro, Slovakia, Slovenia, Ukraine

Climate: temperate; cold, cloudy, humid winters; warm summers

Temperature (F): High/Low Jan. 34/25, Apr. 62/44, July 82/62, Oct. 61/44

Average annual precipitation: 24.2 inches

Terrain: mostly flat to rolling plains; hills and low mountains on the Slovakian border

Highest point is Kekes 1,015 m (3,330 ft)

Natural resources: bauxite, coal, natural gas, fertile soils

Lake Balaton

Natural hazards: levees are common along many streams, but flooding occurs almost every year

People

Population: 10,318,900 (July 1995 est.)

Life expectancy at birth: total population 71.9 years

Nationality: Hungarian

Ethnic division: Hungarian 89.9%, Gypsy 4%, German 2.6%, Serb 2%, Slovak 0.8%, Romanian 0.7%

Religions: Roman Catholic 67.5%, Calvinist 20%, Lutheran 5%, Atheist and other 7.5%

Languages: Hungarian 98.2% other 1.8%

Literacy: total population 99%

Economy

Imports: fuels and energy, raw materials and semi-finished goods, machinery and transport equipment, consumer goods, food and agriculture

Exports: raw materials and semi-finished goods, machinery and transport equipment, consumer goods,, food and agriculture, fuels and energy

Industries: mining, metallurgy, construction materials, processed foods, textiles, chemicals (especially pharmaceuticals), buses, automobiles

Agriculture: forestry; highly diversified crop and livestock farming; principal crops - wheat, corn, sunflowers, potatoes, sugar beets; livestock - hogs, cattle, poultry, dairy products; self-sufficient in food output

Currency: 1 forint (Ft) = 100 filler

forints per US1$ - 112

Transportation
    Railroads: 7,785 km
    Roads: 158,711 km total paved and unpaved
    Ports: Budapest, Dunaujvaros
    Airports: 78 total paved and unpaved. The Ferihegy international airport is
    about 16 km from Budapest

The Press: daily newspapers   **Magyar Hirlap:** 1087 Budapest, Kerepesi ut 29B
    telephone (1) 210-0050   fax (1) 113-0249
    circ 75,000

    Mai Nap: 1087 Budapest, Konyves Kalman krt
    telephone (1) 210-0400   fax (1) 133-9153   circ. 94,000

Tourism: Lake Balaton is the main holiday center for boating, swimming and
    fishing

    Orszagos Idegenforgalmi Hivatal: 1051 Budapest, Vigado u. 6
    telephone (1) 118-0750   fax (1) 118-5241

Diplomatic representation in US:
    chief of mission: Ambassador Gyorgy Banlaki
    chancery: 3910 Shoemaker Street NW, Washington, DC 20008
    telephone: [1] (202) 362-6730
    FAX: [1] (202) 966-8135

US Diplomatic representation:
    chief of mission: Ambassador Donald M. Blinken
    embassy: V. Szabadsag Ter 12, Budapest
    mailing address: AmEmbassy, Unit 1320, Budapest; APO AE 09213-1320
    telephone: [36] (1) 112-6450
    FAX: [36] (1) 132-8934

Iceland

Capital: Reykjavik   longitude: 21.58 W latitude: 64.09 N elevation: 59 ft

Government: republic

Flag: blue with a red cross outlined in white that extends to the edge of the flag; the vertical part of the cross is shifted to the hoist side in the style of the Dannebrog (Danish flag)

Geography

Location: Northern Europe, island between the Greenland Sea and the North Atlantic Ocean, northwest of the UK

Total Area: 103,000 sq km (39,768 sq mi) slightly smaller than Kentucky

Boundaries: no land boundaries

Climate: temperate; moderated by North Atlantic Current; mild, windy winters; damp cool summers

Temperature (F): High/Low Jan. 35/28, Apr. 43/33, July 57/48, Oct. 45/32

Average annual precipitation: 30.7 inches

Terrain: mostly plateau interspersed with mountain peaks, ice fields; coast deeply indented by bays and fjords

Highest point is Hvannadalshnukur 2,119 m (6,952 ft)

Natural resources: fish, hydropower, geothermal power, diatomite

Natural hazards: earthquakes and volcanic activity

Note: strategic location between Greenland and Europe; westernmost European country; more land covered by glaciers than all of continental Europe

People

Population: 266,000 (July 1995 est.)

Life expectancy at birth: total population 78.98 years

Nationality: Icelander

Ethnic division: homogeneous mixture of descendants of Norwegians and Celts

Religions: Evangelical Lutheran 96%, other Protestant and Roman Catholic 3%, none 1%

Languages: Icelandic

Literacy: total population 100%

Economy

Imports: machinery and transportation equipment, petroleum products

Exports: fish and fish products, animal products, aluminum, ferro-silicon, diatomite

Industries: fish processing, aluminum smelting, ferro-silicon production, geothermal power

Agriculture: fishing is the most important economic activity; principal crops - potatoes, turnips; livestock - cattle, sheep

Currency: 1 Icelandic krona (IKr) = 100 aurar
Icelandic kronur per US1$ - 67.76

Transportation

    Railroads: none

    Roads: 11,373 km total paved and unpaved

    Ports: Akureyri, Hornafjordur, Keflavik, Raufarhofn, Reykjavik, Seydhisfjordhur, Straumsvik, Vestmannaeyjar

    Airports: 90 total paved and unpaved

The Press: daily newspapers   **Dagbladid-Visir:** Thverholt 11, POB 5380 Reykjavik telephone (1) 27-022 fax (1) 27-079 circ. 39,500

    Morgunbladid: Kringlan 1, POB 3040, 103 Reykjavik telephone (1) 69-11-00 fax (1) 69-11-81 circ. 52,000

Tourism: Main attractions are the rugged interior with its geysers and thermal springs, Gullfoss waterfall

    Iceland Tourist Board: Laekjargata 3, 101 Reykjavik telephone (1) 27-488 fax (1) 62-47-49

Diplomatic representation in US:

    chief of mission: Ambassador Einar Benediktsson

    chancery: Suite 1200, 1156 15th Street NW, Washington, DC 20005

    telephone: [1] (202) 265-6653 through 6655

    FAX: [1] (202) 265-6656

US Diplomatic representation:

    chief of mission: Ambassador Parker W. Borg

    embassy: Laufasvegur 21, Box 40, Reykjavik

    mailing address: US Embassy, PSC 1003, Box 40 Reykjavik; FPO AE 09728-0340

    telephone: [354] (1) 62-91-00

    FAX: [354] (1) 62-91-39

India

Capital: New Delhi
> longitude: 77.13 E   latitude: 28.37 N   elevation: 714 ft

Government: federal republic

Flag: three equal horizontal bands of orange (top), white, and green with a blue chakra (24-spoked wheel) centered in the white band; similar to the flag of Niger, which has a small orange disk centered in the white band

Geography

Location: Southern Asia, bordering the Arabian Sea and the Bay of Bengal, between Bangladesh and Pakistan

Total Area: 3,287,590 sq km (1,269,339 sq mi) slightly more than one-third the size of the US

Boundaries: Bangladesh, Bhutan, Burma, China, Nepal, Pakistan

Climate: varies from tropical monsoon in south to temperate in north
Temperature (F): High/Low Jan. 70/44, Apr. 97/68, July 96/81, Oct. 93/65
Average annual precipitation: 25.2 inches

Terrain: upland plain (Deccan Plateau) in south, flat to rolling plain along the Ganges, desert in west, Himalayas in north
Highest point is Nanda Devi 7,817 m (25,645 ft)

Natural resources: coal (forth-largest reserves in the world), iron ore, manganese, mica, bauxite, titanium ore, chromite, natural gas, diamonds, petroleum, limestone

Natural hazards: droughts, flash floods, severe thunderstorms common; earthquakes

People

Population: 936,546,000 (July 1995 est.)

Life expectancy at birth: total population 59.04 years

Nationality: Indian

Ethnic division: Indo-Aryan 72%, Dravidian 25%, Monoloid and others 3%

Religions: Hindu 80%, Muslim 14%, Christian 2.4%, Sikh 20%, Buddhist 0.7%, Jains 0.5%, other 0.4%

Languages: English enjoys associate status but is the most important language for national, political, and commercial communication. Hindi the national language and primary tongue of 30% of the people. Other official languages are , Telugu, Marathi, Tamil, Urdu, Gujarati, Malayalam, Kannada, Oriya, Punjabi, Assamese, Kashmiri, Sindhi, Sanskrit; Hindustani a popular variant of Hindu/Urdu, is spoken widely throughout northern India. Note: 24 languages each spoken by a million or more persons; numerous other languages and dialects, for the most part mutually unintelligible

Literacy: total population 52%

Economy

Imports: crude oil and petroleum products, machinery, gems, fertilizer, chemicals

Exports: clothing, gems and jewelry, engineering goods, chemicals, leather manufactures, cotton yarn, and fabric

Industries: textiles, chemicals, food processing, steel, transportation equipment, cement, mining, petroleum, machinery

Agriculture: principal crops - rice, wheat, oilseeds, cotton, jute, tea, sugarcane, potatoes; livestock - cattle, buffaloes, sheep, goats, poultry; India ranks among the top 10 fishing nations

Currency: 1 Indian rupee (Re) = 100 paise
Indian rupees per US1$ - 31.37

Transportation

Railroads: 62,211 km

Roads: 1,970,000 km total paved and unpaved

Ports: Bombay, Calcutta, Cochin, Haldia, Kandla, Madras, Mormugao, New Manglore, Pondicherry, Port Blair (Andaman Islands), Tuticorin, Vishakhapatnam

Airports: 352 total paved and unpaved. There are seven international airports

The Press: daily newspapers   **The Hindustan Times:**
18/20 Kasturba Gandhi Marg, New Delhi 110 001
telephone (11) 331-8201 fax (11) 332-1189
English circ. 326,000

Indian Express: Bahadur Shah Zafar Marg, New Delhi 110 002
telephone (11) 331-1111   fax (11) 371-6037 circ. 551,500

Tourism: Tourist attractions are historic temples, shrines, palaces and forts, scenery and a wide variety of wildlife

Department of Tourism of the Government of India:
Ministry of Tourism, Transport Bhaven, Parliament St.
New Delhi 110 001
telephone (11) 3711-7890   fax (11) 371-0518

Diplomatic representation in US:
chief of mission: Ambassador Siddhartha Shankar Ray
chancery: 2107 Massachusetts Avenue NW, Washington, DC 20008
telephone: [1] (202) 939-7000

US Diplomatic representation:
chief of mission: Ambassador Frank G. Wisner
embassy: Shanti Path, Chanakyapuri 110021, New Delhi
mailing address: use embassy street address
telephone: [91] (11) 60-06-51
FAX: [91] (11) 687-2028

Indian Ocean

Geography

Location: body of water between Africa, Antarctica, Asia, and Australia

Area: 73,600,000 million sq km slightly less than eight times the size of the US; third-largest ocean

Note: includes Arabian Sea, Bass Straight, Bay of Bengal, Great Australian Bight, Gulf of Oman, Persian Gulf, Red Sea, Strait of Malacca, and other tributary water bodies

Climate: northeast monsoon (December to April); southwest monsoon (June to October); tropical cyclones occur during May/June and October/November in the northern Indian Ocean and January/February in the southern Indian Ocean

Terrain: surface dominated by counterclockwise gyre (broad, circular system of currents) in the southern Indian Ocean; unique reversal of surface currents in the northern Indian Ocean, low atmospheric pressure over southwest Asia from hot, rising, summer air results in the southwest monsoon and southwest-to-northeast winds and currents, while high pressure over northern Asia from cold, falling, winter air results in the northeast monsoon and northeast-to-southwest winds and currents; ocean floor is dominated by the Mid-Indian Ocean Ridge and subdivided by the Southeast Indian Ocean Ridge, Southwest Indian Ocean Ridge, and the Ninety East Ridge; maximum depth is 7,258 meters in the Java Trench

Natural resources: oil and gas fields, fish, shrimp, sand and gravel aggregates, placer deposits, polymetallic nodules

Environment

Current issues: endangered marine species include the dugong, seals, turtles, and whales; oil pollution in the Arabian Sea, Persian Gulf, and Red Sea

Natural hazards: ships subject to superstructure icing in extreme south near Antarctica from May to October

Transportation

Ports: Bombay (India), Calcutta (India), Colombo (Sri Lanka), Durban (South Africa), Jakarta (Indonesia), Madras (India), Melbourne (Australia), Richard's Bay (South Africa)

Indonesia

Capital: Jakarta   longitude: 106.45 E latitude: 6.08 S elevation: 26 ft

Government: republic

Flag: two equal horizontal bands of red (top) and white; similar to the flag of Monaco, which is shorter; also similar to the flag of Poland, which is white (top) and red

212

Geography

Location: Southeastern Asia, archipelago between the Indian Ocean and the Pacific Ocean

Total Area: 1,919,440 sq km (714,096 sq mi) slightly less than three times the size of Texas

Boundaries: Malaysia, Papua New Guinea

Climate: tropical; hot, humid; more moderate in highlands

Temperature (F): High/Low Jan. 84/74, Apr. 87/75, July 87/73, Oct. 87/74

Average annual precipitation: 70.8 inches

Terrain: mostly coastal lowlands; larger islands have interior mountains

Highest point is Puncak Jaya 5,030 m (16,503 ft)

Natural resources: petroleum, tin, natural gas, nickel, timber, bauxite, copper, fertile soils, coal, gold, silver

Natural hazards: occasional floods, severe droughts, and tsunamis

People

Population: 203,584,000 (July 1995 est.)

Life expectancy at birth: total population 61.22 years

Nationality: Indonesian

Ethnic division: Javanese, 45%, Sundanese 14%, Madurese 7.5%, coastal Malays 7.5%, other 26%

Religions: Muslim 87%, Protestant 6%, Roman Catholic 3%, Hindu 2%, Buddhist 1%, other 1%

Languages: Bahasa Indonesia (modified form of Malay; official), English, Dutch, local dialects the most widely spoken of which is Javanese

Literacy: total population 82%

Economy

Imports: capital equipment, raw materials, consumer goods, fuels

Exports: manufactures, fuels, foodstuffs, raw materials

Industries: petroleum and natural gas, textiles, mining, cement, chemical fertilizers, plywood, food, rubber

Agriculture: main products are rice, cassava, peanuts, rubber, cocoa, coffee, palm oil, copra, other tropical products, poultry, beef, pork eggs

Currency: 1 Indonesian rupiah (Rp) = 100 sen (sen no longer used)

Indonesian rupiahs per US1$ - 2,203.6

Transportation

Railroads: 6,964 km

Roads: 119,500 km (paved and unpaved NA)

Ports: Cilacap, Cirebon, Jakarta, Kupang, Palembang, Semarang, Surbaya, Ujungpandang

Airports: 450 total paved and unpaved. There are seven international airports.

The Press: daily newspapers **Berita Buana:** Gedung Puri Mandiri, Jalan Warung Buncit Raya 37, Jakarta 12510 telephone (21) 780-0414   circ. 150,000
Suara Merdeka: Jalan Pandanaran 30, Semarang 50241 telephone (24) 41-26-60 fax (24) 41-11-16 circ. 200,000

Tourism: volcanic scenery and religious temples, Lake Toba
Direktorat Jenderal Pariwisata:
81 Jalaan Kramat Raya, Jakarta 10450
telephone (21) 310-3117 fax (21) 310-1146

Diplomatic representation in US:
chief of mission: Ambassador Arifin Mohamad Siregar
chancery: 2020 Massachusetts Avenue NW, Washington, DC 20036
telephone: [1] (202) 775-5200
FAX: [1] (202) 775-5365

US Diplomatic representation:
chief of mission: Ambassador Robert L. Barry
embassy: Medan Merdeka Selatan 5, Box 1, Jakarta
mailing address: APO AP 96520
telephone: [62] (21) 36-03-60
FAX: [62] (21) 386-2259

Capital: Tehran   longitude: 51.26 E   latitude: 35.40 N elevation: 4002 ft
Government: theocratic

Flag: three equal horizontal bands of green (top), white, and red; the national emblem (a stylized representation of the work Allah) in red is centered in the white band; Allah Alkbar (God is Great) in white Arabic script is repeated 11 times along the bottom edge of the green band and 11 times along the top edge of the red band

Geography

Location: Middle East, bordering the Gulf of Oman and the Persian Gulf, between Iraq and Pakistan

Total Area: 1,648,000 million sq km (636,293 sq mi) slightly larger than Alaska

Boundaries: Afghanistan, Armenia, Azerbaijan, Iraq, Pakistan, Turkey, Turkmenistan

Climate: mostly arid or semiarid, subtropical along Caspian coast
Temperature (F): High/Low Jan. 45/27, Apr. 71/49, July 99/72, Oct. 76/53
Average annual precipitation: 9.7 inches

Terrain: rugged, mountainous rim; high, central basin with deserts, mountains; small discontinuous plains along both coasts
Highest point is Damavand 5,601 m (18,376 ft)

Natural resources: petroleum, natural gas, coal, chromium, copper, iron ore, lead, manganese, zinc, sulfur

Natural hazards: periodic droughts, floods; duststorms, sandstorms, earthquakes along the Western border

People

Population: 64,626,000 (July 1995 est.)

Life expectancy at birth: total population 66.97 years

Nationality: Iranian

Ethnic division: Persian 51%, Azerbaijani 24%, Gilaki and Mazandarani 8%, Kurd 7%, Arab 3%, Lur 2%, Baloch 2%, Turkmen 2%, other 1%

Religions: Shi'a Muslim 95%, Sunni Muslim 4%, Zoroastrian, Jewish, Christian, and Baha'i 1%

Languages: Persian and Persian dialects 58%, Turkic and Turkic dialects 26%, Kurdish 9%, Luri 2%, Baloch 1%, Arabic 1%, Turkish 1%, other 2%

Literacy: total population 66%

Economy

Imports: machinery, military supplies, metal works, foodstuffs, pharmaceuticals, technical services, refined oil products

Exports: petroleum, carpets, fruits, nuts, hides

Industries: petroleum, petrochemicals, textiles, cement and other building materials, food processing (particularly sugar refining and vegetable oil production), metal fabricating, armaments and military equipment

Agriculture: principal products - wheat, rice, other grains, sugar beets, fruits, nuts, cotton, dairy products, wool, caviar; not self-sufficient in food

Currency: 10 Iranian rials (IR) = 1 toman note - domestic figures are generally referred to in terms of the toman

Iranian rials per US1$ - 1,749.04

Transportation

Railroads: 4,850 km

Roads: 140,200 km total paved and unpaved

Ports: Abadan, Ahvaz, Bandar Beheshti, Bandar-e'Abbas, Bandar-e Anzali, Bandar-e Bushehr, Bandar-e Khomeyni, Bander-e Mah Shahr, Bandar-e Torkeman, Jazireh-ye Khark, Jazireh-ye Lavan, Jazireh-ye Sirri, Khorramshahr, Now Shahr

Airports: 261 total paved and unpaved. The two main international airports are at Teheran and Abadan

The Press: daily newspapers   **Ettela'at:** Khayyam Street, Teheran
telephone (21) 32-81   fax (21) 311-5530
circ. 500,000

Teheran Times: Nejatullahi Ave, 32 Kouche Bimeh, Teheran
telephone (21) 83-99-00   fax (21) 82-29-51

Tourism: historical sites, Caspian Sea, ancient Persian City of Persepolic

Diplomatic representation in US:

chief of mission: Iran has an Interests Section in the Pakistani Embassy in Washington, DC

chancery: Iranian Interest Section, 2209 Wisconsin Avenue NW, Washington, DC 20007

telephone: [1] (202) 965-4990

US Diplomatic representation: protecting power in Iran is Switzerland

Iraq

Capital: Baghdad   longitude: 44.26 E   latitude: 33.20 N
elevation: 111 ft

Government: republic

Flag: three equal horizontal bands of red (top), white, and black with three green five-pointed stars in a horizontal line centered in the white band; the phrase ALLAHU AKBAR (God is Great) in green Arabic script - Allahu to the right of the middle star and Akbar to the left of the middle star - was added in January 1991 during the Persian Gulf crisis; similar to the flag of Syria that has two stars but no script and the flag of Yemem that has a plain white band; also similar to the flag of Egypt that has a symbolic eagle centered in the white band

Geography

Location: Middle East, bordering the Persian Gulf, between Iran and Kuwait

Total Area: 437,071 sq km (168,753 sq mi) slightly more than twice the size of Idaho

Boundaries: Iran, Jordan, Kuwait, Saudi Arabi, Syria, Turkey

Climate: mostly desert; mild to cool winters with dry, hot cloudless summers; northern mountainous regions along Iranian and Turkish borders experience cold winters with occasionally heavy snows which melt in early spring, sometimes causing extensive flooding in central and southern Iraq
Temperature (F): High/Low Jan. 60/39, Apr. 85/57, July 110/76, Oct. 92/61
Average annual precipitation: 5.5 inches

Terrain: mostly broad plains; reedy marshes alone Iranian border in south; mountains along border with Iran and Turkey
Highest point is Haji Ibrahim 3,600 m (11,811 ft)

Natural resources: petroleum, natural gas, phosphates, sulfur

Natural hazards: duststorms, sandstorms, floods

People

Population: 20,643,769 (July 1995 est.)

Life expectancy at birth: total population 66.52 years

Nationality: Iraqi

Ethnic division: Arab 70%-80%, Kurdish 15%-20%, Turloman, Assyrian or other 5%

Religions: Muslim 97% (Shi'a 60%-65%, Sunni 32%-37%), Christian and other 3%

Languages: Arabic, Kurdiah (official in Kurdish regions). Assyrian, Armenian

Literacy: total population 89%

Economy

Imports: manufactures, food

Exports: crude oil and refined products, fertilizer, sulfur

Industries: petroleum production and refining, chemicals, textiles, construction materials, food processing

Agriculture: principal products - wheat, barley, rice, vegetables, dates, other fruit, cotton, wool; livestock - cattle, sheep; not self-sufficient in food output

Currency: 1 Iraqi dinar (ID) = 1,000 fils

Iraqi dinars per US1$ - 3.2

Transportation

Railroads: 2,457 km

Roads: 45,550 km total paved and unpaved

Ports: Umm Qasr, Khawr az Zubayr, and Al Basrah have limited functionality

Airports: 121 total paved and unpaved. The international airport is at Baghdad

The Press: daily newspapers   **Baghdad Observer:** POB 624, Karantina, Baghdad   circ. 22,000
Ath-Thawra: POB 2009, Aqaba bin Nafi's Square Baghdad   telephone 719-6161   circ. 250,000

Tourism: Baghdad, ruins of Mineveh, "Tower of Babel" ruins at Nimrud

Diplomatic representation in US:

chief of mission: Iraq has an Interest Section in the Algerian Embassy in Washington, DC

chancery: Iraq Interests Section, 1801 P Street NW, Washington, DC 20036

telephone: [1] (202) 483-7500

FAX: [1] (202) 462-5066

US Diplomatic representation:

chief of mission: (vacant); note: operations have been temporarily suspended; a US Interests Section is located in Poland's embassy in Baghdad

embassy: Masbah Quarter (opposite the Foreign Ministry Club), Baghdad

mailing address: PO Box 2447 Alwiyah, Baghdad

telephone: [964] (1) 719-6138, 719-6139, 718-1840, 719-3791

Ireland

Capital: Dublin   longitude: 6.15 W   latitude: 53.20 N   elevation: 154 ft

Government: republic

Flag: three equal vertical bands of green (hoist side), white, orange; similar to the flag of Cote d'Ivoire, which is shorter and has the colors reversed - orange (hoist side), white, and green; also similar to the flag of Italy, which is shorter and has colors of green (hoist side), white, and red

Geography

Location: Western Europe, occupying five-sixths of the island of Ireland in the North Atlantic Ocean, west of Great Britain

Total Area: 70,280 sq km (27,135 sq mi) slightly larger than West Virginia

Boundaries: UK

Climate: temperate maritime; modified by North Atlantic Current; mild winters, cool summers; consistently humid; overcast about half the time Temperature (F): High/Low Jan. 46/34, Apr. 55/39, July 67/52, Oct. 57/43 Average annual precipitation: 30 inches

Terrain: mostly level to rolling interior plain surrounded by rugged hills and low mountains; sea cliffs on west coast

Natural resources: zinc, lead, natural gas, petroleum, barite, copper, gypsum, limestone, dolomite, peat, silver

Natural hazards: NA

People

Population: 3,550,600 (July 1995 est.)

Life expectancy at birth: total population 75.99 years

Nationality: Irishman, Irishwoman, Irish (collective plural)

Ethnic division: Celtic, English

Religions: Roman Catholic 93%, Anglican 3%, none 1%, unknown 2%, other 1%

Languages: Irish (Gaelic), spoken mainly in areas located along the western seaboard, English is the language generally used

Literacy: total population 98%

Economy

Imports: food, animal feed, data processing equipment, petroleum and petroleum products, machinery, textiles, clothing

Exports: chemicals, data processing equipment, industrial machinery, live animals, animal products

Industries: food products, brewing, textiles, clothing, chemicals, pharmaceuticals, machinery, transportation equipment, glass and crystal

Agriculture: principal crops - turnips, barley, potatoes, sugar beets, wheat; livestock - meat and dairy products; self-sufficient in food; food shortages include bread grains, fruits, vegetables

Currency: 1 Irish pound (#Ir) = 100 pence
                        Irish pounds per US1$ - 0.64

Transportation

Railroads: 1,947 km

Roads: 92,327 km total paved and unpaved

Ports: Arklow, Cork, Drogheda, Dublin, Foynes, Galway, Limerick, New Ross, Waterford

Airports: 44 total paved and unpaved. There are international airports at Shannon, Dublin, Cork and Knock, but only the airports at Shannon and Knock are used for transatlantic flights

The Press: daily newspapers

Evening Herald: Independent House, 90 Middle Abbey St, Dublin 1
telephone (1) 873-1666   fax (1) 873-1787
circ. 95,000

Evening Press: Parnell House, Dublin 1,
telephone (1) 671-3333   fax (1) 671-3097   circ. 102,000

Tourism: Killarney Lakes, Kilkenny Castle, the west coast

Dublin Regional Tourism Organization Ltd:
1 Clarinda Park North, Dun Laoghaire, Co Dublin
telephone (1) 280-8571   fax (1) 280-2641
Diplomatic representation in US:
chief of mission: Ambassador Dermot A. Gallagher
chancery: 2234 Massachusetts Avenue NW, Washington, DC 20008
telephone: [1] (202) 462-3939
US Diplomatic representation:
chief of mission: Ambassador Jean Kennedy Smith
embassy: 42 Elgin Road, Ballsbridge, Dublin
mailing address: use embassy street address
telephone: [353] (1) 668-7122
FAX: [353] (1) 668-9946

Israel

Capital: Jerusalem   longitude: 35.13 E   latitude: 31.47 N
elevation: 1,485 ft
Government: republic
Flag: white with blue hexagram (six-pointed linear star) known as the Magen
David (Shield of David) centered between two equal horizontal blue bands
near the top and bottom edges of the flag
Geography
Location: Middle East, bordering the Mediterranean Sea, between Egypt and
Lebanon
Total Area: 20,770 sq km (8,019 sq mi) slightly larger than New Jersey
Boundaries: Egypt, Gaza Strip, Jordan, Lebanon, Syria, West Bank
Climate: temperate; hot and dry in southern and eastern desert areas
Temperature (F): High/Low Jan. 55/41, Apr. 73/50, July 87/63, Oct. 81/59
Average annual precipitation: 20.8 inches

221

Terrain: Negev desert in the south; low coastal plain; central mountains; Jordan Rift Valley

Highest point is Meiran 1,208 m (3,963 ft)

Natural resources: copper, phosphates, bromide, potash, clay, sand, sulfur, asphalt, manganese, small amounts of natural gas and crude oil

Natural hazards: sandstorms may occur during spring and summer

People

Population: 5,433,134 (July 1995 est.)

Note: includes Jewish settlers in the West Bank, in the Israeli-occupied Golan Heights, in the Gaza Strip, and in East Jerusalem

Life expectancy at birth: total population 78.14 years

Nationality: Israeli

Ethnic division: Jewish 82%, (Israel born 50%, Europe/Americas/Oceania born 20%, Africa born 7%, Asia born 5%) non-Jewish 18% (mostly Arab)

Religions: Judaism 82%, Islam 14% (mostly Sunni Muslim), Christian 2%, Druze and other 2%

Languages: Hebrew (official), Arabic used officially for Arab minority, English most commonly used foreign language

Literacy: total population 95%

Economy

Imports: military equipment, investment goods, rough diamonds, oil, other productive inputs, consumer goods

Exports: machinery and equipment, cut diamonds, chemicals, textiles and apparel, agricultural products, metals

Industries: food processing, diamond cutting and polishing, textiles and apparel, chemicals, metal products, military equipment, transport equipment, electrical equipment, miscellaneous machinery, potash mining, high-technology electronics, tourism

Agriculture: citrus and other fruits, vegetables, cotton, beef, poultry, dairy products

Currency: 1 new Israeli shekel (NIS) = 100 new agorot
new Israeli shekels per US1$ - 3.07

Transportation

Railroads: 520 km

Roads: 13,461 km paved

Ports: Ashdod, Ashqelon, Elat, Hadera, Haifa, Tel Aviv-Yafo

Airports: 57 total paved and unpaved. Ben-Gurion International Airport, Tel Aviv

The Press: daily newspapers   **The Jerusalem Post:** POB 81, 91000, Jerusalem
telephone (2) 31-56-66   fax (2) 38-95-27
circ. 30,000 weekdays, 50,000 weekend
Ma'ariv: 2 Carlebach St, Tel Aviv 61200
telephone (3) 563-2111   fax (3)561-0614
circ. 160,000 weekdays, 270,000 weekend

Tourism: the old city of Jerusalem, Mt Zion, Dead Sea
Ministry of Tourism: POB 1018, 24 King George St,
Jerusalem 91000
telephone (2)75-48-ΙΙ   fax (2) 25-08-90

Diplomatic representation in US:
chief of mission: Ambassador Itamar Rabinovich
chancery: 3514 International Drive NW, Washington, DC 20008
telephone: [1] (202) 364-5500
FAX: [1] (202) 364-5610

US Diplomatic representation:
chief of mission: Ambassador Martin Indyk
embassy: 71 Hayarkon Street, Tel Aviv
mailing address: PSC 98, Box 100 Tel Aviv; APO AE 09830
telephone: [972] (3) 517-4338
FAX: [972] (3) 66-34-49

Italy

Capital: Rome   longitude: 12.30 E   latitude: 41.53 N   elevation: 56 ft
Government: republic
Flag: three equal vertical bands of green (hoist side), white, and red; similar
to the flag of Ireland, which is longer and is green (hoist side), white, and
orange; also similar to the flag of Cote d'Ivoire, which has the colors
reversed - orange (hoist side), white, and green

Geography

Location: Southern Europe, a peninsula extending into the central Mediterranean Sea, northeast of Tunisia

Total Area: 301,230 sq km (116,305 sq mi) slightly larger than Arizona
Note: includes Sardinia and Sicily

Boundaries: Austria, France, Holy See (Vatican City), San Marino, Slovenia, Switzerland

Climate: predominantly Mediterranean; Alpine in far north; hot, dry in south
Temperature (F): High/Low Jan. 52/40, Apr. 66/50, July 87/67, Oct. 71/55
Average annual precipitation: 30.1 inches

Terrain: mostly rugged and mountainous; some plains, coastal lowlands
Highest point is Dufourspitze 4,634 m (15,203 ft)

Natural resources: mercury, potash, marble, sulfur, dwindling natural gas and crude oil reserves, fish, coal

Natural hazards: regional risks include landslides, mud flows, avalanches, earthquakes, volcanic eruptions, flooding; land subsidence in Venice

People

Population: 58,262,000 (July 1995 est.)

Life expectancy at birth: total population 77.85 years

Nationality: Italian

Ethnic division: Italian (includes small clusters of German-, French-, and Sloveene-Italians in the north and Albanian-Italians and Greek-Italians in the south), Sicilians, Sardinians

Religions: Roman Catholic 98%, other 2%

Languages: Italian, German (parts of Trentino-Alto Adige region are predominantly German speaking) French (small French-speaking minority in Valle d'Aosta region), Solovene (Slovene-speaking minority in the Trieste-Gorizia area)

Literacy: total population 97%

Economy

Imports: industrial machinery, chemicals, transport equipment, petroleum, metals, food, agricultural products

Exports: metals, textiles and clothing, production machinery, motor vehicles, transportation equipment, chemicals, other

Industries: machinery, iron and steel, chemicals, food processing, textiles, motor vehicles, clothing, footwear, ceramics

Agriculture: self-sufficient in foods other than meat, dairy products, and cereals; principal crops - fruits, vegetables, grapes, potatoes, sugar beets, soybeans, grain, olives; fish

Currency: 1 Italian lira (Lit) = 100 centesimi

Italian lira per US1$ - 1,609.5

Transportation

Railroads: 19,503 km

Roads: 305,388 km total paved and unpaved

Ports: Ancona, Augusta, Bari, Cagliari (Sardinia), Catania, Gaeta, Genoa, La Spezia, Livorno, Naples, Oristano (Sardinia), Palermo (Sicily), Piombino, Porto Torres (Sardinia), Ravenna, Savona, Trieste, Venice

Airports: 138 total paved and unpaved.

The Press: daily newspapers   **I Messaggero:** Via del Tritone 152, 00187 Rome

telephone (6) 47-02-01   circ. 390,000

L'Unita: Via del Taurini 19, 00185 Rome

telephone (6) 40-49-01

circ. 260,000 weekdays   800,000 Sunday

Tourism: sunny climate, Alpine and Mediterranean scenery, medieval and Baroque churches, Renaissance towns and palaces, famous opera houses, paintings, sculptures. The Vatican

Ente Nazionale Italiano per il Turismo:

Via Marghera 2, 00185 Rome

telephone (6) 49-711   fax (6) 496-3379

Diplomatic representation in US:

chief of mission: Ambassador Boris Biancheri-Chiappori

chancery: 1601 Fuller Street NW, Washington, DC 20009

telephone: [1] (202) 328-5500

US Diplomatic representation:

chief of mission: Ambassador Reginald Bartholomew

embassy: Via Vento 119/A, 00187- Rome

mailing address: PSC 59, Box 100, Rome; APO AE 09624

telephone: [39] (6) 46-741

FAX: [39] (6) 488-2672

Jamaica

Capital: Kingston   longitude: 76.48 W   latitude: 17.58 N elevation: 110 ft

Government: parliamentary democracy

Flag: diagonal yellow cross divides the flag into four triangles - green (top and bottom) and black (hoist side and fly side)

Geography

Location: Caribbean, island in the Caribbean Sea, south of Cuba

Total Area: 10,990 sq km (4,243 sq mi) slightly smaller than Connecticut

Boundaries: no land boundaries

Climate: tropical; hot, humid; temperate interior

Temperature (F): High/Low Jan. 86/67, Apr. 87/70, July 90/73, Oct. 88/73

Average annual precipitation: 33.5 inches

Terrain: mostly mountains with narrow, discontinuous coastal plains

Highest point is Blue Mountain Peak 2,256 m (7,402 ft)

Natural resources: bauxite, gypsum, limestone

Natural hazards: hurricanes (especially July to November)

People

Population: 2,574,300 (July 1995 est.)

Life expectancy at birth: total population 74.65 years

Nationality: Jamaican

Ethnic division: African 76.3%, Afro-European 15.1%, East Indian and Afro-East Indian 3%, white 3.2%, Chinese and Afro-Chinese 1.2%, other 1.2%

Religions: Protestant 55.9%, (Church of God 18.4%, Baptist 10%, Anglican 7.1%, Seventh-Day Adventist 6.9%, Pentecostal 5.2%, Methodist 3.1%, United Church 2.7%, other 2.5%), Roman Catholic 5%, other including some spiritual cults 39.1%

Languages: English, Creole

Literacy: total population 82%

Economy

Imports: machinery and transport equipment, construction materials, fuel, food, chemicals

Exports: Alumina, bauxite, sugar, bananas, rum

Industries: bauxite mining, tourism, textiles, food processing, light manufactures

Agriculture: commercial crops - sugarcane, bananas, coffee, citrus, potatoes, vegetables; livestock and livestock products include poultry, goats, milk; not self-sufficient in grain, meat, and dairy products

Currency: 1 Jamaican dollar (J$) = 100 cents

Jamaican dollars per US1$ - 33.19

Transportation

Railroads: 370 km

Roads: 18,200 km total paved and unpaved

Ports: Alligator Pond, Discovery Bay, Kingston, Montego Bay, Ocho Rios, Port Antonio, Longs Wharf, Rocky Point

Airports: 41 total paved and unpaved. The international airports are located near Kingston and at Montego Bay

The Press: daily newspapers

Gleamer: 7 North Street, POB 40, Kingston telephone 922-3400   fax 922-2058 circ. 42,500

Jamaica Herald: 29 Molynes Road, Kingston 10 telephone 968-7721

Tourism: Tourist attractions are beaches, mountains, historic buildings and cultural heritage, ruins of Port Royal

Diplomatic representation in US:

chief of mission: Ambassador Richard Leighton Bernal

chancery: 1520 New Hampshire Avenue NW, Washington, DC 20036

telephone: [1] (202) 452-0660

FAX: [1] (202) 452-0081

US Diplomatic representation:

chief of mission: Ambassador J. Gary Cooper

embassy: Jamaica Mutual Life Center, 2 Oxford Road, 3rd Floor, Kingston

mailing address: use embassy address

telephone: [1] (809) 929-4850 through 4859

FAX: [1] (809) 926-6743

Jan Mayen

10 km

Greenland Sea

Norwegian Sea

Capital: none; administered from Oslo, Norway, through a governor (sysselmann) resident in Longyearbyen (Svalbard)

elevation: 131 ft   longitude: 08.28 W   latitude: 71.01 N

Government: territory of Norway

Geography

    Location: Northern Europe, island between the Greenland Sea and Norwegian Sea, northeast of Iceland

    Total Area: 373 sq km (144 sq mi) slightly more than twice the size of Washington, DC

    Boundaries: no land boundaries

    Climate: arctic maritime with frequent storms and persistent fog

    Temperature (F): High/Low Jan. 31/21, Apr. 31/22, July 46/38, Oct. 39/29

    Average annual precipitation: 21.2 inches

    Terrain: volcanic island, partly covered by glaciers

    Highest point is Beerenberg Peak 2,277 m (7,470 ft)

    Natural resources: none

    Natural hazards: dominated by the Volcano Beerenberg; Volcanic activity resumed in 1970

People

    Population: no permanent inhabitants; note - there are personnel who man the LORAN C base and the weather and coastal services radio station

Economy

    Jan Mayen is a volcanic island with no exploitable natural resources. Economic activity is limited to providing services for employees of Norway's radio and meteorological stations located on the island

Transportation

    Roads: NA

Ports: none; offshore anchorage only

Airports: 1 with unpaved runway

Diplomatic representation in US: none (territory of Norway)

US Diplomatic representation: none (territory of Norway)

Japan

Capital: Tokyo   longitude: 139.45 E   latitude: 35.40 N elevation: 19 ft

Government: constitutional monarchy

Flag: white with a large red disk (representing the sun without rays) in the center

Geography

Location: Eastern Asia, island chain between the North Pacific Ocean and the Sea of Japan, east of the Korean peninsula

Total Area: 377,835 sq km (145,882 sq mi) slightly smaller than California Note: includes Bonin Island (Ogasawara-gunto), Daito-shoto, Minami-jima, Okinotori-shima, Ryukyu Islands (Nansei-shoto) and Volcano Islands (Kazan-retto)

Boundaries: no land boundaries

Climate: varies from tropical in south to cool temperate in north Temperature (F): High/Low Jan. 47/29, Apr. 63/46, July 83/70, Oct. 69/55 Average annual precipitation: 61.6 inches

Terrain: mostly rugged and mountainous Highest point is Mt Fuji   3,776 m (12,389 ft)

Natural resources: negligible mineral resources, fish

Natural hazards: many dormant and some active volcanoes; about 1,500 seismic occurrences (mostly tremors) every year; tsunamis

People

Population: 125,507,000 (July 1995 est.)

Life expectancy at birth: total population 79.44 years

229

Nationality: Japanese

Ethnic division: Japanese 99.4%, other 0.6% (mostly Lorean)

Religions: observe both Shinto and Buddhist 84%, other 16% (including 0.7% Christian)

Languages: Japanese

Literacy: total population 99%

Economy

Imports: manufactures, fossil fuels, foodstuffs and raw material

Exports: manufactures (including machinery, motor vehicles, consumer electronics)

Industries: steel and non-ferrous metallurgy, heavy electrical equipment, construction and mining equipment, motor vehicles and parts, electronic and telecommunication equipment and components, machine tools and automated production systems, locomotives and railroad rolling stock, shipbuilding, chemicals, textiles, food processing

Agriculture: highly subsidized and protected sector, with crop yields among highest in world; principal crops - rice, sugar beets, vegetables, fruit; animal products include pork, poultry, dairy and eggs; about 50% self-sufficient in food production; shortages of wheat, corn, soybeans

Currency: yen (Y)   yen per US1$ - 99.75

Transportation

Railroads: 27,327 km

Roads: 1,111,974 km total paved and unpaved

Ports: Akita, Amagasaki, Chiba, Hachinohe, Hakodate, Higashi-Harima, Himeji, Hiroshima, Kawasaki, Kinuura, Kobe, Kushiro, Mizushima, Moji, Nagoya, Osaka, Sakai, Sakaide, Shimizu, Tokyo, Tomakomai

Airports: 175 total (173 with paved runways). The international airports are Tokyo, Osaka, and Narita

The Press: daily newspapers   **Ashi Evening News:** 7-8-5 Tsukiji, Chuo-ku, Tokyo 104   English   circ. 38,500
telephone (3) 35-467-181 fax (3) 35-431-660
Asahi Shimbun: 5-3-2 Tsukiji, Chou-ku, Tokyo 104-11
telephone (3) 35-450-131 fax (3) 35-450-358
circ. 8.2 million morning, 4.7 million evening

Tourism: Many tourist attractions; The ancient capital of Kyoto, pagodas and temples, forest and mountains, classical Kabuki theater, winter sports, Mt Fuji

Department of Tourism: 2-1-3 Kasumigaseki, Chiyoda-ku, Tokyo 100
telephone (3) 35-804-488   fax (3) 35-807-901

Diplomatic representation in US:

> *chief of mission:* Ambassador Takakazu Kuriyama
> *chancery:* 2520 Massachusetts Avenue NW, Washington, DC 20008
> *telephone:* [1] (202) 939-6700
> *FAX:* [1] (202) 328-2187

US Diplomatic representation:

> *chief of mission:* Ambassador Walter Mondale
> *embassy:* 10-5 Akasaka 1- chome, Minato-ku (107), Tokyo
> *mailing address:* Unit 45004, Box 258, Tokyo; APO AP 96337-0001
> *telephone:* [81] (3) 32-245-000
> *FAX:* [81] (3) 35-051-862

Jarvis Island

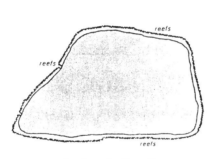

South   Pacific   Ocean

Capital: none; administered from Washington, DC
longitude: 160.01 W   latitude: 0.03 S

Government: unincorporated territory of the US administered by the Fish and
Wildlife Service of the US Department of the Interior as part of the National
Wildlife Refuge System

Geography

> **Location:** Oceania, island in the South Pacific Ocean, about one-half the
> way from Hawaii to the Cook Islands
>
> **Total Area:** 4.5 sq km (1.74 sq mi) about 7.5 times the size of
> The Mall in Washington, DC
>
> **Boundaries:** no land boundaries
>
> **Climate:** tropical; scant rainfall, constant wind, burning sun
>
> **Terrain:** sandy, coral island surrounded by a narrow fringing reef

Natural resources: guano

Note: no natural fresh water resources

Natural hazards: the narrow fringing reef surrounding the island can be a maritime hazard

Note: sparse bunch grass, prostrate vines, and low-growing shrubs; primarily a nesting, roosting, and foraging habitat for seabirds, shorebirds, and marine wildlife; feral cats

People

Population: uninhabited; public entry is by special-use permit only and generally restricted to scientist and educators

Economy

no economic activity

Transportation

Ports: none; offshore anchorage only; note - there is one boat landing area in the middle of the west coast and another near the southwest corner of the island

Note: there is a day beacon near the middle of the west coast

Jersey

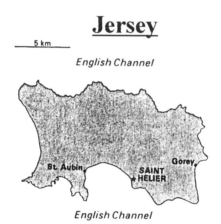

5 km

English Channel

English Channel

Capital: Saint Helier   longitude: 2.03 W   latitude: 49.28 N

Government: British crown dependency

Flag: white with the diagonal red cross of Saint Patrick (patron saint of Ireland) extending to the corners of the flag

Geography

Location: Western Europe, island in the English Channel, northwest of France

Total Area: 117 sq km (45.2 sq mi) about 0.7 times the size of Washington, DC

Boundaries: no land boundaries

Climate: temperate; mild winters and cool summers

Terrain: gently rolling plain with low, rugged hills along north coast

Natural resources: agricultural land

Natural hazards: NA

Note: largest and southernmost of Channel Islands; about 30% of population concentrated in Saint Helier

People

Population: 86,700 (July 1995 est.)

Life expectancy at birth: total population 76.9 years

Nationality: Channel Islander

Ethnic division: UK and Norman-French decent

Religions: Anglican, Roman Catholic, Baptist, Congregational New Church, Methodist, Presbyterian

Languages: English (official), French (official), Norman-French dialect spoken in country districts

Literacy: NA

Economy

Imports: machinery and transport equipment, manufactured goods, foodstuffs, mineral fuels, chemicals

Exports: light industrial and electrical goods, foodstuffs, textiles

Industries: tourism, banking and finance, dairy

Agriculture: potatoes, cauliflowers, tomatoes; dairy and cattle farming

Currency: 1 Jersey pound (#J) = 100 pence

Jersey pounds per US1$ - 0.62

Transportation

Railroads: none

Roads: NA

Ports: Gorey, Saint Aubin, Saint Helier

Airports: 1 with paved runway

Tourism: NA

Diplomatic representation in US: none: (British crown dependency)

US Diplomatic representation: none (British crown dependency)

Johnston Atoli

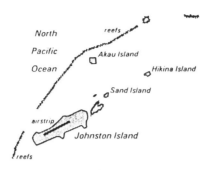

2 km

North Pacific Ocean — reefs — Akau Island — Hikina Island — Sand Island — airstrip — Johnston Island — reefs

Capital: none   longitude: 169.30 W   latitude: 17.00 N

Government: unincorporated territory of the US administered by the US Defense Nuclear Agency and managed cooperatively by US Defense Nuclear Agency and the Fish and Wildlife Service on the US Department of the Interior as part of the National Wildlife Refuge system

Flag: the flag of the United States is used

Geography

Location: Oceania, atoll in the North Pacific Ocean, about one-third of the way from Hawaii to the Marshall Islands

Total Area: 2.8 sq km (1.1 sq mi) about 4.7 times the size of The Mall in Washington, DC

Boundaries: no land boundaries

Climate: tropical; but generally dry; consistent northwest trade winds with little seasonal temperature variation

Terrain: mostly flat with a maximum elevation of 4 meters

Natural resources: guano

Note: no natural fresh water resources

Natural hazards: NA

Note: strategic location in the North Pacific Ocean; Johnston Island and Sand Island are natural islands; North Island (Akau) and East Island (Hikina) are man made islands formed from coral dredgings; closed to public; former nuclear weapons test site; site of Johnston Atoll Chemical Agent Disposal System; some low-growing vegetation

People

Population: 327 (July 1995 est.)

Economy:
> Economic activity is limited to providing services to US military personnel and contractors located on the island. All food and manufactured goods must be imported

Transportation
> **Railroads:** none
> **Roads:** NA
> **Ports:** Johnston Island
> **Airports:** 1 with paved runway

Diplomatic representation in US: none (territory of the US)
US Diplomatic representation: none (territory of the US)

Jordan

Capital: Amman   longitude: 35.56 E latitude: 31.57 N elevation: 2,548 ft
Government: constitutional monarchy
> **Flag:** three equal horizontal bands of black (top), white, and green with a red isosceles triangle based on the hoist side bearing a small white seven-pointed star; the seven points on the star represents the seven fundamental laws of Koran

Geography
> **Location:** Middle East, northwest of Saudi Arabia
> **Total Area:** 89,213 sq km (34,445 sq mi) slightly smaller than Indiana
> **Boundaries:** Iraq, Israel, Saudi Arabia, Syria, West Bank
> **Climate:** mostly arid desert; rainy season in west (November to April)
> Temperature (F): High/Low Jan. 54/39, Apr. 73/49, July 89/65, Oct. 81/57
> Average annual precipitation: 10.9 inches
> **Terrain:** mostly desert plateau in east, highland area in west; Great Rift Valley separates East and West Banks of the Jordan River
> Highest point is Mount Ramm 1,754 m (5,755 ft)

235

Natural resources: phosphates, potash, shale oil

Natural hazards: NA

People

Population: 4,100,709 (July 1995 est.)

Life expectancy at birth: total population 72.27 years

Nationality: Jordanian

Ethnic division: Arab 98%, Circassian 1%, Armenian 1%

Religions: Sunni Muslim 92%, Christian 8%

Languages: Arabic (official), English widely understood among upper and middle classes

Literacy: total population 83%

Economy

Imports: crude oil, machinery, transport equipment, food, live animals, manufactured goods

Exports: phosphates, fertilizers, potash, agricultural products, manufactures

Industries: phosphate mining, petroleum refining, cement, potash, light manufacturing

Agriculture: principal crops - wheat, barley, citrus fruit, tomatoes, melons, olives; sheep, goats, poultry; large net importer of food

Currency: 1 Jordanian dinar (JD) = 1,000 fils

Jordanian dinars per US1$ - 0.69

Transportation

Railroads: 789 km

Roads: 7,500 km total paved and unpaved

Ports: Al'Aqabah

Airports: 17 total paved and unpaved. There are international airports at Amman, Aqaba, and the new Queen Alia International Airport at Zizya

The Press: daily newspapers

Ad-Dustour: POB 591, Amman
telephone 66-41-53   circ. 90,000

Ar-Rai: POB 6710 Amman
telephone 66-71-71   fax 66-12-42   circ. 90,000

Tourism: The US Embassy in Amman is open Sunday through Thursday. Main tourist attractions are biblical sites and ancient cities, Temple of Hercules, Roman Fortress at Azraq

Ministry of Tourism and Antiquities:
POB 224, Amman
telephone 64-23-31   fax 64-84-65

Diplomatic representation in US:

chief of mission: Ambassador Fayiz A. Tarawneh

chancery: 3504 International Drive NW, Washington, DC 20008

telephone: [1] (202) 966-2664

FAX: [1] (202) 966-3110

US Diplomatic representation:

chief of mission: Ambassador Wesley E. Egan, Jr.

embassy: Jabel Amman, Amman

mailing address: POB 354, Amman 11118 Jordan; APO AE 09892-0200

telephone: [962] (6) 82-01-01

FAX: [962] (6) 82-01-59

Juan de Nova Island

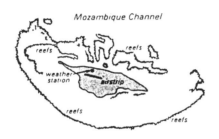

Capital: none; administered by France from Reunion

longitude: 42.50 E   latitude: 16.80 S

Government: French possession administered by Commissioner of the Republic, resident in Reunion

Geography

Location: Southern Africa, island in the Mozambique Channel, about one-third of the way between Madagascar and Mozambique

Total Area: 4.4 sq km (1.7 sq mi) about 7.5 times the size of The Mall in Washington, DC

Boundaries: no land boundaries

Climate: tropical

Terrain: NA

Natural resources: guano deposits and other fertilizers

Natural hazards: periodic cyclones

People

Population: uninhabited

Economy

no economic activity

Transportation

Railroads: NA km; short line going to jetty

Ports: none; offshore anchorage only

Airports: 1 unpaved

Diplomatic representation in US: none (possession of France)

US Diplomatic representation: none (possession of France)

Kazakhstan

Capital: Almaty   longitude: 76.53 E   latitude: 43.16 N elevation: 3,543 ft

Government: republic

Flag: sky blue background representing the endless sky and a gold sun with 32 rays soaring above a golden steppe eagle in the center; on the hoist side is a "national ornamentation" in yellow

Geography

Location: Central Asia, northwest of China

Total Area: 2,717,300 sq km (1,049,150 sq mi) slightly less than four times the size of Texas

Boundaries: China, Kyrgyzstan, Russia, Turkmenistan, Uzbekistan

Climate: continental, cold winters and hot summers, arid and semiarid

Temperature: winter 3 (F), north, 27 (F) south

average summer 66 (F) north, 84 (F) south

Average annual precipitation: 23.5 inches

Terrain: extends from the Volga to the Altai Mountains and from the plains in western Siberia to oasis and desert in Central Asia

Highest point is Belukha Peak 4,506 m (14,783 ft) Alta range

Natural resources: major deposits of petroleum, coal, iron ore, manganese, chrome ore, nickel, cobalt, copper, molybdenum, lead, zinc, bauxite, gold, uranium

Natural hazards: NA

People

Population: 17,377,000 (July 1995 est.)

Life expectancy at birth: total population 68.25 years

Nationality: Kazakhstani

Ethnic division: Kazakh (Qazaq) 41.9%, Russian 37%, Ukrainian 5.2%, German 4.7%, Uzbek 2.1%, Tatar 2%, other 7.1%

Religions: Muslim 47%, Russian Orthodox 44%, Protestant 2%, other 7%

Languages: Kazakh (Qazaq) official language spoken by over 40% of population, Russian (language of inter ethnic communication) spoken by two-thirds of population and used in everyday business

Literacy: total population 98%

Economy

Imports: machinery and parts, industrial materials, oil and gas

Exports: oil, ferrous and nonferrous metals, chemicals, grain, wool, meat, coal

Industries: extractive industries (oil, coal, iron ore, manganese, chromite, lead, zinc, copper, titanium, bauxite, gold, silver, phosphates, sulfur), iron and steel, nonferrous metal, tractors and other agricultural machinery, electric motors, construction materials

Agriculture: principal crops - grain, mostly spring wheat; meat, cotton, wool

Currency: national currency the tenge introduced on 15 November 1993
tenges per US1$ - 54.00

Transportation

Railroads: 14,460 km

Roads: 189,000 km total paved and unpaved

Ports: Aqtau (Shevchenko), Atyrau (Gur'yev), Oskemen (Ust-Kamenogorsk) Pavlodar, Semey (Semipalatinsk)

Airports: 352 total paved and unpaved. One international airport at Almaty

The Press: daily newspapers

Leninshil Zhas: 480044 Almaty, pr. Zhibek zholy 50
telephone (3272) 33-02-19   circ. 270,000

Kazakhstankaya Pravda: Almaty, Gogolya 39
telephone (3272) 63-03-98

Tourism: Almaty, Lake Balkhash

Diplomatic representation in US:
    chief of mission: Ambassador Tuleutai S. Suleymenov
    chancery: (temporary) 3421 Massachusetts Avenue NW,
                           Washington, DC 20008
    telephone: [1] (202) 333-4504 through 4507
    FAX: [1] (202) 333-4509

US Diplomatic representation:
    chief of mission: Ambassador Willian H. Courtney
    embassy: 99/97 Furmanova Street, Almaty, Republic of Kazakhstan 480012
    mailing address: use embassy street address
    telephone: [7] (3272) 63-24-26
    FAX: [7] (3272) 63-38-83

Capital: Nairobi   longitude: 36.50 E   latitude: 1.17 S   elevation: 5,971 ft

Government: republic

    Flag: three equal horizontal bands of black (top), red, and green; the red band is edged in white; a large warrior's shield covering crossed spears is superimposed at the center

Geography

    Location: Eastern Africa, bordering the Indian Ocean, between Somalia and Tanzania

    Total Area: 582,650 sq km (224,961 sq mi) slightly more than twice the size of Nevada

    Boundaries: Ethiopia, Somalia, Sudan, Tanzania, Uganda

    Climate: varies from tropical along coast to arid in interior

    Temperature (F): High/Low Jan. 77/54, Apr. 75/58, July 69/51, Oct. 76/55

    Average annual precipitation: 37.7 inches

Terrain: low plains rise to central highlands bisected by Great Rift Valley; fertile plateau in west

Highest point is Kenya 5,199 m (17,058 ft)

Natural resources: gold, limestone, soda ash, salt barytes, rubies, fluorspar, garnets, wildlife

Natural hazards: NA

People

Population: 28,817,300 (July 1995 est.)

Life expectancy at birth: total population 53.41 years

Nationality: Kenyan

Ethnic division: Kikuyu 22%, Luhya 14%, Luo 13%, Kalenjin 12%, Kamba 11%, Kisii 6%, Meru 6%, Asian, European, and Arab 1%, other 15%

Religions: Protestant (including Anglican) 38%, Roman Catholic 28%, indigenous beliefs 26%, other 8%

Languages: English (official), Swahili (official) numerous indigenous languages

Literacy: total population 71%

Economy

Imports: machinery and transportation equipment, petroleum and petroleum products, iron and steel, raw materials, food and consumer goods

Exports: tea, coffee, petroleum products

Industries: small-scale consumer goods (plastic, furniture, batteries, textiles, soap, cigarettes, flour), processing agricultural products, oil refining, cement, tourism

Agriculture: cash crops - coffee, tea, food products - corn, wheat, sugarcane, fruit, vegetables, dairy products, beef, pork, poultry, eggs

Currency: 1 Kenyan shilling (KSh) = 100 cents

Kenyan shillings per US1$ - 44.47

Transportation

Railroads: 2,650 km

Roads: 64,590 km total paved and unpaved

Ports: Kisumu, Lamu, Mombasa

Airports: 246 total paved and unpaved. Moi International Airport is at Mombasa, and Jomo Kenyatta International Airport is at Nairobi

The Press: daily newspapers   **Kenya Times:** POB 30958, Nairobi
telephone (2) 24-251   circ. 36,000

The Standard: POB 30080, Nairobi
telephone (2) 54-02-80   fax (2) 55-39-39   circ. 70,000

Tourism: attractions are National Parks, wildlife and resorts on the Indian Ocean coast

Kenya Tourist Development Corporation:
Utalii House, Uhuru Highway, POB 42013, Nairobi
telephone (2) 33-08-20   fax (2) 22-78-15

Diplomatic representation in US:
chief of mission: Ambassador Benjamin Edgar Kipkorir
chancery: 2249 R Street NW, Washington, DC 20008
telephone: [1] (202) 387-6101
FAX: [1] (202) 462-3829

US Diplomatic representation:
chief of mission: Ambassador Aurelia Brazeal
embassy: corner of Moi Avenue and Haile Selassie Avenue, Nairobi
mailing address: P O Box 30137, Unit 64100, Nairobi; APO AE 09831
telephone: [254] (2) 33-41-41
FAX: [254] (2) 34-08-38

Kingman Reef

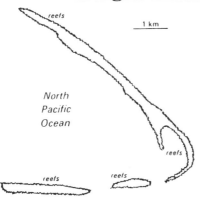

Capital: none; administered from Washington, DC
longitude: 162.3 W   latitude: 7.30 N

Government: unincorporated territory of the US administrated by the US Navy, however it is awash the majority of the time, so it is not usable and is uninhabited

Geography

Location: Oceania, reef in the North Pacific Ocean, about one-half of the way from Hawaii to American Samoa

Total Area: 1 sq km (.38 sq mi) about 1.7 times the size of The Mall in Washington, DC

Boundaries: no land boundaries

Climate: tropical, but moderated by prevailing winds

Terrain: low and nearly level with a maximum elevation of about 1 meter

Natural resources: none

Natural hazards: wet or awash most of the time, maximum elevation of about 1 meter makes this a maritime hazard

People

Population: uninhabited

Economy

no economic activity

Transportation

Ports: none; offshore anchorage only

Diplomatic representation in US: none (territory of the US)

US Diplomatic representation: none (territory of the US)

Kiribati

_1200 km_

North Pacific Ocean

★TARAWA
Banaba
Kiritimati (Christmas)
Kiribati (Gilbert Islands)
Rawaki (Phoenix Islands)
Line Islands

South Pacific Ocean

Capital: Tarawa   longitude: 173.09 E   latitude: 1.23 N

Government: republic

Flag: the upper half is red with a yellow frigate bird flying over a yellow rising sun, and the lower half is blue with three horizontal wavy white stripes to represent the ocean

Geography

Location: Oceania, group of islands in the Pacific Ocean, straddling the equator and the International Date Line, about one-half of the way from Hawaii to Australia

Total Area: 717 sq km (276.8 sq mi) slightly more than four times the size of Washington, DC

Boundaries: no land boundaries

Climate: tropical; marine, hot and humid, moderated by trade winds

Temperature (F): High/Low Jan. 88/74, Apr. 90/75, July 89/74, Oct. 90/74

Terrain: mostly low-lying coral atolls surrounded by extensive reefs

Natural resources: phosphate

Natural hazards: typhoons can occur any time, but usually November to March; occasional tornado

People

Population: 79,400 (July 1995 est.)

Life expectancy at birth: total population 54.16 years

Nationality: I-Kiribati

Ethnic division: Micronesian

Religions: Roman Catholic 52.6%, Protestant (Congregational) 40.9%, Seventh-Day Adventist, Baha'i, Church of God, Mormon 6%

Languages: English (official), Gilbertese

Literacy: NA

Economy

Imports: foodstuffs, machinery and equipment, miscellaneous manufactured goods, fuel

Exports: copra, seaweed, fish

Industries: fishing, handicrafts

Agriculture: subsistence farming predominates; food crops - taro, breadfruit, sweet potatoes, vegetables; not self-sufficient in food

Currency: 1 Australian dollar ($A) = 100 cents

Australian dollars per US1$ - 1.30

Transportation

Railroads: none

Roads: 640 km total paved and unpaved

Ports: Banaba, Betio, English Harbor, Kanton

Airports: 21 total paved and unpaved. There are two international airports, one on Tarawa and the other on Kiritimati.

The Press: weekly newspaper   **Te Uekera:** POB 78, Bairiki, Tarawa

telephone 21-187   circ. 1,600

English and I-Kiribati

Tourism: Main tourist attraction are sites of World War II battles, fishing, bird watching

Kiribati Visitors Bureau:

POB 261, Bikenibeu, Tarawa

telephone 28-288   fax 26-193

Diplomatic representation in US: Kiribati has no mission in the US
US Diplomatic representation: the ambassador to Fiji is accredited to Kiribati

Korea, North

Capital: Pyongyang   longitude: 125.47 E   latitude: 39.00 N
elevation: 89 ft

Government: Communist state; Stalinist dictatorship

Flag: three horizontal bands of blue (top), red (triple width), and blue; the red band is edged in white; on the hoist side of the red band is a white disk with a red five-pointed star

Geography

Location: Eastern Asia, northern half of the Korean peninsula bordering the Korea Bay and the Sea of Japan, between China and Russia

Total Area: 120,540 sq km (46,540 sq mi) slightly smaller than Mississippi

Boundaries: China, South Korea, Russia

Climate: temperate with rainfall concentrated in summer

Temperature (F): High/Low Jan. 27/8, Apr. 60/38, July 83/68, Oct. 64/42

Average annual precipitation: 36.3 inches

Terrain: mostly hilly and mountains separated by deep, narrow valleys; coastal plains wide in west, discontinuous in east

Highest point is Paektu 2,744 m (9,003 ft)

Natural resources: coal, lead, tungsten, zinc, graphite, magnesite, iron ore, copper, gold, pyrites, salt, fluorspar, hydropower

Natural hazards: late spring droughts often followed by severe flooding; occasional typhoons during the early fall

People

Population: 23,486,600 (July 1995 est.)

Life expectancy at birth: total population 70.05 years

Nationality: Korean

Ethnic division: racially homogeneous

Religions: Buddhism and Confucianism, some Christianity and syncretic Chondogy

Languages: Korean

Literacy: total population 99%

Economy

Imports: petroleum, grain, coking coal, machinery and equipment, consumer goods

Exports: minerals, metallurgical products, agricultural and fishery products, manufactures (including armaments)

Industries: machine building, military products, electric power, chemicals, mining, metallurgy, textiles, food processing

Agriculture: principal crops - rice, corn, potatoes, soybeans, pulses; livestock and livestock products - cattle, hogs, pork, eggs; not self-sufficient in grain

Currency: 1 North Korean won (Wn) = 100 chon

North Korean won per US1$ - 2.15

Transportation

Railroads: 4,914 km

Roads: 30,000 km total paved and unpaved

Ports: Ch'ongjin, Haeju, Hungnam (Hamhung), Kimch'aek, Kosong, Najin, Namp'o, Sinuiju, Songnim, Sonbong (formerly Unggi), Ungsang, Wonsan

Airports: 49 total paved and unpaved. The international airport is at Sunan, about 20 km from Pyongyang

The Press: principal newspapers   **Minju Choson:** Pyongyang

6 days a week   circ. 2000,000

Rodong Sinmun: Pyongyang

daily   circ. 1,500,000

Tourism: Moranbong Park, Taesongsan Recreation Ground

Ryohaengsa: (Korea International Travel Company)
Central District, Pyongyang
telephone 22-331   fax 81-76-07

Diplomatic representation in US: none

US Diplomatic representation: none

Korea, South

Capital: Seoul   longitude: 127.00 E   latitude: 37.30 N elevation: 285 ft

Government: republic

Flag: white with a red (top) and blue yin-yang symbol in the center; there is a different black trigram from the ancient I Ching (Book of Changes) in each corner of the white field

Geography

Location: Eastern Asia, southern half of the Korean peninsula bordering the Sea of Japan and the Yellow Sea, south of North Korea

Total Area: 98,480 sq km (38,023 sq mi) slightly larger than Indiana

Boundaries: North Korea

Climate: temperate, with rainfall heavier in summer than winter

Temperature (F): High/Low Jan. 32/15, Apr. 62/41, July 84/70, Oct. 64/42

Average annual precipitation: 49.2 inches

Terrain: mostly hilly and mountains; wide coastal plains in west and south

Highest point is Halla 1,950 m (6,398 ft)

Natural resources: coal, tungsten, graphite, molybdenum, lead, hydropower

Natural hazards: occasional typhoons bring high winds and floods; earthquakes in southwest

People

Population: 45,554,000 (July 1995 est.)

Life expectancy at birth: total population 70.89 years

Nationality: Korean

Ethnic division: homogenous (except for about 20,000 Chinese)

Religions: Christianity 48.6%, Buddhism 47.4%, Confucianism 3%, pervasive folk religion (shamanism) Chondogyo (Religion of the Heavenly Way) 0.2%

Languages: Korean, English widely taught in school

Literacy: total population 96%

Economy

Imports: machinery, electronics and electronic equipment, oil, steel, transport equipment, textiles, organic chemicals, grains

Exports: electronic and electrical equipment, machinery, steel, automobiles, ships, textiles, clothing, footwear, fish

Industries: electronics, automobile production, chemicals, shipbuilding, steel, textiles, clothing, footwear, food processing

Agriculture: principal crops - rice, root crops, barley, vegetables, fruit; livestock and livestock products - cattle, hogs, chickens, eggs; fishing and forestry; self-sufficient in food, except for wheat

Currency: 1 South Korean won (W) = 100 chum (theoretical)

South Korean won per US1$ - 790.48

Transportation

Railroads: 6,763 km

Roads: 63,200 km   (unpaved NA)

Ports: Chinhae, Inch'on, Kunsan, Masan, Mokp'o, Pohang, Pusan, Ulsan, Yosu

Airports: 114 total paved and unpaved. There are international airports at Seoul, Pusan and Cheju

The Press: daily newspapers

Chosun Ilbo: 61, 1-ka, Taepyong-no, Chung-ku, Seoul 100-756
telephone (2) 724-5114   fax (2) 724-5278
circ. 2,000,000

Dong-A Ilbo: 139 Sejong-no, Chongno-ku, Seoul
telephone (2) 721-7114   fax (2) 734- 7742
circ. 1,100,000

Tourism: tourist attractions are mountain scenery, historic sites and popular resorts off the southern coast of Cheju Island. Tokgu Hot Springs

Korea National Tourism Corporation:
KNTC Bldg, 10 Ta-dong, Chung-ku, CPOB 903 Seoul 100
telephone (2) 757-6030   fax (2) 757-5997

Diplomatic representation in US:

chief of mission: Ambassador Pak Kun-u

chancery: 2450 Massachusetts Avenue NW, Washington, DC 20008

telephone: [1] (202) 939-5600

US Diplomatic representation:

chief of mission: Ambassador James T. Laney
embassy: 82 Sejong-Ro, Chongro-ku, Seoul
mailing address: American Embassy, Unit 15550, Seoul;
    APO AP 96205-0001
telephone: [82] (2) 397-4114
FAX: [82] (2) 738-8845

Kuwait

Capital: Kuwait   longitude: 48.00 E latitude: 29.20 N elevation: 16 ft
Government: nominal constitutional monarchy
Flag: three equal bands of green (top), white, and red with a black trapezoid
based on the hoist side
Geography
Location: Middle East, bordering the Persian Gulf, between Iraq
and Saudi Arabia
Total Area: 17,820 sq km (6,880 sq mi) slightly smaller than New Jersey
Boundaries: Iraq, Saudi Arabia
Climate: dry desert; intensely hot summers; short, cool winters
Temperature (F): High/Low Jan. 61/49, Apr. 83/68, July 103/86. Oct. 91/73
Average annual precipitation: 4.9 inches
Terrain: flat to slightly undulating desert plain
Natural resources: petroleum, fish, shrimp, natural gas
Natural hazards: sudden cloudbursts are common from October to April,
they bring inordinate amounts of rain which can damage roads and houses;
sandstorms and duststorms occur throughout the year, but are most common
between March and August

People

Population: 1,817,500 (July 1995 est.)

Life expectancy at birth: total population 75.64 years

Nationality: Kuwaiti

Ethnic division: Kuwaiti 45%, other Arab 35%, South Asian 9%, Iranian 4%, other 7%

Religions: Muslim 85%, (Shi'a 30%, Sunni 45%, other 10%), Christian, Hindu, Parsi, and others 15%

Languages: Arabic (official). English widely spoken

Literacy: total population 74%

Economy

Imports: food, construction materials, vehicles and parts, clothing

Exports: oil

Industries: petroleum, petrochemicals, desalination, food processing, building materials, salt, construction

Agriculture: practically none; extensive fishing in territorial waters and Indian Ocean

Currency: 1 Kuwaiti dinar (KD) = 1,000 fils

Kuwaiti dinars per US1$ - 0.29

Transportation

Railroads: none

Roads: 4,270 km total paved and unpaved

Ports: Ash Shu'aybah, Ash Shuwaykh, Kuwait, Mina' 'Abd Allah, Mina' al Ahmadi, Mina' Su'ud

Airports: 8 total paved and unpaved. The international airport is at Kuwait

The Press: daily newspapers   **Al-Anbaa:** POB 23915, Safat, Kuwait City
telephone 483-0322   circ. 80,000

Arab Times: POB 2270, 13023 Safat, Kuwait City
telephone 481-3566   fax 481-6326   English circ. 45,000

Tourism: The work week in Kuwait is Saturday through Wednesday. Old city of Kuwait, Failaka Island

Department of Tourism: Ministry of Information
POB 193, 13002 Safat, Kuwait City
telephone 243-6644   fax 242-9758

Diplomatic representation in US:

chief of mission: Ambassador Muhammad al-Sabah al-Salim Al Sabah

chancery: 2940 Tilden Street NW, Washington, DC 20008

telephone: [1] (202) 966-0702

FAX: [1] (202) 966-0517

US Diplomatic representation:

chief of mission: Ambassador Ryan C. Crocker

embassy: Bneid al-Gar (opposite the Kuwait International Hotel),
        Kuwait City

mailing address: APO AE 09880-9000

telephone: [965] 242-4151 through 242-4159

FAX: [965] 244-2855

Kyrgyzstan

150 km

Capital: Bishkek   longitude: 74.70 E   latitude: 42.80 N

Government: republic

Flag: red field with a yellow sun in the center having 40 rays representing the 40 Kirghiz tribes; on the obverse side the rays run counterclockwise, on the reverse, clockwise; in the center of the sun is a red ring crossed by two sets of three lines, a stylized representation of the roof of the traditional Kirghi zurt

Geography

Location: Central Asia, west of China

Total Area: 198,500 sq km (76,641 sq mi) slightly smaller than South Dakota

Boundaries: China, Kazakhstan, Tajikistan, Uzbekistan

Climate: dry continental to polar in high Tien Shan; subtropical in southwest (Fergana Valley); temperate in northern foothill zone

251

Temperature: winter low elevation 23 (F), higher elevation 18 (F)

summer low elevation 75 (F), higher elevation 41 (F)

Average annual precipitation: 30 inches

Terrain: peaks of Tien Shan rise to 7,000 meters, and associated valleys and basins encompass entire nation

Highest point is Pobeda Peak 7,439 m (24,406 ft)

Natural resources: abundant hydroelectric potential; significant deposits of gold and rare earth metals; locally exploitable coal, oil and natural gas; other deposits of nepheline, mercury, bismuth, lead, and zinc

Natural hazards: NA

People

Population: 4,770,000 (July 1995 est.)

Life expectancy at birth: total population 68.13 years

Nationality: Kyrgy

Ethnic division: Kirghiz 52.4%, Russian 21.5%, Uzbek 12.9%, Ukrainian 2.5%, German 2.4%, other 8.3%

Religions: Muslim 70%, Russian Orthodox NA

Languages: Kirghiz (Kyrgyz) - official language, Russian widely used

Literacy: total population 97%

Economy

Imports: grain, lumber, industrial products, ferrous metals, fuel, machinery, textiles, footwear

Exports: wool, chemicals, cotton, ferrous and non ferrous metals, shoes, machinery, tobacco

Industries: small machinery, textiles, food-processing industries, cement, shoes, sawn logs, refrigerators, furniture, electric motors, gold, and rare earth metals

Agriculture: wool, tobacco, cotton, livestock (sheep, goats, cattle), vegetables, meat, grapes, fruits and berries, eggs, milk, potatoes

Currency: introduced national currency, the som (10 May 1993)

soms per US1$ - 10.6

Transportation

Railroads: 370 km

Roads: 30,300 km total paved and unpaved

Ports: Ysyk-Kol (Rybach'ye)

Airports: 54 total paved and unpaved. The international airports are located at Bishkek, and Osh

The Press: newspapers   **Kyrgyz Tuusu:** Bishkek

6 papers a week   circ. 180,000

5 papers a week   circ. 120,000

Tourism: Most foreign visitors tend to be mountain climbers.
State Committee for Tourism:
720000 Bishkek, Government House

Diplomatic representation in US:
chief of mission: (vacant); Charge d'Affaires ad interim Almas Chukin
chancery: (temporary) Suite 705, 1511 K Street NW, Washington, DC 20005
telephone: [1] (202) 347-3732, 3733, 3718
FAX: [1] (202) 347-3718

US Diplomatic representation:
chief of mission: Ambassador Eileen A. Malloy
embassy: Erkindik Prospekt #66, Bishkek 720002
mailing address: use embassy street address
telephone: [7] (3312) 22-29-20, 22-27-77, 22-26-31, 22-24-73
FAX: [7] (3312) 22-35-51

Loas

Capital: Vientiane   longitude: 102.38 E   latitude: 17.59 N
elevation: 531 ft

Government: Communist
   Flag: three horizontal bands of red (top), blue (double width), and red with a large white disk centered in the blue band

Geography
   Location: Southeastern Asia, Northeast of Thailand
   Total Area: 236,800 sq km (91,428 sq mi) slightly larger than Utah
   Boundaries: Burma, Cambodia, China, Thailand, Vietnam
   Climate: tropical monsoon; rainy season (May to November); dry season (December to April)

Temperature (F): High/Low Jan. 83/57, Apr. 93/73, July 87/75, Oct. 87/70

Average annual precipitation: 67.5 inches

Terrain: mostly rugged mountains; some plains and plateau

Highest point is Phou Bia 2,820 m (9,252 ft)

Natural resources: timber, hydropower, gypsum, tin, gold, gemstones

Natural hazards: floods, droughts, and blight

People

Population: 4,837,400 (July 1995 est.)

Life expectancy at birth: total population 52.2 years

Nationality: Lao or Laotian

Ethnic division: Lao Loum (lowland) 68%. Lao Theung (upland) 22%, Lao Soung (highland) including the Hmong ("Meo") and the Yao (Mien) 9%, ethnic Vietnamese/Chinese 1%

Religions: Buddhist 60%, animist and other 40%

Languages: Lao (official), French, English, and various ethnic languages

Literacy: total population 50%

Economy

Imports: food, fuel oil, consumer goods, manufactures

Exports: electricity, wood products, coffee, tin, garments

Industries: tin and gypsum mining, timber, electric power, agricultural processing, construction

Agriculture: principal crops - rice, sweet potatoes, vegetables, corn, coffee, sugarcane, cotton; livestock - buffaloes, hogs, cattle, poultry

Currency: 1 new kip (NK) = 100 at

new kips per US1$ - 717

Transportation

Railroads: none

Roads: 14,130 km total paved and unpaved

Ports: none

Airports: 52 total paved and unpaved. The principal airport is at Vientiane

The Press: newspapers   **Pasason:** 80 rue Sethathirath, BP 110, Vientiane
circ. 28,000

Lao Dong: Vientiane

fortnightly   circ. 46,000

Tourism: Xieng Khuane Stone Gardens

National Tourism Department:

Ministry of Trade and Tourism, BP 3556, Vientiane

telephone 32-54 fax 50-25

Diplomatic representation in US:

chief of mission: Ambassador Hiem Phommachanh

chancery: 2222 S Street NW, Washington, DC 20008

telephone: [1] (202) 332-6416, 6417

FAX: [1] (202) 332-4923

US Diplomatic representation:

chief of mission: Ambassador Victor L. Tomseth

embassy: Rue Bartholonie, Vientiane

mailing address: B P 114, Vientiane; American Embassy,

Box V, APO AP 96546

telephone: [856] (21) 21-25-81, 21-25-82, 21-25-85

FAX: [856] (21) 21-25-84

Latvia

Capital: Riga   longitude: 24.10 E   latitude: 56.70 N

Government: republic

Flag: two horizontal bands of maroon (top and bottom), white (middle, narrower than other two bands)

Geography

Location: Eastern Europe, bordering the Baltic Sea, between Estonia and Lithuania

Total Area: 64,100 sq km (24,749 sq mi) slightly larger than West Virginia

Boundaries: Belarus, Estonia, Lithuania, Russia

Climate: maritime; wet, moderate winters

Terrain: low plain

Natural resources: minimal; amber, peat, limestone, dolomite

Natural hazards: NA

People

Population: 2,763,000 (July 1995 est.)

Life expectancy at birth: total population 69.65 years

Nationality: Latvian

Ethnic division: Latvian 51.8%, Russian 33.8%, Byelorussian 4.5%, Ukrainian 3.4%, Polish 2.3%, other 4.2%

Religions: Lutheran, Roman Catholic, Russian Orthodox

Languages: Lettish (official), Lithuanian, Russian, other

Literacy: total population 100%

Economy

Imports: fuels, cars, ferrous metals, chemicals

Exports: oil products, timber, ferrous metals, dairy products, furniture, textiles

Industries: highly diversified - produces buses, vans, street and railroad cars, synthetic fibers, agricultural machinery, fertilizers, washing machines, radios, electronics, pharmaceuticals, processed foods, textiles

Agriculture: principally dairy farming and livestock feeding; products - meat, milk, eggs, grain, sugar beets, potatoes, vegetables; fishing and fish packing

Currency: 1 lat = 100 cents

lats per US1$ - 0.55

Transportation

Railroads: 2,400 km

Roads: 59,500 km total paved and unpaved

Ports: Daugavpils, Liepaja, Riga, Ventspils

Airports: 50 total paved and unpaved. There are two international airports, at Riga and at Jelgava

The Press: daily newspapers

Diena: M. Pils iela 12, Riga 1963
telephone (2) 22-00-19   circ. 110,000

Rigas Balss: Balasta bambis 3, Riga 1081
telephone (2) 46-38-42 fax (2) 46-55-61
circ. 70,000

Tourism: Tourist attractions are winter sports at Sigulda, historic Riga with its medieval and art nouveau buildings, extensive beaches along the Baltic coastline.

Latvian Tourist Board: Pils Lauk. 4, Riga 1050
telephone (2) 22-99-45

Diplomatic representation in US:

chief of mission: Ambassador Ojars Eriks Kalnins

chancery: 4325 17th Street NW, Washington, DC 20011

telephone: [1] (202) 726-8213, 8214

FAX: [1] (202) 726-6785

US Diplomatic representation:

chief of mission: Ambassador Ints M. Silins

embassy: Raina Boulevard 7, Riga 226050

mailing address: use embassy street address

telephone: [371] (2) 21-39-62

FAX: [371] 882-0047 (cellular)

Lebanon

Capital: Beirut   longitude: 35.30 E latitude: 33.52 N elevation: 111 ft

Government: republic

Flag: three horizontal bands of red (top), white (double width), and red with a green and brown cedar tree centered in the white band

Geography

Location: Middle East

Total Area: 10,400 sq km (4,015 sq mi) about 0.8 times the size of Connecticut

Boundaries: Israel, Syria

Climate: Mediterranean; mild to cool, wet winters and hot, dry summers; Lebanon mountains experience heavy winter snows

Temperature (F): High/Low Jan. 62/51, Apr. 72/58, July 87/73, Oct. 81/69

Average annual precipitation: 35.1 inches

Terrain: narrow coastal plain; Al Biqa' (Bekka Valley) separates Lebanon and Anti-Lebanon Mountains

Highest point is Q. es Sauda 3,088 m (10,131 ft)

Natural resources: limestone, iron ore, salt, water-surplus state in a water-deficit region

Natural hazards: duststorms, sandstorms

People

Population: 3,696,000 (July 1995 est.)

257

Life expectancy at birth: total population 69.69 years

Nationality: Lebanese

Ethnic division: Arab 95%, Armenian 4%, other 1%

Religions: Islam 70% (5 legally recognized Islamic groups - Alawite or Nusayri, Druze, Isma'ilite, Shi'a, Sunni), Christian 30%, (11 legally recognized Christian groups - 4 Orthodox Christian, 6 Catholic, 1 Protestant), Judaism negligible %

Languages: Arabic (official), French (official), Armenian, English

Literacy: total population 80%

Economy

Imports: consumer goods, machinery and transport equipment, petroleum products

Exports: agricultural products, chemicals, textiles, precious and semiprecious metals and jewelry, metals and metal products

Industries: banking, food processing, textiles, cement, oil refining, chemicals, jewelry, some metal fabricating

Agriculture: principal products - citrus fruits, vegetables, potatoes, olives, tobacco, hemp (hashish), sheep, goats; not self-sufficient in grain

Currency: 1 Lenanese pound (#L) = 100 piasters

Lebanese pounds per US1$ - 1,644.6

Transportation

Railroads: 222 km (system in disrepair, considered in operable)

Roads: 7,300 km total paved and unpaved

Ports: Al Batrun, Al Mina, An Naqurah, Antilyas, Az Zahrani, Beirut, Jubayl, Juniyah, Shikka Jadidah, Sidon, Tripoli, Tyre

Airports: 9 total paved and unpaved. The principal airport is at Beirut

The Press: daily newspapers   **Al-Anwar:** POB 1038, Beirut
telephone 38-29-92   circ. 76,000

Al-Liwa: POB 2402, Beirut
telephone 86-50-80 circ. 79,000

Tourism: Beirut, sandy beaches, ruins of Byblos, Baalbek, one of the world's oldest city

National Council of Tourism in Lebanon:
POB 11-5344, rue Banque du Liban, Beirut
telephone (1) 86-45-32

Diplomatic representation in US:

chief of mission: Ambassador Riyad Tabbarah

chancery: 2560 28th Street NW, Washington, DC 20008

telephone: [1] (202) 939-6300

FAX: [1] (202) 939-6324

US Diplomatic representation:
   chief of mission: (vacant)
   embassy: Antelias, Beirut
   mailing address: PO Box 70-840, Beirut; PSC 815, Box 2, Beirut;
            FPO AE 09836-0002
   telephone: [961] (1) 40-22-00, 40-33-00, 41-65-02, 42-61-83, 41-77-74
   FAX: [961] (1) 40-71-12

Lesotho

Capital: Maseru   longitude: 27.29 E   latitude: 29.19 S
Government: constitutional monarchy
   Flag: divided diagonally from the lower hoist side corner; the upper half is
   white bearing the brown silhouette of a large shield with crossed spear and
   club; the lower half is a diagonal blue band with a green triangle in the corner
Geography
   Location: Southern Africa, an enclave of South Africa
   Total Area: 30,350 sq km (11,718 sq mi) slightly larger than Maryland
   Boundaries: South Africa
   Climate: temperate; cool to cold, dry winters; hot wet summers
   Temperature (F): High/Low Jan. 86/60, Apr. 73/47, July 61/33, Oct. 78/50
   Terrain: mostly highlands with plateaus, hills, and mountains
   Highest point is 3,482 m (11,425 ft)
   Natural resources: water, agricultural and grazing land, some diamonds and
   other minerals
   Natural hazards: periodic droughts
   Note: landlocked; surrounded by South Africa
People
   Population: 1,993,000 (July 1995 est.)

Life expectancy at birth: total population 62.56 years
Nationality: Mosotho (singular) Basotho (plural)
Ethnic division: Sotho 99.7%, Europeans, Asians
Religions: Christians 80%, rest indigenous beliefs
Languages: Sesotho (southern Sotho), English (official), Zulu, Xhosa
Literacy: total population 59%

Economy

Imports: mainly corn, building materials, clothing, vehicles, machinery, medicines, petroleum
Exports: wool, mohair, wheat, cattle, peas, beans, corn, hides, skins, baskets
Industries: food, beverages, textiles, handicrafts, tourism
Agriculture: exceedingly primitive, mostly subsistence farming and livestock; principal crops - corn, wheat, pulses, sorghum, barley
Currency: 1 loti (L) = 100 lisnte
maloti (M) per US1$ - 3.53

Transportation

Railroads: 2.6 km - owned by, operated by, and included in the statistics of South Africa
Roads: 7,215 km total paved and unpaved (572 km paved)
Ports: none
Airports: 29 total paved and unpaved. The international airport is about 20 km from Maseru

The Press: newspapers   **Lesotho Today:** POB 36, Maseru 100
telephone 32-35-61   fax 31-00-03
English circ. 3,000

The Mirror: Maseru   independent circ. 4,500

Tourism: Major tourist attraction is the scenery.
Lesotho Tourist Board: POB 1378, Maseru 100
telephone 32-37-60   fax 31-01-08

Diplomatic representation in US:

chief of mission: (vacant) Charge d'Affaires ad interim Mokhali A. Lithebe
chancery: 2511 Massachusetts Avenue NW, Washington, DC 20008
telephone: [1] (202) 797-5533 through 5536
FAX: [1] (202) 234-6815

US Diplomatic representation:
chief of mission: Ambassador Myrick Bismarck
embassy: NA, Maseru
mailing address: P O Box 333, Maseru 100, Lesotho
telephone: [266] 31-26-66
FAX: [266] 31-01-16

Liberia

Capital: Monrovia   longitude: 10.46 W   latitude: 6.20 N elevation: 75 ft
Government: republic
 Flag: 11 equal horizontal strips of red (top and bottom) alternating with white; there is a white five-pointed star on a blue square in the upper hoist-side corner; the design was based on the US flag
Geography
 Location: Western Africa, bordering the North Atlantic Ocean, between Cote d'Ivoire and Sierra Leone
 Total Area: 111,370 sq km (43,000 sq mi) slightly larger than Tennessee
 Boundaries: Guinea, Cote d'Ivoire, Sierra Leone
 Climate: tropical; hot, humid, dry winters with hot days and cool to cold nights; wet, cloudy summers with frequent heavy showers
 Temperature (F): High/Low Jan. 86/60, Apr. 87/73, July 80/72, Oct. 78/50
 Average annual precipitation: 202.3 inches
 Terrain: mostly flat to rolling coastal plains rising plateau and low mountains in northwest
 Highest point is Wutivi 1,702 m (5,584 ft)
 Natural resources: iron ore, timber, diamonds, gold
 Natural hazards: dust-laden harmattan winds blow from the Sahara (December to March)

People

Population: 3,073,400 (July 1995 est.)

Life expectancy at birth: total population 58.17 years

Nationality: Liberian

Ethnic division: indigenous African tribes 95% (including Kpelle, Bassa, Gio, Kru, Grebo, Mano, Krahn, Gola, Gbandi, Loma, Kissi, Vai, and Bella), Americo-Liberians 5% (descendants of former slaves)

Religions: traditional 70%, Muslim 20%, Christian 10%

Languages: English (official), Niger-Congo languages group about 20 local languages.

Literacy: total population 40%

Economy

Imports: mineral fuels, chemicals, machinery, transportation equipment, rice and other foodstuffs

Exports: iron ore, rubber, timber, coffee

Industries: rubber processing, food processing, construction material, furniture, palm oil processing, mining (iron ore, diamonds)

Agriculture: principal products - rubber, timber, coffee, cocoa, rice, cassava, palm oil, sugarcane, bananas, sheep, goats; fishing and forestry; not self-sufficient in food

Currency: 1 Liberian dollar (L$) = 100 cents
Liberian dollars per US1$ - 1.00 (official fixed rate)

Transportation

Railroads: 490 km

Roads: 10,087 km total paved and unpaved

Ports: Buchanan, Greenville, Harper, Monrovia

Airports: 59 total paved and unpaved. Roberts International Airport is located at Harbel

The Press: newspapers **Daily Observer:** 117 Broad Street, Crown Hill, POB 1858, Monrovia
telephone 22-35-45   5 a week   circ. 30,000
Sunday Express: Mamba Point, POB 3029, Monrovia weekly

Tourism: beaches, mountain village of Yekepa, virgin tropical forest, diamond mines

Bureau of Tourism: Sinkor, Monrovia

Diplomatic representation in US:

chief of mission: (vacant); Charge d' Affaires Konah K. Blackett

chancery: 5201 16th Street NW, Washington, DC 20011

telephone: [1] (202) 723-0437

US Diplomatic representation:

chief of mission: (vacant); Charge d' Affaires William P. Twaddell

embassy: 111 United Nations Drive, Monrovia

mailing address: P O Box 100098, Mamba Point, Monrovia

telephone: [231] 22-29-91 through 22-29-94

FAX: [231] 22-37-10

Libya

Capital: Tripoli   longitude: 13.07 E latitude: 32.49 N elevation: 72 ft

Government: Jamahiriya (a state of the Masses) in theory, governed by the populace through local councils; in fact, a military dictatorship

Flag: plain green; green is the traditional color of Islam (the state religion)

Geography

Location: Northern Africa, bordering the Mediterranean Sea, between Egypt and Tunisia

Total Area: 1,759,540 sq km (679,358 sq mi) slightly larger than Alaska

Boundaries: Algeria, Chad, Egypt, Niger, Sudan, Tunisia

Climate: Mediterranean along coast; dry, extreme desert interior

Temperature (F): High/Low Jan. 61/47, Apr. 72/57, July 85/71, Oct. 80/65

Average annual precipitation: 15.1 inches

Terrain: mostly barren, flat to undulating plains, plateaus, depressions

Highest point is Bette Peak 2,286 m (7,500 ft)

Natural resources: petroleum, natural gas, gypsum

Natural hazards: hot, dry, dust-laden ghibli is a southern wind lasting one to four days in spring and fall; duststorms, sandstorms

People

Population: 5,248,500 (July 1995 est.)
Life expectancy at birth: total population 64.29 years
Nationality: Libyan
Ethnic division: Berber and Arab 97%, Greeks, Maltese, Italians, Egyptians, Pakistanis, Turks, Indians, Tunisians
Religions: Sunni Muslim 97%
Languages: Arabic, Italian, English, all are widely understood in the major cities
Literacy: total population 60%

Economy

Imports: machinery, transport equipment, food, manufactured goods
Exports: crude oil, refined petroleum products, natural gas
Industries: petroleum, food processing, textiles, handicrafts, cement
Agriculture: cash crops - wheat, barley, olives, dates, citrus fruits, peanuts; 75% of food is imported
Currency: 1 Libyan dinar (LD) = 1,000 dirhams
Libyan dinars per US1$ - 0.33

Transportation

Railroads: Libya has had no railroad in operation since 1965, all previous systems have been dismantled.
Roads: 19,300 km total paved and unpaved
Ports: Al Khums, Banghazi, Darnah, Marsa al Burayqah, Misratah, Ra's Lanuf, Tobruk, Tripoli, Zuwarah
Airports: 146 total paved and unpaved. Tripoli International Airport is located at Ben Gashir, about 30 km from Tripoli

The Press: newspapers

Al-Fajr al-Jadid: POB 2303, Tripoli telephone (21) 33-056   daily   circ. 40,000

Libyan Arab Republic Gazette: Tripoli
weekly   English

Tourism: Tripoli, Greek and Roman ruins, Gulf of Sidra

Department of Tourism and Fairs:
POB 891, Sharia Omar Mukhtar, Tripoli
telephone 32-255

Diplomatic representation in US: none
US Diplomatic representation: none

Liechtenstein

Capital: Vaduz   longitude: 9.32 E   latitude: 47.08 N

Government: hereditary constitutional monarchy

    Flag: two equal horizontal bands of blue (top) and red with a gold crown on the hoist side of the blue band

Geography

    Location: Central Europe, between Austria and Switzerland

    Total Area: 160 sq km (62 sq mi) about 0.9 time the size of Washington, DC

    Boundaries: Austria, Switzerland

    Climate: continental; cold, cloudy winters with frequent snow or rain; cool to moderately warm, cloudy, humid summers

    Temperature (F): High/Low Jan. 35/23, Apr. 57/40, July 77/56, Oct. 58/42

    Terrain: mostly mountainous (Alps) with Rhine Valley in western third

    Highest point is Grauspitze 2,599 m (8,527 ft)

    Natural resources: hydroelectric potential

    Natural hazards: NA

People

    Population: 30,700 (July 1995 est.)

    Life expectancy at birth: total population 77.52 years

    Nationality: Leichtensteiner

    Ethnic division: Alemannic 95%, Italian and other 5%

    Religions: Roman Catholic 87.3%, Protestant 8.3%, unknown 1.6%, other 2.8%

    Languages: German (official), Alemannic dialect

    Literacy: total population 100%

Economy

    Imports: machinery, metal goods, textiles, foodstuffs, motor vehicles

Exports: small specialty machinery, dental products, stamps, hardware, pottery

Industries: electronics, metal manufacturing, textiles, ceramics, pharmaceuticals, food products, precision instruments, tourism

Agriculture: livestock, vegetables, corn, wheat, potatoes, grapes

Currency: 1 Swiss franc, fraken, or franco (SwF) = 100 centimes, rappen, or centesimi

Swiss francs, franken, or franchi per US1$ - 1.28

Transportation

Railroads: 18.5 km; owned, operated, and included in statistics of Austrian Federal Railways

Roads: 323 km all paved

Ports: none

Airports: none

The Press: newspapers **Liechtensteiner Vaterland:** Furst-Franz-Jose-Str. 13, 9490 Vaduz   telephone (75) 232-2826

Monday to Saturday   circ. 9,000

Liechtensteiner Volksblatt: 9494 Schaan

telephone (75) 232-4242   fax (75) 232-2912

Monday to Saturday   circ. 8,500

Tourism: National Museum and Art Gallery at Vadue, Schloss Vadue Prince's Art Collection, Stamp Museum, Malbon Ski Resort

Liechtenstein National Tourist Office:

Postfach 139, 9490 Vaduz

telephone (75) 392-1111   fax (75) 392-1618

Diplomatic representation in US: in routine diplomatic matters, Liechtenstein is represented in the US by the Swiss Embassy

US Diplomatic representation: the US has no diplomatic or consular mission in Liechtenstein, but the US Consul General at Zurich (Switzerland) has consular accreditation at Vaduz

Lithuania

Capital: Vilnius   longitude: 25.60 E   latitude: 55.04 N

Government: republic

Flag: three equal horizontal bands of yellow (top), green, and red

Geography

    Location: Eastern Europe, bordering the Baltic Sea, between Latvia and Russia

    Total Area: 65,200 sq km (25,174 sq mi) slightly smaller than West Virginia

    Boundaries: Belaris, Latvia, Poland, Russia

    Climate: maritime, wet moderate winters and summers

    Terrain: lowland, many scattered small lakes, fertile soil

    Natural resources: peat

    Natural hazards: NA

People

    Population: 3,876,400 (July 1995 est.)

    Life expectancy at birth: total population 71.37 years

    Nationality: Lithuanian

    Ethnic division: Lithuanian 80.1%, Russian 8.6%, Polish 7.7%, Byelorussian 1.5%, other 2.1%

    Religions: Roman Catholic, Lutheran, other

    Languages: Lithuanian (official), Polish, Russian

    Literacy: total population 98%

Economy

    Imports: oil, machinery, chemicals, grain

    Exports: electronics, petroleum products, food, chemicals

Industries: metal-cutting machine tools, electric motors, television sets, refrigerators and freezers; petroleum refining, shipbuilding, furniture making, textiles, food processing, fertilizers, agricultural machinery, optical equipment, electronic components, computers, and amber

Agriculture: sugar, grain, potatoes, sugar beets, vegetables, meat, milk, dairy products, eggs, fish; most developed are the livestock and dairy branches, which depend on imported grain; net exporter of meat, milk, eggs

Currency: introduced the convertible litas in June 1993

litai per US1$ - 4 (fixed rate 1 May 1994)

Transportation

Railroads: 2,010 km

Roads: 44,200 km total paved and unpaved

Ports: Kaunas, Klaipeda

Airports: 96 total paved and unpaved. The international airport is located at Vilnius

The Press: newspapers (5 a week)   **Lietuvos aidas:** Gedimino 12a, Vilnius 2001
telephone (2) 62-26-80 fax (2) 22-76-56
circ. 60,000

Respublika: A. Smetonos 2, Vilnius 2600
telephone (2) 22-31-12   fax (2) 22-35-38
circ. 100,000

Tourism: Main tourist attractions are historic cities and coastal resorts.

State Tourism Department: Gedimino 30/1, Vilnius 2695
telephone (2) 22-67-06   fax (2) 22-68-19

Diplomatic representation in US:

chief of mission: Ambassador Alfonsas Eidintas
chancery: 2622 16th Street NW, Washington, DC 20009
telephone: [1] (202) 234-5860, 2639
FAX: [1] (202) 328-0466

US Diplomatic representation:

chief of mission: Ambassador James W. Swihart, Jr.
embassy: Akmenu 6, Vilnius 2600
mailing address: APO AE 09723
telephone: [370] (2) 22-30-31
FAX: [370] (2) 22-27-79

Luxembourg

Capital: Luxembourg   longitude: 6.09 E   latitude: 49.36 N
elevation: 1,083 ft

Government: constitutional monarchy

Flag: three equal horizontal bands of red (top), white, and light blue; similar to the flag of the Netherlands, which uses a darker blue and is shorter; design was based on the flag of France

Geography

Location: western Europe, between France and Germany

Total Area: 2,586 sq km (998 sq mi) slightly smaller than Rhode Island

Boundaries: Belgium, France, Germany

Climate: modified continental with mild winters, cool summers
Temperature (F): High/Low Jan. 37/29, Apr. 57/40, July 73/55, Oct. 56/43
Average annual precipitation: 30 inches

Terrain: mostly gentle rolling uplands with broad, shallow valleys, uplands to slightly mountainous in the north; steep slope down to Moselle flood plain in the southeast
Highest point is Ardennes Plateau 556 m (1,825 ft)

Natural resources: iron ore (no longer exploited)

Natural hazards: NA

People

Population: 404,800 (July 1995 est.)

Life expectancy at birth: total population 76.95 years

Nationality: Luxembourger

Ethnic division: Celtic base (with French and German blend), Portuguese, Italian, and European

Religions: Roman Catholic 97%, Protestant and Jewish 3%

Languages: Luxembourgisch, German, French, English

269

Literacy: total population 100%

Economy

Imports: minerals, metals, foodstuffs, quality consumer goods

Exports: finished steel products, chemicals, rubber products, glass, aluminum, other industrial products

Industries: banking, iron and steel, food processing, chemicals, metal products, engineering, tires, glass, aluminum

Agriculture: principal products - barley, oats, potatoes, wheat, fruits, wine grapes; cattle raising widespread; forestry

Currency: 1 Luxembourg franc (LuxF) = 100 centimes
Luxembourg francs per US1$ - 31.54

Transportation

Railroads: 371 km

Roads: 5,108 km total paved and unpaved

Ports: Mertert

Airports: 2 both paved. The international airport is near Luxembourg-Ville

The Press: daily newspapers   **Letzebuerger Journal:** 123 rue Adolphe Fischer, POB 2101, 1521 Luxembourg
telephone 49-30-33   fax 49-20-65   circ. 14,000

Tageblatt/Zeitung fir Letzebuerg:
44 rue du Canal, 4050 Eschsur-Alzette
telephone 54-71-31   fax 54-71-30   circ. 30,000

Tourism: Tourist attractions are the ruins of medieval castles, mineral springs at Mondorf-les-Bains, and hiking trails. Moselle wine region

Office National du Tourisme:
77 rue d'Anvers, BP 1001, 1010 Luxembourg
telephone 40-08-08   fax 40-47-48

Diplomatic representation in US:

chief of mission: Ambassador Alphonse Berns
chancery: 2200 Massachusetts Avenue NW, Washington, DC 20008
telephone: [1] (202) 265-4171
FAX: [1] (202) 328-8270

US Diplomatic representation:

chief of mission: Ambassador Clay Constantinou
embassy: 22 Boulevard Emmanuel-Servais, 2535 Luxembourg City
mailing address: PSC 11, Luxembourg City; APO AE 09132-5380
telephone: [352] 46-01-23
FAX: [352] 46-14-01

Macau

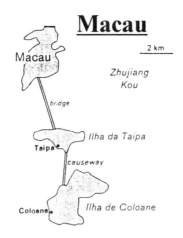

Capital: Macau   longitude: 113.35 E   latitude: 22.12 N

Government: overseas territory of Portugal scheduled to revert to China in 1999

   Flag: the flag of Portugal is used

Geography

   Location: Eastern Asia, bordering the South China Sea and China

   Total Area: 16 sq km (6.2 sq mi) about 0.1 times the size of Washington, DC

   Boundaries: China

   Climate: subtropical; marine with cool winters, warm summers

   Temperature (F): High/Low Jan. 62/53, Apr. 75/72, July 86/84, Oct. 77/75

   Terrain: generally flat

   Natural resources: negligible

   Natural hazards: NA

People

   Population: 491,000 (July 1995 est.)

   Life expectancy at birth: total population 79.86 years

   Nationality: Macanese

   Ethnic division: Chinese 95%, Portuguese 3%, other 2%

   Religions: Buddhist 45%, Roman Catholic 7%, Protestant 1%, none 45.8%, other 1.2%

   Languages: Portuguese (official), Cantonese is the language of commerce

   Literacy: total population 90%

Economy

   Imports: raw materials, foodstuffs, capital goods

   Exports: textiles, clothing, toys

Industries: clothing, textiles, toys, plastic products, furniture, tourism

Agriculture: rice, vegetables; food shortages - rice, vegetables, meat; depends mostly on imports for food requirements

Currency: 1 pataca (P) = 100 avos

patacas per US1$ - 8.03

Transportation

Railroads: none

Roads: 42 km paved

Ports: Macau

Airports: none usable, 1 under construction; 1 seaplane station

Tourism: Macau includes a 16 sq km (6 sq miles) area on the mainland of China bordering the South China Sea, and the small, adjacent islands of Taipa and Coloane. Ruins of Sao Paolo, temples, gardens, casinos

Diplomatic representation in US: none (Chinese territory under Portuguese administration)

US Diplomatic representation: the US has no offices in Macau, and the US interests are monitored by the US Consulate General in Hong Kong

Macedonia

Capital: Skopje   longitude: 21.28 E latitude: 41.59 N elevation: 787 ft

Government: emerging democracy

Flag: 16-point gold sun (Vergina Sun) centered on a red field

Geography

Location: Southeastern Europe, north of Greece

Total Area: 25,333 sq km (9,781 sq mi) slightly larger than Vermont

Boundaries: Albania, Bulgaria, Greece, Serbia and Montenegro

Climate: hot, dry summers and autumns and relatively cold winters with heavy snowfall

Temperature (F): High/Low Jan. 40/26, Apr. 67/42, July 88/60, Oct. 65/43

Average annual precipitation: 19.5 inches

Terrain: mountainous territory covered with deep basins and valleys; there are three lakes, each divided by frontier line; country bisected by Vardar River

Natural resources: chromium, lead, zinc, manganese, tungsten, nickel, low-grade iron ore, asbestos, sulphur, timber

Natural hazards: high seismic risks

People

Population: 2,159,600 (July 1995 est.)

Life expectancy at birth: total population 74 years

Nationality: Macedonian

Ethnic division: Macedonian 65%, Albanian 22%, Turkish 4%, Serb 2%, Gypsies 3%, other 4%

Religions: Eastern Orthodox 67%, Muslim 30%, other 3%

Languages: Macedonian 70%, Albanian 21%, Turkish 3%, Serbo-Croatian 3%, other 3%

Literacy: NA

Economy

Imports: fuels and lubricants, manufactured goods, machinery and transport equipment, food and live animals, chemicals, raw materials, miscellaneous manufactured articles, beverages and tobacco

Exports: manufactured goods, machinery and transport equipment, miscellaneous manufactured articles, raw materials, food (rice) and live animals, beverages and tobacco, chemicals

Industries: low levels of technology predominate, such as, oil refining by distillation only, produces basic liquid fuels, coal, metallic chromium, lead, zinc, and ferro-nickel; light industry produces basic textiles, wood products, and tobacco

Agriculture: meets the basic needs for food; principal crops are rice, wheat, corn, millet; also grown are cotton, sesame, mulberry leaves, citrus fruit, and vegetables; agricultural production is highly labor intensive

Currency: the denar, which was adopted by the Macedonian legislature 26 April 1992, was initially issued in the form of a coupon pegged to the German mark; subsequently repegged to a basket of seven currencies

denar per US1$ - 39.00

Transportation

Railroads: 922 km

Roads: 10.591 km total paved and unpaved

Ports: none

Airports: 16 total paved and unpaved.

The Press: daily newspapers   **Nova Makedonija:** 91000 Skopje,
Mito Hadzivasilev bb   circ. 26,000
telephone (91) 11-20-95 fax (91) 22-48-29
Vecer: 91000 Skopje, Mito Hadzivasilev bb
telephone (91) 11-15-37 fax (91) 23-83-29 circ. 30,000

Tourism: mountain scenery

Diplomatic representation in US: the US recognized the Former Yugoslav
Republic of Macedonia on 8 February 1994
US Diplomatic representation:
chief of mission: Ambassador Victor D. Comras
liaison office: ul. 27 Mart No. 5, 9100 Skoje
mailing address: USLO Skopje, Department of State,
Washington, DC 20521-7120
telephone: [389] (91) 11-61-80
FAX: [389] (91) 11-71-03

Madagascar

Capital: Antananarivo   longitude: 47.30 E   latitude: 18.52 S
elevation: 4,500 ft
Government: republic
    Flag: two equal bands of red (top) and green with a vertical white band of
the same width on hoist side
Geography
    Location: Southern Africa, island in the Indian Ocean, east of Mozambique
    Total Area: 587,040 sq km (226,656 sq mi) slightly less than twice the size
of Arizona
    Boundaries: no land boundaries

Climate: tropical along coast, temperate inland, arid in south
Temperature (F): High/Low Jan. 79/61, Apr. 76/58, July 68/48, Oct. 80/54
Average annual precipitation: 53.3 inches
Terrain: narrow coastal plain, high plateau and mountains in center
Highest point is Maromokotro 2,876 m (9,436 ft)
Natural resources: graphite, chromite, coal, bauxite, salt, quartz, tar sands, semiprecious stones, mica, fish
Natural hazards: periodic cyclones

People

Population: 13,862,400 (July 1995 est.)
Life expectancy at birth: total population 54.45 years
Nationality: Malagasy
Ethnic division: Malayo-Indonesian (Merina and related Betsileo), Cotiers (mixed African, Malayo-Indonesian, and Arab ancestry - Betsimisaraka, Tsimihety, Antaisaka, Sakalava), French, Indian, Creole, Comoran
Religions: indigenous beliefs 52%, Christian 41%, Muslim 7%
Languages: French (official), Malagasy (official)
Literacy: total population 80%

Economy

Imports: intermediate manufactures, capital goods, petroleum, consumer goods, food
Exports: coffee, vanilla, cloves, shellfish, sugar, petroleum products
Industries: agricultural processing (meat canneries, soap factories, breweries, tanneries, sugar refining plants), light consumer goods industries (textiles, glassware), cement, automobiles assembly plant, paper, petroleum
Agriculture: cash crops - coffee, vanilla, sugarcane, cloves, cocoa; food crops - rice, cassava, beans, bananas, peanuts; cattle raising widespread; almost self-sufficient in rice
Currency: 1 Malagasy franc (FMG) = 100 centimes
Malagasy francs per US1$ - 3,718.0

Transportation

Railroads: 1,020 km
Roads: 40,000 km total paved and unpaved
Ports: Antsiranana, Mahajanga, Port Saint-Louis, Toamasina, Toliaria
Airports: 138 total paved and unpaved. The international airport is at Antananarivo

The Press: daily newspapers   **Madagascar Tribune:** Immeuble SME,
rue Ravoninahitriniarivo, BP 659,
Ankorondrano, 101 Antananarivo
telephone (2) 22-635   fax (2) 22-254   circ. 12,500
Nouveau Journal de Madagascar: Cite Batimord;
Ankorondrano, 101 Antananarivo   French and English
circ. 12,000

Tourism: Tourist attractions are unusual varieties of wildlife and unspoiled scenery
1,000 species of orchids
Direction du Tourisme de Madagascar:
Tsimbazaza, BP 610, 101 Antananarivo
telephone (2) 26-298   fax (2) 26-719

Diplomatic representation in US:
chief of mission: Ambassador Pierrot Jocelyn Rajaonarivelo
chancery: 2374 Massachusetts Avenue NW, Washington, DC 20008
telephone: [1] (202) 265-5525, 5526
US Diplomatic representation:
chief of mission: Ambassador Dennis P. Barrett
embassy: 14-16 Rue Rainitovo, Antananarivo, Antananarivo
mailing address: B P 620, Antananarivo
telephone: [261] (2) 21-257, 20-089, 20-718
FAX: [261] (2) 34-539

Malawi

Capital: Lilongwe   longitude: 35.00 E   latitude: 15.46 S
elevation: 3,610 ft

Government: multiparty democracy following a referendum on 14 June 1993; formerly a one-party republic

Flag: three equal bands of black (top), red, and green with a radiant, rising, red sun centered in the black band; similar to the flag of Afghanistan, which is longer and has the national coat of arms superimposed on the hoist side of the black and red bands

Geography

Location: Southern Africa, east of Zambia

Total Area: 118,480 sq km (45,745 sq mi) slightly larger than Pennsylvania

Boundaries: Mozambique, Tanzania, Zambia

Climate: tropical; rainy season (November to May); dry season (May to November)

Temperature (F): High/Low Jan. 80/63, Apr. 80/57, July 74/45, Oct. 86/59

Average annual precipitation: 30.5 inches

Terrain: narrow elongated plateau with rolling plains, rounded hills, some mountains

Highest point is Mulanje 3,000 m (9,843 ft)

Natural resources: limestone, unexploited deposits of uranium, coal, and bauxite

Natural hazards: NA

People

Population: 9,808,400 (July 1995 est.)

Life expectancy at birth: total population 39.01 years

Nationality: Malawian

Ethnic division: Chewa, Nyanja, Tumbuko, Yao, Lomwe, Sena, Tonga, Ngoni, Ngonde, Asain, European

Religions: Protestant 43%, Roman Catholic 20%, Muslim 20%, traditional indigenous beliefs

Languages: English (official), Chichewa (official), other languages important regionally

Literacy: total population 48%

Economy

Imports: food, petroleum products, semi-manufactures, consumer goods, transportation equipment

Exports: tobacco, tea, sugar, coffee, peanuts, wood products

Industries: agricultural processing (tea, tobacco, sugar), sawmilling, cement, consumer goods

Agriculture: cash crops - tobacco, sugarcane, cotton, tea, and corn; subsistence crops - potatoes, cassava, sorghum, pulses; livestock - cattle, goats

Currency: 1 Malawian kwacha (MK) = 100 tambala

Malawian kwacha per US1$ - 7.83

Transportation

Railroads: 789 km

Roads: 13,135 km total paved and unpaved

Ports: Chipoka, Monkey Bay, Nkhata Bay, Nkotakota

Airports: 47 total paved and unpaved. Kamuzu International Airport is located at Lilongwe

The Press: newspapers (in English)
The Daily Times:
Ginnery Corner, Blantyre
telephone 67-15-66
circ. 20,000 Mon.-Fri.

Malawi News: PB 39, Ginnery Corner, Blantyre
weekly circ. 14,500

Tourism: excellent climate, beautiful beaches on Lake Malawi, fine scenery, big game, mountain climbing

Department of Tourism: POB 402, Blantyre
telephone 62-03-00 fax 62-09-47

Diplomatic representation in US:

chief of mission: (vacant) Charge d'Affaires ad interim Patrick Nyasulu

chancery: 2408 Massachusetts Avenue NW, Washington, DC 20008

telephone: [1] (202) 797-1007

US Diplomatic representation:

chief of mission: Ambassador Peter R. Chaveas

embassy: NA, in new capital city development area in Lilongwe

mailing address: P O Box 30016, Lilongwe 3, Malawi

telephone: [265] 78-31-66

FAX: [265] 78-04-71

Malaysia

Capital: Kuala Lumpur   longitude: 101.42 E   latitude: 3.08 N
elevation: 127 ft

Government: constitutional monarchy

Flag: fourteen equal horizontal stripes of red (top) alternating with the white (bottom); there is a blue rectangle in the upper hoist-side corner bearing a yellow crescent and a yellow fourteen-pointed star; the crescent and the star are traditional symbols of Islam; the design was based on the flag of the US

Geography

Location: Southeastern Asia, peninsula and northern one-third on the island of Borneo bordering the Java Sea and the South China Sea, south of Vietnam

Total Area: 329,750 sq km (127,316 sq mi) slightly larger than New Mexico

Boundaries: Brunei, Indonesia, Thailand

Climate: tropical; annual southwest (April to October) and northeast (October to February) monsoons

Temperature (F): High/Low Jan. 90/72, Apr. 91/74, July 90/73, Oct. 89/73

Average annual precipitation: 96.2 inches

Terrain: coastal plains rising to hills and mountains

Highest point is Mt. Kinabalu 4,101 m (13,455 ft)

Natural resources: tin, petroleum, timber, copper, iron ore, natural gas, bauxite

Natural hazards: flooding

People

Population: 19,723,600 (July 1995 est.)

Life expectancy at birth: total population 69.48 years

Nationality: Malaysian

Ethnic division: Malay and other indigenous 59%, Chinese 32%, Indian 9%

Religions: Peninsular Malaysia: Muslim (Malays), Buddhist (Chinese), Hindu (Indians) Sabah: Muslim 38%, Christian 17%, other 45%
Sarawak: tribal religion 35%, Buddhist and Confucianist 24%, Muslim 20%, Christian 16%, other 5%

Languages:
Peninsular Malaysia: Malay (official), English, Chinese dialects, Tamil
Sabah: English, Malay, numerous tribal dialects, Chinese (Mandarin and Hakka dialects predominate)
Sarawak: English, Malay, Mandarin, numerous tribal languages
Literacy: total population 78%

Economy
Imports: machinery and equipment, chemicals, food, petroleum products
Exports: electronic equipment, petroleum and petroleum products, palm oil, wood and wood products, rubber, textiles

Industries:
Peninsular Malaysia: rubber and oil palm processing and manufacturing, light manufacturing industry, electronics, tin mining and smelting, logging and processing timber.
Sabah: logging, petroleum production
Sarawak: agriculture processing, petroleum production and refining, logging

Agriculture:
Peninsular Malaysia: natural rubber, palm oil, rice
Sabah: mainly subsistence, but also rubber, timber, coconut, rice
Sarawak: rubber, timber, pepper; deficit of rice in all areas

Currency: 1 ringgit (M$) = 100 sen
ringgits per US1$ - 2.55

Transportation
Railroads: 1801 km (Peninsular Malaysia 1,665 km; Sabah 136 km; Sarawak 0 km)
Roads: 29,028 km total paved and unpaved (Peninsular Malaysia 23,602 km, Sabah 3,782 km, Sarawak 1,644 km)
Ports: Kota Kinabula, Kuantan, Kuching, Kudat, Lahad Datu, Labuan, Lumut, Miri, Pasir Gudang, Penang, Prot Dickson, Port Kelang, Sandakan, Sibu, Tanjong Berhala, Tanjong Kidurong, Tawau
Airports: 115 total paved and unpaved.

The Press: daily newspapers   **New Straits Times:**
31 Jalan Riong, 59100 Kuala Lumpur
telephone (3) 282-3322 fax 282-1434
circ. 168,000

The Star: 13 Jalan 13/6, 46200 Petaling Jaya,
POB 12474, Selangor circ. 162,000
telephone (3) 757-8811   fax (3) 755-4039

Tourism: the Batu Caves, Cameron Highlands, beaches, wildlife refuge, old
Portuguese Settlement on the spice island route

Diplomatic representation in US:

chief of mission: Ambassador Abdul Majid bin Mohamed

chancery: 2401 Massachusetts Avenue NW, Washington, DC 20008

telephone: [1] (202) 328-2700

US Diplomatic representation:

chief of mission: Ambassador John S. Wolf

embassy: 376 Jalan Tun Razak, 50400 Kuala Lumpur

mailing address: P O Box No. 10035, 50700 Kuala Lumpur;
APO AP 96535-8152

telephone: [60] (3) 248-9011

FAX: [60] (3) 242-2207

Maldives

Capital: Male   longitude: 73.28 E ᶜ⁻ᴳᵃⁿ latitude: 4.10 N

Government: republic

Flag: red with a large green rectangle in the center bearing a vertical white
crescent; the closed side of the crescent is on the hoist side of the flag

Geography

Location: Southern Asia, group of atolls in the Indian Ocean,
south-southwest of India

Total Area: 300 sq km (115.8 sq mi) slightly more than 1.5 times the size of
Washington, DC

Boundaries: no land boundaries

281

Climate: tropical; hot, humid; dry, northeast monsoon (November to March); rainy, southwest monsoon (June to August)

Temperature (F): High/Low Jan. 85/73, Apr. 87/80, July 85/76, Oct. 85/76

Terrain: flat with elevations only as high as 2.5 meters

Natural resources: fish

Natural hazards: low level of islands make them very sensitive to sea level rise

Note: 1,190 coral islands grouped into 26 atolls; archipelago of strategic location astride and along major sea lanes in Indian Ocean

People

Population: 261,400 (July 1995 est.)

Life expectancy at birth: total population 65.49 years

Nationality: Maldivians

Ethnic division: Sinhalese, Dravidian, Arab, African

Religions: Sunni Muslim

Languages: Divehi (dialect of Sinhala; script derived from Arabic), English spoken by most government officials

Literacy: total population 91%

Economy

Imports: consumer goods, intermediate and capital goods, petroleum products

Exports: fish, clothing

Industries: fishing and fish processing, tourism, shipping, boat building, some coconut processing, garments, woven mats, coir (rope), handicrafts

Agriculture: fishing, coconuts, corn, sweet potatoes

Currency: 1 rufiyaa (Rf) = 100 laari

rufiyaa per US1$ - 11.77

Transportation

Railroads: none

Roads: NA

Ports: Gan, Male

Airports: 2 both paved. The airport an Hulue Island near Male, has been expanded and improved to international standards

The Press: newspapers

Haveeru: G. Olympus (North Side)
POB 20103, Male 20-04
telephone 32-36-85   fax 32-31-03
Dhivehi and English   daily   circ. 4,500

Maldives News Bulletin: Maldives News Bureau
Huravee Bldg, Ameer Ahmed Magu, Male 20-05
telephone 32-38-36 fax 32-62-11
weekly, English circ. 600

Tourism: resort islands, white sandy beaches, reef diving, water sports, exotic fish
species

Maldives Association of Tourism Industries:
POB 23, Male   telephone 32-66-40   fax 32-66-41

Diplomatic representation in US: Maldives has no embassy in the US, but does
have a UN mission in New York; Permanent Representative to
the UN, Ahmed Zaki

US Diplomatic representation:
chief of mission: the US Ambassador to Sri Lanka is accredited to Maldives
and makes periodic visits there
consular agency: Midhath Hilmy, Male
telephone: 32-25-81

Mali

Capital: Bamako   longitude: 7.59 W   latitude: 12.40 N
elevation: 1,116 ft

Government: republic
Flag: three equal vertical bands of green (hoist side), yellow, and red; uses
the popular pan-African colors of Ethiopia

Geography
Location: Western Africa, southwest of Algeria
Total Area: 1,240,000 sq km (478,764 sq mi) slightly less than the
size of Texas

Boundaries: Algeria, Burkina, Guinea, Cote d'Ivoire, Mauritania, Niger, Senegal

Climate: subtropical to arid; hot and dry February to June; rainy, humid, and mild June to November; cool and dry November to February

Temperature (F): High/Low Jan. 91/61, Apr. 103/76, July 89/71, Oct. 93/71

Average annual precipitation: 44.1 inches

Terrain: mostly flat to rolling northern plains covered by sand, savanna in south, rugged hills in northeast

Highest point is Hombori Mountains 1,155 m (3,789 ft)

Natural resources: gold, phosphates, kaolin, salt, limestone, uranium, bauxite, iron ore, manganese, tin, and copper deposits are known but not exploited

Natural hazards: hot, dust-laden harmattan haze common during dry season; recurring droughts

People

Population: 9,375,200 (July 1995 est.)

Life expectancy at birth: total population 46.37 years

Nationality: Malian

Ethnic division: Mande 50% (Bambara, Malinke, Sarakole), Peul 17%, Voltaic 12%, Songhai 6%, Tuareg and Moor 10%, other 5%

Religions: Muslim 90%, indigenous beliefs 9%, Christian 1%

Languages: French (official), Bambara 80%, numerous African languages

Literacy: total population 19%

Economy

Imports: machinery and equipment, foodstuffs, construction materials, petroleum, textiles

Exports: cotton, livestock, gold

Industries: minor local consumer goods production and food processing, construction, phosphate and gold mining

Agriculture: mostly subsistence farming; cotton and livestock account for over 70% of exports; other crops - millet, rice, corn, vegetables, peanuts; livestock - cattle, sheep, goats

Currency: 1 CFA franc (CFAF) = 100 centimes

Communaute Financiere Africaine francs per US1$ - 529.43

Transportation

Railroads: 642 km; note - linked to Senegal's rail system through Kayes

Roads: 15,700 km total paved and unpaved

Ports: Koulikoro

Airports: 33 total paved and unpaved. The principal airport is at Bamako-Senou

The Press: daily newspaper   **L'Essor-La Voix du Peuple:** BP 141, Bamako
telephone 22-47-97   circ. 4,000

Tourism: remains of the great Timbuku, cliff top villages, cave paintings, bird
sanctuary

Societe Malienne d'Exploitation des Ressources Touristiques
place de la Republique, BP 222, Bamako   telephone 22-59-42

Diplomatic representation in US:

chief of mission: Ambassador Ibrahim Siragatou Cisse

chancery: 2130 R Street NW, Washington, DC 20008

telephone: [1] (202) 332-2249, 939-8950

US Diplomatic representation:

chief of mission: (vacant)

embassy: Rue Rochester NY and Rue Mohamed V, Bamako

mailing address: B P 34, Bamako

telephone: [223] 22-54-70

FAX: [223] 22-37-12

Malta

Capital: Valletta longitude: 14.32 E latitude: 35.54 N elevation: 233 ft

Government: parliamentary democracy

Flag: two equal vertical bands of white (hoist side) and red; in the upper
hoist-side corner is a representation of the George Cross, edged in red

Geography

Location: Southern Europe, islands in the Mediterranean Sea,
south of Sicily (Italy)

Total Area: 320 sq km (123.6 sq mi) slightly less than twice the size of
Washington, DC

Boundaries: no land boundaries

Climate: Mediterranean with mild, rainy winters and hot, dry summers
Temperature (F): High/Low Jan. 58/50, Apr. 65/56, July 84/72, Oct. 75/66
Average annual precipitation: 20.3 inches
Terrain: mostly low, rocky, flat to dissected plains; many coastal cliffs
Highest point is 240 m (787 ft)
Natural resources: limestone, salt
Natural hazards: NA

People

Population: 369,700 (July 1995 est.)
Life expectancy at birth: total population 77.02 years
Nationality: Maltese
Ethnic division: Arab, Sicilian, Norman, Spanish, Italian, English
Religions: Roman Catholic 98%
Languages: Maltese (official), English (official)
Literacy: total population 84%

Economy

Imports: food, petroleum, machinery and semi-manufactured goods
Exports: machinery and transport equipment, clothing and footwear, printed matter
Industries: tourism, electronics, ship repair yard, construction, food manufacturing, textiles, footwear, clothing, beverages, tobacco
Agriculture: main products - potatoes, cauliflower, grapes, wheat, barley, tomatoes, citrus, cut flowers, green peppers, hogs, poultry, eggs; generally adequate supplies of vegetables, poultry, milk, pork products; seasonal or periodic shortages in grain, animal fodder, fruits, other basic foodstuffs
Currency: 1 Maltese lira (LM) = 100 cents
Maltese lira per US1$ - 0.36

Transportation

Railroads: none
Roads: 1,291 km total paved and unpaved
Ports: Marsaxlokk, Valletta
Airports: 1 The international airport at Luqa about 6 km from Valletta

The Press: daily newspapers   **In-Nazzjon Taghna:** Herbert Ganado St, Pieta
POB 37, Hamrun   circ. 20,000
telephone 24-36-41   fax 24-28-86

The Times: Strickland House, 341 St. Paul Street, POB 328, Valletta
telephone 24-14-64   fax 24-79-01   circ. 24,000

Tourism: Scenic and historical attractions, temples, beautiful beaches.

National Tourism Organization:

280 Republic St. Valletta CMR 02

telephone 23-82-82   fax 22-40-01

Diplomatic representation in US:

    chief of mission: Ambassador Albert Borg Olivier De Puget

    chancery: 2017 Connecticut Avenue NW, Washington, DC 20008

    telephone: [1] (202) 462-3611, 3612

    FAX: [1] (202) 387-5470

US Diplomatic representation:

    chief of mission: Ambassador Joseph R. Paolino, Jr.

    embassy: 2nd Floor, Development House, Saint Anne Street, Floriana, Malta

    mailing address: P O Box 535, Valletta

    telephone: [356] 23-59-60

    FAX: [356] 24-32-29

Man, Isle of

Capital: Douglas   longitude: 4.40 W   latitude: 54.20 N

Government: British crown dependency

    Flag: red with the Three Legs of Man emblem (Trinacria), in the center; the three legs are joined at the thigh and bent at the knee; in order to have the toes pointing clockwise on both sides of the flag, a two sided emblem was used

Geography

    Location: Western Europe, island in the Irish Sea, between Great Britain and Ireland

    Total Area: 588 sq km (227 sq mi) nearly 3.5 time the size of Washington, DC

Boundaries: no land boundaries

Climate: cool summers and mild winters; humid; overcast about half the time

Terrain: hills in north and south bisected by central valley

Natural resources: lead, iron ore

Natural hazards: NA

Note: one small islet, the Calf of Man, lies to the southwest, and is a bird sanctuary

People

Population: 72, 800 (July 1995 est.)

Life expectancy at birth: total population 76.53 years

Nationality: Manxman, Manxwoman

Ethnic division: Manx (Norse-Celtic descent), Briton

Religions: Anglican, Roman Catholic, Methodist, Baptist, Presbyterian, Society of Friends

Languages: English, Manx Gaelic

Literacy: NA

Economy

Imports: timber, fertilizer, fish

Exports: tweeds, herring, processed shellfish, beef, lamb

Industries: financial services, light manufacturing, tourism

Agriculture: cereals and vegetables; cattle, sheep, pigs, poultry

Currency: 1 Manx pound (#M) = 100 pence

Manx pounds per US1$ - 0.63

Transportation

Railroads: 60 km

Roads: 640 km total

Ports: Castletown, Douglas, Peel, Ramsey

Airports: 1 paved. Ronaldsway Airport at Ballasalla

The Press: newspapers   **The Manx Independent:** 20 Duke St, Douglas telephone (624) 62-32-05 fax (624) 67-33-13 Tuesday and Friday circ. 20,000

Peel City Guardian: 14 Douglas St. Peel telephone (624) 84-38-82 fortnightly on Saturday circ. 6,000

Tourism: NA

Department of Tourism: Sea Terminal Buildings, Douglas telephone (642) 68-68-01 fax (624) 68-68-00

Diplomatic representation in US: none (British crown dependency)

US Diplomatic representation: none (British crown dependency)

Marshall Islands

Capital: Majuro   longitude: 171.02 W   latitude: 7.40 N

Government: constitutional government in free association with the US: the Compact of Free Association entered into force 21 October 1986

Flag: blue with two stripes radiating from the lower hoist-side corner - orange (top) and white; there is a white star with four large rays and 20 small rays on the hoist side above the two stripes

Geography

Location: Oceania, group of atolls and reefs in the North Pacific Ocean, about one-half of the way from Hawaii to Papua New Guinea

Total Area: 181.3 sq km (70 sq mi) slightly larger than Washington, DC

Boundaries: no land boundaries

Climate: wet season May to November, hot and humid; islands border typhoon belt

Terrain: low coral limestone and sand islands

Natural resources: phosphate deposits, marine products, deep seabed minerals

Natural hazards: occasional typhoons

Note: two archipelagic island chains of 30 atolls and 1,152 islands; Bikini and Enewetak are former US nuclear test sites; Kwajalein, the famous World War II battleground, is now used as a US missile test range

People

Population: 56,200 (July 1995 est.)

Life expectancy at birth: total population 63.49 years

Nationality: Marshallese

Ethnic division: Micronesian

Religions: Christian (mostly Protestant)

Languages: English (universally spoken and is the official language), two major Marshallese dialects from the Malayo-Polynesian family, Japanese

Literacy: total population 93%

Economy

Imports: foodstuffs, machinery and equipment, beverages and tobacco, fuels

Exports: coconut oil, fish, live animals, trichus shells

Industries: copra, fish, tourism, craft items from shell, wood, and pearls; offshore banking (embryonic)

Agriculture: coconuts, cacao (seed), taro, breadfruit, fruits, pigs, chickens

Currency: 1 United States dollar = 100 cents

US currency is used

Transportation

Railroads: none

Roads: NA

Ports: Majuro

Airports: 16 total paved and unpaved. The main airport is at Majuro

Tourism: Majuro

Tourist Authority: POB 1727, Majuro
telephone (625) 32-18   fax (625) 32-06

Diplomatic representation in US:

chief of mission: Ambassador Wilfred I. Kendall

chancery: 2433 Massachusetts Avenue NW, Washington, DC 20008

telephone: [1] (202) 234-5414

FAX: [1] (202) 232-3236

US Diplomatic representation:

chief of mission: Ambassador David C. Fields

embassy: NA, Majuro

mailing address: P O Box 1379, Majuro,

Republic of the Marshall Islands 96960-1379

telephone: [692] 247-4011

FAX: [692] 247-4012

Martinque

Capital: Fort-de-France   longitude: 61.05 W   latitude: 14.36 N
elevation: 13 ft
Government: overseas department of France
　　Flag: the flag of France is used
Geography
　　Location: Caribbean, island in the Caribbean Sea, north of Trinidad and
　　Tobago
　　Total Area: 1,100 sq km (424.7 sq mi) slightly more than six time the size
　　of Washington, DC
　　Boundaries: no land boundaries
　　Climate: tropical; moderated by trade winds; rainy season (June to October)
　　Temperature (F): High/Low Jan. 83/69, Apr. 86/71, July 86/74, Oct. 87/73
　　Average annual precipitation: 80.4 inches
　　Terrain: mountainous with indented coastline; dormant volcano
　　Highest point is Mont Pelee 1,397 m (4,583 ft)
　　Natural resources: coastal scenery and beaches, cultivable land
　　Natural hazards: hurricanes, flooding, and volcanic activity (an average of
　　one major natural disaster every five years)
People
　　Population: 394,800 (July 1995 est.)
　　Life expectancy at birth: total population 78.67 years
　　Nationality: Martiniquais
　　Ethnic division: African and African-Caucasian-Indian mixture 90%,
　　Caucasian 5%, East Indian, Lebanese, Chinese less than 5%
　　Religions: Roman Catholic 95%, Hindu and pagan African 5%
　　Languages: French, Creole patois
　　Literacy: total population 93%

Economy

Imports: petroleum products, crude oil, foodstuffs, construction materials, vehicles, clothing and other consumer goods

Exports: refined petroleum products, bananas, rum, pineapples

Industries: construction, rum, cement, oil refining, sugar, tourism

Agriculture: fishing, forestry; principal crops - pineapples, avocados, bananas, flowers, vegetables, sugarcane for rum; dependent on imported food, particularly meat and vegetables

Currency: 1 French franc (F) = 100 centimes

French francs per US1$ - 5.29

Transportation

Railroads: none

Roads: 1,680 km total paved and unpaved

Ports: Fort-de-France, La Trinite

Airports: 2 total; 1 unpaved. Martinique's international airport is about 6 km from Fort-de-France

Tourism: The main attractions are mountain and coastal scenery , beaches and the historic town of Fort-de-France

Agence Regionale pour le Developpement du Tourisme en Martinique
Anse Gouraud, 97233 Schoelcher   telephone 61-61-77   fax 61-22-72

Diplomatic representation in US: none (overseas department of France)
US Diplomatic representation: none (overseas department of France)

Mauritania

Capital: Nouakchott   longitude: 15.58 W   latitude: 18.09 N
elevation: 69 ft
Government: republic

Flag: green with a yellow five-pointed star above a yellow, horizontal crescent; the closed side of the crescent is down; the crescent, star, and color green are traditional symbols of Islam

Geography

Location: Northern Africa, bordering the North Atlantic Ocean, between Senegal and Western Sahara

Total Area: 1,030,700 sq km (397,953 sq mi) slightly larger than the size of New Mexico

Boundaries: Algeria, Mali, Senegal Western Sahara

Climate: desert; constantly hot, dry, dusty

Temperature (F): High/Low Jan. 85/57, Apr. 90/64, July 89/74, Oct. 91/71

Average annual precipitation: 6.2 inches

Terrain: mostly barren, flat plains of the Sahara; some central hills

Highest point 906 m (2,972 ft)

Natural resources: iron ore, gypsum, fish, copper, phosphate

Natural hazards: hot, dry, dust/sand-laden sirocco wind blows primarily in March and April; periodic droughts

People

Population: 2,263,300 (July 1995 est.)

Life expectancy at birth: total population 48.54 years

Nationality: Mauritanina

Ethnic division: mixed Maur/black 40%, Maur 30%, Black 30%

Religions: Muslim 100%

Languages: Hasaniya Arabic (official), Pular, Soninke, Wolof (official)

Literacy: total population 35%

Economy

Imports: foodstuffs, consumer goods, petroleum products, capital goods

Exports: iron ore, fish and fish products

Industries: fish processing, mining of iron ore and gypsum

Agriculture: largely subsistence farming and nomadic cattle and sheep herding except in Senegal river valley; crops - dates, millet, sorghum, root crops; fish and fish products number-one export; large food deficit in years of drought

Currency: 1 ouguiya (UM) = 5 khoums
ouguiya per US1$ - 125.91

Transportation

Railroads: 690 km (single track) note: owned and operated by government mining company

Roads: 7,525 km total paved and unpaved

Ports: Bogue, Kaedi, Nouadhibou, Nouakchott, Rosso

Airports: 28 total paved and unpaved. There are international airports at Nouakchott and Nouadhibou

The Press: newspapers   **Ach-Chaab:** BP 371, Nouakchott
telephone 53-523   daily
Journal Officiel: Ministry of Justice, BP 350, Nouakchott
fortnightly

Tourism: French colonial town of St. Louis, Sahara Desert
Direction du Tourisme: BP 246, Nouakchott
telephone 53-337

Diplomatic representation in US:
chief of mission: Ambassador Ismail Ould Iyahi
chancery: 2129 Leroy Place NW, Washington, Dc 20008
telephone: [1] (202) 232-5700
US Diplomatic representation:
chief of mission: Ambassador Dorothy Meyers Sampas
embassy: NA, Nouakchott
mailing address: B P 222, Nouakchott
telephone: [222] (2) 52-660, 52-663
FAX: [222] (2) 51-592

Mauritius

Capital: Port Louis   longitude: 57.30 E   latitude: 20.10 S
elevation: 181 ft
Government: parliamentary democracy
Flag: four equal horizontal bands of red (top), blue, yellow, and green
Geography
Location: Southern Africa, island in the Indian Ocean, east of Madagascar
294

Total Area: 1,860 sq km (718 sq mi) slightly less than 10.5 times the size of Washington, DC

Boundaries: no land boundaries

Climate: tropical; modified by southeast trade winds; warm, dry winters (May to November); hot, wet, humid summer (November to May)

Temperature (F): High/Low Jan. 86/73, Apr. 82/72, July 75/62, Oct. 80/64

Average annual precipitation: 50.6 inches

Terrain: small coastal plain rising to discontinuous mountains encircling central plateau

Highest point 826 m (2,711 ft)

Natural resources: arable land, fish

Natural hazards: cyclones (November to April); almost completely surrounded by reefs that pose a maritime hazard

People

Population: 1,127,200 (July 1995 est.)

Life expectancy at birth: total population 70.84 years

Nationality: Mauritian

Ethnic division: Indo-Mauritian 68%, Creole 27%, Sino-Mauritian 3%, Franco-Mauritian 2%

Religions: Hindu 52%, Christian 28.3%, (Roman Catholic 26%, Protestant 2.3%), Muslim 16.6%, other 3.1%

Languages: English (official), Creole, French, Hindi, Urdu, Hakka, Bojoori

Literacy: total population 80%

Economy

Imports: manufactured goods, capital equipment, foodstuffs, petroleum products, chemicals

Exports: textiles, sugar, light manufactures

Industries: food processing (largely sugar milling), textiles, wearing apparel, chemicals, metal products, transport equipment, non electrical machinery, tourism

Agriculture: about 90% of cultivated land is sugarcane; other products - tea, corn, potatoes, bananas, pulses, cattle, goats, fish; net food importer, especially rice and fish

Currency: 1 Mauritian rupee (MauRs) = 100 cents

Mauritian rupees per US1$ - 17.75

Transportation

Railroads: none

Roads: 1,800 total paved and unpaved

Ports: Port Louis

Airports: 5 total paved and unpaved. Ramgoolam International Airport is located at Plaisance, about 4 km from Mahebourg

The Press: daily newspapers

> **Global News:** Residence des 5 Palmiers, 198 Royal Road, Beau-Bassin
> telephone 454-3353   fax 454-3420
> English and French   circ. 30,000

> **The Sun:** 31 Edith Cavell Street, Port Louis
> telephone 208-9516 fax 208-9517
> English and French   circ. 23,000

Tourism: Tourist are attracted by the climate, beautiful beaches and scenery, bird watching

> **Mauritius Government Tourist Office:**
> Emmanuel Anquetil Bldg.
> Sir Seewoosagur Ramgoolam St, Port Louis
> telephone 201-1703   fax 212-5142

Diplomatic representation in US:

chief of mission: Ambassador Anund Priyay Neewoor

chancery: Suite 441, 4301 Connecticut Avenue NW, Washington, DC 20008

telephone: [1] (202) 244-1491, 1492

FAX: [1] (202) 966-0983

US Diplomatic representation:

chief of mission: Ambassador Leslie M. Alexander

embassy: 4th Floor, Rogers House, John Kennedy Street, Port Louis

mailing address: use embassy street address

telephone: [230] 208-9763 through 9767

FAX: [230] 208-9534

Mayotte

Chissioi M'Zamboro

10 km

Administered by France, claimed by Comoros

MAMOUTZOU

Mayotte

Sada

Île Pamanzi

Bandélé

Mozambique Channel

Capital: Mamoutzou   longitude: 45.06 E   latitude: 12.70 S

Government: territorial collectivity of France

    Flag: the flag of France is used

Geography

    Location: Southern Africa, island in the Mozambique Channel, about one-half of the way from northern Madagascar to northern Mozambique

    Total Area: 375 sq km (145 sq mi) slightly more than twice the size of Washington, DC

    Boundaries: no land boundaries

    Climate: tropical; marine; hot, humid, rainy season during northeastern monsoon (November to May); dry season is cooler (May to November)

    Terrain: generally undulating with ancient volcanic peaks, deep ravines

    Natural resources: negligible

    Natural hazards: cyclones during rainy season

People

    Population: 97,200 (July 1995 est.)

    Life expectancy at birth: total population 58.27 years

    Nationality: Mahorais

    Ethnic division: NA

    Religions: Muslim 99%, Christian (mostly Roman Catholic)

    Languages: Mahorian (a Swahili dialect), French

    Literacy: NA

Economy

    Imports: building materials, transportation equipment, rice, clothing, flour

    Exports: ylang-ylang, vanilla

Industries: newly created lobster and shrimp industry

Agriculture: most important sector; provides all export earnings; crops - vanilla, ylang-ylang, coffee, copra; imports major share of food needs

Currency: 1 French franc (F) = 100 centimes

French francs per US1$ - 5.29

Transportation

Railroads: none

Roads: 42 km total paved and unpaved

Ports: Dzaoudzi

Airports: 1 commercial airstrip at Dzaoudzi

The Press: newspaper   **Le Journal de Mayotte:**

BP 181, Mamoudzou, 97000 Mayotte

telephone 61-16-95   fax 61-08-88   circ. 15,000

Tourism: beautiful natural tropical scenery.

Comite Territorial du Tourisme de Mayotte:

rue de la Pompe, BP 169, Mamoudzou, 97600 Mayotte

telephone 61-09-09   fax 61-03-46

Diplomatic representation in US: none (territorial collectivity of France)

US Diplomatic representation: none (territorial collectivity of France)

Mexico

Capital: Mexico City   longitude: 99.10 W   latitude: 19.25 N

elevation: 7,575 ft

Government: Federal Republic

Flag: three equal vertical bands of green (hoist side), white, and red; the coat of arms (an eagle perched on a cactus with a snake in its beak) is centered in the white band

Geography:

Location: Middle America, bordering the Caribbean Sea and the Gulf of Mexico, between Belize and the US and bordering the North Pacific Ocean, between Guatemala and the US. The United Mexican States is the largest country in Central America.

Total Area: 1,972,550 sq km (751,602 sq mi) slightly less than three time the size of Texas.

Boundaries: Belize and Guatemala

Climate: varies from tropical to desert. Coastal low lands are hot and wet.
Temperature (F): High/Low   Jan. 88/72, Apr. 90/73, July 90/77, Oct. 90/75
Average annual precipitation: 29.5 inches

Terrain: high, rugged mountains, low coastal plains, high plateaus, and desert.
Highest point is Citilaltepetl 5,747 m (18,855 ft)

Natural resources: petroleum, silver, copper, gold, lead, zinc, natural gas, timber

Natural hazards: tsunamis along the Pacific coast, destructive earthquakes in the center and south, and hurricanes on the Gulf and Caribbean coasts.

People

Population: 93,985,900 (July 1995 est.)

Life expectancy at birth: total population 73.43 years

Nationality: Mexican

Ethnic division: mestizo (Indian-Spanish) 60%, Amerindian 30%, Caucasian 9%

Religions: Roman Catholic 89%, Protestant 6%

Languages: Spanish and various Mayan dialects

Literacy: total population 88%

Economy

Imports: metal-working machines, steel mill products, agricultural machinery, electrical equipment, car parts for assembly, repair parts for motor vehicles, aircraft and aircraft parts

Exports: crude oil, oil products, coffee, silver, engines, motor vehicles, cotton, consumer electronics

Industries: food and beverages, tobacco, chemicals, iron and steel, petroleum, mining, textiles, clothing, motor vehicles, consumer durables, tourism

Agriculture: major food crops - corn, wheat, rice, beans; cash crops - cotton, coffee, fruit, tomatoes

Currency: 1 New Mexican Peso (Mex $) = 100 centavos   Mexican peso per
US1$ = 6.74 (average in March 1995)
Note: 1 new peso = 1,000 old pesos

Transportation:
    Railroads: total 24,500 km
    Roads: 242,300 km total paved and unpaved
    Ports: Acapulco, Altamira, Coatzacoalcos, Emsenada, La Paz,
    Lazaro Cardenas, Manazanillo, Mazatlan, Progreso, Salina Cruz, Tampico,
    Topolobampo, Tuxpan, Veracruz
    Airports: total paved and unpaved 2,055
The Press: El Dia: Avda Insurgentes Norte 1210 Col. Capukiklan,
        07370 Mexico, DF. telephone (5) 546-0456   fax (5) 537-6629
        Morning ; circ 75,000
        La Prensa: Basilio Badillo 40, 06030 Mexico, DF.
            telephone (5) 512-0799   Morning   circ 300,000

Tourism: Relics of the Mayan and Aztec civilization, great scenery from the
    coast to the Sierra Madre mountains, Zacatecas, Pyramids of Teotihuacan,
    Floating Gardens of Xochimilco, Copper Canyon
        Secretaria de Turismo:
        Avda Presidente Masarik 172, 3, 11587 Mexico, DF.
        telephone (5) 250-8604; fax (5) 254-0014

Diplomatic representation in US:
    chief of mission: Ambassador Jesus Silvia Herzog Flores
    chancery: 1991 Pennsylvania Avenue NW, Washington, DC 20006
    telephone: (202) 728-1600
US Diplomatic representation:
    chief of mission: Ambassador James R Jones
    embassy: Paseo de la Reforma 305, Colonia Cuauhtemoc,
    06500 Mexico Distrito Federal
    mailing address: P.O. Box 3087, Laredo, Tx 78044-3087
    telephone: [52] (5) 211-0042
    FAX: [52] (5) 511-9980, 208-3373

The Federated States of Micronesia

Yap
Islands
Hall
Islands KOLONIA
Truk
Islands .
·Pohnpei
Kosrae

Kapingamarangi

North Pacific Ocean

Capital: Kolonia (on the island of Pohnpei)
longitude: 140.00 E   latitude: 15.00 N
Government: constitutional government in free association with the US
Flag: light blue with four white five-pointed stars centered; the stars are
arranged in a diamond pattern

Geography

Location: Oceania, island group in the North Pacific Ocean, about
three-quarters of the way from Hawaii to Indonesia
Total Area: 702 sq km (271 sq mi) slightly less than four times the size of
Washington, DC.   Note: includes Pohnpei (Ponape), Truk (Chuuk), Yap,
and Kosrae
Boundaries: no land boundaries
Climate: tropical; heavy year-round rainfall, especially in the eastern islands;
located on southern edge of the typhoon belt with occasional severe damage
Terrain: island vary geologically from high mountainous islands to low,
coral atolls; volcanic outcroppings on Pohnpei, Kosrae, and Truk
Natural resources: forests, marine products, deep-seabed mineral
Natural hazards: typhoons (June to December)

People

Population: 123,000 (July 1995 est.)
Life expectancy at birth: total population 67.81 years
Nationality: Micronesian
Ethnic division: nine ethnic Micronesian and Polynesian groups
Religions: Roman Catholic 50%, Protestant 47%
Languages: English (official and common language)
Literacy: total population 89%

Economy

Imports: food, manufactured goods, machinery and equipment, beverages
Exports: fish, copra, bananas, black pepper

Industries: tourism, construction, fish processing, craft items from shell, wood, and pearls

Agriculture: mainly a subsistence economy; black pepper; tropical fruits and vegetables, coconuts, cassava, sweet potatoes, pigs, chickens

Currency: US Currency used   1 United States dollar (US$) = 100 cents

Transportation

    Railroads: none

    Roads: 226 km total paved and unpaved

    Ports: Colonia (Yap), Kolonia (Pohnpei), Lele, Moen

    Airports: 6 total all paved. There are international airports on Colonia, Kolonia, Chuuk and Kosrae

The Press: **Chuuk News Chronicle:** POB 244, Wenn, Chuuk, Eastern Caroline Islands. FM 96942

    The National Union: POB 490, Kolonia, Pohnpei, Eastern Caroline Islands, FM 96941

    telephone 32-05-48   circ. 5,000   2 a month

Tourism: Excellent conditions for scuba-diving, battle sites and relics of World War II many under water and the ancient ruined city of Nan Madol on Pohnpei.

Diplomatic representation in US:

    chief of mission: Ambassador Jesse B. Marehalau

    chancery: 1725 N Street NW, Washington, DC 20036

    telephone: [1] (202) 223-4383

    FAX: [1] (202) 223-4391

US Diplomatic representation:

    chief of mission: Ambassador March Fong Eu

    embassy: address NA, Kolonia

    mailing address: P. O. Box 1286, Pohnpei, Federated States of Micronesia 96941

    telephone: [691] 320-2187

    FAX: [691] 320-2186

Midway Islands

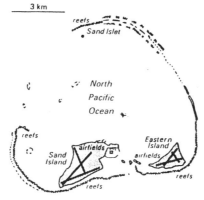

Capital: none; administered from Washington, DC

elevation: 29 ft   longitude: 177.23 W   latitude: 28.13 N

Government: unincorporated territory of the US administered by the US Navy, under Naval Facilities Engineering Command, Pacific Division.

Flag: the US flag is used

Geography

Location: Oceania, atoll in the North Pacific Ocean, about one-third of the way from Honolulu to Tokyo

Total Area: 5.2 sq km (2 sq mi) about 9 times the size of The Mall in Washington, DC

Boundaries: no land boundaries

Climate: tropical. but moderated by prevailing easterly winds

Temperature (F): High/Low Jan. 87/75, Apr. 88/74, July 88/74, Oct. 88/75

Average annual precipitation: 40.7 inches

Terrain: low, nearly level

Natural resources: fish, wildlife

Natural hazards: NA

People

Population: no indigenous inhabitants; note - there are 453 US military personnel (July 1995 est.)

Economy

All food and manufactured goods must be imported

Transportation

Railroads: none

Roads: 32 km

Ports: Sand Island

Airports: 3 total paved and unpaved

Moldova

Capital: Chisinau   longitude: 29.75 W   latitude: 47.20 N

Government: republic

Flag: same color scheme as Romania - 3 equal vertical bands of blue (hoist side), yellow, and red; emblem in center of flag is of a Roman eagle of gold outlined in black with a red beak and talons carrying a yellow cross in its beak and a green olive branch in its right talons and a yellow scepter in its left talons; on its breast is a shield divided horizontally red over blue with a stylized ox head, star, rose, and crescent all in black-outlined yellow

Geography

Location: Eastern Europe, northeast of Romania

Total Area: 33,700 sq km (13,012 sq mi) slightly more than twice the size of Hawaii

Boundaries: Romania, Ukraine

Climate: moderate winters, warm summers

Temperature: average winter (F) 25, Average summer north 67 (F)
                                          "   "   south 72 (F)

Average annual precipitation: 20 inches

Terrain: rolling steppe, gradual slope south to Black Sea

Highest point is Mount Balansi 429 m (1,407 ft)

Natural resources: lignite, phosphorites, gypsum

Natural hazards: NA

People

Population: 4,489,700 (July 1995 est.)

Life expectancy at birth: total population 68.22 years

Nationality: Moldovan

Ethnic division: Moldavian/Romanian 64.5%, Ukrainian 13.8%, Russian 13%, Gagauz 3.5%, Jewish 1.5%, Bulgarian 2%, other 1.7%

Religions: Eastern Orthodox 98.5%, Jewish 1.5%, Baptist

note: the large majority of churchgoers are ethnic Moldavian

Languages: Moldovan (official; virtually the same as the Romanian language), Russian, Gagauz (a Turkish dialect)

Literacy: total population 96%

Economy

Imports: oil. gas, coal, steel machinery, foodstuffs, automobiles, and other consumer durables

Exports: foodstuffs, wine, tobacco, textiles and footwear, machinery, chemicals

Industries: key products are canned food, agricultural machinery, foundry equipment, refrigerators and freezers, washing machines, hosiery, refined sugar, vegetable oil, shoes, textiles

Agriculture: products are vegetables, fruits, wine, grain, sugar beets, sunflower seed, meat, milk, tobacco

Currency: the leu (plural lei) was introduced in late 1993

lei per US1$ - 4.27

Transportation

Railroads: 1,150 km

Roads: 20,000 total paved and unpaved

Ports: none

Airports: 26 total paved and unpaved. The main airport is at Chisinau

The Press: newspapers   **Moldova Suverana:** 277012 Chisinau, St, Puskin 22 telephone (2) 23-35-38   fax (2) 23-35-01 5 a week circ. 100,000

Nezavisimaya Moldova: 277612 Chisinau St, Puskin telephone (2) 23-36-05   fax (2) 23-36-08 5 a week   circ. 62,000

Tourism: NA

Moldova-Tur: 277058 Chisinau, Stefan cel Mare 4 telephone (2) 26-66-79   fax (2) 26-25-86

Diplomatic representation in US:

chief of mission: Ambassador Nicolae Tau

chancery: Suites 329, 333, 1511 K Street NW, Washington, DC 20005

telephone: [1] (202) 783-3012

FAX: [1] (202) 783-3342

US Diplomatic representation:
chief of mission: Ambassador Mary C. Pendleton
embassy: Strada Alexei Mateevich #103, Chisinau
mailing address: use embassy street address
telephone: [373] (2) 23-37-72
FAX: [373] (2) 23-30-44

Monaco

Capital: Monaco   longitude: 7.23 E   latitude: 43.46 N   elevation: 180 ft
Government: constitutional monarchy
Flag: two equal horizontal bands of red (top) and white; similar to the flag of Indonesia which is longer and the flag of Poland which is white (top) and red
Geography
Location: Western Europe, bordering the Mediterranean Sea, on the southern coast of France, near the border with Italy
Total Area: 1.9 sq km (.73 sq mi) about three times the size of The Mall in Washington, DC
Boundaries: France
Climate: Mediterranean with mild, wet winters and hot, dry summers
Temperature (F): High/Low Jan. 54/47, Apr. 61/54, July 78/71, Oct. 68/61
Average annual precipitation: 31.4 inches
Terrain: hilly, rugged, rocky
Natural resources: none
Natural hazards: NA
People
Population: 31,600 (July 1995 est.)
Life expectancy at birth: total population 77.9 years
Nationality: Monacan or Monegasque
Ethnic division: French 47%, Monegasque 16%, Italian 16%, other 21%

Religions: Roman Catholic

Languages: French (official), English, Italian, Monegasque

Literacy: NA

Economy

Imports: full customs integration with France, which collects and rebates Monacan trade duties.

Exports: full customs integration with France, which collects and rebates Monacan trade duties

Industries: NA

Agriculture: none

Currency: 1 French franc (F) = 100 centimes

French francs per US1$ - 5.92

Transportation

Railroads: 1.7 km

Roads: none; city streets

Ports: Monaco

Airports: linked to airport in Nice, France, by helicopter service

The Press: newspapers   **Journal de Monaco:** BP 522, MC 98015

telephone 93-15-80-00   fax 93-15-82-17

Monaco Actualite: 2 rue du Gabia, MC 98000

telephone 92-05-75-36 fax 92-05-75-34 circ. 16,000

Tourism: Monte Carlo, Oceanographic Museum, Exotic Gardens, Monaco Grand Prix, beaches

Direction du Tourisme et des Congres:
2a blvd des Moulins, MC 98030
telephone 92-16-61-16   fax 92-16-60-00

Diplomatic representation in US:

honorary consulate general: Boston, Chicago, Los Angeles, New Orleans, New York, San Francisco, San Huan (Puerto Rico)

US Diplomatic representation: no mission in Monaco, but the US Consul General in Marseille, France, is accredited to Monaco

Mongolia

500 km

Capital: Ulaanbaatar   longitude: 106.52 E   latitude: 47.54 N
elevation: 4,347 ft

Government: republic

Flag: three equal, vertical bands of red (hoist side), blue, and red, centered on the hoist-side red band in yellow is the national emblem ("soyombo" - a columnar arrangement of abstract and geometric representation for fire, sun, moon, earth, water, and yin-yanh symbol)

Geography

Location: Northern Asia, north of China

Total Area: 1,565,000 sq km (604,247 sq mi) slightly larger than Alaska

Boundaries: China, Russia

Climate: desert; continental (large daily and seasonal temperature ranges)
Temperature (F): High/Low Jan. -2/-26, Apr. 44/17, July 71/51, Oct. 43/18
Average annual precipitation: 8.2 inches

Terrain: vast semidesert and desert plains; mountains in west and southwest; Gobi Desert in southeast
Highest point Tabun Bogdo 4,355 m (14,288 ft)

Natural resources: oil, coal, copper, molybdenum, tungsten, phosphates, tin, nickel, zinc, wolfram, fluorspar, gold

Natural hazards: duststorms can occur in the spring

People

Population: 2,493,700 (July 1995 est.)

Life expectancy at birth: total population 66.54 years

Nationality: Mongolian

Ethnic division: Mongol 90%, Kazakh 4%, Chinese 5%, Russian 2%, other 2%

Religions: predominantly Tibetan Buddhist, Mulimm 4%

308

Languages: Khalkha Mongol 90%, Turkic, Russian, Chinese
Literacy: NA
Economy
Imports: machinery and equipment, fuels, food products, industrial consumer goods, chemicals, building materials, sugar, tea
Exports: copper, livestock, animal products, cashmere, wool, hides, fluorspar, other nonferrous metals
Industries: copper, processing of animal products, building materials, food and beverages, mining (particularly coal)
Agriculture: livestock raising predominates (primarily sheep and goats, but also cattle, camels, and horses); crops - wheat, barley, potatoes, forage
Currency: 1 tughrik (Tug) = 100 mongos
tughriks per US1$ - 415.34
Transportation
Railroads: 1,750 km
Roads: 46,700 km total paved and unpaved
Ports: none
Airports: 34 total paved and unpaved. Internal services to most provincial centers.

The Press: newspapers **Ardyn Erh:** Dzasgiyn Gadzryn Ordon, Ulan Bator 12 telephone 32-86-29 circ. 76,000
Ulaanbaatar: Baga Toyrog, Ulan Bator 11
telephone 32-12-94 circ. 32,000

Tourism: The country's main attractions are historical relics, wildlife and scenery, Gobi Desert

Mongolian Foreign Tourism Company:
Chingis Haany Orgon Choloo, Ulan Bator 210543
telephone 32-84-28 fax 32-02-46

Diplomatic representation in US:
chief of mission: Ambassador Luvsandorj Dawaagiw
chancery: 2833 M Street NW, Washington, DC 20007
telephone: [1] (202) 333-7117
FAX: [1] (202) 298-9227

chief of mission: Ambassador Donald C. Johnson

embassy: NA, Ulaanbaatar

mailing address: c/o American Embassy Beijing, Micro Region 11, Big Ring Road; PSC 461, Box 300, FPO AP 96521-0002

telephone: [976] (1) 32-90-95, 32-96-06

FAX: [976] (1) 32-07-76

Montserrat

Capital: Plymouth   longitude: 62.13 W   latitude: 16.43 N   elevation: 130 ft

Government: dependent territory of UK

Flag: blue with the flag of the UK in the upper hoist-side quadrant and the Montserratain coat of arms centered in the outer half of the flag; the coat of arms features a woman standing beside a yellow harp with her arm around a black cross

Geography

Location: Caribbean, island in the Caribbean Sea, southeast of Puerto Rico

Total Area: 100 sq km (38.6 sq mi) about 0.6 times the size of Washington, DC

Boundaries: no land boundaries

Climate: tropical; little daily or seasonal temperature variation

Temperature (F): High/Low Jan. 82/70, Apr. 86/72, July 87/75, Oct. 89/74

Average annual precipitation: 64.5 inches

Terrain: volcanic islands, mostly mountainous, with small coastal lowland

Natural resources: negligible

Natural hazards: severe hurricanes (June to November); volcanic eruptions (there are seven active volcanoes on the island)

People

Population: 12,900 (July 1995 est.)

Life expectancy at birth: total population 75.69 years

Nationality: Montserratian

Ethnic division: black, Europeans

Religions: Anglican, Methodist, Roman Catholic, Pentecostal, Seventh-Day Adventist, other Christian denominations

Languages: English

Literacy: total population 97%

Economy

Imports: machinery and transport equipment, foodstuffs, manufactured goods, fuels, lubricants, and related materials

Exports: electronic parts, plastic bags, apparel, hot peppers, live plants, cattle

Industries: tourism; light manufacturing - rum, textiles, electronic appliances

Agriculture: small-scale farming; food crops - tomatoes, onions. peppers; not self-sufficient in food, especially livestock products

Currency: 1 EC dollar (EC$) = 100 cents

East Caribbean dollars per US1$ - 2.70 (fixed rate since 1976)

Transportation

Railroads: none

Roads: 280 km paved and unpaved

Ports: Plymouth

Airports: 1 This airport is located about 12 km from Plymouth

The Press: newspapers   weekly on Friday

The Montserrat Reporter: Parliament St, Plymouth telephone 491-3600 fax 491-7777 circ. 3,000

The Montserrat Times: POB 28, Plymouth telephone 491-2501   fax 491-6069 circ. 1,200

Tourism: Volcanic activity on the British Island dependency of Montserrat has recently increased and is potentially dangerous. Lush scenery with an abundance of flora and fauna.

Montserrat Tourist Board: Church Road, POB 7, Plymouth telephone 491-2230   fax 491-7430

Diplomatic representation in US: none (dependent territory of the UK)

US Diplomatic representation: none (dependent territory of the UK)

Morocco

Capital: Rabat   longitude: 6.51 W   latitude: 34.02 N   elevation: 213 ft
Government: constitutional monarchy
Flag: red with green pentacle (five-pointed, linear star) known as Solomon's seal in the center of the flag; green is the traditional color of Islam

Geography

Location: Northern Africa, bordering the North Atlantic Ocean and the Mediterranean Sea, between Algeria and Western Sahara
Total Area: 446,550 sq km (172,413 sq mi) slightly larger than California
Boundaries: Algeria, Western Sahara
Climate: Mediterranean, becoming more extreme in the interior
Temperature (F): High/Low Jan. 63/46, Apr. 71/52, July 82/63, Oct. 77/58
Average annual precipitation: 19.8 inches
Terrain: northern coast and interior are mountainous with large areas of bordering plateaus, intermontane valleys, and rich coastal plains
Highest point Mt. Toubkal 4,165 m (13,665 ft)
Natural resources: phosphates, iron ore, manganese, lead, zinc, fish, salt
Natural hazards: northern mountains geologically unstable and subject to earthquakes; periodic droughts

People

Population: 29,169,000 (July 1995 est.)
Life expectancy at birth: total population 68.98 years
Nationality: Moroccan
Ethnic division: Arab-Berber 99.1%, other 0.7%, Jewish 0.2%
Religions: Muslim 98.7%, Christian 1.1%, Jewish 0.2%
Languages: Arabic (official), Berber dialects, French often the languages of business, government, and diplomacy
Literacy: total population 50%

Economy

Imports: capital goods, semiprocessed goods, raw materials, fuel and lubricants, food and beverages, consumer goods

Exports: food and beverages, semiprocessed goods, consumer goods, phosphates

Industries: phosphate rock mining and processing, food processing, leather goods, textiles, construction, tourism

Agriculture: not self-sufficient in food; cereal farming and livestock raising predominate; barley, wheat, citrus fruit, wine, vegetables and olives

Currency: 1 Moroccan dirhams (DH) = 100 centimes

Moroccan dirhams per US1$ - 2.89

Transportation

Railroads: 1,893 km

Roads: 59,474 km total paved and unpaved

Ports: Agadir, Al Jadida, Casablanca, El Jorf Lasfar, Kenitra, Mohammedia, Nador, Rabat, Safi, Tangier; also Spanish-controlled Ceuta and Melilla

Airports: 74 total paved and unpaved. The main international airports are at Casablanca, Rabat, Tangier, Marrakesh, Agadir, Oujda, Al-Hocima abd Fez

The Press: daily newspapers   **Maroc Soir:** 34 rue Muhammad Smiha, Casablanca   circ. 50,000

telephone (2) 26-88-60   fax (2) 26-29-69

Le Matin du Sahara: 88 blvd Muhammad V, Casablanca

telephone (2) 26-88-60 fax (2) 26-29-69 circ. 100,000

Tourism: tourist attractions are the popular resorts on the Atlantic and Mediterranean coasts. Casablanca

Office National Marocain du Tourisme:

31 angle ave al-Abtal and rue Oved Fas, Agdal, Rabat

telephone (7) 77-51-71   fax (7) 77-74-37

Diplomatic representation in US:

chief of mission: Ambassador Mohamed Benaissa

chancery: 1601 21st Street NW, Washington, DC 20009

telephone: [1] (202) 462-7979 through 7982

FAX: [1] (202) 265-0161

US Diplomatic representation:
chief of mission: Ambassador Marc C. Ginsberg
embassy: 2 Avenue de Marrakech, Rabat
mailing address: PSC 74, Box 003, APO AE 09718
telephone: [212] (7) 76-22-65
FAX: [212] (7) 76-56-61

Mozambique

Capital: Maputo   longitude: 32.35 E   latitude: 25.58 S elevation: 194 ft
Government: republic
Flag: three equal horizontal bands of green (top), black, and yellow with a red isosceles triangle based on the hoist side; the black band is edged in white; centered in the triangle is a yellow five-pointed star bearing a crossed rifle and hoe in black superimposed on an open white book

Geography
Location: Southern Africa, bordering the Mozambique Channel, between South Africa and Tanzania
Total Area: 801,590 sq km (309,494 sq mi) slightly less than twice the size of California
Boundaries: Malawi, South Africa, Swaziland, Tanzania, Zambia, Zimbabwe
Climate: tropical to subtropical
Temperature (F): High/Low Jan. 86/71, Apr. 83/66, July 76/55, Oct. 83/64
Average annual precipitation: 29.9 inches
Terrain: mostly coastal lowlands, uplands in center, high plateaus in northwest, mountains in west
Highest point is Mt. Binga 2,436 m   (7,992 ft)
Natural resources: coal, titanium

314

Natural hazards: severe droughts and floods occur in central and southern provinces; devastating cyclones

People

Population: 18,115,600 (July 1995 est.)

Life expectancy at birth: total population 48.95 years

Nationality: Mozambican

Ethnic division: indigenous tribal groups, Europeans about 10,000, Euro-Africans 35,000, Indians 15,000

Religions: indigenous beliefs 60%, Christian 30%, Muslim 10%

Languages: Portuguese (official), indigenous dialects

Literacy: total population 33%

Economy

Imports: food, clothing, farm equipment, petroleum

Exports: shrimp, cashews, cotton, sugar, copra, citrus

Industries: food, beverages, chemicals (fertilizer, soap, paints), petroleum products, textiles, nonmetallic mineral products (cement, glass, asbestos), tobacco

Agriculture: cash crops - cotton, cashews nuts, sugarcane, tea, shrimp; other crops - cassava, corn, rice, tropical fruits; not self-sufficient in food

Currency: 1 metical (Mt) = 100 centavos
meticals per US1$ - 5,220.63

Transportation

Railroads: 3,288 km

Roads: 26,498 km total paved and unpaved

Ports: Beira, Inhambane, Maputo, Nacala, Pemba

Airports: 192 total paved and unpaved. There are three international airports, the main one is at Beira

The Press: daily newspapers

Diario de Mocambique:
Rau D. Joao de Mascarenhas, CP 81, Beira   circ. 16,000
telephone 32-25-01

Noticias: Rau Joaquim Lapa, CP 327, Maputo
telephone 42-01-19   circ. 34,000

Tourism: Maputo, Inhaca Island, beaches

Empresa Nacional de Turismo:
Avda 25 de Setembro 1211, CP 614, Maputo
telephone 25-011

Diplomatic representation in US:

chief of mission: Ambassador Hipolito Pereira Zozimo Patricio
chancery: Suite 570, 1990 M Street NW, Washington, DC 20036
telephone: [1] (202) 293-7146
FAX: [1] (202) 835-0245

US Diplomatic representation:

chief of mission: Ambassador Dennis Coleman Jett
embassy: Avenida Kenneth Kuanda, 193 Maputo
mailing address: P O Box 783, Maputo
telephone: [258] (1) 49-27-97
FAX: [258] (1) 49-01-14

Capital: Windhoek   longitude: 17.06   latitude: 22.34 S
elevation: 5,669 ft

Government: republic

Flag: a large blue triangle with a yellow sunburst fills the upper left section, and an equal green triangle (solid) fills the lower right section; the triangles are separated by a red stripe that is contrasted by two narrow white-edge borders

Geography

Location: Southern Africa, bordering the South Atlantic Ocean, between Angola and South Africa

Total Area: 825,418 sq km (318,694 sq mi) slightly more than half the size of Alaska

Boundaries: Angola, Botswana, South Africa, Zambia

Climate: desert; hot, dry; rainfall sparse and erratic

Temperature (F): High/Low Jan. 85/63, Apr. 77/55, July 68/43, Oct. 84/59

Average annual precipitation: 14.2 inches

316

Terrain: mostly high plateau; Nanib Desert along coast; Kalahari Desert in east

Highest point Brandberg 2,606 m (8,550 ft)

Natural resources: diamonds, copper, uranium, gold, lead, tin, lithium, cadmium, zinc, salt, vanadium, natural gas, fish; suspected deposits of oil, natural gas, coal, iron ore

Natural hazards: prolonged periods of drought

People

Population: 1,652,000 (July 1995 est.)

Life expectancy at birth: total population 62.1 years

Nationality: Namibian

Ethnic division: black 86%, white 6.6%, mixed 7.4%

Note: about 50% of the population belong to the Ovambo tribe and 9% to the Kavangos tribe; other ethnic groups include (with approximate share of total population): Herero 7%, Damara 7%, Nama 5%, Caprivian 4%, Bushmen 3%, Baster 2%, Tswana 0.5%

Religions: 80%-90% Christian (50% Lutheran; at least 30% other Christian denominations)

Languages: English 7% (official), Afrikaans common language of most of the population and about 60% of the white population, German 32%, indigenous languages: Oshivambo, Herero, Nama

Literacy: total population 38%

Economy

Alluvial diamond deposits are among the richest in the world, making Nambia a primary source for gem-quality diamonds.

Imports: foodstuffs, petroleum products and fuel, machinery and equipment

Exports: diamonds, copper, gold, zinc, lead, uranium, cattle, processed fish, karakul skins

Industries: meat packing, fish processing, dairy products, mining (copper, lead, zinc, diamonds, uranium)

Agriculture: livestock raising major source of cash income; crops - millet, sorghum, peanuts; fish

Currency: 1 South African rand (R) = 100 cents

South African rand per US1$ - 3.53

Transportation

Railroads: 2,341 km

Roads: 54,500 km total paved and unpaved

Ports: Luderitz, Walvis Bay

Airports: 135 total paved and unpaved. The international airport is at Windhoek

The Press: daily newspapers

> **The Nambian:** POB 61208, Windhoek
> telephone (61) 36-970 fax (61) 33-980
> Afrikaans, English circ. 15,000
> **The Times of Namibia:** POB 1794, Windhoek
> telephone (61) 22-58-22 fax (61) 22-31-10
> English circ. 10,300

Tourism: Principal tourist attractions are game parks and nature reserves.

> **Namibia Tourism:** Private Bag 13346, Windhoek
> telephone (61) 284-9111 fax (61) 221-930

Diplomatic representation in US:

chief of mission: Ambassador Tuliameni Kalomoh
chancery: 1605 New Hampshire Avenue NW, Washington, DC 20009
telephone: [1] (202) 986-0540
FAX: [1] (202) 986-0443

US Diplomatic representation:

chief of mission: Ambassador Marshall F. McCallie
embassy: Ausplan Building, 14 Lossen St., Windhoek
mailing address: Private Bag 12029 Ausspannplatz, Windhoek
telephone: [264] (61) 22-16-01
FAX: [264] (61) 22-97-92

Nauru

Capital: no official capital; government offices in Yaren District
elevation: 87 ft   longitude: 166.55 E   latitude: 0.32 S

Government: republic

    Flag: blue with a narrow, horizontal, yellow stripe across the center and a large white 12-pointed star below the stripe on the hoist side; the star indicates the country's location in relation to the Equator (the yellow stripe) and the 12 points symbolize the 12 original tribes of Nauru

Geography

    Location: Oceania, island in the South Pacific Ocean, south of the Marshall Islands

    Total Area: 21 sq km (8.1 sq mi) about one-tenth the size of Washington, DC

    Boundaries: no land boundaries

    Climate: tropical; monsoonal; rainy season (November to February)

    Temperature (F): High/Low Jan. 88/74, Apr. 90/75, July 89/74, Oct. 90/74

    Average annual rainfall: 75.1 inches

    Terrain: sandy beaches rises to fertile ring around coral reefs with phosphate plateau in center

    Natural resources: phosphates

    Natural hazards: periodic droughts

    Note: Nauru is one of the three great phosphate rock islands in the Pacific Ocean - the others are Banaba (Ocean Island) in Kiribati and Makatea in French Polynesia; only 53 km south of equator

People

    Population: 10,200 (July 1995 est.)

    Life expectancy at birth: total population 66.68 years

    Nationality: Nauruan

    Ethnic division: Nauruan 58%, other Pacific Islanders 26%, Chinese 8%, European 8%

    Religions: Christian (two-thirds Protestant, one-third Roman Catholic)

    Languages: Nauruan (official; a distinct Pacific Island language), English is widely understood, spoken, and used for most government and commercial purposes

    Literacy: NA

Economy

    Imports: food, fuel, manufactures, building materials, machinery

    Exports: phosphates

Industries: phosphate mining, financial services, coconut products

Agriculture: coconuts; other agricultural activity negligible; almost completely dependent on imports for food and water

Currency: 1 Australian dollar ($A) = 100 cents

Australian dollars per US1$ - 1.30

Transportation

    Railroads: 3.9 km; note - used to haul phosphates from the center of the island to processing facilities on the southwest coast

    Roads: 27 km total paved and unpaved

    Ports: Nauru

    Airports: 1 international airport at Yaren

The Press: newspapers   **Bulletin:** Nauru; weekly; Nauruan and English   circ. 800

        Central Star News: Nauru   fortnightly

Tourism: beaches, coral reefs

Diplomatic representation in US:

    Consulate: Agana (Guam)

US Diplomatic representation: the US Ambassador to Fiji is accredited to Nauru

Navassa Island

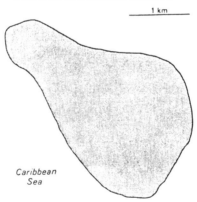

Capital: none; administered from Washington, DC

    longitude: 75.01 W   latitude: 18.65 N

Government: unincorporated territory of the US administered by the US Coast Guard

Geography

    Location: Caribbean, island in the Caribbean Sea, about one-forth of the way from Haiti to Jamaica

    Total Area: 5.2 sq km (2 sq mi) about nine times the size of The Mall in Washington, DC

    Boundaries: no land boundaries

    Climate: marine, tropical

Terrain: raised coral and limestone plateau, flat to undulating; ringed by vertical white cliffs (9 to 15 meters high)

Natural resources: guano

Natural hazards: NA

Note: strategic location 160 km south of the US Naval Base at Guantanamo Bay, Cuba; mostly exposed rock, but enough grassland to support goat herds; dense stands of fig-like trees, scattered cactus

People

Population: uninhabited; note - transient Haitian fishermen and others camp on the island

Economy

No economic activity

Transportation

Ports: none; offshore anchorage only

Nepal

200 km

Capital: Kathmandu   longitude: 85.19 E   latitude: 27.42 N
elevation: 4,388 ft

Government: parliamentary democracy

Flag: red with a blue border around the unique shape of two overlapping right triangles; the smaller, upper triangle bears a white stylized moon and the larger, lower triangle bears a white 12-pointed sun

Geography

Location: Southern Asia, between China and India

Total Area: 140,800 sq km (54,363 sq mi) slightly larger than Arkansas

Boundaries: China, India

Climate: varies from cool summers and severe winters in north to subtropical summers and mild winters in south

Temperature (F): High/Low Jan. 65/35, Apr. 83/53, July 84/68, Oct. 80/56

Average annual precipitation: 56.2 inches

Terrain: Terai or flat river plain of the Ganges in south, central hill region, rugged Himalayas in north

Highest point is Mt. Everest 8,848 m (29,028 ft)

Natural resources: quartz, water, timber, hydroelectric potential, scenic beauty, small deposits of lignite, copper, cobalt, iron ore

Natural hazards: severe thunderstorms, flooding, landslides, drought, and famine depending on timing, intensity, and duration of the summer monsoons

Note: landlocked, strategic location between China and India; contains eight of the world's highest peaks

People

Population: 21,561,000 (July 1995 est.)

Life expectancy at birth: total population 53.09 years

Nationality: Nepalese

Ethnic division: Newars, Indians, Tibetans, Gurungs, Magars, Tamangs, Bhotias, Rais, Limbus, Sherpas

Religions: Hindu 90%, Buddhist 5%, Muslim 3%, other 2%

Note: only official Hindu state in world, although no sharp distinction between many Hindu and Buddhist groups

Languages: Nepali (official), 20 languages divided into numerous dialects

Literacy: total population 26%

Economy

Imports: petroleum products, fertilizer, machinery

Exports: carpets, clothing, leather goods, jute goods, grain

Industries: small rice, jute, sugar, and oil seed mills; cigarette, textile, carpet, cement and brick production; tourism

Agriculture: rice, corn, wheat, sugarcane, root crops, milk, buffalo meat; not self-sufficient in food, particularly in drought years

Currency: 1 Napalese rupee (NR) = 100 paisa

Nepalese rupees per US1$ - 49.88

Transportation

Railroads: 101 km; note - all in Terai close to Indian border

Roads: 7,400 km total paved and unpaved

Ports: none

Airports: 44 total paved and unpaved. Tribhuvan international airport is located about 5 km from Kathmandu

The Press: daily newspapers

Daily News: 7/358 Kohity Bahal, POB 171, Kathmandu   circ. 14,300 telephone 22-31-31   fax 22-55-44

Nepali Hindi Daily: POB 49, Kathmandu
telephone 41-13-74 evening   circ. 45,000

Tourism: Tourist attraction are the Himalaya mountains, including Mt. Everest the
world's highest peak, and Lumbini, the birthplace of Buddha, Temple of the
Living Goddess

Department of Tourism: HM Government of Nepal,
Patan Dhoka, Lalitpur, Kathmandu
telephone 52-36-92   fax 52-78-52

Diplomatic representation in US:
chief of mission: (vacant); Charge d'Affaires ad interim Pradeep Khatiwada
chancery: 2131 Leroy Place NW, Washington, DC 20008
telephone: [1] (202) 667-4550
US Diplomatic representation:
chief of mission: Ambassador Sandra L. Vogelgesang
embassy: Pani Pokhari, Kathmandu
mailing address: use embassy address
telephone: [977] (1) 41-11-79
FAX: [977] (1) 41-99-63

Netherlands Antilles

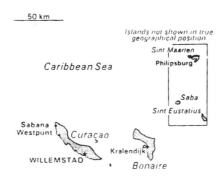

Capital: Willemstad   longitude: 68.56 W   latitude: 12.06 N
elevation: 75 ft
Government: part of the Dutch realm; full autonomy in internal affairs
granted in 1954

Flag: white with a horizontal blue stripe in the center superimposed on a vertical red band also centered; five white five-pointed stars are arranged in an oval pattern in the center of the blue band; the five stars represent the five main islands of Bonaire, Curacao, Saba, Sint Eustatius, and Sint Maarten

Geography

Location: Caribbean, two island groups in the Caribbean Sea - one includes Curacao and Bonaire north of Venezuela and the other is east of the Virgin Islands

Total Area: 960 sq km (371 sq mi) slightly less than 5.5 times the size of Washington, DC

Boundaries: no land boundaries

Climate: tropical; ameliorated by northeast trade winds

Temperature (F): High/Low Jan. 83/75, Apr. 86/76, July 87/77, Oct. 88/78

Average annual precipitation: 23.1 inches

Terrain: generally hilly, volcanic interiors

Natural resources: phosphates (Curacao only), salt (Bonaire only)

Natural hazards: Curacao and Bonaire are south of Caribbean hurricane belt, so rarely threatened; Sint Maarten, Saba, and Sint Eustatius are subject to hurricanes from July to October

People

Population: 203,800 (July 1995 est.)

Life expectancy at birth: total population 76.94 years

Nationality: Netherlands Antillean

Ethnic division: mixed African 85%, Carib Indian, European, Latin, Oriental

Religions: Roman Catholic, protestant, Jewish, Seventh-Day Adventist

Languages: Dutch (official) Papiamento a Spanish-Portuguese-Dutch-English dialect predominates, English widely spoken, Spanish

Literacy: total population 98%

Economy

Imports: crude petroleum, food, manufactures

Exports: petroleum products

Industries: tourism (Curacao and Sint Maarten), petroleum refining (Curacao), petroleum transshipment facilities (Curacao and Bonaire), light manufacturing (Curacao)

Agriculture: chief products - aloes, sorghum, peanuts, vegetables, tropical fruit

Currency: 1 Netherlands Antillean guilder, gulden, or florin (NAf) = 100 cents
Netherlands Antillean gilders, gulden, or florin per US1$ - 1.79

Transportation

Railroads: none

Roads: 950 km total paved and unpaved

Ports: Krakendijk, Philipsburg, Willemstad

Airports: 5 all paved. The international airports are located at Willemstad, on Bonaire, and Philipsburg

The Press: daily newspapers

Extra: W I Compagniestraat 41, Willemstad, Curacao   circ. 20,000
telephone (9) 62-45-95   fax (9) 62-75-75

La Prensa: W I Compagniestraat 41, Willemstad, Curacao
telephone (9) 62-40-86   fax (9) 62-59-83
circ. 12,000

Tourism: Tourist attractions are the white sandy beaches, marine wildlife and diving facilities, casinos

Curacao Tourism Development Foundation:
Pietermaai 19, Willemstad, Curacao
telephone (9) 61-60-00   fax (9) 61-23-05

Diplomatic representation in US: none (self-governing part of the Netherlands)

Diplomatic representation:

chief of mission: Consul General Bernard J. Woerz

consulate general: Saint Anna Boulevard 19, Willemstad, Curacao

mailing address: P O Box 158, Willemstad, Curacao

telephone: [599] (9) 61-30-66

FAX: [599] (9)   61-64-89

Netherlands

Capital: Amsterdam; The Hague is the seat of government

elevation: 5 ft   longitude: 4.54 E   latitude: 52.21 N

Government: constitutional monarchy

Flag: three equal horizontal bands of red (top), white, and blue; similar to the flag of Luxembourg, which uses a lighter blue and is longer

Geography

Location: Western Europe, bordering the North Sea, between Belgium and Germany

Total Area: 37,330 sq km (14,413 sq mi) slightly less than twice the size of New Jersey

Boundaries: Belgium, Germany

Climate: temperate; marine; cool summers and mild winters

Temperature (F): High/Low Jan. 40/31, Apr. 56/40, July 72/55, Oct. 57/44

Average annual precipitation: 25.6 inches

Terrain: mostly coastal lowland and reclaimed land (polders); some hills in southeast

Highest point Vaalserberg 322 m (1,056 ft)

Natural resources: natural gas, petroleum, fertile soil

Natural hazards: the extensive system of dikes and dams, protects nearly one-half of the total area from being flooded

People

Population: 15,453,000 (July 1995 est.)

Life expectancy at birth: total population 77.95 years

Nationality: Dutchman (men) Dutchwoman (women)

Ethnic division: Dutch 96%, Moroccans, Turks, and others 4%

Religions: Roman Catholic 34%, Protestant 25%, Muslim 3%, other 2%, unaffiliated 36%

Languages: Dutch

Literacy: total population 99%

Economy

The Netherlands rank third world wide in value of agricultural exports, behind the US and France

Imports: raw materials and semi-finished products, consumer goods, transportation equipment, crude oil, food products

Exports: metal products, chemicals, processed food and tobacco, agricultural products

Industries: agro-industries, metal and engineering products, electrical machinery and equipment, chemicals, petroleum, fishing, construction, micro electronics

Agriculture: animal production predominates; crops - grains, potatoes, sugar beets, fruits, vegetables; shortage of grain, fats, and oils

Currency: 1 Netherlands guilder, gulden, or florin (f) = 100 cents

Netherlands guilders, gulden, or florins per US1$ - 1.71

Transportation

Railroads: 2,757 km

Roads: 104,831 km total paved and unpaved

Ports: Amsterdam, Delfzijl, Dordrecht, Eemshaven, Groningen, Haarlem, Ijmuiden, Maastricht, Rotterdam, Terneuzen, Utrecht

Airports: 29 total paved and unpaved. The main Dutch airport is at Schiphol, near Amsterdam

The Press: daily newspapers   **De Telegraaf:** POB 376, 1000 EB Amsterdam

telephone (20) 585-9111 fax (20) 585-2113

circ. 744,000

Haagsche Courant: POB 16050, 2500 AA The Hague

telephone (70) 319-0529 fax (70) 319-3480 circ. 152,000

Tourism: Tourist attractions are old towns, the canals, cultivated fields of flowers, art galleries, out-lying islands

Nederlands Bureau voor Toerisme:

POB 458, 2260 MG Leidschendam

telephone (70) 370-5705 fax (70) 320-1654

Diplomatic representation in US:

chief of mission: Ambassador Adriaan Jacobovits De Szeged

chancery: 4200 Linnean Avenue NW, Washington, DC 20008

telephone: [1] (202) 244-5300

FAX: [1] (202) 362-3430

US Diplomatic representation:
    chief of mission: Ambassador Kirk Terry Dornbush
    embassy: Lange Voorhout 102, 2514 EJ The Hague
    mailing address: PSC 71, Box 1000, the Hague; APO AE 09715
    telephone: [31] (70) 310-9209
    FAX: [31] (70) 361-4688

New Caledonia

Islands of Huon and
Chesterfield are not shown.

Capital: Noumea   longitude: 166.27 E   latitude: 22.16 S   elevation: 30 ft
Government: overseas territory of France
    Flag: the flag of France is used
Geography
    Location: Oceania, islands in the South Pacific Ocean, east of Australia
    Total Area: 19,060 sq km (7,360 sq mi) slightly smaller than New Jersey
    Boundaries: no land boundaries
    Climate: tropical; modified by southeast trade winds; hot, humid
    Temperature (F): High/Low Jan. 86/72, Apr. 83/70, July 76/62, Oct. 80/65
    Average annual precipitation: 43.5 inches
    Terrain: coastal plains with interior mountains
    Highest point is Mt Panie 1,650 M (5,413 ft)
    Natural resources: nickel, chrome, iron , cobalt, manganese, silver, gold,
    lead, copper
    Natural hazards: typhoons most frequent from November to March
People
    Population: 184,700 (July 1995 est.)
    Life expectancy at birth: total population 74.02 years
    Nationality: New Caledonian
    Ethnic division: Melanesian 42,5%, European 37.1%, Wallisian 8.4%,
    Polynesian 3,8%, Indonesian 3.6%, Vietnamese 1.6%

Religions: Roman Catholic 60%, Protestant 30%, other 10%

Languages: French, 28 Melanesian-Polynesian dialects

Literacy: total population 91%

Economy

Imports: foods, fuels, minerals, machines, electrical equipment

Exports: nickel metal, nickel ore

Industries: nickel mining and smelting

Agriculture: large area devoted to cattle grazing; coffee, corn, wheat, vegetables

Currency: 1 CFP franc (CFPF) = 100 centimes

Comptoirs Francais du Pacifique francs - 96.25

Transportation

Railroads: none

Roads: 6,340 km total paved and unpaved

Ports: Mueo, Noumea, Thio

Airports: 36 total paved and unpaved. There is an international airport located at Tontouta, about 45 km from Noumea

The Press: daily newspaper   **Les Nouvelles Caledoniennes:**

41-43 rue de Sebastopol, BP 179, Noumea

telephone 27-25-84   fax 28-16-27   circ. 18,000

Tourism: South Pacific Commission Building, St. Joseph's Cathedral, aquarium, Isle of Pines

Destination Nouvelle-Caledonie: Immeuble Manhattan, 39-41 rue de Verdum, BP 688, Noumea

telephone 27-26-32   fax 27-46-23

Diplomatic representation in US: none (overseas territory of France)

US Diplomatic representation: none (overseas territory of France)

New Zealand

Capital: Wellington   longitude: 174.46 E   latitude: 41.16 S
elevation: 415 ft

Government: parliamentary democracy

Flag: blue with the flag of the UK in the upper hoist-side quadrant with four red five-pointed stars edged in white centered in the outer half of the flag; the stars represent the Southern Cross constellation

Geography

Location: Oceania, islands in the South Pacific Ocean, southeast of Australia

Total Area: 268,680 sq km (103,737 sq mi) about the size of Colorado

Boundaries: no land boundaries

Climate: temperate with sharp regional contrasts

Temperature (F): High/Low Jan. 69/56, Apr. 63/51, July 53/42, Oct. 60/48

Average annual precipitation: 47.4 inches

Terrain: predominately mountainous with some large coastal plains

Highest point Mt. Cook 3,764 m (12,349 ft)

Natural resources: natural gas, iron ore, sand, coal, timber, hydropower, gold, limestone

Natural hazards: earthquakes are common, though usually not severe

People

Population: 3,408,000 (July 1995 est.)

Life expectancy at birth: total population 76.65 years

Nationality: New Zealander

Ethnic division: European 88%, Maori 8.9%, Pacific Islander 2.9%, other 2%

Religions: Anglican 24%, Presbyterian 18%, Roman Catholic 15%, Methodist 5%, Baptist 2%, other Protestant 3%, unspecified or none 33%

Languages: English (official), Maori

330

Literacy: total population 99%

Economy

    Imports: machinery and equipment, vehicles and aircraft, petroleum, consumer goods

    Exports: wool, lamb, mutton, beef, fish, cheese, chemicals, forestry products, fruits and vegetables, manufactures

Industries: food processing, wood and paper products, textiles, machinery, transportation equipment, banking and insurance, tourism, mining

Agriculture: livestock predominates; wool, meat, dairy products all export earners; crops - wheat, barley, potatoes, pulses, fruits, vegetables; surplus producer of farm products

Currency: 1 New Zealand dollar (NZ$) = 100 cents

    New Zealand dollars per US1$ - 1.56

Transportation

    Railroads: 4,716 km

    Roads: 92,648 km total paved and unpaved

    Ports: Auckland, Christchurch, Dunedin, Tauranga, Wellington

    Airports: 102 total paved and unpaved. There are international airports at Auckland, Christchurch, and Wellington

The Press: daily newspapers   **New Zealand Herald:**

    46 Albert St. POB 32, Auckland

    telephone (9) 379-5050   fax (9) 366-0146

    circ. 250,000

    The Press: Private Bag 4722, Christchurch

    telephone (3) 379-0940   fax (3) 364-8492 circ. 104,000

Tourism: Main tourist attractions are hot springs and beaches, high mountains, lakes and forests. Stream, lake and deep sea fishing.

    New Zealand Tourism Board: 256 Lambton Quay POB 95, Wellington

    telephone (4) 472-8860   fax (4) 478-1736

Diplomatic representation in US:

    chief of mission: Ambassador Lionel John Wood

    chancery: 37 Observatory Circle NW, Washington, DC 20008

    telephone: [1] (202) 328-4800

US Diplomatic representation:
> *chief of mission:* Ambassador Josiah Horton Beeman
> *embassy:* 29 Fitzherbert Terrace, Thorndon, Wellington
> *mailing address:* P O Box 1190, Wellington;
> PSC 467, Box 1, FPO AP 96531-1001
> *telephone:* [64] (4) 472-2068
> *FAX:* [64] (4) 472-3537

Nicaragua

125 km

Capital: Managua   longitude: 86.18 W   latitude: 12.06 N
elevation: 184 ft

Government: republic

Flag: three equal horizontal bands of blue (top), white, and blue with the
national coat of arms centered in the white band; the coat of arms features a
triangle encircled by the words REPUBLICA DE NICARAGUA on the top
and AMERICA CENTRAL on the bottom; similar to the flag of El Salvador,
which features a round emblem encircled by the words REPUBLICA DE EL
SALVADOR EN LA AMERICA CENTRAL centered in the white band;
also similar to the flag of Honduras, which has five blue stars arranged in an
X pattern centered in the white band

Geography

Location: Middle America, bordering both the Caribbean Sea and the North
Pacific Ocean, between Costa Rica and Honduras

Total Area: 129,494 sq km (49,998 sq mi) slightly larger than
New York State

Boundaries: Costa Rica, Honduras

Climate: tropical in lowlands, cooler in highlands

Temperature (F): High/Low Jan. 88/68, Apr. 93/73, July 88/72, Oct. 88/72

Average annual precipitation: 45.1 inches
Terrain: extensive Atlantic coastal plains rising to central interior mountains; narrow Pacific coastal plain interrupted by volcanoes
Highest point Cerro Mocoton 2,107 m (6,913 ft)
Natural resources: gold, silver, tungsten, lead, zinc, timber, fish
Natural hazards: destructive earthquakes, volcanoes, landslides, and occasionally severe hurricanes

People

Population: 4,207,000 (July 1995 est.)
Life expectancy at birth: total population 64.54 years
Nationality: Nicaraguan
Ethnic division: mestizo (mixed Amerindian and Caucasian) 69%, white 17%, black 9%, Indian 5%
Religions: Roman Catholic 95%, Protestant 5%
Languages: Spanish (official) Note: English-Indian-speaking minorities on Atlantic coast
Literacy: total population 57%

Economy

Imports: consumer goods, machinery and equipment, petroleum products
Exports: meat, coffee, cotton, sugar, seafood, gold, bananas
Industries: food processing, chemicals, metal products, textiles, clothing, petroleum refining and distribution, beverages, footwear
Agriculture: export crops - coffee, bananas, sugarcane, cotton; food crops - rice, corn, cassava, citrus fruit, beans; also produces a variety of animal products - beef, veal, poultry, dairy products; normally self-sufficient in food
Currency: 1 gold cordoba (C$) = 100 centavos
gold cordobas per US1$ - 7.08

Transportation

Railroads: 376 km; note - majority of system is non-operational
Roads: 15,286 km total paved and unpaved
Ports: Bluefields, Corinto, El Bluff, Puerto Cabezas, Puerto Sandino, Rama, San Juan del Sur
Airports: 198 total paved and unpaved. The international airport is at Managua

The Press: daily newspapers

Barricada: Camino del Oriente, del Bolerama, Apdo 576, Managua
telephone (2) 24-291
evenings English circ. 95,000

La Prenza: Km 4 1/2, Carretera Norte, Apdo 192, Managua
telephone (2) 40-139   circ. 75,000

Tourism: ancient city of Leon Viejo, beaches

Instituto Nicaraguense de Turismo:

Avda Bolivar Sur, Apdo 122, Managua

telephone (2) 25-436   fax (2) 25-314

Diplomatic representation in US:

chief of mission: Ambassador Roberto Genaro Mayorga Cortes

chancery: 1627 New Hampshire Avenue NW, Washington, DC 20009

telephone: [1] (202) 939-6570

US Diplomatic representation:

chief of mission: Ambassador John F. Maisto

embassy: Kilometer 4.5 Carretera Sur, Managua

mailing address: APO AA 34021

telephone: [505] (2) 666-010, -013, -015, through 18, 666-026 , 666-027

FAX: [505] (2) 666-046

Niger

500 km

Capital: Niamey   longitude: 2.05 E   latitude: 13.32 N   elevation: 709 ft

Government: republic

Flag: three equal horizontal bands of orange (top), white, and green with a small orange disk (representing the sun) centered in the white band; similar to the flag of India, which has a blue spoked wheel centered in the white band

Geography

Location: western Africa, southeast of Algeria

Total Area: 1,267,000 sq km (489,189 sq mi) slightly less than twice the size of Texas

Boundaries: Algeria, Benin, Burkina, Chad, Libya, Mali, Nigeria

Climate: desert; mostly hot, dry, dusty; tropical in extreme south

Temperature (F): High/Low Jan. 93/58, Apr. 108/77, July 94/74, Oct. 101/74

Average annual precipitation: 21.8 inches

Terrain: predominately desert plains and sand dunes; flat to rolling plains in south; hills in north

Highest point Banguezane 1,900 m (6,234 ft)

Natural resources: uranium, coal, iron ore, tin, phosphates

Natural hazards: recurring droughts

People

Population: 9,281,000 (July 1995 est.)

Life expectancy at birth: total population 45.07 years

Nationality: Nigerien

Ethnic division: Hausa 56%, Djerma 22%, Fula 8.5%, Tuareg 8%, Beri Beri (Kanouri) 4.3%, Arab, Toubou, and Gourmantche 1.2%, about 4,000 French expatriates

Religions: Muslim 80%, remainder indigenous beliefs and Christians

Languages: French (official), Hausa, Djerma

Literacy: total population 11%

Economy

Imports: consumer goods, primary materials, machinery, vehicles and parts, petroleum, cereals

Exports: uranium ore, livestock products, cowpeas, onions

Industries: cement, brick, textiles, food processing, chemicals, slaughterhouses, and a few other small light industries

Agriculture: cash crops - cowpeas, cotton, peanuts; food crops - millet, sorghum, cassava, rice; livestock - cattle, sheep, goats; self-sufficient in food except in drought years

Currency: 1 CFA franc (CFAF) = 100 centimes

Communaute Financiere Africaine francs per US1$ - 529.43

Transportation

Railroads: none

Roads: 39,970 km total paved and unpaved

Ports: none

Airports: 29 total paved and unpaved. There are international airports at Niamey and Agadez

The Press: newspapers   **Journal officiel de la Republique du Niger:** BP 116, Niamey fortnightly circ. 1,000 telephone 72-39-30

Le Sahel: BP 13182, Niamey daily circ. 5,000

Tourism: Lake Chad, ruins of Sokoto Empire at Maradi and Konni
Office National du Tourisme:
ave du President H. Luebke, BP 612, Niamey
telephone 73-24-47

Diplomatic representation in US:
chief of mission: Ambassador Adamou Seydou
chancery: 2204 R Street NW, Washington, DC 20008
telephone: [1] (202) 483-4224 through 4227
US Diplomatic representation:
chief of mission: Ambassador John S. Davison
embassy: Rue Des Ambassades, Naimey
mailing address: B P 11201, Niamey
telephone: [227] 72-26-61
FAX: [227] 73-31-67

Nigeria

Capital: Abuja
Note: on 12 December 1991 the capital was officially moved from Lagos to Abuja; many government offices remain in Lagos pending completion of facilities in Abuja   longitude: 6.93 E   latitude: 9.01 N
Government: military government
   Flag: three equal vertical bands of green (hoist side), white, and green
Geography
   Location: Western Africa, bordering the North Atlantic Ocean, between Benin and Cameroon
   Total Area: 923,770 sq km (356,668 sq mi) slightly more than twice the size of California
   Boundaries: Benin, Cameroon, Chad, Niger

Climate: varies; equatorial in south, tropical in center, arid in north

Temperature (F): High/Low Jan. 88/74, Apr. 89/77, July 83/74, Oct. 85/74

Average annual precipitation: at Lagos, elevation 10 ft (3.24 E - 6.27 N) 72.3 inches

Terrain: southern lowlands merge into central hills and plateaus; mountains in southeast, plains in north

Highest point Dimlang   2,042 m (6,700 ft)

Natural resources: petroleum, tin, columbite, iron ore, coal, limestone, lead, zinc, natural gas

Natural hazards: periodic droughts

People

Population: 101,233,000 (July 1995 est.)

Life expectancy at birth: total population 55.98 years

Nationality: Nigerian

Ethnic division: north: Hausa and Fulani

southwest: Yoruba

southeast: Ibos-non-Africans 27,000

Note: Hausa and Fulani, Yoruba, and Ibos together make up about 65% of population

Religions: Muslim 50%, Christian 40%, indigenous beliefs 10%

Languages: English (official), Hausa, Yoruba, Ibo, Fulani

Literacy: total population 51%

Economy

Imports: machinery and equipment, manufactured goods, food and animals

Exports: cocoa, rubber

Industries: crude oil and mining - coal, tin, columbite; primary processing industries - palm oil, peanut, cotton, rubber, wood, hides and skins; manufacturing industries - textiles, cement, building materials, food products, footwear, chemical, printing, ceramics, steel

Agriculture: cash crops - cocoa, peanuts, palm oil, rubber; food crops - corn, rice, sorghum, millet, cassava, yams; livestock - cattle, sheep, goats, pigs; fishing and forestry resources extensively exploited

Currency: 1 naira (N) = 100 kobo

naira per US1$ - 21.99

Transportation

Railroads: 3,567 km

Roads: 107,990 km total paved and unpaved

Ports: Calabar, Lagos, Onne, Port Harcourt, Sapele, Warri

Airports: 80 total paved and unpaved. The international airports are at Lagos, Kano, Port Harcourt and Calabar

The Press: daily newspapers

> **Daily Times:** New Isheri Road, Agidingbi, PMB 21340, Ikeja, Lagos
> telephone (1) 90-08-50 circ. 400,000
> **Nigerian Tribune:** Imallefalafia St, Oke-Ado, POB 78, Ibadan   telephone (22) 41-08-86 circ. 110,000

Tourism: Tourist attractions are dense forests, coastal scenery, and Nigeria's arts

> **Nigerian Tourism Development Corporation:** Zone 4, PMB 167, Abuja
> telephone (9) 523-0418   fax (9) 523-0962

Diplomatic representation in US:

> *chief of mission*: Ambassador Zubair Mahmud Kazaure
> *chancery:* 1333 16th Street NW, Washington, DC 20036
> *telephone:* [1] (202) 986-8400

US Diplomatic representation:

> *chief of mission:* Ambassador Walter C. Carrington
> *embassy:* 2 Eleke Cresent, Lagos
> *mailing address:* P O Box 554, Lagos
> *telephone:* [234] (1) 261-0097
> *FAX:* [234] (1) 261-0257

Niue

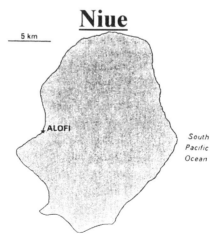

Capital: Alofi   longitude: 170.00 W   latitude: 18.90 S

Government: Self-governing territory in free association with New Zealand; Niue fully responsible for internal affairs; New Zealand retains responsibility for external affairs

Flag: yellow with the flag of the UK in the upper hoist-side quadrant; the flag of the UK bears five yellow five-pointed stars - a large one on a blue disk in the center and a smaller one on each arm of the bold red cross

Geography

Location: Oceania, island in the South Pacific Ocean, east of Tonga

Total Area: 260 sq km (100 sq mi) slightly less than 1.5 times the size of Washington, DC

Boundaries: no land boundaries

Climate: tropical; modified by southeast trade winds

Terrain: steep limestone cliffs along coast, central plateau

Natural resources: fish, arable land

Natural hazards: typhoons

People

Population: 1,850 (July 1995 est.)

Life expectancy at birth: NA

Nationality: Niuean

Ethnic division: Polynesian (with some 200 European, Samoans, and Tongans)

Religions: Ekalesia Nieue (Niuean Church) 75% - a Protestant church closely related to the London Missionary Society, Morman 10%, other 15% (mostly Roman Catholic, Jehovah's Witnesses, Seventh-Day Adventist)

Languages: Polynesian closely related to Tongan and Samoan, English

Literacy: NA

Economy

Imports: food, live animals, manufactured goods, machinery, fuels, lubricants, chemicals, drugs

Exports: canned coconut cream, copra, honey, passion fruit products, pawpaw, root crops, limes, footballs, stamps, handicrafts

Industries: tourism, handicrafts, food processing

Agriculture: coconuts, passion fruit, honey, limes; subsistence crops - taro, yams, cassava (tapioca), sweet potatoes; pigs, poultry, beef cattle

Currency: 1 New Zealand dollar (NZ$) = 100 cents

New Zealand dollars per US1$ - 1.56

Transportation

Railroads: none

Roads: 229 km unpaved; all-weather 123 km; plantation access 106 km

Ports: none; offshore anchorage only

Airports: 1 Hanan International Airport

Diplomatic representation in US: none (self-governing territory in free
association with New Zealand)
US Diplomatic representation: none (self-governing territory in free association
with New Zealand)

Norfolk Island

Capital: Kingston   longitude: 167.40 E   latitude: 28.04 S
Government: Kingston (administrative center); Burnt Pine (commercial center)
    Flag: three vertical bands of green (hoist side), white, and green with a large
    green Norfolk Island pine tree centered in the slightly wider white band
Geography:
    Location: Oceania, island in the south Pacific Ocean, east of Australia
    Total Area: 34.6 sq km (13.4 sq mi) about 0.2 times the size of
    Washington, DC
    Boundaries: no land boundaries
    Climate: subtropical, mild, little seasonal temperature variation
    Average annual precipitation: 53.2 inches
    Terrain: volcanic formation with mostly rolling plains; coast line cliffs
    Natural resources: fish
    Natural hazards: typhoons (especially May to July)
People
    Population: 2,780 (July 1995 est.)
    Life expectancy at birth: NA
    Nationality: Norfolk Islander
    Ethnic division: descendants of the Bounty mutineers, Australian, New
    Zealander
    Religions: Anglican 39%, Roman Catholic 11.7%, Uniting Church of
    Australia 16.4%, Seventh-Day Adventist 4.4%

Languages: English (official) Norfolk a mixture of 18th century English and ancient Tahitian

Literacy: total population 97%

Economy

Imports: NA

Exports: postage stamps, seeds of the Norfolk Island pine and Kentia palm, small quantities of avocados

Industries: tourism

Agriculture: Norfolk Island pine seed, Kentia palm seed, cereals, vegetables, fruit, cattle, poultry

Currency: 1 Australian dollar ($A) = 100 cents

Australian dollars per US1$ - 1.30

Transportation

Railroads: none

Roads: 80 km total paved and unpaved

Ports: none; loading jetties at Kingston and Cascade

Airports: one

The Press: weekly

Norfolk Island Government Gazette:
Kingston, Norfolk Island 2899
telephone 22-001   fax 23-177

Norfolk Islander: Greenways Press, POB 150
Norfolk Island 2899   telephone 22-159   fax 22-948

Tourism: Norfolk Island National Park; a native forest which has unique species of flora including the world's largest fern and fauna such as the Norfolk Island green parrot, the guava bird and the boobook owl

Norfolk Island Government Tourist Board
Burnt Pine, POB 211, Norfolk Island 2899
telephone 22-147   fax 23-109

Diplomatic representation in US: none (territory of Australia)
US Diplomatic representation: none (territory of Australia)

Northern Mariana Islands

Farallon
de Pajaros .

Maug Islands

Asuncion Island

Philippine

Sea

Agrihan

Pagan

North

Pacific

Guguan   Ocean

Sarigan

Anatahan

Farallon de
Medinilla
Saipan SAIPAN
Tinian

Rota

Capital: Saipan   longitude: 145.46 E   latitude: 15.14 N
elevation: 676 ft

Government: commonwealth in political union with the US; self-governing with
locally elected governor, lieutenant governor, and legislature; federal funds to
the Commonwealth administered by the US Department of the Interior,
Office of Territorial and International Affairs

Flag: blue with a white five-pointed star superimposed on the gray silhouette
of a latte stone (a traditional foundation stone used in building) in the center

Geography

Location: Oceania, islands in the North Pacific Ocean, about three-quarters
of the way from Hawaii to the Philippines

Total Area: 477 sq km (184 sq mi) slightly more than 2.5 times the size of
Washington, DC

Boundaries: no land boundaries

Climate: tropical marine; moderated by northeast trade winds, little seasonal
temperature variation; dry season December to June, rainy season July to
October

Temperature (F): High/Low Jan. 81/72, Apr. 83/74, July 83/74, Oct. 83/75

Average annual precipitation: 82.3 inches

Terrain: southern islands are limestone with level terraces and fringing coral
reefs; northern islands are volcanic

Highest point is Mt. Okso'Takpochao on Saipan 471 m (1,545 ft)

Natural resources: arable land, fish

Natural hazards: active volcanoes on Pagan and Agrihan; typhoons
(especially August to November)

People

Population: 51,100 (July 1995 est.)

Life expectancy at birth: total population 67.43 years

Nationality: NA

Ethnic division: Chamorro, Carolinians and other Micronesians, Caucasian, Japanese, Chinese, Korean

Religions: Christian (Roman Catholic majority, although traditional beliefs and taboos may still be found)

Languages: English, Chamorro, Carolinian

Literacy: total population 97%

Economy

Imports: food, construction equipment and materials, petroleum products

Exports: garments

Industries: tourism, construction, light industries, handicraft

Agriculture: coconuts, fruits, cattle, vegetables; food is a major import

Currency: 1 United States dollar (US$) = 100 cents
         US currency is used

Transportation

Railroads: none

Roads: 381 km total paved and unpaved

Ports: Saipan, Tinian

Airports: 8 total paved and unpaved

The Press: newspapers   **Marianas Variety News and Views:**
POB 231, Saipan, MP 96950
circ. 3,000 English and Chamorro Mon.-Fri.
telephone 234-6341   fax 234-9271

Pacific Daily News (Saipan Bureau) POB 822, Saipan, MP 96950
telephone 234-6423   fax 234-5986

Tourism: tourist are mainly attracted by the white, sandy beaches and excellent diving conditions

Marianas Visitors Bureau:
POB 861, Siapan, MP 96950
telephone 234-8325   fax 234-3596

Norway

Capital: Oslo   longitude: 10.45 E   latitude: 59.55 N   elevation: 308 ft

Government: constitutional monarchy

Flag: red with a blue cross outlined in white that extends to the edges of the flag; the vertical part of the cross is shifted to the hoist side in the style of the Dannebrog (Danish flag)

Geography

Location: Northern Europe, bordering the North Sea and the North Atlantic Ocean, west of Sweden

Total Area: 324,220 sq km (125,181 sq mi) slightly larger than New Mexico

Boundaries: Finland, Sweden, Russia

Climate: temperate along coast, modified by North Atlantic current; colder interior; rainy year-round on west coast

Temperature (F): High/Low Jan. 28/19, Apr. 50/34, July 72/55, Oct. 48/38

Average annual precipitation: 28.7 inches

Terrain: glaciated; mostly huge plateaus and rugged mountains broken by fertile valleys; small, scattered plains; coastline deeply indented by fjords; arctic tundra in north

Highest point Glittertinden 2,472 m (8,110 ft)

Natural resources: petroleum, copper, natural gas, pyrites, nickel, iron ore, zinc, lead, fish, timber, hydropower

Natural hazards: NA

Note: about two-thirds mountains; some 50,000 islands off its much indented coastline; strategic location adjacent to sea lanes and air routes in North Atlantic; one of the most rugged and longest coastlines in world.

People

Population: 4,331,000 (July 1995 est.)

Life expectancy at birth: total population 77.61 years

Nationality: Norwegian

Ethnic division: Germanic (Nordic, Alpine, Baltic), Lapps (Sami) 20,000

Religions: Evangelical Lutheran 87.8% (state church), other Protestant and Roman Catholic 3.8%, none 3.2% unknown 5.2%

Languages: Norwegian (official)

Literacy: total population 99%

Economy

Imports: machinery and equipment, chemicals and other industrial inputs, manufactured consumer goods, foodstuffs

Exports: petroleum and petroleum products, metals and products, fish and fish products, chemicals, natural gas, ships

Industries: petroleum and gas, food processing, shipbuilding, pulp and paper products, metals, chemicals, timber, mining, textiles, fishing

Agriculture: among the world's top ten fishing nations; livestock output exceeds value of crops

Currency: 1 Norwegian krone (NKr) = 100 oere

Norwegian krone per US1$ - 6.70

Transportation

Railroads: 4,026 km

Roads: 88,922 km total paved and unpaved

Ports: Bergen, Drammen, Flora, Hammerfest, Harstad, Haugesund, Kristinasand, Larvik, Narvik, Oslo, Porsgrunn, Stavanger, Tromso, Trondheim

Airports: 104 total paved and unpaved. Fornebu International Airport is located at Oslo

The Press: daily newspapers **Aftenposten:** Akersgt, 51 POB 1178 Sentrum, 0107 Oslo

telephone 22-86-30-00   fax 22-42-63-25

circ. morning 278,000 Sunday 226,000

Dagbladet: POB 1184 Sentrum, 0107 Oslo

telephone 22-31-06-00   fax 22-42-95-48 circ. 226,000

Tourism: Norway is a popular resort for winter sports. The 1994 Winter Olympics were held at Lillehammer, The King's Palace at Oslo, Akershus Fortress, museums, fjords

Norta: Head Office, POB 499 Sentrum, 0105 Oslo

telephone 22-42-70-44   fax 22-33-69-98

chief of mission: Ambassador Kjeld Vibe

chancery: 2720 34th Street NW, Washington, DC 20008

telephone: [1] (202) 333-6000

FAX: [1] (202) 337-0870

US Diplomatic representation:

chief of mission: Ambassador Thomas A. Loftus

embassy: Drammensveien 18, 0244 Oslo

mailing address: PSC 69, Box 1000, APO AE 09707

telephone: [47] 22-44-85-50

FAX: [47] 22-44-33-63

Oman

Capital: Muscat   longitude: 58.38 E latitude: 23.37 N elevation: 15 ft

Government: monarchy

Flag: three horizontal bands of white (top, double width), red, and green (double width) with a broad, vertical, red band on the hoist side; the national emblem (a khanjar dagger in its sheath superimposed on two crossed swords in scabbards) in white is centered at the top of the vertical band

Geography

Location: Middle East, bordering the Arabian Sea, Gulf of Oman, and Persian Gulf, between Yemen and the United Arab Emirates

Total Area: 212,460 sq km (82,031 sq mi) slightly smaller than Kansas

Boundaries: Saudi Arabia, Yemen

Climate: dry desert; hot, humid along coast; hot, dry interior; strong southwest summer monsoon (May to September) in far north

Temperature (F): High/Low Jan. 77/66, Apr. 90/78, July 97/87, Oct. 93/80

Average annual precipitation: 3.9 inches

Terrain: vast central desert plain, rugged mountains in north and south

Natural resources: petroleum, copper, asbestos, some marble, limestone, chromium, gypsum, natural gas

Natural hazards: summer winds often raise large sandstorms and duststorms in interior; periodic droughts

Note: Strategic location with small foothold on Musandam Peninsula controlling Strait of Hurmuz, a vital transit point for world crude oil

People

Population: 2,125,800 (July 1995 est.)

Life expectancy at birth: total population 70.25 years

Nationality: Omani

Ethnic division: Arab, Baluchi, South Asian (Indian, Pakistani, Sri Lankan, Bangladeshi)

Religions: Ibadhi Muslim 75%, Sunni Muslim, Shi'a Muslim, Hindu

Languages: Arabic (official), English, Baluchi, Urdu, Indian dialects

Literacy: NA

Economy

Imports: machinery, transportation equipment, manufactured goods, food, livestock, lubricants

Exports: petroleum, re-exports, fish, processed copper, textiles

Industries: crude oil production and refining, natural gas production, construction, cement, copper

Agriculture: largely subsistence farming (dates, limes, bananas, alfalfa, vegetables, camels, cattle), fishing; not self-sufficient in food

Currency: 1 Omani rial (RO) = 1,000 baiza

Omani rials per US1$ - 0.38

Transportation

Railroads: none

Roads: 26,000 km total paved and unpaved

Ports: Mina' al Fahl, Mina' Qabus, Mina' Raysut

Airports: 140 total paved and unpaved. Seeb International Airport is at Salalah. Most towns of any size have landing strips.

The Press: daily newspapers   **Al-Watan:** POB 463, Muscat
telephone 59-19-19 Arabic circ. 24,000
Oman Daily Observer: POB 3002, Ruwi
telephone 70-30-55 English circ. 22,000

Tourism: Sultan's Palace, Portuguese Forts at Muscat

Director of Tourism: Muscat

Diplomatic representation in US:
> *chief of mission:* Ambassador Abdallah bin Muhammad bin Aqil al-Dhahab
> *chancery:* 2535 Belmont Road NW, Washington, DC 20008
> *telephone:* [1] (202) 387-1980 through 1982
> *FAX:* [1] (202) 745-4933

US Diplomatic representation:
> *chief of mission:* Ambassador David J. Dunford
> *embassy:* NA, Muscat
> *mailing address:* P O Box 202, Code No. 115, Muscat
> *telephone:* [968] 69-89-89
> *FAX:* [968] 69-97-79

Pacific Ocean

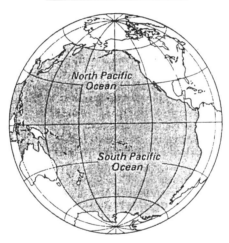

Geography

Location: body of water between Antarctica, Asia, Australia, and the Western Hemisphere

Area: 165,384,000 sq km (63,854,762 sq mi) about 18 times the size of the US; the largest of the world's four oceans

Note: includes Bali Sea, Bellingshausen Sea, Bering Sea, Bering Strait, Coral Sea, East China Sea, Flores Sea, Gulf of Alaska, Gulf of Tonkin, Java Sea, Philippine Sea, Ross Sea, Savu Sea, Sea of Japan, Sea of Okhotsk, South China Sea, Tasman Sea, Timor Sea, and other tributary water bodies

Climate: the western Pacific is monsoonal - a rainy season occurs during the summer months, when moisture-laden winds blow from the ocean over the land, and a dry season during the winter months, when dry winds blow from the Asian land mass back to the ocean

Terrain: surface currents in the northern Pacific are dominated by a clockwise, warm-water gyre (broad circular system of currents) and in the southern Pacific by a counterclockwise, cool-water gyre; in the northern Pacific sea ice forms in the Bering Sea and Sea of Okhotsk in winter; in the southern Pacific sea ice from Antarctica reaches its northernmost extent in October; the ocean floor in the eastern Pacific is dominated by the East Pacific Rise, while the western Pacific is dissected by deep trenches, including the world's deepest, the 10,924 meter Marianas Trench

Natural resources: oil and gas fields, polymetallic nodules, sand and gravel aggregates, placer deposits, fish

Environment

Current issues: endangered marine species include the dugong, sea lion, sea otter, seals, turtles, and whales; oil pollution in Philippine Sea and South China Sea

Natural hazards: surrounded by a zone of violent volcanic and earthquake activity sometimes referred to as the Pacific Ring of Fire; subject to tropical cyclones (typhoons) in southeast and east Asia from May to December (most frequent from July to October); tropical cyclones (hurricanes) may form south of Mexico and strike Central America and Mexico from June to October (most common August to September); southern shipping lanes subject to icebergs from Antarctica; occasional El Nino phenomenon occurs off the coast of Peru when the trade winds slacken and the warm Equatorial Counter current moves south, killing the plankton that is the primary food source for anchovies; consequently, the anchovies move to better feeding grounds, causing resident marine birds to starve by the thousands because of their lost food source; ships subject to superstructure icing in extreme north from October to May and in extreme south from May to October; persistent fog in the northern Pacific can be a maritime hazard from June to December

Transportation

Ports: Bangkok (Thailand), Hong Kong, Los Angles (US), Manila (Philippines), Pusan (South Korea), San Francisco (US), Seattle (US), Shanghai (China), Singapore, Sydney (Australia), Vladivostok (Russia), Wellington (NZ), Yokohama (Japan)

Pakistan

Capital: Islamabad   longitude: 73.08 E   latitude: 33.40 N
elevation 1,644 ft

Government: republic

Flag: green with a vertical white band (symbolizing the role of religious minorities) on the hoist side; a large white crescent and star are centered in the green field; the crescent, star, and color green are traditional symbols of Islam

Geography

Location: Southern Asia, bordering the Arabian Sea, between India and Iran

Total Area: 803,940 sq km (310,401 sq mi) slightly less than twice the size of California

Boundaries: Afghanistan, China, India

Climate: mostly hot, dry desert; temperate in northwest; arctic in north
Temperature (F): High/Low   Jan. 61/36, Apr. 88/59, July 97/77, Oct. 90/59
Average annual precipitation: 37.8 inches

Terrain: flat Indus plain in east; mountains in north and northeast; Balochistan plateau in west
Highest point K2 (Godwin Austen) 8,611 m (28,251 ft)

Natural resources: land, extensive natural gas reserves, limited petroleum, poor quality coal, iron ore, copper, salt, limestone

Natural hazards: frequent earthquakes, occasionally severe especially in north and west; flooding along the Indus after heavy rains (July and August)

People

Population: 131,542,000 (July 1995 est.)

Life expectancy at birth: total population 57.86 years

Nationality: Pakistani

Ethnic division: Punjab, Sindhi, Pashtun (Pathan), Baloch, Muhajir (immigrants from India and their descendants)

Religions: Muslim 97%, (Sunni 77%, Shi'a 20%), Christian, Hindu, and other 3%

Languages: Urdu (official), English (official; lingua franca of Pakistani elite and most government ministries), Punjab 64%, Sindhi 12%, Pashtu 8%, Urdu 7%, Balochi and other 9%

Literacy: total population 35%

Economy

Imports: petroleum, petroleum products, machinery, transportation equipment, vegetable oils, animal fats, chemicals

Exports: cotton, textiles, clothing, rice, leather, carpets

Industries: textiles, food processing, beverages, construction materials, clothing, paper products, shrimp

Agriculture: world's largest contiguous irrigation system; major crops - cotton, wheat, rice, sugarcane, fruits, vegetables; livestock products - milk, beef, mutton, eggs

Currency: 1 Pakistani rupee (PRe) = 100 paisa
                    Pakistani rupees per US1$ - 30.86

Transportation

Railroads: 8,773 km

Roads: 177,410 km total paved and unpaved

Ports: Gwadar, Karachi, Ormaro (under construction), Port Muhammad bin Qasim

Airports: 119 total paved and unpaved. International airports are located at Karachi, Lahore, Rawalpindi, Peshawar, and Quetta. Most towns of any size have landing strips

The Press: daily newspapers

Daily Jang: HQ Printing House, I.I. Chundrigar Road, POB 52, Karachi telephone (21) 21-07-11   circ. 750,000

Nawa-i-Waqt: 4 Sharah-e-Fatima Jinnah, Lahore 54000 telephone (42) 30-20-50 fax (42) 63-67-00 English, Urdu circ. 400,000

Tourism: The Himalayan mountains provides magnificent scenery, mountaineering and winter sports. Historical buildings and archaeological remains

Pakistan Tourism Development Corporation: House #2, St 61, F-7/4, Islamabad 44000 telephone (51) 81-10-01   fax (51) 82-41-73

Diplomatic representation in US:

    chief of mission: Ambassador Maleeha Lodhi

    chancery: 2315 Massachusetts Avenue NW, Washington, DC 20008

    telephone: [1] (202) 939-6200

    FAX: [1] (202) 387-0484

US Diplomatic representation:

    chief of mission: Ambassador John C. Monjo

    embassy: Diplomatic Enclave, Ramna 5, Islamabad

    mailing address: P O Box 1048, PSC 1212, Box 2000, Unit 6220, Islamabad

    telephone: [92] (51) 82-61-61 through 82-61-79

    FAX: [92] (51) 21-42-22

Palau

Capital: Koror   longitude: 134.00 E   latitude: 7.40 N
Note: a new capital is being built about 20 km northeast in eastern Babelthuap

Government: self-governing territory in free association with the US pursuant to Compact of Free Association which entered into force 1 October 1994; Palau is fully responsible for internal affairs; US retains responsibility for external affairs

Flag: light blue with a large yellow disk (representing the moon) shifted slightly to the hoist side

Geography

    Location: Oceania, group of islands in the North Pacific Ocean, southeast of the Philippines

    Total Area: 458 sq km (177 sq mi) slightly more than 2.5 times the size of Washington, DC

    Boundaries: no land boundaries

Climate: wet season May to November; hot and humid

Terrain: about 200 islands varying geologically from high, mountainous main island of Babelthuap to low, coral islands usually fringed by large barrier reefs

Natural resources: forests, minerals (especially gold), marine products, deep-seabed minerals

Natural hazards: typhoons (June to December)

Note: includes World War II battleground of Beliliou (Peleiu) and world-famous rock islands; archipelago of six island groups totaling over 200 islands in the Caroline chain

People

Population: 16,700 (July 1995 est.)

Life expectancy at birth: total population 71.01 years

Nationality: Palauan

Ethnic division: Palauans are a composite of Polynesian, Malayan, and Melanesian races

Religions: Christian (Catholics, Seventh-Day Adventist, Jehovah's Witnesses, the Assembly of God, the Liebenzell Mission, and Latter-Day Saints), Modekngei religion (one-third of the population observes this religion which is indigenous to Palau)

Languages: English (official in all of Palau's 16 states), Sonsorolese (official in the state of Sonsoral), Angaur and Japanese (in the state of Anguar), Tobi (in the state of Tobi), Palauan (in the other 13 states)

Literacy: total population 92%

Economy

Imports: NA

Exports: trochus (type of shellfish), tuna, copra, handicrafts

Industries: tourism, craft items (shell, wood, pearl), some commercial fishing and agriculture

Agriculture: subsistence-level production of coconut, copra, cassava, sweet potatoes

Currency: 1 United States dollar US$ = 100 cents
US currency is used

Transportation

Railroads: none

Roads: 61 km total paved and unpaved

Ports: Koror

Airports: 3 total paved and unpaved

Tourism: beaches, diving

Diplomatic representation in US:
chief of mission: Liaison Officer NA
chancery: 444 North Capital Street NW, Washington, DC 20036
telephone: [1] (202) 624-7793
FAX: NA

US Diplomatic representation:
chief of mission: Liaison Officer Lloyd W. Moss
embassy: Erenguul Street, Koror, Republic of Palau
mailing address: P O Box 6028, Republic of Palau 96940
telephone: [680] 488-2920
FAX: [680] 488-2911

Palmyra Atoll

2 km

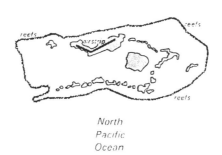

North
Pacific
Ocean

Capital: none; administered from Washington, DC
longitude: 162.10 W   latitude: 6.30 N
Government: incorporated territory of the US; privately owned, but administered by the Office of Territorial and International Affairs, US Department of the Interior
Geography
Location: Oceania, atoll in the North Pacific Ocean, about one-half of the way from Hawaii to American Samoa
Total Area: 11.9 sq km (4.6 sq mi) about 20 times the size of The Mall in Washington, DC
Boundaries: no land boundaries
Climate: equatorial, hot, and very rainy
Terrain: low, with maximum elevations of about 2 meters
Natural resources: none

354

Natural hazards: NA

Note: about 50 islets covered with dense vegetation, coconut trees, and balsa-like trees up to 30 meters tall

People

Population: uninhabited

Economy

no economic activity

Transportation

Roads: much of the road and many causeways built during the war are unserviceable and overgrown

Ports: West Lagoon

Airports: 1 unpaved

Panama

Capital: Panama   longitude: 79.30 W   latitude: 8.57 N   elevation: 118 ft

Government: constitutional republic

Flag: divided into four, equal rectangles; the top quadrants are white (hoist side) with a blue five-pointed star in the center and plain red, the bottom quadrants are plain blue (hoist side) and white with a red five-pointed star in the center

Geography

Location: Middle America, bordering both the Caribbean Sea and the North Pacific Ocean, between Columbia and Costa Rica

Total Area: 78,200 sq km (30,193 sq mi) slightly smaller than South Carolina

Boundaries: Colombia, Costa Rica

Climate: tropical; hot, humid, cloudy; prolonged rainy season (May to January), short dry season (January to May)

355

Temperature (F): High/Low Jan. 88/71, Apr. 87/74, July 87/74, Oct. 85/73
Average annual precipitation: 69.7 inches
Terrain: interior mostly steep, rugged mountains and dissected, upland plains; coastal areas largely plains and rolling hills
Highest point Baru Volcano 3,475 m (11,401 ft)
Natural resources: copper, mahogany forests, shrimp
Natural hazards: NA
Note: strategic location on eastern end of isthmus forming land bridge connecting North and South America; controls Panama Canal that links North Atlantic Ocean via Caribbean Sea with North Pacific Ocean

People

Population: 2,681,000 (July 1995 est.)
Life expectancy at birth: total population 75.2 years
Nationality: Panamanian
Ethnic division: mestizo (mixed Indian and European ancestry) 70%, West Indian 14%, white 10%, Indian 6%
Religions: Roman Catholic 85%, Protestant 15%
Languages: Spanish (official), English
Note: many Panamanians bilingual
Literacy: total population 89%

Economy

Imports: capital goods, crude oil, foodstuffs, consumer goods, chemicals
Exports: bananas, shrimp, sugar, clothing, coffee
Industries: manufacturing and construction, petroleum refining, brewing, cement and other construction materials, sugar milling
Agriculture: crops - bananas, rice, corn, coffee, sugarcane; livestock; fishing; importer of food grains, vegetables
Currency: 1 balboa (B) = 100 centesimos
                 balboas per US1$ - 1.00 (fixed rate)

Transportation

Railroads: 238 km
Roads: 8,530 km total paved and unpaved
Ports: Bahia de las Minas, Balboa, Colon, Cristobal, Panama
Airports: 115 total paved and unpaved. The international airport is located at Panama

The Press: daily newspapers   **La Prenza:**
                                    Avda 11 de Octubre y Calle C. Hato Pintado
                                    Apdo 64586, El Dorado, Panama
                                    telephone 21- 72-22   fax 21-73-28   circ. 45,000

El Siglo: Via Argentina 62, Apdo W, Panama 4
telephone 63-54-01   fax 69-69-54   circ. 42,000

Tourism: Tourist attractions are the ruins of Portobelo, resort at Contadora

Asociacion Panamaena de Agencias de Viajes y Turismo:
Apdo 55-1000 Paitilla, Panama 3
telephone 64-30-29 fax 64-15-70

Diplomatic representation in US:
chief of mission: Ambassador Ricardo Alberto Arias
chancery: 2862 McGill Terrace NW, Washington, DC 20008
telephone: [1] (202) 483-1407

US Diplomatic representation:
chief of mission: (vacant); Charge d'Affaires Oliver P. Garza
embassy: Avenida Balboa and Calle 38, Apartado 6959, Panama City 5
mailing address: American Embassy Panama, Unit 0945; APO AA 34002
telephone: [507] 27-17-77
FAX: [507] 27-19-64

Papua New Guinea

Capital: Port Moresby   longitude: 147.07 E latitude: 9.30 S
elevation 126 ft

Government: parliamentary

Flag: divided diagonally from upper hoist-side corner; the upper triangle is red with a soaring yellow bird of paradise centered; the lower triangle is black with five white five-pointed stars of the Southern Cross constellation centered

357

Geography

Location: Southeastern Asia, group of islands including the eastern half of the island of New Guinea between the Coral Sea and the South Pacific Ocean, east of Indonesia

Total Area: 461,690 sq km (178,259 sq mi) slightly larger than California

Boundaries: Indonesia

Climate: tropical; northwest monsoon (December to March), southeast monsoon (May to October); slight seasonal temperature variation

Temperature (F): High/Low Jan. 89/76, Apr. 87/75, July 83/73, Oct. 86/75

Average annual precipitation: 39.8 inches

Terrain: mostly mountains with coastal lowlands and rolling foothills

Natural resources: gold, copper, silver, natural gas, timber, oil potential

Natural hazards: active volcanism; situated along the Pacific "Rim of Fire"; the country is subject to frequent and sometimes severe earthquakes; mud slides

People

Population: 4,295,000 (July 1995 est.)

Life expectancy at birth: total population 56.85 years

Nationality: Papua New Guinean

Ethnic division: Melanesian, Papuan, Negrito, Micronesian, Polymesian

Religions: Roman Catholic 22%, Lutheran 16%, Presbyterian/Methodist/London Missionary Society 8%, Anglican 5%, Evangelical Alliance 4%, Seventh-Day Adventist 1%, other Protestant sects 10%, indigenous beliefs 34%

Languages: English spoken by 1%-2%, pidgin English widespread, Motu spoken in Papua region

Note: 715 indigenous languages

Literacy: total population 52%

Economy

Imports: machinery and transport equipment, manufactured goods, food, fuels, chemicals

Exports: gold, copper ore, oil, logs, palm oil, coffee, cocoa, lobster

Industries: copra crushing, palm oil processing, plywood production, wood chip production, mining of gold, silver, and copper, construction, tourism

Agriculture: livelihood for 85% of population; fertile soils and favorable climate permits cultivating a wide variety of crops; cash crops - coffee, cocoa, coconuts, palm kernels; other products - tea, rubber, sweet potatoes, fruit, vegetables, poultry, pork; net importer of food for urban centers

Currency: 1 kina (K) = 100 toea

kina per US1$ - 0.85

Transportation

    Railroads: none

    Roads: 19,200 km total paved and unpaved

    Ports: Kieta, Lae, Madang, Port Moresby, Rabaul

    Airports: 505 total paved and unpaved. The International airport is located at Port Moresby.

The Press: newspapers

Papau New Guinea Post-Courier:

POB 85, Port Moresby   telephone 21-25-77

daily   English   circ. 32,000

The Times of Papua New Guinea:

POB 1892, Boroko   telephone 25-25-00   fax 25-25-79

weekly   English   circ. 10,000

Tourism: Baiyer River wildlife sanctuary, anthropology, art, and out of the way adventure, beaches, diving

Tourism Promotions Authority: POB 7144, Boroko

telephone 27-25-21   fax 25-91-19

Diplomatic representation in US:

    chief of mission: Ambassador Kepas Isimel Watangia

    chancery: 3rd Floor, 1615 New Hampshire Avenue NW, Washington, DC 20009

    telephone: [1] (202) 745-3680

    FAX: [1] (202) 745-3679

US Diplomatic representation:

    chief of mission: Ambassador Richard W. Teare

    embassy: Armit Street, Port Moresby

    mailing address: P O Box 1492, Port Moresby, or APO AE 96553

    telephone: [675] 21-14-55, 21-15-94, 21-16-54

    FAX: [675] 21-34-23

Paracel Islands

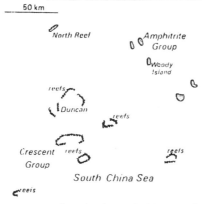

50 km

North Reef

Amphitrite Group

Woody Island

reefs

Duncan

reefs

Crescent Group   reefs   reefs

reefs

South China Sea

reefs

Capital: none   longitude: 112.00 W   latitude: 17.05 N

Government: International disputes: occupied by China, but claimed by Taiwan and Vietnam

Geography

Location: Southeastern Asia, group of small islands and reefs in the South China Sea, about one-third of the way from central Vietnam to the northern Philippines

Total Area: NA

Boundaries: no land boundaries

Climate: tropical

Terrain: NA

Natural resources: none

Natural hazards: typhoons

People

Population: no indigenous inhabitants; note - there are scattered Chinese garrisons

Economy

no economic activity

Transportation

Ports: small Chinese port facilities on Woody Island and Duncan Island being expanded

Airports: 1 with paved runways

Paraguay

Capital: Asuncion longitude: 57.40 W latitude: 25.15 S elevation 456 ft
Government: republic
Flag: three equal horizontal bands of red (top), white, and blue with an emblem centered in the white band unusual flag in that the emblem is different on each side; the obverse (hoist side at the left) bears the national coat of arms (a yellow five-pointed star within a green wreath capped by the words REPUBLICA DEL PARAGUAY, all within two circles); the reverse (hoist side at the right) bears the seal of the treasury (a yellow lion below a red Cap of Liberty and the words Paz y Justicia (Peace and Justice) capped by the words REPUBLICIA DEL PARAGUAY, all within two circles)

Geography
Location: Central South America, northeast of Argentina
Total Area: 406,750 sq km (157,046 sq mi) slightly smaller than California
Boundaries: Argentina, Bolivia, Brazil
Climate: varies from temperate in east to semiarid in far west
Temperature (F): High/Low Jan. 95/71, Apr. 84/65, July 74/53, Oct. 86/62
Average annual precipitation: 51.8 inches
Terrain: grassy plains and wooded hills east of Rio Paraguay; Gran Chaco region west of Rio Paraguay mostly low, marshy plain near the river, and dry forest and thorny scrub elsewhere
Highest point Mirador Nacional 501 m (1,644 ft)
Natural resources: hydropower, timber, iron ore, manganese, limestone
Natural hazards: local flooding in southeast (early September to June); poorly drained plains may become boggy (early October to June)

People
Population: 5,358,800 (July 1995 est.)
Life expectancy at birth: total population 73.58 years
Nationality: Paraguayan

Ethnic division: metizo (mixed Spanish and Indian) 95%, Caucasians plus Amerindians 5%

Religions: Roman Catholic 90%, Mennonite and other Protestant denominations

Languages: Spanish (official), Guarani

Literacy: total population 90%

Economy

Imports: capital goods, foodstuffs, consumer goods, raw materials, fuels

Exports: cotton, soybeans, timber, vegetable oils, meat products, coffee, tung oil

Industries: meat packing, oilseed crushing, milling, brewing, textiles, other light consumer goods, cement, construction

Agriculture: cash crops - cotton, sugarcane, soybeans; other crops - corn, wheat, tobacco, cassava, fruits, vegetables; self-sufficient in most foods

Currency: 1 guarani (G) = 100 centimos
>> guaranies per US1$ - 1,949.6

Transportation

Railroads: 970 km

Roads: 28,300 km total paved and unpaved

Ports: Asuncion, Villeta, San Antonio, Encarnacion

Airports: 929 total paved and unpaved. The international airport is about 12 km from Asuncion

The Press: daily newspapers

ABC Color: Yegros 745, Asuncion
telephone (21) 49-11-60   fax (21) 49-30-59
circ. 75,000

El Diario Noticias: Avda Artigas y Avda Brasilia, Casilla 3017, Asuncion   circ. 55,000
telephone (21) 29-27-21 fax (21) 29-28-40

Tourism: Asuncion, Jesuit Mission Trail, Chaco region

Direccion General de Turismo:
Ministerio de Obras Publicas y Comunicaciones, Palma 468, Asuncion
telephone (21) 44-15-30 fax (21) 91-230

Diplomatic representation in US:

chief of mission: Ambassador Jorge Genaro Andres Prieto Conti

chancery: 2400 Massachusetts Avenue NW, Washington, DC 20008

telephone: [1] (202) 483-6960 through 6962

FAX: [1] (202) 234-4508

US Diplomatic representation:
chief of mission: Ambassador Robert Service
embassy: 1776 Avenida Mariscal Lopez, Asuncion
mailing address: C P 402, Asuncion; Unit 4711, APO AA 34036-0001
telephone: [595] (21) 21-37-15
FAX: [595] (21) 21-37-28

Peru

Capital: Lima   longitude: 77.03 W   latitude: 12.06 S   elevation 394 ft
Government: republic
Flag: three equal, vertical bands of red (hoist side), white, and red with the coat of arms centered in the white band; the coat of arms features a shield bearing a llama, cinchona tree (the source of quinine), and a yellow cornucopia spilling out gold coins, all framed by a green wreath

Geography

Location: Western South America, bordering the South Pacific Ocean, between Chile and Ecuador
Total Area: 1,285,220 sq km (496,223 sq mi) slightly smaller than Alaska
Boundaries: Bolivia, Brazil, Chile, Columbia, Ecuador
Climate: varies from tropical in east to dry desert in west
Temperature (F): High/Low Jan. 82/66, Apr. 80/63, July 67/57, Oct. 71/58
Average annual precipitation: 1.6 inches
Terrain: western coastal plain (costa), high and rugged Andes in center (sierra), eastern lowland jungle of Amazon Basin (selva)
Highest point is Huascaran 6,768 m (22,205 ft)
Natural resources: copper, silver, gold, petroleum, timber, fish, iron ore, coal, phosphate, potash
Natural hazards: earthquakes, tsunamis, flooding, landslides, mild volcanic activity

People

Population: 24,088,000 (July 1995 est.)

Life expectancy at birth: total population 66.07 years

Nationality: Peruvian

Ethnic division: Indians 45%, mestizo (mixed Indian and European ancestry) 37%, white 15%, black, Japanese, Chinese, and others 3%

Religions: Roman Catholic

Languages: Spanish (official), Quechua (official) Aymara

Literacy: total population 82%

Economy

Imports: machinery, transport equipment, foodstuffs, petroleum, iron and steel, chemicals, pharmaceuticals

Exports: copper, zinc, fishmeal, crude petroleum and by-products, lead, refined silver, coffee, cotton

Industries: mining of metals, petroleum, fishing, textiles, clothing, food processing, cement, auto assembly, steel, shipbuilding, metal fabrication

Agriculture: commercial crops - coffee, cotton, sugarcane; other crops - rice, wheat, potatoes, plantains, coca; animal products - poultry, red meats, dairy, wool; not self-sufficient in grain or vegetable oil

Currency: 1 nuevo sol (S/.) = 100 centimos
nuevo sol per US1$ - 2.20

Transportation

Railroads: 1,801 km

Roads: 69,942 km total paved and unpaved

Ports: Callao, Chimbote, Ilo, Iquitos, Matarani, Paita, Pucallpa, Salaverry, San Martin, Talara, Yurimaguas

Note: Iquitos, Pucallpa, and Yurimaguas are all on the upper reaches of the Amazon and its tributaries

Airports: 236 total paved and unpaved. The major international airport is near Lima. Other international airports are at Iquitos, Cuzco, and Arequipa

The Press: daily newspapers   **El Comercio:** Empresa Editora 'El Comercio',
SA, Jiron Antonio Miro Quesada 3000, Lima
telephone (14) 28-76-20   fax (14) 31-08-10
circ. 150,000 weekdays   225,000 Sundays

Ojo: Avda Garcilaso de la Vega, Lima 27
morning   circ. 180,000

Tourism: Tourist attractions are pre-Inca and Inca civilization at Cuzco, Amazon jungle region and Spanish colonial architecture in Lima. Lake Titicaca

364

Viceministerio de Turismo: Calle 1 Oeste,
Corpac, San Isidre, Lima
telephone (14) 40-21-29

Diplomatic representation in US:

chief of mission: Ambassador Ricardo V. Luna Mendoza

chancery: 1700 Massachusetts Avenue NW, Washington, DC 20036

telephone: [1] (202) 833-9860 through 9869

FAX: [1] (202) 659-8124

US Diplomatic representation:

chief of mission: Ambassador Alvin P. Adams, Jr

embassy: corner of Avenida Inca Garcilaso de la Vega
and Avenida Espana, Lima

mailing address: P O Box 1995, Lima 1; American Embassy (Lima)
APO AA 34031

telephone: [51] (14) 33-80-00

FAX: [51] (14) 31-66-82

Philippines

Capital: Manila   longitude: 120.58 E   latitude: 14.37 N   elevation 47 ft

Government: republic

Flag: two equal horizontal bands of blue (top) and red with a white equilateral triangle based on the hoist side; in the center of the triangle is a yellow sun with eight primary rays (each containing three individual rays) and in each corner of the triangle is a small yellow five-pointed star

Geography

Location: Southeastern Asia, archipelago between the Philippine Sea and the South China Sea, east of Vietnam

Total Area: 300,000 sq km (115,830 sq mi) slightly larger than Arizona

365

Boundaries: no land boundaries

Climate: tropical marine; northeast monsoon (November to April); southwest monsoon (May to October)

Temperature (F): High/Low Jan. 86/69, Apr. 93/73, July 88/75, Oct. 88/74

Average annual precipitation: 82 inches

Terrain: mostly mountains with narrow to extensive coastal lowlands

Highest point is Mt. Apo 2,954 m (9,692 ft)

Natural resources: timber, petroleum, nickel, cobalt, silver, gold, salt, copper

Natural hazards: astride typhoon belt, usually affected by 15 and struck by five to six cyclonic storms per year; landslides; active volcanoes, destructive earthquakes

People

Population: 73,266,000 (July 1995 est.)

Life expectancy at birth: total population 65.65 years

Nationality: Filipino

Ethnic division: Christian Malay 91.5%, Muslim Malay 4%, Chinese 1.5%, other 3%

Religions: Roman Catholic 83%, Protestant 9%, Muslim 5%, Buddhist and other 3%

Languages: Philipino (official; based on Tagalog), English (official)

Literacy: total population 94%

Economy

Imports: raw materials, capital goods, petroleum products

Exports: electronics, textiles, coconuts products, copper, fish

Industries: textiles, pharmaceuticals, chemicals, wood products, food processing, electronics assembly, petroleum refining, fishing

Agriculture: major crops - rice, coconuts, corn, sugarcane, bananas, pineapples, mangos; animal products - pork, eggs, beef; net exporter of farm products

Currency: 1 Philippine peso (P) = 100 centavos

Philippine pesos per US1$ - 24.62

Transportation

Railroads: 800 km total; including about 390 km in Luzon

Roads: 160,700 km total paved and unpaved

Ports: Batangas, Cagayan de Oro, Cebu, Davao, Guimaras, Iligan, Iloilo, Jolo, Legaspi, Manila, Masao, Puerto Princesa, San Fernando, Subic Bay, Zamboanga

Airports: 269 total paved and unpaved. The main international airports are at Manila and Mactan (Cebu). Alternate international airports are located at Laoag City, Davao City, Zamboanga City, Puerto Princesa City

The Press: daily newspapers

Manila Bulletin: corner of Muralla and Recoletos Streets, Intramuros, POB 769 Metro Manila telephone (2) 47-36-21 English circ. 260,000
Manila Chronicle: 371 Bonifacio Drive, Port Area, Metro Manila telephone (2) 47-82-61 fax (2) 48-10-85 circ. 165,000

Tourism: Manila, Taal Volcano, beautiful beaches, resorts, Island of Leyte
Philippine Convention and Visitors Corporation: Legaspi Towers, 4th Floor, 300 Roxas Blvd, Metro Manila telephone (2) 57-50-31   fax (2) 521-6165

Diplomatic representation in US:
chief of mission: Ambassador Raul Chaves Rabe
chancery: 1600 Massachusetts Avenue NW, 20036
telephone: [1] (202) 467-9300
FAX: [1] (202) 328-7614
US Diplomatic representation:
chief of mission: Ambassador John D. Negroponte
embassy: 1201 Roxas Boulevard, Ermita Manial 1000
mailing address: APO AP 96440
telephone: [63] (2) 521-7116
FAX: [63] (2) 522-4361

Pitcairn Islands

South Pacific Ocean

Capital: Adamstown   longitude: 130.06 W   latitude: 25.04 S
Government: dependent territory of the UK

Flag: blue with the flag of the UK in the upper hoist-side quadrant and the Pitcairn Islander coat of arms centered on the outer half of the flag; the coat of arms is yellow, green, and light blue with a shield featuring a yellow anchor

Geography

Location: Oceania, islands in the South Pacific Ocean, About one-half of the way from Peru to New Zealand

Total Area: 47 sq km (18.2 sq mi) about 0.3 times the size of Washington, DC

Boundaries: no land boundaries

Climate: tropical; hot, humid, modified by southeast trade winds; rainy season (November to March)

Terrain: rugged volcanic formation; rocky coastline with cliffs

Natural resources: miro trees (used for handicrafts), fish

Natural hazards: typhoons (especially November to March)

People

Population: 73 (July 1995 est.)

Life expectancy at birth: NA

Nationality: Pitcairn Islander

Ethnic division: descendant of the Bounty mutineers

Religions: Seventh-Day Adventist 100%

Languages: English (official), Tahitian/English dialect

Literacy: NA

Economy

Imports: fuel oil, machinery, building materials, flour, sugar, other foodstuffs

Exports: fruits, vegetables, curios

Industries: postage stamps, handicrafts

Agriculture: based on subsistence fishing and farming; wide variety of fruits and vegetables; must import grain products

Currency: 1 New Zealand dollar (NZ$) = 100 cents
New Zealand dollars per US1$ - 1.56

Transportation

Railroads: none

Roads: 6.4 km unpaved

Ports: Bounty Bay

Airports: none

The Press: **Pitcairn Miscellany:** monthly five page news sheet

Tourism: windswept island where Fletcher Christian and the Bounty mutineers stepped ashore in 1790. Their dependents still live on Pitcarin

Diplomatic representation in US: none (dependent territory of the UK)
US Diplomatic representation: none (dependent territory of the UK)

Poland

Capital: Warsaw   longitude: 21.00 E   latitude: 52.15 N   elevation: 361 ft
Government: democratic state
Flag: two equal horizontal bands of white (top) and red; similar to the flags of Indonesia and Monaco which are red (top) and white
Geography
Location: Central Europe, east of Germany
Total Area: 312,680 sq km (120,726 sq mi) slightly smaller than New Mexico
Boundaries: Belarus, Czech Republic, Germany, Lithuania, Russia, Slovakia, Ukraine
Climate: temperate with cold, cloudy, moderately severe winters with frequent precipitation; mild summers with frequent showers and thunderstorms
Temperature (F): High/Low Jan. 32/22, Apr. 53/37. July 75/58, Oct. 55/41
Average annual precipitation: 22 inches
Terrain: mostly flat plain; mountains along southern border
Highest point is Rysy 2,499 m (8,199 ft)
Natural resources: coal, sulfur, copper, natural gas, silver, lead, salt
Natural hazards: NA
People
Population: 38,793,00 (July 1995 est.)
Life expectancy at birth: total population 73.13 years

369

Nationality: noun: Pole (s) adjective: Polish

Ethnic division: Polish 97.6%, German 1.3%, Ukrainian 0.6%, Byelorussian 0.5%

Religions: Roman Catholic 95%, (about 75% practicing), Eastern Orthodox, Protestant, and other 5%

Languages: Polish

Literacy: total population 99%

Economy

Imports: machinery and transport equipment, intermediate goods, chemicals, fuels, miscellaneous manufactures

Exports: intermediate goods, machinery and transport equipment, miscellaneous manufactures, foodstuffs, fuels

Industries: machine building, iron and steel, extractive industries, chemicals, shipbuilding, food processing, glass, beverages, textiles

Agriculture: productivity remains low by European standards; leading European producer of rye, rapeseed, and potatoes; wide variety of other crops and livestock; major exporter of pork products; normally self-sufficient in food

Currency: 1 Zloty (ZI) = 100 groszy

zlotych per US1$ - 2.45

Transportation

Railroads: 25,528 km

Roads: 367,000 km total paved and unpaved (excluding farm, factory and forest roads)

Ports: Gdansk, Gdynia, Gliwice, Kolobrzeg, Szczecin, Swinoujscie, Ustka, Warsaw, Wrocaw

Airports: 134 total paved and unpaved. The international airports are located near Warsaw and at Krakow and Gdansk

The Press: daily newspapers **Gazeta Wyborcza:** 00-732 Warsaw, ul. Czerska 8/10

telephone (22) 41-55-13   fax (22) 41-69-20

circ. 520,000 weekdays,   750,000 weekends

Zycie Warszawy: 00-575 Warsaw, Al. Armii Ludowej 3/5

telephone (2) 625-6990 fax (22) 25-28-29

circ. 250,000 weekdays,   460,000 weekends

Tourism: Warsaw National Museum, Marie Curie Sklodowska Museum, Kampinos Forest, Baltic resorts

Polish Tourist and Country-Lovers Society:

00-075 Warsaw, ul. Senatorska 11

telephone (22) 26-57-35   fax (22) 26-25-05

Diplomatic representation in US:

chief of mission: Ambassador Jerzy Kozminski

chancery: 2640 16th Street NW, Washington, DC 20009

telephone: [1] (202) 234-3800 through 3802

FAX: [1] (202) 328-6271

US Diplomatic representation:

chief of mission: Ambassador Nicholas Andrew Rey

embassy: Aleje Ujazdowskie 29/31, Warsaw

mailing address: American Embassy Warsaw, Box 5010,

Unit 1340, APO AE 09213-1340

telephone: [48] (2) 628-3041

FAX: [48] (2) 628-8298

Portugal

Capital: Lisbon   longitude: 9.08 W latitude: 38.44 N   elevation 253 ft

Government: republic

Flag: two vertical bands of green (hoist side, two-fifths) and red (three-fifths) with the Portuguese coat of arms centered on the dividing line

Geography

Location: Southwestern Europe, bordering the North Atlantic Ocean, west of Spain

Total Area: 92,080 sq km (35,552 sq mi) slightly smaller than Indiana

Note: includes Azores and Madeira islands

Boundaries: Spain

Climate: maritime temperate; cool and rainy in north, plains in south

Temperature (F): High/Low Jan. 57/46, Apr. 67/53, July 81/63, Oct. 72/58

Average annual precipitation: 27.7 inches

Terrain: mountainous north of the Tagus, rolling plains south

Highest point is Malhao da Estrela 1,991 m (6,532 ft)

371

Natural resources: fish, forest (cork), tungsten, iron ore, uranium ore, marble

Natural hazards: Azores subject to severe earthquakes

Note: Azores and Madeira Islands occupy strategic locations along western sea approaches to Strait of Gibraltar

People

Population: 10,563,000 (July 1995 est.)

Life expectancy at birth: total population 75.53 years

Nationality: Portuguese

Ethnic division: homogeneous Mediterranean stock in mainland, Azores, Madeira Islands; citizens of black African decent who immigrated to mainland during decolonization number less than 100,000

Religions: Roman Catholic 97%, Protestant denominations 1%, other 2%

Languages: Portuguese

Literacy: total population 85%

Economy

Imports: machinery and transport equipment, agricultural products, chemicals, petroleum, textiles

Exports: clothing and footwear, machinery, cork and paper products, hides and skins

Industries: textiles and footwear; wood pulp, paper, and cork; metalworking; oil refining; chemicals; fish canning; wine; tourism

Agriculture: small, inefficient farms; imports more than half of food needs; major crops - grain, potatoes, olives, grapes; livestock sector - sheep, cattle, goats, poultry, meat, dairy products

Currency: 1 Portuguese escudo (Esc) = 100 centavos

Portuguese escudos per US1$ - 158.02

Transportation

Railroads: 3,068 km

Roads: 70,176 km total paved and unpaved

Ports: Aveiro, Funchal (Madeira Islands), Horta (Azores), Leixoes, Lisbon, Porto, Ponta Delgada (Azores), Praia da Vitoria (Azores), Setubal, Viana do Castelo

Airports: 65 total paved and unpaved. There are international airports at ˙ Lisbon, Porto, Faro, Funchal on Madeira Island, Santa Maria and Sao Miguel on Azores Islands

The Press: daily newspapers

Diario de Noticias: Av. da Liberdade 266, 1200 Lisbon   circ. 60,000
telephone (1) 56-11-51   fax (1) 53-66-27
Publico: Rua Amilcar, Lote 1, Quinta do Lambert
1700 Lisbon   circ. 75,000
telephone (1) 759-9135 fax (1) 758-7638

Tourism: the Algarve Coast, gardens of Queluz, dramatic landscapes, vinyards, beaches

Secretaria de Estado do Turismo:
Palacio Foz, Praca dos Restauradores, 1200 Lisbon
telephone (1) 346-3580   fax (1) 347-0473

Diplomatic representation in US:
chief of mission: Ambassador Francisco Jose Laco Treichler Knopfli
chancery: 2125 Kalorama Road NW, Washington, DC 20008
telephone: [1] (202) 328-8610
FAX: [1] (202) 462-3726

US Diplomatic representation:
chief of mission: Ambassador Elizabeth Frawley Bagley
embassy: Avenida das Forcas Armadas, 1600 Lisbon
mailing address: PSC 83, Lisbon; APO AE 09726
telephone: [351] (1) 726-6600, 726-6659, 726-8670, 726-8880
FAX: [351] (1) 726-9109

Puerto Rico

Isla Desecheo and
Isla Mona are not shown.

Capital: San Juan   longitude: 66.08 W   latitude: 18.29 N elevation: 82 ft
Government: commonwealth associated with the US

Flag: five equal bands of red (top and bottom) alternation with white; a blue isosceles triangle based on the hoist side bears a large white five-pointed star in the center; design based on the US flag

Geography

Location: Caribbean, island between the Caribbean Sea and the North Atlantic Ocean, east of the Dominican Republic

Total Area: 9,104 sq km (3,515 sq mi) slightly less than three times the size of Rhode Island

Boundaries: no land boundaries

Climate: tropical marine, mild, little seasonal temperature variation
Temperature (F): High/Low Jan. 80/70, Apr. 82/72, July 85/75, Oct. 85/75
Average annual precipitation: 60.8 inches

Terrain: mostly mountains with coastal plain belt in north; mountains precipitous to sea on west coast; sandy beaches along most coastal areas
Highest point is Cerro de Punta 1,338 m (4,389 ft)

Natural resources: some copper and nickel, potential for onshore and offshore crude oil

Natural hazards: periodic droughts

People

Population: 3,813,000 (July 1995 est.)

Life expectancy at birth: total population 75.1 years

Nationality: Puerto Rican (US citizens)

Ethnic division: Hispanic

Religions: Roman Catholic 85%, Protestant denominations and other 15%

Languages: Spanish, English

Literacy: total population 89%

Economy

Imports: chemicals, clothing, food, fish, petroleum products

Exports: pharmaceuticals, electronics, apparel, canned tuna, rum, beverage concentrates, medical equipment, instruments

Industries: manufacturing of pharmaceuticals, electronics, apparel, food products, instruments, tourism

Agriculture: crops - sugarcane, coffee, pineapples, plantains, bananas; livestock - cattle, chickens; imports a large share of food needs

Currency: 1 United States dollar (US$) = 100 cents
US currency is used

Transportation

Railroads: 96 km; rural system used for hauling sugarcane - no passengers

Roads: 13,762 km total all paved

Ports: Guanica, Guayanilla, Guayama, Playa de Ponce, San Juan

Airports: 31 total paved and unpaved

The Press: daily newspapers   **El Nuevo Dia:** 404 Ponce de Leon Ave,
POB 5297, San Juan, PR 00902
telephone (809) 721-7070
El Vocero de Puerto Rico: 206 Ponce de Leon Ave,
POB 3831, San Juan, PR 00904
telephone (809) 721-2300

Tourism: Old San Juan, museum of Puerto Rican Art
Commonwealth of Puerto Rico Tourism Co:
POB 4435, Old San Jaun Station, San Juan, PR 00904
telephone (809) 721-2400   fax (809) 725-4417

Diplomatic representation in US: none (commonwealth associated with the US)
US Diplomatic representation: none (commonwealth associated with the US)

Qatar

Capital: Doha   longitude: 51.32 E   latitude: 25.15 N

Government: traditional monarchy

    Flag: maroon with a broad white serrated band (nine white points) on the
hoist side

Geography

    Location: Middle East, peninsula bordering the Persian Gulf and Saudi
Arabia

    Total Area: 11,000 sq km (4,271 sq mi) slightly smaller than Connecticut

    Boundaries: Saudi Arabia

    Climate: desert; hot, dry; humid and sultry in summer

Temperature (F): High/Low Jan. 71/56, Apr. 85/68, July 100/84, Oct. 91/73

Terrain: mostly flat and barren desert covered with loose sand and gravel

Natural resources: petroleum, natural gas, fish

Natural hazards: haze, dust storms, sandstorms common

People

Population: 534,000 (July 1995 est.)

Life expectancy at birth: total population 73.03 years

Nationality: Qatari

Ethnic division: Arab 40%, Pakistani 18%, Indian 18%, Iranian 10%, other 14%

Religions: Muslim 95%

Languages: Arabic (official), English commonly used as a second language

Literacy: total population 76%

Economy

Imports: machinery and equipment, consumer goods, food, chemicals

Exports: petroleum products, steel, fertilizers

Industries: crude oil production and refining, fertilizers, petrochemicals, steel (rolls reinforcing bars for concrete construction), cement

Agriculture: farming and grazing on a small scale; agricultural area is small and government-owned; commercial fishing is increasing in importance; most food imported

Currency: 1 Qatari riyal (QR) = 100 dirhams
           Qatari riyals per US1$ - 3.64

Transportation

Railroads: none

Roads: 1,190 km total paved and unpaved

Ports: Doha, Halul Island, Umm Sa'id

Airports: 6 total paved and unpaved. The international airport is at Doha and is equipped to receive all type aircraft.

The Press: daily newspapers   **Gulf Times:** POB 288, Doha
                                          telephone 46-66-11   fax 35-04-74
                                          English   circ. 15,000

          Ash-Sharq: POB 3488, Doha
          telephone 86-14-12 fax 66-24-56   Arabic   circ. 40,000

Tourism: Doha National Museum and National Aquarium

Diplomatic representation in US:

chief of mission: Ambassador Abd Al-Rahman bin Saud Fahd Al Thani

chancery: Suite 1180, 600 New Hampshire Avenue NW

Washington, DC 20037

telephone: (202) 338-0111

US Diplomatic representation:

chief of mission: Ambassador Kenton W. Keith

embassy: 149 Ali Bin Ahmed ST., FArig Bin Omran (opposite the television station), Doha

mailing address: P O Box 2399, Doha

telephone: [974] 86-47-01 through 86-47-03

FAX: [974] 86-16-69

Reunion

Capital: Saint-Denis   longitude: 55.28 E   latitude: 20.52 S

Government: overseas department of France

Flag: the flag of France is used

Geography

Location: Southern Africa, island in the Indian Ocean, east of Madagascar

Total Area: 2,510 sq km (969 sq mi) slightly smaller than Rhode Island

Boundaries: no land boundaries

Climate: tropical; but moderates with elevation; cool and dry from May to November, hot and rainy from November to April

Temperature (F): High/Low Jan. 81/78, Apr. 79/75, July 71/69, Oct. 73/71

Terrain: mostly rugged and mountainous; fertile lowlands along coast

Highest point is Piton des Neiges 3,069 m (10,069 ft)

Natural resources: fish, arable land

Natural hazards: periodic, devastating cyclones (December to April) Piton de la Fournaise on the southeastern coast is an active volcano

People

Population: 666,800 (July 1995 est.)

Life expectancy at birth: total population 74.46 years

Nationality: Reunionese

Ethnic division: French, African, Malagasy, Chinese, Pakistani, Indian

Religions: Roman Catholic 94%

Languages: French (official), Creole widely used

Literacy: total population 79%

Economy

Imports: manufactured goods, food, beverages, tobacco, machinery and transportation equipment, raw materials, and petroleum products

Exports: sugar, rum and molasses, perfume essences, lobster, vanilla and tea.

Industries: sugar, rum, cigarettes, several small shops producing handicraft items

Agriculture: cash crops - sugarcane, vanilla, tobacco; food crops - tropical fruits, vegetables, corn; imports large share of food needs

Currency: 1 French franc (F) = 100 centimes

French francs per US1$ - 5.29

Transportation

Railroads: none

Roads: 2,800 km total paved and unpaved

Ports: Le Port, Pointe des Galets

Airports: 2 total. The international airport is at Saint-Denis Gillot

The Press: dailies **Journal de I'lle de la Reunion:** 42 rue Alexis de Villeneuve, BP 166, 97464 Saint-Denis Cedex
telephone 21-32-64 fax 41-09-77 circ. 26,000

Quotidien de la Reunion: BP 303, 97712 Saint-Denis Cedex
telephone 29-10-10 fax 28-25-28 circ. 28,000

Tourism: There is a 'holiday village' in Saint-Gilles

Office du Tourisme: 48 rue Saint-Marie, 97400 Saint-Denis
telephone 41-83-00 fax 21-37-76

Diplomatic representation in US: none (overseas department of France)

US Diplomatic representation: none (overseas department of France)

Romania

200 km

Capital: Bucharest   longitude: 26.07 E   latitude: 44.25 N   elevation: 302 ft

Government: republic

Flag: three equal vertical bands of blue (hoist side), yellow, and red; the national coat of arms that used to be centered in the yellow band has been removed; now similar to the flags of Andorra and Chad

Geography

Location: Southeastern Europe, bordering the Black Sea, between Bulgaria and Ukraine

Total Area: 237,500 sq km (91,699 sq mi) slightly smaller than Oregon

Boundaries: Bulgaria, Hungary, Moldova, Serbia and Montenegro, Ukraine

Climate: temperate; cold, cloudy winters with frequent snow and fog; sunny summers with frequent showers and thunderstorms

Temperature (F): High/Low Jan. 34/19, Apr. 64/41, July 86/60, Oct. 65/43

Average annual precipitation: 23.3 inches

Terrain: central Transylvanian Basin is separated from the Plain of Moldavia on the east by the Carpathian Mountains and separated from the Walachian Plain on the south by Transylvanian Alps

Highest point is Caransebes Peleaga 2,509 m (8,232 ft)

Natural resources: petroleum (reserve declining), timber, natural gas, coal, iron ore, salt

Natural hazards: earthquakes most severe in south and southwest; geologic structure and climate promote landslides

People

Population: 23,198,800 (July 1995 est.)

Life expectancy at birth: total population 72.24 years

Nationality: Romanian

Ethnic division: Romanian 89.1%, Hungarian 8.9%, German 0.4%, Ukrainian, Serb, Croat, Russian, Turk, and Gypsy 1.6%

379

Religions: Romanian Orthodox 70%, Roman Catholic 6% (of which 3% are Uniate), Protestant 6%, unaffiliated 18%

Languages: Romanian, Hungarian, German

Literacy: total population 97%

Economy

Imports: minerals, machinery and equipment, textiles, agricultural goods

Exports: metal and metal products, mineral products, textiles, electric machines and equipment, transport materials

Industries: mining, timber, construction materials, metallurgy, chemicals, machine building, food processing, petroleum production and refining

Agriculture: major wheat and corn producer, other products - sugar beets, sunflower seed, potatoes, milk, eggs, meat, grapes

Currency: 1 lue (L) = 100 bani

> lei per US1$ - 1,776.00

Transportation

Railroads: 1,365 km

Roads: 461,880 km total paved and unpaved

Ports: Braila, Constanta, Galatz, Mangalia, Sulina, Tulcea

Airports: 156 total paved and unpaved. There are international airports at Bucharest, Constanta, and Arad

The Press: daily newspapers

Evenimentul Zilei:
Bucharest, Piata Presei Libere 1
telephone (1) 617-2094 fax (1) 312-8381
circ. 455,000

Romania Libere: 71341 Bucharest, Piata Presei Libere
telephone (1) 617-7849 fax (1) 312-8271
circ. 125,000

Tourism: Bucharest National Art Museum, Cismigiu Gardens, Black Sea resorts, hot springs, mud baths

Ont Carpati SA: 70161 Bucharest, Bd. Magheru 7
telephone (1) 614-5160 fax (1) 312-2594

Diplomatic representation in US:

chief of mission: Ambassador Mihai Horia Botez

chancery: 1607 23rd Street NW, Washington, DC 20008

telephone: [1] (202) 332-4846, 4848, 4851

FAX: [1] (202) 232-4748

US Diplomatic representation:
chief of mission: Ambassador Alfred H. Moses
embassy: Strada Tudor Arghezi 7-9, Bucharest
mailing address: American Consulate General (Bucharest),
Unit 1315, Bucharest; APO AE 09213-1315
telephone: [40] (1) 210-0149, 210-4042
FAX: [40] (1) 210-0395

Russia

2000 km

Capital: Moscow   longitude: 37.42 E   latitude: 55.45 N   elevation 512 ft
Government: federation
Flag: three equal horizontal bands of white (top), blue, and red
Geography
Location: Northern Asia, bordering the Arctic Ocean, between Europe and the North Pacific Ocean
Total Area: 17,075,200 sq km (6,592,735 sq mi) slightly more than 1.8 times the size of the US
Boundaries: Azerbaijan, Belarus, China, Estonia, Finland, Georgia, Kazakhstan, North Korea, Latvia, Lithuania, Mongolia, Norway, Poland, Ukraine
Climate: ranges from steppes in the south through humid continental in much of European Russia; subarctic in Siberia to tundra climate in the polar north; winters vary from cool along the Black Sea coast to frigid in Siberia, summers vary from warm in the steppes to cool along Arctic coast
Temperature (F): High/Low Jan. 15/3, Apr. 50/34, July 73/55, Oct. 48/37
Average annual precipitation: 24.7 inches
Terrain: broad plain with low hills west of Urals; vast coniferous forest and tundra in Siberia; uplands and mountains along southern border regions

Natural resources: wide natural resource base including deposits of oil, natural gas, coal, and many strategic minerals, timber
Note: formidable obstacles of climate, terrain, and distance hinder exploitation of natural resources
Natural hazards: permafrost over much of Siberia is a major impediment to development; volcanic activity in the Kuril Islands; volcanoes and earthquakes on the Kamchatka Peninsula
Note: largest country in the world in terms of area but unfavorably located in relation to major sea lanes of the world; despite its size, much of the country lacks proper soils and climates (either too cold or too dry) for agriculture

People

Population: 149,910,000 (July 1995 est.)

Life expectancy at birth: total population 69.1 years

Nationality: Russian

Ethnic division: Russian 81.5%, Tatar 3.8%, Ukrainian 3%, Chuvash 1.2%, Bashkir 0.9%, Byelorrusian 0.8%, Moldavian 0.7%, other 8.1%

Religions: Russian Orthodox, Muslim, other

Languages: Russian, other

Literacy: total population 98%

Economy

Imports: machinery and equipment, consumer goods, medicines, meat, grain, sugar, semi-finished metal products

Exports: petroleum and petroleum products, natural gas, wood and wood products, metals, chemicals, and a wide variety of civilian and military manufactures

Industries: complete range of mining and extractive industries producing coal, oil, gas, chemicals, and metals; all forms of machine building from rolling mills to high-performance aircraft and space vehicles; ship- building; road and rail transportation equipment; communications equipment; agricultural machinery, tractors, and construction equipment; electric power generating and transmitting equipment; medical and scientific instruments; consumer durables

Agriculture: grain, sugar beets, sunflower seeds, meat, milk, vegetables, fruits; because of its northern location does not grow citrus, cotton, tea, and other warm climate products

Currency: 1 ruble (R) = 100 kopeks
rubles per US1$ - 3,550.00

Transportation

Railroads: 154,000 km; note - 87,000 km in common carrier service, 67,000 km serve specific industries and are not available for common carrier use

Roads: 934,000 km (445,000 km serve specific industries or farms and are not available for common carrier use). Approximately 209,000 km unpaved

Ports: Arkhangel'sk, Astrakhan', Kaliningrad, Kazan', Khabarovsk, Kholmsk, Krasnoyarsk, Moscow, Murmansk, Nakhodka, Nevel'sk, Novorossiysk, Petropavlovsk, St. Petersburg, Rostov, Sochi, Tuapse, Vladivostok, Volgograd, Vostochnyy, Vyborg

Airports: 2,517 total paved and unpaved.

The Press: newspapers

Izvestiya: 103791 Moscow, ul. Tverskaya 18/1 telephone (095) 209-9100 fax (095) 230-2303 circ 1,000,000

Selskaya Zhizm: 125869 Moscow, ul. Pravdy 24 telephone (095) 257-2963   fax (095) 257-2000 3 a week   circ. 1,300,000

Trud: 103792 Moscow, Nastasyinsky per. 4 telephone (095) 292-4947   6 a week   circ. 3,000,000

Tourism: Moscow - Kremlin, Bolshoi Ballet

Intourist: 103009 Moscow, ul. Mokhovaya 13 telephone (095) 292-2260   fax (095) 203-5267

Diplomatic representation in US:

chief of mission: Ambassador Sergey Lavrov

chancery: 2650 Wisconsin Avenue NW, Washington, DC 20007

telephone: [1] (202) 298-5700 through 5704

FAX: [1] (202) 298-5735

US Diplomatic representation:

chief of mission: Ambassador Thomas R. Pickering

embassy: Novinskiy Bul'var 19/23, Moscow

mailing address: APO AE 09721

telephone: [7] (095) 252-2451 through 59

FAX: [7] (095) 956-4261

Rwanda

Capital: Kigali   longitude: 30.04 E   latitude: 1.56 S

Government: republic; presidential system

Flag: three equal vertical bands of red (hoist side), yellow, and green with a large black letter R centered in the yellow band; uses the popular pan-African colors of Ethiopia; similar to the flag of Guinea, which has a plain yellow band

Geography

Location: Central Africa, east of Zaire

Total Area: 26,340 sq km (10,170 sq mi) slightly smaller than Maryland

Boundaries: Burundi, Tanzania, Uganda, Zaire

Climate: temperate; two rainy seasons (February to April, November to January); mild in mountains with frost and snow possible

Temperature (F): High/Low Jan. 77/57, Apr. 77/57, July 79/54, Oct. 79/57

Average annual precipitation: 46.5 inches

Terrain: mostly grassy uplands and hills; relief is mountainous with altitude declining from west to east

Highest point is Karisimbi   4,505 m (14,780 ft)

Natural resources: gold, cassiterite (tin ore), wolframite (tungsten ore), natural gas, hydropower

Natural hazards: periodic droughts; the volcanic Virunga mountains are in the northwest along the border with Zaire

People

Population: 8,606,000 (July 1995 est.)

Life expectancy at birth: total population 38.33 years

Nationality: Rwandan

Ethnic division: Hutu 90%, Tutsi 9%, Twa (Pygmoid) 1%

Religions: Roman Catholic 65%, Protestant 9%, Muslim 1%, indigenous beliefs and other 25%

Languages: Kinyarwands (official), French (official), Kiswahili used in commercial centers

Literacy: total population 50%

Economy

Imports: textiles, foodstuffs, machine and equipment, capital goods, steel, petroleum products, cement and construction material

Exports: coffee, tea, cassiterite, wolframite, pyrethum

Industries: mining of cassiterite (tin ore) and wolframite (tungsten ore), tin, cement, agricultural processing, small-scale beverage production, soap, furniture, shoes, plastic goods, textiles, cigarettes

Agriculture: cash crops - coffee, tea, pyrethrum (insecticide made from chrysanthemums); main food crops - bananas, beans, sorghum, potatoes; stock raising

Currency: 1 Rwandan franc (RF) = 100 centimes

Rwandan franc per US1$ - 144.3

Transportation

Railroads: none

Roads: 4,885 km total paved and unpaved

Ports: Cyangugu, Gisenyi, Kibuye

Airports: 7 total paved and unpaved. The main international airport is at Kigali, a second international airport is at Kamembe, near the Zaire border

The Press: newspapers   **Imvaho:** Office Rwandais d'Information, BP 83, Kigali

telephone 75-724 weekly circ. 52,000

Kinyamateka: 5 blvd de l'OUA, BP 761, Kigali

telephone 76-164 fortnightly circ. 12,000

Tourism: national parks, mountain scenery, Lake Kivu, wild gorilla sanctuaries

Ministry of Environment and Tourism:

BP 2378 Kigali   telephone 77-415 fax 74-834

Diplomatic representation in US:

chief of mission: (vacant); Charge d'Affaires ad interim Joseph W. Mutaboba

chancery: 1714 New Hampshire Avenue NW, Washington, DC 20009

telephone: [1] (202) 232-2882

FAX: [1] (202) 232-4544

US Diplomatic representation:
Note: US Embassy closed indefinitely
chief of mission: Ambassador David P. Rawson
embassy: Boulevard de la Revolution, Kigali
mailing address: B P 28, Kigali
telephone: [250] 75-601 through 03
FAX: [250] 72-128

Saint Helena

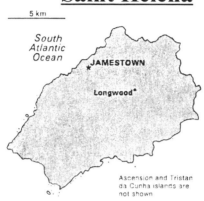

Capital: Jamestown   longitude: 5.43 W   latitude: 15.55 S
elevation: 40 ft

Government: dependent territory of the UK

Flag: blue with the flag of the UK in the upper hoist-side quadrant and the Saint Helenian shield centered on the outer half of the flag; the shield features a rocky coastline and three-masted sailing ship

Geography

Location: Southern Africa, island in the South Atlantic Ocean, West of Angola, about two-thirds of the way from South America to Africa

Total Area: 410 sq km (158.3 sq mi) slightly more than 2.3 times the size of Washington, DC

Boundaries: no land boundaries

Climate: tropical; marine; mild. tempered by trade winds

Temperature (F): High/Low Jan. 80/69, Apr. 81/71, July 72/63, Oct. 73/64

Average annual precipitation: 4.4 inches

Terrain: rugged, volcanic; small scattered plateaus and plains

Natural resources: fish; Ascension is a breeding ground for sea turtles and sooty terns, no minerals

Natural hazards: active volcanism on Tristan da Cunha

People

Population: 6,800 (July 1995 est.)

Life expectancy at birth: total population 75.07 years

Nationality: Saint Helenian

Ethnic division: NA

Religions: Anglican (majority), Baptist, Seventh-Day Adventist, Roman Catholic

Languages: English

Literacy: total population 97%

Economy

Imports: food, beverages, tobacco, fuel oils, animal feed, building materials, motor vehicles and parts, machinery and parts

Exports: fish (frozen and salt-dried skipjack, tuna), handicrafts

Industries: crafts (furniture, lacework, fancy woodwork), fishing

Agriculture: maize, potatoes, vegetables; timber production being developed; crawfishing on Tristan da Cunha

Currency: 1 Saint Helenian pound (#S) = 100 pence

Saint Helenian pounds per US1$ - 0.63

Transportation

Railroads: none

Roads: total: NA (mainland 107 km)

paved: 170 km (mainland 87 km, Ascension 80 km, Tristan da Cunha 3 km)

unpaved: NA (mainland 20 km)

Ports: Georgetown, Jamestown

Airports: 1 with paved runways

The Press: weekly newspaper **St Helena News:** Broadway House, Jamestown

telephone 26-12   fax 25-98

Tourism: rare flora and fauna (about 40 species of flora are unknown in other parts of the world)

Diplomatic representation in US: none (dependent territory of the UK)

US Diplomatic representation: none (dependent territory of the UK)

Saint Kitts and Nevis

Capital: Basseterre   longitude: 62.43 W   latitude: 17.17 N
elevation: 157 ft

Government: constitutional monarchy

Flag: divided diagonally from the lower hoist side by a broad black band bearing two white five-pointed stars; the black band is edged in yellow; the upper triangle is green, the lower triangle is red

Geography

Location: Caribbean, islands in the Caribbean Sea, about one-third of the way from Puerto Rico to Trinidad and Tobago

Total Area: 269 sq km (104 sq mi) slightly more than 1.5 times the size of Washington, DC

Boundaries: no land boundaries

Climate: subtropical tempered by constant sea breezes; little seasonal temperature variation; rainy season (May to November)
Temperature (F): High/Low Jan. 83/73, Apr. 85/75, July 86/78, Oct. 86/76
Average annual precipitation: 50.9 inches

Terrain: volcanic with mountainous interiors
Highest point is Mt. Misery 1,315 m (4,314 ft)

Natural resources: negligible

Natural hazards: hurricanes (July to October)

People

Population: 41,200 (July 1995 est.)

Life expectancy at birth: total population 66.51 years

Nationality: Kittsian (s), Nevisian (s)

Ethnic division: black African

Religions: Anglican, other Protestant sects, Roman Catholic

Languages: English

Literacy: total population 97%

Economy

Imports: machinery, manufactures, food, fuels

Exports: machinery, food, electronics, beverages and tobacco

Industries: sugar processing, tourism, cotton, salt, copra, clothing, footwear, beverages

Agriculture: cash crop - sugarcane; subsistence crops - rice, yams, vegetables, bananas; fishing potential not fully exploited

Currency: 1 East Caribbean dollar (EC$) = 100 cents

East Caribbean dollars per US1$ - 2.70

Transportation

Railroads: 58 km on Saint Kitts for sugarcane

Roads: 300 km total paved and unpaved

Ports: Basseterre, Charlestown

Airports: 2 with paved runways. Golden Rock International Airport is about 4 km from Basseterre

The Press: weekly on Saturday newspaper   **The Democrat:**

Cayon Street, POB 30, Basseterre

telephone 465-2091   circ. 3,000

Tourism: Attractions are excellent beaches, mountain scenery and the historical Brimstone Hill Fort on Saint Christopher

Saint Kitts - Nevis Tourist Board:

Treasury Pier, POB 132, Basseterre   telephone 465-4040

Diplomatic representation in US:

chief of mission: Ambassador Erstein Mallet Edwards

chancery: suite 608, 2100 M Street NW, Washington, DC 20037

telephone: [1] (202) 833-3550

FAX: [1] (202) 833-3553

US Diplomatic representation: no official presence; covered by embassy in Bridgetown, Barbados

Saint Lucia

Capital: Castries   longitude: 60.59 W   latitude: 14.01 N   elevation: 10 ft

Government: parliamentary democracy

Flag: blue with a gold isosceles triangle below a black arrowhead; the upper edges of the arrowhead have a white border

Geography

Location: Caribbean, island in the Caribbean Sea, north of Trinidad and Tobago

Total Area: 620 sq km (239 sq mi) slightly less than 3.5 times the size of Washington, DC

Boundaries: no land boundaries

Climate: tropical, moderated by northeast trade winds; dry season from January to April, rainy season from May to August

Temperature (F): High/Low Jan. 82/69, Apr. 87/71, July 87/74, Oct. 87/72

Average annual precipitation: 86.6 inches

Terrain: volcanic and mountainous with some broad, fertile valleys

Highest point is Mt. Gimie 950 m (3,117 ft)

Natural resources: forests, sandy beaches, minerals (pumice), mineral springs, geothermal potential

Natural hazards: hurricanes and volcanic activity

People

Population: 156,600 (July 1995 est.)

Life expectancy at birth: total population 69.88 years

Nationality: Saint Lucian

Ethnic division: African descent 90.3%, mixed 5.5%, East Indian 3.2%, Caucasian 0.8%

Religions: Roman Catholic 90%, Protestant 7%, Anglican 3%

Languages: English (official). French patois

Literacy: total population 67%

390

Economy

Imports: manufactured goods, machinery and transportation equipment, food and live animals, chemicals, fuels

Exports: bananas, clothing, cocoa, vegetables, fruits, coconut oil

Industries: clothing, assembly of electronic components, beverages, corrugated cardboard boxes, tourism, lime processing, coconut processing

Agriculture: crops - bananas, coconuts, vegetables, citrus fruit, root crops, cocoa; import food for the tourist industry

Currency: 1 East Caribbean dollar (EC$) = 100 cents

East Caribbean dollars per US1$ - 2.70

Transportation

Railroads: none

Roads: 760 km total paved and unpaved

Ports: Castries, Vieux Fort

Airports: 3 with paved runways. The international airports are located at Vieux Fort and Castries

The Press: newspapers

The Crusader: 19 St. Louis Street, Castries
telephone 452-2203 weekly circ. 4,000

The Voice of St. Lucia: Odessa Bldg, Darling Road, POB 104, Castries
telephone 452-2490 fax 453-1453
3 a week circ. 5,000

Tourism: Attraction are sandy beaches, scenery, historical sites, bird life, sulfur baths, and other exciting events

Saint Lucia Tourist Board:
Pointe Seraphine, POB 221, Castries
telephone 452-5968 fax 453-1121

Diplomatic representation in US:

chief of mission: Ambassador Dr. Joseph Edsel Edmunds

chancery: 3216 New Mexico Avenue NW, Washington, DC 20016

telephone: [1] (202) 364- 6792 through 6795

FAX: [1] (202) 364-6728

US Diplomatic representation: no official presence since the Ambassador resides in Bridgetown (Barbados)

Saint Pierre and Miquelon

Capital: Saint-Pierre   longitude: 56.20 W   latitude: 47.00 N

Government: territorial collectivity of France

    Flag: the flag of France is used

Geography

    Location: Northern North America, islands in the North Atlantic Ocean, south of Newfoundland (Canada)

    Total Area: 242 sq km (93.4 sq mi) slightly less than 1.5 times the size of Washington, DC

    Boundaries: no land boundaries

    Climate: cold and wet, with much mist and fog; spring and autumn are windy. Winters are cold with average temperatures -4F, summer to 68F

    Terrain: mostly barren rock

    Natural resources: fish, deepwater ports

    Natural hazards: persistent fog throughout the year can be a maritime hazard

People

    Population: 6,800 (July 1995 est.)

    Life expectancy at birth: total population 76 years

    Nationality: Frenchman (men) Frenchwoman (woman)

    Ethnic division: Basques and Bretons (French fishermen)

    Religions: Roman Catholic 98%

    Languages: French

    Literacy: total population 99%

Economy

    Imports: meat, clothing, fuel, electrical equipment, machinery, building materials

    Exports: fish and fish products, fox and mink pelts

Industries: fish processing and supply base for fishing fleets; tourism

Agriculture: vegetables, cattle, sheep, pigs for local consumption
Currency: 1 French franc (F) = 100 centimes
> French francs per US1$ - 5.29

Transportation
>   **Railroads:** none
>   **Roads:** 120 km total paved and unpaved
>   **Ports:** Saint-Pierre
>   **Airports:** 2 total. The commercial airport is located on Saint-Pierre

Tourism: NA
> **Agence Regionale du Tourisme:**
> rue du 11 Novembre, Bp 4274, 97500 Saint-Pierre
> telephone 41-22-22 fax 41-33-55

Diplomatic representation in US: none (territorial collectivity of France)
US Diplomatic representation: none (territorial collectivity of France)

Saint Vincent and the Grenadines

Capital: Kingstown   longitude: 61.14 W   latitude: 13.12 N
Government: constitutional monarchy
>   **Flag:** three vertical bands of blue (hoist side), gold (double width), and
>   green; the gold band bears three green diamonds arranged in a V pattern

Geography
>   **Location:** Caribbean, islands in the Caribbean Sea, north of Trinidad and
>   Tobago
>   **Total Area:** 340 sq km (131 sq mi) slightly less than twice the size of
>   Washington, DC
>   **Boundaries:** no land boundaries

Climate: tropical; little seasonal temperature variation; rainy season (May to November)

Temperature (F): High/Low Jan. 83/70, Apr. 86/72, July 86/74, Oct. 86/73

Terrain: volcanic, mountainous; Soufriere Volcano on the island of Saint Vincent

Highest point is Soufriere 1,219 m (4,000 ft)

Natural resources: negligible

Natural hazards: hurricanes; Soufriere volcano is a constant threat

People

Population: 117,700 (July 1995 est.)

Life expectancy at birth: total population 72.66 years

Nationality: Saint Vincentian

Ethnic division: African descent, Caucasian, East Indian, Carib Indian

Religions: Anglican, Methodist, Roman Catholic, Seventh-Day Adventist

Languages: English, French patois

Literacy: total population 96%

Economy

Imports: foodstuffs, machinery and equipment, chemicals and fertilizers, minerals and fuels

Exports: bananas, eddooes and dasheen (taro), arrowroot starch, tenis racquets

Industries: food processing, cement, furniture, clothing, starch

Agriculture: provides bulk of exports; products - bananas, sweet potatoes, spices; small number of cattle, sheep, hogs, goats; small fish catch used locally

Currency: 1 East Caribbean dollar (EC$) = 100 cents

East Caribbean dollars per US1$ - 2.70

Transportation

Railroads: none

Roads: 1,000 km total paved and unpaved

Ports: Kingstown

Airports: 6 with paved runways. There is a civilian airport just outside of Kingstown

The Press: newspapers　　　　**The News:** Grenville St. POB 1078, Kingstown
telephone 456-2942　fax 456-2941

The Vincentian: Paul's Ave, POB 592, Kingstown
telephone 456-1123　weekly　circ. 5,600

Tourism: Superior yachting facilities are available. Caribbean picture rocks, beaches, snorkeling

Department of Tourism: POB 834, Kingstown
telephone 457-1502 fax 456-2610
Diplomatic representation in US:
    chief of mission: Ambassador Kingsley C.A. Layne
    chancery: 1717 Massachusetts Avenue NW, Washington, DC 20036
    telephone: [1] (202) 462-7806, 7846
    FAX: [1] (202) 462-7807
US Diplomatic representation: no official presence since the Ambassador resides in Bridgetown (Barbados)

San Marino

Capital: San Marino   longitude: 12.28 E   latitude: 43.55 N
Government: republic
    Flag: two equal horizontal bands of white (top) and light blue with the national coat of arms superimposed in the center; the coat of arms has a shield (featuring three towers on three peaks) flanked by a wreath, below a crown and above a scroll bearing the word LIBERTAS (Liberty)
Geography
    Location: Southern Europe, an enclave in central Italy
    Total Area: 60 sq km (23 sq mi) about 0.3 times the size of Washington, DC
    Boundaries: Italy
    Climate: Mediterranean; mild to cool winters; warm, sunny summers
    Temperature (F): High/Low Jan. 42/33, Apr. 62/49, July 81/66, Oct. 65/53
    Terrain: rugged mountains
    Natural resources: building stone
    Natural hazards: air pollution

Note: landlocked; smallest independent state in Europe after the Holy See and Monaco; dominated by the Apennines

People

Population: 24,600 (July 1995 est.)

Life expectancy at birth: total population 81.27 years

Nationality: Sammarinese

Ethnic division: Sammarinese, Italian

Religions: Roman Catholic

Languages: Italian

Literacy: total population 96%

Economy:

Imports: wide variety of consumer goods

Exports: building stone, lime, wood, chestnuts, wheat, wine, baked goods, hides, and ceramics

Industries: tourism, textiles, electronics, ceramics, cement, wine

Agriculture: products - wheat, grapes, maize, olives, meat, cheese, hides; small number of cattle, pigs, horses

Currency: 1 Italian lire (Lit) = 100 centesimi; note - also mints its own coins
Italian lire per US1$ - 1,609.5

Transportation

Railroads: none

Roads: 104 km total paved and unpaved

Ports: none

Airports: none

The Press: there are no daily newspapers

Tourism: San Marino City, medieval fortresses

Ufficio di Stato per il Turismo:

Contrada Omagnano 20, 47031 San Marino
telephone 88-24-00   fax 99-03-88

Diplomatic representation in US:

honorary consulate general: Washington, DC, New York and Detroit

US Diplomatic representation: no mission in San Marino, but the Consul General in Florence (Italy) is accredited to San Marino

Sao Tome and Principe

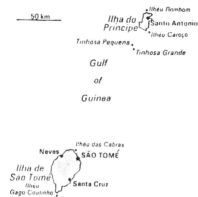

Capital: Sao Tome   longitude: 6.43 E latitude: 0.12 N elevation: 16 ft

Government: republic

Flag: three horizontal bands of green (top), yellow (double width), and green with two black five-pointed stars placed side by side in the center of the yellow band and a red isosceles triangle based on the hoist side; uses the popular pan-African colors of Ethiopia

Geography

Location: Western Africa, island in the Atlantic Ocean, straddling the equator, west of Gabon

Total Area: 960 sq km (371 sq mi) slightly less than 5.5 times the size of Washington, DC

Boundaries: no land boundaries

Climate: tropical; hot, humid; one rainy season (October to May)

Temperature (F): High/Low Jan. 86/73, Apr. 86/73, July 82/69, Oct. 84/71

Average annual precipitation: 38 inches

Terrain: volcanic, mountainous

Highest point is Pico 2,024 m (6,640 ft)

Natural resources: fish

Natural hazards: NA

People

Population: 140,700 (July 1995 est.)

Life expectancy at birth: total population 63.65 years

Nationality: Sao Tomean

Ethnic division: mestica, angolares (descendants of Angolan slaves), forros (descendants of freed slaves), servicais (contract laborers from Angola, Mozambique, and Cape Verde), tongas (children of servicais born on the islands), Europeans (primarily Portuguese)

Religions: Roman Catholic, Evangelical Protestant, Seventh-Day Adventist

397

Languages: Portuguese (official)

Literacy: total population 73%

Economy

Imports: machinery and electrical equipment, food products, petroleum

Exports: cocoa, copra, coffee, palm oil

Industries: light construction, shirts, soap, beer, fisheries, shrimp processing

Agriculture: cash crops - cocoa, coconuts, palm kernels, coffee; food products - bananas, papaya, beans, poultry, fish; not self-sufficient in food grain and meat

Currency: 1 dobra (Db) = 100 centimos
dobras per US1$ - 129.59

Transportation

Railroads: none

Roads: 300 km total paved and unpaved. Roads on Principe are mostly unpaved and in need of repair

Ports: Santo Antonio, Sao Tome

Airports: 2 with paved runways. The principal airport is at Sao Tome

The Press: newspapers   **Diario da Republica:** Imprensa Nacional, CP 28, Sao Tome   telephone   21-530   weekly

Povo: Rua Tres de Fevereiro, Predio da Flebe, Sao Tome telephone   22-375   weekend newspaper and magazine

Tourism: The high level of rainfall during most of the year limits the duration of the tourist season. Spectacular scenery, unique species of wildlife and flora. sandy uncrowded beaches, extinct volcanoes

Diplomatic representation in US: Sao Tome and Principe has no embassy in the US, but does have a Permanent Mission to the UN, headed by First Secretary Domingos Augusto Ferreira, located at 122 East 42nd Street, Suite 1604, New York, NY 10168, telephone [1] (212) 697-4211

US Diplomatic representation: ambassador to Gabon is accredited to Sao Tome and Principe on a nonresident basis and makes periodic visits to the islands

Saudi Arabia

Capital: Riyadh   longitude: 46.46 E   latitude: 24.39 N   elevation: 1,938 ft

Government: monarchy

Flag: green with large white arabic script (that may be translated as There is no God but God; Muhammad is the Messenger of God) above a white horizontal saber (the tip points to the hoist side); green is the traditional color of Islam

Geography

Location: Middle East, bordering the Persian Gulf and the Red Sea, north of Yemen

Total Area: 1,960,582 sq km (756,981 sq mi) slightly less than one-fourth the size of the US

Boundaries: Iraq, Jordan, Kuwait, Oman, Qatar, United Arab Emirates, Yemen

Climate: harsh, dry desert with extremes of temperature

Temperature (F): High/Low Jan. 70/46, Apr. 89/64, July 107/78, Oct. 94/61

Average annual precipitation: 3.2 inches

Terrain: mostly uninhabited, sandy desert

Highest point is Mount Subh 1,372 m (4,501 ft)

Natural resources: petroleum, natural gas, iron ore, gold, copper

Natural hazards: frequent sand and dust storms

Note: extensive coastlines on Persian Gulf and Red Sea provide great leverage on shipping (especially crude oil) through Persian Gulf and Suez Canal

People

Population: 18,730,000 (July 1995 est.)

Life expectancy at birth: total population 68.5 years

Nationality: Saudi

Ethnic division: Arab 90%, Afro-Asian 10%

Religions: Muslim 100%

Languages: Arabic

Literacy: total population 62%

Economy

Saudi Arabia has the largest reserves of petroleum in the world and ranks as the largest exporter of petroleum

Imports: machinery and equipment, chemicals, foodstuffs, motor vehicles, textiles

Exports: petroleum and petroleum products

Industries: crude oil production, petroleum refining, basic petrochemicals, cement, two small steel-rolling mills, construction, fertilizer, plastic

Agriculture: products - wheat, barley, tomatoes, melons, dates, citrus fruit, mutton, chickens, eggs, milk; approaching self-sufficiency in food

Currency: 1 Saudi riyal (SR) = 100 halalah

Saudi riyals per US1$ - 3.74

Transportation

Railroads: 1,390 km

Roads: 151,530 km total paved and unpaved

Ports: Ad Dammam, Al Jubayl, Duba, Jiddah, Jizan, Rabigh, Ras al Khafji, Ras al Mishab, Ras Tanura, Yanbu' al Bahr, Yanbu' al Sinaiyah

Airports: 211 total paved and unpaved. The main airport is "King Khalid International Airport" at Riyadh. There are two other international airports.

The Press: daily newspapers

Arab News: POB 4556, Jeddah
telephone (2) 669-1888 fax (2) 667-1650
circ. 110,000 English

Ar-Riyadh: POB 851, Riyadh
telephone (1) 442-0000 fax (1) 441-7580
circ. 150,000 Sat.- Thur. 90,000 Friday Arabic

Tourism: The workweek in Saudi Arabia is Saturday through Wednesday. All devout Muslims try to make at least one visit to the holy cities of Medina, the burial place of Muhammad, and Mecca, his birthplace. Red Sea, oil industry installations

Saudi Hotels and Resort Areas Co:
POB 5500, Riyadh 11422
telephone (1) 465-7177 fax (1) 465-7172

Diplomatic representation in US:

chief of mission: Ambassador Bandar bin Sultan Abd al-Aziz Al Saud

chancery: 601 New Hampshire Avenue NW, Washington, DC 20037

telephone: [1] (202) 342-3800

US Diplomatic representation:
chief of mission: Ambassador Raymond E. Mabus, Jr.
embassy: Collector Road M, Diplomatic Quarter, Riyadh
mailing address: American Embassy, Unit 61307, Riyadh;
International Mail; PO Box 94309, Riyadh 11693; APO AE 09803-1307
telephone: [966] (1) 488-3800
FAX: [966] (1) 482-4364

Senegal

Capital: Dakar   longitude: 17.27 E   latitude: 14.38 N   elevation: 131 ft
Government: republic under multiparty democratic rule
   Flag: three equal vertical bands of green (hoist side), yellow, and red with a
   small green five-pointed star centered in the yellow band; uses the popular
   pan-African colors of Ethiopia
Geography
   Location: western Africa, bordering the North Atlantic Ocean, between
   Guinea-Bissau and Mauritania
   Total Area: 196,190 sq km (75,749 sq mi) slightly smaller than
   South Dakota
   Boundaries: The Gambia, Guinea, Guinea-Bissau, Mali, Mauritania
   Climate: tropical; hot, humid, rainy season (December to April) has strong
   southeast winds; dry season (May to November) dominated by hot, dry
   harmattan wind
   Temperature (F): High/Low Jan. 79/64, Apr. 81/65, July 88/76, Oct. 89/76
   Average annual precipitation: 21.3 inches
   Terrain: generally low, rolling, plains rising to foothills in southeast
   Highest point is Futa Jallon 500 m (1,640 ft)
   Natural resources: fish, phosphates, iron ore
   Natural hazards: lowlands seasonally flooded; periodic droughts

People

Population: 9,008,000 (July 1995 est.)

Life expectancy at birth: total population 57.16 years

Nationality: Senegalese

Ethnic division: Wolof 36%, Fulani 17%, Serer 17%, Toucouleur 9%, Diola 9%, Mandingo 9%, European and Lebanese 1%, other 2%

Religions: Muslim 92%, indigenous beliefs 6%, Christian 2%, (mostly Roman Catholic)

Languages: French (official), Wolof, Pulaar, Diola, Mandingo

Literacy: total population 27%

Economy

Imports: food and beverages, consumer goods, capital goods, petroleum

Exports: fish, ground nuts (peanuts), petroleum products, phosphates, cotton

Industries: agricultural and fish processing, phosphate mining, petroleum refining, building materials

Agriculture: major crops - peanuts (cash crop), millet, corn, sorghum, rice, cotton, tomatoes, green vegetables; estimated two-thirds self-sufficient in food

Currency: 1 CFAF franc = 100 centimes

Communaute Financiere Africaine francs per US1$ - 529.43

Transportation

Railroads: 905 km

Roads: 14,007 km total paved and unpaved

Ports: Dakar, Kaolack, Matam, Podor, Richard-Toll, Saint-Louis, Ziguinchor

Airports: 24 total paved and unpaved. The international airport is at Dakar

The Press: daily newspapers

Le Soleil: BP 92, Dakar
telephone 32-46-92 fax 32-03-81
circ. 45,000

Sud au Quotidien: Immeuble Fahd, BP 4130, Dakar
telephone 22-53-93 fax 22-52-90 circ. 30,000

Tourism: Tourist attractions are fine beaches and six national parks.

Ministry of Tourism and Air Transport:
23 rue Calmette, BP 4049, Dakar
telephone 23-65-02 fax 22-94-13

Diplomatic representation in US:

chief of mission: Ambassador Mamadou Mansour Seck

chancery: 2112 Wyoming Avenue NW, Washington, DC 20008

telephone: [1] (202) 234-0540, 0541

US Diplomatic representation:
chief of mission: Ambassador Mark Johnson
embassy: Avenue Jean XXIII at the corner of Avenue Kleber, Dakar
mailing address: B P 49, Dakar
telephone: [221] 23-42-96, 23-34-24
FAX: [221] 22-29-91

Serbia and Montenegro

Capital: Belgrade   longitude: 20.02 E   latitude: 44.48 N   Elevation: 433 ft
Government: republic
Flag: three equal horizontal bands of blue (top), white, and red
Geography

Location: Southeastern Europe, bordering the Adriatic Sea, between Albania and Bosnia and Herzegovina

Total Area: 102,350 sq km (39,517 sq mi) slightly larger than Kentucky

Boundaries: Albania, Bosnia and Herzegovina, Bulgaria, Croatia, Hungary, The Former Yugoslav Republic of Macedonia, Romania

Climate: in the north, continental climate (cold winter and hot, humid summers with well distributed rainfall); central portion, continental and Mediterranean climate; to the south, Adriatic climate along coast, hot, dry summers and autumns and relatively cold winters with heavy snowfall inland Temperature (F): High/Low   Jan. 37/26, Apr. 64/45, July 83/62, Oct. 64/47 Average annual precipitation: 27.7 inches

Terrain: extremely varied; to the north, rich fertile plains; to the east, limestone ranges and basins; to the southeast, ancient mountains and hills; to the southwest, extremely high shoreline with no islands off the coast

Natural resources: oil, gas, coal, antimony, copper, lead, zinc, nickel, gold, pyrite, chrome

Natural hazards: destructive earthquakes

People

Population: 11,102,000 (July 1995 est.)

Life expectancy at birth: total population

Montenegro: 79.56 years

Serbia: 73.68 years

Nationality: Serb (s) and Montenegrin (s)

Ethnic division: Serbs 63%, Albanian 14%, Montenegrins 6%, Hungarians 4%, other 13%

Religions: Orthodox 65%, Muslim 19%, Roman Catholic 4%, Protestant 1%, other 11%

Languages: Serbo-Croatian 95%, Albanian 5%

Literacy: NA

Economy

Imports: prior to the breakup of the federation, Yugoslavia imported machinery and transport equipment, fuels and lubricants, manufactured goods, chemicals, food and live animals, raw materials including coking coal for the steel industry

Exports: prior to the breakup of the federation, Yugoslavia exported machinery and transport equipment, manufactured goods, chemicals, food and live animals, raw materials

Industries: machine building (aircraft, trucks, and automobiles; armored vehicles and weapons; electrical equipment; agricultural machinery), metallurgy (steel, aluminum, copper, lead, zinc, chromium, antimony, bismuth, cadmium), mining (coal. bauxite, nonferrous ore, iron ore, limestone), consumer goods (textiles, footwear, foodstuffs, appliances), electronics, petroleum products, chemicals, and pharmaceuticals

Agriculture: the fertile plains of Vojvodina produce 80% of the cereal production of the former Yugoslavia and most of the cotton, oilseeds, and chicory; Vojvodina also produces fodder crops to support intensive beef and dairy production; Serbia proper, although hilly, has a well-distributed rainfall and a long growing season; produces fruit, grapes, and cereals; in this area, livestock production (sheep and cattle) and dairy farming prosper; Kosovo produces fruits, vegetables, tobacco, and a small amount of cereals; the mountainous pastures of Kosovo and Montenegro support sheep and goat husbandry; Montenegro has only a small agriculture sector, mostly near the coast where a Mediterranean climate permits the culture of olives, citrus, grapes, and rice

Currency: 1 Yugoslav New Dinar (YD) = 100 paras

Yugoslav New Dinars per US1$ - 102.6

Transportation

Railroads: 3,960

Roads: 46,019 km total paved and unpaved

Ports: Bar, Belgrade, Kotor, Novi Sad, Pancevo, Tivat

Airports: 54 total paved and unpaved. There are international airports at Bekgrade and Podgorica

The Press: daily newspapers   **Politika:** 11000 Belgrade, Makedonska 29 telephone (11) 322-1836   fax (11) 324-9395 circ. 200,000

Vecernje novosti: 11000 Belgrade, trg Nikole Pasica 7 telephone (11) 334-531   fax (11) 344-913   circ. 170,000

Tourism: mountain scenery, historic centers

Yugotours: 11000 Belgrade, Kneza Mihaila 50 telephone (11) 18-78-22   fax (11) 18-07-45

Diplomatic representation in US: US and Serbia and Montenegro do not maintain full diplomatic relations; the Embassy of the former Socialist Federal Republic of Yugoslavia continues to function in the US

US Diplomatic representation:

chief of mission: (vacant) Charge d'Affaires Rudolf V. Perina

embassy: NA, Belgrade

mailing address: Box 5070, Unit 1310, APO AE 09213-1310

telephone: [381] (11) 64-56-55

FAX: [381] (11) 64-52-21

Seychelles

Capital: Victoria   longitude: 55.28 E   latitude: 4.38 S   elevation: 15 ft

Government: republic

> **Flag:** three horizontal bands of red (top), white (wavy), and green; the white band is the thinnest, the red band is the thickest

Geography

> **Location:** Eastern Africa, group of islands in the Indian Ocean, northeast of Madagascar
>
> **Total Area:** 455 sq km (176 sq mi) slightly less than 2.5 times the size of Washington, DC
>
> **Boundaries:** no land boundaries
>
> **Climate:** tropical marine; humid; cooler season during southeast monsoon (late May to September); warmer season during northwest monsoon (March to May)
>
> Temperature (F): High/Low Jan. 83/76, Apr. 86/77, July 81/75, Oct. 83/75
>
> Average annual precipitation: 92.5 inches
>
> **Terrain:** Mahae Group is granitic, narrow coastal strip, rocky, hilly; others are coral. flat, elevated reefs
>
> Highest point is Morne Seychellois 912 m (2,993 ft)
>
> **Natural resources:** fish, copra, cinnamon trees
>
> **Natural hazards:** lies outside the cyclone belt, so severe storms are rare; short droughts possible

People

> **Population:** 72,800 (July 1995 est.)
>
> **Life expectancy at birth:** total population 70.08 years
>
> **Nationality:** Seychellois
>
> **Ethnic division:** Seychellois (mixture of Asians, Africans, Europeans)
>
> **Religions:** Roman Catholic 90%, Anglican 8%, other 2%
>
> **Languages:** English (official), French (official), Creole
>
> **Literacy:** total population 58%

Economy

> **Imports:** manufactured goods, food, petroleum products, tobacco, beverages, machinery and transportation equipment
>
> **Exports:** fish, cinnamon bark, copra, petroleum products (re-exports)

Industries: tourism, processing of coconut and vanilla, fishing, coir rope factory, boat building, printing, furniture, beverage

Agriculture: mostly subsistence farming; cash crops - coconuts, cinnamon, vanilla; other products - sweet potatoes, cassava, bananas; broiler chickens; large share of food needs imported; expansion of tuna fishing under way

Currency: 1 Seychelles rupee (SRe) = 100 cents

Seychelles rupees per US1$ - 4.93

Transportation
    Railroads: none
    Roads: 260 km total paved and unpaved
    Ports: Victoria
    Airports: 14 total paved and unpaved.

The Press: newspapers   **The Seychelles Nation:** POB 321, Victoria
    telephone 22-41-61   fax 22-10-06
    Mon. - Sat. English, French and Creole circ 3,500

Tourism: Tourist attraction are fine beaches, more than 500 varieties of flora and
    many rare species of birds
        Seychelles Tourist Board:
        Independence House, POB 92 Victoria
        telephone 22-53-33

Diplomatic representation in US:
    chief of mission: Ambassador Marc R. Marengo
    chancery: (temporary) 820 Second Avenue, Suite 900F,
        New York, NY 10017
    telephone: [1] (212) 687-9766, 9767
    FAX: [1] (212) 922-9177

US Diplomatic representation:
    chief of mission: Ambassador Carl Burton Stokes
    embassy: 4th Floor, Victoria House, Box 251, Victoria, Mahe
    mailing address: Box 148, Unit 62501, Victoria, Seychelles;
        APO AE 09815-2501
    telephone: [248] 22-52-56
    FAX: [248] 22-51-89

Sierra Leone

Capital: Freetown   longitude: 13.17 W latitude: 8.30 N   elevation: 37 ft

Government: military government

Flag: three horizontal bands of light green (top), white, and light blue

Geography

Location: Western Africa, bordering the North Atlantic Ocean, between Guinea and Liberia

Total Area: 71,740 sq km (27,699 sq mi) slightly smaller than South Carolina

Boundaries: Guinea, Liberia

Climate: tropical; hot, humid; summer rainy season (May to December); winter dry season (December to April)

Temperature (F): High/Low Jan. 85/75, Apr. 87/77, July 83/74, Oct. 85/74

Average annual precipitation: 135.2 inches

Terrain: coastal belt of mangrove swamps, wooded hill country, upland plateau, mountains in east

Highest point is Loma Mountains 1,947 m (6,390 ft)

Natural resources: diamonds, titanium ore, bauxite, iron ore, gold, chromite

Natural hazards: dry, sand-laden harmattan winds blow from the Sahara (November to May); sandstorms, dust storms

People

Population: 4,754,000 (July 1995 est.)

Life expectancy at birth: total population 46.94 years

Nationality: Sierra Leonean

Ethnic division: 13 native African tribes 99% (Temne 30%, Mende 30%, other 39%), Creole, European, lebanese, and Asian 1%

Religions: Muslim 60%, indigenous beliefs 30%, Christian 10%

408

Languages: English (official; regular use limited to literate minority), Mende (principal vernacular in the south), Temne (principal vernacular in the north), Krio (the language of re-settled ex-slave population of the Freetown area and is lingua franca)

Literacy: total population 21%

Economy

Imports: foodstuffs, machinery and equipment, fuels

Exports: rutile (titanium dioxide), bauxite, diamonds, coffee, cocoa, fish

Industries: mining (diamonds, bauxite, rutile), small-scale manufacturing (beverages, textiles, cigarettes, footwear), petroleum refinery

Agriculture: largely subsistence farming; cash crops - coffee, cocoa, palm kernels; harvest of food staple rice meets 80% of domestic needs

Currency: 1 leone (Le) = 100 cents
leones per US1$ - 617.67

Transportation

Railroads: 84 km mineral line is used on a limited basis because the mine at Marampa is closed

Roads: 7,400 km total paved and unpaved

Ports: Bonthe, Freetown, Pepel

Airports: 11 total paved and unpaved. There is an international airport at Lungi

The Press: **Daily Mail:** 29-31 Rawdon St. POB 53 Freetown
telephone (22) 22-31-91   circ. 10,000
newspaper (appears irregularly)
            Weekend Spark: 7 Lamina Sankoh St. Freetown
telephone (22) 22-33-97 weekly periodical circ. 20,000

Tourism: Main tourist attractions are beaches, mountain and game reserves
            National Tourist Board: International Conference Center,
Aberdeen Hill, POB 1435, Freetown
telephone (22) 27-25-20   fax (22) 27-21-97

Diplomatic representation in US:

chief of mission: Ambassador Thomas Kahota Kargbo
chancery: 1701 19th Street NW, Washington, DC
telephone: [1] (202) 939-9261

US Diplomatic representation:
  chief of mission: Ambassador Lauralee M. Peters
  embassy: Corner of Walpole and Siaka Stevens Streets, Freetown
  mailing address: use embassy street address
  telephone: [232] (22) 22-64-81, through 22-64-85
  FAX: [232] (22) 22-54-71

Singapore

Capital: Singapore   longitude: 103.51 E   latitude: 1.17 N   elevation: 33 ft
Government: republic within Commonwealth
  Flag: two equal horizontal bands of red (top) and white; near the hoist side of the red band, there is a vertical, white crescent (closed portion is toward the hoist side) partially enclosing five white five-pointed stars arranged in a circle

Geography
  Location: Southeastern Asia, islands between Malaysia and Indonesia
  Total Area: 633 sq km (242 sq mi) slightly less than 3.5 times the size of Washington, DC
  Boundaries: no land boundaries
  Climate: tropical; hot, humid, rainy; no pronounced rainy or dry seasons; thunderstorms occur on 40% of all days (67% of days in April)
  Temperature (F): High/Low Jan. 86/73, Apr. 88/75, July 88/75, Oct. 87/74
  Average annual precipitation: 95 inches
  Terrain: lowland; gently undulating central plateau contains water catchment area and nature preserve
  Highest point is Bukit Timah 177 m (581 ft)
  Natural resources: fish, deepwater ports
  Natural hazards: NA

410

People

Population: 2,891,000 (July 1995 est.)

Life expectancy at birth: total population 76.16 years

Nationality: Singaporean

Ethnic division: Chinese 76.4%, Malay 14.9%, Indian 6.4%, other 2.3%

Religions: Buddhist (Chinese), Muslim (Malays), Christian, Hindu, Sikh, Taoist, Confucianist

Languages: Chinese (official), Malay (official and national), Tamil (official), English (official)

Literacy: total population 89%

Economy

Imports: aircraft, petroleum, chemicals, foodstuffs

Exports: computer equipment, rubber and rubber products, petroleum products, telecommunications equipment

Industries: petroleum refining, electronics, oil drilling equipment, rubber processing and rubber products, processed food and beverages, ship repair, entrepot trade, financial services, biotechnology

Agriculture: minor importance in the economy; self-sufficient in poultry and eggs; must import much of other food; major crops - rubber, copra, fruit, vegetables

Currency: 1 Singapore dollar (S$) = 100 cents

Singapore dollars per US1$ - 1.45

Transportation

Railroads: 38.6 km

Roads: 2,883 km total paved and unpaved

Ports: Singapore

Airports: 10 with paved runways. Singapore Changi Airport

The Press: daily newspapers

The Straits Times: Times House
390 Kim Seng Road, Singapore 0923
telephone 737-0011   fax 732-0131
circ. 360,000   English

Lianhe ZaoBao: News Center, 82 Genting Land, Singapore 1334
telephone 743-8800   fax 748-652
circ. 206,000   Chinese

Tourism: Excellent shopping facilities, Chinatown, Tiger Balm Gardens, Sri Mariamman Temple, botanical gardens

Singapore Tourist Promotion Board:
Raffles City Tower 36-04, 250 North Bridge Road,
Singapore 0617   telephone 339-6622   fax 339-9423

Diplomatic representation in US:

   chief of mission: Ambassador Sellapan Rama Nathan

   chancery: 3501 International Place NW, Washington, DC 20008

   telephone: [1] (202) 537-3100

   FAX: [1] (202) 537-0876

US Diplomatic representation:

   chief of mission: Ambassador Timothy A. Chorba

   embassy: 30 Hill Street, Singapore 0617

   mailing address: FPO AP 96534

   telephone: [65] 338-0251

   FAX: [65] 338-4550

Slovakia

Capital: Bratislava   longitude: 17.02 E   latitude: 48.02 N

Government: Parliamentary democracy

   Flag: three equal horizontal bands of white (top), blue, and red superimposed with the Slovak cross in a shield centered on the hoist side; the cross is white centered on a background of red and blue

Geography

   Location: Central Europe, south of Poland

   Total Area: 48,845 sq km (18,859 sq mi) about twice the size of New Hampshire

   Boundaries: Austria, Czech Republic, Hungary, Poland, Ukraine

   Climate: temperate; cool summers; cold, cloudy, humid winters

   Terrain: rugged mountains in central and northern part and lowlands in the south

   Natural resources: brown coal and lignite; small amounts of iron ore, copper and manganese ore; salt

   Natural hazards: NA

People

Population: 5,433,000 (July 1995 est.)

Life expectancy at birth: total population 73.24 years

Nationality: Slovak

Ethnic division: Slovak 85.7%, Hunbgarian 10.7%, Gypsy 1.5%, Czech 1%, Ruthenian 0.3%, Ukrainian 0.3%, German 0.1%, Polish 0.1%, others 0.3%

Religions: Roman Catholic 60.3%, atheist 9.7%, Protestant 8.4%, Orthodox 4.1%, other 17.5%

Languages: Slovak (official), Hungarian

Literacy: NA

Economy

Imports: machinery and transport equipment; fuels and lubricants; manufactured goods; raw materials; chemicals; agricultural products

Exports: machinery and transport equipment; chemicals; fuels, minerals, and metals; agricultural products

Industries: metal and metal products; food and beverages; electricity, gas, and water; coking, oil production; chemical and man made fibers; machinery; paper and printing; earthware and ceramics; transport vehicles; textiles; electrical and optical apparatus; rubber products

Agriculture: largely self-sufficient in food production; diversified crop and livestock production, including grains, potatoes, sugar beets, hops, fruit, hogs, cattle, and poultry; exporter of forest products

Currency: 1 koruna (Sk) = 100 halierov

koruny per US1$ - 31.14

Transportation

Railroads: 3,660 km

Roads: 17,650 km total paved and unpaved

Ports: Bratislava, Komarno

Airports: 37 total paved and unpaved. There are five international airports in Slovakia. Bratislava, Kosice, Piest'any, Poprad, Sliac

The Press: daily newspapers

Nov'y cas: Gorkeho 5, 812 78 Bratislava
telephone (7) 36-30-70 fax (7) 36-31-04
circ. 250,000

Pravda: Pribinova 25, 819 08 Bratislava
telephone (7) 36-75-03 fax (7) 210-4759 circ. 235,000

Tourism: Tourist attractions are the many spa resorts with thermal and mineral springs, ski resorts, numerous castles and historic towns

Slovakoturist: Volgogradska 1, Bratislava
telephone (7) 55-247

413

Diplomatic representation in US:

    chief of mission: Ambassador Branislav Lichardus
    chancery: (temporary) Suite 380, 2201 Wisconsin Avenue NW,
    Washington, DC 20007
    telephone: [1] (202) 965-5161
    FAX: [1] (202) 965-5166

US Diplomatic representation:

    chief of mission: Ambassador Theodore E. Russell
    embassy: Hviezdoslavovo Namestie 4, 81102 Bratislava
    mailing address: use embassy address
    telephone: [42] (7) 33-08-61, 33-33-38
    FAX: [42] (7) 33-00-96

Slovenia

75 km

    Capital: Ljubljana   longitude: 14.31 E   latitude: 46.04 N
    elevation: 981 ft

Government: emerging democracy

    Flag: three equal horizontal bands of white (top), blue, and red with the
    Slovenian seal (a shield with the image of Triglav in white against a blue
    background at the center, beneath it are two wavy blue lines depicting seas
    and rivers, and around it, there are three six-sided stars arranged in an
    inverted triangle); the seal is located in the upper hoist side of the flag
    centered in the white and blue bands

Geography

    Location: Southeastern Europe, bordering the Adriatic Sea, between Croatia
    and Italy
    Total Area: 20,296 sq km (7,836 sq mi) slightly larger than New Jersey
    Boundaries: Austria, Croatia, Italy, Hungary

Climate: Mediterranean climate on the coast, continental climate with mild to hot summers and cold winters in the plateaus and valleys to the east
Temperature (F): High/Low Jan. 36/25, Apr. 60/40, July 80/57, Oct. 59/43
Average annual precipitation: 54.6 inches
Terrain: a short coastal strip on the Adriatic, an alpine mountain region adjacent to Italy, mixed mountain and valleys with numerous rivers to the east
Natural resources: lignite coal, lead, zinc, mercury, uranium, silver
Natural hazards: flooding and earthquakes

People

Population: 2,052,000 (July 1995 est.)
Life expectancy at birth: total population 74.73 years
Nationality: Slovene
Ethnic division: Slovene 91%, Croat 3%, Serb 2%, Muslim 1%, other 3%
Religions: Roman Catholic 96% (including Uniate), Muslim 1%, other 3%
Languages: Slovenian 91%, Serbo-Croatian 7%, other 2%
Literacy: NA

Economy

Imports: machinery and transport equipment, intermediate manufactured goods, chemicals, raw materials, fuels and lubricants, food
Exports: machinery and transport equipment, intermediate manufactured goods, chemicals, food, raw materials, consumer goods
Industries: ferrous metallurgy and rolling mill products, aluminum reduction and rolled products, lead and zinc smelting, electronics (including military electronics), trucks, electric power equipment, wood products, textiles, chemicals, machine tools
Agriculture: stock breeding (sheep and cattle) and dairy farming; main crops - potatoes, hops, hemp, flax; an export surplus in those commodities; Slovenia must import many other agricultural products and has a negative overall trade balance in this sector
Currency: 1 tolar (SIT) = 100 stotins
tolars per US1$ - 127.0

Transportation

Railroads: 1,210 km
Roads: 14,726 km total paved and unpaved
Ports: Izola, Koper, Piran
Airports: 14 total paved and unpaved. There are three international airports in Slovenia, Ljubljana, Maribor, Portoroz

The Press: daily newspapers

Delo: 61000 Ljubljana, Dunajska 5
telephone (61) 131-8255 fax (61) 133-4032
circ. 90,000

Vecer: 62000 Maribor, Svetozarevska 14
telephone (62) 22-42-21 fax (62) 22-77-36   circ. 65,000

Tourism: Tourist attractions are Alp mountains, beaches and more than 6,000
  caves

Tourist Association of Slovenia: 61000 Ljubljana, Milosiceva 38
telephone (61) 12-01-41   fax (61) 30-15-70

Diplomatic representation in US:
chief of mission: Ambassador Ernest Petric
chancery: 1525 New Hampshire Avenue NW, Washington, DC 20036
telephone: [1] (202) 667-5363
FAX: [1] (202) 667-4563

US Diplomatic representation:
chief of mission: Ambassador E. Allan Wendt
embassy: P O Box 254, Prazakova 4, 61000 Ljubljana
mailing address: American Embassy, Ljubljana, Department of State,
Washington, DC 20521-7140
telephone: [386] (61) 301-427, 472, 485
FAX: [386] (61) 301-401

Solomon Islands

Capital: Honiara   longitude: 159.57 E   latitude: 9.26 S
Government: parliamentary democracy

Flag: divided diagonally by a thin yellow stripe from the lower hoist-side corner; the upper triangle (hoist side) is blue with five white five-pointed stars arranged in an X pattern; the lower triangle is green

Geography

Location: Oceania, group of islands in the South Pacific Ocean, east of Papua New Guinea

Total Area: 28,450 sq km (10,985 sq mi) slightly larger than Maryland

Boundaries: no land boundaries

Climate: tropical monsoon; few extremes of temperature and weather
Temperature (F): High/Low Jan. 88/76, Apr. 87/76, July 85/74, Oct. 88/75
Average annual precipitation: 119.5 inches

Terrain: mostly rugged mountains with some low coral atolls
Highest point is Mount Popomanatseu 2,331 m (7,647 ft)

Natural resources: fish, forests, gold, bauxite, phosphates, lead, zinc, nickel

Natural hazards: typhoons, but they are rarely destructive; geologically active region with frequent earth tremors; volcanic activity

People

Population: 399,800 (July 1995 est.)

Life expectancy at birth: total population 70.84 years

Nationality: Solomon Islander

Ethnic division: Melanesian 93%, Polynesian 4%, Micronesian 1.5%, European 0.8%, Chinese 0.3%, other 0.4%

Religions: Anglican 34%, Roman Catholic 19%, Baptist 17%, United (Methodist/Presbyterian) 11%, Seventh-Day Adventist 10%, other Protestant 5%, traditional beliefs 4%

Languages: Melanesian pidgin in much of the country is lingua franca, English spoken by 1%-2% of population
Note: 120 indigenous languages

Literacy: NA

Economy

Imports: plant and machinery, manufactured goods, food and live animals, fuel

Exports: fish, timber, palm oil, cocoa, copra

Industries: copra, fish (tuna)

Agriculture: mostly subsistence farming; cash crops - cocoa, beans, coconuts, palm kernels, timber; other products - rice, potatoes, vegetables, fruit, cattle, pigs; not self-sufficient in food grains

Currency: 1 Solomon Island dollar (SI$) = 100 cents
Solomon Island dollars per US1$ - 3.31

417

Transportation

    Railroads: none

    Roads: 1,300 total paved and unpaved.

    Note: in addition, there are 800 km of private logging and plantation roads of varied construction

    Ports: Aola Bay, Honiara, Lofung, Noro, Viru Harbor, Yandina

    Airports: 31 total paved and unpaved. The principal international airport is located about 12 km from Honiara

The Press: weekly newspaper   **Solomon Star:** POB 255, Honiara

        telephone 22-913   fax 21-572

        English circ. 4,000

        Solomon Voice: POB 1235, Honiara

    telephone 22-275   fax 20-090   circ. 10,000

Tourism: beaches, coral reefs, rain forest

        Solomon Islands Tourist Authority:

        POB 321, Honiara   telephone 22-442   fax 23-986

Diplomatic representation in US: ambassador traditionally resides in Honiara (Solomon Islands)

US Diplomatic representation: embassy closed July 1993; the ambassador to Papua New Guinea is accredited to the Solomon Islands

Somalia

Capital: Mogadishu   longitude: 45.21 E   latitude: 2.02 N   elevation: 39 ft

Government: none

    Flag: light blue with a large white five-pointed star in the center; design based on the flag of the UN (Italian Somaliland was a UN trust territory)

Geography

Location: Eastern Africa, bordering the Gulf of Edan and the Indian Ocean, east of Ethiopia

Total Area: 637,660 sq km (246,201 sq mi) slightly smaller than Texas

Boundaries: Djibouti, Ethiopia, Kenya

Climate: principally desert; December to February - northeast monsoon, moderate temperatures in north and very hot in south; May to October - southwest monsoon, torrid in the north and hot in the south, irregular rainfall, hot and humid periods (tangambili) between monsoons

Temperature (F): High/Low Jan. 86/73, Apr. 90/78, July 83/73, Oct. 88/75

Average annual precipitation: 16.4 inches

Terrain: mostly flat to undulating plateau rising to hills in north

Highest point is Simbir Berris 2,408 m (7,900 ft)

Natural resources: uranium and largely unexploited reserves of iron ore, tin, gypsum, bauxite, copper, salt

Natural hazards: recurring droughts; frequent dust storms over eastern plains in summer

People

Population: 7,348,000 (July 1995 est.)

Life expectancy at birth: total population 55.74 years

Nationality: Somali

Ethnic division: Somali 85%, Bantu, Arabs 30,000

Religions: Sunni Muslim

Languages: Somali (official), Arabic, Italian, English

Literacy: total population 24%

Economy

Imports: petroleum products, foodstuffs, construction materials

Exports: bananas, live animals, fish, hides

Industries: a few small industries, including sugar refining, textiles, petroleum refining (mostly shut down) (1994)

Agriculture: dominant sector, led by livestock rising (cattle, sheep, goats); crops - bananas, sorghum, corn, mangoes, sugarcane, not self-sufficient in food; distribution of food disrupted by civil strife; fishing potential largely unexploited

Currency: 1 Somali shilling (So. Sh.) = 100 cents

Somali shillings per US1$ - approximately 5,000

Transportation

Railroads: none

Roads: 22,500 km. 2,700 km paved.

Ports: Bender Cassin (Boosasso), Berbera, Chisimayu (Kismaayo), Merca, Mogadishu

Airports: 76 total paved and unpaved. The international airport is at Mogadishu

The Press: daily newspapers

The Country: POB 1178, Mogadishu
telephone 21-206

Xiddigta Oktobar: POB 1178, Mogadishu
telephone 21-206

Tourism: Mogadishu, beaches, skin diving, wildlife

Diplomatic representation in US: Somalian Embassy ceased operation
8 May 1991

US diplomatic representation:

Note: the US Embassy in Mogadishu was evacuated and closed indefinitely in January 1991; Ambassador Daniel Simpson, ambassador to Kenya, represents US interests in Somalia

liason office; US Embassy, Nairobi, Kenya

address: corner of Moi Avenue and Haile Selassie Avenue, Nairobi

mailing address: P O Box 30137, Unit 64100, Nairobi or APO AE 09831

telephone: [254] (2) 33-41-41

FAX: [254] (2) 34-08-38

South Africa

Capital: Pretoria (administrative); longitude: 28.12 E latitude: 25.45 S
elevation: 4,491 ft   Cape Town (legislative) elevation: 56 ft
  Bloemfontrin (judicial) elevation: 4,665 ft

Government: republic

Flag: two equal width horizontal bands of red (top) and blue separated by a central green band which splits into a horizontal Y, the arms of which end at the corner of the hoist side, embracing a black isosceles triangle from which the arms are separated by narrow yellow bands; the red and blue bands are separated from the green band and its arms by narrow white stripes

Geography

Location: Southern Africa, at the tip of the continent of Africa

Total Area: 1,219,912 sq km (471,008 sq mi) slightly less than twice the size of Texas

Boundaries: Botswana, Lesotho, Mozambique, Namibia, Swaziland, Zimbabwe

Climate: mostly semiarid; subtropical along east coast; sunny days, cool nights

Temperature (F): High/Low Jan. 78/58, Apr. 72/50, July 63/39, Oct. 77/53

Average annual precipitation: 30.9 inches

Terrain: vast interior plateau rimmed by rugged hills and narrow coastal plain

Highest point is Injasuti 3,408 m (11,182 ft)

Natural resources: gold, chromium, antimony, coal, iron ore, manganese, nickel, phosphates, tin, uranium, gem diamonds, platinum, copper, vanadium, salt, natural gas

Natural hazards: prolonged drought

People

Population: 45,096,000 (July 1995 est)

Life expectancy at birth: total population 65.42 years

Nationality: South African

Ethnic division: black 75.2%, white 13.6%, Colored 8.6%, Indian 2.6%

Religions: Christian (most whites and Colored and about 60% of blacks), Hindu (60% of Indians), Muslim 2%

Languages: eleven official languages, including Afrikaans, English, Ndebele, Pedi, Sotho, Swazi, Tsonga, Tswana, Venda, Xhosa, Zulu

Literacy: total population 76%

Economy

Imports: machinery, transport equipment, chemicals, oil, textiles, scientific instruments

Exports: gold, other minerals and metals, food, chemicals

Industries: mining (world's largest producer of platinum, gold, chromium), automobiles assembly, metal working, machinery, textile, iron and steel, chemical, fertilizer, foodstuffs

Agriculture: diversified agriculture, with emphasis on livestock; products - cattle, poultry, sheep, wool, mild, beef, corn, wheat, sugarcane, fruits, vegetables; self-sufficient in food

Currency: 1 rand (R) = 100 cents

rand per US1$ - 3.53

Transportation

Railroads: 20,638 km

Roads: 188,309 km total paved and unpaved

Ports: Cape Town, Durban, East London, Mosselbaai, Port Elizabeth, Richards Bay, Saldanha

Airports: 853 total paved and unpaved. The international airport is at Johannesburg

The Press: daily English newspapers **The Pertoria News:** 216 Vermeulen St, Pretoria 0002

telephone (12) 325-5382 fax (12) 325-7300

circ. 26,000 (Mon-Fri) 16,000 (Sat)

The Star: 47 Sauer St. POB 1014, Johannesburg 2000

telephone (11) 633-9111 fax (11) 836-8398

circ. 210,000 (Mon-Fri), 156,000 (Sat), 90,000 (Sun)

Tourism: game parks, Durban's Snake Park, Centenary Aquarium

South African Tourism Board: 442 Rigel Ave South, Frasmusrand 0181, Private Bag X164, Pretoria 0001

telephone (12) 347-0600   fax (12) 45-47-68

Diplomatic representation in US:

chief of mission: Ambassador Franklin Sonn

chancery: 3051 Massachusetts Avenue NW, Washington, DC 20008

telephone: [1] (202) 232-4400

US Diplomatic representation:

chief of mission: Ambassador Princeton N. Lyman

embassy: 877 Pretorius Street, Arcadia 0083

mailing address: P O Box 9536, Pretoria 0001

telephone: [27] (12) 342-1048

FAX: [27] (12) 324-2244

South Georgia and the South Sandwich Islands

Capital: none; Grytviken on South Georgia is the garrison town
longitude: 37.40 W   latitude: 54.00 S

Government: dependent territory of the UK

Geography

Location: Southern South America, islands in the South Atlantic Ocean, east of the tip of South America

Total Area: 4,066 sq km (1,570 sq mi) slightly larger than Rhode Island

Note: includes Shag Rocks, Clerke Rocks, Bird Island

Boundaries: no land boundaries

Climate: variable, mostly westerly winds throughout the year, interspersed with periods of calm; nearly all precipitation falls as snow

Terrain: most of the islands, rising steeply from the sea, are rugged and mountainous; South Georgia is largely barren and has steep, glacier-covered mountains; the South Sandwich Islands are of volcanic origin with some active volcanoes

Natural resources: fish

Natural hazards: the South Sandwich Islands have prevailing weather conditions that generally make them difficult to approach by ship; they are also subject to active volcanism

Note: the north coast of South Georgia has several large bays, which provide good anchorage; reindeer, introduced early in this century, live on south Georgia

423

People

> **Population:** no indigenous population; there is a small garrison on south Georgia, and the British Antarctic Survey has a biological station on Bird Island; the Sandwich Islands are uninhabited

Economy

> Some fishing takes place in adjacent waters. There is a potential source of income from harvesting fin fish and krill. The islands receive income from postage stamps produced in the UK

Transportation

> **Roads:** NA
>
> **Ports:** Grytviken
>
> **Airports:** none

Diplomatic representation in US: none (dependent territory of the UK)

US Diplomatic representation: none (dependent territory of the UK)

Spain

Capital: Madrid   longitude: 3.43 W latitude: 40.25 N elevation: 2,165 ft

Government: parliamentary monarchy

> **Flag:** three horizontal bands of red (top), yellow (double width), and red with the national coat of arms on the hoist side of the yellow band; the coat of arms includes the royal seal framed by the Pillars of Hercules, which are the two promontories (Gibraltar and Ceuta) on either side of the eastern end of the Strait of Gibraltar

Geography

> **Location:** Southwestern Europe, bordering the Bay of Biscay, Mediterranean Sea, and North Atlantic Ocean, southwest of France
>
> **Total Area:** 504,750 sq km (194,884 sq mi) slightly more than twice the size of Oregon

424

Note: includes Balearic Islands, Canary Islands, and five places of sovereignty (plazas de soberania) on and off the coast of Morocco - Ceuta, Mellila, Islas Chafarinas, Penon de Alhucemas, and Penon de Velez de la Gomera

Boundaries: Andorra, France, Gilbraltar, Portugal

Climate: temperate; clear, hot summers in interior, more moderate and cloudy along coast; cloudy, cold winters in interior, partly cloudy and cool along coast

Temperature (F): High/Low Jan. 47/35, Apr. 65/45, July 87/63, Oct. 65/49
Average annual precipitation: 17.5 inches

Terrain: large, flat to dissected plateau surrounded by rugged hills; Pyrenees in north

Highest point is Pico de Teide 3,710 m (12,172 ft)

Natural resources: coal, lignite, iron ore, uranium, mercury, pyrites, fluorspar, gypsum, zinc, lead, tungsten, copper, kaolin, potash, hydropower

Natural hazards: periodic droughts

People

Population: 39,405,000 (July 1995 est.)

Life expectancy at birth: total population 77.91 years

Nationality: Spaniard

Ethnic division: composite of Mediterranean and Nordic types

Religions: Roman Catholic 99%, other sects 1%

Languages: Castilian Spanish, Catalan 17%, Galician 7%, Basque 2%

Literacy: total population 96%

Economy

Imports: machinery, transport equipment, fuels, semi-finished goods, foodstuffs, consumer goods, chemicals

Exports: car and trucks, semi-finished manufactured goods, foodstuffs, machinery

Industries: textiles and apparel (including footwear), food and beverages, metals and metal manufactures, chemicals, shipbuilding, automobiles, machine tools, tourism

Agriculture: major products - grain, vegetables, olives, wine grapes, sugar beets, citrus fruit, beef, pork, poultry, dairy; largely self-sufficient in food

Currency: 1 paseta (Pta) = 100 centimes
pesetas per US1$ - 132.61

Transportation

Railroads: 14,400 km

Roads: 331,961 km total paved and unpaved

Ports: Aviles, Barcelona, Bilboa, Cadiz, Cartagena, Castellon de la Plana, Ceuta, Huelva, La Coruna, Las Palmas (Canary Islands), Malaga, Melilla, Pasajes, Puerto de Gijon, Santa Cruz de Tenerife (Canary Island), Santander, Tarragona, Valencia, Vigo

Airports: 106 total paved and unpaved. More than 20 airports are equipped for international flights

The Press: daily newspapers

El Periodico: Consell de Cent 425-427, 08004 Barcelona
telephone (3) 265-5353 fax (3) 484-6512
circ. 190,000,   380,000 Sunday

Diario: Albasanz 14, 28037 Madrid
telephone (1) 396-5000   fax (1) 396-5146
circ. 179,000   210,000 Sunday

Tourism: Madrid, Royal Palace, museums, historic cities, Basque fishing village, badlands of the Pyrenees, Ordesa National Park, beaches

Secretaria General de Turismo:
Maria de Molina 50, 28006 Madrid
telephone (1) 411-4014   fax (1) 563-8638

Diplomatic representation in US:
chief of mission: Ambassador Jaime De Ojeda Eiseley
chancery: 2375 Pennsylvania Avenue NW, Washington, DC 20037
telephone: [1] (202) 452-0100,   728-2340
FAX: [1] (202) 833-5670

US Diplomatic representation:
chief of mission: Ambassador Richard N. Gardner
embassy: Serrano 75, 28006 Madrid
mailing address: APO AE 09642
telephone: [34] (1) 577-4000
FAX: [34] (1) 577-5735

Spratly Islands

Capital: none   longitude: 112.30 E   latitude: 8.40 N

Government: International disputes: all of the Spratly Islands are claimed by
China, Taiwan, and Vietnam; part of them are claimed by Malaysia and the
Philippines; in 1984, Brunei established and exclusive economic zone, which
encompasses Louisa Reef, but has not publicly claimed the island

Geography

Location: Southeastern Asia, group of reefs in the South China Sea, about
two-thirds of the way from Vietnam to the southern Philippines

Total Area: NA sq km but less than 5 sq km (1.9 sq mi)

Note: includes 100 or so islets, coral reefs, and sea mounts scattered over the
South China Sea

Boundaries: no land boundaries

Climate: tropical

Terrain: flat

Natural resources: fish, guano, undetermined oil and natural gas potential

Natural hazards: typhoons; serious maritime hazard because of numerous
reefs and shoals

People

Population: no indigenous inhabitants; there are scattered garrisons

Economy

Economic activity is limited to commercial fishing. The proximity to nearby
oil- and gas-producing sedimentary basins suggests the potential for oil and
gas deposits, but the region is largely unexplored, and there are no reliable
estimates of potential reserves; commercial exploitation has yet to be
developed

Industries: none

Transportation
   Ports: none
   Airports: 4 total paved and unpaved

Sri Lanka

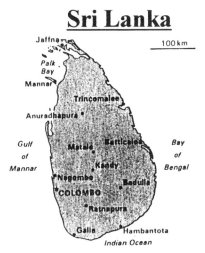

   Capital: Colombo   longitude: 79.52 E   latitude: 6.55 N   elevation: 24 ft
Government: republic
   Flag: yellow with two green panels; the smaller hoist-side panel has two
   equal vertical bands of green (hoist side) and orange; the other panel is a
   large dark rectangle with a yellow lion holding a sword, and there is a yellow
   bo leaf in each corner; the yellow field appears as a border that goes around
   the entire flag and extends between the two panels
Geography
   Location: Southern Asia, island in the Indian Ocean, south of India
   Total Area: 65,610 sq km (25,332 sq mi) slightly larger than West Virginia
   Boundaries: no land boundaries
   Climate: tropical monsoon; northeast monsoon (December to March);
   southwest monsoon (June to October)
   Temperature (F): High/Low Jan. 86/72, Apr. 88/76, July 85/77, Oct. 85/75
   Average annual precipitation: 92.3 inches
   Terrain: mostly low, flat to rolling plain; mountains in south-central interior
   Highest point is Pidurutalagala 2,524 m (8,281 ft)
   Natural resources: limestone, graphite, mineral sands, gems, phosphates,
   clay
   Natural hazards: occasional cyclones and tornadoes
People
   Population: 18,343,000 (July 1995 est)
   Life expectancy at birth: total population 72.14 years
   428

Nationality: Sri Lankan

Ethnic division: Sinhalese 74%, Tamil 18%, Moor 7%, Burgher, Malay, and Vedda 1%

Religions: Buddhist 69%, Hindu 15%, Christian 8%, Muslim 8%

Languages: Sinhala (official and national language) 74%, Tamil (national language) 18%

Literacy: total population 88%

Economy

Imports: textiles and textiles materials, machinery and equipment, transport equipment, petroleum, building materials

Exports: garments and textiles, teas, diamonds, other gems, petroleum products, rubber products, other agricultural products, marine products, graphite

Industries: processing of rubber, tea, coconuts, and other agricultural commodities; clothing, cement, petroleum refining, textiles, tobacco

Agriculture: field crops - rice, sugarcane, grains, pulses, oilseeds, roots, spices; cash crops - tea, rubber, coconuts; animal products - milk, eggs, hides, meat; not self-sufficient in rice production

Currency: 1 Sri Lankan rupee (SLRe) = 100 cents
Sri Lankan rupee per US1$ - 50.11

Transportation

Railroads: 1,948 km

Roads: 75,263 km total paved and unpaved

Ports: Colombo, Galle, Jaffna, Trincomalee

Airports: 14 total paved and unpaved

The Press: daily newspapers   **The Island:** 223 Bloemendhal Road, Colombo, 13   telephone (1) 24-001   circ. 80,000 daily 200,000 Sunday

Sun: 5 Gunasena Mawatha, POB 226, Colombo, 12 telephone (1) 23-864   circ. 60,000 daily, 80,000 Sunday

Tourism: natural scenery, ancient monuments, Buddhist festivals, zoological gardens, beaches

Celon Tourist Board: 78 Stuart Place, POB 1504, Colombo 3   (verify) telephone (1) 43-70-59   fax (1) 43-79-53

Diplomatic representation in US:

chief of mission: Ambassador Jayantha Dhanapala

chancery: 2148 Wyoming Avenue NW, Washington, DC 20008

telephone: [1] (202) 483-4025 through 4028

FAX: [1] (202) 232-7181

US Diplomatic representation:

chief of mission: Ambassador Teresita C. Schaffer

embassy: 210 Galle Road, Colombo 3

mailing address: P O Box 106, Colombo

telephone: [94] (1) 44-80-07

FAX: [94] (1) 43-73-45

Sudan

Capital: Khartoum   longitude: 32.32 E   latitude: 15.33 N
elevation: 1,279 ft

Government: ruling military junta - Revolutionary Command Council - dissolved on 16 October 1993 and government civilianized

Flag: three equal horizontal bands of red (top), white, and black with a green isosceles triangle based on the hoist side

Geography

Location: Northern Africa, bordering the Red Sea, between Egypt and Eritrea

Total Area: 2,505,810 sq km (967,493 sq mi) slightly more than one-quarter the size of the US

Boundaries: Central African Republic, Chad, Egypt, Eritrea, Ethiopia, Kenya, Libya, Uganda, Zaire

Climate: tropical in south; arid desert in north; rainy season (April to October)

430

Temperature (F): High/Low Jan. 90/59, Apr. 105/72, July 101/77, Oct. 104/75

Average annual precipitation: 6.2 inches

Terrain: generally flat, featureless plain; mountains in east and west
Highest point is Mount Marra 3,070 m (10,073 ft)

Natural resources: small reserves of petroleum, iron ore, copper, chromium ore, zinc, tungsten, mica, silver, gold

Natural hazards: dust storms

Note: largest country in Africa; dominated by the Nile and its tributaries

People

Population: 30,121,000 (July 1995 est.)

Life expectancy at birth: total population 54.71 years

Nationality: Sudanese

Ethnic division: black 52%, Arab 39%, Beja 6%, foreigners 2%, other 1%

Religions: Sunni Muslim 70% (in north), indigenous beliefs 25%, Christian 5% (mostly in south and Khartoum)

Languages: Arabic (official), Nubian, Ta Bedawie, diverse dialects of Nilotic, Nilo-Hamitic, Sudanic languages, English

Literacy: total population 32%

Economy

Imports: foodstuffs, petroleum products, manufactured goods, machinery and equipment, medicines and chemicals, textiles

Exports: gum arabic, livestock/meat, cotton, sesame, peanuts

Industries: cotton ginning, textiles, cement, edible oils, sugar, soap distilling, shoes, petroleum refining

Agriculture: major products - cotton, oilseeds, sorghum, millet, wheat, gum arabic, sheep, marginally self-sufficient in most foods

Currency: 1 Sudanese pound (#Sd) = 100 piastres
official rate - Sudanese pounds per US1$ - 434.8
Note - the commercial rate is 300 Sudanese pounds per US1$

Transportation

Railroads: 5,516 km

Roads: 20,703 km total paved and unpaved

Ports: Juba, Khartoum, Kusti, Malakal, Nimule, Port Sudan, Sawakin

Airports: 70 total paved and unpaved. The international airport is at Khartoum

The Press: daily newspapers   **Sudan Times:** Khartoum; English
                                    Al-Khartoum: Khartoum; Arabic

Tourism: Khartoum, Mahdi's Tomb, Khalifa's House at Suakin, National Park at Dinder, Red Sea

Public Corporation of Tourism and Hotels:
POB 7104, Khartoum   telephone 81-764

Diplomatic representation in US:
chief of mission: Ambassador Ahmad Sulayman
chancery: 2210 Massachusetts Avenue NW, Washington, DC 20008
telephone: [1] (202) 338-8565 through 8570
FAX: [1] (202) 667-2406

US Diplomatic representation:
chief of mission: Ambassador Donald K. Petterson
embassy: Shar'ia Ali Abdul Latif, Khartoum
mailing address: P O Box 699, Khartoum: APO AE 09829
telephone: 74-700, 74-611 (operator assistance required)

Suriname

Capital: Paramaribo   longitude: 55.14 W   latitude: 5.52 N elevation: 12 ft

Government: republic

Flag: five horizontal bands of green (top, double width), white, red (quadruple width), white, and green (double width); there is a large yellow five-pointed star centered in the red band

Geography

Location: Northern South America, bordering North Atlantic Ocean, between French Guiana Guyana

Total Area: 163,270 sq km (63,039 sq mi) slightly larger than Georgia

Boundaries: Brazil, French Guiana, Guyana

Climate: tropical; moderated by trade winds

432

Temperature (F): High/Low Jan. 85/72, Apr. 86/73, July 87/73, Oct. 91/73
Average annual precipitation: 91 inches
Terrain: mostly rolling hills; narrow coastal plain with swamps
Highest point is Julianatop 1,280 m (4,200 ft)
Natural resources: timber, hydropower potential, fish, shrimp, bauxite, iron ore, and small amounts of nickel, copper, platinum, gold
Natural hazards: NA

People

Population: 429,900 (July 1995 est.)
Life expectancy at birth: total population 69.76 years
Nationality: Surinamer
Ethnic division: Hindustani (also known as "East" Indians; their ancestors emigrated from northern India in the latter part of the 19th century) 37%, Creole (mixed European and African ancestry) 31%, Javanese 15.3%, "Bush Black" (also known as "Bush Creole" whose ancestors were brought to the country in the 17th and 18th century as slaves) 10.3%, Amerindian 2.6%, Chinese 1.7%, Europeans 1%, other 1.1%
Religions: Hindu 27.4%, Muslim 19.6%, Roman Catholic 22.8%, Protestant 25.2% (predominantly Moravian), indigenous beliefs 5%
Languages: Dutch (official), English (widely spoken), Sranang Tongo (Surinamese, sometimes called Taki-Taki, is native language of Creoles and much of the younger population and is lingua franca among others), Hindustani (a dialect of Hindu), Javanese
Literacy: total population 95%

Economy

Imports: capital equipment, petroleum, foodstuffs, cotton, consumer goods
Exports: alumina, aluminum, shrimp and fish, rice, bananas
Industries: bauxite mining, alumina and aluminum production, lumbering, food processing, fishing
Agriculture: paddy rice planted on 85% of arable land and represents 60% of total farm output; other products - bananas, palm kernels, coconuts, plantains, peanuts, beef, chickens; shrimp and forestry products of increasing importance; self-sufficient in most foods
Currency: 1 Surinamese guilder, gulden, or florins (Sf) = 100 cents
Surinamese, guilders, gulden, or florin per US1$ - 1.78

Transportation

Railroads: 166 km
Roads: 8,800 km total paved and unpaved
Ports: Albina, Moengo, Nieuw Nickerie, Paramaribo, Paranam, Wageningen

Airports: 46 total paved and unpaved. The international airport is located about 40 km from Paramaribo

The Press: daily newspapers　　**De Ware Tijd:** Malebatrumstraat 11,
POB 1200, Paramaribo　telephone 72-823
De West: Dr J.C. de Mirandastraat 2-6
POB 176, Paramaribo
telephone 73-338　fax 70-322　circ. 18,000

Tourism: Tourist attractions are nature reserves and parks. Unspoiled interior with many species of animals, birds and plants.
Suriname Tourism Department: Cornelis Jongbawstraat 2, Paramaribo;　telephone 41-03-57

Diplomatic representation in US:
chief of mission: Ambassador Willem A. Udenhout
chancery: Suite 108, 4301 Connecticut Avenue NW, Washington, DC 20008
telephone: [1] (202) 244-7488, 7490 through 7492
FAX: [1] (202) 244-5878

US Diplomatic representation:
chief of mission: Ambassador Roger R. Gamble
embassy: Dr. Sophie Redmondstraat 129, Paramaribo
mailing address: P O Box 1821, Paramaribo
telephone: [597] 47-29-00, 47-78-81, 47-64-59
FAX: [597] 41-00-25

Svalbard

Capital: Longyearbyen　longitude: 15.30 E　latitude: 78.10 N
elevation 23 ft

Government: territory of Norway administered by the Ministry of Industry, Oslo, through a governor (sysselmann) residing in Longyearbyen, Spitsbergen; by treaty (9 February 1920) sovereignty was given to Norway

Flag: the flag of Norway is used

Geography

Location: Northern Europe, islands between the Arctic Ocean, Barents Sea, Greenland Sea, and Norwegian Sea, north of Norway

Total Area: 62,049 sq km (23,957 sq mi) slightly smaller than West Virginia

Boundaries: no land boundaries

Climate: arctic, tempered by warm North Atlantic Current; cool summers, cold winters; North Atlantic Current flows along west and north coasts of Spitsbergen, keeping water open and navigable most of the year

Temperature (F): High/Low Jan. 19/9, Apr. 22/11, July 45/39, Oct. 31/23

Average annual precipitation: 13.3 inches

Terrain: wild, rugged mountains; much of high land ice covered; west coast clear of ice about half the year; fjords along west and north coast

Natural resources: coal, copper, iron ore, phosphate, zinc, wildlife, fish

Natural hazards: ice floes often block up the entrance to Bellsund (a transit point for coal export) on the west coast and occasionally make parts of the northeastern coast inaccessible to maritime traffic

Note: northernmost part of the Kingdom of Norway; consists of nine main islands; glaciers and snowfields cover 60% of the total area

People

Population: 2,950 (July 1995 est.)

Life expectancy at birth: NA

Nationality: NA

Ethnic division: Russian 64%, Norwegian 35%, other 1%

Religions: NA

Languages: Russian, Norwegian

Literacy: NA

Economy

Imports: coal

Exports: NA

Industries: coal mining

Agriculture: NA

Currency: 1 Norwegian krone (NKr) = 100 oere

Norwegian kroner per US1$ - 6.70

Railroads: none

Roads: NA

Ports: Barentsburg, Longyearbyen, Ny-Alesund, Pyramiden

Airports: 4 total, one with paved runway, others unpaved

Tourism: expeditions, tourists, scientific studies

Office of the Governor: Kontoret til Sysselmannen pa Svalbard,
9170 Longyearbyen, Svalbrd
telephone 79-02-31-00   fax 79-02-11-66

Diplomatic representation in US: none (territory of Norway)

US Diplomatic representation: none (territory of Norway)

Swaziland

Capital: Mbabane (administrative) longitude: 31.08 E latitude: 26.20 S
Lobamba (legislative)   elevation: 3,816 ft

Government: monarchy; independent member of Commonwealth

Flag: three horizontal bands of blue (top), red (triple width), and blue; the red band is edged in yellow; centered in the red band is a large black and white shield covering two spears and a staff decorated with feather tassels, all placed horizontally

Geography

Location: Southern Africa, between Mozambique and South Africa

Total Area: 17,360 sq km (6,703 sq mi) slightly smaller than New Jersey

Boundaries: Mozambique, South Africa

Climate: varies from tropical to near temperate

Temperature (F): High/Low Jan. 77/59, Apr. 74/53, July 67/42, Oct. 75/54

Average annual precipitation: 55.2 inches

Terrain: mostly mountains and hills; some moderately sloping plains

Highest point is Emlembe 1,862 m (6,109 ft)

Natural resources: asbestos, coal, clay, cassiterite, hydropower, forests, small gold and diamond deposits, quarry stone, and talc

Natural hazards: NA

People

Population: 967,000 (July 1995 est.)

Life expectancy at birth: total population 56.84 years

Nationality: Swazi

Ethnic division: African 97%, European 3%

Religions: Christian 60%, indigenous beliefs 40%

Languages: English (official; government business conducted in English), siSwati (official)

Literacy: total population 67%

Economy

Imports: motor vehicles, machinery, transport equipment, petroleum products, foodstuffs, chemicals

Exports: sugar, edible concentrates, wood pulp, cotton yarn, asbestos

Industries: mining (coal and asbestos), wood pulp, sugar

Agriculture: mostly subsistence agriculture; cash crops - sugarcane, cotton, maize, tobacco, rice, citrus fruit, pineapples; other crops and livestock - corn, sorghum, peanuts, cattle, goats, sheep; not self-sufficient in grain

Currency: 1 lilangeni (E) = 100 cents

emalangeni per US1$ - 3.53

Note: the Swazi emalangeni is at par with the South African rand

Transportation

Railroads: 297 km; includes 71 km which are not in use

Roads: 2,853 km total paved and unpaved

Ports: none

Airports: 18 total paved and unpaved. Scheduled passenger and cargo services are from the airport at Matsapa

The Press: daily English newspapers **Swaziland Observer:** Swazi Plaza, POB A385, Mbabane telephone 23-383 circ 10,000

The Times of Swaziland: Allister Miller St, POB 156, Mbabane circ. 11,500 telephone 42-220 fax 42-438

Tourism: Tourist attractions are game reserves and beautiful mountain scenery, Matenga Falls

437

Diplomatic representation in US:
chief of mission: Ambassador Madzandza Mary Khanya
chancery: 3400 International Drive NW, Washington, DC 20008
telephone: [1] (202) 362-6683, 6685
FAX: [1] (202) 244-8059
US Diplomatic representation:
chief of mission: Ambassador John T. Sprott
embassy: Central Bank Building, Warner Street, Mbabane
mailing address: P O Box 199, Mbabane
telephone: [268] 46-441 through 46-445
FAX: [268] 45-959

Sweden

Capital: Stockholm   longitude: 18.05 E latitude: 59.20 N elevation: 144 ft
Government: constitutional monarchy
Flag: blue with a yellow cross that extends to the edges of the flag; the vertical part of the cross is shifted to the hoist side in the style of the Dannebrog (Danish flag)
Geography
Location: Northern Europe, bordering the Baltic Sea, Gulf of Bothnia, and Skagerrak, between Finland and Norway
Total Area: 449,964 sq km (173,731 sq mi) slightly smaller than California
Boundaries: Finland, Norway

Climate: temperate in south with cold, cloudy winters and cool. partly cloudy summers; subarctic in north

Temperature (F): High/Low Jan. 30/23, Apr. 47/34, July 71/57, Oct. 49/41

Average annual precipitation: 21.9 inches

Terrain: mostly flat or gently rolling lowlands; mountains in west

Highest point is Kebnekaise 2,117 m (6,946 ft)

Natural resources: zinc, iron ore, lead, copper, silver, timber, uranium, hydropower potential

Natural hazards: ice floes in the surrounding waters, especially in the Gulf of Bothnia, can interfere with maritime traffic

People

Population: 8,822,000 (July 1995 est.)

Life expectancy at birth: total population 78.43 years

Nationality: Swede

Ethnic division: white, Lapp (Sami), foreign born or first-generation immigrants 12% (Finns, Yugoslavs, Danes, Norwegians, Greeks, Turks)

Religions: Evangelical Lutheran 94%, Roman Catholic 1.5%, Pentecostal 1%, other 3.5%

Languages: Swedish

Note: small-Lapp and Finnish-speaking minorities; immigrants speak native languages

Literacy: total population 99%

Economy

Imports: machinery, petroleum and petroleum products, chemicals, motor vehicles, foodstuffs, iron and steel, clothing

Exports: machinery, motor vehicles, paper products, pulp and paper, iron and steel products, chemicals, petroleum and petroleum products

Industries: iron and steel, precision equipment (bearings, radio and telephone parts, armaments), wood pulp and paper products, processed foods, motor vehicles

Agriculture: animal husbandry predominates, with milk and dairy products accounting for 37% of farm income; main crops - grains, sugar beets, potatoes; 100% self-sufficient in grains and potatoes; Sweden is about 50% self-sufficient in most products

Currency: 1 Swedish krona (SKr) = 100 oere

Swedish kronor per US1$ - 7.46

Transportation

Railroads: 12,000 km (includes 953 km of privately owned railways)

Roads: 135,859 km total paved and unpaved

Ports: Gavle, Goteborg, Halmstad, Helsingborg, Hudiksvall, Kalmar, Karlshamn, Malmo, Solvesborg, Stockholm, Sundsvall

Airports: 253 total paved and unpaved. The main international airport is at Arlanda, about 40 km from Stockholm. Other international airports are at Landvetter, and Sturup

The Press: daily newspapers

Goteborgs-Posten: Polhemsplatsen 5, 405 02 Goteborg
telephone (31) 62-40-00   fax (31) 80-27-69
circ. 275,00 weekdays, 320,000 Sundays

Dagens Nyheter: 105 15 Stockholm
telephone (8) 738-1000   fax (8) 619-0811
circ. 386,000 weekdays   448,000 Sundays

Tourism: Tourist attractions are white sandy beaches, many lakes and forests, mountains of the "Midnight Sun". Drottningholm Palace, Gota canal trip

Svenska Turistforeningen: Drottninggt 31-33, POB 25, 101 20 Stockholm
telephone (8) 790-3100   fax (8) 20-13-32

Diplomatic representation in US:

chief of mission: Ambassador Carl Henrik Sihver Liljegren
chancery: 1501 M Street NW, Washington, DC 20005
telephone: [1] (202) 467-2600
FAX: [1] (202) 467-2699

US Diplomatic representation:

chief of mission: Ambassador Thomas L. Siebert
embassy: Strandvagen 101, S-115 89 Stockholm
mailing address: use embassy street address
telephone: [46] (8) 783-5300
FAX: [46] (8) 661-1964

Switzerland

Capital: Bern   longitude: 7.26 E latitude: 46.57 N   elevation: 1,877 ft

Government: federal republic

   Flag: red square with a bold, equilateral white cross in the center that does not extend to the edges of the flag

Geography

   Location: Central Europe, east of France

   Total Area: 41,290 sq km (15,942 sq mi) slightly more than twice the size of New Jersey

   Boundaries: Austria, France, Italy, Liechtenstein, Germany

   Climate: temperate, but varies with altitude; cold, cloudy, rainy/snowy winters; cool to warm, cloudy, humid summers with occasional showers Temperature (F): High/Low Jan. 38/29, Apr. 59/42, July 77/58, Oct. 58/44 Average annual precipitation: 38.5 inches

   Terrain: mostly mountains (Alps in south, Jura in northwest) with a central plateau of rolling hills, plains, and large lakes Highest point is Dufourspitze 4,634 m (15,203 ft)

   Natural resources: hydropower potential, timber, salt

   Natural hazards: avalanches, landslides, flash floods

People

   Population: 7,085,000 (July 1995 est.)

   Life expectancy at birth: total population 78.36 years

   Nationality: Swiss

   Ethnic division: German 65%, French 18%, Italian 10%, Romansch 1%, other 6%

   Religions: Roman Catholic 47.6%, Protestant 44.3%, other 8.1%

   Languages: German 65%, French 18%, Italian 12%, Romansch 1%, other 4%

   Literacy: total population 99%

441

Economy

Imports: agricultural products, machinery and transportation equipment, chemicals, textiles, construction materials

Exports: machinery and equipment, precision instruments, metal products, foodstuffs, textiles and clothing

Industries: machinery, chemicals, watches, textiles, precision instruments

Agriculture: dairy farming predominates; less than 50% self-sufficient in food; must import fish, refined sugar, fats and oils (other than butter), grains, eggs, fruits, vegetables, meat

Currency: 1 Swiss franc, franken, or franco (SwF) = 100 centimes, rappen, or centesimi

Swiss francs, franken, or franchi per US1$ - 1.28

Transportation

Railroads: 5,763 km

Roads: 71,118 km (all paved)

Ports: Basel

Airports: 69 (one unpaved). Principal airports are located at Zurich, Geneva, and Basel-Mulhouse

The Press: daily newspapers

Berner Zeitung: Nordring, Postfach 1147, 3001 Berne
telephone (31) 41-46-46   circ. 125,000

Le Matin: 33 ave de la Gare, 1001 Lausanne
telephone (21) 49-49-49 fax (21) 49-41-10
circ. 55,000 Sunday 160,000

Tourism: Winter sports, mountaineering, beautiful lakes, lake resorts, and the Alp mountains.

Swiss National Tourist Office: Bellariastr. 38, 8027 Zurich
telephone (1) 288-1111   fax (1) 288-1205

Diplomatic representation in US:

chief of mission: Ambassador Carlo Jagmetti

chancery: 2900 Cathedral Avenue NW, Washington, DC 20008

telephone: [1] (202) 745-7900

FAX: [1] (202) 387-2564

US Diplomatic representation:
> *chief of mission:* Ambassador M. Larry Lawrence
> *embassy:* Jubilaeumstrasse 93, 3005 Bern
> *mailing address:* use embassy street address
> *telephone:* [41] (31) 357-7011
> *FAX:* [41] (31) 357-7344

Syria

Capital: Damascus   longitude: 36.19 E   latitude: 33.30 N
elevation: 2,362 ft

Government: republic under left-wing military regime since March 1963

Flag: three equal horizontal bands of red (top), white, and black with two small green five-pointed stars in a horizontal line centered in the white band; similar to the flag of Yemen, which has a plain white band and of Iraq, which has three green stars (plus an Arabic inscription) in a horizontal line centered in the white band also similar to the flag of Egypt, which has a symbolic eagle centered in the white band

Geography

Location: Middle East, bordering the Mediterranean Sea, between Lebanon and Turkey

Total Area: 185,180 sq km (71,498 sq mi) slightly larger than North Dakota

Boundaries: Iraq, Israel, Jordan, Lebanon, Turkey

Climate: mostly desert; hot, dry, sunny summers (June to August) and mild, rainy winters (December to February) along coast; cold weather with snow or sleet periodically hits Damascus

Temperature (F): High/Low Jan. 53/36, Apr. 75/49, July 96/64, Oct. 81/54

Average annual precipitation: 8.6 inches

Terrain: primarily semiarid and desert plateau; narrow coastal plain; mountains in west

443

Highest point is Hermon 2,814 m (9,232 ft)

Natural resources: petroleum, phosphates, chrome and manganese ores, asphalt, iron ore, rock salt, marble, gypsum

Natural hazards: dust storms, sandstorms

Note: there are 42 Jewish settlements and civilian land use sites in the Israeli-occupied Golan Heights

People

Population: 15,452,000 (July 1995 est.)

Life expectancy at birth: total population 66.81 years

Nationality: Syrian

Ethnic division: Arab 90.3%, Kurds, Armenians, and others 9.7%

Religions: Sunni Muslim 74%, Alawite, Druze, and other Muslim sects 16%, Christian (various sects) 10%, Jewish (tiny communities in Damascus, Al Qamishli, and Aleppo)

Languages: Arabic (official), Kurdish, Armenian, Aramaic, Circassian, French widely understood

Literacy: total population 64%

Economy

Imports: foodstuffs, metal products, machinery

Exports: petroleum, textiles, cotton, fruit and vegetables, wheat, barley, chickens

Industries: textiles, food processing, beverages, tobacco, phosphate rock mining, petroleum

Agriculture: all major crops (wheat, barley, cotton, lentils, chickpeas) grown mainly on rain-watered land causing wide swing in production; animal products - beef, lamb, eggs, poultry, milk; not self-sufficient in grain or livestock products

Currency: 1 Syrian pound (#S) = 100 piastres

Syrian pounds per US1$ - 11.2

Transportation

Railroads: 1,998 km

Roads: 31,569 km total paved and unpaved

Ports: Baniyas, Jablah, Latakia, Tartus

Airports: 107 total paved and unpaved. The international airport is at Damascus

The Press: daily newspapers   **Al-Baath:** BP 9389, Mezze Autostrade, Damascus   circ. 65,000

telephone (11) 66-46-00 fax (11) 24-00-99

Ath-Thawra: Al-Wihdat Press, BP 2448, Damascus circ. 55,000

Tourism: The work week in Syria is Saturday through Thursday. The U.S. Embassy is open Sunday through Thursday. Tourist attractions are the Mediterranean coastline, town bazaars and the antiquities of Damascus and Palmyra

Ministry of Tourism: rue Victoria, Damascus
telephone (11) 21-59-16

Diplomatic representation in US:
chief of mission: Ambassador Walid Mualem
chancery: 2215 Wyoming Avenue NW, Washington, DC 20008
telephone: [1] (202) 232-6313
FAX: [1] (202) 234- 9548

US Diplomatic representation:
chief of mission: Ambassador Christopher W.S. Ross
embassy: Abou Roumaneh, Al-Mansur Street No. 2, Damascus
mailing address: P O Box 29, Damascus
telephone: [963] (11) 333-2814,   333-3788
FAX: [963] (11) 224-7938

China (Taiwan)

Capital: Taipei   longitude: 121.32 E   latitude: 25.05 N   elevation: 30 ft

Government: multiparty democratic regime

Flag: red with a dark rectangle in the upper hoist-side corner bearing a white sun with 12 rays

Geography

Location: Eastern Asia, islands bordering the East China Sea, Philippine Sea, South China Sea, and Taiwan Strait, north of the Philippines, off the southeastern coast of China

Total Area: 35,980 sq km (13,892 sq mi) slightly larger than Maryland and Delaware combined

Boundaries: no land boundaries

Climate: tropical; marine; rainy season during southwest monsoon (June to August); cloudiness is persistent and extensive all year

Temperature (F): High/Low Jan. 66/54, Apr. 77/63, July 92/76, Oct. 81/67

Average annual precipitation: 83.8 inches

Terrain: eastern two-thirds mostly rugged mountains; flat to gently rolling plains in west

Natural resources: small deposits of coal, natural gas, limestone, marble, and asbestos

Natural hazards: earthquakes and typhoons

People

Population: 21,501,000 (July 1995 est.)

Life expectancy at birth: total population 75.47 years

Nationality: Chinese

Ethnic division: Taiwanese 84%, mainland Chinese 14%, aborigine 2%

Religions: mixture of Buddhist, Confucian, and Taoist 93%, Christian 4.5%

Languages: Mandarin Chinese (official), Taiwanese (Min), Hakka dialects

Literacy: total population 86%

Economy

Imports: machinery and equipment, electronic products, chemicals, iron and steel, crude oil, foodstuffs

Exports: electrical machinery, electronic products, textiles, footwear, foodstuffs, plywood and wood products

Industries: electronics, textiles, chemicals, clothing, food processing, plywood, sugar milling, cement, shipbuilding, petroleum refining

Agriculture: major crops - vegetables, rice, fruit, tea; livestock - hogs, poultry, beef, milk

Currency: 1 New Taiwan dollar (NT$) = 100 cents

New Taiwan dollars per US1$ - 26.20

Transportation

Railroads: 4,600 km

Roads: 20,041 km total paved and unpaved

Ports: Chi-lung (Keelung), Hua-lien, Kao-hsiung, Su-ao, Tai-chung

Airports: total 41. There are two international airports, Chiang Kai-shek at Taoyuan, and Hsiaokang in Kaohsiung

The Press: daily newspapers

Central Daily News: 260 Pa Teh Road, Sec. 2, Taipei   circ. 600,000
telephone (2) 776-3322   fax (2) 777-5835

Chinese Times Express: 132 Da Li Street, Taipei
telephone (2) 308-2221   fax (2) 304-8138
circ. 400,000

Tourism: Taipei, National Palace Museum, Sun Moon Lake
Taiwan Visitors' Association:
5th Floor, 9 Minchaun East Road,
Sec. 2, Taipei
telephone (2) 594-3261 fax (2) 594-3265

Diplomatic representation in US: none; unofficial commercial and cultural relations with the people of the US are maintained through a private instrumentality, the Taipei Economic and Cultural Representative Office with headquarters in Taipei and field offices in Washington, DC

US Diplomatic representation: none; unofficial commercial and cultural relations with the people of Taiwan are maintained through private institution, the American Institute in Taiwan, which has offices in Taipeo at #7, Lane 134, Hsin Yi Road, Section 3, telephone [886] (2) 709-2000

Tajikistan

150 km

Capital: Dushanbe   longitude: 68.70 E   latitude: 42.40N
Government: republic
Flag: three horizontal stripes of red (top), a wider stripe of white, and green; a crown surmounted by seven five-pointed stars is located in the center of the white stripe

Geography
Location: Central Asia, west of China
Total Area: 143,100 sq km (55,251 sq mi) slightly smaller than Wisconsin
Boundaries: Afghanistan, China, Kyrgyzstan, Uzbekistan

Climate: mid-latitude continental, hot summers, mild winters; semiarid to polar in Pamir Mountains

Temperature: average winter (F) 28 to 36, average summer (F) 86

Average annual precipitation: 63 inches in mountains, 6 inches elsewhere

Terrain: Pamir and Altay mountains dominate landscape; western Fergana Valley in north, Kofarnihon and Vakhsh Valleys in southwest

Highest point is Communism Peak 7,495 m (24,590 ft)

Natural resources: significant hydropower potential, some petroleum, uranium, mercury, brown coal, lead, zinc, antimony, tungsten

Natural hazards: NA

People

Population: 6,156,000 (July 1995 est.)

Life expectancy at birth: total population 69.03 years

Nationality: Tajik

Ethnic division: Tajik 64.9%, Uzbek 25%, Russian 3.5% (declining because of emigration), other 6.6%

Religions: Sunni Muslim 80%, Shi'a Muslim 5%

Languages: Tajik (official) Russian widely used in government and business)

Literacy: total population 98%

Economy

Imports: fuel, chemicals, machinery and transport equipment, textiles, foodstuffs

Exports: cotton, aluminum, fruits, vegetable oil, textiles

Industries: aluminum, zinc, lead, chemicals and fertilizers, cement, vegetable oil, metal-cutting machine tools, refrigerators and freezers

Agriculture: cotton, grain, fruits, grapes, vegetables; cattle, sheep and goats

Currency: 1 ruble (R) = 100 kopeks

U.S. exchange rate not available

Transportation

Railroads: 480 km in common carrier service; does not include industrial lines

Roads: 29,900 km total paved and unpaved

Ports: none

Airports: 59 total paved and unpaved. The main international airport is at Dushanbe

The Press: newspapers   **Narodnaya Gazeta:** Dushanbe   5 a week

Sadoi mardum: Dushanbe   5 a week

Tourism: scenic mountains

State Committee for Youth, Sport and Tourism: Dushanbe

Diplomatic representation in US:
> *chief of mission:* NA
> *chancery:* NA
> *telephone:* NA
> *FAX: NA*

US Diplomatic representation:
> *chief of mission:* Ambassador Stanley T. Escudero
> *embassy:* Interim Chancery, #39 Ainii Street, Oktyabrskaya Hotel, Dushanbe
> *mailing address:* use embassy street address
> *telephone:* [7] (3772) 21-03-56

Tanzania

Capital: Dar es Salaam   longitude: 39.18E latitude: 6.51 S elevation 47 ft

Government: republic
> **Flag:** divided diagonally by a yellow-edged black band from the lower hoist-side corner; the upper triangle (hoist side) is green and the lower triangle is blue

Geography
> **Location:** Eastern Africa, bordering the Indian Ocean, between Kenya and Mozambique
>
> **Total Area:** 945,090 sq km (364,899 sq mi) slightly larger than twice the size of California
>
> **Boundaries:** Burundi, Kenya, Malawi, Mozambique, Rwanda, Uganda, Zambia
>
> **Climate:** varies from tropical along coast to temperate in highlands

Temperature (F): High/Low Jan. 87/77, Apr. 86/73, July 83/66, Oct. 85/69
Average annual precipitation: 41.9 inches
Terrain: plains along coast; central plateau; highlands in north, south
Highest point is Kilmanjaro   5,895 m   (19,340 ft)
Natural resources: hydropower potential, tin, phosphates, iron ore, coal,
diamonds, gemstones, gold, natural gas, nickel
Natural hazards: the tsets fly and lack of water limit agriculture; flooding
on the central plateau during the rainy season

People

Population: 28,702,000 (July 1995 est.)

Life expectancy at birth: total population 42.53 years

Nationality: Tanzanian

Ethnic division:

Mainland: native African 99%, (consisting of well over 100 tribes),
Asian, European, and Arab 1%

Zanzibar: NA

Religions:

Mainland: Christians 45%, Muslim 35%, indigenous beliefs 20%

Zanzibar: Muslim 99% plus

Languages: Swahili (official; widely understood and generally used for
communication between ethnic groups and is used in primary education),
English (official; primary language of commerce, administration, and higher
education)

Note: first language of most people is one of the local languages

Literacy: total population 59%

Economy

Imports: manufactured goods, machinery and transportation equipment,
cotton piece goods, crude oil, foodstuffs

Exports: coffee, cotton, tobacco, tea, cashew nuts, sisal

Industries: primarily agricultural processing (sugar, beer, cigarettes, sisal twine),
diamond and gold mining, oil refining, shoes, cement, textiles, wood
products, fertilizer

Agriculture: cash crops - coffee, sisal, tea, cotton, pyrethrum (insecticide made
from chrysanthemums), cashews, tobacco, cloves
(Zanzibar); food crops - corn, wheat, cassava, bananas, fruits, vegetables;
small number of cattle, sheep, and goats; not self-sufficient in food grain
production

Currency: 1 Tanzanian shilling (TSh) = 100 cents
Tanzanian shillings per US1$ - 523.40

Transportation

Railroads: 2,600 km

Roads: 81,900 km total paved and unpaved

Ports: Bukoba, Dar es Salaam, Kigoma, Lindi, Mkoma, Mtoani, Mtwara, Musoma, Mwanza, Tanga, Wete, Zanzibar

Airports: 108 total paved and unpaved. The major international airport is located just out side of Dar es Salaam. The other international airports are at Kilimanjaro and Zanzibar

The Press: daily newspapers   **Daily News:** POB 9033 Dar es Salaam

telephone (51) 25-318   circ. 50,000

Uhuru: POB 9221, Dar es Salaam

telephone (51) 64-341   circ. 100,000

Tourism: About one-third of Tanzania's land has been set aside for national parks, forest, and game reserves. Mount Kilimanjaro, Olduvai Gorge

Tanzania Tourist Board: IPS Bldg, Maktaba St.

POB 2485, Dar es Salaam

telephone (51) 27-671 fax (51) 46-780

Zanzibar Tourist Corporation: POB 216, Zanzibar

telephone (54) 32-344   fax (54) 33-430

Diplomatic representation in US:

chief of mission: Ambassador Charles Musama Nyirabu

chancery: 2139 R Street NW, Washington, DC 20008

telephone: [1] (202) 939-6125

FAX: [1] (202) 797-7408

US Diplomatic representation:

chief of mission: Ambassador Brady Anderson

embassy: 36 Laibon Road (off Bagamoyo Road), Dar es Salaam

mailing address: P O Box 9123, Dar es Salaam

telephone: [255] (51) 66-010 through 66-015

FAX: [255] (51) 66-701

Thailand

400 km

Capital: Bangkok   longitude: 100.30 E   latitude: 13.44 N elevation: 7 ft

Government: Constitutional monarchy

 Flag: five horizontal bands of red (top), white, blue (double width), white, and red

Geography

 Location: Southeastern Asia, bordering the Andaman Sea and the Gulf of Thailand, southeast of Burma

 Total Area: 514,000 sq km (198,455 sq mi) slightly more than twice the size of Wyoming

 Boundaries: Burma, Cambodia, Laos, Malaysia

 Climate: tropical; rainy, warm, cloudy southwest monsoon (mid-May to September); dry, cool monsoon (November to mid-March); southern isthmus always hot and humid

 Temperature (F): High/Low Jan. 89/68, Apr. 86/73, July 83/66, Oct. 85/69 Average annual precipitation: 55 inches

 Terrain: central plain; Khorat plateau in the east; mountains elsewhere Highest point is Doi Inthanon 2,576 m (8,452 ft)

 Natural resources: tin, rubber, natural gas, tungsten, tantalum, timber, lead, fish, gypsum, lignite, fluorite

 Natural hazards: land subsidence in Bangkok are resulting from the depletion of the water table; droughts

People

 Population: 60,272,000 (July 1995 est)

 Life expectancy at birth: total population 68.42 years

 Nationality: Thai

 Ethnic division: Thai 75%, Chinese 14%, others 11%

 Religions: Buddhism 95%, Muslim 3.8%, Christianity 0.5%, Hinduism 0.1%, other 0.6%

452

Languages: Thai, English the secondary language of the elite, ethnic and regional dialects

Literacy: total population 93%

Economy

Imports: capital goods, intermediate goods and raw material, consumer goods

Exports: machinery and manufactures, agricultural products and fisheries

Industries: tourism is the largest source of foreign exchange; textiles and garments, agricultural processing,. beverages, tobacco. cement, light manufacturing, such as jewelry; electric appliances and components, integrated circuits, furniture, plastics; world's second-largest tungsten producer and third-largest tin producer

Agriculture: leading producer and exporter of rice and cassava (tapioca); other crops - rubber, corn, sugarcane, coconuts, soybeans; except for wheat, self-sufficient in food

Currency: 1 baht (B) = 100 satang

bath per US1$ - 25.07

Transportation

Railroads: 3,940 km

Roads: 77,697 km total paved and unpaved

Ports: Bangkok, Laem Chabang, Pattani, Phuket, Sattahip, Si Racha, Songkhla

Airports: 105 total paved and unpaved. The main international airport is near Bangkok. There are several other airports of international standards

The Press: daily newspapers

Daily News: 1/4 Thanon Vibhavadi Rangsit, Bangkok; Thai Language
telephone (2) 579-0220 fax (2) 561-1343 circ. 650,000

Bangkok Post: Bangkok Post Bldg. 136 Soi Na Ranong, Klongtoey, Bangkok 10110   English Language
telephone (2) 240-3700   fax (2) 240-3666   circ. 54,000

Tourism: Attractions are temples, palaces and pagodas, beach resorts

Tourist Authority of Thailand:
372 Thanon Bamrung Muang, Bangkok 10100
telephone (2) 226-0060 fax (2) 224-6221

Diplomatic representation in US:

    chief of mission: Ambassador Manatphat Chuto

    chancery: 1024 Wisconsin Avenue NW, Washington, DC 20007

    telephone: [1] (202) 944-3600

    FAX: [1] (202) 944-3611

US Diplomatic representation:

    chief of mission: Ambassador David F. Lambertson

    embassy: 95 Wireless Road, Bangkok

    mailing address: APO AP 96546

    telephone: [66] (2) 252-5040

    FAX: [66] (2) 254-2990

Togo

Capital: Lome   longitude: 1.21 E   latitude: 6.10 N   elevation: 72 ft

Government: republic under transition to multiparty democratic rule

    Flag: five equal horizontal bands of green (top and bottom) alternating with yellow; there is a white five-pointed star on a red square in the upper hoist-side corner; uses the popular pan-African colors of Ethiopia

Geography

    Location: Western Africa, bordering the North Atlantic Ocean, between Benin and Ghana

    Total Area: 56,790 sq km (21,927 sq mi) slightly smaller than west Virginia

    Boundaries: Benin, Burkina, Ghana

    Climate: tropical, hot, humid in south; semiarid in north

    Temperature (F): High/Low Jan. 84/74, Apr. 86/77, July 80/74, Oct. 83/75

    Average annual precipitation: 31 inches

    Terrain: gently rolling savanna in north; central hills; southern plateau; low coastal plain with extensive lagoons and marshes

    Highest point is Agou 1,050 m (3,445 ft)

Natural resources: phosphates, limestone, marble

Natural hazards: hot, dry harmattan wind can reduce visibility in north during winter; periodic droughts

People

Population: 4,411,000 (July 1995 est.)

Life expectancy at birth: total population 57.42 years

Nationality: Togolese

Ethnic division: 37 tribes; largest and most important are Ewe, Mina, and Kabye, European and Syrian-Lebanese under 1%

Religions: indigenous beliefs 70%, Christian 20%, Muslim 10%

Languages: French (official and the language of commerce), Ewe and Mina (the two major African languages in the south), Dagomba and Kabye (the two major African languages of the north)

Literacy: total population 43%

Economy

Imports: machinery and equipments, consumer goods, food, chemical products

Exports: phosphates, cotton, cocoa, coffee

Industries: phosphate mining, agricultural processing, cement, handicrafts, textiles, beverages

Agriculture: cash crops - coffee, cocoa, cotton; food crops - yams, cassava, corn, beans, rice, millet, sorghum; livestock production not significant

Currency: 1 CFA franc (CFAF) = 100 centimes

Communaute Financiere Africaine francs per US1$ - 529.43

Transportation

Railroads: 532 km

Roads: 5,462 km total paved and unpaved

Ports: Kpeme, Lome

Airports: 9 total paved and unpaved. The international airports are at Tokoin, near Lome, and at Niamtougou

The Press: daily newspaper   **Togo-Presse:**   BP 891, Lome
                                                                   telephone 21-37-18 circ. 15,000

Tourism: Lome, Palime, (Kpalime), Lama Kara, Togoville

Direction des Professions Touristiques:
BP 1289, Lome   telephone 21-56-62

Diplomatic representation in US:

    chief of mission: Charge d'Affaires Edem Frederic Hegbe

    chancery: 2208 Massachusetts Avenue NW, Washington, DC 20008

    telephone: [1] (202) 234-4212

    FAX: [1] (202) 232-3190

US Diplomatic representation:

    chief of mission: Ambassador Johnny Young

    embassy: Rue Pelletier Caventou and Rue Vauban, Lome

    mailing address: B P 852, Lome

    telephone: [228] 21-77-17, 21-29-91, through 21-29-94

    FAX: [228] 21-79-52

Tokelau

Capital: none; each atoll has its own administrative center

        longitude: 173.00 W   latitude: 8.85 S

Government: territory of New Zealand

    Flag: the flag of New Zealand is used

Geography

    Location: Oceania, group of islands in the South Pacific Ocean, about one-half of the way from Hawaii to New Zealand

    Total Area: 10 sq km (3.86 sq mi) about 17 times the size of The Mall in Washington, DC

    Boundaries: no land boundaries

    Climate: tropical; moderated by trade winds (April to November)

    Terrain: coral atolls enclosing large lagoons

    Natural resources: negligible

    Natural hazards: lies in Pacific typhoon belt

People

    Population: 1,550 (July 1995 est.)

Life expectancy at birth: NA

Nationality: Tokelauan

Ethnic division: Polynesian

Religions: Congregational Christian Church 70%, Roman Catholic 28%, other 2%

Note: on Atafu, all Congregational Christian Church of Samoa; on Nukunonu, all Roman Catholic; on Fakaofo, both denominations

Languages: Tokelauan (a polynesian language), English

Literacy: NA

Economy

Imports: foodstuffs, building materials, fuel

Exports: stamps, copra, handicrafts

Industries: small-scale enterprises for copra production, wood work, plaited craft goods; stamps, coins; fishing

Agriculture: coconuts, copra; basic subsistence crops - breadfruit, papaya, bananas; pigs, poultry, goats

Currency: 1 New Zealand dollar (NZ$) = 100 cents

New Zealand dollars per US1$ - 1.56

Transportation

Railroads: none

Roads: NA

Ports: none; offshore anchorage only

Airports: none; lagoon landings by amphibious aircraft from Western Samoa

Diplomatic representation in US: none (territory of New Zealand)

US Diplomatic representation: none (territory of New Zealand)

Tonga

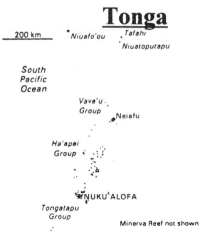

Capital: Nuku'alofa longitude: 175.14 W latitude: 21.09 S

Government: hereditary constitutional monarchy

Flag: red with a bold red cross on a white rectangle in the upper hoist-side corner

Geography

Location: Oceania, archipelago in the South Pacific Ocean, about two-thirds of the way from Hawaii to New Zealand

Total Area: 748 sq km (289 sq mi) slightly more than four times the size of Washington, DC

Boundaries: no land boundaries

Climate: tropical; modified by trade winds; warm season (December to May), cool season (May to December)

Temperature (F): High/Low Jan. 86/75, Apr. 86/75, July 85/74, Oct. 85/75

Average annual precipitation: 112.3 inches

Terrain: most islands have limestone base formed from uplifted coral formations; others have limestone overlying volcanic base

Highest point is 1,033 m (3,389 ft)

Natural resources: fish, fertile soil

Natural hazards: cyclones (October to April); earthquakes and volcanic activity on Fonuafo'ou

Note: archipelago of 170 islands (36 inhabited)

People

Population: 105,800 (July 1995 est.)

Life expectancy at birth: total population 68.16 years

Nationality: Tongan

Ethnic division: Polynesian, Europeans about 300

Religions: Christian (Free Wesleyan Church claims over 30,000 adherents)

Languages: Tongan, English

Literacy: total population 100%

Economy

Imports: food products, machinery and transport equipment, manufactures, fuels, chemicals

Exports: squash, vanilla, fish, root crops, coconut oil

Industries: tourism, fishing

Agriculture: dominated by coconut, copra, and bananas production; vanilla beans, cocoa, coffee, ginger, black pepper

Currency: 1 pa'anga (T$) = 100 seniti

pa'anga per US1$ - 1.26

Transportation

Railroads: none

Roads: 366 km total

Paved: 272 km (198 km on Tongatapu; 74 km on Vava'u)

Unpaved: 94 km (usable only in dry weather)

Ports: Neiafu, Nuku'alofa, Pangai

Airports: 6 total paved and unpaved. Tonga is served by Fua'amotu Airport, about 20 km from Nuku'alofa

The Press: newspapers   **The Times of Tonga/Koe Taimi'o Tonga:**
Nuku'alofa   weekly, English, local news

Tonga Chronicle/Kalonikali Tonga:
POB 197, Nuku'alofa   telephone 21-300   weekly

circ. 6,000 (Tongan),   1,200 (English)

Tourism: Scenic beauty and mild climate, grove of the bats, Lakafa'anga cliffs

Tonga Visitors Bureau: Vuna Road,
POB 37, Nuku'alofa
telephone 23-366   fax 22-129

Diplomatic representation in US: Ambassador Sione Kite, resides in London

US Diplomatic representation: the US has no offices in Tonga; the ambassador to Fiji is accredited to Tonga

Trinidad and Tobago

Capital: Port-of-Spain   longitude: 61.31 W   latitude: 10.38 N

Government: parliamentary democracy

Flag: red with a white-edged black diagonal band from the upper hoist side

Geography

Location: Caribbean, islands between the Caribbean Sea and the North Atlantic Ocean, northeast of Venezuela

Total Area: 5,103 sq km (1,970 sq mi) slightly smaller than Delaware

Boundaries: no land boundaries

Climate: tropical; rainy season (June to December)

Temperature (F): High/Low Jan. 87/69, Apr. 90/69, July 88/71, Oct. 89/81
Average annual precipitation: 64.1 inches
Terrain: mostly plains with some hills and low mountains
Highest point is Mt. Aripo 940 m (3,084 ft)
Natural resources: petroleum, natural gas, asphalt
Natural hazards: outside usual path of hurricanes and other tropical storms

People

Population: 1,272,000 (July 1995 est.)
Life expectancy at birth: total population 70.14 years
Nationality: Trinidadian
Ethnic division: black 43%, East Indian (a local term-primarily immigrants from northern India) 40%, mixed 14%, white 1%, Chinese 1%, other 1%
Religions: Roman Catholic 32.2%, Hindu 24.2%, Anglican 14.4%, other Protestant 14%, Muslim 6%, none or unknown 9.1%
Languages: English (official), Hindi, French, Spanish
Literacy: total population 97%

Economy

Imports: Machinery, transportation equipment, manufactured goods, food, live animal
Exports: petroleum and petroleum products, chemicals, steel products, fertilizer, sugar, cocoa, coffee, citrus, flowers
Industries: petroleum, chemicals, tourism, food processing, cement, beverage, cotton textiles
Agriculture: major crops - cocoa, sugarcane; sugarcane acreage is being shifted to rice, citrus, coffee, vegetables; poultry sector most important source of animal protein; must import large share of food needs
Currency: 1 Trinidad and Tobago dollar (TT$) = 100 cents
Trinidad and Tobaga dollars per US1$ - 5.87

Transportation

Railroads: minimal agricultural railroad system near San Fernando
Roads: 8,000 km total paved and unpaved
Ports: Pointe-a-Pierre, Point Fortin, Point Lisas, Port-of Spain, Scarborough, Tembladora
Airports: 6 total paved and unpaved. The main international airport is located about 20 km from Port-of-Spain

The Press: daily newspapers   **Trinidad Guardian:** POB 122, Port-of-Spain
telephone 623-8870   circ. 55,000

Trinidad and Tobago Express: 35 Independence Square, Port-of-Spain   telephone 623-1711   circ. 65,000

Tourism: Caroni Bird Sanctuary (exotic birds), Arena Forest, with giant tropical trees, beaches

Triniday and Tobago Hotel and Tourism Association: POB 243, Port-of-Spain   telephone 624-3928

Diplomatic representation in US:
chief of mission: Ambassador Corinne Averille McKnight
chancery: 1708 Massachusetts Avenue NW, Washington, DC 20036
telephone: [1] (202) 467-6490
FAX: [1] (202) 785-3130

US Diplomatic representation:
chief of mission: Ambassador Brian Donnelly
embassy: 15 Queen's Park West, Port-of-Spain
mailing address: P O Box 752, Port-of-Spain
telephone: [1] (809) 622-6372 through 6376, 6176
FAX: [1] (809) 628-5462

Tromelin Island

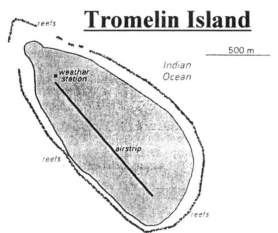

Capital: none; administered by France from Reunion
longitude: 54.60 E   latitude: 6.01 S

Government: French possession administered by Commissioner of the Republic, resident in Reunion

Geography

Location: Southern Africa, island in the Indian Ocean, east of Madagascar
Total Area: 1 sq km (0.386 sq mi) about 1.7 time the size of The Mall in Washington, DC
Boundaries: no land boundaries
Climate: tropical
Terrain: sandy

461

Natural resources: fish

Natural hazards: NA

Note: climatologically important location for forecasting cyclones; wildlife sanctuary

People

    Population: uninhabited

Economy

    no economic activity

Transportation

    Ports: none; offshore anchorage only

    Airports: 1 with paved runways under 914 m

Diplomatic representation in US: none (possession of France)

US Diplomatic representation: none (possession of France)

Tunisia

Capital: Tunis   longitude: 10.13 E latitude: 36.50 N   elevation: 217 ft

Government: republic

    Flag: red and white disk in the center bearing a red crescent nearly encircling a red five-pointed star; the crescent and the star are traditional symbols of Islam

Geography

    Location: Northern Africa, bordering the Mediterranean Sea, between Algeria and Libya

    Total Area: 163,610 sq km (63,170 sq mi) slightly larger than Georgia

    Boundaries: Algeria, Libya

    Climate: temperate in north with mild, rainy winters and hot, dry summers; desert in south

Temperature (F): High/Low Jan. 58/43, Apr. 70/51, July 90/68, Oct. 77/59
Average annual precipitation: 16.5 inches
Terrain: mountains in north; hot, dry central plain; semiarid south merges into the Sahara
Highest point is Mount Chambi 1,544 m (5,066 ft)
Natural resources: petroleum, phosphates, iron ore, zinc, salt
Natural hazards: NA

People

Population: 8,880,000 (July 1995 est.)
Life expectancy at birth: total population 73.25 years
Nationality: Tunisian
Ethnic division: Arab-Berber 98%, European 1%, Jewish less than 1%
Religions: Muslim 98%, Christian 1%, Jewish 1%
Languages: Arabic (official and one of the languages of commerce), French (commerce)
Literacy: total population 57%

Economy

Imports: industrial goods and equipment, hydrocarbons, food, consumer goods
Exports: hydrocarbons, agricultural products, phosphates and chemicals
Industries: petroleum, mining (particularly phosphate and iron ore), tourism, textiles, footwear, food, beverages
Agriculture: output subject to severe fluctuations because of frequent droughts; export crops - olives, dates, oranges, almonds; other products - grain, sugar beets, wine grapes, poultry, beef, dairy; not self-sufficient in food
Currency: 1 Tunisian dinar (TD) = 1,000 millimes
Tunisian dinars per US1$ - 0.98

Transportation

Railroads: 2,260 km
Roads: 29,183 km total paved and unpaved
Ports: Bizerte, Gabes, La Goulette, Sfax, Sousse, Tunis, Zarzis
Airports: 31 total paved and unpaved. There are international airports at Tunis-Carthagfe, Sfax, Djerba, Monastir, Tabarka and Tozeur
The Press: daily newspapers   **Al-Amal:** 15 rue 2 Mars 1934, Tunis
telephone 26-48-99   circ. 50,000   Arabic
La Presse de Tunisie: 6 rue Ali Bach-Hamba, Tunis
telephone 34-10-66   fax 34-97-20 circ. 40,000 French

Tourism: Tunisia contains the site of the ancient Phoenician city of Carthage. Moorish architecture and remains of the Roman Empire. Beautiful beaches

Office National du Tourisme Tunisien:
1 ave Muhammad V, Tunis
telephone 34-10-77   fax 35-09-97

Diplomatic representation in US:
chief of mission: Ambassador Mohamed Azzouz Ennaifer
chancery: 1515 Massachusetts Avenue NW, Washington, DC 20005
telephone: [1] (202) 862-1850

US Diplomatic representation:
chief of mission: Ambassador Mary Ann Casey
embassy: 144 Avenue de la Liberte, 1002 Tunis-Belvedere
mailing address: use embassy street address
telephone: [216] (1) 78-25-66
FAX: [216] (1) 78-97-19

Turkey

400 km

Black Sea

Mediterranean
Sea

Capital: Ankara   longitude: 32.53 E   latitude: 39.57 N   elevation: 2,825 ft
Government: republican parliamentary democracy
Flag: red with a vertical white crescent (the closed portion is toward the hoist side) and white five-pointed star centered just outside the crescent opening
Geography
Location: Southwestern Asia, bordering the Black Sea, between Bulgaria and Georgia, and bordering the Aegean Sea and the Mediterranean Sea, between Greece and Syria
Total Area: 780,580 sq km (301,382 sq mi) slightly larger than Texas
Boundaries: Armenia, Azerbaijan, Bulgaria, Georgia, Greece, Iraq, Syria

Climate: temperate; hot dry summers with mild; wet winters; harsher in interior

Temperature (F): High/Low Jan. 39/24, Apr. 63/40, July 86/59, Oct. 69/44

Average annual precipitation: 13.6 inches

Terrain: mostly mountains; narrow coastal plain; high central plateau (Anatolia)

Highest point is Ararat 5,165 m (16,946 ft)

Natural resources: antimony, coal, chromium, mercury, copper, borate, sulphur, iron ore

Natural hazards: very severe earthquakes, especially in northern Turkey, along an arc extending from the Sea of Marmara to Lake Van

Note: strategic location controlling the Turkish Straits (Bosporus, Sea of Marmara, Dardanelles) that link Black and Aegean Seas

People

Population: 63,406,000 (July 1995 est.)

Life expectancy at birth: total population 71.48 years

Nationality: Turk

Ethnic division: Turkish 80%, Kurdish 20%

Religions: Muslim 99.8%, (mostly Sunni), other 0.2% (Christian and Jews)

Languages: Turkish (official), Kurdish, Arabic

Literacy: total population 79%

Economy

Imports: manufactured goods, fuels, foodstuffs

Exports: manufactured products, foodstuffs, mining products

Industries: textiles, food processing, mining (coal, chromite, copper, boron), steel, petroleum, construction, lumber, paper

Agriculture: products - tobacco, cotton, grain, olives, sugar beets, pulses, citrus fruit, variety of animal products; self-sufficient in food most years

Currency: 1 Turkish lira (TL) = 100 kurus

Turkish lira per US1$ - 37,444.1

Transportation

Railroads: 10,413 km

Roads: 320,611 km total paved and unpaved

Ports: Gemlik, Hopa, Iskenerun, Istanbul, Izmir, Izmit, Mersin, Samsun, Trabzon

Airports: 116 total paved and unpaved. The international airports are located at Istanbul, Ankara, Izmir and Trabzon

The Press: daily newspapers **Milliyet:** Nurnosmaniye Cad 65, Istanbul telephone (212) 511-4410 fax (212) 513-8742 circ. 340,000

Sabah: Atakan Sok. 14 Mecidekoy, Istanbul
telephone (212) 275-2200   circ. 508,000

Tourism: Ancient monuments, Temple of Artemis, beautiful beaches
Ministry of Tourism: Ismet Inonu Bul. 5, Bahcelievler, Ankara
telephone (312) 212-8300   fax (312) 212-8391

Diplomatic representation in US:
chief of mission: Ambassador Nuzhet Kandemir
chancery: 1714 Massachusetts Avenue NW, Washington, DC 20036
telephone: [1] (202) 659-8200

US Diplomatic representation:
chief of mission: Ambassador Marc Grossman
embassy: 110 Ataturk Boulevard, Ankara
mailing address: PSC 93, Box 5000, Ankara; APO AE 09823
telephone: [90] (312) 468-6110 through 6128
FAX: [90] (312) 467-0019

Turkmenistan

300 km

Capital: Ashgabat   longitude: 58.25 E   latitude: 37.90 N
Government: republic

Flag: green field, including a vertical stripe on the hoist side, with a claret vertical stripe in between containing five white, and orange carpet guls (an assymetrical design used in producing rugs) associated with five different tribes; a white crescent and five white stars in the upper left corner to the right of the carpet guls

Geography

Location: Central Asia, bordering the Caspian Sea, between Iran and Kazakhstan

Total Area: 488,100 sq km (188,455 sq mi) slightly larger than California

Boundaries: Afghanistan, Iran, Kazakhstan, Uzbekistan

Climate: subtropical desert

Temperature (F): average temperature in January is 25F (as low as -27F) average temperature in July is 82F (summer temperatures often reach 122F) Average annual precipitation: 4 inches, 16 inches in mountains

Terrain: flat to rolling sandy desert with dunes rising to mountains in the south; low mountains along border with Iran; borders Caspian Sea in west Highest point is Kugitangtau Peak 3,139 m (10,299 ft)

Natural resources: petroleum, natural gas, coal, sulphur, salt

Natural hazards: NA

People

Population: 4,076, 000 (July 1995 est.)

Life expectancy at birth: total population 65.35 years

Nationality: Turkmen

Ethnic division: Turkmen 73.3%, Russian 9.8%, Uzbek 9%, Kazakh 2% other 5.9%

Religions: Muslim 87%, Eastern Orthodox 11%, unknown 2%

Languages: Turkmen 72 %, Russian 12%, Uzbek 9%, other 7%

Literacy: total population 98%

Economy

Imports: machinery and parts, grain and food, plastics and rubber, consumer durables, textiles

Exports: natural gas, cotton, petroleum products, electricity, textiles, carpets

Industries: natural gas, oil, petroleum products, textiles, food processing

Agriculture: cotton, grain, animal husbandry

Currency: Turkmenistan introduced its national currency, the manat, on 1 November 1993.

manats per US1$ - multiple rate system: 10 (official) and 230 (permitted in transactions between the government and individuals)

Transportation

Railroads: 2,120 km in common carrier service; does not include industrial lines

Roads: 23,000 km total paved and unpaved

Ports: Turkmenbashi (formerly Krasnowodsk)

Airports: 64 total paved and unpaved. The main airport is at Ashgabat

The Press: newspapers   **Turkmenskaya iskra:** Ashgabat 6 a week (Russian)
> **Syyasy sokhbetdesh:** 744014 Ashgabat 14,
> ul. Gogolya 28 weekly circ. 14,500
> telephone (3632) 25-12-12

Tourism: Tourist attractions are the bazaar at Ashgabat and the hot sulfurous
> springs at Bacharden
> > **Ministry of Culture and Tourism:**
> > Ashgabt telephone (3632) 25-35-60

Diplomatic representation in US:
> *chief of mission:* Ambassador Khalil Ugur
> *chancery:* 1511 K Street NW, Suite 412, Washington, DC 20005
> *telephone:* [1] (202) 737-4800
> *FAX:* [1] (202) 737-1152

US Diplomatic representation:
> *chief of mission:* Ambassador Joseph S. Hulings III
> *embassy:* 6 Teheran Street, Yubilenaya Hotel, Ashgabat
> *mailing address:* use embassy street address
> *telephone:* [7] (3632) 24-49-25, 24-49-22
> *FAX:* [7] (3632) 25-53-79

Turks and Caicos Islands

Capital: Grand Turk longitude: 71.07 W latitude: 21.29 N
elevation: 11 ft

Government: dependent territory of the UK

> **Flag:** blue with the flag of the UK in the upper hoist-side quadrant and the
> colonial shield centered on the outer half of the flag; the shield centered on
> the outer half of the flag; the shield is yellow and contains a conch shell,
> lobster, and cactus

Geography

Location: Caribbean, two island groups in the North Atlantic Ocean, southeast of The Bahamas

Total Area: 430 sq km (166 sq mi) slightly less than 2.5 times the size of Washington, DC

Boundaries: no land boundaries

Climate: tropical; marine; moderated by trade winds; sunny and relatively dry

Temperature (F): High/Low Jan. 81/70, Apr. 84/73, July 88/77, Oct. 87/76

Average annual precipitation: 30.5 inches

Terrain: low, flat limestone; extensive marshes and mangrove swamps

Natural resources: spiny lobsters, conch

Natural hazards: frequent hurricanes

Note: 30 islands (eight inhabited)

People

Population: 14,300 (July 1995 est.)

Life expectancy at birth: total population 75.37 years

Nationality: none

Ethnic division: African

Religions: Baptist 41.2%, Methodist 18.9%, Anglican 18.3%, Seventh-Day Adventist 1.7%, other 19.9%

Languages: English (official)

Literacy: total population 98%

Economy

Imports: food and beverages, tobacco, clothing, manufactures, construction materials

Exports: lobster, dried and fresh conch, conch shells

Industries: fishing, tourism, offshore financial services

Agriculture: subsistence farming prevails, based on corn and beans; fishing more important than farming; not self-sufficient in food

Currency: 1 United States dollar (US$) = 100 cents

US currency is used

Transportation

Railroads: none

Roads: 121 km paved and unpaved

Ports: Cockburn Harbour, Grand Turk, Providenciales, Salt Cay

Airports: 7 total paved and unpaved. There are international airports on Grand Turk, South Caicos, North Caicos and Providenciales

The Press: newspapers   **Conch News:** Mission Folly, POB 17, Grand Turk
telephone 946-2923   weekly
Turks and Caicos News: Central Square, Providenciales
telephone 946-4664   fax 946-4661   weekly
Tourism: Beautiful unspoilt beaches, diving
Turks and Caicos Islands Tourist Board:
Pond Street, POB 128, Grand Turk
telephone 946-2321 fax 946-2733
Diplomatic representation in US: none (dependent territory of the UK)
US Diplomatic representation: none (dependent territory of the UK)

Tuvalu

Nanumea
.Niutao
.Nanumanga   150 km
.Nui
.Vaitupu
Nukufetau
FUNAFUTI
Funafuti
*South
Pacific
Ocean*   Niulakita

Nurakita

Capital: Funafuti   longitude: 179.12 E   latitude: 8.30 S
Government: democracy; began debating republic status in 1992
Flag: light blue with the flag of the UK in the upper hoist-side quadrant; the
outer half of the flag represents a map of the country with nine yellow
five-pointed stars symbolizing the nine islands

Geography
Location: Oceanic, island group consisting of nine coral atolls in the South
Pacific Ocean, about one-half of the way from Hawaii to Australia
Total Area: 26 sq km (10 sq mi) about 0.1 times the size of
Washington, DC
Boundaries: no land boundaries
Climate: tropical; moderated by easterly trade winds (March to November);
westerly gales and heavy rain (November to March)
Temperature (F): High/Low Jan. 85/81, Apr. 85/81, July 84/82, Oct. 84/81
Terrain: very low-lying and narrow coral atolls
Highest point is 4.6 m (15 ft)
Natural resources: fish

Note: Tuvalu's nine coral atolls have enough soil to grow coconuts and support subsistence agriculture

Natural hazards: severe tropical storms are rare

People

Population: 10,300 (July 1995 est.)

Life expectancy at birth: total population 63.15 years

Nationality: Tuvaluan

Ethnic division: Polynesian 96%

Religions: Church of Tuvalu (Congregationalist) 97%, Seventh-Day Adventist 1.4%, Baha'i 1%, other 0.6%

Languages: Tuvaluan, English

Literacy: NA

Economy

Imports: food, animals, mineral fuels, machinery, manufactured goods

Exports: copra

Industries: fishing, tourism, copra

Agriculture: coconuts and fish

Currency: 1 Tuvaluan dollar ($T) or 1 Australian dollar ($A) = 100 cents Tuvaluan dollars or Australian dollars per US1$ - 1.30

Transportation

Railroads: none

Roads: 8 km gravel

Ports: Funafuti, Nukufetau

Airports: 1 with unpaved runways

The Press: newspaper   **Tuvalu Echoes:** Vaiaku, Funatuti
telephone 731   English   circ. 1,200

Tourism: beaches and coral beaches

Ministry of Commerce and Natural Resources: Vaiaku, Funafuti   telephone 737

Diplomatic representation in US: Tuvalu has no mission in the US

US Diplomatic representation: none

Uganda

Capital: Kampala   longitude: 32.35 E   latitude: 0.20 N   elevation: 4,304 ft

Government: republic

Flag: six equal horizontal bands of black (top), yellow, red, black, yellow, and red; a white disk is superimposed at the center and depicts a red-crested crane (the national symbol) facing the staff

Geography

Location: Eastern Africa, west of Kenya

Total Area: 236,040 sq km (91,135 sq mi) slightly smaller than Oregon

Boundaries: Kenya, Rwanda, Sudan, Tanzania, Zaire

Climate: tropical; generally rainy with two dry season (December to February, June to August); semiarid in northeast

Temperature (F): High/Low Jan. 83/65, Apr. 79/64, July 72/62, Oct. 81/63

Average annual precipitation: 46.2 inches

Terrain: mostly plateau with rim mountains

Highest point is Margherita 5,119 m (16,795 ft)

Natural resources: copper, cobalt, limestone, salt

Natural hazards: NA

People

Population: 19,574,000 (July 1995 est.)

Life expectancy at birth: total population 36.58 years

Nationality: Ugandan

Ethnic division: Baganda 17%, Karamojong 12%, Basogo 8%, Iteso 8%, Langi 6%, Rwanda 6%, Bagisu 5%, Acholi 4%, Lugbara 4%, Bunyoro 3%, Batobo 3%, European, Asian, Arab 1%, others 23%

Religions: Roman Catholic 33%, Protestant, 33%, Muslim 16%, indigenous belief 18%

Languages: English (official), Luganda, Swahili, Bantu languages, Nilotic language

472

Literacy: total population 56%

Economy

    Imports: petroleum products, machinery, cotton piece goods, metals, transportation equipment, food

    Exports: coffee, cotton, tea

Industries: sugar, brewing, tobacco, cotton textiles, cement

Agriculture: mainly subsistence; cash crops - coffee, tea, cotton, tobacco; food crops - cassava, potatoes, corn, mullet, pulses; livestock products - beef, goat meat, milk, poultry; self-sufficient in food

Currency: 1 Ugandan shilling (USh) = 100 cents

              Ugandan shillings per US1$ - 1,195.00

Transportation

    Railroads: 1,300 km

    Roads: 26,200 km total paved and unpaved

    Ports: Entebbe, Jinja, Port Bell

    Airports: 29 total paved and unpaved. Uganda's international airport is at Entebbe, about 40 km from Kampala

The Press: newspapers

    The Monitor: POB 12141, Kampala
    telephone (41) 25-13-53 fax (41) 25-13-52
    biweekly, English circ. 34,000

    New Vision: POB 9815, Kampala
    telephone (41) 23-58-46 fax (41) 23-52-21
    daily, English circ. 37,000

Tourism: Tourist attractions are the forests, lakes and wildlife

    Uganda Tourist Development Corporation
    Plot 6, 2nd Street, POB 7211, Kampala
    telephone (41) 24-52-61

Diplomatic representation in US:

    chief of mission: Ambassador Stephen Kapimpina Katenta-apuli
    chancery: 5911 16th Street NW, Washington, DC 20011
    telephone: [1] (202) 726-7100 through 7102, 0416
    FAX: [1] (202) 726-1727

US Diplomatic representation:

    chief of mission: Ambassador E. Michael Southwick
    embassy: Parliament Avenue, Lampala
    mailing address: P O Box 7007, Kampala
    telephone: [256] (41) 25-97-92, 25-97-93, 25-97-95
    FAX: [256] (41) 25-97-94

Ukraine

250 km

Capital: Kiev (Kyyiv) longitude: 30.27 E latitude: 50.24 N elevation: 587 ft

Government: republic

Flag: two equal horizontal bands of azure (top) and golden yellow represents grainfields under a blue sky

Geography

Location: Eastern Europe, bordering the Black Sea, between Poland and Russia

Total Area: 603,700 sq km (233,089 sq mi) slightly smaller than Texas

Boundaries: Belarus, Hungary, Moldova, Poland, Romania, Russia, Slovakia

Climate: temperate continental; Mediterranean only on the southern Crimean coast; precipitation disproportionately distributed, highest in the west and north, lesser in the east and southeast; winters vary from cool along the Black Sea to cold farther inland; summers are warm across the greater part of the country, hot in the south

Temperature (F): High/Low Jan. 24/14, Apr. 56/41, July 77/59, Oct. 56/42

Average annual precipitation: 26.7 inches

Terrain: most of Ukraine consists of fertile plains (steppes) and plateaux, mountains being found only in the west (the Carpathians), and in the Crimean Peninsula in the extreme south

Highest point is Mount Goverl 2,061 m (6,762 ft)

Natural resources: iron ore, coal manganese, natural gas, oil, salt, sulphur, graphite, titanium, magnesium, kaolin, nickel, mercury, timber

Natural hazards: NA

People

Population: 51,868,000 (July 1995 est.)

Life expectancy at birth: total population 70.11 years

474

Nationality: Ukrainian

Ethnic division: Ukrainian 73%, Russian 22%, Jewish 1%, other 4%

Religions: Ukrainian Orthodox - Moscow Patriarchate, Ukrainian Catholic Ukrainian Orthodox - Kiev Patriarchate, Ukrainian Autocephalous Orthodox, (Uniate), Protestant, Jewish

Languages: Ukrainian, Russian, Romanian, Polish, Hungarian

Literacy: total population 98%

Economy

Imports: energy, machinery and parts, transportation equipment, chemical, textiles

Exports: coal, electric power, ferrous and nonferrous metals, chemicals, machinery and transport equipment, grain, meat

Industries: coal, electric power, ferrous and nonferrous metals, machinery and transport equipment, chemicals, food processing (especially sugar)

Agriculture: grain, vegetables, meat, milk, sugar beets

Currency: Ukraine withdrew the Russian ruble from circulation on 12 November 1992 and declared the Karbovanets (plural karovantsi) sole legal tender in Ukrainian markets; Ukrainian officials claim this is an interim move toward introducing a new currency - the hryvnya

Karbovansti per US1$ - 107,900

Transportation

Railroads: 23,350 km

Roads: 273,700 km total paved and unpaved

Ports: Berdyans'k, Illichivs'k, Izmayil, Kerch, Kherson, Kiev (Kyyiv), Mariupol, Mykolayiv, Odesa, Pivdenne, Reni

Airports: 706 total paved and unpaved (163 with paved runways)

The principal international airport is at Kiev

The Press: newspapers

News from Ukraine: 252107 Kiev, vul. O. Shmidta 35/37
English   circ. 20,000

Silski Visti: 252047 Kiev, Peremohy pr. 50
telephone (44) 441-8333   circ. 550,000

Tourism: Resorts on the Black Sea coast, historical attractions at Kiev and Odesa

Association of Foreign Tourism:
Kiev, Yaroslaviv val 36
telephone (44) 212-5570

United Arab Emirates

Capital: Abu Dhabi   longitude: 54.25 E   latitude: 24.28 N

Government: federation with specified powers delegated to the UAE central government and other powers reserved to member emirates

Flag: three equal horizontal bands of green (top), white, and black with a thicker vertical red band an the hoist side

Geography

    Location: Middle East, bordering the Gulf of Oman and the Persian Gulf, between Oman and Saudi Arabia

    Total Area: 75,581 sq km (29,182 sq mi) slightly less than Maine

    Boundaries: Oman, Saudi Arabia

    Climate: desert; cooler in eastern mountains

    Temperature (F): High/Low Jan. 74/54, Apr. 86/65, July 100/82, Oct. 92/71

    Average annual precipitation: 4.3 inches

    Terrain: flat, barren coastal plain merging into rolling sand dunes of vast desert wasteland; mountains in east

    Natural resources: petroleum, natural gas

Natural hazards: frequent sand and dust storms

Note: strategic location along southern approaches to Strait of Hormuz, a vital transit point for world crude oil

People

Population: 2,925,000 (July 1995 est.)

Life expectancy at birth: total population 72.51 years

Nationality: Emirian

Ethnic division: Emirian 19%, other Arab 23%, South Asian 50%, other expatriates (includes Westerners and East Asians) 8%

Religions: Muslim 96% (Shi'a 16%), Christian, Hindu, and others 4%

Languages: Arabic (official), Persian, English, Hindi, Urdu

Literacy: total population 71%

Economy

Imports: manufactured goods, machinery and transport equipment, food

Exports: crude oil, natural gas, re-exports, dried fish, dates

Industries: petroleum, fishing, petrochemicals, construction materials, some boat building, handicrafts, pearling

Agriculture: cash crop - dates; food products - vegetables, watermelons, poultry, eggs, dairy, fish; only 25% self-sufficient in food

Currency: 1 Emitian dirham (Dh) = 100 fils

Emirian dirham per US1$ - 3.67

Transportation

Railroads: none

Roads: 2,000 km total paved and unpaved

Ports: Ajman. Al Fujayrah, Das Island, Khawr Fakkan, Mina' Jabal' Ali, Mina' Khalid, Mina' Rashid, Mina' Saqr, Mina' Zayid, Umm al Qiwain

Airports: 41 total paved and unpaved. There are five international airports, Abu Dhabi, Dubai, Fujayrah, Ras al-Khaimah and Sharjah

The Press: daily newspapers　　**Khaleej Times:** POB 3082, Abu Dhabi
telephone 33-60-00　fax 33-642　circ. 60,000

Gulf News: POB 6519, Dubai
telephone (4) 44-71-00　fax (4) 44-16-27
English circ. 80,000

Tourism: Abu Dhabi, South Hajar Mountains, Persian Gulf

Sharjah Department of Tourism: POB 8, Sharjah
telephone (6) 58-11-11　fax (6) 58-11-67

Diplomatic representation in US:

chief of mission: Ambassador Muhammad bin Husayn al-Shaali

chancery: suite 600, 3000 K Street NW, Washington, DC 20007

telephone: [1] (202) 338-6500

US Diplomatic representation:

chief of mission: Ambassador Willian A. Rugh

embassy: Al-Sudan Street, Abu Dhabi

mailing address: P O Box 4009, Abu Dhabi; American Embassy Abu Dhabi

telephone: [971] (2) 43-66-91, 43-66-92

FAX: [971] (2) 43-47-71

United Kingdom

Capital: London   longitude: 0.10 W latitude: 51.30 N elevation: 16 ft

Government: constitutional monarchy

Flag: blue with the red cross of Saint George (patron saint of England) edged in white superimposed on the diagonal red cross of Saint Patrick (patron saint of Ireland) which is superimposed on the diagonal white cross of Saint Andrew (patron saint of Scotland); known as the Union Flag or Union Jack; the design and colors (especially the Blue Ensign) have been the basis for a number of other flags including dependencies, Commonwealth countries, and others

Geography

Location: Western Europe, islands including the northern one-sixth of the island of Ireland between the North Atlantic Ocean and the North sea, northwest of France

Total Area: 244,820 sq km (94,525 sq mi) slightly smaller than Oregon

Boundaries: Ireland

Climate: temperate; moderated by prevailing southwest winds over the North Atlantic Current; more than half of the days are overcast

Temperature (F): High/Low Jan. 43/36, Apr. 56/42, July 71/56, Oct. 58/46

Average annual precipitation: 23.3 inches

Terrain: mostly rugged hills and low mountains; level to rolling plains in east and southeast

Highest point is Ben Nevis 1,343 m (4,406 ft)

Natural resources: coal, petroleum, natural gas, tin, limestone, iron ore, salt, clay, chalk, gypsum. lead, silica

Natural hazards: NA

Note: lies near vital North Atlantic sea lanes; only 35 km from France and now linked by tunnel under the English Channel; because of heavily indented coastline, no location in more than 125 km (78 mi) from tidal waters

People

Population: 58,296,000 (July 1995 est.)

Life expectancy at birth: total population 77 years

Nationality: Briton (s) British (collective plural)

Ethnic division: English 81.5%, Scottish 9.6%, Irish 2.4%, Welsh 1.9%, Ulster 1.8%, West Indian, Indian, Pakistani, and other 2.8%

Religions: Anglican 27 million, Roman Catholic 9 million, Muslim 1 million, Presbyterian 800,000, Methodist 760,000, Sikh 400,000, Hindu 350,000, Jewish 300,000

Note: the UK does not include a question on religion in its census

Languages: English, Welsh (about 26% of the population of Wales), Scottish form of Gaelic (about 60,000 in Scotland)

Literacy: total population 99%

Economy

Imports: manufactured goods, machinery, semi-finished goods, foodstuffs, consumer goods

Exports: manufactured goods, machinery, fuels, chemicals, semi-finished goods, transport equipment

Industries: production machinery including machine tools, electric power equipment, automation equipment, railroad equipment, shipbuilding, aircraft, motor vehicles and parts, electronic and communications equipment, metals, chemicals, coal, petroleum, paper and paper products, food processing, textiles, clothing, and other consumer goods

Agriculture: wide variety of crops and livestock

Currency: 1 British pound (#) = 100 pence

British pounds per US1$ - 0.63

Transportation

Railroads: 16,888 km

Roads: 360,047 km (includes Northern Ireland) all paved.

Ports: Aberdeen, Belfast, Bristol, Cardiff, Grangemouth, Hull, Leith, Liverpool, London, Manchester, Medway, Sullom Voe, Tees, Tyne

Airports: 505 total paved and unpaved. The principal international airport is Heathrow, located just outside of London, others are Gatwick, Stansted, Luton, Manchester and Glasgow

The Press: daily newspapers　　**Daily Mirror:** 33 Holborn, London, EC1P 1DQ
telephone (71) 353-0246 fax (71) 822-3405
circ. 2,750,000

Daily Telegraph: 1 Canada Square
Canary Wharf, London, E14 5AR
telephone (71) 538-5000 circ. 1,250,000

The Times: 1 Pennington St, Wapping, London, E1 9XN
telephone (71) 782-5000 fax (71) 488-3242
circ. 380,000

Tourism: historic land marks - from Roman, Norman, Medieval, Tudor, and Georgian times, castles, cathedrals, monuments, birthplace of Shakespeare, luscious countrysides

British Tourist Authority:
Thames Tower, Black's Road, London, W6 9EL
telephone (81) 846-9000   fax (81) 563-0302

Diplomatic representation in US:
chief of mission: Ambassador Sir Robin William Renwick
chancery: 3100 Massachusetts Avenue NW, Washington, DC 20008
telephone: [1] (202) 462-1340
FAX: [1] (202) 898-4255

US Diplomatic representation:
chief of mission: Ambassador Adm. William W. Crowe
embassy: 24/31 Grosvenor Square, London W. 1A1AE
mailing address: PSC 801, Box 40, FPO AE 09498-4040
telephone: [44] (71) 499-9000
FAX: [44] (71) 409-1637

United States

Capital: Washington, DC   longitude: 77.00 W   latitude: 38.55 N

Government: federal republic; strong democratic tradition

Flag: thirteen equal horizontal stripes of red (top and bottom) alternation with white; there is a blue rectangle in the upper hoist-side corner bearing 50 small white five-pointed stars arranged in nine offset horizontal rows of six stars (top to bottom) alternating with rows of five stars; the 50 stars represent the 50 states, the 13 stripes represent the 13 original colonies; known as Old Glory; the design and colors have been the basis for a number of other flags including Chile, Liberia, Malaysia, and Puerto Rico

Geography

Location: North America, bordering both the North Atlantic Ocean and the North Pacific Ocean, between Canada and Mexico

Total Area: 9,372,610 sq km (3,618,765 sq mi)

Comparative area: about half the size of Russia; about three-tenths the size of Africa; about one-half the size of South America (or slightly larger than Brazil); slightly smaller than china; about two and one-half times the size of Western Europe.

Note: includes only the 50 states and the District of Columbia

Boundaries: Canada, Cuba (US Naval Base at Guantanamo Bay), Mexico

Climate: mostly temperate, but tropical in Hawaii and Florida and arctic in Alaska, semiarid in the great plains west of the Mississippi River and arid in the Great Basin of the southwest; low temperatures in the northwest are ameliorated occasionally in January and February by warm chinook winds from the eastern slopes of the Rocky Mountains

Temperature (F): see individual states

Terrain: vast central plain, mountains in west, hills and low mountains in east; rugged mountains and broad river valleys in Alaska; rugged, volcanic topography in Hawaii

481

Highest point is Mount McKinley (Alaska) 20,320 ft

Natural resources: coal, copper, lead, molybdenum, phosphates, uranium, bauxite, gold, mercury, nickel, potash, silver, tungsten, zinc, petroleum, natural gas, timber

Natural hazards: tsunamis, volcanoes, and earthquakes activity around Pacific Basin; hurricanes along the Atlantic coast; tornadoes in the midwest; mud slides in California; forest fires in the west; flooding; permafrost in northern Alaska is a major impediment to development

Note: world's fourth- largest country (after Russia, Canada, and China)

People

Population: 263,815,000 (July 1995 est.)

Life expectancy at birth: total population 75.99 years

Nationality: American

Ethnic division: white 83.4%, black 12.4%, Asian 3.3%, Native American 0.8%

Religions: Protestant 56%, Roman Catholic 28%, Jewish 2%, other 4%, none 10%

Languages: English, Spanish (spoken by a sizable minority)

Literacy: total population 97%

Economy

Imports: crude oil and refined petroleum products, machinery, automobiles, consumer goods, industrial raw materials, food and beverages

Exports: capital goods, automobiles, industrial supplies and raw materials, consumer goods, agricultural products

Industries: leading industrial power in the world, highly diversified and technologically advanced; petroleum, steel, motor vehicles, aerospace, telecommunications, chemicals, electronics, food processing, consumer goods, lumber, mining

Agriculture: favorable climate and soils support a wide variety of crops and livestock production; world's second largest producer and number one exporter of grain; surplus food producer

Currency: 1 United States dollar (US$) = 100 cents

Transportation

Railroads: 240,000 km mainline route (non government owned)

Roads: 6,243,163 km total paved and unpaved

Ports: Anchorage, Baltimore, Boston, Charleston, Chicago, Duluth, Hampton Roads, Honolulu, Huston, Jacksonville, Los Angles, New Orleans, New York, Philadelphia, Port Canaveral, Portland (Oregon), Prudhoe Bay, San Francisco, Savannah, Seattle, Tampa, Toledo

Airports: 15,032 total paved and unpaved.

UNITED STATES

Alabama

Capital: Montgomery   **Elevation:** 183 ft.

Longitude: 90.30 W   **Latitude:** 32.21 N

Organized as Territory: March 3, 1817

Statehood: December 14, 1819, the 22nd state

Land area: 50,750 sq miles, the 29th state in area

Terrain: coastal plains give way to hills, broken terrain.

Boundaries: Mississippi, Tennessee, Georgia, Florida, Gulf of Mexico

Highest point: Cheaha Mountain 2,407 ft.

Number of counties: 67

Motto: *Audemus jura nostra defendere* (We dare defend our rights)

Nickname: Yellowhammer State

State bird: Yellowhammer   **State flower:** Camellia

State forests: 21 (48,000 acres)

State parks: 24 (45,614 acres)

Resident population: 4,187,000 (1993 est.)

Temperature: High/Low; Jan. 58/38, Apr. 76/52, July 92/72, Oct. 79/54
        Average annual precipitation: 49.16 inches

Industries: paper products, textiles, chemicals, rubber, fabricated metal products

Agriculture: greenhouse and nursery products, dairy products, poultry, cattle, hogs,
        soybeans, peanuts, corn, wheat, cotton, vegetables, fruit

Mining: coal, petroleum, natural gas, crushed stone, limestone

The Press: daily newspapers

Birmingham News: North Fourth Ave, POB 2553, Birmingham, Al 35202-2553 tel. (205) 325-2222; fax (205) 325-3246 circ. 169,000 evening, 213,000 Sunday

Montgomery Register: 304 Government Street, POB 1000, Montgomery, Al 36101-1000 tel. (205) 262-1611; fax (205) 261-1501 circ. 54,000 morning, 61,000 Sunday

Tourism: Civil War Sites, U.S.Space and Rocket Center in Huntsville, Robert Trent Golf Train stretches from Mobile to Huntsville, Talladega Super speedway, Montgomery Zoo, relics of Indian and Old South History at Tuscaloosa, historic southern homes and mansions, covered bridges. White beaches on the Gulf Coast

Alabama Tourism/Bureau of Travel
P O Box 4927   401 Adams Avenue
Montgomery, Al 36103-4927
tel. [1] (334) 242-4169, (1) 800-252-2262
fax [1] (334) 242-4554

http://www.alaweb.asc.edu/

Alaska

Capital: Juneau   **Elevation:** 12 ft
Longitude: 134.35 W   **Latitude:** 58.22 N
Organized as Territory: 1912
Statehood: Jan. 3, 1959, the 49th state
Land area: 591,004 sq miles, the first (#1) and largest of all the states
Terrain: Pacific and Arctic mountains, central plateau
Boundaries: Canada, Arctic Ocean, North Pacific Ocean
Highest point: Mount McKinley 20,320 ft
Number of boroughs: 27
Motto: North to the Future
Nickname: "The Last Frontier" or "Land of the Midnight Sun"
State bird: Willow ptarmigan   **State flower:** Forget-me-not
State forests: none
National parks: 15
State parks: 117   (322 million acres)
Resident population: 599,000 (1993 est.)
Temperature: High/Low   Jan. 30/18, Apr. 47/31, July 64/48, Oct. 47/36
        Average annual precipitation: 53.95 inches
Industries: fisheries, lumber, pulp and other forest products, furs, aerospace
        (launching polar-orbit rockets and satellites at the University of Alaska's
        Poker Flat Research Range near Fairbanks), tourism
Agriculture: Greenhouse, dairy products, potatoes, hay
Mining: petroleum, natural gas, coal, silver, gold, zinc

The Press: daily newspaper   **Anchorage News:** POB 149001,
                Anchorage, Ak 99514-9001
                tel. (907) 257-4200; fax (907) 258-2157
                circ. 76,000 morning, 98,000 Sunday

Tourism: Alaska isn't just a place you visit, its a feeling you experience. The landscape borders two oceans and has 47,300 miles of coastline. Over three million lakes, 3,000 rivers and more than 100,000 glaciers. Attractions; Alaska's northern lights, the *aurora borealis*. Katmai National Park and Preserve, volcanoes, Mount McKinley, wildlife, over 355 different species of birds. Federal and state campgrounds are available. Kodiak Island, home of Alaska's largest fishing fleet. Past the tip of Alaska Peninsula the Aleutian Islands begin their 1,500 mile sweep towards Asia. These beautiful wind sweep isles are now the location of numerous national wildlife refuges. Historic Russian churches at Unalaska and Dutch Harbor

Note: Juneau, Alaska, is the only state capital in the U.S. which has no road access and can only be reached by air or water

> Alaska Tourism & Marketing
> Department 201 POB 110801
> Juneau, AK 99811
> tel. [1] (907) 465-2010
> fax [1] (907) 465-2287

http://www.state.ak.us/

Arizona

Capital: Phoenix   **Elevation:** 1,117 ft
Longitude: 112.01 W   **Latitude:** 33.26 N
Organized as Territory: Feb. 24, 1863
Statehood: Feb. 14, 1912, the 48th state
Land area: 114,000 sq miles, the 6th state in area
Terrain: Colorado plateau in north (including the Grand Canyon), Sonoran dessert in southwest, Mexican highlands run northwest to southeast
Boundaries: California, Nevada, Utah, Colorado, New Mexico, Mexico
Highest point: Humphreys Peak 12,643 ft
Number of counties: 15
Motto: *Ditat Deus* (God enriches)
Nickname: Grand Canyon State
State bird: Cactus Wren   **State flower:** Flower of saguaro cactus
State forests: none
State parks: 24
Resident population: 3,936,000 (1993 est.)

Temperature: High/Low   Jan. 65/38, Apr. 84/52, July 105/76, Oct. 88/57
    Average annual precipitation: 7.41 inches

Industries: electrical equipment and communications, transportation equipment, scientific instruments, aeronautical items

Agriculture: cattle, dairy products, cotton, vegetables, fruit

Mining: copper, gold

The Press: daily newspapers   **Arizona News:** 4850 South Park Ave, POB 26807, Tucson, Az 85726
tel. (602) 573-4220; fax (602) 573-4107
circ. 88,000 morning, 166,000 Sunday

Arizona Republic: 120 East Van Buren Street, POB 1950, Phoenix, AZ 85001
tel. (602) 271-8000, fax (602) 271-8500
circ. 363,000 morning, 595,000 Sunday

Tourism: Arizona's Grand Canyon, over two billion years in the making. Petrified Forest National Park. Petrified remains of ancient trees and other plants, dinosaur fossils, and indian ruins. Painted Desert, named for its rippling mounds of purple, red, and grey sediments. Hoover Dam. The 727 foot-high structure is the highest concrete dam in the U.S. Jerome, picturesque historic copper-mining town.

Phoenix, the Desert Botanical Garden and the Phoenix Zoo in a natural setting

Arizona Tourism Office
1100 West Washington Street
Phoenix, AZ 85007
tel. [1] (800) 842-8257 [1] (602) 542-8687
fax [1] (602) 542-4068

http:www.state.az.us/

Arkansas

Capital: Little Rock   **Elevation:** 257 ft
Longitude: 92.14 W   **Latitude:** 34.44 N
Organized as Territory: March 2, 1819
Statehood: June 15, 1836, the 25th state
Land area: 53,187 sq miles, the 27th state in area

Terrain: northwest highlands (Ozark mountains), southern lowlands, eastern delta and prairie

Boundaries: Texas, Oklahoma, Missouri, Tennessee, Mississippi, Louisiana

Highest point: Magazine Mountain 2,753 ft

Number of counties: 75

Motto: *Regnat populus* (The people rule)

Nickname: "The Natural State"

State bird: Mockingbird   **State flower:** Apple Blossom

State forests: none

State parks: 47

Resident population: 2,424,000 (1993 est.)

Temperature: High/Low   Jan. 50/29, Apr. 74/50, July 93/70, Oct. 76/49
Average annual precipitation: 47.18 inches

Industries: steel, clothing, furniture, prepared foods, chemicals, boats, electric motors, machine tools, fabricated metal products, pulp and paper products, tourism

Agriculture: cotton, rice, soybeans, feed grains, vegetables, watermelons, fruits, cattle ranching and dairy farms; poultry; (Arkansas is number-one in broiler chicken industry), turkeys, eggs

Aquaculture: commercial production of catfish, crawfish and minnow crops

Mining: petroleum, natural gas, bromine, quartz crystals, diamonds

The Press: newspaper   **Arkansas Democrat Gazette:**
121 East Capitol Street, POB 2221,
Little Rock, AR 72203
tel. (501) 378-3400, fax (501) 378-3591
circ. 177,000 morning, 236,000 Sunday

Tourism: Victorian architecture and attractions at Eureka Springs. Spa resorts at Hot Springs National Park. Fort Smith historical sites. Little Rock - seat of government, finance, commerce and culture. Helena - Victorian homes and the Delta Cultural Center. Over 600 lakes, hunting and fishing Murfreesboro is the home of the only diamond mine open to the public on the North American continent

Arkansas Tourism Department
One Capitol Mall
Little Rock, AR 72201
tel. [1] (800) 628-8725   [1] (501) 682-7777
fax [1] (501) 682-1364

http://www.state.ar.us/

California

Capital: Sacramento   **Elevation:** 17 ft

Longitude: 121.30 W   **Latitude:** 38.35 N

Statehood: Sept. 9, 1850, the 31st state

Land area: 158,706 sq miles, the 3rd state in area

Terrain: continuous coastline mountains west, Sierra Nevada mountains on the east, rugged mountains north, desert basins of the southern interior

Boundaries: Oregon, Nevada, Arizona, Mexico, North Pacific Ocean

Highest point: Mount Whitney 14,495 ft

Number of counties: 58

Motto: *Eureka*   (I have found it)

Nickname: Golden State

State bird: California valley quail   **State flower:** Golden poppy

State forests: 8, (70,238 acres)

State parks and beaches: 180 (723,000 acres)

Resident population: 31,211,000 (1993 est.)

Temperature: High/Low   Jan. 53/37, Apr. 71/45, July 93/58, Oct. 77/50
Average annual precipitation: 17.33 inches

Industries: transportation equipment, aircraft, machinery, electronic equipment, biotechnology, food processing, wine, tourism

Agriculture: greenhouse and nursery products, dairy products, cattle, poultry, vegetables, fruit, nuts, cotton

Mining: petroleum, natural gas

The Press: daily newspapers   **Los Angeles Times:**
Times Mirror Square
tel. (213) 237-3999, fax (213) 237-4712
circ. 1,243,000 daily, 1,576,000 Sunday
San Francisco Chronicle: 901 Mission Street
San Francisco, CA 94103
tel. (415) 777-1111, fax (415) 512-8196
circ. 570,000 morning,   704,000 Sunday

Tourism: Death Valley is 282 feet below sea level, the main commerce is at Furnace Creek (it gets hot, record temperature was set July 10,1913 at 134 degrees F (57 C). Lassen National Volcanic National Park with over 50 wilderness lakes and an active volcano. Yosemite National Park, spectacular attractions, particularly Yosemite Falls, the fifth highest waterfall on earth.

San Diego, historic buildings, beautiful beaches, three world-famous animal parks. Universal Studios Hollywood, Disneyland, Knotts Berry Farm, Golden Gate Bridge in San Francisco, Redwood National Park contains the world's tallest trees, some surpassing 300 feet in height

California Office of Tourism
P O Box 1499
Sacramento, CA 95812
tel. [1] (800) 862-2543   [1] (916) 322-2881 ext 100
fax [1] (916) 322-3402

http://www.ca.gov/

Colorado

Capital: Denver   **Elevation:** 5,283 ft
Longitude: 105.00 W   **Latitude:** 39.45 N
Organized as Territory: Feb 28, 1861
Statehood: Aug 1, 1876, the 38th state
Land area: 104,091 sq miles the 8th state in area
Terrain: eastern high with dry plains, central plateau hills to mountainous, high ranges of Rocky Mountains west, with broad valleys and deep canyons
Boundaries: Utah, Arizona, New Mexico, Oklahoma, Kansas, Nebraska, Wyoming
Highest point: Mount Elbert 14,433 ft
Number of counties: 63
Motto: *Nil sine Numine* (Nothing without Providence)
Nickname: Centennial State
State bird: Lark bunting   **State flower:** Rocky Mountain columbine
State forests: 1 (71,000 acres)
State parks: 44
Resident population: 3,566,000 (1993 est.)
Temperature: High/Low Jan. 44/16, Apr. 61/34, July 87/59, Oct. 67/37
Average annual precipitation: 14.60 inches
Industries: scientific instruments, machinery, fabricated metal products, electrical equipment, printing and publishing, food processing, tourism
Agriculture: cattle, dairy products, corn, wheat, hay
Mining: petroleum, coal, natural gas

The Press: daily newspapers

Denver Post: 1560 Broadway
Denver, CO 80202
tel. (303) 820-1010, fax (303) 820-14406
circ. 285,000 morning, 440,000 Sunday

Denver Rocky Mountain News:
400 West Colfax Ave, Denver, CO 80204
tel. (303) 892-5000, fax (303) 892-5081
circ. 374,000 morning, 433,000 Sunday

Tourism: Rocky Mountain National Park, Mesa Verde National Park, the Great
Sand Dunes and Dinosaur National Park, the Black Canyon
Colorado Association of Campgrounds, Cabins & Lodges
5101 Pennsylvania Avenue
tel. [1] (303) 499-9343
fax [1] (303) 499-9333

http://www.state.co.us/

Connecticut

Capital: Hartford   **Elevation:** 169 ft
Longitude: 72.41 W   **Latitude:** 41.56 N
Statehood: Jan. 9, 1788, the 5th state
Land area: 5,018 sq miles, the 48th state in area
Terrain: hilly eastern upland, narrow central lowland, western upland, mountains
in the north
Boundaries: Long Island Sound, Rhode Island, Massachusetts, New York
Highest point: Mount Frissell, on south slope 2,380 ft
Number of counties: 8
Motto: *Qui transtulit sustinet* (He who transplanted still sustains)
Nickname: Nutmeg State
State bird: American Robin   **State flower:** Mountain Laurel
State forests: 30 (143,067 acres)
State parks: 92 (31,423 acres)
Resident population: 3,281,000 (1993 est.)
Temperature: High/Low Jan. 33/16, Apr. 59/48, July 84/61, Oct. 64/41
Average annual precipitation: 43.00 inches
Industries: submarines, weapons, jet engines, helicopters, electrical equipment,
scientific instruments, printed materials, motors, hardware and tools, ball
bearings, cutlery, fabricated metal products, tourism

Agriculture: greenhouse and nursery products, dairy products, poultry, tobacco, vegetables, fruits

Mining: crushed stone

The Press: daily newspapers

Hartford Courant: 285 Broad Street
Hartford, CT 06115
tel. (203) 241-6200, fax (203) 241-3865
circ. 231,000 morning, 320,000 Sunday

New Haven Register: Long Wharf, 40 Sargent Drive
New Haven, CT 06511
tel. (203) 789-5200 fax (203) 865-7894
circ. 101,000 morning, 134,000 Sunday

Tourism: Long Island Sound shoreline offers many uncrowded beaches, lighthouses, historic sites. New Haven's Peabody Museum. Explore the historic Old New-Gate Prison and Copper Mine in East Granby. Mystic Seaport with its marine life aquarium, tour the USS Nautilus at Groton, Bridgeport's Barnum Museum, other; Yale University's Gallery of Fine Arts, Winchester Gun, and American Clock and Watch

Connecticut Department of Tourism
865 Brook Street
Rocky Hill, CT 06067
tel. [1] (800) 282-6863   [1] (203) 258-4355
fax [1] (302) 563-4877

http://www.state.ct.us/

Delaware

Capital: Dover

Wilmington   **Elevation:** 74 ft

Longitude: 75.36 W   **Latitude:** 39.40 N

Statehood: Dec 7, 1787, the 1st state

Land area: 2,044 sq miles, the 49th in area

Terrain: plateau in northern tip, sloping to a near sea-level coastal plain

Boundaries: Pennsylvania, Maryland, New Jersey, Atlantic Ocean, Delaware Bay

Highest point: On Ebright Road 442 ft

Number of counties: 3

Motto: Liberty and independence

Nickname: Diamond State; First State; Small Wonder

State bird: Blue Hen chicken   **State flower:** Peach blossom
State forests: 3 (6,149 acres)
State parks: 12
Resident population: 700,000 (1993 est.)
Temperature: (Wilmington) High/Low Jan. 40/24, Apr. 63/42, July 86/66,
        Oct. 68/47
        Average annual precipitation: 43.63 inches
Industries: transportation equipment, chemicals, food processing, fishing, tourism
Agriculture: poultry (broilers), dairy products, corn, soybeans, potatoes, hay, fruit
Mining: sand and gravel, magnesium compounds

The Press: daily newspaper   **News-Journal:** 950 West Basin Road,
                                    POB 15505, New Castle, DE 19720
                                    tel. (302) 324-2617, fax (302) 324-5518
                                    circ. 119,000 morning, 140,000 Sunday

Tourism: Delaware is best known for its blue water and white sandy beaches. Reboboth Beach/Dewey Beach, the largest of three Delaware seashores areas, has been popular since the 1870s. The Kalmar Nyckel Shipyard and Museum commemorates the original 1638 settlement of Wilmington by the Swedes and their captain Peter Minuet (Minuet bought Manhattan Island from the Indians). Brandywine River Museum. Longwood Gardens with over 11,000 different kinds of plants.

Delaware Tourism Office
99 Kings Highway
P O Box 1401
Dover, DE 19903
tel. [1] (800) 441-8846 [1] (302) 739-4271
fax [1] (302) 739-5749

http://www.state.de.us/

Florida

Capital: Tallahassee   **Elevation:** 55 ft
Longitude: 84.22 W   **Latitude:** 30.23 N
Organized as Territory: March 20, 1822
Statehood: March 3, 1845, the 27th state
Land area: 58,664 sq miles, the 22th state in area
Terrain: land is flat to rolling, highest point is in the northwest

Boundaries: Alabama, Georgia, Gulf of Mexico, Atlantic Ocean
Highest point: Britton Hill 345 ft.
Number of counties: 67
Motto: In God we trust
Nickname: Sunshine State
State bird: Mockingbird   **State flower:** Orange blossom
State forests: 4 (306,881 acres)
State parks: 145 (215,820 acres)
Resident population: 13,608,000 (1993 est.)
Temperature: High/Low Jan. 64/41, Apr. 80/56, July 91/72, Oct. 81/58
    Average annual precipitation: 58.75 inches
Industries: transportation equipment, electrical equipment, chemicals, scientific
    instruments, food processing, international trade, tourism
Agriculture: greenhouse and nursery products, dairy products, cattle, calves, forest
products, sugarcane, oranges, grapefruit, tomatoes, potatoes, melons, strawberries
Mining: phosphate rock

The Press: daily newspapers   **Miami Herald:** One Herald Plaza
    Miami, FL 33132-1693
    tel. (305) 350-2111, fax (305) 376-2677
    circ. 445,000 morning, 553,000 Sunday
St Petersburg Times: 490 First Avenue South
POB 1121, St Petersburg, FL 33731
circ. 352,000 morning, 452,000 Sunday
Tourism: Florida is a haven for watersports enthusiasts with over 1,200 miles of
    coastline. St Augustine, the oldest permanent city in the U.S. (founded in
    1565). Kennedy Space Center (NASA). Everglades National Park. Universal
    Studios at Orlando. Disney World's, Magic Kingdom Park.
    Florida Department of Tourism
    126 Van Buren Street
    Tallahassee, FL 32399
    tel. [1] (904) 487-1462
    fax. [1] (904) 921-9158

http://www.state.fl.us/

Georgia

Capital: Atlanta   **Elevation:** 1,010 ft

Longitude: 84.26 W   **Latitude:** 33.39 N

Statehood: Jan 2, 1788, the 4th state

Land area: 58,910 sq miles, the 21st state in area

Terrain: Blue Ridge Mountains cover northeast and north central, central plain slope south, coastal plain levels to coast flatland

Boundaries: South Carolina, North Carolina, Tennessee, Alabama, Florida, Atlantic Ocean

Highest point: Brasstown Bald 4,784 ft

Number of counties: 159

Motto: Wisdom, justice, and moderation

Nickname: Peach State, Empire State of the South

State bird: Brown thrasher   **State flower:** Cherokee rose

State forests: 25,258,000 acres (67 % of total state area)

State parks: 53 (42,600 acres)

Resident population: 6,917,000 (1993 est.)

Temperature: High/Low Jan. 51/33, Apr. 71/51, July 86/69, Oct. 73/52 Average annual precipitation: 48.66 inches

Industries: transportation equipment, paper and paper products, electrical equipment, textiles, chemicals (resins and turpentine), food processing, apparels, tourism

Agriculture: cattle, poultry, dairy products, peanuts, corn, cotton, tobacco, soybeans, peaches

Mining: marble, kaolin, barite, bauxite, clays, crushed stone

The Press: daily newspapers

Atlanta Journal-Constitution:
72 Marietta St. NW, Atlanta, GA 30303
tel (404) 526-5193
circ. 330,000 morning, 701,000 Sunday

Macon Telegraph: 120 Broadway, POB 4167, Macon, GA 31208 tel. (912) 744-4200 fax (912) 744-4269 circ. 75,000 morning, 100,000 Sunday

Tourism: The Carter Presidential Center, over 27 million documents, memorabilia, and displays. Cotton Exchange Welcome Center and Museum, Okefenokee National Wildlife Refuge, has hiking, canoeing and camping.

Kennesaw Mountain National Battlefield Park, Cumber!and Island National Park, guided tour of local heritage sites. Historic Savannah

Georgia Tourism Division
P O Box 1776
Atlanta, GA 30301
tel. [1] (800) 847-4842   [1] (404) 656-3590
fax [1] (404) 651-9063

http://www.state.ga.us/

Hawaii

Capital: Honolulu   **Elevation:** 7 ft
Longitude: 157.55 W   **Latitude:** 21.20 N
Organized as Territory: 1990
Statehood: Aug 21, 1959, the 50th state
Land area: 6,471 sq miles, the 47th state in area
Terrain: eight main islands, volcanic and mountainous with some broad fertile valleys
Boundaries: no land boundaries
Highest point: Mauna Kea 13,796 ft
Number of counties: 4 plus one non-functioning county (Kalawao)
Motto: Ua Mau Ke Ea O Ka Aina I Ka Pono
          (The life of the land is perpetuated in righteousness)
Nickname: Aloha State
State bird: Nene (hawaiian goose)   **State flower:** Hibiscus (yellow)
State parks and historic sites: 77
Resident population: 1,172,000 (1993 est.)
Temperature: High/Low Jan. 79/65, Apr. 81/68, July 87/73, Oct. 86/72
          Average annual precipitation: 24.05 inches
Industries: food processing, petroleum products (refineries on Oahu processes petroleum imported from Indonesia), tourism
Agriculture: chief products - pineapple, sugarcane; tropical fruits, coffee, nuts, vegetables, bananas, flowers
Mining: crushed stone

The Press: daily newspaper

Honolulu Star-Bulletin:
605 Kapiolani Blvd, Honolulu, HI 96813
tel. (808) 525-8000, fax (808) 525-8037
circ. 89,000 evening, 203,000 Sunday

Tourism: Polynesian Cultural Center, U.S.S Arizona Memorial at Pearl Harbor, Bishop Museum, Waikiki Beach, all on Oahu. Haleakala National Park (Maui), Hawaii Volcanoes National Park (Hawaii)

Hawaii Visitors Bureau
2270 Kalakaua Ave   Suite 801
Honolulu, HI 96815
tel. [1] (800) 847-4844   [1] (808) 923-1811
fax [1] (808) 922-8991

http://www.hawaii.edu/

Idaho

Capital: Boise   **Elevation:** 2,838 ft
Longitude: 116.13 W   **Latitude:** 43.34 N
Organized as Territory: March 3, 1863
Entered Union: July 3, 1890, the 43rd state
Land area: 83,564 sq miles, the 13th state in area
Terrain: plains in south, mountains, canyons and gorges in the central area, subalpine in the north
Boundaries: Washington, Oregon, Nevada, Utah, Wyoming, Montana
Highest point: Borah Peak 12,662 ft
Number of counties: 44, plus small part of Yellowstone National Park
Motto: Esto perpetua (Let it be perpetual)
Nickname: Gem State; Spud State; Panhandle State
State bird: Mountain bluebird   **State flower:** Syringa
State forests: 881,000 acres
State parks: 22 (44,177 acres)
Resident population: 1,099,000 (1993 est.)
Temperature: High/Low Jan. 36/21, Apr. 61/37, July 91/59, Oct. 65/39
    Average annual precipitation: 11.97 inches
Industries: machinery, electrical equipment, chemicals, timber, wood products, food processing, tourism, winter sports
Agriculture: cattle, dairy products, produces about one-fourth of the nation's potato crop; wheat, fruit, corn, barley, hay, sugar beets, and hops

mercury, and gold

The Press: daily newspaper

Idaho Stateman: 1200 North Curtis Road,
POB 40, Boise, ID 83707
tel. (208) 377-6200, fax (208) 377-6309
circ. 60,000 morning, 80,000 Sunday

Tourism: Craters of the Moon National Park, State Historical Museum at Boise,
sites visited by Lewis and Clark

Idaho Tourism and Travel Council
700 West State Street
Boise, ID 83720
tel. [1] (800) 635-7820 [1] (208) 334-2470
fax [1] (208) 334-2631

http://www.state.id.us/

Illinois

Capital: Springfield **Elevation:** 588 ft
Longitude: 89.40W **Latitude:** 39.50 N
Organized as Territory: Feb. 3, 1809
Entered Union and rank: Dec. 3, 1818, the 21st state
Land area: 56,345 sq miles, the 24th state in area
Terrain: flat prairies and fertile plains throughout hills in the southern region
Boundaries: Iowa, Missouri, Kentucky, Indiana, Lake Michigan, Wisconsin
Highest point: Charles Mound 1,235 ft
Number of counties: 102
Motto: State sovereignty, national union
Nickname: Prairie State
State bird: Cardinal **State flower:** Violet
Public use areas: 187 (275,000 acres) includes state parks, memorials, forests and
conservation areas
Resident population: 11,697,000 (1993 est.)
Temperature: High/Low Jan. 35/19, Apr. 64/43, July 87/66, Oct. 68/45
Average annual precipitation: 35.48 inches
Industries: iron and steel producer, chemicals, electrical equipment, machinery,
printed material, meat packaging, railroad cars, clothing, furniture, tractors,
liquor, watches, farm implements, railroad center, Great Lakes port

498

Agriculture: Illinois ranks third in the export of corn, soybeans, and hog

Agriculture: Illinois ranks third in the export of corn, soybeans, and hog production; other crops - corn, oats, wheat, barley, rye; truck vegetables; dairy products, greenhouse and nursery products

Mining: coal, petroleum, crushed stone, sand and gravel

The Press: daily newspapers

Chicago Sun-Times:
401 North Wabash Ave, Chicago, IL 60611
tel. (312) 321-3000 fax (312) 321-3084
circ. 538,000 morning, 559,000 Sunday

Chicago Tribune: 435 North Michigan Ave,
Chicago, IL 60611 tel. (312) 222-3232
circ. 734,000 morning, 1,133,000 Sunday

Tourism: Chicago: Art Institute, Shedd Aquarium, Museum of Science and Industry, Adler Plantarium, Merchandise Mart. Springfield: historic sites, home of Lincoln

Illinois Office of Tourism
620 East Adam Street
Springfield, IL 62701
tel. [1] (800) 226-6632
fax [1] (312) 814-6175

http://www.state.il.us/

Indiana

Capital: Indianapolis

Elevation: 792 ft

Longitude: 86.17 W

Latitude: 39.44 N

Organized as Territory: May 7, 1800

Entered Union: Dec. 11, 1816, the 19th state

Land area: 36,185 sq miles, the 38th state in area

Terrain: flat, fertile rolling plains, hilly southern region

Boundaries: Illinois, Kentucky, Ohio, Michigan, Lake Michigan

Highest point: Wayne county 1,257 ft

Number of counties: 92

Motto: The Crossroads of America

Nickname: Hoosier State

State bird: Cardinal

State flower: Peony

State parks: 20 (56,806 acres)

State memorials: 16 (941,977 acres)

Resident population: 5,713,000 (1993 est.)

Temperature: High/Low Jan. 36/20, Apr. 63/42, July 85/65, Oct. 67/44
Average annual precipitation: 39.98 inches

Industries: automobile parts and accessories, mobile homes and recreational vehicles, truck and bus bodies, aircraft engines, farm machinery, chemicals, machinery, electrical equipment, iron and steel, fabricated steel, office furniture, pharmaceuticals

Agriculture: The principal crop is corn; other crops - soybeans, wheat, oats, rye, tomatoes, onions; poultry, hogs

Mining: coal, limestone, crushed stone

The Press: daily newspapers

Indianapolis Star: 307 North Pennsylvania St
Indianapolis, IN 46204
tel. (317) 633-1240 fax (317) 633-1174
Circ. 232,000 morning, 417,000 Sunday

Journal-Gazette: 600 West Main St. POB 88,
Fort Wayne, IN 46801
tel. (219) 461-8333 fax (219) 461-8648
circ. 63,000 morning, 139,000 Sunday

Tourism: Indianapolis Motor Speedway, Indiana Dunes National Lakeshore, mineral springs at west Baden, and French Lick, Wyandotte Cave, one of the largest in the U.S. George Rogers Clark National Historical Park

Indiana Department of Commerce
Tourism Development Division
One North Capitol, Suite 700
Indianapolis, IN 46204
tel. [1] (800) 289-6646 [1] (317) 232-8860
fax [1] (317) 232-8995

http://www.state.in.us/

Iowa

Capital: Des Moines   **Elevation:** 938 ft

Longitude: 93.39 W   **Latitude:** 41.32 N

Organized as Territory: June 12, 1838

Entered Union: Dec. 28, 1846, the 29 state

Land area: 56,275 sq miles, the 23rd state in area

Terrain: flat and level fertile land

Boundaries: South Dakota, Nebraska, Missouri, Illinois, Wisconsin, Minnesota

Highest point: North boundary of Osceola County 1,670 ft

Number of counties: 99

Motto: Our liberties we prize and our rights we will maintain

Nickname: Hawkeye State

State bird: Eastern goldfinch   **State flower:** Wild rose

State forests: 5 (28,000 acres)

State parks: 84 (49,237 acres)

Resident population: 2,814,000 (1993 est.)

Temperature: High/Low Jan. 28/11, Apr. 60/39, July 85/65, Oct. 65/44
   Average annual precipitation: 31.49 inches

Industries: food processing, non-electrical machinery, farm machinery, electrical
   equipment, fabricated products, printing and publishing, chemicals, forest
   products (hardwood lumber), cement, tourism

Agriculture: corn, soybeans; livestock; cattle (grain-fed), hogs

Mining: limestone, sand and gravel, gypsum, coal

The Press: daily newspapers   **Des Moines Register:** 715 Locus St,
   POB 957, Des Moines, IA 50304
   tel. (515) 284-8000 fax (515) 284-8103
   circ. 206,000 mornings   345,000 Sunday

Sioux City Journal: 515 Pavonia St, Sioux City, IA 51102
   tel. (712) 279-5068 fax (712) 279-5059 circ. 50,000 morning

Tourism: Fort Dodge Historical Museum, Effigy Mounds National Monument at
   Marquette, a prehistoric Indian burial site, Herbert Hoovers birthplace and
   library near West Branch

   Iowa Economic Development
   Division of Tourism
   200 East Grand Avenue
   Des Moines IA 50309
   tel. [1] (800) 345-4692 [1] (515) 242-4705
   fax [1] (515) 242-4749

http://www.state.ia.us/

Kansas

Capital: Topeka   **Elevation:** 877 ft

Longitude: 95.38 W   **Latitude:** 39.04 N

Organized as Territory: May 30, 1854

Statehood: Jan. 29, 1861, the 34th state

Land area: 82,277 sq miles, the 13th state in area

Terrain: hilly plains in the east, level prairie and rolling hills in the central region, high plains in the west

Boundaries: Nebraska, Colorado, Oklahoma, Missouri

Highest point: Mount Sunflower 4,039 ft

Number of counties: 105

Motto: *Ad astra per aspera* (To the stars through difficulties)

Nickname: Sunflower State; Jayhawk State

State bird: Western Meadowlark   **State flower:** Sunflower

State parks: 22 (14,394 acres)

Resident population: 2,531,000 (1993 est.)

Temperature: High/Low Jan. 38/18, Apr. 63/43, July 89/67, Oct. 70/45
Average annual precipitation: 33.38 inches

Industries: petroleum products, aircraft manufacturing, machinery, transportation equipment, chemicals, printed material, milling, meat processing;

Agriculture: wheat, corn, oats, barley, sorghum, soybeans, potatoes, hay, cattle, hogs

Mining: petroleum, natural gas, coal, zinc, salt, lead, helium production

The Press: daily newspapers

Topeka Capital-Journal:
616 Jefferson St, Topeka, KS 66607-1120
tel. (913) 295-1111 fax (913) 295-1198
circ. 67,000 morning 74,000 Sunday

Wichita Eagle: 825 East Douglas St, Wichita, KS 67202
tel. (316) 268-6000 fax (316) 268-6609
circ. 122,000 morning, 199,000 Sunday

Tourism: Eisenhower Memorial Museum and Presidential Library, at Abilene, Fort Levenworth, Fort Riley, Kansas Museum of History at Topeka, John Brown's cabin at Osawatomie

Kansas Department of Commerce
Division of Travel and Tourism
700 SW Harrison   Suite 1300
Topeka, KS 66603
tel. [1] (800) 252-6727 [1] (913) 296-2009
fax [1] (913) 296-6988

http://falcon.cc.ukans.edu/~nsween/europa.html

Kentucky

Capital: Frankfort

Lexington   **Elevation:** 966 ft

Longitude: 84.36 W   **Latitude:** 38.02 N

Statehood: June 1, 1792, the 15th state

Land area: 40,409 sq miles, the 36th state in area

Terrain: mountainous in the east, hilly northern region, fertile rolling plains in central and southwest regions

Boundaries: Missouri, Tennessee, Virginia, West Virginia, Ohio, Indiana, Illinois

Highest point: Black mountain 4,145 ft

Number of counties: 120

Motto: United we stand, divided we fall

Nickname: Bluegrass State

State bird: Kentucky cardinal   **State flower:** Goldenrod

State forests: 9 (44,173 acres)

State parks: 43 (40,574 acres)

Resident population: 3,789,000 (1993 est.)

Temperature: (Lexington) High/Low Jan. 41/25, Apr. 66/44, July 86/66, Oct. 69/47

Average annual precipitation: 43.81 inches

Industries: motor vehicles, automotive parts, machinery, iron and steel products, tobacco products, electronic equipment, chemicals, printed material, aluminum ware, furniture, apparel, textiles, lumber products, brooms, whiskey

Agriculture: corn, soybeans, wheat, fruit, tobacco; dairy products; cattle, hogs, horses

Mining: petroleum, natural gas, coal, flourspar, clay, stone

The Press: daily newspapers

Courier-Journal: 525 West Broadway, Louisville, KY 40202
tel. (502) 582-4011 fax (502) 582-4075
circ. 238,000, 329,000 Sunday

Lexington Herald-Leader: 100 Midland Ave Lexington, KY 40508
tel. (606) 231-3100   fax (606) 231-3494
circ. 123,000 morning 165,000 Sunday

Tourism: Mammoth Cave, Fort Knox, Old Fort Harrod State Park, Kentucky
Derby at Churchhill Downs,

Kentucky Department of Travel
Capital Plaza Tower   22nd Floor
Frankfort, KY 40601
tel. [1] (800) 225-8747   [1] (502) 564-4930
fax [1] (502) 564-5695

http://name1.state.ky.us/

Louisiana

Capital: Baton Rouge   **Elevation:** 64 ft

Longitude: 91.08 W   **Latitude:** 30.32 N

Organized as Territory: March 26, 1804

Statehood: April 30, 1812, the 18th state

Land area: 47,751 sq miles, the 31st state in area

Terrain: marshes and lowland in the Mississippi River flood plains, rolling hills
north

Boundaries: Texas, Arkansas, Mississippi, Gulf of Mexico

Highest point: Driskill Mountain 535 ft

Number of parishes (counties): 64

Motto: Union, justice, and confidence

Nickname: Pelican State; Sportsman's Paradise; Creole State; Sugar State

State bird: Brown Pelican   **State flower:** Magnolia

State forests: 1 (8,000 acres)

State parks: 30 (13,932 acres)

Resident population: 4,295,000 (1993 est.)

Temperature: High/Low Jan. 62/41, Apr. 79/58, July 91/73, Oct. 80/57
Average annual precipitation: 56.73 inches

Industries: transportation equipment; petroleum products, paper products, lumber
and lumber products, apparel, food processing

Agriculture: sweet potatoes, corn, rice, soybeans, sugarcane, cotton, pecans, cattle,
dairy products.
Note: Louisiana marshes supply most of the nation's furs (muskrat, opossum,
raccoon, mink and otter), large numbers of game birds

Mining: petroleum, natural gas, salt, sulfur

The Press: daily newspapers

Advocate: 525 Lafayette St,
Baton Rouge, LA 70802-5494
tel. (504) 383-1111 fax (504) 388-0129
circ. 102,000 morning, 329,000 Sunday

Times-Picayune: 3800 Howard Ave, New Orleans, LA 70140
tel. (504) 826-3279 fax (504) 826-3007
circ. 272,000 daily, 324,000 Sunday

Tourism: New Orleans, French Quarter, and the Superdome, plantation homes and "Tabasco" (hot sauce) at New Iberia. Mississippi delta region, cajun country, Chalmette National Historical Park

Louisiana Office of Tourism
PO Box 94291 Department TPG5
Baton Rouge, LA 70804
tel. [1] (800) 633-6970 [1] (504) 342-8390
fax [1] (504) 342-8390

http://www.state.la.us/

Maine

Capital: Augusta
Portland   **Elevation:** 43 ft
Longitude: 70.19 W   **Latitude:** 43.39 N
Statehood: March 15, 1820, the 23rd state
Land area: 33,265 sq miles, the 39th state in area
Terrain: Appalachian Mountains extend through state, rugged terrain west, sandy beaches southern coast, mainly rocky northern coast
Boundaries: Canada, New Hampshire, Atlantic Ocean
Highest point: Mount Katahdin   5,268 ft
Number of counties: 16
Motto: *Dirigo* (I lead)
Nickname: Pine Tree State
State bird: Chickadee   **State flower:** White pine cone and tassel
State forests: 1 (21,000 acres)
State parks: 26 (247,627 acres)
Resident population: 1,239,000 (1993 est.)
Temperature: High/Low Jan. 31/12, Apr. 53/33, July 79/57, Oct. 60/38
Average annual precipitation: 42.15 inches

Industries: pulp-paper products, timber and timber products, transportation equipment, electrical equipment, leather products, footwear, food processing, fish and lobster processing, tourism

Agriculture: apples, blueberries, potatoes, vegetables, dairy products, poultry

The Press: daily newspapers

Bangor News: 491 Main St, Bangor, ME 04402-1239
tel. (207) 990-8000   fax (207) 941-0885
circ. 76,000 morning

Portland Press Herald: 390 Congress St, POB 1460, Portland, ME 04101
tel. (207) 780-9000 fax (207) 780-9499
circ. 52,000 morning, 142,000 Sunday

Tourism: St. Croix Island National Monument, Bar Harbor, Wadsworth-Longfellow House in Portland, mountain resorts, 2,500 lakes, seacoast beaches

Maine Tourism Office
PO Box 2300
Hallowell, ME 04347
tel. [1] (800) 533-9595   [1] (207) 623-0363
fax [1] (207) 623-0388

http://www.state.me.us/

Maryland

Capital: Annapolis

Baltimore   **Elevation:** 148 ft

Longitude: 76.38 W   **Latitude:** 39.18 N

Statehood: April 28, 1788, the 7th state

Land area: 10,460 sq miles, the 42nd state in area

Terrain: coastal plains south, Chesapeake Bay, hilly upland region north

Boundaries: Pennsylvania, West Virginia, Virginia, Chesapeake Bay, Delaware

Highest point: Backbone Mountain 3,360 ft

Number of counties: 23, and 1 independent city

Largest county: Montgomery

Motto: *Fatti maschii, parole femine* (manly deeds, womanly words)

Nickname: Free State; Old Line State

State bird: Baltimore oriole   **State flower:** Black-eyed Susan

State forests: 13 (132,944 acres)

State parks: 47 (87,670 acres)

Resident population: 4,965,000 (1993 est.)

Temperature: (Baltimore) High/Low Jan. 42/25, Apr. 65/42, July 87/67, Oct. 68/46

Average annual precipitation: 41.62 inches

Industries: seafood (oysters, clams, crabs, fish); primary metals, transportation equipment, food processing, instruments, chemicals, printing and publishing, cement

Agriculture: greenhouse and nursery products; wheat, corn, soybeans, vegetables, melons, dairy products, poultry

Mining: coal, sand and gravel, clay, crushed stone

The Press: daily newspaper

Baltimore Sun: 501 North Calvert St
Baltimore, MD 21278
tel. (301) 332-6300
circ. 238,000 daily, 492,000 Sunday

Tourism: Goddard Space Center, Fort Henry National Monument, Maryland Science Center at Baltimore's Inner Harbor, U.S. Naval Academy in Annapolis, Jefferson Patterson Historical Park and Museum at St. Mary's City

Maryland Office of Tourism
217 East Redwood Street
Baltimore, MD 21202
tel. [1] (800) 543-1036   [1] (410) 333-6611
fax [1] (410) 333-6643

http://www.gov.state.md.us/

Massachusetts

Capital: Boston

Elevation: 15 ft

Longitude: 71.50 W

Latitude: 42.21 N

Statehood: Feb 6, 1788, the 6th state

Land area: 8,284 sq miles, the 45th state in area

Terrain: rolling hills north, central region flat with stony upland pastures, jagged indented coast from Rhode Island to Cape Cod

Boundaries: New Hampshire, Vermont, New York, Connecticut, Rhode Island, Atlantic Ocean

Highest point: Mount Greylock 3,491 ft

Number of counties: 14

Motto: *Ense petit placidam sub liberate quietem*
       (By the sword we seek peace, but peace only under liberty)

Nickname: Bay State; Old Colony State

State bird: Chickadee   **State flower:** Mayflower

State forests and parks: 129 (242,000 acres)

Resident population: 6,012,000 (1993 est.)

Temperature: High/Low Jan. 36/23, Apr. 56/41, July 81/65, Oct. 63/48
    Average annual precipitation: 41.55 inches

Industries: electronics and communication equipment, electric equipment,
    scientific instruments, printed material, fabricated steel products,
    transportation equipment, greenhouse and nursery products, fisheries
    (flounder and scallops), textiles, footwear, tourism

Agriculture: cranberries, vegetables, fruit, dairy products, poultry

Mining: sand and gravel, crushed stone

The Press: daily newspapers   **Boston Globe:** POB 2378 Boston, MA 02107
          tel. (617) 929-2000
          circ. 517,000 morning, 798,000 Sunday
        Boston Herald: One Harold Square, Boston, MA 02106
          tel. (617) 426-3000
          circ. 328,000 morning, 223,000 Sunday

Tourism: Minute Man National Historical Park, USS Constitution, John F
    Kennedy Library and Museum, Boston Symphony summer concerts, Old
    Sturbridge Village

        Massachusetts Office of Travel and Tourism
        100 Cambridge Street   13th Floor
        Boston, MA 02202
        tel. [1] (800) 447-6277   [1] (617) 727-3201
        fax [1] (617) 727-6525

http://www.state.ma.us/

Michigan

Capital: Lansing   **Elevation:** 841 ft

Longitude: 84.36 W   **Latitude:** 42.47 N

Organized as Territory: Jan 11,1805

Statehood: Jan. 26, 1837, the 26th state

Land area: 58,527 sq miles, the 23rd state in area

Terrain: lower peninsula low rolling hills, upper peninsula is level in the east with swampy areas, western region is higher and more rugged

Boundaries: Lake Michigan, Wisconsin, Lake Huron, Canada, Ohio, Indiana, Lake Erie

Highest point: Mount Curwood 1,980 ft

Number of counties: 83

Motto: *Si quaeris peninsulam amoenam circumspice*
(If you seek a pleasant peninsula, look about you)

Nickname: Wolverine State

State bird: Robin   **State flower:** Apple blossom

State parks and recreational areas: 82 (250,000 acres)

Resident population: 9,478,000 (1993 est.)

Temperature: High/Low Jan. 29/15, Apr. 57/36, July 83/59, Oct. 62/41
Average annual precipitation: 30.77 inches

Industries: motor vehicles and parts, airplane parts, machine tools, steel springs, refrigerators, hardware, prepared cereals, timber and wood products, food processing, cement, fishing, tourism

Agriculture: fruits (apples, grapes, pears, cherries), corn, potatoes, beans, sugar beets, greenhouse and nursery products, dairy products, cattle

Mining: iron ore, copper, gypsum, salt, lime, gravel, iodine, bromine

The Press: daily newspapers   **Detroit Free Press:** 321 West Lafayette Blvd, Detroit, MI 48231
tel. (313) 222-6400, fax (313) 678-6400
circ. 622,000 morning, 1,215,000 Sunday
Flint Journal: 200 East First St, Flint, MI 48502
tel. (313) 766-6100 fax (313) 767-7518
circ. 106,000 evening, 124,000 Sunday

Tourism: automobile plants in Dearborn, Detroit, Flint, Lansing, and Pontiac. Pictured Rocks and Sleeping Bear Dunes National Lakeshore, many summer resorts along the Great Lakes, 3,288 miles of shoreline. Hunting, fishing, camping; over 10,000 inland lakes

Michigan Travel Bureau
Department TPS
PO Box 30226
Lansing, MI 48909
tel. [1] (800) 543-2937   [1] (517) 373-0670
fax [1] (517) 373-0059

http://web.mde.state.mi.us/lcgis/state.html

Minnesota

Capital: St. Paul   **Elevation:** 834 ft

Longitude: 93.13 W   **Latitude:** 44.53 N

Organized as Territory: March 3, 1849

Statehood: May 11, 1858, the 32nd state

Land area: 84,402 sq miles, the 12th state in area

Terrain: mountainous north, rocky ridges in the northeast, rolling plains northwest to the south

Boundaries: North Dakota, South Dakota, Iowa, Wisconsin, Lake Superior, Canada

Highest point: Eagle Mountain 2,301 ft

Number of counties: 87

Motto: *L'Etoile du Nord* (The North Star)

Nickname: North Star State; Gopher State; Land of 10,000 Lakes

State bird: Common loon (also called Great Northern Diver)

State flower: Showy lady slipper

State forests: 56 (3,200,000 + acres)

State parks: 66 (226,000 acres)

Resident population: 4,517,000 (1993 est.)

Temperature: High/Low Jan. 21/3, Apr. 56/35, July 82/61, Oct. 61/39
Average annual precipitation: 26.62 inches

Industries: electronics computers, scientific instruments, non-electrical machinery, plastics, flour-mill products, food processing, plastics, printing and paper products, fabricated metal products, tourism

Agriculture: corn, wheat, rye, soybeans, oats, barley, alfalfa, sugar beets, potatoes, green peas, cattle, hogs

Mining: iron ore

The Press: daily newspapers

Star Tribune: 425 Portland Ave, Minneapolis, MN 55488
tel. (612) 673-4000 fax (612) 673-4359
circ. 408,000 daily, 678,000 Sunday

St Paul Pioneer Press: 345 Cedar St, St Paul, MN 55101
tel. (612) 222-5011, fax (612) 228-5500
circ. 212,000 daily, 277,000 Sunday

Tourism: St. Paul Winter Carnival, Walker Art Center, and Minnehaha Park, Minnesota Zoological Gardens, hunting, fishing, water sports, more than 10,000 lakes

Minnesota Office of Tourism
100 Metro Square
121 7th Place East
St. Paul, MN 55101
tel. [1] (800) 657-3700 [1] (612) 296-5029
fax [1] (612) 296-7095

http:www.state.mn.us/

Mississippi

Capital: Jackson   **Elevation:** 310 ft
Longitude: 90.12 W   **Latitude:** 32.20 N
Organized as Territory: April 7, 1798
Statehood: Dec. 10, 1817, the 20th state
Land area: 47,689 sq miles, the 32nd state in area
Terrain: flat north, rugged sandy hills in the northeast, low fertile delta south, sandy gulf coastal area
Boundaries: Arkansas, Louisiana, Gulf of Mexico, Alabama, Tennessee
Highest point: Woodall Mountain 806 ft
Number of counties: 82
Motto: *Virtute et armis* (By valor and arms)
Nickname: Magnolia State
State bird: Mockingbird
State flower: magnolia
State forests: 1 (1,760 acres)
State parks: 27 (16,763 acres)
Resident population: 2,643,000 (1993 est.)

Temperature: High/Low Jan. 58/36, Apr. 78/53, July 93/71, Oct. 80/52

Average annual precipitation: 50.96 inches

Industries: transportation equipment, electrical equipment, wood products, paper products, apparel, furniture, tourism

Agriculture: cotton, soybeans, corn, rice, cereal grains, sweet potatoes, sugarcane; fodder, cattle, dairy products, poultry, approximately 100,00 acres of catfish ponds

Mining: petrolcum, natural gas

The Press: daily newspaper

Clarion-Ledger: 311 East Pearl Street
POB 40, Jackson, MS 39205
tel. (601) 961-7000   fax (601) 961-7047
circ. 108,000 evening, 127,000 Sunday

Tourism: Pre-Civil War mansions, Tupelo National Battlefield, historical landmarks

Mississppi Tourism Division
PO Box 1705
Ocean Springs, MS 39566
tel. [1] (800) 927-6378   [1] (601) 359-3297
fax [1] (601) 359-2832

http://www.state.ms.us/

Missouri

Capital: Jefferson City

St. Louis   **Elevation:** 535 ft

Longitude: 90.12 W   **Latitude:** 38.35 N

Organized as Territory: June 4, 1812

Statehood: Aug, 10, 1821, the 24th state

Land area: 69,697 sq miles, the 19th state in area

Terrain: rolling hills, fertile plains north, Ozarks mountains south with hills and deep narrow valleys, plains with low elevation in west

Boundaries: Nebraska, Kansas, Oklahoma, Arkansas, Tennessee, Kentucky, Illinois, Iowa

Highest point: Taum Sauk Mountain 1,772 ft

Number of counties: 114, plus 1 independent city

Motto: *Salus populi suprema lex esto*

(The welfare of the people shall be the supreme law)

Nickname: Show-me State

State bird: Bluebird   **Floral emblem:** Hawthorn

State parks and historic sites: 79 (126,072 acres)

Resident population: 5,234,000 (1993 est.)

Temperature: (St. Louis) High/Low Jan. 40/23, Apr. 67/46, July 88/69, Oct. 70/48

Average annual precipitation: 36.70 inches

Industries: transportation equipment, motor vehicles and parts, defense and aerospace technology, chemicals, fabricated metal products, machinery, printed material, food processing, beverages, food processing; tourism;

Agriculture: hay, corn, soybeans, wheat, oats, barley, rice, sorghum, tobacco, grapes for wine, cattle, hogs

Mining: lead, limestone, coal

The Press: daily newspapers   **Kansas City Star:** 1729 Grand Ave, Kansas City, MO 64108
tel. (816) 234-4141, fax (816) 234-4926
circ. 289,000 evening, 423,000 Sunday

St Louis Post-Dispatch: 900 North Tucker Blvd
St Louis, MO 63101 tel. (314) 340-8000 fax (314) 240-3050
circ. 391,000 morning, 586,000 Sunday

Tourism: country music shows at Branson, Gateway Arch at the Jefferson National Expansion at St. Louis, Harry S. Truman home and library, Pony Express and Jesse James museums, Mark Twain's boyhood home and cave, historic sites, fishing

Missouri Division of Travel
Truman State Office Building
PO Box 1055
Jefferson City, MO 65102
tel. [1] (800) 535-3210 [1] (314) 751-4133
fax [1] (314)-751-5160

http://www.ecodev.state.mo.us/

Montana

Capital: Helena   **Elevation:** 3,828 ft
Longitude: 112.2 W   **Latitude:** 46.35 N
Organized as Territory: May 26, 1864
Statehood: Nov. 8, 1889, the 41st state
Land area: 147,046 sq miles, the 4th state in area
Terrain: Rocky Mountains in west, gentle rolling Great Plains in east
Boundaries: Canada, Idaho, Wyoming, South Dakota, North Dakota
Highest point: Granite Peak 12,799 ft
Number of counties: 56, plus small part of Yellowstone National Park
Motto: *Oro y plata* (Gold and Silver)
Nickname: Treasure State
State bird: Western meadowlark   **State flower:** Bitterroot
State forests: 7 (214,000 acres)
State parks and recreational areas: 110 (18,273 acres)
Resident population: 839,000 (1993 est.)
Temperature: High/Low Jan. 28/8, Apr. 55/30, July 84/52, Oct. 59/32
      Average annual precipitation: 12.26 inches
Industries: fabricated metal products, wood products, food processing
Agriculture: wheat, barley, oats, flaxseed, sugar beets, potatoes, hay, sheep, cattle
Mining: coal, copper, lead, zinc, silver, gold, petroleum

The Press: daily newspaper

Billings Gazette: 401 North Broadway, POB 2507, Billings, MT 59103 tel. (406) 657-1200, fax (406) 657-1345 circ. 54,000 morning, 61,000 Sunday

Tourism: Glacier National Park, is very scenic with over 60 glaciers, 200 lakes and many streams with good trout fishing, Custer Battlefield National Monument, Yellowstone National Park, historical sites

Montana Travel Promotion Division
Department of Commerce
1424 9th Avenue
Helena, MT 59620
tel. [1] (800) 541-1447 [1] (406) 444-2654
fax [1] (406) 444-1800

http://www.mt.gov/

Nebraska

Capital: Lincoln   **Elevation:** 1,178 ft

Longitude: 96.40 W   **Latitude:** 40.50 N

Organized as Territory: May 30, 1854

Statehood: March 1, 1867, the 37th state

Land area: 77,355 sq miles, the 15th state in area

Terrain: central lowland plains in east, rising to the Great Plains and rolling hill country of the north and northwest

Boundaries: Wyoming, Colorado, Kansas, Missouri, Iowa, South Dakota

Highest point: southwestern Kimball County 5,426 ft

Number of counties: 93

Motto: Equality before the law

Nickname: Cornhusker State; Beef State; The Tree Planter State

State bird: Western Meadowlark   **State flower:** Goldenrod

State forests: none

State parks: 86 areas, historical and recreational

Resident population: 1,607,000 (1993 est.)

Temperature: High/Low Jan. 33/12, Apr. 63/39, July 89/66, Oct. 68/44 Average annual precipitation: 27.70 inches

Industries: food processing, electronic components, auto accessories, farm machinery, instruments, mobile homes, transportation equipment, chemicals, pharmaceuticals, apparel, tourism

Agriculture: corn, soybeans, rye, wheat, fodder, cattle, hogs

Mining: petroleum, natural gas

The Press: daily newspaper   **Omaha World-Herald:** World-Herald Square Omaha, NE 68102 tel. (402) 444-1000 fax (402) 345-0138 circ. 127,000 morning, 289,000 Sunday

Tourism: Chimney Rock National Historic Site, Agate Fossil Beds, Sheldon Memorial Art Gallery,

Nebraska Travel and Tourism
Department of Economic Development
PO Box 98913
Lincoln, NB 68509
tel. [1] (800) 228-4307   [1] (402) 471-3794
fax [1] (402) 471-3026

http://www.ded.state.ne.us/tourism.html

Nevada

Capital: Carson City
　　　Reno　　　　　**Elevation:** 4,404 ft
Longitude: 119.47 W　　**Latitude:** 39.30 N
Organized as Territory: March 2, 1861
Statehood: Oct. 31, 1864, the 36th state
Land area: 110,561 sq miles, the 7th state in area
Terrain: desert, rugged mountain ranges north to south, Mojava Desert in southeast
Boundaries: California, Arizona, Utah, Idaho, Oregon
Highest point: Boundary Peak 13,140 ft
Number of counties: 16 plus 1 independent city
Motto: All for our country
Nickname: Sagebrush State; Silver State; Battle-born State
State bird: Mountain bluebird　　　**State flower:** Sagebrush
State forests: none
State parks: 20 (150,000 acres, including leased land)
Resident population: 1,389,000 (1993 est.)
Temperature: (Reno) High/Low Jan. 45/18, Apr. 64/27, July 91/47, Oct. 70/31
　　Average annual precipitation: 7.61 inches
Industries: Nevada is the gambling and entertainment capital of the U.S. Gaming equipment, irrigation equipment, seismic monitoring devices, machinery, food processing, titanium products, speciality printing
Agriculture: Nevada is the driest state in the nation with an average annual rainfall of only 7.61 inches, much of Nevada is uninhabited, sage-brush-covered desert. Principal crops - hay, alfalfa seed, wheat, barley, potatoes, cattle
Mining: gold and silver

The Press: daily newspapers

Las Vegas Review-Journal:
1111 West Bonanza, Las Vegas, NV 89106
tel. (702) 383-0211
circ. 54,000 morning, 61,000 Sunday
Reno Gazette Journal: POB 22000, Reno, NV 89520
tel. (702) 788-6200 fax (702) 788-6458
circ. 67,000 morning 84,000 Sunday

Tourism: Major resorts areas are Reno, Lake Tahoe, and Las Vegas, Hoover Dam, Pyramid Lake, Virginia City, Great Basin Nation Park, Carson City Mint, Historical sites

Nevada Tourism Commission
State Capital Complex
Carson City, NV 89710
tel. [1] (800) 237-0774 [1] (702) 4322
fax [1] (702) 687-6779

http://www.state.nv.us/

New Hampshire

Capital: Concord   **Elevation:** 342 ft
Longitude: 70.30 W   **Latitude:** 43.12 N
Statehood: June 21, 1788, the 9th state
Land area: 9,279 sq miles, the 44th state in area
Terrain: rolling hills to mountains rising from the central plateau, low rolling coast
Boundaries: Maine, Canada, Vermont, Massachusetts, Atlantic Ocean
Highest point: Mount Washington 6,288 ft
Number of counties: 10
Motto: Live free or die
Nickname: Granite State
State bird: Purple finch   **State flower:** Purple lilac
State forests and parks: 175 (96,975 acres)
Resident population: 1,125,000 (1993 est.)
Temperature: High/Low Jan. 31/10, Apr. 57/32, July 83/57, Oct. 62/36
Average annual precipitation: 38.18 inches
Industries: machinery, electrical equipment, scientific instruments, printed material, fabricated metal products, food processing, pulp and paper products, clay products, tourism
Agriculture: corn, potatoes, vegetables, fruit, hay, poultry, dairy farming

Mining: sand and gravel, clay

The Press: daily newspaper

Union Leader: POB 9555,
Manchester, NH 03108
tel. (603) 668-4321   fax (603) 668-0382
circ. 71,000 morning, 99,000 Sunday

Tourism: Daniel Webester's birthplace near Franklin, Strawberry Banke, restored
building of the original settlement at Portsmouth, Lake Winnipesaukee,
largest of over 1,300 lakes, "Old Man of the Mountain" granite head profile
(the state's official emblem) at Francxonia

New Hampshire Office of Travel and Tourism
PO Box 1856
Concord, NH 03302
tel. [1] (800) 386-4664   [1] (603) 271-2343
fax [1] (603) 271-2629

http://www.state.nh.us/

New Jersey

Capital: Trenton   **Elevation:** 56 ft
Longitude: 74.46 W   **Latitude:** 40.13 N
Statehood: Dec 18, 1787, the 3rd state
Land area: 7,787 sq miles, the 46th state in area
Terrain: Appalachian Valley in the northwest, mountain ranges northeast to
southwest, coastal plain rising to gentle slopes in southeast
Boundaries: New York, Pennsylvania, Delaware, Atlantic Ocean
Highest point: High Point 1,803 ft
Number of counties: 21
Motto: Liberty and prosperity
Nickname: Garden State
State bird: Eastern goldfinch   **State flower:** Purple violet
State forests: 11
State parks: 35 (67,111 acres)
Resident population: 7,879,000 (1993 est.)
Temperature: High/Low Jan. 38/25, Apr. 62/43, July 85/67, Oct. 66/48
Average annual precipitation: 43.85 inches

Industries: pharmaceuticals, machinery, electrical equipment, scientific instruments, chemicals, food processing, apparel, printed material, tourism, legalized casino gambling in Atlantic City

Agriculture: greenhouse and nursery products, tomatoes, corn, asparagus, poultry, dairy farming

Mining: oil refining, crushed stone, sand and gravel

The Press: daily newspapers

Star-Ledger: Star-Ledger Plaza, Newark, NJ 07101
tel. (201) 877-4141 fax (201) 643-7248
circ. 485,000 morning 707,000 Sunday

The Times: 500 Perry Street, POB 847, Trenton, NJ 08605
tel. (609) 396-3232 fax (609) 396-3633
circ. 81,000 morning, 94,000 Sunday

Tourism: casino and gambling, Walt Whitman House in Camden, Edision National Historic Site in West Orange, New Jersey State Aquarium in Camden

New Jersey Division of Travel and Tourism
CN 826
Trenton, NJ 08625
tel. [1] (800) 537-7379 [1] (609) 292-2470
fax [1] (609) 633-7418

http://www.state.nj.us/

New Mexico

Capital: Santa Fe
Albuquerque   **Elevation:** 5,311
Longitude: 106.39 W   **Latitude:** 35.05 N
Organized as Territory: Sept. 9, 1850
Statehood: Jan, 6, 1912, the 47th state
Land area: 121,593 sq miles, the 5th state in area
Terrain: Great Plains east, Rocky Mountains in the central area, high plateau west
Boundaries: Mexico, Texas, Oklahoma, Colorado, Utah, Arizona
Highest point: Wheeler Peak 13,161 ft
Number of counties: 33
Motto: *Crescit eundo* (It grows as it goes)
Nickname: Land of Enchantment; Sunshine State
State bird: Roadrunner   **State flower:** Yucca

State forests: 933,000 acres
State parks: 29 (105,012 acres)
Resident population: (1993 est.)
Temperature: (Albuquerque) High/Low   Jan. 47/24, Apr. 70/41, July 92/65,
   Oct. 72/45
   Average annual precipitation: 8.33 inches
Industries: transportation equipment, electrical equipment, machinery, scientific
   instruments, chemicals, lumber, printed materials, stone-clay-glass products,
   food processing, tourism
Agriculture: cotton, corn, sorghum, beans, onions, chile, lettuce, pecans,
   peanuts, dairy products, cattle
Mining: copper, gold, silver, lead, zinc, molybdenum, potassium salts,
   uranium, coal, petroleum, natural gas

The Press: daily newspaper

Albuquerque Journal: PO Drawer JT,
Albuquerque, NM 87109
tel. (505) 823-3393, fax (505) 823-3369
circ. 123,000 morning, 162,000 Sunday

Tourism: Carlsbad Caverns National Park, Chaco Culture National Historic Park,
   the ruins at Fort Union, Inscription Rock at El Morro National Monument,
   White Sands and Gila Cliff Dwellings National Monument

New Mexico Department of Tourism
Room 751 Lamy Building
491 Old Santa Fe Trail
Santa Fe, NM 87503
tel. [1] (800) 545-2040   [1] (505) 827-0299
fax [1] (505) 827-7402

http://www.state.nm.us/

New York

Capital: Albany   **Elevation:** 275 ft
Longitude: 73.45 W   **Latitude:** 42.40 N
Statehood: July 26, 1788, the 11th state
Land area: 49,108 sq miles, the 30th state in area

Terrain: Adirondack Mountains in the northeast, lowlands from Lake Ontario northeast along the Canadian border, Atlantic coastal plains in the southeast, Appalachian Highlands and Catskill Mountains west, Lake Erie-Ontario lowland plateau

Boundaries: Canada, Lake Ontario, Lake Erie, Pennsylvania, New Jersey, Atlantic Ocean, Connecticut, Massachusetts, Vermont

Highest point: Mount Marcy 5,344 ft

Number of counties: 62

Motto: Excelsior (Ever upward)

Nickname: Empire State

State bird: Bluebird   **State flower:** Rose

State forest preserves: Adirondacks, 2,500,000 acres, Catskills, 250,000 acres

State parks: 150 (250,000 acres)

Resident population: 18,197,000 (1993 est.)

Temperature: High/Low Jan. 30/13, Apr. 58/36, July 84/60, Oct. 63/40
Average annual precipitation: 36.46 inches

Industries: foreign trade, banking, printing and publishing, theatrical productions, apparel, leather products, instruments manufacturing, chemical, electronic equipment, machinery, wineries, tourism

Agriculture: corn, grains, vegetables, fruit, dairy products, poultry, cattle

Mining: crushed stone

The Press: daily newspapers   **New York Daily News:** 220 East 42nd Street, New York, Ny 10017
tel. (212) 210-2100 fax (212) 210-2049
circ. 782,000 morning, 983,000 Sunday

New York Times: 229 West 43rd Street, New York, NY 100002
tel. (212) 556-1234
circ. 1,146,000 morning, 1,762,000 Sunday

Tourism: United Nations, skyscrapers, museums, theaters, Central Park, Grant's Tomb, in New York City. Statue of Liberty National Monument, Niagara Falls, National Historic Sites that include Franklin D. Roosevelt's home at Hyde Park

New York State Department of Economic
Development/ Tourism
One Commerce Plaza
Albany, NY 12245
tel. [1] (800) 225-5697 [1] (518) 474-4116
fax [1] (518) 486-6416

http://www.state.ny.us/

North Carolina

Capital: Raleigh   **Elevation:** 434 ft
Longitude: 78.39 W   **Latitude:** 35.46 N
Statehood: Nov. 21, 1789, the 12th state
Land area: 52,669 sq miles, the 28th state in area
Terrain: gentle to rugged mountains north to southwest, central plateau, coastal
    plain and tidewater east
Boundaries: Atlantic Ocean, Virginia, Tennessee, Georgia, South Carolina
Highest point: Mount Mitchell 6,684 ft
Number of counties: 100
Motto: *Esse quam videri* (to be, rather than to seem)
Nickname: Tar Heel State
State bird: Cardinal   **State flower:** Flowering Dogwood
State forests: 1
State parks: 30 (125,000 acres)
Resident population: 6,945,000 (1993 est.)
Temperature: High/Low Jan. 51/30, Apr. 73/47, July 88/67, Oct. 72/48
    Average annual precipitation: 45.30 inches
Industries: paper and paper products, chemicals, iron and steel products, tobacco
    products, machinery, electrical equipment, furniture, textiles, brick, tourism
Agriculture: tobacco, corn, cotton, vegetables, peanuts, hay, poultry (broilers,
    turkeys), hogs
Mining: phosphate rock, mica, lithium, crushed stone

The Press: daily newspapers   **Charlotte Observer:** 600 South Tryon St
                                        POB 32188, Charlotte, NC 28232
                                        tel. (704) 379-6300 fax (704) 358-5036
                                        circ. 239,000 morning, 299,000 Sunday

News and Observer: 215 South McDowell St,
Raleigh, NC 27602
tel. (919) 829-4500   fax (919) 829-4808
circ. 141,000 morning, 181,000 Sunday
Tourism: Wright Brothers National Memorial at Kitty Hawk, Great Smokey
Mountains, Carl Sandberg's home near Hendersonville, Old Salem
Restoration in Winston-Salem, fresh and salt water fishing, mountain resorts,
golfing

North Caroling Division of Travel & Tourism
430 N Salisbury Street
Raleigh NC 27611
tel. [1] (800) 847-4862   [1] (919) 733-4171
fax [1] (919) 733-8582

http://www.sips.state.nc.us/nchome.html

North Dakota

Capital: Bismarck   **Elevation:** 1,647 ft
Longitude: 100.45 W   **Latitude:** 46.46 N
Organized as Territory: March 2, 1861
Statehood: Nov. 2, 1889, the 39th state
Land area: 70,703 sq miles, the 17th state in area
Terrain: prairie, central lowlands east, Missouri plateau of the Great Plains west
Boundaries: Canada, Montana, Wyoming, South Dakota, Minnesota
Highest point: White Butte 3,506 ft
Number of counties: 53
Motto: Liberty and union, now and forever: one and inseparable
Nickname: Sioux State; Flickertail State; Peace Garden State
State bird: Western Meadowlark   **State flower:** Wild Prairie Rose
State forests: none
State parks: 14 (14,922 acres)
Resident population: 635,000 (1993 est.)
Temperature: High/Low Jan. 19/-3, Apr. 55/31, July 84/57, Oct. 60/33
Average annual precipitation: 16.14 inches
Industries: farm equipment, food processing,
Agriculture: durum wheat, barley, rye, flaxseed, sunflower seeds, sugar beets,
beans (dry), hay: beef cattle, sheep, hogs
Mining: petroleum, natural gas, coal, clay, sand and gravel, salt

The Press: daily newspaper

The Forum: 101 5th Street, POB 2020, Fargo, ND 58107
tel. (701) 235-7311   fax (701) 241-5487
circ. 55,000 daily, 70,000 Sunday

Tourism: Fort Union Trading Post National Historic Site, Badlands, Theodore Roosevelt National Park, fishing, hunting, tourism

North Dakota Tourism Promotion
Liberty Memorial Building
State Capitol Grounds
Bismarck, ND 58505
tel. [1] (800) 435-5663   [1] (701) 328-2525
fax [1] (701) 328-4878

http://www.state.nd.us/

Ohio

Capital: Columbus   **Elevation:** 812 ft
Longitude: 83.10 W   **Latitude:** 40.00 N
Statehood: March 1, 1803, the 17th state
Land area: 41,330 sq miles, the 35th state in area
Terrain: central plain in the west, Allegheny plateau in the east
Boundaries: Lake Erie, Michigan, Indiana, Kentucky, West Virginia, Pennsylvania
Highest point: Campbell Hill 1,550 ft
Number of counties: 88
Motto: With God, all things are possible
Nickname: Buckeye State
State bird: Cardinal   **State flower:** Scarlet carnation
State forests: 19 (172,744 acres)
State parks: 71 (198,027 acres)
Resident population: 11,091,000 (1993 est.)
Temperature: High/Low Jan. 36/20, Apr. 63/40, July 85/62, Oct. 66/42
Average annual precipitation: 36.98 inches
Industries: transportation equipment, machinery, auto assembly, auto equipment (parts, glass), steel mills, roller bearings, jet engines, machine tools, chemicals, office machines, heating, refrigeration and air conditioners, food processing, lime production, cement, tourism
Agriculture: corn, oats, soybeans, clover, grapes, dairy products, sheep, hogs, cattle

Mining: coal, petroleum, natural gas, gypsum, clay, sand and gravel, salt,

The Press: daily newspapers

Cincinnati Enquire: 617 Vine St,
Cincinnati, OH 45292
tel. (513) 721-2700 fax (513) 369-1079
circ. 201,000 morning, 347,000 Sunday

Columbus Dispatch: 34 South Third St,
Columbus, OH 43215
tel. (614) 461-5000 fax (614) 461-7580
circ. 268,000 morning, 403,000 Sunday

Tourism: Historic sites and the homes of Presidents Grant, Taft, Hayes, Harding, and Garfield. Indian burial grounds at Mound City Group National Monument

Ohio Office of Travel and Tourism
PO Box 1001
Columbus, OH 43216
tel. [1] (800) 282-5393 [1] (614) 466-8844
fax [1] (614) 466-6744

http://www.state.oh.us/

Oklahoma

Capital: Oklahoma City   **Elevation:** 1,285
Longitude: 97.36 W   **Latitude:** 35.24 N
Organized as Territory: May 2, 1890
Statehood: Nov. 16, 1907, the 46th state
Land area: 69,956 sq miles, the 18th state in area
Terrain: central plains, high plains in the west, small mountains in the east
Boundaries: Texas, Arkansas, Missouri, Kansas, Colorado, New Mexico
Highest point: Black Mesa 4,973 ft
Number of counties: 77
Motto: *Labor omnia vincit* (Labor conquers all things)
Nickname: Sooner State
State bird: Scissor-tailed flycatcher   **State flower:** Mistletoe
State forests: none
State parks: 36 (57,487 acres)
Resident population: 3,231,000 (1993 est.)

Temperature: High/Low Jan. 48/26, Apr. 72/49, July 93/70, Oct. 74/51
    Average annual precipitation: 31.71 inches
Industries: petroleum, refining, natural gas, construction and oil equipment,
    machinery, transportation equipment, electrical equipment, rubber and plastic
    products, food processing, meat packing, helium
Agriculture: greenhouse and nursery products, wheat, cotton, hay, sorghum,
    peanuts, dairy products, cattle, poultry
Mining: coal, copper, zinc, silver, gypsum

The Press: daily newspapers   **Oklahoman:** POB 25125,
                    Oklahoma City, OK 73125
                    tel. (405) 232-3311
                    circ. 232,000 morning, 335,000 Sunday
              Tulsa World: 315 South Boulder Ave,
              POB 1770, Tulsa, OK 74102
              tel. (918) 581-8300 circ. 134,000 morning, 241,000 Sunday
Tourism: Will Roger's Memorial in Claremore, Fort Gibson Stockade, Cherokee
    Cultural Center, National Cowboy Hall of Fame in Oklahoma City
                    Oklahoma Tourism & Recreation Services
                    500 Will Rogers Building
                    Oklahoma City, OK 73105
                    tel. [1] (800) 652-6552   [1] (405) 521-2464
                    fax [1] (405) 521-3992

http://www.oklaosf.state.ok.us/

Oregon

Capital: Salem   **Elevation:** 196 ft
Longitude: 123.01 W   **Latitude:** 44.55 N
Organized as Territory: Aug. 14, 1848
Statehood: Feb. 14, 1859, the 33rd state
Land area: 97,073 sq miles, the 10th state in area
Terrain: rugged coast range, fertile central valley, Cascade Mountains east of the
    valley, desert plateau east of Cascades
Boundaries: Pacific Ocean, California, Nevada, Idaho, Washington
Highest point: Mount Hood 11,239 ft
Number of counties: 36
Motto: "*Alis volat propriis*" (" She flies with her own wings")

Nickname: Beaver State
State bird: Western meadowlark   **State flower:** Oregon grape
State forests: 820,000 acres
State parks: 240 (93,330 acres)
Resident population: 3,038,000 (1993 est.)
Temperature: High/Low   Jan. 45/32, Apr. 61/37, July 82/51, Oct. 64/42
Average annual precipitation: 40.49 inches
Industries: lumber and plywood, metal products, pulp and paper, machinery,
    electronic equipment, aluminum, chemicals, food processing, nickel
    smelting, salmon-fishing and hatchery, dairy products, cheese
Agriculture: greenhouse and nursery products, wheat, hay, berries (blackberries,
    boysenberries, loganberries, strawberries, raspberries), peppermint (oil), grass
    seeds, hazelnuts (filberts), hops, fruits (cherries, apples, prunes), beans,
    onions, christmas trees, cattle, sheep
Mining: nickel, crushed rock, sand and gravel

The Press: daily newspapers   **The Oregonian:** 1320 SW Broadway
    Portland, OR 97201
    tel. (503) 221-8327 fax (503) 294-4199
    circ. 338,000 morning, 441,000 Sunday
        Statesman Journal: 280 Church St, NE
    POB 13009, Salem, OR 97309
    tel. (503) 399-6611   fax (503) 399-6808
    circ. 60,000 morning, 69,000 Sunday
Tourism: Mount Hood ski lodge, Bonneville Dam, Oregon Dunes National
    Recreational Area, Oregon Caves National Monument, Columbia River
    Gorge, John Day Fossil Beds, Newberry Volcanic National Monument and
    East Lake

    Oregon Tourism Department
    775 Summer Street. NE
    Salem, OR 97310
    tel [1] (800) 547-7842 [1] (503) 986-0000
    fax [1] (503) 986-0001

http://www.state.or.us/

Pennsylvania

Capital: Harrisburg   **Elevation:** 338 ft

Longitude: 76.51 W   **Latitude:** 40.13 N

Statehood: Dec. 12, 1787, the 2nd state

Land area: 45,308 sq miles, the 33 rd state in area

Terrain: Allegheny Mountains run southwest to northeast, northwest rugged plateau falls to Lake Erie lowland

Boundaries: New York, Lake Erie, Ohio, West Virginia, Maryland, Delaware, New Jersey

Highest point: Mount Davis 3,213 ft

Number of counties: 67

Motto: Virtue, liberty, and independence

Nickname: Keystone State

State bird: Ruffed grouse   **State flower:** Mountain laurel

State forests: 1,991,526 acres

State parks: 114 (277,164 acres)

Resident population: 12,048,000 (1993 est.)

Temperature: High/Low Jan. 38/23, Apr. 64/42, July 87/65, Oct. 67/45 Average annual precipitation: 37.96 inches

Industries: alloy steel, chemicals, machinery, electrical equipment, transportation equipment, printed material, data processing, fabricated metal products, cement, glass, tiles, brick, tourism

Agriculture: greenhouse and nursery products, sweet corn, potatoes, mushrooms, beans, maple syrup, fruit, Christmas trees, hay, dairy products (milk, cheese), cattle, poultry

Mining: coal, natural gas, slate, limestone, crushed stone

The Press: daily newspapers

Philadelphia Inquire: 400 North Broad St, Philadelphia, PA 19101 tel. (215) 854-2000 fax (215) 854-4794 circ. 516,000 morning, 983,000 Sunday

Pittsburg Post-Gazette: 34 Blvd of the Allies, Pittsburg, PA 15222 tel. (412) 263-1100   fax (412) 263-2014 circ. 245,000 morning, 455,000 Sunday

Tourism: Gettysburg National Military Park, Valley Forge National Historical Park, Eisenhower farm near Gettysburg, Independence National Historical Park in Philadelphia,

Pennsylvania Travel Development
Department of Commerce
416 Forum Building
Harrisburg, PA 17120
tel. [1] (800) 847-4872   [1] (717) 787-5453
[1] (800) 237-4363
fax [1] (717) 234-4560

http://www.state.pa.us/

Rhode Island

Capital: Providence   **Elevation:** 51 ft
Longitude: 71.24 W   **Latitude:** 41.50 N
Statehood: May 29, 1790, the 13th state
Land area: 1,212 sq miles, the 50th state in area (smallest of all the states)
Terrain: east is the lowlands of Narragansett Basin, west is flat with some rolling
          hills
Boundaries: Atlantic Ocean, Massachusetts, Connecticut
Highest point: Jerimoth Hill 812 ft
Number of counties: 5
Motto: Hope
Nickname: The Ocean State
State bird: Rhode Island Red   **State flower:** Violet
State forests: 11 (20,900 acres)
State parks: 17 (8,200 acres)
Resident population: (1993 est.)
Temperature: High/Low Jan. 36/21, Apr. 57/38, July 80/63, Oct. 64/43
          Average annual precipitation: 40.90 inches
Industries: greenhouse and nursery products, jewelry and silverware
          manufacturing, electronics, plastic products, fabricated metal products, boat
          and ship construction; health research, tourism
Agriculture: small scale farming; wine grapes, turf grass, nursery stock,
          fishing (clams, lobster, squid)

The Press: daily newspaper   **Providence Journal-Bulletin:** 75 Fountain St
          Providence, RI 02902
          tel. (401) 277-7847 fax (401) 277-7461
          circ. 190,000 daily, 265,000 Sunday

Tourism: General Nathanael Greene Homestead in Coventry, Samual Slater's Mill in Pawtucket, Touro Synagogue (1763) is the oldest in the U.S. Newport, summer capital of society

Rhode Island Tourism Division
Department of Economic Development
7 Jackson Walkway
Rhode Island, RI 02903
tel. [1] (800) 556-2484   [1] (401) 277-2601
fax [1] (401) 277-2102

http://.www.state.ri.us/

South Carolina

Capital: Columbia   **Elevation:** 213 ft

Longitude: 81.07 W   **Latitude:** 33.57 N

Statehood: May 23, 1788, the 8th state

Land area: 31,113 sq miles, the 40th state in area

Terrain: mountainous in the northwest, central plains, coastal plains

Boundaries: Atlantic Ocean, North Carolina, Georgia

Highest point: Sassafras Mountain 3,560 ft

Number of counties: 46

Motto: *Animis opibusque parati* (prepared in mind and resources)
    Dum spiro spero (While I breathe, I hope)

Nickname: Palmetto State

State bird: Carolina wren   **State flower:** Carolina jessamine

State forests: 4 (124,052 acres)

State parks: 50 (61,726 acres)

Resident population: 3,643,000 (1993 est.)

Temperature: High/Low Jan. 57/34, Apr. 77/51, July 92/70, Oct. 77/51
    Average annual precipitation: 45.26 inches

Industries: textiles, wood pulp, paper products, fabricated steel products, machinery, chemicals, electrical equipment, apparel, tourism

Agriculture: tobacco, cotton, peanuts, sweet potatoes, soybeans, corn, oats, peaches, dairy products, cattle, poultry

Mining: asbestos, granite, limestone

The Press: daily newspapers

The Post Courier: 134 Columbus St,
Charleston, SC 29403
tel. (803) 298-4100 fax (803) 853-5673
circ. 112,000 morning, 122,000 Sunday

The State: POB 1333, Columbia, SC 29202
tel. (803) 771-6161   fax (803) 771-8430
circ. 145,000 morning, 173,000 Sunday

Tourism: Fort Sumter National Monument, the aircraft carrier USS Yorktown in
Charleston Harbor, Cypress Gardens, Cowpens National Battlefield, Hilton
Head resorts

South Carolina Tourism
Department of Parks
1205 Pendleton Street
Columbia, SC 29201
tel. [1] (800) 346-3634   [1] (803) 734-0122
fax [1] (803) 734-0138

http://www.state.sc.us/

South Dakota

Capital: Pierre
Sioux Falls   **Elevation:** 1,814 ft
Longitude: 96.44 W   **Latitude:** 43.33 N
Organized as Territory: March 2, 1861
Statehood: Nov 2, 1889, the 40th state
Land area: 77,116 sq miles, the 16th state in area
Terrain: mountains in the southwest corner, prairie plains with rolling hills
Boundaries: Montana, Wyoming, Nebraska, Iowa, Minnesota, North Dakota
Highest point: Harney Peak 7,242 ft
Number of counties: 67 (64 county governments)
Motto: Under God the people rule
Nickname: Mount Rushmore State; Coyote State
State bird: Ringnecked Pheasant   **State flower:** American pasqueflower
State forests: none
State parks: 13, plus 39 recreational areas (87,269 acres)
Resident population: (1993 est.)
Temperature: (Sioux Falls) High/Low Jan. 25/4, Apr. 58/34, July 85/62,
Oct. 63/38

Average annual precipitation: 25.26 inches

Industries: lumber and wood products, machinery, scientific instruments, farm equipment, food processing, tourism

Agriculture: oats, rye, flaxseed, sunflower seed, corn, wheat, hay, dairy products, cattle, hogs

Mining: petroleum, gold, silver, beryllium, betonite, uranium, granite

The Press: daily newspaper

Argus Leader: 200 South Minnesota Ave
POB 5034, Sioux Falls, SD 57117
tel. (605) 331-2200 fax (605) 331-2371
circ. 48,000 morning, 70,000 Sunday

Tourism: the Black Hills and Mount Rushmore, a memorial to Crazy Horse is being carved in granite near Custer, the Badlands, the Wall Drug Store in Wall, Deadwood where Wild Bill Hickok was killed in 1876, and now has legalized casino gambling. The world's only Corn Palace in Mitchell

South Dakota Tourism
711 Wells Avenue
Pierre, SD 57501
tel. [1] (800) 732-5682   [1] (605) 773-3301
fax [1] (605) 773-3256

http://www.state.sd.us/

Tennessee

Capital: Nashville   **Elevation:** 590 ft
Longitude: 86.41 W   **Latitude:** 36.07 N
Statehood: June 1, 1796, the 16th state
Land area: 42,144 sq miles, the 34th state in area
Terrain: rugged mountains in the east, slightly rolling interior plateau, swamp and flood plain in the extreme west
Boundaries: Missouri, Arkansas, Mississippi, Alabama, Georgia, North Carolina, Virginia, Kentucky
Highest point: Clingmans Dome 6,643 ft
Number of counties: 95
Motto: "Agriculture and Commerce"
Nickname: Volunteer State
State bird: Mockingbird   **State flower:** Iris
State forests: 13 (150,000 acres)

State parks: 50 (133,000 acres)

Resident population: 5,099,000 (1993 est.)

Temperature: High/Low   Jan. 48/29, Apr. 71/49, July 92/69, Oct. 73/49
   Average annual precipitation: 46.61 inches

Industries: transportation equipment, electrical equipment, machinery, fabricated
   metal products, lumber and hard wood flooring, furniture, chemicals, textiles,
   leather goods, rubber products, apparel, food processing, tourism

Agriculture: corn, soybeans, cotton, tobacco, hay, dairy products, cattle, hogs

Mining: coal, zinc, pyrites, marble, clay, crushed stone

The Press: daily newspapers

The Commercial Appeal: 495 Union Ave
   Memphis, TN 38103
   tel. (901) 529-2211   fax (901) 529-2522
   circ. 208,000 morning   289,000 Sunday

The Tennessean: 1100 Broadway
   Nashville, TN 37203
   tel. (615) 259-8333   fax (615) 259-8820
   circ. 135,000 morning   269,000 Sunday

Tourism: Andrew Jackson National Historic Site, American Museum of Atomic
   Energy at Oak Ridge, Rock City Gardens near Chattanooga, Great Smokey
   Mountains National Park, Grand Ole Opera in Nashville

   Tennessee Tourist Development
   320 6th Avenue, North Suite 500
   Nashville, TN 37202
   tel. [1] (800) 836-6200 [1] (615)-741-2159
   fax [1] (615) 741-7225

http://www.state.tn.us/

Texas

Capital: Austin   **Elevation:** 597

Longitude: 97.42 W   **Latitude:** 30.18 N

Statehood: Dec. 29 1845, the 28th state

Land area: 266,807 sq miles, the 2nd state in area

Terrain: mountains northwest, Gulf Coast plain in the south and southeast, prairie
   interior

Boundaries: Gulf of Mexico, Louisiana, Arkansas, Oklahoma, New Mexico, Mexico

Highest point: Guadalupe Peak 8,751 ft

Number of counties: 254

Motto: Friendship

Nickname: Lone Star State

State bird: Mockingbird   **State flower:** Bluebonnet

State forests: 5 (7,609 acres)

State parks: 218 (206 developed)

Resident population: 18,031,000 (1993 est.)

Temperature: High/Low Jan. 60/39, Apr. 79/58, July 95/74, Oct. 80/57
Average annual precipitation: 33.30 inches

Industries: oil refining, petroleum products, chemicals, transportation equipment, machinery, food processing, cement, helium, tourism

Agriculture: cotton, rice, pecans, peanuts, sorghum, fruits, vegetables, poultry, cattle, sheep

Mining: petroleum, natural gas, sulfur, salt, graphite, bromine, clay

The Press: daily newspapers

Austin American-Statesman:
POB 670, Austin, TX 78767
tel. (512) 445-3745 fax (512) 445-3800
circ. 177,000 daily, 269,000 Sunday

Dallas Morning News: POB 665237, Dallas, TX 75265
tel. (214) 977-8222   fax (214) 977-8638
circ. 394,000 morning, 618,000 Sunday

Tourism: the Alamo in San Antonio, Gulf Coast resort area, Lyndon B. Johnson Space Center in Houston, Big Bend and Guadalupe Mountains National Park, Aircraft carrier in Corpus Christi Harbor, Bouncing lights in west Texas

Texas Travel and Information Center
PO Box 5064
Austin, TX 78763
tel. [1] (800) 888-8839   [1] (512) 467-3719
fax [1] (512) 483-3793

http://www.state.tx.us/

Utah

Capital: Salt Lake City   **Elevation:** 4,220 ft

Longitude: 111.58 W   **Latitude:** 40.46 N

Organized as Territory: Sept. 9, 1850

Statehood: Jan. 4, 1896, the 45th state

Land area: 84,899 sq miles, the 11th state in area

Terrain: Great Salt Lake and the Bonneville salt flats in the northwest, Rocky Mountains in the northeast, brilliantly colored canyons in the southeast, interior desert

Boundaries: Idaho, Nevada, Arizona, New Mexico, Colorado, Wyoming

Highest point: Kings Peak 13,528 ft

Number of counties: 29

Motto: Industry

Nickname: Beehive State

State bird: Sea gull   **State flower:** Sego lily

State forests and parks: 44 (64,097 acres)

Resident population: 1,879,000 (1993 est.)

Temperature: High/Low Jan. 37/19, Apr. 63/37, July 93/61, Oct. 66/38 Average annual precipitation: 15.63 inches

Industries: transportation equipment, machinery, fabricated metal products, aerospace, biomedical, and computer related businesses, computer software, tourism

Agriculture: winter wheat, beans, alfalfa, dairy products, poultry, cattle, sheep, (Utah's farmlands and crops require extensive irrigation)

Mining: petroleum, natural gas, gold, silver, copper, lead, zinc, molybdenum

The Press: daily newspapers

Desert News: 30 East First St South, POB 1257, Salt Lake City, UT 84110 tel. (801) 237-2100 fax (801) 237-2121 circ. 65,000 evenings, 69,000 Sunday

Salt Lake Tribune: 143 South Main St, POB 867, Salt Lake city, UT 84110 tel. (801) 237-2800 fax (801) 521-9418 circ. 112,000 morning, 145,000 Sunday

Tourism: Bryce Canyon, Zion National Parks, Rainbow Bridge National
Monuments, the Mormon Tabernacle in Salt Lake City, fishing

Utah Travel Council
Council Hall, Capitol Hill
Salt Lake City, UT 84114
tel. [1] (800) 200-1160   [1] (801) 538-1030
fax [1] (801) 538-1399

http://www.state.ut.us/

Vermont

Capital: Montpelier   **Elevation:** 525 ft
Longitude: 72.32 W   **Latitude:** 44.15 N
Statehood: March 4, 1791, the 14th state
Land area: 9,614 sq miles, the 43rd state in area
Terrain: mountainous
Boundaries: Canada, New York, Massachusetts, New Hampshire
Highest point: Mount Mansfield 4,393 ft
Number of counties: 14
Motto: Vermont, Freedom, and Unity
Nickname: Green Mountain State
State bird: Hermit thrush   **State flower:** Red clover
State forests: 34 (113,953 acres)
State parks: 45 (31,325 acres)
Resident population: 576,000 (1993 est.)
Temperature: High/Low Jan. 26/8, Apr. 53/33, July 81/59, Oct. 59/39
        Average annual precipitation: 32.54 inches
Industries: electrical equipment, fabricated metal products, printing and
        publishing, paper and paper products, food processing, tourism
Agriculture: fruit, maple syrup, truck farming, dairy products. (rugged, rocky
        terrain discourages extensive farming)
Mining: monument granite, marble, talc

The Press: daily newspaper   **The Free Press:** 191 College St
                                    Burlington, VT 05401
                                    tel. (802) 863-3441 fax (802) 862-5622
                                    circ. 54,000 morning, 66,000 Sunday

Tourism: Bennington Battle Monument, Calvin Coolidge Homestead at Plymouth, Marble Exhibit in Proctor, hunting and fishing

Vermont Travel Division
Box 37   134 State Street
Montpelier, VT 05601
tel. [1] (800) 837-6668   [1] (802) 828-3236
fax [1] (802) 828-3233

http://www.state.vt.us/

Virginia

Capital: Richmond   **Elevation:** 164 ft

Longitude: 77.29 W   **Latitude:** 37.33 N

Statehood: June 25, 1788, the 10th state

Land area: 40,767 sq miles, the 36th state in area

Terrain: Blue Ridge mountains and valleys in the west, rolling plateau interior, coastal plain and tidewater eastern shore

Boundaries: Tennessee, North Carolina, Atlantic Ocean, Maryland, West Virginia, Kentucky

Highest point: Mount Rogers 5,729 ft

Number of counties: 95, plus 41 independent cities

Motto: *Sic semper tyrannis* (Thus always to tyrants)

Nickname: The Old Dominion; Mother of Presidents

State bird: Cardinal   **State flower:** American dogwood

State forests: 8 (49,556 acres)

State parks and recreational parks: 27 (42,722 acres)

Resident population: 6,491,000 (1993 est.)

Temperature: High/Low   Jan. 47/28, Apr. 70/45, July 88/68, Oct. 71/47
Average annual precipitation: 43.77 inches

Industries: transportation equipment, electrical equipment, electronic, industrial machinery and equipment, chemicals, tobacco products, lumber and wood products, furniture, textiles, apparel, food processing

Agriculture: corn, barley, tomatoes, tobacco, peanuts, potatoes, sweet potatoes, vegetables, apples, dairy products, poultry (turkeys). Famous for Smithfield hams

Mining: coal, lime, kyanite, stone

The Press: daily newspapers

Richmond Times-Dispatch:
333 East Grace St, POB 85333,
Richmond, VA 23293
tel. (804) 649-6000   fax (804) 775-8059
circ. 143,000 daily, 254,000 Sunday

Virginian-Pilot: 150 West Brambleton Ave,
Norfolk, VA 23510
tel. (804) 446-2000 fax (804) 626-1375
circ. 155,000 morning, 238,000 Sunday

Tourism: Shenandoah National Park, Booker T. Washington's birthplace near
Raonoke, Robert E. Lee Memorial, Williamsburg, the restored Colonial
capital, Monticello, home of Thomas Jefferson, Arlington Cemetery, beaches,
fishing, crabbing

Virginia Division of Tourism
901 East Byrd Street
Richmond, VA 23219
tel. [1] (800) 248-4833   [1] (804) 786-2051
fax [1] (804) 786-1919

http://www.state.va.us/

Washington

Capital: Olympia   **Elevation:** 195 ft
Longitude: 122.54 W   **Latitude:** 46.58 N
Organized as Territory: March 2, 1853
Statehood: Nov. 11, 1889, the 42nd state
Land area: 68,138 sq miles, the 20th state in area
Terrain: coast range mountains, interior rolling plateau to Cascade Mountains,
fertile plains east of the Cascades, some desert
Boundaries: Canada, Pacific Ocean, Oregon, Idaho
Highest point: Mount Rainier 14,410 ft
Number of counties: 39
Motto: *Al-Ki* (Indian word meaning "by and by")
Nickname: Evergreen State; Chinook State
State bird: Willow goldfinch   **State flower:** Coast Rhododendron
State forest lands: 1,922,880 acres
State parks: 215 (231,861 acres)
Resident population: 5,255,000 (1993 est.)

Temperature: High/Low Jan. 44/30, Apr. 60/37, July 78/49, Oct. 61/40
Average annual precipitation: 51.11 inches

Industries: aircraft and missiles, electric power generation, shipbuilding, transportation equipment, machinery, fabricated metal products, aluminum producer, chemicals, lumber, paper products, commercial fishing, food processing, tourism

Agriculture: fruit (apples, pears, cherries, apricots, grapes), wheat, lentils, peas, asparagus, potatoes, spearmint and peppermint oil, dairy products, cattle

The Press: daily newspapers
Seattle Post-Intelligencer: 101 Elliott Ave West
POB 1909, Seattle, WA 98119
tel. (206) 44808000   fax (206) 448-8165
circ. 209,000 morning, 521,000 Sunday
Seattle Times: Fairview Ave North and John St
POB 70, Seattle, WA 98111
tel. (206) 464-2994   fax (206) 464-2261
circ. 238,000 evening, 515,000 Sunday

Tourism: Whitman Mission and Fort Vancouver National Historic Sites, Pacific Science Center and Space Needle in Seattle, Mt. Rainier, Mt. St. Helens (erupted May 18, 1980), Neah Bay, fishing, hunting, hiking

Washington State Tourism
101 General Admission Building
PO Box 42500
Olympia, WA 98504
tel. [1] (800) 544-1800   [1] (360) 753-5601
fax [1] (360) 753-4470

http://www.wa.gov/wahome.html

Washington, D.C.

Washington, D.C.   **Elevation:** 25 ft
Longitude: 77.27 W   **Latitude:** 38.57 N
Created municipal corporation: Feb. 21, 1871
Land area: 69 sq miles
Terrain: low hills north, slope west toward the Potomac River and south
Boundaries: Maryland, Virginia
Motto: *Justitia omnibus* (Justice to all)

Tree: Scarlet oak   **Flower:** American beauty rose
City parks: 753 (7,725 acres)
Resident population: 598,000 (1991 est.)
Temperature: High/Low   Jan. 44/28, Apr. 67/46, July 88/69, Oct. 70/50
     Average annual precipitation: 40.00 inches
Airport: Dulles International

The Press: daily newspapers   **Washington Post:** 1150 15th Street NW
                    Washington, DC 20071 tel. (202) 334-6000
                    circ. 839,00 morning, 1,166,000 Sunday
          Washington Times: 3600 New York Avenue NW
          Washington, DC 20002
          tel. (202) 636-3028 fax (202) 269-3419
          circ. 90,000 morning

Tourism: What to see: Philip Randolph Statue, Art, Science & Technology
Institute, Holography Museum of the 3rd Dimension, Jefferson Memorial,
Banneker Circle & Fountain, Bureau of Engraving & Printing, Congressional
Cemetery, Bumbarton House, Ebenezer Methodist Church, Emancipation Statue,
Federal Bureau of Investigation, Folger Shakespeare Library, Ford's Theatre &
Lincoln Museum, Franciscan Monastery, Frederick Douglass National Historic Site,
Georgetown Park, Hillwood Museum, Jewish Historical Society of Greater
Washington, Kenilworth Aquatic Gardens, John F. Kennedy Center for the
Performing Arts, Library of Congress, Lincoln Memorial, National Aboretum,
National Archives & Records Administration, National Art Gallery, National
Geographic Society, National Museum of Health & Medicine, Navy Museum, The
Octagon Museum, Supreme Court of the United States, U.S. Capitol, Union
Station, United States Botanic Gardens, Washington Monument, Washington
National Cemetery, The Washington Post, White House, White House Visitors
Center, Smithsonian Institution,
          District of Columbia
          Washington, DC Convention and Visitors Association
          1212 New York Avenue, NW
          Washington, DC 20005
          tel. [1] (800) 635-6338   [1] (202) 789-7000
          fax [1] (202) 789-7037

     http://dcpages.ari.net/

West Virginia

Capital: Charleston   **Elevation:** 939 ft
Longitude: 81.38 W   **Latitude:** 38.31 N
Statehood: June 20, 1863, the 35th state
Land area: 24,231 sq miles, the 41 state in area
Terrain: hilly to mountainous
Boundaries: Ohio, Kentucky, Virginia, Maryland, Pennsylvania
Highest point: Spruce Knob 4,863 ft
Number of counties: 55
Motto: *Montani semper liberi* (Mountaineers are always free)
Nickname: Mountain State
State bird: Cardinal   **State flower:** Rhododendron
State forests: 9 (79,502 acres)
State parks: 34 (74,508 acres)
Resident population: 1,820,000 (1993 est.)
Temperature: High/Low   Jan. 44/25, Apr. 68/44, July 86/64, Oct. 69/45
     Average annual precipitation: 43.66 inches
Industries: fabricated metal products, steel, aluminum, chemicals, glass products, hardwood lumber, quarry products, tourism
Agriculture: apples, hay, alfalfa, dairy products, poultry (broilers, turkeys, eggs), cattle
Mining: coal, petroleum, natural gas, stone, clay

The Press: daily newspaper   **Charleston Daily Mail:** 1001 Virginia St East, Charleston, WV 25331
     tel. (304) 348-5140 fax (304) 348-4847
     circ. 104,000 evenings,   104,000 Sunday
Tourism: Harper's Ferry, The Greenbrier and Berkeley Spring Resorts, historic homes in the Eastern Panhandle
                    West Virginia Division of Tourism Marketing
                    Capitol Complex PO Box 50305
                    Charleston, WV 25305
                    tel. [1] (800) 225-5982   [1] (304) 558-2286
                    fax [1] (304) 558-0108

http://access.K12.wv.us/

Wisconsin

Capital: Madison   **Elevation:** 858 ft
Longitude: 89.20 W   **Latitude:** 43.08 N
Organized as Territory: July 4, 1836
Statehood: May 29, 1848, the 30th state
Land area: 56,153 sq miles, the 26th state in area
Terrain: northern highland, Lake Superior lowland, rolling sandy interior plain
Boundaries: Minnesota, Iowa, Illinois, Lake Michigan, Michigan, Lake Superior
Highest point: Timms Hill 1,952 ft
Number of counties: 72
Motto: Forward
Nickname: Badger State
State bird: Robin   **State flower:** Wood violet
State forests: 9 (476,004 acres)
State parks and scenic trails: 45 parks, 14 trails (66,185 acres)
Resident population: 5,021,000 (1993 est.)
Temperature: High/Low Jan. 25/8, Apr. 56/35, July 81/59, Oct. 61/39
          Average annual precipitation: 30.59 inches
Industries: automobiles, transportation equipment, fabricated metal products, machinery, electrical equipment, paper products, furniture, food processing, beer, tourism
Agriculture: dairy products (milk, cheese), corn, oats, potatoes, peas, beans, cranberries, hay, cattle
Mining: crushed stone, sand and gravel

The Press: daily newspapers

Green Bay Press-Gazette:
435 East Walnut St, POB 19430,
Green Bay, WI 54307
tel. (414) 435-4411 fax (414) 431-8308
circ. 59,000 evening, 65,000 Sunday
Milwaukee Journal: 333 West State St,
POB 661, Milwaukee, WI 53201
tel. (414) 224-2000   fax (414) 224-2485
circ. 240,000 evening, 491,000 Sunday
Tourism: Apostle Islands National Lakeshore, Ice Age National Scientific Reserve, Circus World Museum at Baraboo, over 14,000 lakes, water sports, hunting, fishing

Wyoming

Capital: Cheyenne   **Elevation:** 6,126 ft
Longitude: 104.49 W   **Latitude:** 41.09 N
Organized as Territory: May 19, 1869
Statehood: July 10, 1890, the 44th state
Land area: 97,809 sq miles, the 9th state in area
Terrain: Rocky mountains west, Great Plains east
Boundaries: Idaho, Montana, South Dakota, Nebraska, Colorado, Utah
Highest point: Gannett Peak 13,804 ft
Number of counties: 23 plus Yellowstone National Park
Motto: Equal rights
Nickname: Equality State; "The Cowboy State"
State bird: Meadowlark   **State flower:** Indian paintbrush
State forests: none
State parks and historic sites: 23 (58,498 acres)
Resident population: 469,200 (1993 est.)
Temperature: High/Low Jan. 30/15, Apr. 55/30, July 84/55, Oct. 62/34
    Average annual precipitation: 14.48 inches
Industries: chemicals, wool production, tourism
Agriculture: sheep and cattle, wheat, oats, corn, barley, sugar beets, potatoes, alfalfa
Mining: petroleum, natural gas, coal, sodium carbonate (natrona) deposits, uranium

The Press: daily newspaper   **Star-Tribune:** POB 80, Casper, WY 82602
    tel. (307) 266-0500   fax (307) 266-0501
    circ. 34,000 morning, 38,000 Sunday

Tourism: Yellowstone National Park, with the Rocky Mountains steaming with geysers, bubbling with mud pots and abounding with wildlife. America's first national monument, Devil's Tower. Over 600 species of free-ranging wildlife inhabit the mountains, deserts and plains. Archaeological sites, historical sites, mansions, petroglyphs, geological museums, mines. Hunting, fishing, camping

Wyoming Division of Tourism
Interstate 25 at College Drive
Cheyenne, WY 82002
tel. [1] (800) 225-5996, [1] (307) 777-7777
fax [1] (307) 777-6904

http://www.state.wy.us/

Uruguay

125 km

Capital: Montevideo   longitude: 56.10 W   latitude: 34.55 S   elevation: 72 ft

Government: republic

Flag: nine equal horizontal stripes of white (top and bottom) alternating with blue; there is a white square in the upper hoist-side corner with a yellow sun bearing a human face known as the Sun of May and 16 rays alternately triangular and wavy

Geography

Location: Southern South America, bordering the South Atlantic Ocean, between Argentina and Brazil

Total Area: 176,220 sq km (68,039 sq mi) slightly smaller than Washington State

Boundaries: Argentina, Brazil

Climate: warm temperate; freezing temperatures almost unknown
Temperature (F): High/Low Jan. 83/62, Apr. 71/53, July 58/43, Oct. 68/49
Average annual precipitation: 37.4 inches

Terrain: mostly rolling plains and low hills; fertile coastal lowland
Highest point is Mirador Nacional 501 m (1,644 ft)

Natural resources: soil, hydropower potential, minor minerals

Natural hazards: seasonally high winds (the pampero is a chilly and occasional violent wind which blows north from the Argentine pampas), droughts, floods; because of the absence of mountains, which act as weather barriers, all locations are particularly vulnerable to rapid changes in weather fronts

People

Population: 3,223,000 (July 1995 est.)

Life expectancy at birth: total population 74.46 years

Nationality: Uruguayan

Ethnic division: white 88%, mestizo 8%, black 4%

Religions: Roman Catholic 66%, (less than half adult population attends church regularly), Protestant 2%, Jewish 2%, non-professing or other 30%

Languages: Spanish, Brazilero (Portuguese-Spanish mix on the Brazilian frontier)

Literacy: total population 96%

Economy

Imports: machinery and equipment, vehicles, chemicals, minerals, plastics

Exports: wool and textile manufactures, beef and other animal products, leather, rice

Industries: meat processing, wool and hides, sugar, textiles, footwear, leather apparel, tires, cement, petroleum refining, wine

Agriculture: large area devoted to livestock grazing; wheat, rice, corn, sorghum; fishing; self-sufficient in most basic foodstuffs

Currency: 1 Uruguayan peso ($Ur) = 100 centesimos

Uruguayan pesos per US1$ - 5.6

Transportation

Railroads: 3,000 km

Roads: 49,900 km total paved and unpaved

Ports: Fray Bentos, Montevideo, Nueva Palmira, Paysandu, Punta del Este

Airports: 85 total paved and unpaved. The main airport is at Carrasco, about 20 km from Montevideo

The Press: daily newspapers **El Diario:** Rio Negro 1028, Montevideo
telephone (2) 92-02-48 fax (2) 92-13-26
circ. 80,000

La Hora Popular: Yatay 1446 casi Marcelino Sosa, Montevideo
telephone (2) 20-50-02   circ. 30,000

Tourism: Sandy beaches, interior forests with a variety of wildlife and vegetation, Lobos Island

Direccion Nacional de Turismo:
Agraciada 1409, 4,5, and 6, Montevideo
telephone (2) 90-41-48

Diplomatic representation in US:

chief of mission: Ambassador Eduardo Macgillycuddy

chancery: 1918 F Street NW, Washington, DC 20006

telephone: [1] (202) 331-1313 through 1316

US Diplomatic representation:

chief of mission: Ambassador Thomas J. Dodd

embassy: Lauro Muller 1776, Montevideo

mailing address: APO AA 34035

telephone: [598] (2) 23-60-61, 48-77-77

FAX: [588] (2) 48-86-11

Uzbekistan

Capital: Tashkent   longitude: 69.18 E latitude: 41.20 N
elevation: 1,569 ft

Government: republic

Flag: three equal horizontal bands of blue (top), white, and green separated by red fimbriations with a crescent moon and 12 stars in the upper hoist-side quadrant

Geography

Location: Central Asia, north of Afghanistan

Total Area: 447,400 sq km (172,741 sq mi) slightly larger than California

Boundaries: Afghanistan, Kazakhstan, Kyrgyzstan, Tajikistan, Turkmenistan

Climate: mostly mid-latitude desert, long, hot summers, mild winters; semiarid grassland in east

Temperature (F): High/Low Jan. 37/21, Apr. 65/47, July 92/64, Oct. 65/41

Average annual precipitation: 14.7 inches

Terrain: mostly flat-to-rolling sandy desert with dunes; broad, flat intensely irrigated river valleys along course of Amu Darya and Sirdaryo Rivers; Fergana Valley in east surrounded by mountainous Tajikistan and Kyrgyzstan; shrinking Aral Sea in west

Highest point is in the Gissar Range 4,643 m (15,233 ft)

Natural resources: natural gas, petroleum, coal, gold, uranium, silver, copper, lead and zinc, tungsten, molybdenum

Natural hazards: NA

People

Population: 23,090,000 (July 1995 est.)

Life expectancy at birth: total population 68.79 years

Nationality: Uzbek

Ethnic division: Uzbek 71.4%, Russian 8.3%, Tajik 4.7%, Kazakh 4.1%, Tatar 2.4%, Karakalpak 2.1%, other 7%

Religions: Muslim 88%, (mostly Sunnis), Eastern Orthodox 9%, other 3%

Languages: Uzbek 74.3%, Russian 14.2%, Tajik 4.4%, other 7.1%

Literacy: total population 97%

Economy

Uzbekistan is the world's third largest cotton exporter.

Imports: grain, machinery and parts, consumer durables, other foods

Exports: cotton, gold, natural gas, mineral fertilizers, ferrous metals, textiles, food

Industries: textiles, food processing, machine building, metallurgy, natural gas

Agriculture: cotton, vegetables, fruits, grain, livestock

Currency: som

soms per US1$ - 25.0

Transportation

Railroads: 3,460 km in common carrier service; does not include industrial lines

Roads: 78,400 km total paved and unpaved

Ports: Termiz

Airports: 261 total paved and unpaved. Major airport is located at Tashkent

The Press: newspapers   **Molodets Uzbekistana:**
700083 Tashkent, ul. Matbuochilar 32
telephone (3712) 32-56-51
5 a week in Russian   circ. 30,000
Turkiston: 700083 Tashkent, ul Matbuochilar 32,
telephone (3712) 33-89-61   3 a week   circ. 70,000

Tourism: Cities of the ancient "Silk Route"

Uzbektourism: 700027 Tashkent, ul. Khorezmskaya 47
telephone (3712) 33-54-14   fax (3712) 32-79-48

Diplomatic representation in US:

chief of mission: Ambassador Fatikh Teshabayev

chancery: (temporary) Suites 619 and 623, 1511 K Street NW, Washington, DC 20005

telephone: [1] (202) 638-4266, 4267

FAX: [1] (202) 638-4268

US Diplomatic representation:

chief of mission: Ambassador Henry L. Clarke

embassy: 82 Chilanzarskaya, Tashkent

mailing address: use embassy street address

telephone: [7] (3712) 77-14-07, 77-10-81

FAX: [7] (3712) 77-69-53

Vanuatu

Capital: Port-Vila   longitude: 168.18 E   latitude: 17.45 S

Government: republic

Flag: two equal horizontal bands of red (top) and green with a black isosceles triangle (based on the hoist side) all separated by a black-edged yellow stripe in the shape of a horizontal Y (the two points of the Y face the hoist side and enclose the triangle); centered in the triangle is a boar's tusk encircling two crossed namele leaves, all in yellow

Geography

Location: Oceania, group of islands in the South Pacific Ocean, about three-quarters of the way from Hawaii to Australia

Total Area: 14,760 sq km (5,699 sq mi) slightly larger than Connecticut

Boundaries: no land boundaries

Climate: tropical; moderated by southeast trade winds

Temperature (F): High/Low Jan. 80/78. Apr. 84/78, July 74/73, Oct. 78/75

Terrain: mostly mountains of volcanic origin; narrow coastal plains
Highest point is Mt. Tabwemasana 1,879 m (6,165 ft)
Natural resources: manganese, hardwood forests, fish
Natural hazards: tropical cyclones or typhoons (January to April);
volcanism causes minor earthquakes

People

Population: 174,000 (July 1995 est.)
Life expectancy at birth: total population 59.71 years
Nationality: Ni-Vanuatu
Ethnic division: indigenous Melanesian 94%, French 4%, Vietnamese,
Chinese, Pacific Islanders
Religions: Presbyterians 36.7%, Anglican 15%, Catholic 15%, indigenous
beliefs 7.6%, Seventh-Day Adventist 6.2%, Church of Christ 3.8%, other
15.7%
Languages: English (official), French (official), pidgin (known as Bislama
or Bichelama)
Literacy: total population 53%

Economy

Imports: machine and vehicles, food and beverages, basic manufactures,
raw materials and fuels, chemicals
Exports: copra, beef, cocoa, timber, coffee
Industries: food and fish freezing, wood processing, meat canning
Agriculture: export crops - coconuts, cocoa, coffee, fish; subsistence crops - taro,
yams, coconuts, fruits, vegetables
Currency: 1 vatu (VT) = 100 centimes
vatu per US1$ - 112.42

Transportation

Railroads: none
Roads: 1,027 km total paved and unpaved
Ports: Forari, Port-Vila, Santo (Espiritu Santo)
Airports: 31 total paved and unpaved. The principal airports are at Efate and
Espiritu Santo

The Press: newspaper

Vanuatu Weekly: PMB 049, Port-Vila
telephone 22-999
English and French circ. 1,800

What's Doing in Vanuatu: Port-Vila
Tourist information - in English

Tourism: The capital is Port-Vila, located on the island of Efate. Beautiful beaches

National Tourism Office of Vanuatu

Kumul Highway, POB 209, Port-Vila   telephone 22-685

Diplomatic representation in US: Vanuatu does not have a mission in the US

US Diplomatic representation: the ambassador to Papua New Guinea is
accredited to Vanuatu

Venezuela

400 km

Capital: Caracas   longitude: 66.56 W latitude: 10.35 N elevation: 3,418 ft

Government: republic

Flag: three equal bands of yellow (top), blue, and red with the coat of arms
on the hoist side of the yellow band and an arc of seven stars white
five-pointed stars centered in the blue band

Geography

Location: Northern South America, bordering the Caribbean Sea and the
North Atlantic Ocean, between Columbia and Guyana

Total Area: 912,050 sq km (352,143 sq mi) slightly more than twice the size
of California

Boundaries: Brazil, Colombia, Guyana

Climate: tropical; hot, humid; more moderate in highlands

Temperature (F): High/Low Jan. 75/56, Apr. 81/60, July 78/61, Oct. 79/61

Average annual precipitation: 32.9 inches

Terrain: Andes Mountains and Maracaibo Lowlands in northwest; central
plains (llanos); Guiana Highlands in southeast

Highest point is Pico Bolivar 5,007 m (16,427 ft)

Natural resources: petroleum, natural gas, iron ore, gold, bauxite, other
minerals, hydropower, diamonds

Natural hazards: subject to floods, rock slides, mudslides; periodic droughts

People

    Population: 21,005,000 (July 1995 est.)

    Life expectancy at birth: total population 73.31 years

    Nationality: Venezuelan

    Ethnic division: mestizo 67%, white 21%, black 10%, Amerindians 2%

    Religions: nominally Roman Catholic 96%, Protestant 2%

    Languages: Spanish (official), native dialects spoken by about 200,000 Amerindians in the remote interior

    Literacy: total population 90%

Economy

    Imports: raw materials, machinery and equipment, transport equipment, construction materials

    Exports: petroleum, bauxite and aluminum, steel, chemicals, agricultural products, basic manufactures

Industries: petroleum, iron-ore mining, construction materials, food processing, textiles, steel, aluminum, motor vehicle assembly

Agriculture: products - corn, sorghum, sugarcane, rice, bananas, vegetables, coffee, beef, pork, milk, eggs, fish; not self-sufficient in food other than meat

Currency: 1 bolivar (Bs) = 100 centimos

                    bolivares per US1$ - 169.57

Transportation

    Railroads: 542 km

    Roads: 81,000 km total paved and unpaved

    Ports: Amuay, Bajo Grande, El Tablazo, La Guaira, La Salina, Maracaibo, Matanzas, Palua, Puerto Cabello, Puerto la Cruz, Puerto Ordaz, Puerto Sucre, Punta Cardon

    Airports: 431 total paved and unpaved. The main international airport is located about 10 km from Caracas

The Press: daily newspapers

    Meridiano: Edif. Bloque Dearmas, final Avda San Martin cruce on Avda La Paz Caracas 1020
    telephone (2) 443-1066   circ. 300,000

    El Mundo: Torre de la Prensa, Puente Trinidad a Panteon, Apdo 192, Caracas
    telephone (2) 81-49-31   circ. 196,000

Tourism: Guayana highlands, exotic birds and butterflies, lush rain forests, Angle Falls, swimming and snorkeling, the Andes

Diplomatic representation in US:

chief of mission: Ambassador Pedro Luis Echeverria

chancery: 1099 30th Street NW, Washington, DC 20007

telephone: [1] (202) 342-2214

US Diplomatic representation:

chief of mission: Ambassador Jeffery Davidow

embassy: Avenida Francisco de Miranda and Avenida Principal de la Floresta, Caracas

mailing address: P O Box 62291, Caracas 1060-A   APO AA 34037

telephone: [58] (2) 285-2222,   3111

FAX: [58] (2) 285-0366

Vietnam

Capital: Hanoi   longitude: 105.52 E   latitude: 21.01 N   elevation: 53 ft

Government: Communist state

Flag: red with a large yellow five-pointed star in the center

Geography

Location: Southeastern Asia, bordering the Gulf of Thailand, Gulf of Tonkin, and South China Sea. between China and Cambodia

Total Area: 329,560 sq km (127,243 sq mi) slightly larger than New Mexico

Boundaries: Cambodia, China, Laos

Climate: tropical in south; monsoonal in north with hot, rainy season (mid-May to mid-September) and warm, dry season (mid-October to mid-March)

Temperature (F): High/Low Jan. 68/56, Apr. 82/69, July 91/78, Oct. 84/71

Average annual precipitation: 66.2 inches
Terrain: low, flat delta in south and north; central highlands; hilly, mountainous in far north and northwest
Highest point is Fan Si Pan 3,142 m (10,308 ft)
Natural resources: phosphates, coal, manganese, bauxite, chromate, offshore oil deposits, forests
Natural hazards: occasional typhoons (May to January) with extensive flooding

People

Population: 74,394,000 (July 1995 est.)
Life expectancy at birth: total population 65.72 years
Nationality: Vietnamese
Ethnic division: Vietnamese 85%-90%, Chinese 3%, Muong, Thai, Meo, Khmer, Man, Cham
Religions: Buddhist, Taoist, Roman Catholic, indigenous beliefs, Islam, Protestant
Languages: Vietnamese (official), French, Chinese, English, Khmer, tribal languages (Mon-Khmer and Malayo-Polynesian)
Literacy: total population 88%

Economy

Imports: petroleum products, machinery and equipment, steel products, fertilizer, raw cotton, grain
Exports: petroleum, rice, agricultural products, marine products, coffee
Industries: food processing, textiles, machine building, mining, cement, chemical fertilizer, glass, tires, oil
Agriculture: paddy rice, corn, potatoes; commercial crops - (rubber, soybeans, coffee, tea, bananas) and animal products, fish; self-sufficient in food staple rice. note - the third largest exporter of rice in the World, behind the US and Thailand
Currency: 1 new dong (D) = 100 xu
new dong per US1$ - 11,000

Transportation

Railroads: 3,059 km (including 224 km not restored to service after war damage)
Roads: 85,000 km total paved and unpaved
Ports: Da Nang, Haipong, Ho Chi Minh City, Hon Gai, Qui Nhon, Nha Trang
Airports: 48 total paved and unpaved. The principal international airports are at Ho Chi Minh City and Hanoi

The Press: daily newspapers   **Nhan Dan:** 71 Hang Trong, Hanoi
telephone 25-42-31   circ. 200,000
Saigon Giai Phong: 432 Xo Viet Nghe Tinh,
Ho Chi Minh City   telephone 29-59-42   circ. 85,000

Tourism: Ho Chi Minh City, Marble Mountain, Hanoi
Viet Nam Tourism: 30a Ly Thuong Kiet, Hanoi
telephone 26-41-54   fax 25-75-83

Diplomatic representation in US:
chief of mission: Liaison Officer Le Van Bang
liaison office: NA
telephone: NA
FAX: NA
Note: negotiations between representatives of the US and Vietnam concluded
28 January 1995 with the signing of an agreement to establish liaison
offices in Hanoi and Washington, DC
US Diplomatic representation:
chief of mission: Liaison Officer James Hall
liaison office: NA
mailing address: NA
telephone: NA
FAX: NA

Virgin Islands

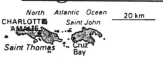

Capital: Charlotte Amalie longitude: 64.56 W latitude: 18.21 N
Government: organized, unincorporated territory of the US administered by the
Office of Territorial and International Affairs, US Department of the Interior

Flag: white with a modified US coat of arms in the center between the large blue initials V and I; the coat of arms shows an eagle holding an olive branch in one talon and three arrows in the other with a superimposed shield of vertical red and white stripes below a blue panel

Geography

Location: Caribbean, islands between the Caribbean Sea and the North Atlantic Ocean, east of Puerto Rico

Total Area: 352 sq km (135 sq mi) slightly less than twice the size of Washington, DC

Boundaries: no land boundaries

Climate: subtropical. tempered by easterly tradewinds, relatively low humidity, little seasonal temperature variation; rainy season May to November

Temperature (F): High/Low Jan. 79/75, Apr. 80/77, July 83/80, Oct. 83/80

Terrain: mostly hilly to rugged and mountainous with little level land Highest point is Crown Mountain on St. Thomas 474 m (1,556 ft)

Natural resources: sun, sand, sea, surf

Natural hazards: rarely affected by hurricanes; frequent and severe droughts, floods, and earthquakes

People

Population: 97,800 (July 1995 est.)

Life expectancy at birth: total population 75.29 years

Nationality: Virgin Islander

Ethnic division: black 80%, white 15%, other 5%

Religions: Baptist 42%, Roman Catholic 34%, Episcopalian 17%, other 7%

Languages: English (official) Spanish, Creole

Literacy: NA

Economy

One of the world's largest petroleum refineries is at Saint Croix

Imports: crude oil, foodstuffs, consumer goods, building materials

Exports: refined petroleum products

Industries: tourism, petroleum refining, watch assembly, rum distilling, construction, pharmaceuticals, textiles, electronics

Agriculture: truck gardens, food crops (small scale), fruit, sorghum, Senepol cattle

Currency: 1 United States dollar (US$) = 100 cents
US currency is used

Transportation

Railroads: none

Roads: 856 km

Ports: Charlotte Amalie, Christiansted, Cruz Bay, Port Alucroix
Airports: 2 with paved runways
Note: international airports on Saint Thomas and Saint Croix

Tourism: Fort Christian, Crown House, Coral World, orchidarium, beaches

Diplomatic representation in US: none (territory of the US)
US Diplomatic representation: none (territory of the US)

Wake Island

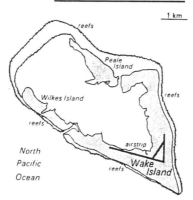

Capital: none; administered from Washington, DC
longitude: 166.30 W   latitude: 19.10 N
Government: unincorporated territory of the US administered by the US Army and
Strategic Defense Command
Flag: the US flag is used

Geography

Location: Oceania, island in the North Pacific Ocean, about two-thirds of
the way from Hawaii to the Northern Mariana Islands
Total Area: 6.5 sq km (2.51 sq mi) about 11 times the size of the
Mall in Washington, DC
Boundaries: no land boundaries
Climate: tropical
Terrain: atoll of three coral islands built up on an underwater volcano;
central lagoon is former crater, islands are part of the rim; average elevation
less than 4 meters
Natural resources: none
Natural hazards: occasional typhoons
Note: strategic location in the North Pacific Ocean; emergency landing
location for transpacific flights

People

    Population: 302 (July 1995 est.)

Economy

    Overview: Economic activity is limited to providing services to US military personnel and contractors located on the island. All food and manufactured goods must be imported

Transportation

    Railroads: none

    Ports: none; two offshore anchorages for large ships

    Airports: 1 with paved runways

Diplomatic representation in US: none (territory of the US)

US Diplomatic representation: none (territory of the US)

Note: formerly an important commercial aviation base, now used by US military, some commercial cargo planes, as well as the US Army Space and Strategic Defense Command for missile launches

Wallis and Futuna

50 km

MATA-UTU
Île Uvéa

South Pacific Ocean

Île Futuna
Leava
Île Alofi

Capital: Mata-Utu (on Ile Uvea)   longitude: 177.30 W latitude: 12.42 S

Government: overseas territory of France

    Flag: the flag of France is used

Geography

    Location: Oceania, islands in the South Pacific Ocean, about two-thirds of the way from Hawaii to New Zealand

    Total Area: 274 sq km (105.8 sq mi) slightly larger than Washington, DC

    Boundaries: no land boundaries

    Climate: tropical; hot, rainy season (November to April); cool, dry season (May to October). Temperatures are generally between 73 F and 86F

    Terrain: volcanic origin; low hills

Natural resources: negligible

Natural hazards: NA

People

Population: 14,600 (July 1995 est.)

Life expectancy at birth: total population 72.24 years

Nationality: Wallisian, Futunan, or Wallis and Futuna Islanders

Ethnic division: Polynesian

Religions: Roman Catholic

Languages: French, Wallisian (indigenous Polynesian language)

Literacy: total population 50%

Economy

Imports: foodstuffs, manufactured goods, transportation equipment, fuel, clothing

Exports: copra, handicrafts

Industries: copra, handicrafts, fishing, lumber

Agriculture: dominated by coconut production, with subsistence crops of yams, taro, bananas, and herds of pigs and goats

Currency: 1 CFP franc = 100 centimes

Comptoirs Francais du Pacifique francs per US1$ - 96.25

Transportation

Railroads: none

Roads: 120 km total paved and unpaved

Ports: Leava, Mata-Utu

Airports: 2 (one unpaved). There is an international airport in Hihifo district on Uvea, about 4 km from Mata-Utu

Tourism: Facilities for tourism are limited in Mata-Utu. No tourist facilities are available on Futuna

Diplomatic representation in US: none (overseas territory of France)

US Diplomatic representation: none (overseas territory of France)

West Bank

50 km

The West Bank is Israeli occupied with interim status subject to Israeli/Palestinian negotiations -- final status to be determined.

Nābulus

Ram Allah •
Jerusalem• •Jericho
Bethlehem•

Dead Sea

• Hebron

Capital: NA   longitude: 35.25 E   latitude: 32.00 N

Government: Under the Israeli-PLO Declaration of Principles on Interim Self-Government Arrangements, Israel agreed to transfer certain powers and responsibilities to the Palestinian Authority, and subsequently to an elected Palestinian Council, as part of interim self-governing arrangements in the West Bank and Gaza Strip

Flag: NA

Geography

Location: Middle East, west of Jordan

Total Area: 5,860 sq km (2,263 sq mi) slightly larger than Delaware

Note: includes West Bank, Latrun Salient, and the northwest quarter of the Dead Sea, but excludes Mt. Scopus; East Jerusalem and Jerusalem No Man's Land are also included only as a means of depicting the entire area occupied by Israel in 1967

Boundaries: Israel, Jordan

Climate: temperate, temperature and precipitation vary with altitude, warm to hot summers, cool to mild winters

Terrain: mostly rugged dissected upland, some vegetation in west, but barren in east

Natural resources: negligible

Natural hazards: NA

Note: landlocked; highlands are main recharge area for Israel's coastal aquifers.

People

Population: 1,320,000 (July 1995 est.)

Life expectancy at birth: total population 71.42 years

Nationality: NA

Ethnic division: Palestinian Arab and other 83%, Jewish 17%

560

Religions: Muslim 75% (predominantly Sunni), Jewish 17%, Christian and other 8%

Languages: Arabic, Hebrew (spoken by Israeli settlers), English (widely understood)

Literacy: NA

Economy

Imports: food, consumer goods, construction materials

Exports: olives, fruit, vegetables

Industries: generally small family businesses that produce cement, textiles, soap, olive-wood carvings, and mother of pearl souvenirs; the Israelis have established some small-scale modern industries in the settlements and industrial centers

Agriculture: olives, citrus and other fruits, vegetables, beef, and dairy products

Currency: 1 new Israeli shekel (NIS) = 100 new agorot;
1 Jordanian dinar (JD) = 1,000 fils
new Israeli shekels per US1$ - 3.02
Jordanian dinars per US1$ - 0.67

Transportation

Railroads: none

Roads: NA

Note: small road network; Israelis have developed many highways to service Jewish settlements

Ports: none

Airports: 2 with paved runways

Western Sahara

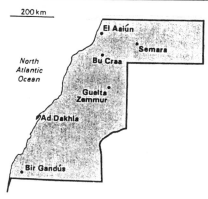

Capital: none   longitude: 13.20 E   latitude: 25.00 N

Government: legal status of territory and question of sovereignty unresolved; territory contested by Morocco and Mauritania

Administration divisions: none (under de facto control of Morocco)

Flag: NA

Geography

Location: Northern Africa, bordering the North Atlantic Ocean, between Mauritania and Morocco

Total Area: 266,000 sq km (102,703 sq mi) slightly smaller than Colorado

Boundaries: Algeria, Mauritania, Morocco

Climate: hot, dry desert; rain is rare; cold offshore air current produce fog and heavy dew

Terrain: mostly low, flat desert with large areas of rocky or sandy surfaces rising to small mountains in south and northeast

Highest point is 823 m (2,700 ft)

Natural resources: phosphates, iron ore

Natural hazards: hot, dry, dust/sand-laden sirocco wind can occur during winter and spring; widespread harmattan haze exists 60% of time, often severely restricting visibility

People

Population: 217,800 (July 1995 est.)

Life expectancy at birth: total population 46.31 years

Nationality: Sahrawi

Ethnic division: Arab, Berber

Religions: Muslim

Languages: Hassaniya Arabic, Moroccan Arabic

Literacy: NA

Economy

Imports: fuel for fishing fleet, foodstuffs

Exports: phosphates

Industries: phosphate mining, handicraft

Agriculture: limited largely to subsistence agriculture and fishing; some barley is grown in non drought years; fruit and vegetables are grown in the few oasis; food imports are essential; camels, sheep, and goats are kept by the nomadic natives

Currency: 1 Moroccan dirham (DH) = 100 centimes

Moroccan dirhams per US1$ - 8.89

Transportation

Railroads: none

Roads: 6,200 km paved and unpaved

Ports: Ad Dakhla, Cabo Bojador, El Aaium
Airports: 14 total paved and unpaved

Diplomatic representation in US: none
US Diplomatic representation: none

Western Samoa

Capital: Apia   longitude: 171.45 W   latitude: 13.48 W   elevation: 7 ft
Government: constitutional monarchy under native chief
Flag: red with a blue rectangle in the upper hoist-side quadrant bearing five white five-pointed stars representing the Southern Cross constellation
Geography
Location: Oceania, group of islands in the South Pacific Ocean, about one-half of the way from Hawaii to New Zealand
Total Area: 2,860 sq km (1,104 sq mi) slightly smaller than Rhode Island
Boundaries: no land boundaries
Climate: tropical; rainy season (October to March), dry season (May to October)
Temperature (F): High/Low Jan. 86/75, Apr. 85/76, July 85/74, Oct. 85/75
Average annual precipitation: 114.3 inches
Terrain: narrow coastal plain with volcanic, rocky, rugged mountains in interior
Highest point is Mt. Silisili 1,857 m (6,094 ft)
Natural resources: hardwood forests, fish
Natural hazards: occasional typhoons; active volcanism
People
Population: 209,800 (July 1995 est.)
Life expectancy at birth: total population 68.38 years
Nationality: Western Samoan

Ethnic division: Samoan 92.6%, Euronesians 7%, (persons of European and Polynesian blood), Europeans 0.4%

Religions: Christian 99.7% (about one-half of population associated with the London Missionary Society; includes Congregational, Roman Catholic, Methodist, Latter Day Saints, Seventh-Day Adventist)

Languages: Samoan (Polynesian), English

Literacy: total population 97%

Economy

Imports: intermediate goods, capital goods

Exports: coconut oil and cream, taro, copra, cocoa

Industries: timber, tourism, food processing, fishing

Agriculture: coconuts, fruit (including bananas, taro, yams)

Currency: 1 tala (WS$) = 100 sene

                            tala per US1$ - 2.46

Transportation

Railroads: none

Roads: 2,042 km (375 km paved) balance unpaved

Ports: Apia, Asau, Mulifanua, Saleologa

Airports: The international airport is at Faleolo

The Press: newspapers

The Samoa Observer: POB 1572, Apia
telephone 21-099   fax 23-078
5 times a week   English   circ. 4,800

The Samoa Times: POB 1160, Apia
telephone 20-945   weekly

Tourism: Fuipisia Falls, Savai Island, beaches, turquoise lagoons, dugout canoes, open markets, tapa cloth

Western Samoa Visitors' Bureau: POB 862, Apia
telephone 20-878   fax 22-848

Diplomatic representation in US:

chief of mission: Ambassador Tuiloma Neroni Slade

chancery: 820 Second Avenue, Suite 800, New York, NY 10017

telephone: [1] (212) 599-6196, 6197

FAX: [1] (212) 599-0797

US Diplomatic representation:

chief of mission: the ambassador to New Zealand is accredited to Western Samoa

embassy: 5th floor, Beach Road, Apia

mailing address: P O Box 3430, Apia

telephone: [685] 21-631

FAX: [685] 22-030

World

Government Administrative divisions: 265 nations, dependent areas, other, and miscellaneous entries

Geography

Total Area: 510,072,000 sq km (196,938,800 sq mi)

land area: 148,940,000 sq km (57,505,734 sq mi). Land area about 16 times the size of the US

water area: 361,132,000 sq km (139,433,065 sq mi)

Note: 70.8% of the world is water, 29.2% is land

Land Boundaries: the land boundaries in the world total 250,883.64 km (not counting shared boundaries twice)

Coastline: 356,000 km

Climate: two large areas of polar climates separated by two rather narrow temperate zones from a wide equatorial band of tropical to subtropical climates

Terrain: highest elevation is Mt. Everest at 8,848 meters and the lowest depression is the Dead Sea at 392 meters below sea level; greatest ocean depth is the Marianas Trench at 10,924 meters

Natural resources: the rapid using up of non-renewable mineral resources, the depletion of forest areas and wetlands, the extinction of animals and plant species, and the deterioration in air and water quality pose serious long-term problems that governments and peoples are only beginning to address

Environment

Current issues: large areas subject to overpopulation, industrial disasters, pollution (air, water, acid rain, toxic substances), loss of vegetation (overgrazing, deforestation, desertification), loss of wildlife, soil degradation, soil depletion, erosion

Natural hazards: large areas subject to severe weather (tropical cyclones), natural disasters (earthquakes, landslides, tsunamis, volcanic eruptions)

People:

Population: 5,733,690,000 (July 1995 est.)

Circumference: Equatorial = 40,075 km (24,902 miles)

Polar = 40,007 km (24,860 miles)

Distance from the Sun: Maximum is 152,000,000 km (94,600,000 miles)

Minimum is 147,000,000 km (91,300,000 miles)

Yemen

Capital: Sanaa   longitude: 44.14 E   latitude: 15.24 N

Government: republic

Flag: three equal horizontal bands of red (top), white, and black; similar to the flag of Syria which has two green stars and of Iraq which has three green stars (plus an Arabic inscription) in a horizontal line centered in the white band; also similar to the flag of Egypt which has a symbolic eagle centered in the white band

Geography

Location: Middle East, bordering the Arabian Sea, Gulf of Aden, and Red Sea, between Oman and Saudi Arabia

Total Area: 527,970 sq km (203,849 sq mi) slightly larger than twice the size of Wyoming

Note: includes Perim, Socotra, the former Yeman Arab Republic (YAR or North Yemen), and the former People's Democratic Republic of Yemen (PDRY or South Yemen)

Boundaries: Oman, Saudi Arabia

Climate: mostly desert; hot and humid along west coast; temperate in western mountains affected by seasonal monsoon; extraordinarily hot, dry, harsh desert east

Temperature (F): High/Low Jan. 82/72, Apr. 89/77, July 97/83, Oct. 91/76
Average annual precipitation: 0.9 inches

Terrain: narrow coastal plain backed by flat-topped hills and rugged mountains; dissected upland desert plains in center slope into the desert interior of the Arabian Peninsula

Natural resources: petroleum, fish, rock salt, marble, small deposits of coal, gold, lead, nickel, and copper, fertile soil in west

Natural hazards: sandstorms and dust storms in summer

Note: controls Bab el Mandeb, the strait linking the Red Sea and the Gulf of Aden, one of the world's most active shipping lanes

People

Population: 14,729,000 (July 1995 est.)

Life expectancy at birth: total population 62.51 years

Nationality: Yemeni

Ethnic division: predominantly Arab; Afro-Arab concentrations in western coastal locations; South Asians in southern regions; small European communities in major metropolitan areas

Religions: Muslim including Sha'fi (Sunni) and Zaydi (Shi'a), small numbers of Jewish, Christian, and Hindu

Languages: Arabic

Literacy: total population 38%

Economy:

Imports: textiles and other manufactured consumer goods, petroleum products, sugar, grain, flour, other foodstuffs, cement, machinery, chemicals

Exports: crude oil, cotton, coffee, hides, vegetables, dried and salted fish

Industries: crude oil production and petroleum refining; small- scale production of cotton textiles and leather goods; food processing; handicrafts; small aluminum products factory; cement

Agriculture: products - grain, fruits, vegetables, qat (mildly narcotic shrub), coffee, cotton, dairy, poultry, meat, fish; not self-sufficient in grain

Currency: Yemeni rial (new currency); 1 North Yemeni riyal (YR) = 100 fils; 1 South Yemeni dinar (YD) = 1,000 fils

Note: following the establishment of the Republic of Yemen on 22 May 1990, the North riyal and South Yemeni Dinar are to be replaced with the new Yemeni rial

Yemeni rials per US1$ - 12.0

Transportation

Railroads: none

Roads: 51,390 km total paved and unpaved

Ports: Aden, Al Hudaydah, Al Mukalla, Mocha, Nishtun

Airports: 46 total paved and unpaved. There are six international airports.

The Press: daily newspaper   **Ar-Rabi' 'Ashar Min Uktubar:**
POB 4227, Crater, Aden   (no Saturdays)

Tourism: Cities of Sanaa, Aden, Hadeida, Taiz, history, culture, art, architecture, monuments to the Queen of Sheba, Archaeological finds and Royal Artifacts
Yemen Tourist Co: POB 1526, Sanaa

Diplomatic representation in US:

chief of mission: Ambassador Mushsin Ahmad al-Ayni

chancery: Suite 705, 2600 Virginia Avenue NW, Washington, DC 20037

telephone: [1] (202) 965-4760, 4761

FAX: [1] (202) 337-2017

US Diplomatic representation:

chief of mission: Ambassador David Newton

embassy: Dhahr Himyar Zone, Sheraton Hotel District, Samaa

mailing address: P O Box 22347 Sanaa; Sanaa,

Department of Washington, DC 20521-6330

telephone: [967] (1) 23-88-43 through 23-88-52

FAX: [967] (1) 25-15-63

Zaire

500 km

Capital: Kinshasa   longitude: 15.18 E   latitude: 4.18 S   elevation: 1,066 ft
Government: republic with a strong presidential system
   Flag: light green with a yellow disk in the center bearing a black arm holding a red flaming torch; the flames of the torch are blowing away from the hoist side; uses the popular pan-African colors of Ethiopia
Geography
   Location: Central Africa, northeast of Angola
   Total Area: 2,345,410 sq km (905,563 sq mi) slightly more than one-quarter the size of the US
   Boundaries: Angola, Burundi, Central African Republic, Congo, Rwanda, Sudan, Uganda, Zambia
   Climate: tropical; hot and humid in equatorial river basin; cooler and drier in southern highlands; cooler and wetter in eastern highlands; north of Equator - wet season April to October, dry season December to February; south of Equator - wet season November to March, dry season April to October
   Temperature (F): High/Low Jan. 87/70, Apr. 89/71, July 81/64, Oct. 88/70
   Average annual precipitation: 53.4 inches
   Terrain: vast central basin is a low-lying plateau; mountains in east
   Highest point is Margherita 5,119 m (16,795 ft)
   Natural resources: cobalt, copper, cadmium, petroleum, industrial and gem diamonds, gold, silver, zinc, manganese, tin, germanium, uranium, radium, bauxite, iron ore, coal, hydropower potential
   Natural hazards: periodic droughts in south; volcanic activity
   Note: straddles Equator; very narrow strip of land that controls the lower Congo River and is only outlet to South Atlantic Ocean; dense tropical rain forest in central river basin and eastern highlands
People
   Population: 44,061,000 (July 1995 est.)
569

Life expectancy at birth: total population 47.54 years

Nationality: Zairian

Ethnic division: over 200 African ethnic groups, the majority are Bantu; four largest tribes - Mongo, Luba, (all Bantu), and the Mangbetu-Azande (Hamitic) make up about 45% of the population

Religions: Roman Catholic 50%, Protestant 20%, Kimbanguist 10%, Muslim 10%, other syncretic sects and traditional beliefs 10%

Languages: French, Lingala, Swahili, Kingwana, Tshiluba

Literacy: total population 72%

Economy

Imports: consumer goods, mining and other machinery, transport equipment, fuels

Exports: copper, coffee, diamonds, cobalt, crude oil

Industries: mining, mineral processing, consumer products (including textiles, footwear, cigarettes, processed foods and beverages), cement, diamonds

Agriculture: cash crops - coffee, palm oil, rubber, quinine; food crops - cassava, bananas, root crops, corn

Currency: 1 zaire (Z) = 100 makuta

new zaires per US1$ - 3,275.71

Note: on 22 October 1993 the new zaire, equal to 3,000,000 old zaires, was introduced

Transportation

Railroads: 5,138 km;

Note: severely reduced trackage use because of civil strife

Roads: 146,500 km total paved and unpaved

Ports: Banana, Boma, Bukavu, Bumba, Goma, Kalemie, Kindu, Kinshasa, Kisangani, Matadi, Mbandaka

Airports: 270 total paved and unpaved. There are international airports at Ndjili, Luano, Bukavu, Goma, and Kisangani

The Press: daily newspapers

L'Analyste: 129 ave du Bas-Zaire, BP 91, Kinshasa-Gombe telephone (12) 80-987

Mjumbe: BP 2474, Lubumbashi, Shaba telephone (2) 25-348

Tourism: Extensive lakes and mountain scenery, national parks

Office National du Tourisme:
2a/2b ave des Orangers, BP 9502,
Kinshasa-Gombe   telephone (12) 30-070

Diplomatic representation in US:

    chief of mission: Ambassador Tatanene Manata

    chancery: 1800 New Hampshire Avenue NW, Washington, DC 20009

    telephone: [1] (202) 234-7690, 7691

US Diplomatic representation:

    chief of mission: (vacant); Charge d'Affaires John M. Yates

    embassy: 310 Avenue des Aviateurs, Kinshasa

    mailing address: Unit 31550, Kinshasa;   APO AE 09828

    telephone: [243] (12) 21-532, 21-628

    FAX: [243] (12) 21-534 ext. 2308, 21-535 ext. 2308; (88) 43-805, 43-467

Zambia

Capital: Lusaka   longitude: 28.16 E latitude: 15.28 S elevation: 4,191 ft

Government: republic

    Flag: green with a panel of three vertical bands of red (hoist side), black, and orange below a soaring orange eagle, on the outer edge of the flag

Geography

    Location: Southern Africa, east of Angola

    Total Area: 752,610 sq km (290,583 sq mi) slightly larger than Texas

    Boundaries: Angola, Malawi, Mozambique, Namibia, Tanzania, Zaire, Zimbabwe

    Climate: tropical; modified by altitude; rainy season (October to April)

    Temperature (F): High/Low Jan. 78/63, Apr. 79/59, July 73/49, Oct. 88/70

    Average annual precipitation: 32.9 inches

    Terrain: mostly high plateau with some hills and mountains

    Highest point is Sunzu 2,067 m (6,782 ft)

    Natural resources: copper, cobalt, zinc, lead, coal, emeralds, gold, silver, uranium, hydropower potential

Natural hazards: tropical storms (November to April)

People

Population: 9,446,000 (July 1995 est.)

Life expectancy at birth: total population 42.88 years

Nationality: Zambian

Ethnic division: African 98.7%, European 1.1%, other 0.2%

Religions: Christian 50%-75%, Muslim and Hindu 24%-49%, indigenous beliefs 1%

Languages: English (official)

Note: about 70 indigenous languages

Literacy: total population 73%

Economy

Imports: machinery, transportation equipment, foodstuffs, fuels, manufactures

Exports: copper, zinc, cobalt, lead, tobacco

Industries: copper mining and processing, construction, foodstuffs, beverages, chemicals, textiles, and fertilizers

Agriculture: crops - corn (food staple), sorghum, rice, peanuts, sunflower, tobacco, cotton, sugarcane, cassava; cattle, goats, beef, eggs

Currency: 1 Zambian kwacha (ZK) = 100 ngwee

Zambian Kwacha per US1$ - 672.8

Transportation

Railroads: 1,273 km

Roads: 36,370 km total paved and unpaved

Ports: Mpulungu

Airports: 113 total paved and unpaved. The international airport is located about 24 km from Lusaka

The Press: daily newspapers

The Times of Zambia:
POB 30394, Lusaka
telephone (1) 22-90-76 fax (1) 22-28-80
circ. 65,000   English

Zambia Daily Mail: POB 31421, Lusaka
telephone (1) 21-17-22 circ. 40,000   English

Tourism: Attractions are national parks with wildlife and unspoilt scenery, Victoria Falls

Zambia Naational Tourist Board:
Century House, Cairo Road, POB 30017 Lusaka
telephone (1) 22-90-87

Diplomatic representation in US:

chief of mission: Ambassador Dunstan Weston Kamana

chancery: 2419 Massachusetts Avenue NW, Washington, DC 20008

telephone: [1] (202) 265-9717 through 9719

FAX: [1] (202) 332-0826

US Diplomatic representation:

chief of mission: Ambassador Roland K. Kuchel

embassy: corner of Independence Avenue and United Nations Avenue, Lusaka

mailing address: P O Box 31617, Lusaka

telephone: [260] (1) 22-85-95, 22-86-01, 22-86-03

FAX: [260] (1) 26-15-38

Zimbabwe

Capital: Harare   longitude: 31.03 E   latitude: 17.50 S   elevation: 4,831 ft

Government: parliamentary democracy

Flag: seven equal horizontal bands of green, yellow, red, black, red, yellow, and green with a white equilateral triangle edged in black on the hoist side; a yellow Zimbabwe bird is superimposed on a red five-pointed star in the center of the triangle

Geography

Location: Southern Africa, northeast of Botswana

Total Area: 390,580 sq km (150,803 sq mi) slightly larger than Montana

Boundaries: Botswana, Mozambique, South Africa, Zambia

Climate: tropical; moderated by altitude; rainy season (November to March)

Temperature (F): High/Low Jan. 78/60, Apr. 78/55, July 70/44, Oct. 83/58

Average annual precipitation: 32.6 inches

Terrain: mostly high plateau with higher central plateau (high veld); mountains in east

Highest point is Mt Inyangani 2,596 m (8,517 ft)

Natural resources: coal, chromium ore, asbestos, gold, nickel, copper, iron ore, vanadium, lithium, tin, platinum group metals

Natural hazards: recurring droughts; floods and severe storms are rare

People

Population: 11,139,961 (July 1995 est.)

Life expectancy at birth: total population 41.35 years

Nationality: Zimbabwean

Ethnic division: African 98% (Shona 71%, Ndebele 16%, other 11%), white 1%, mixed and Asian 1%

Religions: syncretic (part Christian, part indigenous beliefs) 50%, Christian 25%, indigenous beliefs 24%, Muslim and other 1%

Languages: English (official), Shona, Sindebele

Literacy: total population 78%

Economy

Imports: machinery and transportation equipment, other manufactures, chemicals, fuels

Exports: agricultural (tobacco and other), manufactures, gold, ferrochrome, textiles

Industries: mining, steel, clothing and footwear, chemicals, foodstuffs, fertilizer, beverage, transportation equipment, wood products

Agriculture: 40% of the land area divided into 4,500 large commercial farms and 42% in communal lands; crops - corn (food staple), cotton, tobacco, wheat, coffee, sugarcane, peanuts; livestock - cattle, sheep, goats, pigs; self-sufficient in food

Currency: 1 Zimbabwean dollar (Z$) = 100 cents

Zimbabwean dollars per US1$ - 8.37

Transportation

Railroads: 2,745 km

Roads: 85,237 km total paved and unpaved

Ports: Binga, Kariba

Airports: 471 total paved and unpaved. The major international airport is at Harare. Domestic air service connect most of the larger towns

The Press: daily newspapers

Daily Gazette: POB 66070, Kopje, Harare
telephone 73-87-22
The Herald: POB 396, Harare
telephone 79-57-71   fax 79-13-11
circ. 135,000   English

Tourism: Hwange National Park is one of a few great elephant sanctuaries left in Africa; over one hundred different species of animals and four hundred different species of birds. Lake Kariba supports over forty different species of fish, as well as hippo and crocodiles. Vumba Botanical Gardens, rain forests, Victoria Falls, one of the most spectacular natural wonders of the world

Zimbabwe Tourist Development Corporation:
POB 286, Causeway, Harare
telephone 79-36-66 fax 79-36-69

Diplomatic representation in US:
chief of mission: Ambassador Amos Bernard Muvengwa Midzi
chancery: 1608 New Hampshire Avenue NW, Washington, DC 20009
telephone: [1] (202) 332-7100
FAX: [1] (202) 483-9326

US Diplomatic representation:
chief of mission: Ambassador Johnny Carson
embassy: 172 Herbert Chitepo Avenue, Harare
mailing address: P O Box 3340, Harare
telephone: [263] (4) 79-45-21
FAX: [263] (4) 79-64-88

APPENDIX

01. U.S. Department of State - Bureau of Consular Affairs
Automated Fax System
There are four indexes of publication and documents available.
1) List of Countries and Travel Warnings
2) Travel, Passport and Visa information
3) Judicial Assistance and Citizenship
4) Children's issues

To receive the index, dial (202) 647-3000. When instructed to do so, press the "star" key. Then, enter the number for the index you wish to obtain and then press the start/connect button to begin transmission.

02. World Business Directory. Detailed information on more than 140,000 business involved in international trade.
World Trade Centers Association
1 World Trade Center, Suite 35 North
New York, NY 10048
1-800-937-8886, in New York City (212) 435-2552

03. International Measurements

1 kilometer (km) = 0.6214 mile	1 mile = 1.609 kilometer
1 meter (m) = 39.37 inches	1 yard = 0.9144 meter
= 3.2808 feet	1 foot = 0.3048 meter
= 1.0936 yard	
1 centimeter (cm) = 0.3937 inch	

1 square kilometer = 0.3861 square miles = 247.1 acres
1 square mile = 2.5899 square kilometers

1 liter = 0.2642 U.S. gallon	1 U.S. gallon = 3.785 liters
1 kilogram (kg) = 2.2046 pounds	1 pound = 0.4536 kilogram
	1 pound = 453.6 grams

04. Temperature conversion:
Degrees Fahrenheit = 9 X degrees Celsius (Centigrade) divided by 5 + 32
Degrees Celsius (Centigrade) = 5 X (degrees F - 32) divided by 9
(temperatures shown in this book are for the capital cities unless noted)

05.	Latitude: describes a position on the earth's surface in relation to the equator and is measured in degrees. Any point on the equator has a latitude of zero degrees. The North Pole has a latitude of 90 degrees north and the South Pole has a latitude of 90 degrees south. 1 degree is about 60 nautical (sea or air) miles, or 69 statute (land) miles.

06.	Longitude: lines of longitude run north and south along the surface of the earth and is divided into 360 equal parts. An imaginary line running through Greenwich, a borough of London, lies at 0 degrees longitude. The earth is divided into two parts, or hemispheres, of east and west longitude. Each hemisphere is has 180 degrees. Degrees longitude are used to measure east and west distances on the maps.

The earth turns once on its axis every 24 hours, thus, giving us the following calculations

24 hours of time = 360 degrees of longitude.

1 hour of time = 15 degrees of longitude.

4 minutes of time = 1 degree of longitude.

1 minute of time = 15 seconds of longitude.

1 second of time = 15 minutes of longitude.

NOTE:

While every effort has been made to ensure the accuracy of the information contained in this book, the author cannot accept responsibility for errors that may appear

INFORMATION SOURCE:

01.	Foreign Country Embassies
02.	State Department Travel Advisory
03.	CIA World Fact Book
04.	United Nations Library
05.	Travel Brochures

Glossary

- A -

alluvial   found in, or made up of, alluvium
                  alluvium is sand, clay, etc. gradually deposited by moving
                  water, as along a river bed or the shore of a lake

aloes   any of a large genus (*aloe*) of plants of the lily family, native to
                  South Africa, with fleshy leaves that are spiny along the edge 2.
                  bitter, laxative drug made from the juice of certain aloe leaves

altitude   the height of a thing above the earth's surface or above sea level

animism   the doctrine that all life is produced by a spiritual force
                  separate from matter; the belief that all natural phenomena
                  have souls independent of their physical being; a belief in
                  existence of spirits, demons, etc

arable   suitable for plowing and, hence, for producing crops

archaeology   the scientific study of the life and culture of ancient
                  peoples, as by the excavation of ancient cities, relics, artifacts,
                  etc

archipelago a sea with many islands; a group or chain of many islands

arctic   characteristic of, or near the North Pole or the region around it;
                  very cold, frigid

arctic climate   no warm season; warmest month below 50F (10C)

atheist   the belief that there is no God, or denial that God or gods exist

atmosphere   the gaseous envelope (air) surrounding the earth; it
                  consists of oxygen and nitrogen and other gases, and rotates
                  with the earth

atoll   a ring shaped coral island nearly, or completely surrounding a
                  lagoon

avalanche   a mass of loosened snow, earth, rocks, etc. suddenly and swiftly
             sliding down a mountain, often growing as it descends

- B -

Berber (religion)   1. any of a Moslem people living in northern Africa 2.
                  their language, a subfamily of the Afro-asiatic family of
                  languages

barren   not producing crops or fruit; having little or no vegetation;
                  unproductive land

bog (boggy)   wet, spongy ground; a small swamp or marsh

capital goods	assets which are capable of generating income and which have themselves been produced; machines, plants, buildings
cash crop	a crop grown for sale, generally for export rather than for domestic consumption
cassava	a tropical plant of the spurge family, having edible starchy roots; used in making bread and tapioca
catchment	a reservoir or other basin for collecting water, especially rainfall
chicle	a gum like substance made from the milky juice of the sapodilla tree and used in making chewing gum
chicory	a perennial weedy plant, its root roasted and ground for mixing with coffee or for use as a coffee substitute
circumference	the line bounding a circle, a rounded surface, or an area suggesting a circle
coir	the prepared fiber of the husks of coconuts, used to make rope, etc.
commonwealth	the association of independent states comprising the UK and most of its dependencies
conch	the large spiral, one piece shell of any of various sea mollusk, often edible
confederation	independent nations or states joined in a league or confederacy whose central authority is usually confined to common defense or foreign relations
coniferous	cone bearing trees and shrubs, mostly evergreens
continental climate	hot summers, cold winters: typical of the interior of a continent. Coldest month below 32 degrees F; warmest month above 50 degrees F
copra	dried coconut meat, the source of coconut oil
coral	the hard, stony skeleton secreted by certain marine polyps and often deposited in extensive masses forming reefs and atolls in tropical seas
coupon	a certificate or ticket entitling the holder to a specified right, as redemption for cash or gifts, reduced purchase price, etc.
cowpeas	of the legume family, the edible seed of this plant, cooked as a vegetable
cults (cultist)	a system of religious worship or ritual
cultural	of the training and refinement of the mind, interests, tastes, skills, arts, etc.
cyclone	a windstorm with a violent, whirling movement

delta — a deposit of sand and soil, usually triangular, formed at the mouth of some rivers, as of the Nile

democracy — government in which the people hold the ruling power either directly or through elected representatives

dependency — a foreign territory governed by another country

desert — a dry, barren, sandy region, naturally incapable of supporting almost any plant or animal life

dialects — the form or variety of a spoken language peculiar to a region, community, social group, etc.

diatomite — an earthly deposit formed mainly of siliceous shells of diatoms and used in a finely pulverized state as an abrasive, absorbent, filter, etc.; also diatomaceous earth

drought — a prolonged period of dry weather; lack of rain

dune — a rounded hill or ridge of sand heaped up by the action of the wind

earthquake — a shaking or trembling of the crust of the earth, caused by underground volcanic forces or by breaking and shifting of rock beneath the surface

ecosystem — a system made up of a community of animals, plants, and bacteria and its interrelated physical and chemical environment

El Nino — a warm inshore current annually flowing south along the coast of Ecuador and, about every seven years, extending down the coast of Peru where it has a devastating effect on the ecology

equatorial — of or near the earth's equator

escarpment — a steep slope or cliff formed by erosion

essence — a substance that keeps, in concentrated form, the flavor, fragrance, or other properties of the plant, drug, food etc. from which it is extracted, such as perfume

ethnic — designating or of any of the basic groups or divisions of mankind or of a heterogeneous population, as distinguished by customs, characteristics, language, common history, etc.

fauna — the animals of a specified region or time

federation — (government) the act of uniting or of forming a union of states, groups, etc. by agreement of each member to subordinate its power to that of the central authority in common affairs

fjords   a narrow inlet or arm of the sea bordered by steep cliffs, especially in Norway

flora   the plants of a specified region or time

fog   a large mass of water vapor condensed to fine particles, at or just above the earth's surface; thick obscuring mist

frost frozen dew or vapor; moisture frozen as a white, crystalline coating on a surface

- G -

geothermal of or relating to the earth's internal heat

geysers   a spring from which boiling water and steam gush into the air at intervals

ghibli   (Libya)   ghibli is a southern wind lasting one to four days

glacial weather   freezing; frigid

glacier   a large mass of ice and snow that forms in areas where the rate of snowfall exceeds the rate at which snow melts

ground water   water found underground in porous rock strata and soils

guano   manure of sea birds: it is used as a fertilizer

gyre   broad, circular system of current

- H -

harmattan a dry, dust wind that blows from the interior of Africa toward the Atlantic, especially from November to March

haze   a thin vapor of fog, smoke, dust, etc. in the air that reduces visibility

humid   full of water vapor; damp; moist

hurricane a violent tropical cyclone with winds moving at 73 or more miles per hour, often accompanied by torrential rains

- I -

indigenous (beliefs, inhabitants)

- J -

jute   a strong glossy fiber used for making burlap, sacks, mats, rope, etc.

- K -

kaolin   a fine white clay used in making porcelain, as a filter in textiles, paper, rubber, etc., and in medicine in the treatment of diarrhea

karakul   broad tailed sheep

khamsin   a hot south wind from the Sahara that blows in the Near East, especially Egypt, from late March until early May

- L -

lagoon   a shallow lake or pond, especially one connected with a larger body of water; the area of water enclosed by circular coral reef, or atoll

lingua franca	any hybrid language used for communication between different peoples, as pidgin English

- M -

mangrove	trees and shrubs that inhibit tidal marshes and river mouths in the tropics
manioc	same as cassava
maritime climate	a climate with both a small annual and daily range of temperature found on most coasts
marsh	a tract of low, wet, soft land; swamp; bog
medieval	characteristic of, or suggestive of the Middle Ages
mediterranean climate	hot summers, warm winters, affected by trade winds in summer, westerlies in winter. It occurs on the west side of large land masses between latitudes 30 - 60 degrees
mestizo	a person of mixed parentage; especially, in the western U.S. and in Latin American countries, the offspring of a Spaniard or Portuguese and an American Indian
minority	a racial, religious, ethnic, or political group smaller than and differing from the larger, controlling group in a community, nation, etc.
monarchy	the single or sole ruler of a state; a government or state headed by a monarch
monsoon	the season during which this wind blows from the southwest, characterized by heavy rains
mulatto	a person who has one negro parent and one white parent

- N -

nomad	a member of a tribe or people having no permanent home, but moving about constantly in search of food, pasture, etc.

- O -

okoume	a tropical softwood
oceania	islands in the Pacific Ocean

- P -

parliamentary	based on or conforming to the customs and rules of a parliament or other public assembly
patois	a form of a language differing generally from the accepted standard, as a provincial or local dialect
pawpaws	of the custard-apple family, having an oblong, yellowish, edible fruit with many seeds
peninsula	any land area projecting out into water

permafrost   permanently frozen subsoil

pidgin (language)   a mixed language, or jargon; any jargon intermixed with English

plateau   an elevated tract of more or less level land; tableland

polar   relating to, or near the North or South Pole

possession   territory ruled by an outside country

pozzolana   volcanic rock

prevailing (winds)   superior in strength, influence, or effect

prostrate   (bot. growing on the ground; trailing)

protectorate   the relation of a strong state to a weaker state under its control and protection; a state or territory so controlled and protected

pulse   any member of the legume family; a pottage made of meal or pulse (peas, beans, lentils, etc.)

pumice   a spongy, light, porous, volcanic rock used in solid or powered form for scouring, smoothing, and polishing

pyrethrum   (insecticide made from chrysanthemums)

- Q -

qat   found in Africa and Arabia; the fresh leaf is chewed for its stimulating effects

- R -

rape (seed grain)   an annual old-world plant of the mustard family, whose seeds yield an oil and whose leaves are used for fodder

rare earth   any of certain basic oxides much alike in physical and chemical properties

realm   a region, sphere; area, any of the primary biogeographic regions of the earth

republic   a state or nation in which the supreme power rests in all the citizens entitled to vote

- S -

savanna   a treeless plain or a grassland characterized by scattered trees, especially in tropical or subtropical regions having seasonal rains

seismic   having to do with, or caused by an earthquake or earthquakes

semiarid   characterized by little yearly rainfall and by the growth of short grasses and shrubs; climate or region

shea nuts   of the sapodilla family, whose seeds yield a thick, white fat used as a food, in soap, etc.

shoals   a shallow place in a river, sea, etc., a sand bar or piece of rising ground forming a shallow place that is a danger to navigation

583

sirocco   a hot, steady, oppressive wind blowing from the Libyan deserts across the Mediterranean into south Europe, often bringing dust, and sometimes accompanied by rain

sisal   a strong fiber from the leaves of an agave, used for making rope, sacking, insulation, etc.

sorghum   any of a genus of tropical old-world grasses that produce glossy seeds: grown for grain, syrup, fodder, etc.

sovereignty   supreme and independent political authority

sub arctic   designation or of the area immediately surrounding the Arctic Circle

subtropical climate   Warmest month above 72 degrees F (22 C); coolest month between 32 F and 65 F.   (0 C to 18 C)

syncretic   the merging into one or two or more differently inflected forms; to combine or unite

- T -

taboo (Northern Mariana Islands - religion)   prohibited or forbidden by tradition, convention, etc

temperate climate   mild winters, warm summers, rainfall through the year. Coolest month above 32 F but below 65 F (0C to 18 C); warmest month above 50 F and below 72 F (10C to 22C)

territory   a state under the control of another

theocratic (government)   government by priests claiming to rule with divine authority

thunderstorms   a storm accompanied by thunder and lighting

tornado   a violently whirling column of air extending downward from a cumulonimbus cloud; almost always seen as a rapidly rotating, slender funnel-shaped cloud that usually destroys everything along its narrow path

trade winds   a wind that blows steadily toward the equator from the northeast in the tropics north of the equator and from the southeast in the tropics south of the equator

tundra   any of the vast, nearly level, treeless plains of the arctic regions

trochus   (type of shellfish)

tropical climate   very hot and generally humid. No winter; coolest month above 64 degrees F (18 C)

tsetse fly   any of two small, two winged flies of central and south Africa, including species that carry the trypanosomes that causes nagana and sleeping sickness

tsunami	a huge sea wave caused by a submarine disturbance, as earthquake or volcanic eruption
typhoon	any violent tropical cyclone originating in the west Pacific, especially the South China Sea

-U -

Uniate	a member of any Eastern Christian Church in union with the Roman Catholic Church but with its own rite, custom, etc.

- V -

volcano	a vent in the earth's crust through which molten rock (lava), rock fragments, gases, ashes, etc. are ejected from the earth's interior
Voodoo (religion)	a primitive religion based on a belief in sorcery and in the of charms, fetishes, etc.

- W -

wetlands	swamps or marshes

- Y -

ylang-ylang	an East Indian tree of the custard-apple family, with fragrant, greenish-yellow flowers. The oil obtained from these flowers, used in perfumes

Chauncey Shattuck resides in Reno, Nevada and has a great interest in foreign countries and world events. His engineering background and technical writing experience has been especially helpful in researching and writing this informational guide handbook. Travel assignments have taken him throughout the Philippines, Japan, Canada, Mexico, and every state in the United States